Handbook of Research on Threat Detection and Countermeasures in Network Security

Alaa Hussein Al-Hamami
Amman Arab University, Jordan

Ghossoon M. Waleed Al-Saadoon
Applied Science University, Bahrain

A volume in the Advances in Information Security,
Privacy, and Ethics (AISPE) Book Series

An Imprint of IGI Global

Managing Director:	Lindsay Johnston
Managing Editor:	Austin DeMarco
Director of Intellectual Property & Contracts:	Jan Travers
Acquisitions Editor:	Kayla Wolfe
Production Editor:	Christina Henning
Development Editor:	Erin O'Dea
Typesetter:	Amanda Smith
Cover Design:	Jason Mull

Published in the United States of America by
Information Science Reference (an imprint of IGI Global)
701 E. Chocolate Avenue
Hershey PA, USA 17033
Tel: 717-533-8845
Fax: 717-533-8661
E-mail: cust@igi-global.com
Web site: http://www.igi-global.com

Copyright © 2015 by IGI Global. All rights reserved. No part of this publication may be reproduced, stored or distributed in any form or by any means, electronic or mechanical, including photocopying, without written permission from the publisher. Product or company names used in this set are for identification purposes only. Inclusion of the names of the products or companies does not indicate a claim of ownership by IGI Global of the trademark or registered trademark.

Library of Congress Cataloging-in-Publication Data

Library of Congress Cataloging-in-Publication Data

Al-Hamami, Alaa Hussein, 1948-
  Handbook of research on threat detection and countermeasures in network security / Alaa Hussein Al-Hamami and Ghossoon M. Waleed Al-Saadoon, editors.
      pages cm
  Includes bibliographical references and index.
  ISBN 978-1-4666-6583-5 (hardcover) -- ISBN 978-1-4666-6584-2 (ebook) -- ISBN 978-1-4666-6586-6 (print & perpetual access) 1. Computer networks-Security measures. I. Al-Saadoon, Ghossoon M. Waleed, 1969- II. Title.
  TK5105.59.A393 2015
  005.8--dc23
                             2014029335

This book is published in the IGI Global book series Advances in Information Security, Privacy, and Ethics (AISPE) (ISSN: 1948-9730; eISSN: 1948-9749)

British Cataloguing in Publication Data
A Cataloguing in Publication record for this book is available from the British Library.

All work contributed to this book is new, previously-unpublished material. The views expressed in this book are those of the authors, but not necessarily of the publisher.

For electronic access to this publication, please contact: eresources@igi-global.com.

Advances in Information Security, Privacy, and Ethics (AISPE) Book Series

ISSN: 1948-9730
EISSN: 1948-9749

MISSION

As digital technologies become more pervasive in everyday life and the Internet is utilized in ever increasing ways by both private and public entities, concern over digital threats becomes more prevalent.

The **Advances in Information Security, Privacy, & Ethics (AISPE) Book Series** provides cutting-edge research on the protection and misuse of information and technology across various industries and settings. Comprised of scholarly research on topics such as identity management, cryptography, system security, authentication, and data protection, this book series is ideal for reference by IT professionals, academicians, and upper-level students.

COVERAGE

- Computer ethics
- Tracking Cookies
- Privacy Issues of Social Networking
- Technoethics
- Electronic Mail Security
- Information Security Standards
- Global Privacy Concerns
- IT Risk
- CIA Triad of Information Security
- Cyberethics

IGI Global is currently accepting manuscripts for publication within this series. To submit a proposal for a volume in this series, please contact our Acquisition Editors at Acquisitions@igi-global.com or visit: http://www.igi-global.com/publish/.

The Advances in Information Security, Privacy, and Ethics (AISPE) Book Series (ISSN 1948-9730) is published by IGI Global, 701 E. Chocolate Avenue, Hershey, PA 17033-1240, USA, www.igi-global.com. This series is composed of titles available for purchase individually; each title is edited to be contextually exclusive from any other title within the series. For pricing and ordering information please visit http://www.igi-global.com/book-series/advances-information-security-privacy-ethics/37157. Postmaster: Send all address changes to above address. Copyright © 2015 IGI Global. All rights, including translation in other languages reserved by the publisher. No part of this series may be reproduced or used in any form or by any means – graphics, electronic, or mechanical, including photocopying, recording, taping, or information and retrieval systems – without written permission from the publisher, except for non commercial, educational use, including classroom teaching purposes. The views expressed in this series are those of the authors, but not necessarily of IGI Global.

Titles in this Series

For a list of additional titles in this series, please visit: www.igi-global.com

Handbook of Research on Emerging Developments in Data Privacy
Manish Gupta (State University of New York at Buffalo, USA)
Information Science Reference • copyright 2015 • 507pp • H/C (ISBN: 9781466673816) • US $325.00 (our price)

Handbook of Research on Securing Cloud-Based Databases with Biometric Applications
Ganesh Chandra Deka (Ministry of Labour and Employment, India) and Sambit Bakshi (National Institute of Technology Rourkela, India)
Information Science Reference • copyright 2015 • 434pp • H/C (ISBN: 9781466665590) • US $335.00 (our price)

Information Security in Diverse Computing Environments
Anne Kayem (Department of Computer Science, University of Cape Town, South Africa) and Christoph Meinel (Hasso-Plattner-Institute for IT Systems Engineering, University of Potsdam, Potsdam, Germany)
Information Science Reference • copyright 2014 • 354pp • H/C (ISBN: 9781466661585) • US $245.00 (our price)

Network Topology in Command and Control Organization, Operation, and Evolution
T. J. Grant (R-BAR, The Netherlands) R. H. P. Janssen (Netherlands Defence Academy, The Netherlands) and H. Monsuur (Netherlands Defence Academy, The Netherlands)
Information Science Reference • copyright 2014 • 320pp • H/C (ISBN: 9781466660588) • US $215.00 (our price)

Cases on Research and Knowledge Discovery Homeland Security Centers of Excellence
Cecelia Wright Brown (University of Baltimore, USA) Kevin A. Peters (Morgan State University, USA) and Kofi Adofo Nyarko (Morgan State University, USA)
Information Science Reference • copyright 2014 • 357pp • H/C (ISBN: 9781466659469) • US $215.00 (our price)

Multidisciplinary Perspectives in Cryptology and Information Security
Sattar B. Sadkhan Al Maliky (University of Babylon, Iraq) and Nidaa A. Abbas (University of Babylon, Iraq)
Information Science Reference • copyright 2014 • 443pp • H/C (ISBN: 9781466658080) • US $245.00 (our price)

Analyzing Security, Trust, and Crime in the Digital World
Hamid R. Nemati (The University of North Carolina at Greensboro, USA)
Information Science Reference • copyright 2014 • 281pp • H/C (ISBN: 9781466648562) • US $195.00 (our price)

Research Developments in Biometrics and Video Processing Techniques
Rajeev Srivastava (Indian Institute of Technology (BHU), India) S.K. Singh (Indian Institute of Technology (BHU), India) and K.K. Shukla (Indian Institute of Technology (BHU), India)
Information Science Reference • copyright 2014 • 279pp • H/C (ISBN: 9781466648685) • US $195.00 (our price)

www.igi-global.com

701 E. Chocolate Ave., Hershey, PA 17033
Order online at www.igi-global.com or call 717-533-8845 x100
To place a standing order for titles released in this series, contact: cust@igi-global.com
Mon-Fri 8:00 am - 5:00 pm (est) or fax 24 hours a day 717-533-8661

To the soul of my parents, my family and my students with love and appreciation.

Prof. Alaa

To the soul of my lovely mother, dearest father and my family with love and appreciation.

Dr. Ghossoon

Editorial Advisory Board

Hussein Al-Bahadil, *University of Petra, Jordan*
Abbas Al-Bakry, *Babylon University, Iraq*
Wasim A. Al-Hamdani, *Kentucky State University, USA*
Sattar Almaliky, *Babylon UniversityIraq*
Hasan L. Al-Saedy, *British Institute of Technology and E-Commerce, UK*
Imad Fakhri Alshaikhli, *International Islamic University of Malaysia,* Malaysia
S. Karthik, *College of Technology, India*
Abdul Monem Rahma, *University of Technology, Iraq*
Abdelbadeeh M. Salem, *Ain Shams University, Cairo, Egypt*
Ali Shamim, *India*

List of Reviewers

Nidhal El Abbadi, *University of Kufa, Iraq*
Abdelbadeeh M. Salem, *Ain Shams University, Egypt*
Alaa Hussein Al-Hamami, *Amman Arab University, Jordan*
Ghosson Mohammed Waleed Al-Saadoon, *Applied Science University, Bahrain*
 Imad Fakhri Alshaikhli, *International Islamic University of Malaysia , Malaysia*

List of Contributors

Table of Contents

Detailed Table of Contents

The techniques and tools available for the attackers and protectors are decisive and the main cause for deciding the leading and winning side. This chapter discusses the main concepts, developments, and future trends of security. There are three main reasons for security development and its innovation. The first reason is: Perfect security does not exist; this will lead the researcher to develop more and more methods to defend against new attacks and to support the existence security systems. The second reason is: New technology always brings new threats, which means new countermeasures against those threats is always a necessity. The third reason is: There is no single countermeasure that can be used to ensure security for our systems, and there are many new threats and attacks need to be defeated. For these reasons, security is very active subject and needs more financial support for research and system development, thoughts, technologies, tools, and skilled people to ensure and maintain security for our systems.

This chapter aims to build a proposed Wire/Wireless Network Intrusion Detection System (WWNIDS) to detect intrusions and consider many of modern attacks which are not taken in account previously. The proposal WWNIDS treat intrusion detection with just intrinsic features but not all of them. The dataset of WWNIDS will consist of two parts; first part will be wire network dataset which has been constructed from KDD'99 that has 41 features with some modifications to produce the proposed dataset that called modern KDD and to be reliable in detecting intrusion by suggesting three additional features. The second part will be building wireless network dataset by collecting thousands of sessions (normal and intrusion); this proposed dataset is called Constructed Wireless Data Set (CWDS). The preprocessing process will be done on the two datasets (KDD & CWDS) to eliminate some problems that affect the detection of intrusion such as noise, missing values and duplication.

Chapter 3

Ghossoon M. Waleed Al-Saadoon, Applied Science University, Bahrain

The computer sciences and their applications are developing continuously. This growth should be protected. One of the methods to fulfill this approach by using the encryption method 'Rijndael Advanced Encryption Standard' is applied for security information DBs, to prevent an unauthorized user from accessing any stored information. The security method determines the resources that agents are able to have an access and to give permission to other agents. Security and security assurance are special integrity in agent system to enable it to cooperate or to complete the application and where agent system may not be trustful to visiting agents. Ideas of this chapter of using multi agent framework is to design the proposed Automatic Intrusion Detection model and to secret multi agent preservation using authentication measurement network threat. This approach uses statistical models to correlate and analyse data in the network. It takes the decisions to control both local and global agent's data bases perceptively. Also it adopts the security problem authentication and authorization by providing a secure distributed agent system.

Chapter 4

Zuhoor Al-Khanjari, Sultan Qaboos University, Oman
Asaad Abdulrahman Nayyef, Sultan Qaboos University, Oman

The increase of attacks on e-Government infrastructures led to the emergence of several information security techniques. Insider threat is one of the most complex problems in information security. It requires a sophisticated response to detect and protect the un-authorized use. This chapter provides a framework for developing a high level security management for e-Government website. The framework is based on the sensors and detectors, which consist of relatively small amounts of source code to detect all attacks in e-Government website against all threats in real time. In this chapter, the authors also provide a full illustration of how to design and protect all files used to implement a secure e-Government websites. This should contain a self- audit of the file and represent a kind of processes that are used to protect data in different types of files including: image, sound, string or any file within e-Government website.

Chapter 5

Wasim A. Al-Hamdani, Kentucky State University, USA

Enterprise Resource Planning (ERP) software is business-management software that allows an organization to use a system of integrated applications to manage the business. ERP software often contains highly confidential information that is vital to a firm's competitiveness, so it is critically important that appropriate security be implemented to reduce its vulnerability. In this chapter, security issues are presented that could arise when ERP software is integrated with many systems and with web environments. The security issue is one of the major issues with ERP software, and it has not been a major focus of the developers of the software, who leave this issue to different components of the system and to vendor implementation. In this chapter, The author presents a new security model for ERP software. The author also presents a new authentication model that consists of the following layers: Role base, Data mining, Risk-based access control, and PKI.

Chapter 6

Imad Fakhri Alshaikhli, International Islamic University of Malaysia, Malaysia
Mohammad Abdulateef AlAhmad, PAAET, Kuwait

Cryptographic hash function verifies data integrity and sender identity or source of information. The task is accomplished by taking a variable bit patterns as an input then produces a fixed bit patterns of output. This chapter provides a detailed overview to include classification, properties, constructions, attacks, applications and an overview of a selected dedicated cryptographic hash function.

Chapter 7

Hussein Zedan, Applied Science University, Bahrain
Meshrif Alruily, De Montfort University, UK

Digital forensics aims to examine a wide range of digital media in a "forensically" sound manner. This can be used either to uncover rationale for a committed crime and possible suspects, prevent a crime from taken place or to identify a threat so that it can be dealt with. The latter is firmly rooted within the domain of intelligence counter measures. The authors call the outcome of the analyses subject profiling where a subject can be a threat or a suspect. In this Chapter the authors outline a process for profiling based on Self-organizing Map (SOM) and evaluating our technique by profiling crimes using a multi-lingual corpus. The development and application of a Crime Profiling System (CPS) is also presented. The system is able to extract meaningful information (type of crime, location and nationality), from Arabic language crime news reports. The system has two unique attributes; firstly, information extraction depends on local grammar, and secondly, automatic generation of dictionaries. It is shown that the CPS improves the quality of the data through reduction where only meaningful information is retained. Moreover, when clustering, using Self Organizing Map (SOM), we gain efficiency as the data is cleansed by removing noise. The proposed system is validated through experiments using a corpus collated from different sources; Precision, Recall and F-measure are used to evaluate the performance of the proposed information extraction approach. Also, comparisons are conducted with other systems.

Chapter 8

Alaa Hussein Al-Hamami, Amman Arab University, Jordan

Through commercial networks and across the Internet, there are data files, millions of images and videos, and trillions of messages flow each day to drive the world economy. This vast electronic infrastructure is what our nation depends on. To commit crime by using a computer and communication to forge a person's identity, illegal imports or malicious programs, the computer here is used as an object or subject for the cybercrime. Most of the online activities are vulnerable to intrusion and can compromise personal safety just as effectively as common everyday crimes. This chapter concentrates on explaining and discussing the terms of cyber security, cybercrimes, and cyber-attacks. A history for each term has been given and the problems of cyber security have been discussed. Finally, a proposed solution has been suggested and future trends have been forecasted, and at the end of the chapter a conclusion will be given.

The financial cost of cyber crime now has an annual cost estimated in the UK in eleven figures. In this chapter an ethic based definition of cyber crime is introduced and cyber crimes are classified. The impact of each class of cyber crime on society, individual, government and international security is highlighted. The cost of cyber crime is evaluated and a technique to prevent and mitigate the effect of these crimes on individual, government and international security and world peace is indicated. The forensic techniques and tools used in cyber crime evidence gathering and prosecuting procedure is also indicated. Finally, recommendations and suggestion are given to mitigate the impact of cyber crime on individuals, societies, world finance and international security.

Chapter 10

Cyberspace is known as the digital electronic medium for the knowing range of securing in the cyberspace. Therefore the importance of inferring the reference measure in the form of assessment procedure to improve the knowledge and making the decision for the e- government services. A series of the standards build on the application of data mining methods specifically represented as decision tress model, Logistic regression, association rules model, Bayesian network for making reference measurements, to measure the extent of securing the data, and the provided services. The authors discuss various types of cyber-attacks describing how data mining helps in detection and prevention of these attacks. A comparative analysis between a set of selected frameworks is presented. Finally this chapter imparts numbers of applications for the data mining Methodologies in Cyber Security. Results applied on the site of the authority for cleaning and beautifying Cairo governorate in Egypt.

The terms biometrics and biometry have been used to refer to the field of development of statistical and mathematical methods applicable to data analysis problems in the biological sciences. Recently biometrics refers to technologies and applications applied for personal identification using physical and behavioral parameters. Biometric security systems ensuring that only the authorized persons are permitted to access a certain data, because it is difficult to copy the biometric features pattern for a specific person. Biometrics is playing an important role in applications that are centric on identification, verification and classification. This chapter focuses on biometric security in their types, specifications, technologies and algorithms. Some algorithms of biometric security are also included in this chapter. Finally latest and future aspects of biometric system and merging technologies are also mentioned, including more details of system structures and specifications and what constitution will shape biometric security of in the future.

The security of information exchange is very important on the network. Authentication and information hiding have also become important issues. Information hiding techniques are acquiring an increasing importance due to the widespread diffusion of multimedia contents. The aim of this chapter is to focus on the Singular Value Decomposition (SVD) transform, with the aim of providing an exhaustive overview on those steganography, image cryptography and watermarking techniques leveraging on the important properties of such a transform. Despite the attention it has received in the last years, SVD in image processing and security is still in its infancy. Many SVD characteristics are still unutilized in image processing. In this chapter the author tries to highlight the basic properties of SVD and some of their applications in the field of security to encourage researchers to discover more about SVD properties which are not yet utilized.

Chapter 13

This unauthorized intrusion has cost time and money for businesses and users. The exponential growth of spam emails in recent years has resulted in the necessity for more accurate and efficient spam filtering. This chapter focuses on creating a text-based anti-spam system using back-propagation neural network for Malay Language emails that efficiently and effectively counter measure spam problems. The proposed algorithm consists of three stages; pre-processing, implementation and evaluation. Malay language emails are collected and divided into spam and non-spam. Features are extracted and document frequency as dimension reduction technique is calculated too. Classifiers are trained to recognize spam and non-spam emails using training datasets. After training, classifiers are tested to check whether they can predict spam (or non-spam) emails accurately with the testing datasets. The result of this classification in terms of accuracy, precision, and recall are evaluated, compared and analyzed, thus providing the best anti-spam solution to counter measure spam problem of Malay language emails.

Chapter 14

The aim of server virtualization is to eliminate the Hardware equipment in the Datacenter and maximize the utilization of the existing resources. This helps companies in achieving the business goals and objectives in cost effective manner and better support and integration. Virtualization technology changes the protection way of security, as most of hardware and software become after virtualization such as servers, switches, Logical Unit Numbers (LUNs) etc. and it's no longer trying to protect a physical hardware, (Hurwitz & et al, 2013). The overall objective of this chapter is to find out the solution for reducing the keep regular increasing recurring cost and risk involved in information technology management and maintenance. The chapter is about finding out the solution from which it's possible to ultimately lower the cost, speed deployment, provide additional disaster recovery options, and ease testing and developing, and provide unprecedented mobility, flexibility and reliability.

Mohammad Alaa Hussain Al-Hamami, Applied Science University, Bahrain

Big Data is comprised systems, to remain competitive by techniques emerging due to Big Data. Big Data includes structured data, semi-structured and unstructured. Structured data are those data formatted for use in a database management system. Semi-structured and unstructured data include all types of unformatted data including multimedia and social media content. Among practitioners and applied researchers, the reaction to data available through blogs, Twitter, Facebook, or other social media can be described as a "data rush" promising new insights about consumers' choices and behavior and many other issues. In the past Big Data has been used just by very large organizations, governments and large enterprises that have the ability to create its own infrastructure for hosting and mining large amounts of data. This chapter will show the requirements for the Big Data environments to be protected using the same rigorous security strategies applied to traditional database systems.

S. Karthik, SNS College of Technology, India
A. Rajiv Kannan, College of Engineering, India

Distributed denial-of-service attacks are a serious threat to the stability and availability of the Internet. Several traceback schemes are available to mitigate these attacks. Along with several IP traceback schemes, a latest one is the DGT in which the tracking is relying on geographical information. Segment direction ratios (SDR) a novel scheme to overcome the directional limitations of 23 DGT is proposed. This scheme is generalized to 2n DGT (n $\geq$ 4).The concepts of DR, DRS and NDRS at a Router point is introduced based on uniqueness theorem. Three dimensional, multi-directional geographical traceback, using direction ratio algorithm (DRA) is proposed to remove the limitations. To overcome directions, dimensions and storage space deficiency, three dimensional multidirectional geographical IP traceback direction ratio sampling algorithm (DRSA) traceback is proposed.

Alaa Hussein Al-Hamami, Amman Arab University, Jordan
Rafal A Al-Khashab, Amman Arab University, Jordan

Cloud computing provides the full scalability, reliability, high performance and relatively low cost feasible solution as compared to dedicated infrastructure. These features make cloud computing more attractive to users and intruders. It needs more and complex security measures to protect user privacy and data centers. The main concern in this chapter is security, privacy and trust. This chapter will give a discussion and a suggestion for using cloud computing to preserve security and privacy. The malicious hacker and other threats are considering the major cause of leaking security of the personal cloud due to centralized location and remote accesses to the cloud. According to attacks, a centralized location can be easier target rather than several goals and remote access is insecure technologies which offer a boundary of options for attackers to infiltrate enterprises. The biggest concern is attackers that will use the remote connection as a jumping point to get deeper into an organization.

Wireless ad hoc networks are susceptible to attacks by malicious nodes that could easily bring down the whole network. Therefore, it is important to have a reliable mechanism for detecting and isolating malicious nodes before they can do any harm to the network. Trust-based routing protocols are one possible mechanism as they locate trusted routes dynamically to conform to network environment. However, such algorithms require reliable and effective trust determination algorithm. This chapter presents a detail description and evaluation of the trust determination algorithm, namely, the Neighbor-Weight Trust Determination (NWTD) algorithm. The performance of the algorithm is evaluated through simulation using the Mobile Ad hoc Network (MANET) simulator (MANSim). The simulation results demonstrated the effectiveness and reliability of the algorithm in isolating any maliciously behaving node(s) in a timely manner.

These days, peoples expected to move around carrying their mobile devices, talking to friends, completing their work, accessing emails etc. His/her pictures, work, study, even relationship (friends, and family) all is in the mobile device. Therefore, mobile devices (especially smart phones) become an ideal target for different attacks. Mobile computing also becomes important in enterprises and organizations. Therefore, it is important to illustrate the state of art on vulnerabilities and threats on mobile device. This chapter is addressed to explain mobile computing concept, features, architecture, operating systems, and risks to mobile devices. Mobile operating system structureand characteristicsare demonstrated. The author also illustrates mobile security issues, and type of threats to mobile devices. Finally, features and security models of two popular smartphone operating systems, Android and iOS, are illustrated. It was found that the security models of these two smartphones is immature and do not meet the enterprises security policies.

Chapter 20

Because of its importance, social media became a main target in cyber war and for criminals as well. The attacker can gain a lot of valued information from social media. This chapter will discuss the security impacts on social media and their effects on individuals, companies, and governments. This chapter, also will explain risks of using Internet, the importance of social media for attackers, what could go wrong in social media, examples of methods used by attackers, why attackers success in their attacks, social media problems from a legal point of view, social media security environment, general security model for social media web sites, data that could be mined, points of attack, security defenses against attacks, methods of security attacks, reasons of attacking social media, social media programming flaws, social media security strategy and policy, social media privacy and governments, social media security new trends, and the best practice in social media.

Chapter 21

Due to the swift growth of the using of the digital multimedia in the internet these days, the security in digital images has become a very important issue. Lately, significant attentions are given by many researchers in the field of the security for digital images, and several image encryption techniques have been developed to improve the security levels of these images. Different techniques can be applied to protect intellectual property rights for digital images and prohibit illegal copying. The aim of this chapter is to introduce the most important techniques that have been developed to implement the security in digital images such as digital watermarking and image steganography.

Preface

Nowadays, the field of security is facing more challenges than ever due to the fact that "Perfect Security does not exist" and to the innovation in e-business applications which need more security and trust in doing business. There is also a fact concerning the new technology: "New technology brings new threats". Also there is "No one single solution for several threat types". So security will continue its mission of promoting high level research efforts and novel applications of specialized research issues. Security constitutes many important topics for novel and future oriented research.

Computer security theories are widely-used in investigating the performance of existing and proposed computer networks security, protocols, algorithms, models, applications, etc. The application of network security can potentially improve the quality and effectiveness of security mechanisms and modeling. It is clear that testing and evaluating security application implementations with real hardware is quite complex in terms of manpower, time, and other resources. The main challenge to counter threats is to model the process as close as possible to reality; otherwise it could produce entirely different performance characteristics from the ones discovered during actual use.

The main objectives of this comprehensive and timely book is to: present state-of-the-art methodologies in networks security, implementation, application and modeling of threats detections and countermeasures; illustrate the benefits of detection and prevention threats applications in computer networks, modeling, and analysis; identify the main issues that face efficient and effective countermeasures implementation in network security; demonstrate by examples how the performance of computer network security can be evaluated; provide cutting edge research on threat detections, preventions and countermeasures of computer security; present different trends in countermeasures (modeling, application, analysis, etc.); discuss the main features of current security applications; point- out the main trends in security evaluation and tools; introduce the most popular academic and professional computer networks security; and finally, provide a complete compilation of the potential problems that may arise during the use of network security and the solutions applied to them.

This book props original material concerned with all aspects of security on network threats detection and prevention, security countermeasures and applications, algorithms analysis, management, implementation, theories, and performance evaluation. The primary mission of the book is to enhance development of the theory and practice of countermeasures in network security and its theories, algorithms, applications and modeling, which are normally appealing to academics, researchers, and professionals. In the information technology age, and with tremendous advancement in computer and communication technologies, network security has become an integral part of many applications and organizations. It is our further aim to provide ample examples to educate organizations in how they can benefit from network security, evaluate the performance, and manage these valuable resources.

Threat Detection and Countermeasures in Network Security is composed of 21 chapters written by highly qualified scholars discussing a wide range of topics, including security concepts, developments and future trends, network intrusion detection system, secret multi agent, authentication model, cryptographic hash function, cybercrime, biometric security, data hiding schemes, cloud computing security, and security in digital images.

Chapter 1, *Security Concepts, Developments, and Future Trends*, discusses the main concepts, developments and future trends of security. There are three main reasons for security development and its innovation. The first reason is: Perfect security does not exist; this will lead the researcher to develop more and more methods to defend against new attacks and to support the existence security systems. The second reason is: New technology always brings new threats, which means new countermeasures against those threats is always a necessity. The third reason is: There is no single countermeasure that can be used to ensure security for our systems, and there are many new threats and attacks need to be defeated. For these reasons, security is very active subject and needs more financial support for research and system development, thoughts, technologies, tools, and skilled people to ensure and maintain security for our systems.

Chapter 2, *Enhance Network Intrusion Detection System by Exploiting BR Algorithm as an Optimal Feature Selection*, aims to build a proposed Wire/Wireless Network Intrusion Detection System (WW-NIDS) to detect intrusions and consider many of modern attacks that are not taken in account previously. The proposed WWNIDS treats intrusion detection with just intrinsic features but not all of them.

Chapter 3, *Automatic Intrusion Detection and Secret Multi Agent Preservation Using Authentication Measurement Network Threat*. The aim of using multi agent framework is to design the proposed automatic intrusion detection model and secret multi agent preservation using authentication measurement network threat. This approach uses statistical models to correlate and analysis data, and takes the decisions to control both local and global agent's data bases perceptively. This chapter also adopts the security problem authentication and authorization by providing a secure distributed agent system.

Chapter 4, *Real Time Internal Intrusion Detection: A Case Study of Embedded Sensors and Detectors in E-Government Websites*, provides a detailed description of a framework for designing, analyzing, deploying, and enforcing high level security management for e-Government website. This is done by using internal sensors and detectors, which are placed at critical points inside the e-Government website source code.

Chapter 5, *Authentication Model for Enterprise Resource Planning Network*. The security issue is one of the major issues with Enterprise Resource Planning (ERP) network software, and it has not been a major focus of the software developers, who leave this issue to different components of the system and to vendor implementation. This chapter presents a new security model for ERP software. It presents a new authentication model that consists of the following layers: role base, data mining, risk-based access control, and public key infrastructure (PKI).

Chapter 6, *Cryptographic Hash Function: A High Level View*. Cryptographic hash function verifies data integrity and sender identity or source of information. The task is accomplished by taking a variable bit patterns as an input then produces a fixed bit patterns of output. This chapter provides a detailed overview to include classification, properties, constructions, attacks, applications, and a selected dedicated cryptographic hash function.

Chapter 7, *Crime Profiling System*, outlines a process for profiling based on self-organizing map (SOM) and evaluating the proposed technique by profiling crimes using a multi-lingual corpus. The development and application of a crime profiling system (CPS) is also presented. The system is able to extract meaningful information (type of crime, location and nationality), from Arabic language crime news reports. The system has two unique attributes; firstly, information extraction depends on local grammar, and secondly, automatic generation of dictionaries.

Chapter 8, *Proposals to Win the Battle against Cyber Crime*, concentrates on explaining and discussing the terms of cyber security, cybercrimes, and cyber-attacks. A history for each term has been given and the problems of cyber security have been discussed. A methodology for the cybercrime is explained. Finally, a proposed solution is suggested and future trends are forecasted, and at the end of the chapter a conclusion is given.

Chapter 9, *Cyber Crimes: Types, Sizes, Defense Mechanism and Risk Mitigation*, an ethic based definition of cyber crime is introduced and cyber crimes are classified. The impact of each class of cyber crime on society, individual, government and international security is highlighted. The cost of cyber crime is evaluated and a technique to prevent and mitigate the effect of these crimes on individual, government and international security and world peace is indicated. The forensic techniques and tools used in cyber crime evidence gathering and prosecuting procedure is also indicated. Finally, recommendations and suggestion are given to mitigate the impact of cyber crime on individuals, societies, world finance and international security.

Chapter 10, *Cyber Space Security Assessment Case Study*, focuses on a variety of techniques, approaches for predicting the cyber security threats which are helpful and marked as the important field of data mining technologies in cyber security. Also it discusses various types of cyber-attacks describing how data mining helps in detection and prevention of these attacks. A comparative analysis between a set of selected frame works is presented. Finally this chapter imparts multiple applications for the data mining methodologies in cyber security.

Chapter 11, *Biometric Security*, focuses on biometric security in their types, specifications, technologies and algorithms. Some algorithms of biometric security are also included in this chapter. Finally latest and future aspects of biometric system and merging technologies are mentioned, including more details of system structures and specifications and what constitution will shape biometric security in the future.

Chapter 12, *Data Hiding Schemes Based on Singular Value Decomposition*, discusses how information hiding techniques are becoming increasingly important, due to the widespread diffusion of multimedia contents. This chapter have tried to highlights the basic properties of singular value decomposition (SVD) and some of its applications in the field of security to encourage researchers to discover more about SVD properties which are not yet utilized.

Chapter 13, *Malay Language Text-Based Anti-Spam System Using Neural Network*, focuses on creating a text-based anti-spam system using back-propagation neural network for Malay Language emails that efficiently and effectively counter measure spam problems. The proposed algorithm consists of three stages; pre-processing, implementation and evaluation. Malay language emails are collected and divided into spam and non-spam. Features are extracted and document frequency as dimension reduction technique is calculated too. Classifiers are trained to recognize spam and non-spam emails using training datasets. After training, classifiers are tested to check whether they can predict spam (or non-spam) emails accurately with the testing datasets. The result of this classification in terms of accuracy, precision, and recall are evaluated, compared and analyzed, thus providing the best anti-spam solution to counter measure spam problem of Malay language emails.

Chapter 14, *Virtualization Technology and Security Challenges*. The aim of server virtualization is to eliminate the hardware equipment in the datacenter and maximize the utilization of the existing resources. One of the most concerns of companies and organizations is how secure is the new environment after transforming into virtualized infrastructure. Many new potential threats and vulnerabilities have to be understood and well managed. Virtualization technology changes the protection way of security, as most of hardware and software become after virtualization such as servers, switches. The overall objective of this chapter is to find out the solution for reducing the keep regular increasing recurring cost and risk involved in information technology management and maintenance. The chapter is about finding out the solution from which it's possible to ultimately lower the cost, speed deployment, provide additional disaster recovery options, and ease testing and developing, and provide unprecedented mobility, flexibility and reliability.

Chapter 15, *The Impact of Big Data on Security*. Big data is very important because most organizations now are accessing and using it. In the past big data has been used just by very large organizations, governments and large enterprises that have the ability to create its own infrastructure for hosting and mining large amounts of data. Big data environments need to be protected using the same rigorous security strategies applied to traditional database systems, such as databases and data warehouses, to support compliance requirements and prevent breaches. This chapter tries to explain the meaning of big data, its importance, its value, the reason behind its emergence, the role of big data in security, security awareness in big data environments, big data security and privacy challenges and issues.

Chapter 16, *16-Directional Geographic Trace Back with Generalization to Three Dimensional Multidirectional Geographic IP Trace Back*. Distributed denial of service (DDoS) attacks, breaking into hundreds of machines all over the Internet, typically exhaust bandwidth, router processing capacity or network stack resources, by breaking network connectivity to the victims. So distributed denialofservice attacks are a serious threat to the stability and availability of the Internet. To thwart these attacks, IP trace back has been proposed where one attempts to reconstruct entire attack path, the attack packets have traversed or focusing only on the source of attack packets, no matter which path they take for assault.

Chapter 17, *A New Approach in Cloud Computing User Authentication*. The main concern in this chapter is security, privacy and trust. This chapter gives a discussion and a suggestion for using cloud computing to preserve security and privacy. This chapter deals with personal cloud which is the basic of the other type of cloud computing deployment, so the security of the personal cloud is the core for the other types of cloud computing deployment models. The malicious hacker and other threats are considering the major cause of leaking security of the personal cloud due to centralized location and remote accesses to the cloud. According to attacks, a centralized location can be easier to target rather than several goals and remote access is insecure technologies which offer a boundary of options for attackers to infiltrate enterprises. The biggest concern is attackers that will use the remote connection as a jumping point to get deeper into an organization.

Chapter 18, *Trust Determination in Wireless Ad Hoc Networks*. Wireless ad hoc networks are susceptible to attack by malicious nodes that could easily bring down the whole network. Therefore, it is important to have a reliable mechanism for detecting and isolating malicious nodes before they can do any harm to the network. Trust-based routing protocols are one possible mechanism as they locate trusted routes dynamically to conform to network environment. However, such algorithms require reliable and effective trust determination algorithm. This chapter presents a detail description and evaluation of the trust determination algorithm, namely, the neighbor-weight trust determination (NWTD) algorithm. The performance of the algorithm is evaluated through simulation using the mobile ad hoc network (MANET) simulator (MANSim). The simulation results demonstrated the effectiveness and reliability of the algorithm in isolating any maliciously behaving node(s) in a timely manner.

Chapter 19, *Security in Mobile Computing*. Mobile computing is a combination of wireless network and computing portability that allows information accessing anytime, from any place, using any mobile device. Mobile computing requires software (mobile application requirements, and data encryptions), hardware (mobility devices and components), and mobile communication issues (network infrastructure, protocols, and communication properties). The main characteristics of mobile computing are portability, data connection, social interactivity, and individuality. Generally, mobile computing suffers from series of specific problems and limitations including scarcity of bandwidth, security standards, power consumption, transmission interferences: potential health hazards and human interface with device. This chapter overviews Android and iOS mobile operating systems which are illustrated along with their security issues and exposing threats to mobile devices. The security model of iOS and Android is constructed based on, authentication, source of application, data encryption, data isolation, authorization access control Securing mobile devices is important to consumers and enterprises, but it is a challenging task. We should always remember that developing highly secured mobile system is very hard task. This is due to the significant increase of vulnerabilities targeting the services and communication channels of mobile devices.

Chapter 20, *The Security Impacts on Social Media Platforms*, discusses the security impacts on social media and their effects on individuals, companies, and government. This chapter, also explains the types of social media, risks of using Internet, the importance of social media for attackers, what could go wrong in social media, examples of methods used by attackers, why attackers success in their attacks, and social media problems from a legal point of view. Also, this chapter discusses social media security environment, general security model for social media web sites, data that could be mined, points of attack, security defenses against attacks, methods of security attacks, reasons of attacking social media, social media programming flaws, social media security strategy and policy, social media privacy and Governments, social media security new trends, and the best practice in social media.

Chapter 21, *Security in Digital Images: From Information Hiding Perspective.*

Due to the swift growth of using the digital multimedia in the internet these days, the security in digital images has become a very important issue. Lately, significant attentions are given by many researchers in the field of the security in digital images, and several image encryption techniques have been developed to improve the security levels of these images. Different techniques can be applied to protect intellectual property rights for digital images and prohibit illegal copying. The aim of this chapter is to introduce the most important techniques that have been developed to implement the security in digital images such as: digital watermarking and image steganography.

Acknowledgment

The editors would like to take this opportunity to express their deep appreciation to the IGI Global team for their significant support and patience. We also like to thank Ms. Jan Travers, director of Intellectual property and Contracts at IGI Global for her support and encouragement. Likewise the editors would like to extend their appreciation to the Development Division at IGI Global, namely Mr. Joel A. Gamon, Development Editor, Editorial Content department, and Ms. Erin O'Dea, Editorial assistant, Development Division.

The editors would like to extend their deep appreciation to Associate Professor Dr. Hussein Al-Bahadili for his help and assistant for all phases in the preparation of the book. The editors conveys their thanks to the Editorial Advisory Board and reviewers for their relentless work and for their constant demand for perfection.

It was our dream to tell the story of security, and it came true in editing this book. We shared our dream with distinguished colleagues who contributed nice and scientific chapters for different topics concerning security. We tried to collect together several topics such as security attacks, threats, and detection and prevention systems. Also this book contains different security applications with different tools such as biometrics, steganography, images, mobile computing, and cryptography. This book is like a garden contains many roses.

Our heartiest thanks and appreciation to the distinguished authors for submitting such valuable and excellent chapters and for their patience during the editing process. We extend our sincerely thanks to the Advisory Board and reviewers for their magnanimous support and for their demand for perfection.

Finally and more importantly we sincerely thank almighty Allah for the gracious presence throughout our life.

Alaa H. Al-Hamami
Amman Arab University, Jordan

Ghossoon M. Waleed Al-Saadoon
Applied Science University, Bahrain

Chapter 1
Security Concepts, Developments, and Future Trends

Alaa Hussein Al-Hamami
Amman Arab University, Jordan

Ghossoon M. Waleed Al-Saadoon
Applied Science University, Bahrain

ABSTRACT

The techniques and tools available for the attackers and protectors are decisive and the main cause for deciding the leading and winning side. This chapter discusses the main concepts, developments, and future trends of security. There are three main reasons for security development and its innovation. The first reason is: Perfect security does not exist; this will lead the researcher to develop more and more methods to defend against new attacks and to support the existence security systems. The second reason is: New technology always brings new threats, which means new countermeasures against those threats is always a necessity. The third reason is: There is no single countermeasure that can be used to ensure security for our systems, and there are many new threats and attacks need to be defeated. For these reasons, security is very active subject and needs more financial support for research and system development, thoughts, technologies, tools, and skilled people to ensure and maintain security for our systems.

INTRODUCTION

These days are called the knowledge era, and every day we hear about new development and an invented new technology. New technology is always brings new threats; this will lead to invent a new counter measure to protect our society from these new threats. Perfect security does not exist, and security strength depends on the weakest ring in the security chain.

Computers and communications are still suffering from their poor security systems that can't stand against the risks of losing or destroying their data files and folders, intrusion of the unauthor-

DOI: 10.4018/978-1-4666-6583-5.ch001

Copyright © 2015, IGI Global. Copying or distributing in print or electronic forms without written permission of IGI Global is prohibited.

ized users and the malfunction of the instruments. These risks can't be ignored; in most organizations protection is still far away from serious actions due to the following reasons (Tanenbaum and Wetherall, 2010):

- **Un-Proper Security Systems:** Most techniques that distinguish authorized users are of equal effect on hindering the unauthorized users.
- **Some Organizations Pride that They Are Protected:** Several computer crimes are uncovered because organization managers hide such crimes to keep the image of their organizations undistorted.
- **Downloading the Technique for Security Problem:** It should be always recognized that security is human problem rather that a technological one.
- **Threat from Inside the Organization:** Most of computer and data threats come from inside the organizations rather than from outside. The computer hackers are most likely one of your employees that receive his/her salary from your organization and not a person who lives away from you.
- The other threat may come from an employee who previously was working for your organization recently, therefore the best security techniques do not usually depend on the technology but depend and focus on the human element.
- Precaution from the problem is not enough, instead, as usual, it is essential to take one step towards the problem-solving given that such step should not be the last one.
- There are always persons believe that there is no issue that is so called "security".

Of course, professionals are still enjoying an important responsibility because they should determine the nature of their organizations data and threat types that face their organizations. Also, they should set and execute plans to protect their

data from such threats. These are the important objectives and they always need a high level of technological knowledge. In the realms of computers and communications, even when completing such high professional objectives, they are insufficient to keep computers and communications security (Stallings, 2004).

BASIC PRINCIPLES IN SECURITY SYSTEM DESIGN

Before discussing the basic principles of the security system design, the common goals that contribute in setting the essential corner stone for the security system design should be identified. The following points may represent essential principles when designing security system:

- The idea of non-existence of integrative security system, and there exist several gaps that should be filled-removed-through taking all possibilities at design stage and set security system review measures at implementation phase that all should be thoroughly recognized.
- Access cost to the information by the intruder should be higher than the cost of information themselves. In this case, deterring is more in preventing the intruder to try access the information.
- The cost and complexity of the designed security system shall be in balance with the value of information protected by it, as much as information value is high, security system will be more complex, and vice versa.
- Information for whom needs: it is necessary to demonstrate as least information as possible that is required to the authenticated person(s), and when transmitting such information from one computer to another.
- Security system shall be able to protect itself from intruder and shall have different

levels of protection in case one level failed, the whole system sustains but one part of it fails and the other parts stay effective.

- Know your enemy: intruders are distinguished in computers by being hackers who have the advanced potentials and high experience in intruding protection systems depending on the modern techniques in design to face such substantial challenge.
- Protection priorities: priorities shall be set for information to be protected and means of protection to be provided. Do not be short-sighted to think in the information stored in your organization only, but think of information sent and received via your organization, as well.

PROTECTION SYSTEM DESIGN

Computer crimes are conducted by people not by machines, therefore, there shall be strong contexts and methods, to face this human element and for the purpose of other security measures. The advanced information age has introduced a new integrative challenge to the managers interested in computers security. Security problem has become public issue that needs serious and integrative methods to solve it. These methods may include (Stallings, 2011).

1. Consider information as a material that has a value to be protected exactly as any other property.
2. Identify the threat for such property (information), determine the type of this information, and the type of threat and by whom?
3. Choose the suitable methods and techniques to face the specific threat.

To design any information security system, a number of typical steps must be applied in identifying the problems and problem solving techniques; these steps may include, but not limited to:

Security Threats

Threats must be identified to prepare the correct precaution and the right measure. In general, it should be remembered that, there is no one measure for all the threats since the technical deficiency in addition to the high cost. For this reason simple threats must be identified so that their treatments would be simple and inexpensive for the invaluable information. Furthermore, some complex threats that their defying methods are complex, as well as, because the information to be protected are of confidential nature and of a high value.

In the statistical yearly reports issued by the National Center for Computers Crime Data (NCCCD), it was found out the business computer crimes in America are billions of US$ per year, and this figure does not include an expected loss of thousands years from individual time or tens of years from computer's time. This cost will be increased due to the continuous development in technology and the invention of new technology. The invention of technology will lead to new types of threats.

There are many types of threats due to the variety of causes for these threats. Some of these types are the following (Douligeris and Serpanos, 2007):

- Infringe (intrude) by a computer especially by employees who work with the affected companies themselves or by x-employees in the company. These attacks are called sometimes as Logical Bombs.
- **Industrial Snooping and the Loss of Industrial Markets:** This threat becomes very important and valuable. Most of the companies pay a lot of money just to countermeasure this threat.
- **Use/Misuse of Money E-Transference:** E-payments now are very reliable due to the high technology used and due to the development and deployed of the E-Commerce.

- **Computer Fails and Data Corruption:** Data integrity plays a key role in decision support system. The correct and right decision is depend on reliable information.
- **Possible Intruding of Privacy:** Using e-mails in business will be encouraged by assuring privacy.

There are several methods to execute the above-mentioned threats; therefore, suitable solution must be applied for each threat. Solution for one of threats might be improper for other threats, for example to solve the company workers threat who are considered (authorized) to use information, control systems must be applied to them but not making them feel that they are untrusted, and at the same time, such systems catch all workers mistakes and misuses.

Also, if the system relies on a communication network, simulation plays an important role in hiding the sent information from intruders. Even for the electromagnetic radiation transmitted from the monitor, it is now possible to recompose what is edited on the screen remotely by cheap devices that can be purchased from local markets for some countries, therefore electromagnetic eaves spread must be prevented by several methods. Some of these methods are: starting from using simple materials such as applying metal networks in the computer hall walls, up to using developed techniques such as (Tempest) to prevent radiation transmitting from monitoring.

For Virus threat, there are several familiar means to fight viruses and destroy them including: Discovery and killing programs (SW), using material cards installed inside the computer, and applying other means such as stimulation to help in discovering and destroying viruses.

Security System Cost

Information value plays a great role in security system design, as much as information value is high, security system will be complex and ex-

pensive. Here, the important rule which says that access cost of such information by the intruder must be more than the information value itself. Some information is extremely important, so in this case assistance should be asked from the advanced technologies of security system design. Cost, effort and complexity are the real cost of protecting such information.

Security system cost remains proportional with the protected information value as security system complexity increases as much as the increase of information (data) value. Complex security system design shall not be exaggerated that require big efforts by the authorized persons in passing through the fire-wall designed by such security system that induce boring at users which in turn leads to the failure of the used application for the lack of flexibility and impeding the course of action. Furthermore, trust must not be adopted as means of protection since security system design should be proportional with the protected information value as the instilled idea among designers that the simple means used in security system protection is sufficient to prevent intruders and protect the information.

Detection

In the security system, detection applicability against intrusion should be available which operates usually simultaneously with security system protection, for example: Security system may provide protection against intrusion or un-authorized log in (Access), also it records failed access attempts to detect the harmful activities and persons who performed such activities, as well. Usually, security system includes a file that records the failed access attempts to the system.

Prevention

Prevention means taking all measures and necessary precautions to prevent stealing or destroying information. Prevention is considered one of the most important theoretical concepts (virtual) that is difficult to important practically because of high relevant precautions costs. Nevertheless, it is considered one of the most important phases of security system design.

Prevention includes many vocabularies starting from erecting firefighting systems, electric generators, stable electrical systems and files copy store unit up to erecting complete computers centers to be alternative to the destroyed centers because of explosion, fire, flood, or other natural disasters such as earth quack.

Deterrence

Proper deterrence must be available for destruction activities because this may lead the destroyers fear detection and accountability against them. This is done through detecting the destructive action and does the proper action to stop the destructive action and take actions against the doers. The first action might be disconnection and inform those in charge (Security Officers) voluntarily through the security system to take the proper measure with documenting the incidence to prove the criminal evidence. Deterrence benefit may appear in the following:

- Reveal Security system potency to detect the detected destructive actions; and also
- To prove that there is a follow-up in taking actions against negligent so that the detected destructive action will not pass without punishment because if this happens, it will encourage intruders to repeat attempts to succeed finally in one intrusion attempt.

System Correction

Weakness points must be detected in security system and continuously correcting such weakness points setting out from the principle that there is no ideal security system without weakness points through which intruders may sneak into therefore,

security system shall be practically tested to detect its points of weakness and treat them. The effectiveness of security system relies on the weakest cycle in it so as much as its cycles (phases) are strong (effective), its composing series will be effective to. On the other hand, if one cycle of security system is weak, it will be easier for the whole security system to fail down.

Trust

Since network security is all about protecting network property and entities from untrustworthy parties, it may sound against logic to discuss the concept 'trust' in network security. A network security scheme can provide the claimed protections from untrustworthy parties only when it is based on a well-defined and realistic trust model.

A trust model is a set of assumptions with respect to each related parties and their relationships. A trust model will identify trusted parties. No security can be provided without depending on at least one trusted party or one trusted condition. Trust is a relative concept. A trusted party is relative to one or multiple other parties. A party could be trusted by others in many different ways and to variable extents. A trusted party must be defined as in which aspects, to which extents, and by whom it is trusted. The relationship between two parties will include whether they can communicate securely in the sense whether they can establish a protected channel via cryptography methods (Ramteke et al, 2013).

A trust model is also a practical concept. It is often, if not always, determined by business relations. For example, a service provider may play the role of a trusted party for the customers. Cryptography keys are distributed based on service registrations. In this case, the trusted party may maintain keys together with other information. Sometimes, a party is called trusted "third" party because it is an independent service and trusted by the other parties.

A trust model for network security must consider its threat environment. That is, in order to establish a trust model, a sensible assessment must be in place regarding what an untrustworthy party can do to attack the network property and each network entity. The assessment may be not precise, since network threat will never appear exactly the same as what we can expect. The assessment must take the physical environment into account. A network may extend to very weird and deserted areas where an attacker can have unlimited potential to access network properties and entities.

In current network security practice, trust models are not usually explicitly defined but extensively used as the bases. Some of the network security protocols with their trust models can be listed as the following:

- **Access Authentication:** It is very important for a service provider to make sure that only eligible users can access the resource.
- **Security Link Establishment:** In network security, the protection methods and cryptography keys between two network nodes may be established through a protocol.
- **Access Domain Mobility:** Mobility makes security not easy. For a cellular network, across-service-domain access authentication is handled by a roaming agreement.

Security Aspects

Security objectives are accomplished through security policies and services. A security policy is the set of criteria that define the provision of security services, where a security service is a service which provided by a layer of communicating open systems, in order to ensure adequate security of the systems or of the data transfers. The security services are implemented by security mechanisms which are in general mechanisms that can be used to technically enforce and implement a security service.

The Open System Interconnection (OSI) security architecture focuses on security attacks, mechanisms, and services. These can be defined briefly as follows:

- **Security Attack:** Any action that compromises the security of information owned by a system or an organization.
- **Security Mechanism:** A process (or a device incorporating such a process) that is designed to detect, prevent, countermeasure or recover from a security attack.
- **Security Service:** A processing or communication service that enhances the security of the data processing systems of an organization. The services are intended to counter security attacks, and they make use of one or more security mechanisms to provide the service.

In the literature, the terms 'threat' and 'attack' are commonly used to mean more or less the same thing. In summary, 'threat' is defined as a potential for violation of security, which exists when there is a circumstance, capability, action, or event that could breach security and cause harm. That is, a threat is a possible danger that might exploit vulnerability. While 'attack' is defined as an assault on system security that derives from an intelligent threat; that is, an intelligent act that is a deliberate attempt (especially in the sense of a method or technique) to evade security services and violate the security policy of a system.

It is possible to define the computer security as: the protection afforded to an automated information system in order to attain the applicable objectives of preserving the integrity, availability and confidentiality of information system resources (includes hardware, software, firmware, information/data, and telecommunications) (Tanenbaum and Wetherall, 2010).

Computer security is both fascinating and complex. Some of the reasons follow:

- Computer security is not as simple as it might first appear to the novice. The requirements seem to be straightforward, but the mechanisms used to meet those requirements can be quite complex and subtle.
- In developing a particular security mechanism or algorithm, one must always consider potential attacks (often unexpected) on those security features. Hence procedures used to provide particular services are often counterintuitive.
- Computer security is essentially a battle of wits between a perpetrator who tries to find holes and the designer and administrator who tries to close them.
- In developing a particular security mechanism or algorithm, one must always consider potential attacks (often unexpected) on those security features. Hence procedures used to provide particular services are often counterintuitive.
- Having designed various security mechanisms, it is necessary to decide where to use them.
- Security mechanisms typically involve more than a particular algorithm or protocol, but also require participants to have secret information, leading to issues of creation, distribution, and protection of that secret information.
- Computer security is essentially a battle of wits between a perpetrator who tries to find holes and the designer and administrator who tries to close them.
- There is a natural tendency on the part of users and system managers to perceive little benefit from security investment until a security failure occurs.
- Security requires regular monitoring, difficult in today's short-term environment.
- Security is still too often an afterthought - incorporated after the design is complete.

- Many users/security administrators view strong security as an impediment to efficient and user-friendly operation of an information system or use of information.

Security Services

The basic security services in communications include the following:

- **Authentication:** It is the assurance that communicating entity is the one claimed using the identification code, and this is very important in network application where the communication is remotely. Authentication Protocols are used to convince parties of each other's identity and to exchange session keys. This service may be used to prove that the claimed identity of a communicating entity is valid (peer entity authentication) or that the claimed source of data unit is valid (data origin authentication). To prevent masquerade and to prevent compromise of session keys, essential identification and session key information must be communicated in encrypted form. This requires the prior existence of secret or public keys that can be used for this purpose.
- **Access Control: Data Confidentiality:** It is characteristic of stopping exposure of information to unauthorized persons or systems and it invents preservation of the privacy users in relating with their information.There are many methods to preserve privacy such as authentication, digital signature, or biometrics (Finger print). This service may include: connectionless confidentiality (when it provides confidentiality in a connectionless service data unit), selective field confidentiality (when it protects selective fields of the data), connection confidentiality (when

it involves all the layers of the communication), and traffic flow confidentiality (when it protects information that could be potentially derived from observation of traffic flows).

- **Data Integrity:** It is the assurance that data received is unchanged by unknown or unauthorized entity as sent by an authorized entity. This service may have several forms. Connection integrity with recovery provides integrity of the data and also detects modification, insertion, deletion, and replay of data. Selective field connection integrity provides integrity for selective data fields within a connection.

- **Nonrepudiation:** It is the protection against denial by one of the parties in a communication and this is very important in e-commerce applications. The security procedures offer many methods to prove the correctness of the process and prevent any denial from any one of the parties to the contract. This service may take one or both of two forms. With nonrepudiation with proof of delivery the sender of data is provided with proof of the delivery of data, so that the receiver cannot later deny having received the particular data. With nonrepudiation with proof of origin the recipient of data is provided with the proof of the origin of data, so that the sender cannot later deny that he or she sent the particular data.

Security Mechanisms

Mechanism is a feature designed to detect, prevent, or recover from a security attack. No single mechanism that will support all services required. Security mechanisms are the specific means of implementing one or more security services. These can also be divided into several categories:

- **Authentication Mechanisms:** Data Authentication refers to protecting the source(s) of information from the modification or alteration by an adversary. With data authentication, one can distinguish between the original message sent by the intended sender and adversary. Authentication mechanisms may be based on cryptographic techniques and trust infrastructures such as Public Key Infrastructure (PKI), Biometrics, passwords, and smart cards.

- **Encryption Mechanisms:** The encryption mechanisms can complement a number of other security mechanisms. These mechanisms provide data privacy services by transforming the data to forms not readable by unauthorized entities. The encryption algorithms are generally divided into symmetric (or single key), where the same single key is used for both encryption and decryption, and asymmetric (or public key), where two keys are used. The public key for the encryption and the private key for decryption.

- **Digital Signatures:** Digital Signatures (DSs) are the electronic equivalent of ordinary signatures in electronic data. Such mechanisms are constructed by properly applying asymmetric ciphering. The deciphering of a data unit with the private key of an entity corresponds to the signature procedure of the data unit. The result is the digital signature of the particular data unit produced by the holder of the private key. The ciphering of the generated digital signature with the corresponding public key of the particular entity corresponds to the verification procedure. DSs provide the ability to: verify author, date and time of signature, authenticate message contents. DS can be verified by third parties to resolve disputes. DS can be used to provide peer entity authentication and data origin authentication, data integrity, and nonrepudiation services. DS must depend on the message signed, must use information unique to sender (to prevent both forgery and denial), must be relatively easy to produce, and must be relatively easy to recognize and verify. DS must be computationally infeasible to forge (with new message for existing digital signature and with fraudulent digital signature for given message), and must be practical save DS in storage.

- **Data Integrity Mechanisms:** These mechanisms provide data integrity services by appending some kind of checksums to the data which may prove alteration of the data. Data integrity may involve a single data unit or field or a stream of data units or fields. The Message Authentication Codes (MACs) and the DSs can be used as data integrity mechanisms.

- **Access Control Mechanisms:** The access control mechanisms are used to provide access control services. The access control mechanisms may also report unauthorized access attempts as part of a security audit trail. These mechanisms may use the authenticated identity of an entity or other information related with an entity (e.g., membership, or capabilities of the entity) in order to determine and enforce the access rights of the entity.

- **Traffic-Padding Mechanisms:** These mechanisms can be effective only if the traffic padding is protected by a confidentiality service. These mechanisms provide protection from traffic analysis attacks. Several network protocols and security mechanisms include padding mechanisms to protect the exchanged communication.

- **Routing Control Mechanisms:** Hackers, viruses, and malicious programs frequently exploit the security vulnerabilities of routing protocols in order to launch network

security attacks (Subashini and Kavitha, 2011). These mechanisms allow the selection of a specific route for the communicating data, either dynamically or statistically through prearranged routes. Moreover, by applying security policies, data carrying certain security labels may be routed through certain sub-networks, relays, or links.

- **Notarization Mechanisms:** Notarization mechanisms are used to assure the integrity, the source or destination, and the time of sending or delivering of transmitted data. A notarization mechanism may be supported by other mechanisms such as digital signatures, encryption or integrity mechanisms.Such assurance mechanisms may be part of the networking protocols in use and/or of a trusted third party which may be used to assure the communication consistency and nonrepudiation.

Security Attacks

It is any action that compromises the security of information owned by an organization. Information security is about how to prevent attacks, or failing that. To detect attacks on information-based systems often 'threat' and 'attack' used to mean same thing have a wide range of attacks can focus of generic types of attacks passive and active.

Threats and attacks may involve any layer in the OSI architecture, from the physical to the application. It is possible that a successful attack in one layer may render useless the security measures taken in the other layers. Some basic security attacks are described in the following (Kotzanikolaou et al, 2006):

- **Spoofing Attacks:** Spoofing is the act of a subject asserting an identity that the subject has no right to use. A simple instance of this type of attacks is Internet Protocol (IP) spoofing, through which a system is convinced that it is communicating with a known entity and thus provides access to the attacker. The attacker sends a packet with an IP source address of a known trusted host by altering the packet at the transport layer. The target host may be delivered and accept the modified packet as valid.

- **Eavesdropping Attacks:** These attacks consist of the unauthorized interception of network communication and the disclosure of the exchanged information. This can be performed in several different layers – for example, in the network layer by sniffing into the exchanged packets or in the physical layer by physically wire-tapping the access medium (cabling or wireless medium).
- **Logon Abuse Attacks:** A successful logon abuse attack would bypass the authentication and access control mechanisms and allow a user to obtain access with more privileges than authorized.
- **Intrusion Attacks:** These types of attacks focus on unauthorized users gaining access to a system through the network. Such an attack would target specific vulnerabilities in assets. For example, a typical Web server intrusion attack is a buffer overflow attack, which occurs when a Web service receives more data than it has been programmed to handle and thus reacts in unexpected and unpredicted ways.
- **Hijacking Attacks:** These attacks are essentially attempts to gain unauthorized access to a system by using a legitimate entity's existing connection. For example, at the session layer, if a user leaves an open session, this can be subject to session hijacking by an attacker. An example of session hijacking is the TCP sequence number attack: this attack exploits the communication session which was established between the target host and a legitimate host

that initiated the session. The attacker hijacks the session of the legitimate host by predicting a sequence number selected by the target host, which is used by the TCP.

- **Denial-of-Service (DoS) Attacks:** These attacks attempt to exhaust the network or server resources in order to render it useless for legitimate hosts and users. A more advance type is the Distributed Denial-of-Service (DdoS) attacks, where the attacker uses resources from a distributed environment against a target host. Some well-known DoS attacks are as follows:
- **Application-Level Attacks:** Examples of these attacks include malicious software attacks (viruses, Trojans, etc), Structure Query Language (SQL) injection, and cross-site scripting (XXS). These attacks are concerned with the exploitation of weakness in the application layer and really focus on intrusion attacks in most cases- for example, security weaknesses in the Web server, in the specific technology used in the website, or in faulty controls in the filtering of an input on the server side.
  - **Ping of Death:** This is an early DoS attack in which an attacker sends a ping request that is larger than 65536 bytes, which is the maximum allowed size for the IP, causing the system to crash or restart. Such attacks are not in use today, since most operating systems have implemented measures against it.
  - **SYN Attack:** This causes the attacked system to crash, while waiting for the proper acknowledgments of the initial requests. In a SYN attack, the attacker exploits the inability of a server process to handle unfinished connection requests, but it does not respond when the server answers those requests.

SECURITY APPLICATIONS

Security is very important part of our life and an essential integral part of our society. Life becomes very difficult without security. Applications couldn't survive without security. We mean by security is to preserve privacy, authenticity, rights and duties of people. We will introduce some of the security applications and of course there are many could be mentioned under this title. Some of these applications are:

Secure Architectures with Active Networks

Active networking is a relatively new networking technology that adds programming capability to network nodes and to datagram traveling in the network. The result is a dynamic, adaptive network that can offer a number of advantages such as dynamic creation and execution of network services, customized network functions, interoperability, user control and programmability, and distributed processing and management. Applications that can benefit from active networks include online cashing such as for auction systems and stock servers, network management, congestion control, multicasting, and intelligent mobile agents.

The aim of this application is to make the active networking used in deploying security effectively and how can secure technologies be used to make active network applications more secure. Active networking technology has been used to design two secure architectures. The first is an adaptive Virtual Private Network (VPN) framework that can offer flexible, portable services and customizable VPN mechanisms to provide on-demand secure tunnels in a dynamic environment. The second is a novel architecture for deploying secure multicasting on a VPN through the use of active networks. The secure active multicast architecture implements four modules for handling the security issues in multicasting: group management, authentication, stream handling, and secure packets delivery (Gehrmann et al, 2004).

Security in E-Services and Applications

Electronic Service (e-service) computing is an evolution of Internet Computing. The e-service paradigm, leveraging a service-oriented architecture, focuses on building reliable service environments through strong relationships between participants. The paradigm shift from goods-based services to service-based services has significant implications for new security requirements for e-service that shift the focus from data to process (people). Thus, it is essential to identify the impact of e-services on individuals, organizations, and society and to understand requirements of the infrastructure and technologies needed for providing secure e-services.

In order to ensure the execution of secure e-service through the interactions over the networks and the integrity of the involved participants, the important security issues are identified as follows: from the primitive (e.g., authentication, data integrity, data confidentiality) to the more complex (e.g., nonrepudiation, trust) and from the participant's perspective (e.g., privacy, user anonymity, user location traceability) to the process's (auditability, subsequent service requirement). It is possible to explore the challenging research issues on e-service security using actual instances of applications to e-finance, e-government, and so on.

E-service security is still an open and emerging topic, and thus a final review cannot be given yet. Consequently, we exemplarily present current solutions through existing applications and outline a possible model of the requirements for e-service security and the general e-service paradigm with its problems and its potential (Bashar et al, 2011).

In the future, the requirement for more complex e-services will emerge for a wide variety of applications. In addition, many new applications and constraints will be introduced. More reliable emerging technologies such as biometric authentication and smart cards should be incorporated in future e-services for better authentication and nonrepudiation services. An integrated electronic solution (e-solution) with multiple interdependent e-services from a single provider will be common practice in future e-solution.

As the world is already in the wireless era, the demand for use of e-services from mobile phones or Personal Digital Assistants (PDA) will be seen in near future (m-commerce, m-government, etc.). For comprehensive security of the systems, physical security of the mobile devices will play a vital role. Cloning of Subscriber Identity Modules (SIMs) in the cellular phones has been a threat to cellular phone service providers in the past. In order to protect the cryptographic keys and other secret information, secure, tamper-proof hardware will be essential.

Security in Web Services

Web services connect computer and devices with each other using widely accepted standards such as HTTP (Hyper Text Transfer Transport protocol) and XML (eXtensible markup Language) aimed at addressing interoperability issues between different domains within independent environments. Web services can be defined as software objects that can be assembled over the Internet using standard protocols to perform functions or execute business processes. The key in offering Web services is the ability to create on-the-fly services through the use of loosely coupled, reusable software components (Shama and Ojha, 2010).

Web services offer application-to-application interaction via defined formats and protocols in a platform-independent and language-neutral manner. The term Web services is also often used to denote a set of base protocols (related technologies) such as SOAP, WSDL, and UDDI, which form the initial specification for Web services (Bashar et al, 2011):

- **Simple Object Access Protocol (SOAP):** Defines the run time message that contains the service request and response. SOAP is independent of any particular transport and implementation technology.

- **Web Services Description Language (WSDL):** Describes a Web service and the SOAP messages it understands. WSDL provides a structured way to describe what a service does, paving the way for automation.

- **Universal Discovery, Description, Integration (UDDI):** UDDI is a cross-industry initiative to create a standard for service discovery together with a registry facility that facilitates the publishing and discovery processes.

In today's software infrastructures there is a need for a comprehensive Web services security architecture providing end-to-end message security to cope with all security issues related to the above objectives. End-to-end message security is established when a message that traverse multiple application intermediaries within and between different security domains is secure over the entire route. This approach can be used by itself or it can be combined with an existing transport-level security solution offering point-to-point security such as Secure Socket Layer (SSL)/Transport Layer Security (TLS) providing a comprehensive suite of security capabilities (Al-Bakri et al, 2011).

It is possible to put a framework of more specific Web services security mechanisms and standards which are in the process of being developed by the industry in order to address gaps between existing security standards and Web services. These Web services security specifications address single-message, end-to-end security by providing a general-purpose mechanism for associating security tokens with messages.

Secure Multicasting

The vast majority of traffic in computer networks is unicast traffic, meaning that each packet has exactly one source and one destination. For applications that require the same data being distributed to many recipients, a more suitable form of communication is multicast. Multicast traffic has one source but its destination is not a single host but instead a group of hosts. When a node on the network joins a multicast group, it will receive all the data sent to that group.

Multicast communication is a very efficient method of distributing data to a group of recipients over a computer network. The dominant services of the Internet today are based on unicast networking, but there is a growing need for the adoption of Internet Protocol (IP) multicast as it is much better suited for various modern applications when a very large number of users is involved. One of the main reasons for the limited adoption of multicast is the lack of reliable security mechanisms for the protection of the transmitted data. Applications (but also providers and users) that use multicast networking often have the same security requirements as their unicast counterparts, namely the assurance for data integrity, authentication, and confidentiality depending on the nature of the application (Wood and Stankovic, 2002).

The advantage of using multicast instead of unicast is that packets are replicated only when this is needed in order to minimize the load on the network, the routers, and the sender (commonly a server). Each router receives only one version of the data for each multicast group.

Voice over IP Security

With the rapid expansion of computer networks during the past few years, transferring voice over the data network has gained quick popularity. Voice over Internet Protocol (VoIP) is a rapidly emerging technology for voice communication that uses the ubiquity of IP-based network to deploy VoIP –enabled devices in enterprise and home environments. VoIP-enabled device such as desktop and mobile IP phones and gateways, decrease the cost of voice and data communication, enhance existing features, and add compelling new telephony features and services.

SECURITY ALGORITHMS

There are many algorithms can be used in design, implementation, application, test, and evaluation for the security systems. These algorithms assist in making easy life for the designer and the security implementers. Most of the donkey works in computer systems will be done by those algorithms.

There was a great interest between researchers to generate search algorithms that find near-optimal solutions in reasonable running time. The Swarm-based Algorithm is a search algorithm capable of locating good solutions efficiently. The algorithm could be considered as belonging to the category of Intelligent Optimization Tools.

If an optimization problem has a single optimum, Swarm-based Optimization Algorithm (SOA) population members can be expected to join to that optimum solution. If an optimization problem has multiple optimal solutions, SOA can be used to capture them in its final populations. SOA includes (Bashar et al, 2011):

- The Ant Colony Optimization (ACO) algorithm.
- Ant Colony Optimization (ACO) Bees Algorithm (BA).

ACO is a very successful algorithm which emulates the behavior of real ants. Ants are capable of finding the shortest path from the food source to their nest using a chemical substance called pheromone to guide their search. A passing lost ant will follow this trail depends on the quality of the pheromone laid on the ground as the ants move. Example of ACO algorithms are:

- **The Particle Swarm Optimization (PSO) Algorithm:** It is an optimization procedure based on the social behavior of group of organizations (for example the flocking of birds and the schooling of fish). Individual solutions in a population are viewed as "particles" that evolve or change their positions with time. Some researchers proposed a Particle swarm Optimizer as a tool for Data Mining. They found that Particle Swarm Optimizers proved to be a suitable candidate for classification tasks.

- **The Genetic Algorithm (GA):** GA is based on natural selection and genetic recombination. It works by choosing solutions from the current population and then apply genetic operations (such as mutation and crossover) to create a new population. GA exploits historical information to speculate on new search areas with improved performance. GA performs global search.

Data Mining, Artificial Immune system, steganography, cryptography, and other algorithms are used in security applications for the intrusion or protection or both. We can use several algorithms such as Data Mining or Ant colony in Intrusion detection and prevention. We can use Cryptography and steganography in preserving security, privacy, Integrity, and Non-repudiation.

NEW SECURITY DIRECTIONS

Security is a hot topic and developed very fast due to many reasons such as: it is a challenge between the bad and good guise. Most of the electronic applications need security in their implementations and operations. There is a necessity for the security new developments, concepts, and techniques. We have to invent new methods and algorithms to protect our society and public. We can list the following thoughts for the researchers to concentrate for developing reliable security systems:

- Develop hybrid algorithms that combine more than one algorithm to develop single efficient algorithm through the excluding all disadvantages of the individual algorithms and use the advantages of them.

- It is possible for the researchers and developers to use Software Engineer in designing the security programs by making these programs immune for violations and have their own protection. Also these programs must have their commands and reactions to the accidents by making them more intelligent and independent.

- We have to educate people that security is very important subject and make them following all the security instructions in their used applications or dealing with the databases.

- Designing a security system for any application must be follows the stated characteristics in previous sections. Cost is very important and must be balanced with the information value.

- More and more of algorithms will be used in the developed security systems. The purpose is to reduce the cost of searching, processing, and auditing. This reduction in cost will make the application faster, less cost, and applicable for more people or organizations.

- Most of the end users will use Mobile device; developers must pay attention to this device by improving the security application on it. The important thing is to combine the owner characteristic with the applications to have an authorized access; otherwise it is normal to lose the mobile device and can be used by another person easily.

- We suggest that security system is including within the desired application, and user here is just to open it by his/her magic tool (may be a simple password, Digital signature, Finger print, a combination of two tools,……etc).

- Threat always comes from inside the organization; developers must consider the importance of the auditing systems and make the security systems tied with business rules and recording every transaction in addition to applying the security standards.

- The new developments in applications and services such as GRID Network, Cloud Computing, etc., force the developers to find new methods and techniques against the new threats.
- Distribution of enforcement functionality allows more flexibility in defining security policies that accurately map the needs of organization. At the same time, the complexity of managing such security policies increases considerably. The increasing use of wireless networks that topologically reside inside an organization's security perimeter further complicates management.
- IPSec is a promising Internet security solution that is likely to be widely deployed over the Internet in the near future due to its capability, superiority over transport- and applications-level security solutions, and it's easier large-scale deployment as it requires far fewer IPSec-complaint devices compared to the number of devices in the Internet.

REFERENCES

Al-Bakri, S. H., Mat Kiah, M. L., Zaidan, B. B., & Gazi, M. A. (2011). Securing peer-to-peer mobile communications using public key cryptography: New security strategy. *International Journal of the Physical Sciences*, 6(4), 930–938.

Bashar, A., Almohammad, , & Gheorghita, G. (2011). Information hiding in SOAP messages: A steganographic method for web services. *International Journal for Security Research*, 1(1/2), 61–70.

Douligeris, C., & Serpanos, D. N. (2007). *Network Security: Current Status and Future Directions*. New York, USA: John Wiley & Sons, Inc. doi:10.1002/0470099747

Gehrmann, C., Mitchell, C., & Nyberg, K. (2004). Manual Authentication for wireless devices. *CryptoBytes*, 7(1), 29–37.

Kotzanikolaou, P., Mavropodi, R., Douligeris, C., & Chrissikopoulos, V. (2006). Secure distributed intelligent networks. *Elsevier Computer Communications*, 29(3), 325–336.

Ramteke, S. P., Karemore, P. S., & Golait, S. S. (2013). Privacy preserving and access control to intrusion detection in cloud system. *International Journal of Innovative Research in Computer and communication Engineering*, 1(1), 21–29.

Sharma, A., & Ojha, A. (2010). Implementation of cryptography for privacy preserving data mining. *International Journal of Database Management Systems*, 2(3), 57–65. doi:10.5121/ijdms.2010.2306

Stallings, W. (2004). *Network security essentials: Applications and standards* (4th ed.). Upper Saddle River, NJ: Prentice-Hall.

Stallings, W. (2011). *Cryptography and network security: Principle and practices* (5th ed.). Upper Saddle River, NJ: Prentice-Hall.

Subashini, S., & Kavitha, V. (2011). A Survey on security issues in service delivery models of cloud computing. *Journal of network and Computer Application*, 34(1), 1-11.

Tanenbaum, A. S., & Wetherall, D. J. (2010). *Computer Networks* (5th ed.). Upper Saddle River, NJ: Prentice-Hall.

Wood, A. D., & Stankovic, J. A. (2002). Denial of service in sensor networks. *IEEE Computer*, 35(10), 54–62. doi:10.1109/MC.2002.1039518

Xiaohui, L., & Chun, C. (2011). The Study on Privacy Preserving Data Mining for Information Security. *International Conference on Future Information Technology (IPCSIT)*, Vol. 13.

KEY TERMS AND DEFINITIONS

Computer Security: A generic name for the collection of tools designed to protect data and to thwart hackers.

Intrusion Prevention: Prevention means taking all measures and necessary precautions to prevent stealing or destroying information.

Protection: The measure to be taken against any threats.

Security System Cost: A balance between the complexity of the security system and the value of the assets.

Security Techniques: Any technique used to stop the attack.

Threats: Detection applicability against intrusion should be available which operates usually simultaneously with security system protection.

Trust: The resistance of the security system to the threats.

Chapter 2
Enhance Network Intrusion Detection System by Exploiting BR Algorithm as an Optimal Feature Selection

Soukaena Hassan Hashem
University of Technology, Iraq

ABSTRACT

This chapter aims to build a proposed Wire/Wireless Network Intrusion Detection System (WWNIDS) to detect intrusions and consider many of modern attacks which are not taken in account previously. The proposal WWNIDS treat intrusion detection with just intrinsic features but not all of them. The dataset of WWNIDS will consist of two parts; first part will be wire network dataset which has been constructed from KDD'99 that has 41 features with some modifications to produce the proposed dataset that called modern KDD and to be reliable in detecting intrusion by suggesting three additional features. The second part will be building wireless network dataset by collecting thousands of sessions (normal and intrusion); this proposed dataset is called Constructed Wireless Data Set (CWDS). The preprocessing process will be done on the two datasets (KDD & CWDS) to eliminate some problems that affect the detection of intrusion such as noise, missing values and duplication.

INTRODUCTION

Intrusion is any set of deliberate, unauthorized, inappropriate, and/or illegal activities by perpetrators either inside or outside an organization, which can be deemed a system penetration, that attempt to compromise the integrity, confidentiality or availability of a system resource (Hashem, 2013). An Intrusion Detection is a security mechanism that monitors and analyzes network or computer system events to provide real-time warnings for unauthorized access to system resources or to archive log and traffic information for later analysis. The detection of intrusion (intrusion attempts) operates on logs or other information available from the computer system or the network. ID is an important component of infrastructure of protection mechanisms (Majeed et al, 2013).

DOI: 10.4018/978-1-4666-6583-5.ch002

Copyright © 2015, IGI Global. Copying or distributing in print or electronic forms without written permission of IGI Global is prohibited.

Intrusion Detection System is software, hardware or a combination of both that monitors and collects system and network information and analyzes it to determine if an intrusion has occurred. Snort is an open source IDS available to the general public. IDS may have different capabilities depending upon how complex and sophisticated the components are. Inevitably, the best intrusion prevention system will fail. Thus a system's second line of defense is IDS, and this had Bee Ranker (BR) n which is the focus of much research in recent years (Majeed et al, 2013).

Data Mining-based ID techniques generally fall into two main categories: 'misuse detection' and 'anomaly detection'. In misuse detection systems, patterns of well-known attacks are used to match and identify known intrusion. These techniques are able to automatically retrain ID models on different input data that include new types of attacks, as long as they have BR n labeled appropriately. Unlike signature-based IDSs, models of misuse are created automatically, and can be more sophisticated and precise than manually created signatures. A base stone of misuse detection techniques strength is their high degree of Precision in detecting known attacks and their variations. Misuse detection techniques in general are not effective contra new attacks that have no matched rules or models yet. Anomaly detection, on the other hand, builds models of normal behavior, and flags observed activities that deviate significantly from the established normal usage profiles as anomalies, that is, possible intrusions. Anomaly detection techniques thus identify new types of intrusions as diversions from usual usage. Anomaly detection techniques can be effective contra unknown or new attacks since no *a priori* knowledge about fixed intrusions are required. However, anomaly-based IDSs tend to generate more false alarms than misuse-based IDSs because an anomaly can just be a new normal behavior. Some IDSs use both anomaly and misuse detection techniques (Zhou & Zhao, 2013).

DARPA'99 "KDD'99 dataset" which represents the most widely used dataset for the evaluation of ID methods since 1999. This dataset is prepared by Stolfo et al. and is built based on the data captured in DARPA'98 IDS evaluation program. The most used is 10% KDD'99 dataset, available in Notepad format at (Bensefia and Ghoualmi, 2011) and it consists of thousands connection session. Each session has 41 features and is labeled as either normal or an intrusion, with exactly one specific attack type. There are four attacks categories these are: Denial of Service Attack (DoS), User to Root Attack (U2R), Remote to Local Attack (R2L), and Probing Attack. KDD'99 features can be classified into three groups: Basic features, Content features, and Traffic features (Lee et al, 1999; The UCI, 1999).

Feature selection, also known as "subset selection" or "variable selection", is an important pre-processing step used in data mining and machine learning because it treat huge no. of data with many attributes, where a subset of the features available from the original data are selected for posterior application of a learning algorithm. Feature selection is the most critical step in constructing intrusion detection models since it tend to reduce, if possible, number of features (attributes) and select the most intrinsic of these features in the classification decision, and hence to reduce the computation time of implementing the classification algorithms. Feature selection was proven to have a significant impact on the performance of the classifiers, since it can reduce the building and testing time of a classifier by reasonable percent that according many of previous experiments and researches (Majeed et al, 2013).

The Bee Ranker (BR) Algorithm is a new population-based search algorithm that mimics the food foraging behavior of swarms of honey BR s. In its basic version, the algorithm performs a kind of 'neighborhood search' combined with 'random search' and can be used for optimization problems (Hashem et al, 2013).

WLANs suffer from a lot of security weakness points, some of these weakness points are already found in usual wired networks and others weakness points are new as a consequent to the broadcast connection medium. These weakness points include confidentiality, integrity and availability vulnerabilities. There are many security enhancements for WLAN were added to the IEEE 802.11 standards such as: Wired Equivalent Privacy (WEP), Wi-Fi Protected Access (WPA) and IEEE 802.11i (WPA2). These protocols can protect the data of frames only to provide the confidentiality and the integrity security principles. The management and control frames still suffer from weakness in security (Barhoo, & Elshami, 2011).

Many of weakness point are founded in link layer level of the 802.11 protocol. Many 802.11-specific attacks were analyzed and characterized to introduce a real threat to network availability. Most of the attacks on WLAN are:

- **Deauthentication Attack:** The attacker imitates a deauthentication frame as if it had originated from the base station (Access Point). Up on reception, the station disconnects and tries to reconnect to the base station again. This process is repeated indefinitely to keep the station disconnected from the base station.
- **ChopChop Attack:** The attacker intercepts an encryption frame and uses the Access Point to estimate the clear text. The attack is performed as follows: The intercepted encrypted frame is chopped from the last byte. Then, the attacker builds a new frame 1 byte smaller than the original frame.
- **Fragmentation Attack:** The attacker sends a frame as a successive set of fragments. The access point will assemble them into a new frame and send it back to the wireless network.

- **Duration Attack:** The attacker exploit a weakness points in the virtual carrier-sense mechanism and sends a frame with the NAV field set to a high value (32 ms) (Tulasi & Ravikanth, 2011 ; Lalli & Palanisamy, 2013).

LITERATURE REVIEW

- In (Ahmad et al, 2011) Ahmad I. et al, suggest to select features with combination of two methods and these are Principle Component analysis (PCA) and Genetic Algorithm (GA) is used to search the principal feature space for genetic eigenvectors that offers a subset of features with optimal power. Using both of PCA and GA for feature selection and Multilayer Preceptor MLP for classification purpose. Consequently, that gives effective intrusion detection which is capable to reduce number of features and raise the detection rates.
- In (Reedy et al, 2011) Reddy E. K. et al, give a view about network security technology and point to modern intrusion detection applications facing complex problem, because these applications must be reliable, scalable, management easy, and have no high cost for maintenance. Data mining used in intrusion detection systems, since it demonstrated high accuracy, good generalization to novel types of intrusion, and robust behavior in a changing environment. There are many significant weakness points exist in the production quality of IDSs.
- In (Bensefia & Ghoualmi, 2011) Bensefia H. et al., suggest a strategy to adapting NIDS using both Simple Connectionist Evolving System (SECOS) and a Winner-Takes-All (WTA) hierarchy of XCS (modern Classifier System). They integrate

(SECOS and WTA) to put in relief an adaptive hybrid intrusion detection core that plants the adaptability as an intrinsic and native functionality in the IDS.

- In (Vaarandi, 2011) Vaarandi R., suggested a proposed unsupervised machine learning using data mining as dependable method for NIDS classification. With data mining all pattern is mined from NIDS logs and treated automatically, in order to build an careful classifier. The classifier is then used in online environment for distinctive important IDS alerts from highly occurring false positives and events of low importance.

- In (Vaarandi & Podins, 2010) Vaarandi R. et al., they introduce a new unsupervised machine learning real time warn classification strategy which is based on high occurrence item set mining and data clustering techniques. Their method applies a frequent item set mining algorithm to past IDS alert logs, in order to find patterns that describe redundant alerts. After that, data clustering methods are used for finding detailed sub patterns for each detected pattern. Finally, the detected knowledge is explained and used for real time classification of IDS alerts, in order to characterize critical alerts from irrelevant ones.

- In (Mohammad et al, 2011) Mohammad M. N. et al., introduce an enhanced method for IDS based on combining data mining and expert system aim to design and develop intelligent data mining-based intrusion detection system and its base stone a composite detection strategy with both anomaly and misuse detection work serially to detect the user's activity in turn. The system collects the data of database audit system in real time, analyzes the audit data, judges that it is a normal behavior, abnormal behavior or aggressive behavior and responds to the result

obtained by the operation behavior and finally reports the result to the manager in a comprehensible form.

- In (Guojun et al, 2011) Guojun Z. et al., presented NIDS based on IPv6 to address the challenges of this new environment, system is four dimensions: tracking the flow of data and analysis, capturing packets and rules matching, disaster recovery, and blocking. The technique of ID is introduced into the system for realizing the coordination control among parts. The system has a perfect detection rating.

- In (Al-Janabi & Saeed, 2011), They proposed an anomaly based IDS that can promptly detect and classify various attacks. Anomaly-based IDSs need to be able to learn the unstable behavior of users or systems. The proposed IDS experimenting with packet behavior as parameters in anomaly ID. There are several methods to assist IDSs to learn system's behavior, the proposed IDS uses a back propagation Artificial Neural Network (ANN) to learn system's behavior and uses the KDD CUP'99 dataset in its experiments and the obtained results satisfy the work objective.

- In (Haldar et al, 2010), Haldar N. et al presented IDS which employs usage of classification methods to model the usage patterns of authenticated users and uses it to detect intrusions in wireless networks. The key idea behind the proposed IDS is the identification of discriminative features from user's activity data and using them to identify intrusions in wireless networks. The detection module uses statistical methods to accumulate interested statistical variables and compares them with the thresholds derived from users' activities data. When the variables exceed the predestined thresholds, an alarm is put forward to alert about a sensible intrusion in the network.

- In (Baig & Kumar, 2011), they introduced proposal for feature selection using IGR ranking as a means to compute the relevance of each feature and the k-means classifier to select the optimal set of 802.11 MAC layer features that can improve the detection rate of intrusion detection systems while minimize the learning time of learning algorithm. The reducing of the feature set for wireless intrusion detection systems will improve the performance and learning time of different types of classifiers. They try three types of ANN architectures, the results are concentrate on high accuracy of NIDS obtained by detection engine based on intrinsic features of 802.11 MAC layer.

- In (Neelakantan et al, 2011) Neelakantan N. P. et al., introduced a proposed NIDS for wireless network 802.11, but without using the features of MAC layers just depend on transport layer and network layer. the results were reasonable but some of attacks, especially those related to data link layer cannot be recognized and never detected.

- In (Gupta et al, 2011) Gupta V. et al., analyze attacks that deny channel access by causing pockets of congestion in mobile ad hoc networks. Such attacks would essentially prevent one or more nodes from accessing or providing specific services. In particular, we focus on the properties of the popular medium access control (MAC) protocol, the IEEE 802.11x MAC protocol, which enable such attacks. They consider various traffic patterns that an intelligent attacker(s) might generate in order to cause denial of service. They show that conventional methods used in wire-line networks will not be able to help in prevention or detection of such attacks. Our analysis and simulations show that providing MAC layer fairness alleviates the effects of such attacks.

- In (Lakhina et al, 2010) Lakhina S. et al, presented a new hybrid algorithm (principal component analysis neural network algorithm) is used to reduce the number of computer resources, both memory and CPU time required to detect attack. The PCA (Principal Component Analysis) transform used to reduce the feature and trained neural network is used to identify the any kinds of new attacks. Test and comparison are done on NSL-KDD dataset. It is a new version of KDD99.

- In (Peddabachigaria et al, 2005) Peddabachigaria S. et al., presents two hybrid approaches for modeling IDS. Decision Trees (DT) and Support Vector Machines (SVM) are combined as a hierarchical hybrid intelligent system model (DT–SVM) and an ensemble approach combining the base classifiers. The hybrid intrusion detection model combines the individual base classifiers and other hybrid machine learning paradigms to maximize detection accuracy and minimize computational complexity. Empirical results illustrate that the proposed hybrid systems provide more accurate intrusion detection systems.

- In (Depren et al, 2005) Depren O. et al., propose a novel Intrusion Detection System (IDS) use hybrid anomaly and misuse detection technique. This hybrid IDS contain an anomaly detection engine, a misuse detection engine and a decision support system combining the results of these two detection engines.

ANALYSIS FOR CRITICAL POINTS IN CURRENT NIDS

From our survey of traditional and current NIDS there are number of significant drawbacks, we see these critical issues must be taken in consideration to construct our proposed model, these drawbacks are:

1. Dataset KDD'99 is widely used dataset for the intrusion detection. But this dataset has huge no. of records and high no. of redundant records. That makes selecting subsets of records for training and testing exhausting for researchers and effect on accuracy of IDSs.

2. NIDS are usually aim to detect known network level attacks. This leaves them vulnerable to novel malicious attacks.

3. Data seems to be growing rapidly. Depending on the intrusion detection tools constructed by an organization and its size there is the possibility for logs to reach millions of records per day.

4. False positives, occurs when normal attack is mistakenly classified as malicious and treated accordingly.

5. False negatives, this is the case where IDS does not generate an alert when an intrusion is actually taking place.

6. In anomaly detection the subject's normal behavior is modeled on the basis of the (audit) data collected over a period of normal operation. If undiscovered intrusive activities occur during this period, they will be considered normal activities. Because of some technical reasons, the current anomaly detection approaches usually suffer from a high false-alarm rate.

7. Misuse detection engine work better than anomaly detection engine for known intrusion patterns. Misuse engine detect known attacks more best and generate lower false warns. This high performance due to misuse detection engine takes characteristics of explicit knowledge of the intrusions.

8. There is no available standard dataset for wireless intrusion detection as in wire networks, where KDD'99 presents the benchmark dataset for training and testing.

9. Noise limits intrusion detection systems effectiveness. Corrupted packets generated from software bugs, data become spoiled, and native packets that flee can create a significantly high false-warns rate.

PROPOSAL OF WWNIDS

This chapter introduces a proposal WWNIDS to advance NIDS across improving two important stages these are: Construct integrated training and testing datasets and optimize feature space to include intrinsic features. Algorithm WWNIDS will explain the sequential stages, to advance NIDS to control the security of wire and wireless networking:

Algorithm WWNIDS

Input: KDD'99, wireless sessions, wire sessions present most modern attacks, and new features.

Output: Accurate WWNIDS.

Steps:

1. Build modern KDD dataset to have various sessions from KDD'99 (normal and all classes of intrusions).

2. Vaccinate the proposed modern KDD dataset by new collected sessions, those introduce most modern intrusions.

3. Concatenate new features due to the vaccinated sessions which are present intrusions not yet considered in KDD'99.

4. Preprocessing of the proposed KDD dataset since it is a collection of sessions from more than one resource of data and the three added feature, so there is no integrity. The problems related to get data integrity are noise, incomplete values of attributes.

5. Build wireless dataset CWDS consist of all features taken from data link layer especially from the sublayer Media Access Control of 802.11.

6. Proposing BR algorithm (one of most important swarm intelligence algorithms) for ranking the features depending two statistical ranking methods. By applying proposed BR algorithm on modern KDD features will register two cases 44 features and top eight features. By applying BR algorithm

on CWDS register two cases 17 features and top eight features.

7. Suggest two classifiers ANN and SVM on modern KDD dataset after preprocessing step. Apply them two times depending on the two cases; the all features and the subset features considered with BR algorithm. And on CWDS two times depending on the two cases the all features and the subset features with BR algorithm. That is to evaluate the proposed WWNIDS with various classifiers on all cases with and without of BR algorithm.

8. Allow the enhanced WWNIDS to be adaptive by reporting the new sessions the classifiers not trained on then analyze these sessions to extract the new patterns present the new unknown intrusion. Finally add these sessions to the training and testing datasets.

9. End.

MODERN KDD DATASET (VACCINATE SESSIONS AND FEATURES)

Most of, nearly 70%, sessions in the proposed modern KDD dataset are from KDD'99. About 30% of the created dataset is vaccinated by connection sessions that have most modern intrusions come from continues development networking environment, such as IPv6, mobil-

ity and cloud computing. The proposed modern KDD dataset will be divided into two subsets, one for training and other for testing. These two subsets have 600,000 records, 450,000 records for training and 150,000 for testing. Most of these records are selected in very precise way to have various types of normal and intrusion connections. The new types of attacks taken into account are:

1. Fishing attacks.
2. Various types of worms.
3. Various types of Trajan horses.

These types of attacks could be taken under one proposed name called Modern Attack which is present most new attacks that not correlated with the famous four types of attack in KDD'99 dataset. The proposal increases the no. of features which are important to be added because it intrinsic to the modern attacks added as a connection session to KDD dataset. These new features are:

Knowledge-based connection features obtained using some knowledge of connection environment (wire or wireless), connection protection (encrypted or unencrypted) and connection media (graphics, image, video, sound and text).

By these new features the no. of all features will be 41 features with 3 added, and no. of general classes will be six. These Classes are: normal connections, four known attacks of KDD'99 and Modern Attacks, Table 1.

Table 1. Modern KDD architecture

Session ID	KDD'99 features (41)	New (3) Features
1	KDD'99 sessions	Filled with proposed encoded values
.	Vaccinated Sessions for modern intrusion (41+3) features	

MODERN DATASET PREPROCESSING

In addition to the vaccinated sessions there were filling values of new three added features along with all parts of dataset (parts taken from KDD'99), since these three features are filled automatically with part of new sessions added. Surely the proposed modern dataset has a rate of noise come from getting data from more than one resource; noise is the big problem in constructing WWNIDS since it depends on data mining as a tool for detection, the data mining very sensitive to noise. Noise causes a bias in detection rate. The following steps introduce the preprocessing steps applied on proposed modern KDD dataset.

1. Missing values of attributes treated by filling values with the most frequent attribute value in the dataset. Missing values in the proposal are these three features added in the sessions vaccinated, which they don't found in the sessions taken from KDD'99.
   a. Connection types in modern KDD filled with 1 if type is wire and 2 if wireless.
   b. Connection security in modern KDD filled 1 if encrypted and 2 with unencrypted.
   c. Connection media in modern KDD filled with 1 if text, 2 if image, 3 if sound and 4 if video.
2. Redundant records are removed by keeping unique record from them in dataset (many of added sessions were redundant). Removing redundant records reduce time of training and increase accurate of detection rate.
3. The incomplete attribute avoided by adding the three features which are basics in solving new attacks are not considered in KDD'99.
4. The misclassified records labeled with a true classification, in the proposal the treating done by classify the record according the nearest classified records.

CWDS DESCRIPTION

The data will use to train and test the classifiers were collected from a WLAN 802.11. The 802.11 network is composed of seven wireless stations and access points. Two machines are used to generate normal traffic of WWW protocols and download/upload protocols. The other four machines transmit in parallel data uploaded from four types of wireless intrusions. The seventh machine is used to get and store all types of traffic (normal and intrusive (type of intrusion). The intrusions will used to test proposed WWNIDS; these intrusions are the four types of WLAN attacks. A benchmark wireless dataset are not available so in this proposal will customize the dataset depending on the features of datalink layer especially MAC sublayer. By using Wireshark tool collect 3000 frames. From each frame we extract the following features, all of these features are directly extracted from the header and the last feature extracted implicitly from analyzing the frames; see Figure 1.

- Two bits detect which version of the 802.11 MAC is contained in the rest of the frame.
- Detect the type of the frame.
- Detect the Subtype of the frame.
- Detect if a frame is destined to the Distribution System.
- Detect if a frame is non final fragment or not.
- Detect whether a frame is non final fragment or not.
- Detect if the frame is retransmitted frame.
- Detect whether the station is active or in Power Saving Mode.
- Detect whether an access point has buffered frames for a dozing station.
- Detect if the frame is processed by the WEP protocol.
- Detect if the "strict ordering" delivery is employed.
- Detect number of microseconds the medium is expected to be busy.

Figure 1. Frame WLAN 802.11 with details

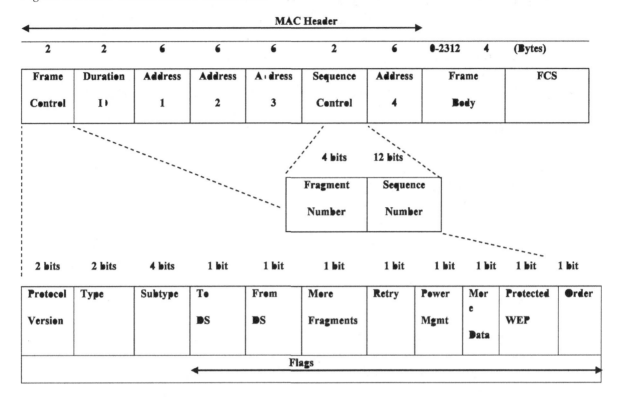

- Detect MAC address of the receiving station.
- Detect MAC address of the transmitting station.
- Detect MAC address of the sending, Destination or Base Station.
- Detect frame Check Sequence, which contains a 32 bit CRC.
- Detect Casting type, Unicast Multicast Broadcast.

The data collected were grouped in two sets: training and testing sets. The training set contains the input with its desired output. Testing dataset are necessary to avoid the effect of over fitting, it should be able to predict the output of each entry of the testing data set.

FEATURE SELECTION (PROPOSE BR RANKING METHOD)

The most important step in constructing WWNIDS is how to recognize the important features they will be base stone in raise detection rate and optimize the trigger of warns (reduce false positive warns, reduce low important warns, and reduce false negative warns). By minimize features the data space will also minimized, so the training dataset and training time will be more efficient for classification models deal with online real time environment.

The proposal introduce swarm algorithm (BR) as a feature ranking that by making the following assumptions:

1. The weights of KDD features and modern features will be taken by its correlation to the 6 classes; this correlation will be measured by average of two ranking methods Relief Measure and Gain Ratio.

2. Some parameters' names in BR algorithm will be replaced according to the proposal of feature selection, these are:
   a. bee is called Agent-Ranker (AR).
   b. n the scout ARs will be; n no. of KDD features and modern features.
   c. m sites and e best sites will be; m selected features and e best features.
   d. nep no. of ARs recruited will be; nep weight given to e best features.
   e. nsp no. of ARs recruited will be; nsp weight given to (m-e) features.
   f. Patches will be; features set.
   g. Neighborhood for features will be; other features in the same type (as in the WWNIDS there are 6 types) then features in other feature type's subset.

After interpretations in the points above the proposal BR ranking for feature selection will be introduced by Algorithm-BR.

Algorithm Bee Ranker

Parameters:
1. *n*: Number of all known features.
2. *m*: Number of features selected out of *n* *visited* features.
3. *e*: Number of best features out of *m* selected features.
4. *nep*: Weight given for best *e* features (high).
5. *nsp*: Weight given for other (*m-e*) selected features (low).
6. *ngh*: Initial size of features set which includes features and its neighborhood features and stopping criterion.

Steps:
1. Initialize population with random features. (*n* features are placed randomly in the search space).
2. Evaluate fitness of the population. Fitness calculation for features obtained from average of two ranking measures 'Chi-Square' and 'Gain Ratio'.
3. While (stopping criterion not fit). While no more new ranking for features.

```
// Construct new population.
```

4. Select features for neighborhood search. (Feature that have the highest fitness are chosen as "selected" and features from same type subset are chosen for neighborhood search (after complete the features from same type subset algorithm will begin with the other feature type subset)).
5. Weighted selected feature (more weights for features in best *e* features) and evaluate fitness.
6. Select the fittest feature from each feature set. (For each feature set, only the feature with the highest fitness will be selected to form the next feature population).
7. Assign remaining features to search randomly and evaluate their fitness.
8. End While.
9. End.

WWNIDS CLASSIFIER CONSTRUCTING

The proposed is WWNIDS aim to construct NIDS protect both wire and wireless, this mean it will deal with three layers; transport, Internet and data link layers. That by construct two NIDS separately one for wire NIDS and the second for wireless NIDS then integrate them to construct the WWNIDS, as in the following consequences steps:

Table 2. Truth table of final INIDS according wire-NIDS and wireless-NIDS

Action	Wire-NIDS	Wireless-NIDS	INIDS
Action1	Pass	Pass	Pass
Action2	Pass	Alarm	Alarm
Action3	Alarm	Pass	Alarm
Action4	Alarm	Alarm	Alarm

1. Wire NIDS Model is DM-based IDS for training and testing will depend on KDD'99 dataset, using proposed BR ranking as a feature extraction and both ANN and SVM as classifiers.

2. Wireless NIDS Model is DM-based IDS for training and testing will depend on CWDS collected on WLAN 802.11, using proposed BR ranking as a feature extraction and both ANN and SVM as classifiers.

3. WWNIDS is a Wire NIDS and Wireless NIDS done by the following strategy:

   a. Entering real-time data, frames of WLAN 802.11.

   b. Separate the packet (transport layer and internet layers) from datalink layer.

   c. Process packet with Wire NIDS and process datalink with Wireless NIDS.

   d. Apply the logical truth table of (AND operation) for deciding the frames (connections with three layers) to pass or trig alarm to recorded as intrusion, see Table 2.

Always IDS have database either has all signatures of known attack which support the misuse intrusion detection or has all the normal behavior which support the anomaly intrusion detection. The proposal support IDS with database has both normal and attacks in all its variations to decide if that attack or not,

if it was attack then it determines its type. The research record detecting intrusions using most of strong data mining algorithms used in last year: Artificial Neural Network (ANN), see algorithm ANN and Support Vector Machine (SVM), see algorithm SVM. These learning algorithms implemented in proposed VB.NET environment to evaluate the optimization of modern KDD and CWDS with proposed BR ranking feature selection.

Algorithm Suggested: ANN

Input: Modern KDD and CWDS for training and testing.

Output: Optimal ANN (classifier model).

Steps:

1. Main Assumption for the Training Process of MLP:

   a. Learning method: Quasi Newton BFGS and Levenberg-Marquardt

   b. Number of Epochs: 1000.

   c. MSE (Mean Square error): 0.01.

   d. Learning rate: 0,9.

   e. Activation function: log-signoid.

   f. Number of neurons in the Input layer: (41 or according no. of SVM set).

   g. Number of neurons in the hidden layer: (21 for 41 input neurons and with no. of SVM set equal to half of this no.).

   h. Number of neurons in the output layer: (6 cause no. of intrusions classes are 4, unknown intrusion and the normal class).

   i. Update of weights – batch mode (after presentation of the entire training data set).

2. Train and Test on W dataset to construct final ANN model for WNIDS.

3. End.

Algorithm Suggested: SVM

Input: modern KDD and CWDS for training and testing.
Output: Optimal SVM (classifier model).
Steps:

1. Initialize all points in training dataset as (Xi, Yj) where X is a vector of data x1, ..., xn and Y is vector of classes.
2. Initialize vector of weight W.
3. Distribute all points (x, y) and extract the hyper plane separator.
4. If the hyper plane give optimal separation then depend hyper plane as classifier model to classify testing dataset and go End.
5. Else must do the following steps.
6. Maximize the hyper plan using equation of Getting Maximum Margin:

$$MM = 2 / \|w\| \tag{6}$$

7. For minimum using equation same as maximizing

$$\Phi(w) = \frac{1}{2} w^t w \tag{7}$$

8. Initialize Lagrange multiplier α_i vector $\alpha_1 \ldots \alpha_n$ using equation

$$Q(\alpha) = \Sigma \alpha_i - \frac{1}{2} \Sigma \Sigma \alpha_i \alpha_j y_i y_j x_i^T x_j \tag{8}$$

9. Apply classification function using equation

$$f(x) = S a_i y_i x_i^T x + b \tag{9}$$

10. Determine the support vectors xi with non-zero α_i (support vectors are the points determine the area of hyper plan).
11. Depend the hyper plan resulted after determining support vectors as the classifier model to classify testing dataset.
12. End.

EXPERIMENTAL WORK AND RESULTS

This section will explain the experimental work and results of WWNIDS, with wire NIDS the number of features increased to be 44 features and types of connection increased to be 6 general classes. Table 3 displays the number of training and testing examples of modern dataset. For wireless NIDS collect 3000 frames using wireshark tools to construct, from these frames we construct wireless dataset which conducted by selecting 2000 (1500 for training and 500) for testing) frame with optimal features' values (no missing values, no noisy and no redundant) and then distribute the data collected to training and testing and specify no. of frames for normal and each attacks in both training and testing as in Table 4.

The set of intrinsic features obtained by applying BR ranking on modern KDD training dataset, this subset is {Protocol_type, Service, Flag, count, srv_count, same_srv_rate, dst_host_srv_count, dst_host_same_srv_rate, dst_host_same_src_port_rate}.The set of intrinsic features obtained by applying BR ranking on CWDS training dataset, this subset is { Type, Subtype, To DS, More Fragmentation, Retry, Protected Wep, Duration, Casting type}.

Training which consist two classifiers (SVM and ANN) on *Training dataset* has been done with two sets of features (*All_Features*, *BR _Features*), so the

Table 3. Number of examples for training and testing

Connection Types	Training Examples	Testing Examples
Normal	95,000	20,000
Denial of Services	85,000	40,000
Remote to User	103,000	20,000
User to Root	57,000	20,000
Probing	70,000	30,000
Modern	40,000	20,000
No. of Examples	450,000	150,000

Table 4. No. of records selected from CWDS for training and testing

No. of Records/Type of Records	Training Examples	Testing Examples
Deauthentication	300	100
Chopchop	300	100
Duration	300	100
Fragmentation	300	100
Normal	300	100
No. of Examples	1500	500

proposed system has been experimented (i.e., trained and tested) for two times to assess the accuracy of the classifiers. Performed three different experiments and selected subsets of eight features in both datasets modern KDD and proposed CWDS that indicates better performance as compared to complete set of features. The aim is to select minimum features that produce optimal results in accuracy. This definitely impact on overall performance of the system. The features are reduced to 8 from the 44 and 8 from 17 raw features set. The experiments show that optimal features increased accuracy, reduced training and computational overheads and simplified the architecture of intrusion analysis engine.

Results of three conducted experiments (Exp1, Exp2, Exp3), which producing the most accurate results, have been presented in this section. Four classification models have been constructed in each

of these three experiments. Next these models have been applied on the same *Testing dataset*, which has been constructed during Exp1, to assess the validation and accuracy of these constructed models on the same testing dataset. The classification results of testing are either TP (intrusion), TN (normal), false positive (FP) (misclassified as intrusion), false negative (FN) (misclassified as normal), Unknown (new user behavior or new attack). From classification results we calculate the detection rate (DR) of IDS is the ratio between the number of TP and the total number of intrusion patterns presented in the testing dataset. It has been calculated using

$$DR = \frac{TP}{TP + FN + Unknown2} * 100\% \quad (10)$$

and the false alarm rate (FAR) of an IDS is the ratio between number of "normal" patterns classified as attacks (FP) and the total number of "normal" patterns presented in the testing dataset. It has been computed using

$$FAR = \frac{FP}{TN + FP + Unknown1} * 100\%$$
$$(11)$$

Values for both of DR and FAR for each classifier in the three experiments have been illustrated in Table 5.

Table 5. DRs and FARs of both of them SVM and ANN classifiers

SVM Classifier				ANN Classifier			
Feature Selection Measure	Experiment No.	DR	FAR	Feature Selection Measure	Experiment No.	DR	FAR
BR	1	1	0	BR	1	0.999	0
	2	0.998	0		2	0.999	0
	3	0.999	0		3	0.999	0
ALL	1	0.995	0.02	ALL	1	0.994	0.03
	2	0.996	0.03		2	0.988	0.03
	3	0.995	0.07		3	0.995	0.03

Table 6. Accuracy of SVM and ANN classifiers

Classifier	Experiment No.	BR_F	ALL_F
SVM	1	1	0.995
	2	1	0.996
	3	0.999	0.997
ANN	1	1	0.994
	2	0.999	0.997
	3	0.999	0.995

DR are higher with SVM anomaly classifiers and also with ANN misuse classifiers and FAR often ranging between (0 - 0.07) with SVM classifiers and ANN classifiers. It is very clear from these that SVM classifiers are better with anomaly detection and ANN classifiers are better with misuse detection. Selection of the best classification model would be done significantly according to its classification accuracy, which is introduced as the ratio between the number of the correctly classified patterns (TP, TN) and the total number of patterns of the testing dataset. The accuracy (Accu) of each classifier has been calculated using

$$Accu = \frac{TP + TN}{TP + FP + TN + FN + unknown} * 100\%$$

(12)

Table 6 Summarizes *Accu* of both SVM and ANN classifiers with *BR_F and ALL_F* in the three experiments. According to these results, the classifiers SVM and ANN were more accurate with *BR_F Accu*.

CONCLUSION

From results obtained in implementing the WWNIDS reached to the following conclusions:

1. Updating KDD by a proposed created dataset to has new vaccinated sessions, make it reliable and novel since it will contain most modern attacks not appear in KDD'99.

2. Because of vaccination there is three features added to be 44 features. This makes dataset suffer from missing values. But by applying preprocessing to dataset make the constructed classifier dependable and truth.

3. Optimizing no. of features to consider the critical feature will make the classifier constructing optimized in time and space. Also make the classifier work more speed as real-time system, since no. of features will be checked much less than original numbers of all features.

4. Data mining are introduced for helping WWNIDS to detect intrusions correctly, and accordingly WWNIDSs have shown to be successful in detecting known attacks.

5. Feature selection is an important task of Network Intrusion application. Using BR feature selection approach, intrusions are detected with less error rate and high accuracy.

6. Usage of ANN and SVM for anomaly detection with the input data from the modern KDD and proposed CWDS gives good performance of WWNIDS as comparison with depended related works.

7. Tables (5 and 6 present results of detection for SVM and ANN separately where notice the higher rates of detection and very less rates of false alarms especially with BR set of features.

REFERENCES

Ahmad, I., Abdulah, A. B., Alghamdi, A. S., Alnfajan, K., & Hussain, M. (2011). Feature subset selection for network intrusion detection mechanism using genetic eigen vectors. In *Proceedings of the 2011 International Conference on Telecommunication Technology and Applications*. *IACSIT Press*: *Singapore*.

Al-Janabi, S. T., & Saeed, H. A. (2011). A Neural Network Based Anomaly Intrusion Detection System. 2011 Developments in E-systems Engineering, (pp. 221-226) IEEE Computer Society.

Baig, M. N., & Kumar, K. K. (2011). Intrusion detection in wireless networks using selected features. *International Journal of Computer Science and Information Technologies*, 2(5), 1887–1893.

Barhoo, T. S., & ElShami, E. (2011). Detecting WLANs' DoS Attacks Using Back propagate Neural Network. *Journal of Al Azhar University-Gaza*, 13, 83–92

Bensefia, H., & Ghoualmi, N. (2011). A New Approach for Adaptive Intrusion Detection, In *2011 Seventh International Conference on Computational Intelligence and Security*. doi:10.1109/CIS.2011.220

Depren, O., Topallar, M., Anarim, E., & Ciliz, M. K. (2005). An intelligent intrusion detection system (IDS) for anomaly and misuse detection in computer networks. *Expert Systems with Applications*, 29(4), 713–722. doi:10.1016/j.eswa.2005.05.002

Guojun, Z., Liping, C., & Weitao, H. (2011). The Design of Cooperative Intrusion Detection System, IEEE *Computer Society, 2011 Seventh International Conference on Computational Intelligence and Security, pp.* 764-766. doi:10.1109/CIS.2011.173

Gupta V., Krishnamurthy S., & Faloutsos M, (2011). *Denial of Service Attacks at the MAC Layer in Wireless Ad Hoc Networks*. This material is based upon work supported by the National Science Foundation under Grant No. 9985195, DARPA award N660001-00-18936

Haldar, N. A., Abulaish, M., & Pasha, S. A. (2010). An Activity Pattern Based Wireless Intrusion Detection System, IEEE Computer Society, In *2012 Ninth International Conference on Information Technology- New Generations*, pp. 846-847.

Hashem, S. H. (2013). Efficiency Of SVM And PCA To Enhance Intrusion Detection System. *Journal Of Asian Scientific Research*, 3(4), 381–395.

Hashem, S. H., Habr, B. S., & Khalil, B. M. (2013). Enhance network intrusion detection system using BR algorithm, *Madinat Aleleem Journal 5*(1).

Lakhina, S., Joseph, S., & Verma, B. (2010). Feature reduction using principal component analysis for effective anomaly–based intrusion detection on NSL-KDD. *International Journal of Engineering Science and Technology*, 2(6), 1790–1799.

Lalli, & Palanisamy. (2013). Modernized intrusion detection using enhanced apriori algorithm. *International Journal of Wireless & Mobile Networks, 5*(2).

Lee, W., Stolfo, S. J., & Mok, K. W. (1999). A data Mining Framework for Building Intrusion Detection Models, In *Proceeding of IEEE Symposium on Security and Privacy*, pp 120-132.

Majeed, S. K., Hashem, S. H., & Gbashi, I. K. (2013). Propose HMNIDS hybrid multilevel network intrusion detection system. *IJCSI International Journal of Computer Science Issues, 10*(5).

Mohammad, M. N., Sulaiman, N., & Muhsin, O. A. (2011). A novel intrusion detection system by using intelligent data mining in weka environment. *Procedia Computer Science*, *3*, 1237–1242. doi:10.1016/j.procs.2010.12.198

Neelakantan, N. P., Nagesh, C., & Tech, M. (2011). Role of feature selection in intrusion detection systems for 802.11 networks. *International Journal of Smart Sensors and Ad Hoc Networks*, *1*(1).

Peddabachigaria, S., Abraham, A., Grosanc, C., & Thomas, O. (2005). Modeling intrusion detection system using hybrid intelligent systems. *Journal of Network and Computer Applications*, *30*(1), 114–132. doi:10.1016/j.jnca.2005.06.003

Reddy, E. K., Reddy, V. N., & Rajulu, P. G. (2011). A Study of Intrusion Detection in Data Mining, *Proceedings of the World Congress on Engineering 2011* Vol III WCE *2011, July 6 - 8, London, U.K.*

Suebsing, A., & Hiransakolwong, N. (2011), Euclidean-based Feature Selection for Network Intrusion Detection, *2009 International Conference on Machine Learning and Computing IPCSIT* vol.3 *(2011), IACSIT Press, Singapore*.

Tulasi, R. L., & Ravikanth, M. (2011). Impact of feature reduction on the efficiency of wireless intrusion detection systems. *International Journal of Computer Trends and Technology*.

University of California Irvine. (1999). *KDD Cup 1999 Data*. Retrieved July 14, 2013 from http://kdd.ics.uci.edu/databases/kddcup99/kddcup99.html

Vaarandi, R. (2011). Real-Time Classification of IDS Alerts with Data Mining Techniques. In *Proceedings of the 28th IEEE conference on Military communications (MILCOM'09)*, pp.1786-1792.

Vaarandi, R., & Podinš, K. (2010). Network IDS Alert Classification with Frequent Itemset Mining and Data Clustering, In *The 2010 International IEEE Conference on Network and Service Management, pp. 451-456.*

Zhou, Q., & Zhao, Y. (2013). The design and implementation of intrusion detection system based on data mining technology. *Journal of Applied Sciences. Engineering and Technology*, *5*(14), 3824–3829.

KEY TERMS AND DEFINITIONS

Artificial Neural Networks: The most important one algorithm of machine learning used in classification and clustering.

Bee Algorithm: One of famous swarm intelligence algorithms, used in many applications for optimizing solution.

BR s Algorithm: A new population-based search algorithm that mimics the food foraging behavior of swarms of honey BR s.

Feature Selection: A techniques applied by using many algorithms to optimize search space by reducing features into most important features by ranking or transformation to the most correlated features.

Intrusion Detection System: IT is a software, hardware or a combination of both that monitors and collects system and network information and analyzes it to determine if an intrusion has occurred.

Support Vector Machine: The famous new algorithm used in classification since it search about the most critical point in search space to distinguish the patterns.

WLANs Suffer: From a lot of security weakness points, some of these weakness points are already found in usual wired networks and others weakness points are new as a consequent to the broadcast connection medium. These weakness points include confidentiality, integrity, and availability vulnerabilities.

Chapter 3
Automatic Intrusion Detection and Secret Multi Agent Preservation Using Authentication Measurement Network Threat

Ghossoon M. Waleed Al-Saadoon
Applied Science University, Bahrain

ABSTRACT

The computer sciences and their applications are developing continuously. This growth should be protected. One of the methods to fulfill this approach by using the encryption method 'Rijndael Advanced Encryption Standard' is applied for security information DBs, to prevent an unauthorized user from accessing any stored information. The security method determines the resources that agents are able to have an access and to give permission to other agents. Security and security assurance are special integrity in agent system to enable it to cooperate or to complete the application and where agent system may not be trustful to visiting agents. Ideas of this chapter of using multi agent framework is to design the proposed Automatic Intrusion Detection model and to secret multi agent preservation using authentication measurement network threat. This approach uses statistical models to correlate and analyse data in the network. It takes the decisions to control both local and global agent's data bases perceptively. Also it adopts the security problem authentication and authorization by providing a secure distributed agent system.

INTRODUCTION

Over the years computer systems have successfully evolved from centralized monolithic computing devices supporting static application to distributed computing by Networks, therefore in this chapter the systems are becoming more opened and subjected to set of security threats. Thus, a key challenge is to provide all computer systems with the appropriate mechanisms to offer security

DOI: 10.4018/978-1-4666-6583-5.ch003

Copyright © 2015, IGI Global. Copying or distributing in print or electronic forms without written permission of IGI Global is prohibited.

services such as authentication, secret preservation and automatic attacks detection commonly known as Intrusion Detection.

Security is crucial to the success of active networking especially when the current network is characterized by a dynamic nature and increasing distribution. Traditional network relies on security mechanisms and policies deployed on the underlying operating system. Nevertheless, these measures are insufficient and they present, in general, a set of flows that result security vulnerabilities. The field of automated computer security intrusion detection gives result to secret multi agent preservation using authentication measurement network threat. The goal of this chapter is to analyze events on the network and identify manifestations of attacks. Commercial solutions are generally centralized and suffer from significant limitations when used in high-speed networks. The identification of distributed intrusions threats requires cooperation of different sensors so it is advisable to consider mobile devices as a challenge to intrusion detection. To distribute automatic intrusion detection can use mobile and intelligent multi agents throughout the measurement Authentication Network.

Multi agent systems are used in various applications such as workflow, scheduling and optimization. An agent is a physical or logical entity characterized by many attributes. In a traditional approach, each component represents a different Network Management (NM) function that may or may not be autonomous. When a new network technology is introduced or an old technology is upgraded, each network management component must be accessed, changed, debugged, and the filtered mechanisms for processing data must be reevaluated, The advantage of the new approach in this chapter is, when a new method of analyzing data is developed, this method can be incorporated into the architecture as a new multi agent. The adjustments are then limited to register that multi agent and giving the multi agent ability to produce and evaluate agent-to-agent messages. Thus, the overhead for changes is much less than with traditional approaches (seminarproject, 2010).

An agent can be a person, a machine, a piece of software, or a variety of other things. The basic dictionary definition of agent is one who acts. However, for developing Information Technology (IT) systems, such a definition is too general: IT-related agents need additional properties. Some of the properties that agents may possess in various combinations include the following (Coursehero, 2013):

- **Reducing Network Load:** Existing Intrusion Detection System (IDS) are faced with the problem of performing a huge amount of data over transfer. Abstracted forms of this data are usually sent from all locations in the network to the central site in order to process. Sending a huge amount of data causes an increase of a network loads. Mobile agents offer the opportunity to overcome this problem by eliminating the need of so much data transfer. The processing program (agent) can be dispatched to the host containing crucial data. This will reduce network traffic since an agent is smaller than the processed data.

- **Overcoming Network Latency:** Mobile agents are able to dispatch from a host to carry out operations directly to the remote point of interest, thus agent scans provide an appropriate response faster than a hierarchical IDS that has to communicate with a central coordinator based elsewhere on the network.

- **Asynchronous Execution and Autonomy:** Agents can be stopped and started without disturbing the rest of the IDS. Notice that the mobile agents are able to continue to operate autonomously even if the host platform -where it was created -is not available or is disconnected from the network. Mobile agent framework provides IDS with the possibility of continuing to work even when a central controller is down.

- **Dynamic Adaptation:** Mobile agents can be retracted, cloned, dispatched, killed or put to sleep as network's configuration; topology and traffic characteristics change over time. As the number of nodes in the network increases, agents can be cloned and dispatched to these new computing elements.
- **Robust Behavior:** Mobile agents have the ability to react dynamically to security conditions making it easier to build robust distributed systems.
- **Scalability:** Distributed mobile agents IDS are one of the several options that allow computational load and diagnostic responsibilities to be distributed through the network. This improves scalability and maintains fault-resistance behavior.

NETWORK SECURITY ISSUES

Networks have security problems for the following reasons:

- **Sharing:** Because of the resource and workload sharing of networks, more users have the potential to an access networked systems than single computers, perhaps worse, access is afforded to more systems, so that access controls for single systems may be inadequate in networks.
- **Complexity of System:** A network combines two or more possibly dissimilar operating systems. Therefore, a network operating control system is likely to be more complex than an operating system for a single computing system.
- **Unknown Perimeter:** The expandability of a network also implies uncertainty about the network boundary. One host may be a node on two different networks, so that resources on one network are accessible to the users of other network as well.

- **Many Points of Attack:** A simple computing system is a self-contained unit. Access controls on one machine preserve the security of data on the processor. However, when a file is stored in a network host remote from the user, the file may pass through many hosts to get to the user. Although the administrator of one host may enforce rigorous security policies, that administrator has no control over other hosts in the network. The user has to depend on the access control mechanisms of all these systems.
- **Anonymity:** An attacker can mount an attack from thousands of miles away and thus never have to touch the system attacked or come into contact with any of its administrators or users (http://www.coursehero.com/file/4039109/SecurityOverview).

Multi Agent System

Multi Agent System (MAS) architectures can be considered organizations composed of autonomous and proactive agents that interact with one another in order to cooperate and then achieve either a common goal or simply their own goals (Margus and et al, 2001). This definition applies to complex agents only. The Object Management Group (OMG) has a more general definition that applies to both simple and complex agents. According to them, multi-agent systems are: Systems composed of agents, coordinated through their relationships with one another. The following definition redefines multi-agent systems in terms of agencies. A multi-agent system is a collection of interacting agencies. A design methodology of MAS should help the designer to represent information about a changing environment and its effects on the MAS, an aspect of the modeling task which is currently lacking from agent design methodologies .A multi-agent system is defined as a system consisting of a number of agents that share a common environment (Hamed, 2005; Eipgog, 2012).

The main difference between Multi Agent and single agent systems is that in MAS several agents exits, and they are aware of each other goals and actions besides being aware of each other intentions and behavior, in multi-agent system, each agent can communicate with another, either to help an individual agent achieves its goal, or in a rare case, prevents it.

Multi-agent systems are composed of several autonomous entities, which have the following general characteristics:

- Each agent has incomplete capabilities to solve the problem.
- There is no global control.
- Data is decentralized.

Agent Management

The management of agents is recognized to be an important part of an agent platform. This certainly holds for large-scale multiage systems deployed on heterogeneous and open systems.

In multi-agent system literature, different aspects of management are addressed. The concept management service is mentioned in the range of functionalities in the Core Agency. Core Agencies represent the minimal functionality required by an agency in order to support the execution of agents. Support for human interaction is provided by the management services, to monitor and control agents and places.

Some descriptions of agent platform management systems do not explicitly include life cycle models, but do recognize agent states.

For example, the Agent Management System (AMS) recognizes the following states:

- Creation,
- Suspension,
- Resumption,
- Termination,
- Migration,
- Localization.

Other descriptions of management systems recognize "Actions" on agents, which seem to be derived from a (hidden) life cycle model (Mobach and et al, 2001).

Security Agent

The security of a distributed application can be an important issue. The level of security depends on the sensitivity of the information in the system. System information includes information communicated between agents, as well as the information stored with each agent. With distributed applications that interface to external systems, there may be issues of agent authenticity and source verification. A distributed application may need to authenticate the identity of an agent, assign permissions that define the level of access an agent has, and encrypt information passed between agents.

Computer security is a major concern for organizations. Whilst security violations can be caused by external users (hackers), some scientists have shown that the primary threat comes from individuals inside the organization. Hence much more emphasis has to be placed on internal security mechanisms .External network attacks can be categorized into IP spoofing attacks, Packet-sniffing, sequence number prediction attacks and trust-access attacks. Categories of internal attack include passwords attacks, session hijacking attacks, shared library attacks, social engineering attacks, and technological vulnerability attack (Mobach and et al, 2001).

Security and privacy are growing concerns in the open distributed software systems community because of the Internet's rapid growth and the desired secure transactions over it. This desire has led to the advent of many security architectures and protocols which deal with authentication, cryptography, and authorization. One of the biggest risks to Internet survivability is the growing number of distributed and automated attacks by malicious intruders. The security industry has so far concentrated solely on the development of automated security programs that analyze the attacks within a single isolated system (Buchanan, 2011).

COMPUTER NETWORK SECURITY

Computer network security programs can be categorized as follows:

- **Security Enhancement Software:** This enhances or replaces an operating system's built-in security software (for example, Mangle It, Passwd+ and Shadow).
- **Authentication and Encryption Software:** This encrypts and decrypts computer files.
- **Security Monitoring Software Monitor:** This monitors different operations of a computer network and outputs the results sents to system administrators.
- **Network Monitoring Software:** This monitors user's behavior or monitors incoming or outgoing traffic (Mobach and et al, 2001).

APPLICATIONS OF AGENT

Agents are the next major computing paradigm and will be pervasive in every market. There are several orthogonal dimensions along which agent applications could be classified. The type of the agent can classify them, by the technology used to implement the agent, or by the application domain itself.

These are the simple agents focus on what is defined as "intelligent agents", some examples are: Autonomous robots for sample gathering in space missions, software agents that are programmed to search for the Internet information.

There are eight broad categories of agent using (Ross, 2001):

1. Personal Computer (PC).
2. Network management.
3. Information and Internet access.
4. Mobility management.
5. E- Commerce.
6. Computer user interface.
7. Application development.
8. Military application.

AGENT-BASED DEVELOPMENT ENVIRONMENT

Some examples of freeware agent environments that will be looked at for the use in experiments, are:

1. Agent builder incorporates the use of a graphical toll to aid the construction process of intelligent software agents.
2. FIPA-OS (Foundation for Intelligent Physical Agents) focuses on software agents, communication and inter-operability between agents, external behavior not how agents process information they receive, and agents in heterogeneous environments.
3. JADE (Java Agent Development Framework) is a development framework. This framework is aimed at two main aspects: developing multi-agent systems and applications, which conform to FIPA standards for intelligent agents.
4. OAA (Open Agent Architecture) allows for the provision of software services through the co-operative efforts of distributed autonomous agents.

CLASSIFICATION OF INTRUSION DETECTION SYSTEM

The "standard" classifications of IDSs include the following categories:

1. Statistical anomaly detection, rule-based anomaly detection, and rule-based penetration identification.
2. The IDSs can be characterized by:
   a. Where they live,
   b. What you have to tell them,
   c. What they look for,
   d. Which technologies they use,
   e. What they tell you.
3. Employs signature detection to discriminate between anomaly or attack patterns (signatures) and known intrusion detection signatures.

The data processing techniques used in IDS:

- **Expert Systems Using Set of Rules Describing an Attack:** All security related events incorporated in an audit trail are translated in terms of if-then-else rules. Examples are Wisdom & Sense and Computer Watch (developed at AT and T).
- **Signature Analysis Similarly to Expert System Approach:** This method is based on the attack knowledge. They transform the semantic description of an attack into the appropriate audit trail format. Thus, the attack signatures can be found in logs or input data streams in a straightforward way. An attack scenario can be described, for example, as a sequence of audit events that a given attack generates or patterns of searchable data that are captured in the audit trail. This method uses abstract equivalents of audit trail data. Detection is accomplished by using common text string matching mechanisms. Typically, it is a very powerful technique and as such very

often it employed in commercial systems (for example Stalker, Real Secure, Net Ranger, and Emerald expert-BSM). Such as:

- ◦ Colored Petri Nets.
- ◦ State-transition analysis.
- ◦ Statistical analysis.
- ◦ Neural Networks.
- ◦ Computer immunology.
- ◦ Machine learning.
- ◦ Data mining (Proctor, 2001; Detection, 2011; Ijarcsce, 2012).

Attacks of Unauthorized Third Parties

Possible threats result from wiretapping, eavesdropping, message tampering and replay, as countermeasures, conventional security functions for protected communication via insecure networks are appropriate (construction of secure channels, mutual authentication, use of cryptographic mechanisms and time stamps).

Attacks Among Agent Systems

Agent systems form the platform for the creation, interpretation, execution, transfer, co-ordination and co-operation as well as the termination and extermination of agents. They are generally bound to a host and thus not the mobile. Exactly as less than 1, the conventional concepts for security in distributed systems are applicable to recognize and classify possible attacks to take appropriate countermeasures.

Attacks of Agents on Agents

In addition to spying out data and code and their manipulation by other agents, there are the threats of unauthorized use of services of an agent (e.g. by the unauthorized call of methods), of masquerading the own identity, spamming or repudiation of activities. Furthermore, agents can ignore authorized calls for service and deny service itself. For countermeasures against the mentioned threats the agents themselves are, on one hand, responsible for example (implementation of an access control mechanism, authentication of the communication partner) and, on the other hand, the agent system as the execution platform (e.g. auditing and accounting). The programming language used (encapsulation, information hiding, and prevention of memory manipulation) and the processing model (isolated memory, sandboxing, access prohibition) is of particular importance.

Attacks of Agents on Agent Systems

In addition to the attacks characterized so far, there are spying out, unauthorized use and the manipulation of resources which are managed by the agent system. That's why the agent system has to authenticate agents (especially mobile agents prior to their arrival) as well as to reliably limit the resources useable by agents on the basis of access control mechanisms. Furthermore, secure programming languages of agents (or languages extended by security concepts) and a secure processing model (code inspection prior to execution, sandboxing) serves the countering attacks of agents on agent systems.

Attacks of Agent Systems on Agents

The problem of the 'malicious host' is one of the current topics of research in the field of security in agent applications. It cannot be treated with conventional mechanisms because there are no such attacks in traditional distributed systems. In addition to the spying out and the manipulation of code and data brought by the agent, a possible attack could be denying the execution/ interpretation of the all or part of the agent code. Basically it is assumed that a complete solution of the problem is not possible as long as trustworthy hardware or realization

of agent systems which is not used. There for proposals exits for individual branches which, however, need further intensive research. In addition to the mentioned hardware-oriented approach, the following methods are essential using encrypted functions, code mess up and time stamp, achievement of trustworthiness (of the agent system) through reputation and social control.

INTRUSION PREVENTION

The 1st when intrusions occur, possible problems are included:

1. Loss of data;
2. Modification of data, which can be more serious than loss of data;
3. Misuse of equipment;
4. Loss of employee time and/or CPU time;
5. Time spent assessing damage and cleaning up;
6. Embarrassment to the company/project/individual.

The 2nd watching and intrusion detection system should be reported, because the biggest security threat is legitimate users having their login information sniffed at a remote site, need to watch for unusual activity for each user. For example, if a user typically uses a computer for editing, compiling, and running FORTRAN programs, and suddenly begins using Internet Relay Chat (IRC), we need to be notified.

Following the activity patterns of users requires monitoring the commands they issue, which meant a network keystroke logger was needed. Port scanning is very popular and because we need to watch other network services (in addition to those that the keystroke logger has been pick up).

The 3rd suspect an intrusion occurs, possible actions are:

1. Remove compromised machine from the network,
2. Setup additional monitoring,
3. Deny access to effected machines and/or subnets,
4. Deny access to specific users,
5. Notify essential personnel (Thomas, 2001).

AGENT SECURITY

In an open network environment, intentional attacks on both machines and agents will start as soon as the system is deployed, and even in the closed network environment with trusted users, there is still the danger of misprogrammed agents, which can do significant damage accidentally. Hence, security is perhaps the most critical issue in a migrated agent system.

As stated system is made of group of machines, which provide a running environment for group of agents. The following points address the problems of protecting these different parts of the system from one another:

Protecting the Machine from the Agent

The machine should be able to authenticate the agent's owner, assign resource limited based on this authentication, and prevent any violation of the resource limits. To prevent thief or damage of sensitive attacks, the resource limits must include access right (reading certain file).

Protecting Agents from Agents

An agent should not be able to interfere with another agent to steal agent's resources. This problem can be viewed as a sub problem of protecting the machines, since as long as an agent cannot subvert the agent communication machines and cannot consume or hold excessive system resources. It will be unable to affect agents unless that agent chooses to communicate with it.

Protecting the machine and other agents involves two tasks:

- **Authentication:** Verify the identity of agent owner, and
- **Authorization and Enforcement:** Assign resource limited to the agent based on this identity and enforce those resources limits.

EXAMPLE OF AUTOMATIC INTRUSION DETECTION AND SECRET PRESERVATION MULTI AGENT USING AUTHENTICATION MEASUREMENT NETWORK THREAT

This chapter includes the example to Automatic Intrusion Detection and Secret Preservation Multi Agent Using Authentication Measurement Network Threat through the design and the implemention a special Framework for security in a distributed heterogeneous data bases networks depending on Multi agent system, this is type of protection agents from machine.

The framework can provide distributed, adaptive and automated for complex Databases. Multi agents seem more convenient to executed it through internet (remotely globally) and intranet (locally), and analyze login file through the analysis data.

A machine should be able to tamper with an agent or pull sensitive information out of the agent without the agent's cooperation. Protecting an agent from a malicious machine is the most difficult security problem (unless trusted hardware is available on each agent server), something which is extremely unlikely in the near future, there is no way to prevent a malicious machine from examining or modifying any part of the agents that visit it.

The automatic intrusion detection can preser secret multi agent using authentication measurement network threat that proposed system security multi agent distributed system to design a platform security in order to be applied in distributed system by using the multi agent systems and applying intrusion detection security measurement method (Rijndael encryption) to prevent it.

One of the important measurement used in the proposed security system is 'simple object access protocol message' (for more security through applying Rijndael encryption) and uses the 'cookies principle' (for keeping the information when exchange the data between websites for one mint only) also used 'session principle' (to keep more secure of the present system 'platform' to check any intruder need to reduce information by clearing all the authorized users after one second) the distributed system platform will be applied through the internet environments (E-Government), which is used for one time for testing only.

The management of heterogeneous networks requires the capabilities to combine different types of data and to account events. No single network management methodology is likely to satisfy the diverse needs of networks so as to maintain a desirable level of analysis data –based performance through Globally reports (Integrity monitoring of full reports, Fail Log, Success Log and the DB implementation) and Locally reports in the same Local server agent (Fail Login and Success User login).

The object-oriented paradigm has led to the concept of 'objects' distributed around the network, where these objects may consist of data and code embedded in SOAP Message.

An agent is an encapsulated computer system that is situated in some environments, and that is capable flexible, autonomous action and dynamic Fail over (for set the backup web service, fielded of global administrator accurse then the other path automatically discovers this problem) in that environment in order to meet its design objectives. The architecture of the automated system is able to support the Multi agent distributed, communication between agents, access to server resources, security mechanisms, appropriate efficiency, and ability to run on platform.

Once a security policy has been lain down, the distributed system platform will be more secue becomes it has been enforced. Important security mechanisms are (Encryption, Authentication, Authorization and Auditing).

PROPOSED SECURITY MULTI AGENT DISTRIBUTED SYSTEM

The proposed platform can provide distributed, scalability adaptive and automated multi agent network management for today's complex networks. This model is based on the use of the agents system that uses semantic model (behavior) to correlate and analyze data; control decisions (authenticated and authorized) are made both locally and globally from a analysis data perspective.

Architecture of Secret Multi Agent for the Proposed System is used one of the important Measurement to prevent authentication attack in the Network.

Security Multi Agent Management

Security agent's management policies specify that actions must be performed when certain events occur and provide the ability to respond to the changing circumstances if there is a need to do so to keep the system secure. Security agent management policies specify what actions must be specified when security violations occur and who must execute those actions; what auditing and logging activities must be performed, when and by whom. Its can be used to handle cases of intrusion detection; policies can be set up to respond to the monitoring of security related activities, report suspicious activity and enact further surveillance or increase security measures in case of intrusions or attempted security violations. it might enable or disable access control policies accordingly to increase the degree of security provided by the system.

Therefore must be login the (User name & password) to check who users have used the login (administrator or local web server).

Security Intrusion Detection and Prevention

Computing is heading towards another major revolution with the maturing of distributed object technology that will allow applications to be distributed across heterogeneous machines anywhere in the world. Simultaneously, this approach aims to secure the architecture of distributed object technologies using agents system, and how they are progressing. In particular, the roles of ASP.net and V.Basic.net. One of the security encryption methods which are used in distributed system is principle of Cookie. The Cookie keeps the precise integrity information for one second between sites and then Cookie clears itself.

The intruder can be prevented from distributed system either by addressing and guiding it to the global Security Agent, or by failing in Security (authorization and authentication) i.e. (User name and Password), for three times and recording in the global login file by using Rijndael encryption. Intrusion Prevention is differing from an Intrusion Detection System (IDS).

Security Agent Policy

Security agent management in large systems with millions of objects is impossible without the ability to group security policies and structures them to reflect organizational structure, preserve the natural way system administrators operate or simply provide reusability of common definitions, easing the task of policy administrators divided into (global agent features and local agent).

Global Agent Features

The administrator agents have the main task with XML web services as shown in Figure 1.

1. Setting Security and privileges.
2. Detecting Service Statues.
3. Supervising DB inquiries.
4. Generating reports.
5. Sending status E-Mails.
6. Failed over.
7. The log history for each activity includes only the administrator agent functionality.

The administrator of agents is recognized to be an important part of an Agent Platform (AP). This certainly holds for large-scale agents system deployed on heterogeneous Data Base (DB). There are main activities for administrator agents:

1. Determining the Roles for creating the privileges for all Global server and Local servers (hosts) need the (DB, Access file) for Read, modify or full control. Has different privilege access and security.
2. Creating local system administrator then broadcast to the global (supervised) server.
3. Exist in groups.
4. Creating User.
5. Administrator can associate user to access remote server, give user dynamic roles.
6. The log history for each activity includes only the administrator agent functionality.
7. Site management system (add new site that all local servers can communicate with it)
8. The E-Mail sending will provide the required services and developments for notifications to users.

Algorithm and Data Flow

The data flow processing in the distributed system platform, and the algorithm for data processing in SADS platform describes how the system process of data will be (dynamic, autonomy and flexible):

Input: User Name and Password authentication.
Output: Intrusion detections and prevent all intruder.

Figure 1. Data flow in the proposed system

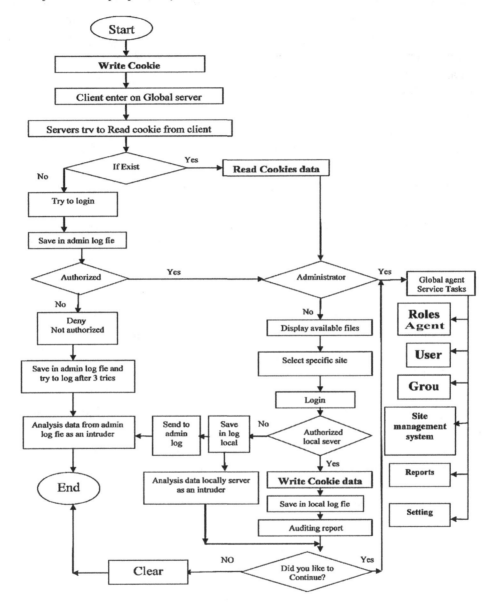

1. Start to log in the SADS platform to implement the simulation of E-Government application through the specific path (Seminar, 2012).

2. Write cookie (the cookie used to keep the data at one second and clear itself after this time when exchange data done between websites).

3. *Client agent* (user) tries to login *Global agent* through the application (cookie keeps for data to detected whether its authorized or not).

4. If (Exist) before that time, then read the cookie information from the administrator agent (the same data).

Otherwise: Session clear information.

5. If authorized, now the system Global administrator agent check through the SOAP message translator as an administrator (user) or not: **If** administrator is true then the system will be already connected automatically with the website administrator agent, which includes all the tasks:

    a. Determined Roles agent for local server (hosts)

    b. Specified Groups agent (which user belongs to deal with which group)

    c. Identify users in the Local server agent (authentication).

    d. Allow administrator to add new websites (Site management system) belongs to system (E-Government), these available links used from local servers agent.

    e. Log history is also the functionality controlled and executed from Global admin agent (saved in Global login agent) to generated reports:

        i. Full of general login report monitoring.

        ii. Specific for all intruders in the Global and Local system.

        iii. Fail Login and Success Login.

        iv. DB implementation.

    f. E-Mail sending if any fail over accurse in any local system (may be stopped) then the administrator sends warning messages for all the other local server agents to change this path automatically.

Else not administrator (local server user), the local user may be as (Local server agent or general user...etc), then can connect autonomy and more flexible according to (user name and password permission) immediately after check authentication.

a. Write cookie, if authenticated then can access to deal with all links available websites, and save all activities in log file the local server.

b. Generate analysis data (general local report for local server and specific report for an intruder in the local server).

c. Send reports if Global administrator agent needed form local servers including the intruders only), another report for access write user activities, stop.

6. **Else** (Not authorized), the wrong (incorrect name or password), the application allow to try log in 3 time only), and save all activities in the Integrity monitoring, to analysis data for intruder.

7. Generate reports activities for global administrator agent.

8. E-Mail sending if any local agent servers fail over then discovered automatically by Global administrator agent through change the path. Notes that the SADS system dynamically check (Global administrator agent has fail over or not) this problem autonomy solved through define new path automatically without any interrupt of SADS system has detected from other local server agent.

9. Stop.

CONCLUSION

From the implementation of the proposed system and the effects of the performance results, it leads to the following conclusions:

1. One of the main conclude of agent system can be satisfied in the architecture, the agent can be adapted and autonomy in the system.

2. The cookie mechanism keeps the client information when exchanged between websites naming service, access control, flexible distributed computing, and system wide monitor.

3. The SADS platform can provide flexibility for:
   a. Distribution of the Agent concepts and implementation in the E-Government system.
   b. Agent checking the authority of programs inside and outside the network.
   c. Prevention of an intrusion to the heterogeneous Data Bases.

4. Log history monitoring which provides a set of administrative methods that include:
   a. Access to all existing registration users where their names on a local server agent (host).
   b. Adding and removing users and administrators.
   c. Obtaining a list of currently registrations servers.
   d. Obtaining a list of failed machines.
   e. Obtaining failed over (when the fail in the system occurs, it can be automatically discover the problem by changing the path without any local web service(s) agent knows, or when the path for local server is changed).

5. Data Encryption Standard substitutes characters and rearranges their order on the basis of an encryption key provided to authorize users via a secure mechanism.

6. The control agent communicates with local agents and other control agents to give local and global perspectives of the QoS network.

7. Combine Agents in one system (architecture and policy) to form one complete Agent Security system.

SUGGESTIONS FOR FUTURE WORKS

As one knows in practice, it is impossible to produce a complete and consistent documented requirements and applications. Many things could be added and suggested to the proposed system in order to be more reliable and applicable. The following ideas may be suggested for future works:

1. Try to choose different approach in the Agent design (adding new features by expanding the permission under the control of Local server's agents in the Security Agent Distributed System platform.

2. Combine the proposed system with Wireless Application Protocol (WAP) to be more flexible. Using Wireless Application with proposed system will give the flexibility and reliability for the hybrid system. This gives the power to the proposed system and makes it easy to use. This idea could be extended by using Mobile system by adding a proxy to the proposed system.

3. Using a mathematical Model to improve the Quality of Service (QoS) for the Network.

4. Using a Multi-Lingual Interface to make the system available to everybody.

REFERENCES

Askguru. (2011). Retrieved March 12, 2011 from http://askguru.net/newreply.php?tid=11752&pid=46273

Buchanan, W. J., Naylor, M., Mannion, M., Pikoulas, J., & Scott, A. (2011). *Agent Technology*. Retrieved July 5, 2013 from http://buchananweb.co.uk/research/agent2.PDF

Cissyr. (2013). Retrieved July 17, 2012 from http://www.cis.syr.edu/~wedu/Teaching/cis758/LectureNotes/Security_Overview.docCissyrCissyr

Coursehero. (2013). Retrieved August 14, 2013 from http://www.coursehero.com/file/4039109/SecurityOverview

Das, S. K. (2012). *Seminar Report on Intrusion Detection System*. Retrieved August 21, 2012 from: http://www.123seminarsonly.com/Seminar-Reports/006/73557476-Intrusion-Detection-System.doc

Detection. (2011). Retrieved June 10, 2011 from http://int-detection.fotopages.com

Eipgov. (2012). Retrieved May 5, 2012 from: http://www.eip.gov.eg/Upload/ConferenceDocs/4/4.pdf

Guijarro, M., Rubén, F.-F., & Pajares, G. (2011). A multi-agent system architecture for sensor networks. In F. Alkhateeb (Ed.), *Multi-Agent Systems: Modeling, Control, Programming, Simulations and Applications*. InTech; doi:10.5772/14309

Hamed, S. M. (2005). *Design and Implementation of a Secure Distributed Agent System*. PhD thesis, University of Technology, Iraq.

Ijarcsse. (2012). Retrieved May 25, 2012 from: http://www.ijarcsse.com/docs/papers/Volume_3/7_July2013/V3I7-0225.pdf

Letsch, T. (2001). *Agents and system agents 2001-02-21*. Retrieved October 10, 2013 from http://www.tagents.org/thesis/node3.html

Mobach, D. G. A., Overeinder, B. J., Wijngaards, N. J. E., & Brazier, F. M. T. (2001). *Managing Agent Life Cycles in Open Distributed Systems*. Retrieved from http://www.soc.napier.ac.uk/~bill/research/dist_c26.PDF

Ojaa, M., Tammb, B., & Taveterc, K. (2001).. . *Agent-Based Software Design.*, 7(1), 5–21.

Proctor Paul, E. (2001). *The Practical Intrusion Detection Hand Book*. Nottingham, England: Prentice Hall.

Ross, J. A. (2001). *Security Engineering: A Guide to building Dependable Distributed Systems*. New York, USA: John Wiley.

Seminarproject. (2010). Retrieved April 8, 2011 from http://seminarprojects.com/Thread-mobile-agent-based-distributed-intrusion-detection-system.

Tom, W. (2000). *Agent-based system architecture and organization*. Retrieved from http://www.enel.ucalgary.ca/People/far/Lectures/SENG697/PDF/tutorials/2002/Agent-Based_System_Archit

Warnier, M., Brazier, F. M. T., & Oskamp, A. (2008, March). Security of distributed digital criminal dossiers. *Journal of Software*, 3(3).

Warnier, M., Oey, M. A., Timmer, R. J., Overeinder, B. J., & Brazier, F. M. T. (2009). Enforcing integrity of agent migration paths by distribution of trust. *International Journal of Intelligent Information and Database Systems*, 3(4).

Weyns, D. (2010). *Architecture-Based Design of Multi-Agent Systems*. Springer.

KEY TERMS AND DEFINITIONS

Agent Platform: The management of agents is recognized to be an important part of an agent platform. This certainly holds for large-scale multiage systems deployed on heterogeneous and open systems.

Automatic Intrusion Detection: The automatic intrusion detection can preservation secret multi agent using authentication measurement network threat that proposed system security multi agent distributed system to design a platform for security in order to be applied in distributed system by using the multi agent systems and applying intrusion detection security measurement method (Rijndael encryption) to prevent it.

Intrusion Detection System (IDS): Faced with the problem of performing a huge amount of data over transfer.

Intrusion Prevention: When any problem accord the system watching and intrusion detection system should be reported to us, because our biggest security threat is legitimate users having their login information sniffed at a remote site, we need to watch for unusual activity for each user. For example, if a user typically uses a computer for editing, compiling, and running FORTRAN programs, and suddenly begins using Internet Relay Chat (IRC), we need to be notified.

Multi Agent System (MAS): Architectures can be considered organizations composed of autonomous and proactive agents that interact with one another in order to cooperate and then achieve either a common goal or simply their own goals.

Multi Agent Systems: Used in various applications such as workflow, scheduling and optimization. An agent is a physical or logical entity characterized by many attributes.

Security Agent: The security of a distributed application can be an important issue. The level of security depends on the sensitivity of the information in the system. System information includes information communicated between agents, as well as the information stored with each agent. With distributed applications that interface to external systems.

Chapter 4
Real Time Internal Intrusion Detection:
A Case Study of Embedded Sensors and Detectors in E-Government Websites

Zuhoor Al-Khanjari
Sultan Qaboos University, Oman

Asaad Abdulrahman Nayyef
Sultan Qaboos University, Oman

ABSTRACT

The increase of attacks on e-Government infrastructures led to the emergence of several information security techniques. Insider threat is one of the most complex problems in information security. It requires a sophisticated response to detect and protect the un-authorized use. This chapter provides a framework for developing a high level security management for e-Government website. The framework is based on the sensors and detectors, which consist of relatively small amounts of source code to detect all attacks in e-Government website against all threats in real time. In this chapter, the authors also provide a full illustration of how to design and protect all files used to implement a secure e-Government websites. This should contain a self- audit of the file and represent a kind of processes that are used to protect data in different types of files including: image, sound, string or any file within e-Government website.

INTRODUCTION

Insider threat is one of the most complex problems in information security it requires a sophisticated response to detect the subtle variations in access patterns that separate intentional misuse from authorized use.

Historically, the detection technology dated back to 1980. Anderson introduced the concept of intrusion detection. Anderson proposed a "security surveillance system" involving formal examination of a system's audit logs. In examining the system threats, Anderson also introduced the notion of categorizing intruders based upon their

DOI: 10.4018/978-1-4666-6583-5.ch004

Copyright © 2015, IGI Global. Copying or distributing in print or electronic forms without written permission of IGI Global is prohibited.

access to a system, and he defined the internal intruders with permissions to access the system and external intruders without any permission (Anderson, 1980).

In this chapter, the authors advocate improving the embedded sensors for real time internal intrusion detection system. This involves adding code to the e-Government website where monitoring will take place. The sensors check for specific conditions that indicate an attack is taking place, or an intrusion has occurred. Embedded sensors have advantages over other intruder detection techniques (usually implemented as separate processes) in terms of reduced host impact, resistance to attack, efficiency and effectiveness of detection.

The authors describe the use of embedded sensors in general, and their application to the detection of website attacks to protect all files in e-Government website. The Design and development of the sensors have been done in the real website hosting. Our tests show a high success rate in the detection of the attacks. The work we propose is divided into four stages:

1. Designing infrastructure for the development of the sensors.
2. Implementing sensors for detecting intrusions.
3. Performing analysis on the data obtained in step (2) and validating if the existing sensors can be used to detect new attacks.
4. Connecting to other ISP to open same e-Government website.

A method is proposed to detect internal intrusion for protecting e-Government website using Java language. This is done by dealing with the classes of the HTML file. This file contains all programmable steps to detect internal intrusion and protect all files, which deal with that site from unauthorized changing by an intruder inside ISP. Automatic audit for all files provides high security to the site protection without using any other protection programs. These programs might

be used to detect intruder inside e-Government website in ISP. With this method we can protect all files, which are dealing with the e-Government website, and automatically check for all files inside class file. This method differs from other methods by not providing the program code inside the HTML file. Therefore, it is difficult to discover and analyze the proposed method because it is inside the class file.

By using real time technique, we can use our method to detect internal intruder and protect all kinds of files inside e-Government website and all those which deal with them without returning to or getting the help of the ISP and without stopping the site for service in case of intrusion through operating an alternative site from another ISP.

This chapter is organized as follows. Section 2 provides the background and related work on the intrusion detection. Section 3 explains the Intrusion Detection System (IDS) and methods of intrusion detection, intrusion tools and defense techniques. Section 4 discusses types of attack, methods of attack, vectors for attack and types of defenses. Section 5 describes the Sensors, detectors and embedded sensors for intrusion detection. This section also provides the main functions of the proposed system and the infrastructure of the internal embedded sensor. Section 6 provides concluding remarks of the work. Section 7 presents our suggestions for future work.

RELATED WORK

Intrusion detection in e-Government website is performed through strong auditing. By enabling auditing for files and objects that are critical to security, you can track exactly which users have accessed sensitive objects and in what manner. The major difference between anonymous hacking from the Internet and abuse by valid users is that you can easily determine the identity of valid users and hold them legally accountable for their behavior. Intrusion detection in production private computers is simpler but less effective than intrusion detection in public sites. Internal users won't be fooled by decoys they know the network architecture. They also have no need for the signature attacks like port scanners used by hackers, because they know exactly where servers are and what they perform. Securing public Internet servers is very difficult because you are inviting the public to use your computers in a specific context. The goal of Internet security is to ensure that the public cannot use your servers in any manner that you don't specifically invite. To keep your public servers secure, you need to follow these four security practices:

- Restrict access to all protocols except public protocols that you intend to serve.
- Harden public protocols so that they cannot be exploited.
- Ensure that legitimate remote users cannot be impersonated.
- Monitor all access to determine that the first three practices are successful.

An intrusion detection system is an important component to enhance security in e-Government website. The security environment in e-Government website differs from other websites that are used for browsing the internet (Al-Khanjari & Alanee, 2013). Paez et al. (2013) proposed some techniques in order to provide internal security for the agents belonging to the system and works with a multi agent platform and each component inside the infrastructure is verified using security techniques in order to provide integrity Song et al. (2010) focused on provides metrics to measure the effectiveness of modern polymorphic engines and provide insights into their designs. We describe methods to evade statistics-based IDS sensors and present suggestions on how to defend against them. Park and Salvatore (2012) described the isolate the proprietary source code from such theft using fake source code as decoys. Also in his paper addresses the two research problems. The

first: How to generate fake (bogus) software. The second: How to detect software exfiltration and unauthorized use. Chou (2011) describes in his paper an ensemble design for cyber security threats detection, which fuses the results from multiple classifiers together to make a final assessment decision. For promoting both speed and accuracy in the detection performance. Also in his paper he is used the data mining techniques to reduce the number of false alarms. His results indicate that our ensemble approach achieves higher detection rates than that of using a full feature set of classifiers. Zhang and Gu (2011) proposed an anomaly based network intrusion detection system based on Multilayer perceptron with single hidden layer trained by Back propagation learning algorithm. The system operation was divided into three stages: Input Data Collection and Preprocessing, Training, and Detection stage. The result for the proposed module was 95% detection rate. Ajith et al. (2013) discussed in detail the overview of port-scan attack and the response of IDS are studied. Sumit et al. (2012) in his work presents a situation-aware intrusion detection model that integrates these heterogeneous data sources and builds a semantically rich knowledge-base to detect cyber threats/vulnerabilities. Also he described a semantically rich framework for a situation aware intrusion detection system which can harvest the advantages of heterogeneous data sources to detect the threats. Jonny et al. (2012) presented the results of deploying a knowledge-based system for detection, identification, and disambiguation of various sensor and system faults in an electromechanical actuator system. Furthermore, in his paper presented some approaches for mitigation of the most common sensor faults: bias, drift, scaling and dropout. Based on the sensitivity analysis, the KB system performance showed similar results compared to a NN-based inference system implemented previously. In addition, the system expanded on the previous work in three aspects. First, the KB system broadened the scope, both in terms of sensor/fault combinations and functionality (i.e. the system can handle more sensor-fault pairs without significant modifications). Secondly, the KB system demonstrated robustness of fault detection in the presence of sensor dropouts since it was able to reason about system fault cases even when a key sensor signal was absent. Thirdly, the KB system was able to calculate fault parameters and correct sensor fault signals for the fault types discussed.

INTRODUCTION TO THE INTRUSION DETECTION SYSTEM (IDS)

In the last few years, a number of Intrusion Detection Systems (IDS) have been developed both in the commercial and academic sectors. These systems use various approaches to detect unauthorized activity and have given us some insight into the problems that still have to be solved before we can have intrusion detection systems that are useful and reliable in production settings for detecting a wide range of intrusions in website. The systems should be so well protected. In this case an attack would require so much time and effort that this helps us in giving the attacker hard time and might according the attacker before gaining access. Ideally, a company should have the proper Intrusion Detection System (IDS) in place so that it can detect an attack and protect against it before it does any damage. An intrusion detection system (IDS) is software that is used to detect unauthorized activity and usually configured to log and alert you on your website or network.

There are several different ways in which IDS might be implemented. Here is a general list of how they are implemented and used:

- **Network Intrusion Detection System (NIDS):** Used to discover attackers on your network and it is important to gather the host information of the intruder. A NIDS monitors network traffic and traffic patterns that can be used to discover someone attempting a denial-of-service attack, port scans, or attempts to guess the password to a secured resource (Zeng & ZhiChen, 2010).
- **System Integrity Verifier (SIV):** Monitors a single system's file structure to determine if (and when) an attacker modifies, deletes, or changes a system file. Implementation of Trusted Computing in providing a mechanism to check whether hardware, software or application running on a platform "behaves as expected" without a need for further validation (Isa et al., 2012).
- **Log File Monitor (LFM):** Parses system log entries to identify possible system attacks or compromises. This allows for aggregating low-level metrics from operating systems, to higher-level application-specific metrics derived from services, databases or application log files (Konig et al., 2012).

Intrusion Detection

Intrusion detection and assessment systems are an integral part of any physical protection system. Detection and assessment provide a basis for the initiation of an effective security response. Intrusion Detection Systems (IDSs) should be designed to facilitate the detection of attempted and actual unauthorized entry into designated areas and should complement the security response by providing the security force with prompt notification of the detected activity from which an assessment can be made and a response initiated (U.S. Nuclear Regulatory Commission, 2011; Ojugo, Eboka, Okonta, Yoro & Aghware, 2012).

Intruder

A person who is the perpetrator of a computer security incident often referred to as hackers or crackers. An intruder is a vandal who may be operating from within the boundaries of an organization or attacking it from the outside. Intruders may enter a computer system in order to: Inspect Insert, Modify and Delete. Data which would normally be under the control of the legitimate users of the system and the ultimate purpose of intruders may be to (Robin, 2013):

- Prevent the legitimate users from using the system.
- Reveal confidential information.
- Use the system as a stepping stone to attack other systems.

There are two types of intruders:

- **External Intruders:** Who have no authorized access to network resources.
- **Internal Intruders:** Who have authorized access to network resources.

Intrusion

Intrusion is the set of actions that attempts to compromise integrity, confidentiality or availability of network resources; while an intruder is any user or group of users who initiates such intrusive action. Intrusion generally refers to unauthorized access by outside parties, whereas misuse is typically used to refer to unauthorized access by internal parties.

Methods of Intrusion Detection

Intrusion detection may be managed by two basic methods: knowledge-based and behavior-based detection. Knowledge-based detection relies on the identification of known attack signatures and events that should never occur within a network. Behavior-based detection involves the use of established usage patterns and baseline operation to identify variations that may pinpoint unauthorized access attempts.

Knowledge-Based IDS

The most common form of IDS detection involves knowledge-based identification of improper, unauthorized, or incorrect access and use of network resources. The identification of known attack signatures allows for few false alarms a known attack pattern is almost always a good sign of a danger to the network. Because the signature identifies a known method of attack, you can use detailed planning to counter and recover from the attack (Smith, Matthews, Anupam, & Tim, 2012). Knowledge-based IDS has several limitations, including the following:

- The maintenance of the knowledge library to include newly identified signatures can become a complex and time-consuming task.
- Knowledge-based detection of internal misuse is difficult because most misuse involves an improper utilization of a normal form of access or privilege.
- As new exploits are identified, it will take some time before an identified signature for the attack can be prepared and distributed. During this time, knowledge-based IDS cannot identify attacks of the new type.
- Knowledge-based IDS is closely tied to the technologies used within a particular network. As new technologies are integrated, or evolutionary changes are made to the network environment, knowledge-based systems may be unable to provide support for all potential avenues of attack created by the changes.

Behavior-Based IDS

One of the most common workstation-level compromise-detection methods involves a user noticing an unusual pattern of behavior, the ability to detect anomalies from normal patterns of operation makes it possible to identify new threats that may bypass knowledge-based IDS. Highly secure environments may use complex patterns of behavior analysis (Christopher & Audrey, 2002).

Although more flexible than knowledge-based IDS, behavior-based detection has several limitations, including the following:

- The most common drawback to behavior-based IDS is the high incidence of false alarms. Because anything falling outside of the established behavior profile is considered a potential sign of attack, any action that varies from the norm may generate an alert.
- Behavior profiles must be regularly updated to include changes in technology, changes in network configuration, and changes to business practices that may affect the normal order of operations. In systems that maintain detailed user access profiles, even a simple promotion within the business structure might require administrative action to update the usage profile of the user involved.
- Because of the need for periodic updates to behavior profiles, behavior-based IDS might not provide identification of threats during the update cycle and may even identify an ongoing attack pattern as part of the normal pattern of use, thus creating a potential area for later exploitation.

Intrusion Tools and Techniques

Hackers use a variety of tools and techniques to attack networks. Assuming that the intruder begins with no information about your site. Hackers rummaging through the Internet looking for targets of opportunity. Hacking attempts usually proceed as follows (Dabbagh et al. 2011; Al-Haidari et al., 2012):

- **IP Address Scans:** Scan across the network range, if any, to find service hosts. Hackers usually scan at least the entire range of IP addresses around your host and may use reverse DNS lookup to determine if those other hosts are registered to your network.
- **Port Scans:** Scan across responding hosts to find running services. This information tells the hacker what services are running on each publicly reachable host.
- **Services Evaluation:** Determine the operating system type of each host.
- **Target Selection:** Selects the weakest found host. Hackers will usually target the host with the most running services, in the assumption that little to no work has gone into securing that host's default configuration.
- **Automated Password Attacks:** Used against services like FTP, HTTP or others that allow access to the file system or a remote console. Hackers employ software specifically written to perform a high rate of logon attempts using dictionaries of common passwords.

Intruder Detection and Defense Techniques

The following are the three main types of intruder detection and defense techniques (Chao et al., 2012; Esposito et al., 2013):

Active Detection

Active detection is analogous to a security guard walking down the hallway rattling doors. The guard is checking for a break-in. Special network software can search for hackers trying known attack methods, including suspicious activity as they travel over the network. Some sophisticated active systems actually take action, such as shutting down the communications sessions that the hacker is using, as well as e-mailing or paging you. Some packages actually go as far as trying to cripple the computer from which the hacker is attacking; the active detection involves some actions to be taken by the intrusion detection system in response to a suspicious activity or an intrusion.

Passive Detection

Video cameras are an example of passive intrusion-detection systems. Their counterparts in networking are files that log events that occur on the network. Tripwire for UNIX systems is one of the earliest programs of this type. With passive detection systems, files and data are looked at, and checksums are calculated for each file and piece of data. These checksums are then stored in a log file. If the network administrator notices a security breach on the network, he or she can access the log files to find clues regarding the security breach.

Proactive Defense

The main feature of the proactive defense is to make sure your network is invulnerable to attack. You can do this through research and maintenance. You must stay current on all known security holes on your network. You can use tools such as SA-TAN to find the holes in your security walls and plug them with software patches. Unfortunately, before you can patch a hole, it must be discovered and the war against attackers must be ongoing. As soon as you patch a hole, the hacker will find and exploit two other weaknesses. It usually takes some time for apatch to be developed and, at that time, companies lose resources to a hacker.

THREAT WEBSITE

To prepare and protect your Website in order to preserve the authenticity, confidentiality, integrity, and availability, you need to understand the multiple types of attacks.

Types of Attack

The seriousness of a hacking event is determined mostly by whether you are a random target of opportunity or you have been specifically targeted (Hoang & Uyen, 2012).

- A random attack does not indicate a specific, malicious intent against your web site and it is unlikely to result in a sustained hacking effort.
- A targeted attack is perpetrated specifically against your organization. It requires vigilance to prevent and research to determine who is perpetrating the attack.

Specifically, you need to prepare for the following three types of attacks:

- **Automated Attacks:** Also referred to as "worms," automated attacks are perpetrated by virus-like software that exploits a known weakness in specific Internet service software, such as a Web server or an e-mail server.
- **Target of Opportunity Attacks:** Random target-of-opportunity attacks are the typical "hacking" events that occur on the Internet.
- **Targeted Attacks:** Attacks specifically targeted against your organization are very rare and far more serious. These attacks are unlikely to happen to most businesses, but attackers who carry them out are more persistent and likely to use any means possible to gain access or cause a denial of service. In exceptionally rare cases, these attacks might be perpetrated by an experienced hacker looking for a technical challenge.

There are many ways to categorize these attackers; all attackers share certain characteristics. They don't want to be caught, so they try to conceal themselves, their identity and real geographic location. If they gain access to your system, they will certainly attempt to preserve that access.

- **Joyriders:** Are bored people looking for amusement. They break in because they think you might have interesting data, or because it would be amusing to use your computers, or because they have nothing better to do. They might be out to learn about the kind of computer you have or about the data you have. They're curious but not actively malicious.
- **Vandals:** Are out to do damage, either because they get their kicks from destroying things, or because they don't like you. Vandals are a big problem if you're somebody that the Internet underground might think of as The Enemy or if you tend to annoy people who have computers and time. In most circumstances, deleting your data, or even ruining your computer equipment, is not the worst thing somebody could do to you, but it is what vandals do.
- **Scorekeepers:** Many intruders are engaging in an updated version of an ancient tradition. They're gaining bragging rights, based on the number and types of systems they've broken into. Like joyriders and vandals, scorekeepers may prefer sites of particular interest. Breaking into something well known, well defended, or otherwise especially cool is usually worth more points to them. However, they'll also attack anything they can get at; they're going for quantity as well as quality. They don't have to want anything you've got or care in the least about the characteristics of your site. They may or may not do damage on the way through. They'll certainly gather information and keep it for later use (perhaps using it to barter with other attackers). They'll probably try to leave themselves

ways to get back in later. And, if at all possible, they'll use your machines as a platform to attack others.

- **Spies:** Most people who break into computers do so for the same reason people climb mountains because they're there. While these people are not above theft, they usually steal things that are directly convertible into money or further access (e.g., credit card, telephone, or network access information). If they find secrets they think they can sell, they may try to do so, but that's not their main business.

Methods of Attacks

There are many types of attacks (Zhang, 2013; Sanmorino & Yazid, 2013). They are discussed as follows:

- **Denial of Service (DOS) Attacks:** These attacks exploit the nature of Internet protocols to prevent valid users from reaching a service. These attacks do not attempt to gain access to a system; they seek only to prevent others from using it.
- **Exploitation Attacks:** Frequently referred to as "buffer overruns," this type of attack seeks to connect anonymously to a service and then elevate the attacker's privileges on the system to that of a valid user or an administrator. This type of attack exploits a weakness in the server code allowing attackers to execute arbitrary code that they've sent to the service. The code elevates their privileges and allows them to gain direct access.
- **Information Gathering Attacks:** Information gathering attacks are not exploits or denial of service attacks; they themselves do nothing harmful to the target. These attacks are used to provide information for further intrusion into a system. Hackers routinely employ these methods to obtain and identify targets.

- **Disinformation Attacks:** Disinformation deceives the attack target to plant incorrect information. This information paves the way for future attacks.
- **Impersonation Attacks:** These attacks occur when a user without valid access uses a valid user account to gain access by either discovering a password or performing a brute-force password attack that reveals an account password. Disgruntled former employees or illicit competitors typically perpetrate these attacks, but hackers looking for a challenge might perpetrate them. These attacks are very serious because they indicate specific, malicious intent directed against your company.

Vectors for Attacks

The following are the ways for a hacker to access your website or network (Benjamin & Hsinchun, 2013):

- By using a computer on your network directly.
- By remote control server.
- By connecting over the Internet.
- By connecting to your network directly.

There are only a few ways an attacker can reach a computer as discussed below:

- **Direct Attack:** A direct attack occurs when a hacker attempts to exploit a computer directly from the computer's console. These attacks are exceptionally rare and are typically performed only by disgruntled employees or employees performing pranks on others who leave their computers logged on.
- **Wireless:** These attacks occur when hackers directly connect to the interior of the network using wireless services intended for legitimate users and begin attacking from inside the perimeter of the network.

- **Internet:** The Internet is the most common vector for attacks. The vast majority of businesses and many consumers worldwide have.
- **Internet Access:** This level of connectivity and the anonymous nature of lower-level Internet protocols create the perfect environment for hacking and invite abuse.

Types of Defenses Techniques

Education

Perhaps the most important thing that can be done to enhance network security is to promote education of network security issues by training or self-study. Network administrators are not the only ones who should be concerned about education, but users, IT managers, and executives should also have an appropriate understanding (Hahn et al., 2013; Khan et al., 2010).

Application Security

Various client and server applications have security settings that will help prevent unauthorized access and violation of system integrity. Web browsers, for instance, can be configured to implement certain restrictions depending on the Web site being viewed.

Physical Security

Access to wiring closets, server rooms, and even offices by unauthorized users presents a tremendous security risk. Keeping doors locked and unused network ports disabled are the starting points. Many corporate buildings have security personnel and require badges for access. If the enforcement of building access is lax, intruders won't need to attack via the Internet; they will just walk in and attach a laptop computer at a vacant desk.

Firewall

Firewalls keep your Internet connection as secure as possible by inspecting and then approving or rejecting each connection attempt made between your internal network and external networks like the Internet. Strong firewalls protect your network at all software layers from the Data Link layer up through the Application layer.

Firewalls function primarily to using three fundamental methods:

- Packet Filtering rejects TCP/IP packets from unauthorized hosts and rejects connection attempts to unauthorized services.
- Network Address Translation (NAT) translates the IP addresses of internal hosts to hide them from outside monitoring. You may hear of NAT referred to as IP masquerading.
- Proxy Services make high level application connections on behalf of internal hosts in order to completely break the network layer connection between internal and external hosts.

Most firewalls also perform two other important security services:

- **Encrypted Authentication:** Allows users on the public network to prove their identity to the firewall, in order to gain access to the private network from external locations.
- **Virtual Private Networking:** Establishes a secure connection between two private networks over a public medium like the Internet. This allows physically separated networks to use the Internet rather than leased line connections to communicate.

PURPOSE OF THE DEVELOPMENT OF THE SENSORS

We discuss the development of the sensors and the results obtained to protect Class, Image and other files in e-Government website. The two hypotheses that underlined in this chapter are practical in nature. First, they intend to show that it is feasible to build an intrusion detection system in e-Government website using both internal sensors and embedded detectors. Second, it can be used to detect both known and new attacks.

The internal embedded sensor was also used to confirm the possibility to building e-Government website security. Therefore, Designing infrastructure for the development of the sensors e-Government website was a center point for the development of this chapter.

What are Sensors and Detectors?

An internal sensor is a piece of code built into an e-Government website that monitors a specific variable or condition of that site. By being built into the program that it is monitoring, an internal sensor can perform direct monitoring on the system, which allows it to obtain information that is reliable (very difficult to modify) and real-time (obtained almost at the moment it is generated). An embedded detector is a piece of code built into an e-Government website that looks for specific signs of specific attacks or intrusions. An embedded detector bases its decisions on an internal sensor, explicitly (when the sensor is clearly differentiable from the detector).

Embedded sensors operate in a different manner in comparison to other intrusion detection systems. The sensors are themselves resistant to attack. They are also effective in detecting attacks in real-time with minimal impact on website performance. Sensor code is internal to the website, executable code. Sensors are also placed at specific and critical points in the execution path of running code. An attacker is unable to bypass the sensor, because the sensor is part of the code that it protects, therefore it is difficult to extract or remove it. This limits ways in which an attacker can disable a specific sensor. Sensors are only active when checking specific areas of code where attacks occur; they do not run all the time or as independent agents. Sensor code is not executed until the vulnerable code is about to be executed. Sensors do not impact the normal operation of the web site. The attack is detected at the exact moment that the vulnerability is exploited. An attack is immediately detected thus allowing administrators to have more time to deal with the issue. Because attack detection is real-time, an embedded sensor does not require storage and analysis of data.

Embedded Sensors for Intrusion Detection

An embedded sensor is defined as a piece of code in e-Government website that monitors a specific variable, activity or condition of a host. Because the sensor monitors the system directly (real-time) and not through an audit trail or through packets on a network. We say that it performs direct monitoring, and since the sensor is part of the e-Government website program or system it monitors, it is said that it is an internal sensor.

Embedded sensors are built by modifying the source code of the program that will be monitored. Sensors should be added to the code at the point where a security problem can be detected in the most efficient way by using the data available at that moment. If implemented correctly, the sensor will be able to determine whether an attack is taking place by performing very simple checks.

Advantages of Embedded Sensors in E-Government Website

Using embedded sensors for e-Government website in an internal intrusion detection system has the following advantages over using external sensors (implemented as separate programs):

- Data in e-Government website is never stored on an external medium before the sensor obtains them. Therefore, the possibility of an intruder modifying the data to hide its tracks.
- Embedded sensors are part of the code in e-Government website they monitor. Therefore, they cannot be disabled (as it is possible with an external sensor, which can be disabled) and they are very difficult to modify to produce incorrect results.
- Embedded sensors can analyze the data (at real time). Therefore, reducing impact on the host.
- They can obtain data at its source, or at the place where it is more convenient to obtain. Data does not have to traverse through an external program interface for the sensor to get it. This is because the internal sensor in website can read it directly off the program's data structures. This reduces the delay between the generation of the data and when the intrusion detection system can make use of it.
- Embedded sensors in e-Government website are only executed when the task they perform is required the section of code which includes themis executed.This indicates that they are not executed as separate processes or threads, but as part of the monitored program e-Government website.
- Embedded sensors in e-Government website can look for very specific conditions that signal attacks, instead of reporting generic data for analysis.

- This means that the amount of data that needs to be reported, collected and analyzed by higher level analysis engines is much smaller.

Disadvantages of Embedded Sensor in E-Government Website

Embedded sensors in e-Government website have the following disadvantages with respect to external sensors:

- They are more difficult to implement, because they require modifications to the source code of the e-Government website.
- Their implementation requires having access to the source code of the e-Government website
- They have to be implemented in the same language as the e-Government website program in which they are being incorporated.
- Improperly implemented sensors can have detrimental effects on the performance of the e-Government website.

The Main Function of the Proposed System

The proposed system operation starts by initializing the request signal of website through internet browser for controlling the e-Government website inside ISP. After initialization stage; the proposed system starts checking the collected information about the site. The first stage checks the watermark inside the e-Government website. The information about copyright protection will be detected and analyzed for accepting to check other files in e-Government website before opening it. The internal embedded sensor receives the request and tries to detect any threats inside ISP. If there is an attack, then the internal embedded sensor will try to stop this attack by sending signal to other ISP to open the same e-Government

website and sending Email to the administrator or the supervisor site, which contains a changed file. The main stages of the internal embedded sensor are:

- **Initialization Stage:** This stage includes the following:
  - ○ Initializing the request signal of e-Government website through internet browser
  - ○ Checking the watermark or copyright protection
  - ○ Initializing the analysis phase.
- **Analysis Stage:** This stage involves checking all files used in the e-Government website.

Figure 1 shows the basic flowchart of the proposed system.

Check Image File

After determining the initialization stage and checking watermark (copyright protection), the proposed system starts the second stage to check the Image file as URL if it exists, get the length, width and height of the Image and create crop filters Image from original Image. After that, the system converts the original Image file to Byte Array output Stream to draw Image in e-Government website. Otherwise, send signal to other ISP to open same e-Government website.

Check Sound File

After determining the initialization stage and checking Image file, the proposed system continues to read the Sound file as URL if it exists. It checks the length inside the ISP site if the sound file equals to original Sound Length then play the sound in e-Government website. Otherwise send signal to other ISP to open same e-Government website.

Figure 1. Flowchart of the proposed system

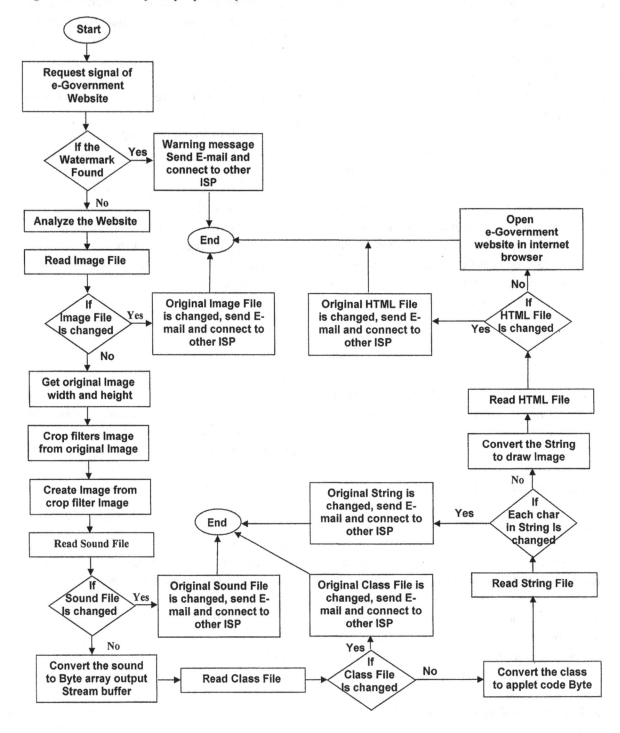

Figure 2. The original image file and crop filter image of SQU logo

Check Class File

In this step the proposed system checks the class file and opens it to applet's class file. Then it converts the original class file to temporary container for checking. After that it converts the original Class file to the temporary buffer to the byte array output stream buffer and checks other file in e-Government website.

Check String Text

In this step the proposed system checks the string text static. Then it gets the Length of each char, and shifts the length of each char in string text by any number. Then it determines the position to draw string in e-Government website.

Check HTML File

In this step the proposed system checks the length of HTML file. After that it converts the original HTML file to temporary buffer and then from temporary buffer to byte array output stream buffer to open the e-Government website in internet browser. Otherwise send signal to other ISP to open same e-Government website.

Infrastructure Internal Embedded Sensor

The main aim of the proposed system is to design real time internal intrusion detection in website to detect the intruder that tries to attack the website. The first step of the working proposed system is start up checking the watermark (copyright protection) as sending parameter from HTML file to Class file.

The proposed system will check other files step by step. After checking the watermark copyright protection the system will check Image file. Figure 2 shows the original image file and crop filter Image from original image of Sultan Qaboos University (SQU) logo.

If the Image has been changed, then the proposed system will send Email to supervisor site and send signal to other ISP to open same e-Government website.

When the proposed system checks the image file, it will check Sound file. If sound file has been changed then the proposed system will send an Email to supervisor site and send a signal to other ISP to open same e-Government website. When the proposed system finds that watermark, image and sound files have not been changed; it will check the Text String.

By using any program attack to change the text inside web site for example we used hex editor program to change original text. Then try to change the first word in text (Real). It can be replaced with numbers (1234) in HxD Hex Editor Software inside the ISP then the program asks for accepting to change original Text. After accepting to change the text inside website, the proposed system will send an Email to supervisor of the e-Government website and Security Officer. Also, it sends signal to other ISP to open the same e-Government website.

CONCLUSION

This chapter has proposed an architecture based on using internal sensors built into the source code of the programs. These sensors are monitored by real time and able to extract information from e-Government website inside the ISP in which they are generated or used. Furthermore, those internal sensors are expandedwith decision-making logic. Also, this chapter has provided an architectural and practical framework in which future study of internal sensors and embedded detectors in intrusion detection could be based in e-Government website. It has also presented a classification of the data source types for internal intrusion detection and a description of the characteristics and types of internal sensors and embedded detectors which are used inside e-Government website like image, sound, text, class and HTML file.The internal sensor has been introduced as an approach for the development of real time internal intrusion detection in e-Government website and Transition Analysis Technique is used to detect internal intruder in e-Government website. The work supports efficient development of new internal intrusion detection sensors because the main mechanism is used to detect any internal intruder on e-Government website in real time. However, in practice, the

design of an internal intrusion detection system may not follow the functional model. In most cases, the designers of the intrusion detection system face constraints imposed by the environment in which the intrusion detection system is going to operate.

We have shown how internal sensors for intrusion detection attacks are used in e-Government website. The following points are concluded from the proposed system.

- The internal sensors have been the simplest in the cases where they embedded themselves in all files on website and checked all attacks.
- This internal intrusion detection system can operate without any external components.
- The prototype implemented is able to detect previously unknown attacks.
- The proposed method detects internal intrusion for protecting an e-Government website using Java language for dealing with the classes.
- Using automatic audit for all files provides high security to the site protection without using any other protection programs.
- By using the real time technique, we can use our method to detect internal intruder and protect all kinds of files inside e-Government website and all those which deal with them without returning to or getting the help of the ISP and without making the site stops providing service in case of intrusion through operating an alternative site from another ISP.
- Hacker cannot attack the e-Government website from memory because the Java applet makes garbage collection to the memory.
- The proposed method to detect the internal intrusion and protect files using Java language is very flexible in dealing with any kind of operating systems.

SUGGESTIONS FOR FUTURE WORK

The work presented in this chapter has explored the basic concepts of using internal sensors for intrusion detection by showing their feasibility. However, there is a considerable amount of work that needs to be done to further study and characterize their properties. Future work could also explore improving the detection of new attacks in Database by implementing internal detectors for a larger number of records inside Database. Another possibility would be the automatic generation of components that could be used by programmers to insert sensors and detectors in their source code.

This chapter has explored the feasibility of extracting information about the behavior of a computer system that is more complete and reliable than any data that had been available before to intrusion detection systems. This availability opens multiple possibilities for future exploration and research, and may lead to the design and development of more efficient, reliable and effective intrusion detection systems.

REFERENCES

Ajith, A., Prachi, D., Aggarwal, A., Sharma, S. C., & Sateesh, P. (2013). Distributed port-scan attack in cloud environment. IEEE, 27-31.

Al-Haidari, F., Sqalli, M. H., & Salah, K. (2012). Enhanced EDoS-Shield for Mitigating EDoS Attacks Originating from Spoofed IP Addresses. In *Security and Privacy in Computing and Communications, IEEE 11th International Conference*, (pp. 1167–1174). Liverpool, UK.

Al-Khanjari, Z., Alanee, A., Kraiem, N., & Jamoussi, Y. (2013). Proposing a real time internal intrusion detection system towards a secured development of e-government web site. *European Scientific Journal*, (3), 27-37.

Anderson, J. P. (1980). Computer Security Threat Monitoring and Surveillance. Fort Washington, USA: Technical Report, James P. Anderson Co.

Benjamin, V. A., & Hsinchun, C. (2013). Machine learning for attackvector identification in malicious source code, *Intelligence and Security Informatics (ISI), 2013 IEEE International Conference,* Seattle, Washington USA: IEEE Conference publications, 21–23.

Chao, Y., Yimin, S., & Guofei, G. (2012). Active User-Side Evil Twin Access Point Detection Using Statistical Techniques. Information Forensics and Security. IEEE Transactions.

Chou, T. C. (2011). Cyber security threats detection using ensemble architecture. International Journal of Security and Its Applications, 5(2), 17–32.

Christopher, A., & Audrey, D. (2002). Managing Information Security Risks. USA: Addison Wesley.

Dabbagh, M., Ghandour, A. J., Fawaz, K., & Hajj, W. (2011). Slow port scanning detection, In *Proceedings of the Information Assurance and Security (IAS), 7th International Conference IEEE* (pp. 228-233). doi:10.1109/ISIAS.2011.6122824 doi:10.1109/ISIAS.2011.6122824

Esposito, S., Fallavollita, P., Corcione, M., & Balsi, M. (2013). Experimental Validation of an Active Thermal Landmine Detection Technique. *Geoscience and Remote Sensing Society, IEEE Transactions,* 99.

Hahn, A., Ashok, A., Sridhar, S., & Govindarasu, M. (2013). Cyber-physical security testbeds: Architecture, application, and evaluation for smart grid. Smart Grid IEEE Transactions, 4(2), 847–855.

Hoang, L., & Uyen, T. (2012). A study of different types of attacks in mobile ad hoc networks. In *Electrical & Computer Engineering (CCECE), 2012 25th IEEE Canadian Conference*, (pp. 149-161). Montreal Canada.

Isa, M., Hashim, H., Manan, J. A., Mahmod, R., & Othman, H. (2012). Integrity Verification Architecture (IVA) Based Security Framework for Windows Operating System. In *Trust, Security and Privacy in Computing and Communications, IEEE 11th International Conference*, (pp. 1304-1309). Liverpool, UK.

Jonny, C., Abhinav, S., & Edward, B. (2012). A knowledge-based system approach for sensor fault modeling, detection and mitigation. *Elsevier, 39*(12), 10977–10989.

Khan, B., Khan, M. K., Mahmud, M., & Alghathbar, K. S. (2010). Security Analysis of Firewall Rule Sets in Computer Networks, Emerging Security Information Systems and Technologies *(SECURWARE), 2010 Fourth International Conference, IEEE Conference publications*, Venice Italy, 51-56.

König, B., Alcaraz Calero, J. M., & Kirschnick, J. (2012). Elastic monitoring framework for cloud infrastructures. IET Communications, 6(10), 1306–1315. doi:10.1049/iet-com.2011.0200 doi:10.1049/iet-com.2011.0200

Office of Nuclear Security and Incident Response. (2011). Intrusion Detection Systems and Subsystems: Technical information for NRC licensees. Washington, D.C: U.S. Nuclear Regulatory Commission.

Ojugo, E., Eboka, A. O., Okonta, O. E., Yoro, R. E., & Aghware, F. O. (2012). Genetic Algorithm Rule-Based Intrusion Detection System. Journal of Emerging Trends in Computing and Information Sciences, 3(8), 1182–1194.

Paez, R., Uribe, M. Y., & Torres, M. (2013). Internal Security on an IDS based on agents. International Journal of Network Security and Its Applications, 5(4), 129–142. doi:10.5121/ijnsa.2013.5410 doi:10.5121/ijnsa.2013.5410

Park, Y. P., & Salvatore, J. (2012). Software Decoys for Insider Threat. Anomaly Detection at Multiple Scales The Defense Advanced Research Projects Agency (DARPA). New York, USA: Columbia University.

Robin, S. (2013). Intrusion Detection and Protection Systems, Intrusion Detection. Technical University of Denmark.

Sanmorino, A., & Yazid, S. (2013). DDoS Attack detection method and mitigation using pattern of the flow, *Information and Communication Technology (ICoICT), 2013 International Conference*, Indonesia: IEEE Conference publications, 12–16.

Song, Y. S., Locasto, M. E., Stavrou, A., Keromytis, A. D., & Stolfo, S. J. (2010). On the infeasibility of modeling polymorphic shellcode. Re-thinking the role of learning in intrusion detection systems (pp. 179–205). New York: Springer.

Sumit, M., Matthews, M., Anupam, J., & Tim, F. (2012). A Knowledge-Based Approach to Intrusion Detection Modeling (pp. 1–7). IEEE Computer Society.

Zeng, B., & Yao, L. & ZhiChen, C. (2010).A network intrusion detection system with the snooping agents. In *Computer Application and System Modeling (ICCASM).* IEEE Conference Publications, 3, 232-236.

Zhang, F. (2011). Mitigating Distributed Denial-of-Service Attacks: Application-Defense and Network-Defense Methods, Computer Network Defense (EC2ND), *2011 Seventh European Conference, IEEE Conference publications*, Gothenburg Sweden, 58-69.

Zhang, G., & Gu, U. (2011). The research and implementation of intelligent intrusion detection system based on artificial neural network. IEEE, 5, 3178-3182.

KEY TERMS AND DEFINITIONS

E-Government: Refers to government's use of information and communication technology (ICT) to exchange information and services with citizens and businesses.

Embedded Sensors: A piece of code added to a program that will be monitored.

Hackers: Used a variety of tools and techniques to attack the websites or networks.

Intruder: A person who is the perpetrator of a computer security incident often referred to as hackers or crackers.

Intrusion Detection System (IDS): A device or software application that monitors network or system activities for malicious activities or policy violations and produces reports to a management station.

Intrusion Detection: The problem of identifying individuals who are using a computer system without authorization.

Intrusion: The set of actions that attempts to compromise integrity, confidentiality or availability of network resources.

Port Scans: Scan across responding hosts to find running services.

Chapter 5
Authentication Model for Enterprise Resource Planning Network

Wasim A. Al-Hamdani
Kentucky State University, USA

ABSTRACT

Enterprise Resource Planning (ERP) software is business-management software that allows an organization to use a system of integrated applications to manage the business. ERP software often contains highly confidential information that is vital to a firm's competitiveness, so it is critically important that appropriate security be implemented to reduce its vulnerability. In this chapter, security issues are presented that could arise when ERP software is integrated with many systems and with web environments. The security issue is one of the major issues with ERP software, and it has not been a major focus of the developers of the software, who leave this issue to different components of the system and to vendor implementation. In this chapter, The author presents a new security model for ERP software. The author also presents a new authentication model that consists of the following layers: Role base, Data mining, Risk-based access control, and PKI.

INTRODUCTION

Enterprise Resource Planning is a business integration approach; it was first developed by the Gartner Group in 1990 as the next generation of manufacturing business system and manufacturing resource planning software. Today, ERP software is considered to be "the price of entry for running a business" (Kumar, 2000).ERP software integrates internal and external information across an entire organization, including finance, accounting, manufacturing, sales and service, customer-relationship management, and others. ERP software computerize these activities with a unified software application. The objectivesare to facilitate the flow of information between all business functions inside the limits of the organization and to manage the connections outside the organization (Bidgoli, 2003). ERP software can be used to manage and modernize all the resources in an enterprise, and it incorporates the business processes within and across the functional boundaries in the organization. With ERP

DOI: 10.4018/978-1-4666-6583-5.ch005

Copyright © 2015, IGI Global. Copying or distributing in print or electronic forms without written permission of IGI Global is prohibited.

software, an enterprise can systematize its central and essential business applications; decrease the-complexity and cost of collaboration; ensure that the enterprise takes part in the BPR to optimize its operations, and become a successful business (She, 2007; Thuraisingham, 2006). ERP softeware allows enterprises to share information systems with trusted associates over supply chain management, and the number of authorized users and operators continues to rise. The ERP approach represents a new way of managing business systems that is beyond the perimeter of conventional IT security. Enterprises must trust the actions of employees and trust their partners' employees and perimeter security. For most ERP systems, security starts with user-based controls, which limit a user's access to the system based on her or his individual, customized, authorization level. The fact that security is a big issue is evidenced by the following statement:"When you consider that the average business loses 3 percent to 6 percent of annual revenue due to fraud, most agree that the ERP security features listed above are not working" (Holsbac & Johnson, 2004).

In this work, The general architucture of ERP software has been presented, and security issues are presented that could arise when ERP software is integrated with many systems and with web environments. The work is focused on current issues in ERP, such as:

- Role-Based Access Control;
- Security in SAP R/3;
- Baan Security.

The major contribution of this chapter is a new authentication model that consists of the following layers:

- Role base,
- Data mining,
- Risk base access control,
- PKI.

These layers are presented in:

ERP SYSTEMS AND APPLICATIONS

Enterprise Resource Planning (ERP) is an industry expression for the wide set of accomplishments that assist and manage the significant parts of a business. The information is presented through an ERP system that provides great assistance in meeting the industry's objectives. ERP software applications can be used to purchase parts, manage product planning, provide customer service, assess inventories, interact with suppliers, and track orders. ERP software can also include applications for the finance and human resources aspects of a business. Classically, an ERP system uses a relational database system or is integrated with such a system. The deployment of an ERP system includes significant business process analysis, employee retraining, and new work procedures.

The history of ERP began in the 1960s, when organizations developed mainframe computing systems for use in automatically managing the company's inventories. In the 1970s, these systems were based mainly on programming languages, such as COBOL. The evolution from simple inventory tracking systems to Material Requirements Planning (MRP) software permitted the planning of production and the required supplies of raw materials by working back from sales forecasts. Consequently, the controller first looked at Marketing and Sales' forecast of demand, then looked at the manufacturing timetable required to meet that demand, calculated the raw materials required to meet production, and projected the quantities of raw materials that should be purchased. For a company with many products, managing the raw materials sharing production resources would be impossible without a computer to keep track of various inputs.

The fundamental functions of MRP were conducted by mainframe computers. Electronic Data Interchange (EDI) is a paperless exchange of business information using electronic mail (e-mail), computer bulletin boards, Electronic Funds Transfer (EFT), and other similar technologies.

The direct computer-to-computer exchange of typical business documents allowed companies to handle purchasing electronically, eliminating the costs and delays that resulted from chapter purchase orders and invoice systems. The functional area now known as Supply Chain Management (SCM) began with the allocation of long-range production schedules between manufacturers and their suppliers (Monk & Wagner, 2013).

ERP has a wide range of applications in both industrial and government systems, such as banking, aerospace, defense, consumer products, construction, healthcare, education and research, insurance, raw and processed materials, logistics, transportation, wholesale, public sectors, and telecommunications, Figure 1 shows the overall ERP functionality.

In the early days after ERP was deployed, maintaining an ERP system was costly and time consuming. However, due to the decreased cost of hardware infrastructure, the implementation and maintenance costs of ERP system were reduced significantly. Currently, many small, light-weight ERP applications have been developed for small and medium companies. Several business-related products, including SAP, Oracle, and Baan, are now available in the marketplace. In addition, web services and service-oriented designs are the major underlying technologies for the emerging ERP systems.

There are several key benefits to ERP technology, including (Bortolus, 2012):

- **Integration of Applications:** They share a single definition and source of all information.
- **Common Data Processing Methods:** All applications update data in real time rather than batching transactions for periodic updates.
- **Distributed Data Processing:** Information can be updated at the source, which is different from sending chapter forms or emails to a central data entry point.

- **Shared Look to the System:** All users navigate the system the same way, regardless of which application they are using.
- Organizational goals can be added as data and used to drive transaction processing.

Because applications share common definitions for information, the system must be developed with rules built into the database. Development of screens and reports can be minimized because each application does not need to duplicate shared data update capabilities. For instance, defining departments can be done in one place and shared by all applications. There is no need to create departments individually, (Bortolus, 2012).

Business logic in ERP uses client/server architecture to establish a distributed computing environment. There are three layers in this client/server architecture (see Figure 1):

- **Front (Presentation) Layer:** A Graphical User Interface (GUI) or browser mechanism that collects input, generates requests, and returns the results to the user.
- **Middle (Application) Layer:** Application programs that collect the requests from the front layer and process the requests based on rules, functions, or logics.
- **Back (Database) Layer:** DBMS that control the operational and business data throughout the enterprise and users' access to this information. This layer may also include the operating system and the related hardware (Sprott, 2000).

Particular systems could be developed by the enterprise itself; however, others could be developed by different vendors using different technologies, databases, and languages. Different systems used for implementation could cause difficulty in upgrading the organization's businesses, strategy, and information technologies efficiently.

Figure 1. Overall functionality of ERP

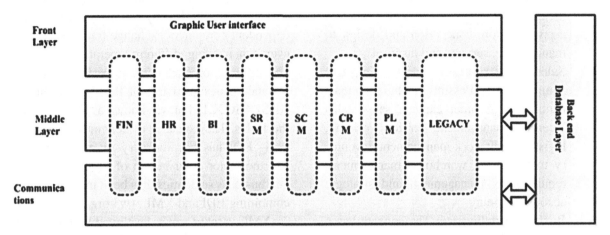

A typical ERP system should have at least the following features:

- **Subdivide:** Different enterprise functionalities are designed as distinct components.
- **Real Time:** All functions operate in real time, online, and batch processing as well.
- **Integrated:** Components are integrated, and the seamless data flow between components allows them to collaborate as one function.
- **Flexible:** The system is expandable and compatible with the old systems, making changes in business processes and strategies easy to implement.
- **Adaptability:** The system must be easy to configure according to the business needs.
- **Profitable:** The system should reduce costs or increase profits.
- **Secured:** The system must be enforced to protect different business resources regardless of whether it is appropriate or sufficient (Glass, 1998).

ERP is a big umbrella under which different vendors provide different ERP components; however, the core procedures and functions are essentially the same. These functionalities include (Bakry & Barky, 2005):

- **Human Resource Management:** Possibly include other components such as payroll management, learning management, benefits, recruitment, self-service, time and labor management, and compensation management.
- **Financial Management:** Possibly include components such as payables and receivables management, assets management, properties management, collection and payment management, cash-flow management, loans, investments management, financial alliance, treasury management, and planning and budgeting.
- **Manufacturing Management:** Possibly include components such as distinct manufacturing, manufacturing flow processes, manufacturing, manufacturing scheduling, shop management, and floor management.
- **Customer Relationship Management (CRM):** Possibly include components such as collecting, storing, and analyzing customer information, feedback information, and evaluation information
- **Supplier Relationship Management (SRM):** Similar to CRM, SRM manages the supplier relationships by storing, collecting, and analyzing supplier information.

- **Product Lifecycle Management:** Possibly include components such as life cycle of a product from conception and design to manufacture, service, and disposal.
- **Sales, Distribution, and Logistics Management:** Possibly include components such as order capture, sales, sales incentive management, services, pricing, logistics, bulk-stock management, inventory management, warehouse management, requirements management, and strategic account planning.
- **Business Intelligence:** The concept has a wide range of concealment of all the processes and conducts analysis and/or evaluation of the work at the strategic level, tactical level, or operational level by providing direction for optimizing business performance.
- **Demand Management:** Can be classified into this category.
- **Supply Chain Management (SCM):** This concept has some overlap with the components above. An SCM possibly includes components such as business processes, e.g., CRM and SRM, manufacturing management, demand management, and production planning.

These business processes have to be connected across organizations in order for a business success of supply chain. These processes are inter-organizational, thus may be either included in or excluded from the scope of ERP. With the definition of extended ERP, we no longer consider ERP as internal within an organization. (She, 2007 ; Thuraisingham, 2006).

"ERP" is sometimes confused with "e-commerce, but ERP is extra concerned with the internal functionalities in an organization, whereas e-commerce (e-business) focuses on the business across companies.

Electronic data interchange (EDI) (paperless exchange) is a method by which two or more independent computers exchange transaction data even when using different operating systems. The information exchanged is performed using a standard designed format that is now called ANSI ASC X.12 but was known as EDIFACT in the 1980s. The exchange of documents and data using EDI has become very prominent today, and the major contribution of EDI technology, i.e., business semantics, has been maintained by combining EDI and XML. (w3.org, 2012).

XML, a text format developed by the World Wide Web Consortium (W3C), was designed to transport and store data. It is a simplification of Standard Generalized Markup Language (SGML). The advantage of XML over other descriptive languages (such as HTML) is its ability to represent the data format using Document Type Declaration (DTD) schema or XML schema, whereas HTML was designed to display data.

Currently, we are in the third generation of ERP systems; the first generation related to manufacturing applications; the second generation addressed specialized applications, such as supply-chain management; and the third generation was based on web services (Thuraisingham, 2006).

Web service is defined as "a software system designed to support inter-operable, machine-to-machine interaction over a network." (Some people define web service as a network-accessible interface to application functionality, built using standard Internet technologies (Costello). Web services are frequently just web APIs that can be accessed over a network, such as the Internet, and executed on a remote system that is hosting the requested services.

The web services that we see deployed on the Internet today are HTML web sites in which application services, i.e., the mechanisms for publishing, managing, searching, and retrieving content, are accessed through the use of standard protocols and data formats, i.e., HTTP and HTML. Client applications (web browsers) that understand these standards can interact with the application services to perform tasks, such as ordering books, sending greeting cards, and reading news.

The definition of W3C web service encompasses many different systems, but, in common usage, the term refers to clients and servers that communicate over the HTTP protocol used on the web. Such services tend to fall into one of two categories, i.e., Big Web Services and RESTful Web Services (w3. org, Web services architecture, 2012). Big Web Services use XML messages that follow the SOAP standard and that have been popular with traditional enterprises. In such systems, there is often a machine-readable description of the operations offered by the service written in the web services description language (WSDL). The latter is not a requirement of a SOAP endpoint, but it is a prerequisite for automated, client-side code generation in many Java and .NET SOAP frameworks, with notable exceptions including frameworks such as spring, Apache Axis2, and Apache CXF. Some industry organizations, such as the WS-I, mandate both SOAP and WSDL in their definition of a web service. More recently, RESTful Web services (w3.org, 2012) have been gaining in popularity, particularly with Internet companies. These also meet the W3C definition, and they often are better integrated with HTTP than SOAP-based services. They do not require XML.

Because of the abstraction provided by the standards-based interfaces, it does not matter whether the application services are written in Java and the browser is written in C++ or whether the application services are deployed on a UNIX box while the browser is deployed on Windows. Web services allow for cross-platform interoperability in a way that makes the platform irrelevant. The web-services architecture is implemented through the layering of five types of technologies, organized into layers that build upon one another, i.e., discovery, description, packaging, transport, and network. It should come as no surprise that this stack is very similar to the TCP/IP network model used to describe the architecture of Internet-based applications.

There are many ways that a requester might use a web service. In general, the following broad steps are required (w3.org, 2013):

1. The requester and provider become known to each other (or at least one becomes known to the other).
2. The requester and provider (somehow) agree on the service description and semantics that will govern the interaction between the requester's and the provider's agents.
3. The service description and semantics are understood by the requester's and provider's agents.
4. The requester's and provider's agents exchange messages, thus performing some task on behalf of the requester and the provider, i.e., the exchange of messages with the provider's agent represents the concrete manifestation of interacting with the provider's web service. Some of these steps may be automated, and others may be performed manually.

The basic web services platform is XML + HTTP. The HTTP protocol is the most-used Internet protocol. XML provides a language that can be used between different platforms and programming languages and that can still express complex messages and functions. The web services platform elements are:

- **SOAP (Simple Object Access Protocol):** SOAP is a simple, XML-based protocol that allows applications to exchange information over HTTP. More simply stated, SOAP is an independent platform and protocol for accessing a web service; SOAP stands for Simple Object Access Protocol, and it is a communication protocol via Internet and a W3C standard.
- **Universal Description, Discovery, and Integration (UDDI):** UDDI is a directory service with which businesses can register

and search for web services; UDDI is for storing information about web services and interfaces described by WSDL. It communicates via SOAP and is built into the Microsoft .NET platform.

- **Web Services Description Language (WSDL):** WSDL is an XML-based language for describing web services and how to access them; it also is used to locate web services and a W3C standard.

SAP stands for Systems Applications and Products in data processing, which were designed and developed by five IBM engineers during the 1970s as standards-based software substitutes for custom-built ERP software. SAP emphasizes the development of application software for real-time business processing, beginning with its first software developed in 1973. SAP was designed to run on the mainframe and initially was called Release 2 (R/2). SAP quickly apprehended on the client server model with a later release R/3, and this was the most popular version of SAP. After R/3, SAP releases were referred to as "Enterprise Central Component" (ECC).

Oracle developed additional ERP software, such as strategic procurement, self-service applications, financial consolidation, and flow manufacturing. Oracle's ERP system is now known as Oracle E-business Suite, which has more than 50 different components that cover many areas, including finance, projects, supply-chain management, accounting, manufacturing, human resources, and front office.

SECURITY IN ERP

Security is significant for ERP systems, since they are used in defense, intelligence, medical, and financial applications. Hughes and Beer specified in (Hughes & Beer, 2007) that "It was clear that security issues generally fell into one of two areas:

- It has become extremely difficult to understand how to securely configure an ERP system and the myriad of products purchased to integrate with it—products like report generators, data warehouses, learning management systems, imaging systems, portals, and others.
- The overhead of managing access and authorization roles—for both the ERP and third-party software integrated with the ERP—is huge. Institutions said they had backed off from using role-based security because the overhead of managing it was just too high. For example, rather than setting up fine-grained role access so that only biology faculty can see the records of biology majors, an institution might set up one role called "faculty" and allow all faculty to see the records of all students, thus increasing the opportunity for data misuse and violations of data privacy."

The aspects of security in an ERP system can be summarized (She, 2007; Thuraisingham, 2006) as shown below:

- Security policy and administrator.
- User authentication.
- Separation of duties.
- Authorization.
- Time restriction.
- Log and trace.
- Database security.

Current Directions for Secure ERP

There are many trends to achieve security in ERP, and they are summarized in the following sections.

Role-Based Access Control

The basic concept of Role-Based Access Control (RBAC) is that users are appointed to roles, permissions are appointed to roles, and users get permissions by being associates of roles. Core RBAC includes conditions in which user-role and permission-role responsibility can be many-to-many. Therefore a user can be appointed to many roles and a single role can have many users.

Rationale: Core RBAC captures the features of traditional group-based access control as implemented in operating systems through the current generation. As such, it is a widely deployed and familiar technology. The features required of Core RBAC are essential for any form of RBAC. The main issue in defining Core RBAC is to determine which features to exclude. This proposed standard has deliberately kept a very minimal set of features in Core RBAC.

In particular, these features accommodate traditional, but robust, group-based access control. Not every group-based mechanism qualifies because of the requirements given above. One of the features omitted as mandatory for Core, (Ferraiolo et al, 2001).

Role-base access control has the following concepts (DoD, 1985; NCSC, 1988):

- **Subject:** An active entity, it could be a person, a process, or a device that causes information to flow among objects or change the system.
- **Object:** A passive entity that holds or receives information.
- **Access:** A specific type of interface between a subject and object that results in the flow of information from one to the other.
- **Access Control:** The process of limiting access to resources of a system only to authorized programs, processes, or other systems.
- **Group:** Set of users.
- **User:** Any person who interacts directly with a computer system.

- **Administration Role:** A role that includes granting permission to modify the set of users' roles or permission or to modify the user assignment or permission assignment relationships.
- **Constraint:** A relationship between or among roles.
- **Permission:** A description of the type of authorized intersections a subject can have within an object.
- **Resource:** Anything used or consumed while performing a function. The categories of resources are time, information, object, or process.
- **Role:** A job function within the organization that describes the authority and responsibility conferred on a user assigned to the role.
- **Role Hierarchy:** Partial order relationship established among roles.
- **Session:** A mapping between a user and an activated subset of the set of roles the user is assigned to.
- **System Administrator:** The individual who establishes the system's security policies, performs the administrator's roles, and reviews the system audit trail RBAC provides a useful level of abstraction to endorse security administration at the enterprise level rather at the user-identity level. The basic concepts are: establish permissions created based on the efficient role in the enterprise and then correctly assign users to roles or sets of roles. With RBAC decisions are based on the roles of users have as part of an enterprise. Roles could characterize the task, responsibilities, duties, and qualifications associated within the definition of the enterprise. RBAC provides a great mechanism for reducing the complexity, difficulty, cost, and potential for error when allocating user permissions within the enterprise, because the roles within the enterprise are reasonably

persistent with respect to user turnover and task re-assignment. Since roles classically have had overlapping permissions, RBAC often includes the characteristic of establishing role hierarchies, where a given role can include all permissions of another role. RBAC allows for specification and enforcement of protection policies, which can be tailored on a business-by-business basis. RBAC is a rich and open-ended concept that ranges from being very simple at one extreme to being fairly complex and sophisticated at the other extreme (Sandhu et al, 2000).

- ◦ Flat RBAC.
- ◦ Hierarchical RBAC.
- ◦ Constrained RBAC.
- ◦ Symmetrical RBAC.

Security in SAP R/3

The most important aspects of establishing and implementing a security policy for R/3 are the business demands and the significance of security. For some businesses, security means:

- Unauthorized persons do not have access to certain data.
- No one can retrieve information by unauthorized means.
- Activities must be recorded so that they can be reconstructed.
- Individuals can be held responsible for actions that they perform using R/3

Generally, all systems are subject to some threats, including:

- Angry or frustrated employees.
- Eavesdroppers or "hackers" who want to access sensitive data.
- Users' errors or carelessness.
- Software errors.
- Lack of infrastructure security.

- Lack of physical security.
- Lack of continuity plans.
- Disaster recovery.
- Incident response plans.
- Inadequate policies.

Some of the concepts involved in the authorization of a SAP R/3 system (Bakry, 2005) are provided below:

- **Authorization Object:** This represents the authorization model and contains of some authorization fields.
- **Authorization:** An instance of one authorization object that expresses the acceptable value range of each authorization field of the authorization object
- **Authorization Profile:** Contains selected authorizations that are assigned to the user by the administrator.
- **Authorization Check:** Used to protect the transactions or data and is embedded in the program logic
- **User's Master Record:** Enables users to log on to the system and be granted limited access to the transactions and data.
- **Profile Generator:** Helps the administrators generate, create, and assign permission profiles using activity groups and users. A profile generator may have the following components:
- **Activity Group:** A group of events, such as reports, tasks, and transactions. It usually represents a job function in the business, and it may have several users assigned to it; a user can be assigned to many different activity groups. An activity group can be appointed to the subsequent types of users, i.e., user's ID, job, and position. Job represents the general classification of duties. Job is just the title, and position is the function of the job.
- **Composite Activity Group:** Set of several activity groups.

- **User's Assignment:** Work that assigns one or more roles/users/ positions to one or more activity groups or complex activity groups.

Baan Security

Baan security architecture is based on the RBAC model. The Baan security solution uses a tool called 'Dynamic Enterprise Modeler' (DEM) to assist the security configuration of Baan. There are four concepts in Baan's security solution: User, Employee, Role, and Process.

UCON Model

Some articles have suggested that the UCON model could possibly be used in the future for security purposes (Bakry, 2005). The UCON model is the latest, enhanced model based on traditional, access-control models, which enable the flexibility of subject and object attributes and provide stable oversight of the usage of resources. In the UCON model, the decision to approve access is based on three factors, i.e., authorizations, obligations, and conditions. Authorizations and obligations are necessities that must be satisfied by the subject and the object. However, conditions are subject- and object-independent obligations that must be satisfied by the environment.

A Security Model for ERP

The new model is based on four levels:

1. Role-based access control.
2. Access-control risk assessments.
3. Data mining on role-based access control.
4. Multi-level of PKI with each level based on need to know.
5. Figure 2. shows the overall security model for ERP.

A user entering the system will be questioned about his role in the system, and, if he or she has only a single role in the ERP, he or she can access the data through lock the view. Otherwise, the system will run a data mining procedure to determine the user's:

1. History of access,
2. Previous access of data,
3. Level of clearance,
4. Level of need to know.

This data mining on the user's access behavior will point out the level of risk associated with this user. If he or she has a low risk to system data, then he or she can access the data within one control, i.e., "conflict of interest," with the data being accessed.

A multi-role, high risk user must go through second risk evaluation based on need to know. If the user passes this evaluation, her or his need to know will have a public key and a private key for each level of need to know. These PKI could work as follows:

To update a file on need to know level 1, one needs:

$K^1_{Symmetric}$: To encrypt the file

$K^1_{Private}$: To sign the file

K^1_{Public} : Sent to the ERP and used for verification.

To read a file, one needs:

$K^1_{Symmetric}$: To allow the user to decrypt the file

K^1_{Public} : To check the integrity of the file; If the signature is correct, only a user with the correct private key could have encrypted and signed the file.

To create a file, the user must complete the following steps:

Figure 2. Overall security model for ERP

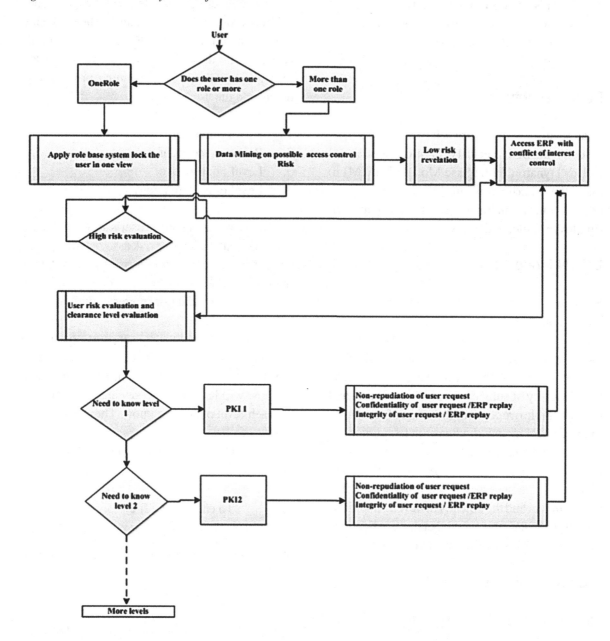

- Generate the symmetric key.
- Generate the public-private key pair.
- Encrypt the file with the symmetric key:
  $$C=K^{1}_{Symmetric}(M)$$
- Sign the encrypted file:
  $$DS = Sing_{privatekey}(C)$$
- Send $\{C.DS.K^{1}_{Public}\}$ to the server.

If the following equation is true, the ERP will save the file:

$$hash(C)\,? = Vpublickey(DS)$$

The verification is made to ensure the integrity of the file. To read a file, the client requests $\{C,DC\}$ from the server. The integrity is satisfied if equation (1) is true. Then, the client can decrypt the file using:

$$M = DK^1_{Symmetric}(C)$$

Before a file can be updated, it will normally be read from the server. The updating process is almost the same as the process involved in creating a file. The only difference is that the client will not need to create keys or send the public key to the server. In other words, the client:

- Encrypts the file with the symmetric key: $C = EK^1_{Symmetric}(M)$
- Signs the file with the private key: $DS = S_{private}(C)$
- Sends $\{C, DS\}$ to the server.

Figure 3. Overall security model for ERP with checker

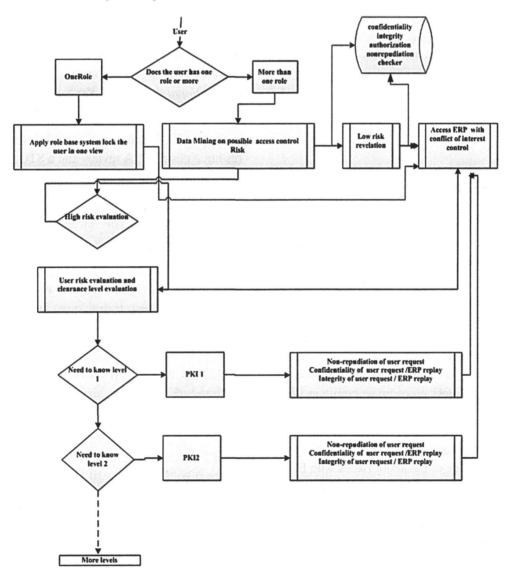

Again, the server checks equation (1) using the stored public key and overwrites the encrypted file (C) and the signature (DS) if the integrity of the user is verified.

System Evaluation

The system has a weakness in that a "trusted user" can conduct most functions with only recording history without having her or his integrity checked and other issues, such as non-repudiation. If this issue has been classified as a weakness, a new level of access evaluation could be implemented, and Figure 3 shows that this checker has been added.

Through the primary system simulation, the system suffers from slow access for risky users. This issue is a normal behavior because the system must balance security and speed of usability. The system shows that going in two three level of high risk need to know slows access to the data by 27% if the PKI is used properly.

CONCLUSION

ERP is business management software that permits an organization to use a system of integrated applications to manage the business. ERP software integrates all facets of an operation, including development, manufacturing, sales, and marketing.

ERP software consists of many enterprise modules that an enterprise would purchase, based on what best meets its specific needs and technical capabilities. Each ERP module is focused on one area of business procedures; common ERP modules include those for product planning, material purchasing, inventory control, distribution, accounting, marketing, finance, and HR.

Security is one of the major issues with ERP, and it has not been a major focus of ERP as one unites. Rather, it has been left to different components of the system and their vendor implementation chapter, so we have presented a new security model for ERP.

The major emphasis of this chapter is to present a new authentication model, which consists of the following layers:

- Role–based,
- Data mining,
- Risk-based access control, and
- PKI.

The model has proven to be effective, but it is slow due to the requirements of the security verification process.

REFERENCES

Bakry, A. H., & Bakry, S. H. (2005). Enterprise resource planning - a review and a STOPE view. *International Journal of Network Management*, *15*(15), 363–370. doi:10.1002/nem.584

Bakry, A. H., & Bakry, S. H. (2005). Enterprise resource planning: A review and a STOPE view. *International Journal of Network Management*, *15*(5), 363–370. doi:10.1145/1110960.1110967

Bidgoli, H. (2003). *The Internet Encyclopedia*. John Wiley & Sons, Inc.

Bortolus, D. (2012). *What Is ERP Technology?* Retrieved from http://www.ehow.com/about_6665167_erp-technology_.html

DoD. (1985). *Trusted Computer System Evaluation Criteria.* DoD 5200.28-STD, Department of Defense. Retrieved from http://fas.org/irp/nsa/rainbow/std001.htm

Ferraiolo, D., Sandhu, R., Gavrila, S., & Kunh, D. (2001). Proposed NIST Standard for Role-Based. *ACM Transactions on Information and System Security*, *4*(3), 224–274. doi:10.1145/501978.501980

Glass, R. L. (1998). Enterprise Resource Planning - Breakthrough or Term. *The Data Base for Advances in Information Systems*, *29*(2), 13–16. doi:10.1145/298752.298755

Holsbeck, M. V., & Johnson, J. Z. (2004). *Security in an ERP World*. Retrieved from http://www.net-security.org/article.php?id=691

Hughes, J. R., & Beer, R. (2007). *A Security Checklist for ERP Implementations*. (educause.edu) Retrieved from http://www.educause.edu/ero/article/security-checklist-erp-implementations

Kumar, K. a. (2000). ERP Experiences and Evolution, 43(4).

Monk, E. F., & Wagner, B. J. (2013). *Concepts in Enterprise Resource Planning*. USA: Cengage Learning.

NCSC. (1988.). *National Computer Security Center, "Glossary of Computer Security Terms"*. Retrieved from http://csrc.nist.gov/publications/secpubs/rainbow/tg004.txt

Sandhu, R., Ferraiolo, D., & Kuhn, R. (2000). *The NIST Model for Role-Base Access Control: Towards A Unified Standard*. Retrieved from http://csrc.nist.gov/rbac/sandhu-ferraiolo-kuhn-00.pdf

She, W., & Thuraisingham, B. (2007). Security for Enterprise Resource Planning Systems. *Information Systems Security*, *16*(3), 152–163. doi:10.1080/10658980701401959

Sprott, D. (2000). Componentizing the Enterprise Application Packages. *Communications of the ACM*, *43*(3).

Thuraisingham, B. (2006). *Assured information sharing: Technology challenges and directions*. UTD Technical Report UTDCS-43-06, the University of Texas at Dallas.

w3.org. (2012). *Web services architecture*. Retrieved from http://www.w3.org/

w3.org. (2013). *XML*. Retrieved from http://www.w3.org/XML/

KEY TERMS AND DEFINITIONS

Access Control: The selective restriction of access to a physical or logical resource.

Authentication: Any process by which a system verifies the identity of a User who wishes to access it. Since Access Control is normally based on the identity of the User who requests access to a resource.

Authorization Check: Used to protect the transactions or data and is embedded in the program logic.

Business Intelligence: The concept has a wide range of concealment of all the processes and conducts analysis and/or evaluation of the work at the strategic level, tactical level, or operational level by providing direction for optimizing business performance.

ERP: Enterprise Resource Planning is business process management software that allows an organization to use a system of integrated applications to manage the business and automate back office functions.

Permission: A description of the type of authorized intersections a subject can have within an object.

PKI: An arrangement that binds public keys with respective user identities by means of a certificate authority (CA). The user identity must be unique within each CA domain.

Chapter 6
Cryptographic Hash Function:
A High Level View

Imad Fakhri Alshaikhli
International Islamic University of Malaysia, Malaysia

Mohammad Abdulateef AlAhmad
PAAET, Kuwait

ABSTRACT

Cryptographic hash function verifies data integrity and sender identity or source of information. The task is accomplished by taking a variable bit patterns as an input then produces a fixed bit patterns of output. This chapter provides a detailed overview to include classification, properties, constructions, attacks, applications and an overview of a selected dedicated cryptographic hash function.

INTRODUCTION

A message digest $\{0,1\}^n$ is an algorithm H that uses a un-constant size message as input $\{0,1\}^*$ to produce a constant size output (sometimes called a digital fingerprint, imprint, hash result, hash code, hash value, or purely hash). All above alterative names were actually functions which made to play a fundamental role in modern cryptography practical applications, for example, a digital signature (Goldwasser et al, 1988), digital time stamp (Haber & Stornetta, 1991), message authentication code (or MAC) (Krawczyk et al, 1997), public key encryption (Cramer & Shoup, 2003), tamper detection of files and many more. Due to the application versatility it deserved the nickname "Swiss army knife of cryptography".

DOI: 10.4018/978-1-4666-6583-5.ch006

Background

Cryptology is the science of hiding and revealing information. This term is subdivided into two categories; cryptography and cryptanalysis. Cryptography is the science of studying the information security. Where, its opposite term is cryptanalysis, which refers to the science of violating the information security. While, cryptographer studies the techniques needed to achieve and protect the information between any communication channels, cryptanalyst studies the techniques needed to understand the meaning of secret information and attempts to break them. More precisely, Whitfield Diffie and Martin Hellman, in their seminal paper on "New Directions in Cryptography" (Diffie

Copyright © 2015, IGI Global. Copying or distributing in print or electronic forms without written permission of IGI Global is prohibited.

& Hellman, 1976), they have given birth to many concepts that are widely used these days by clearly distinguishing between privacy and authentication. Their definition of cryptography is "Cryptography is the study of mathematical systems for solving two kinds of security problems: privacy and authentication". Where, privacy of information ensures the secrecy of the information, and authenticity proves sender's identity. Another new definition proposed by Ronald Rivest (Rivest, 1991), he noted in chapter "Cryptography" in the "Handbook of Theoretical Computer Science" that cryptography is about communication in the presence of adversaries. The adversary is the enemy or opponent who aims to prevent the cryptographers of the cryptosystems to achieve their protection security goals. The adversaries can be in form of humans, computers operated or programmed by humans. The modern cryptography concept presented new directions of security measurements that should be considered when designing a cryptosystem. More precisely, modern cryptography is all about constructing and analyzing protocols that overcome adversaries' threats that are related to information security. Where, information security falls into four measurements: data confidentiality, data integrity, authenticity and non-repudiation. To achieve the information security measurements, modern cryptography can be divided into several area of study. Cryptographic hash function is one branch of the cryptography family tree. Cryptographic hash function is a function that takes an arbitrary length as an input and produces a fixed size of an output. The viability of using keyed cryptographic hash function is to verify data integrity and sender identity or source of information. Consequently, the digital Holy Quran requires a keyed cryptographic hash function as protection method from any alteration or modification. Next sections will overview cryptographic hash functions in more details.

CLASSIFICATION, PROPORITIES, CONSTRUCTIONS, AND ATTACKS OF HASH FUNCTIONS

1. Classification of Hash Functions

Figure 1 classifies our research model function into two main categories unkeyed and keyed. The first one takes a un-constant span message as a single input and outputs a constant hash digest, $Y:\{0,1\}^* \to \{0,1\}^n$. It is also known as a Modification Detection Code (MDC). Where the later accepts an random span message and a set span secret key as two inputs then outputs a set span hash digest., $Y_K: \{0,1\}^k \times \{0,1\}^* \to \{0,1\}^n$. It is also known as Message Authentication Codes (MACs). Looking down at the unkeyed route stems out a subclass of three algorithms as shown in Figure 1. Below is the MDC super class hierarchy (OWHF), then (CRHF), and finally (UOWHF) (Naor & Yung, 1989).

CRHF commonly works with longer segment hash values. An unkeyed hash function is used with a set of absolute integer n that contain at least the below characteristics:

Figure 1. Classification of cryptographic hash function
(Naor & Yung, 1989).

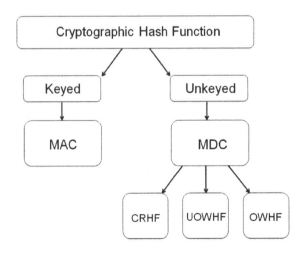

1. **Compression:** Given x as an input of an unequal limited size of bits mapped by the function h, to produce an output result of finite span of bits n.
2. **Ease of Computation:** The function introduced in the above property is easy to compute.

Modification Detection Codes are classified as follows:

1. An OWHF is an algorithm that returns a result which is difficult for a pre-specified hash digest of some given input.
2. A CRHF is an algorithm that returns a difficult hash digest for finding any two given inputs.

In a UOWHF, for haphazardly selected (input, key) respectively (x, k) and applied to H_k, the result of $y = x$ would be hard to find when applying $H_k(x) = H_k(y)$ (Naor & Yung, 1989).

The main purpose of keyed hash function algorithm is to authenticate message code (MAC) as shown in Figure 1. The below characteristics must be guaranteed:

1. **Compression:** If an input x was mapped by a function H along with a key k of randomly limited bit span, could get an output $H_k(x)$ of a set bit span n.
2. **Easiness to Compute:** Assume an H common function was passed a measurable piece of value k along with another measurable piece of input x, it is simple to work out $H_k(x)$ and give a result called MAC value (Naor & Yung, 1989).

Block ciphers, modular arithmetic, and dedicated hash functions are other classifications separately from the above mentioned classification.

2. Properties of Hash Functions

Today application security use hash functions as a major tool. Applications usually are stuck to security requirements that can be receive from various properties that belong to Hash functions. The following are the explanation of the computational feasibility for the three such famous security properties:

1. **Preimage Resistance:** Suppose for a given code h, when applying the hash function H using x, H(x) computationally not reasonable to equal h.
2. **Second Preimage Resistance:** Suppose a given input m, finding $y \neq m$ with H(y) is computationally not reasonable to equal H(m).
3. **Collision Resistance:** Assume a plot of any two pair of values (m,y), their corresponding separate functions H(y) and H(x) is computationally infeasible (Naor & Yung, 1989).

Figure 2 illustrates the definitions of hash function security proprieties.

The preimage resistance property can be described as the inability to learn about the contents of the input data from its hash digest. The second preimage resistance property can be expressed as the inability to learn about the content of the second preimage from the given first preimage such that both of these preimages have the same hash digest. The collision resistance property can be interpreted when two different and separate contents of inputs yield to the same hash digest.

3. Construction of Hash Functions

Building hash functions can be achieved by using various constructions such as Merkle-Damgård or sponge constructions. Merkle-Damgård construction was introduced by R. Merkle's PhD. It

Figure 2. Hash function security proprieties

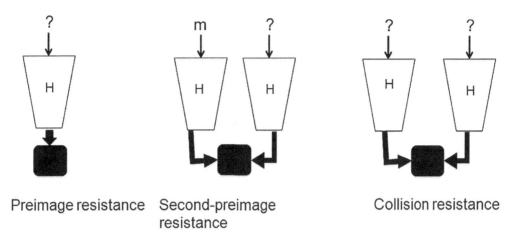

Preimage resistance   Second-preimage
resistance

Collision resistance

represented way of constructing devoted hash algorithms from compression algorithms. In 2007, sponge construction was introduced in SHA-3 competition by Guido Bertoni, Joan

Daemen, Micheal Peeter and Gilles Van Assche to represent the compression function introduced by the innovative SHA-3 standard (Keccak algorithm).

3.1 The Merkle-Damgård (MD) Construction

A Ph.D. thesis (Damgård, 1990) was submitted in 1979 to describe a construction. As Figure 3 shows the construction that iterates sequentially a chaining transformation that grabs two inputs a message block beside the previous chaining value. The string x is divided into a number of blocks t with each block with size i=r depicted $x1=_{x2}=.....=x_t$ each of r bits that should match to the length of the input of preferred compression function f. The algorithm steps of MD construction as follows:

Break the input x into blocks $x_1, x_2.....x_t$.

If needed, 0-bits are padded to the ending block x_t to achieve the multiple length of r.

Creating a new block x_{t+1} with an r bits to construct the right justified of x bit pattern for overall bit-length (MD strengthen).

Inputting $x_1, x_2.....x_t$ to the compression function (iterated processing) to produce an intermediate value of Hi.

Figure 3. Detailed view of MD construction (Damgård, 1990).

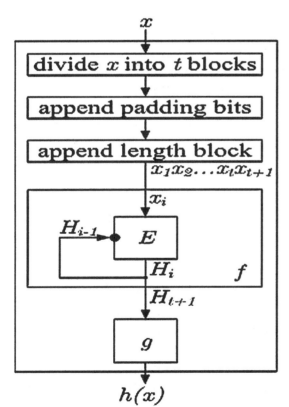

Figure 4. MD strengthening
(Damgård, 1990).

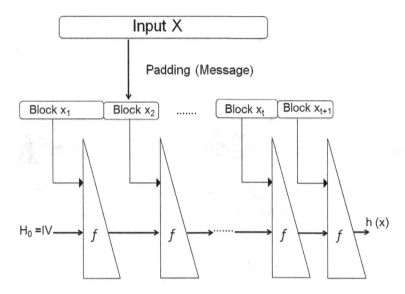

Each iteration requires a block xi and a previous function value H(i-1) as a feedback. Thus, an initial function value H0 must exist with an r length for the first iteration. After processing all the input blocks by the function in previous step, it is transformed by another function ending with the final hash-value with preferred length of bits. The later function is the identity (Damgård, 1990).

The most distinctive and special part of MD construction is that it simplifies the design to reduce it from collision-resistance to collision-resistance compression. In other words, the property of security between the compression function and hash function is not reflexive and it is transformed from the first to the second (compression to hash).

The well-known MD construction (Damgård, 1990) has determined the basic structure of iterated hash functions. MD iterates sequentially a chaining of input message blocks and the previous chaining value to produce the final hash digest h(x). Figure 4 shows the MD strengthen overall design. Padding is an algorithm to extend the input length to become a multiple length of r. the algorithm adds at the end of the input a single

digit '1' and as many '0' digits as needed to attain the preferred length r. This approach called MD strengthens or length padding which makes the construction secure.

The most famous function of all functions are MD5, SHA-1, -2 are based in there construction design the MD design. However, it is quite well studied and discovered several weaknesses named generic attacks such as multi-collisions (Joux, 2004), long-message second preimage and differentiability (Maurer et al, 2004) have been shown for this construction. Due to the structural weakness discovered from these attacks, two intermediate MD construction versions were developed as follow:

3.2 Wide Pipe Hash Construction

Stefan lucks (Lucks, 2004) introduced the wide pipe hash construction as an intermediate version of MD to improve the structural weaknesses of MD design. Figure 5 shows the wide pipe hash construction. The process is similar to MD algorithm steps except of having a larger internal state size, which means the final hash digest is smaller than the internal state size of bit length.

Figure 5. The wide pipe hash construction
(Lucks, 2004).

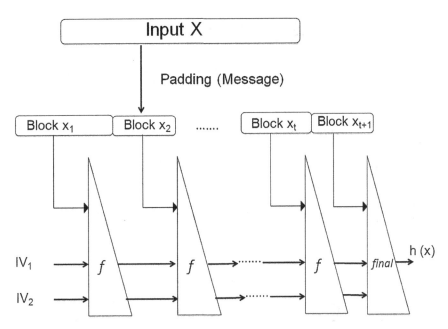

Also, the final compression function compresses the internal state length (for ex, 2n- bit) to output a hash digest of n-bit. This simply can be achieved by discarding the last half of 2n-bit output.

3.3 Fast Wide Pipe Construction

Mridul Nandi and Souradyauti Paul proposed the fast wide pipe construction. It is twice faster than the wide pipe construction. Figure 6 shows the fast wide pipe construction. As the Figure shows, the input (IVs) for each compression function is divided into halves.

The compression function takes two halves input, the first half is processed and its output is reprocessed again with the XOR of the second half for the original function. The process of feed- forwarding is the tip of in accelerating the overall design. Hence, faster process is obtained. The final output of the hash digest can be truncated to the desired digest length using the final compression function.

3.4 The Sponge Construction

An iterative construction design named Sponge introduced by Guido Bertoni, Joan Daemen, Micheal Peeter and Gilles Van Assche to replace MD construction. Mapping an inconsistent length of an input to an inconsistent length output. Namely, by applying a set-length transformation that operates on a fixed number of b = bit rate + capacity as illustrated in Figure 7. At the start point, a filling algorithm pads an input and divides it into equal sections of bits r. Then, the b bits of the state are initialized to zero (Bertoni et al, 2007). The following points and Figure illustrate the sponge construction:

1. **Absorbing Phase:** XORs the sections of bit r with the initial r bits of the state of the function F. After processing all sections, the phase will start.
2. **Squeezing Phase:** The starting r bits of the state will go again as output section of the function F. lastly, the number of output sections the user will chose the number of output sections (Bertoni, et al., 2007).

Figure 6. The fast wide pipe hash construction
(Nandi & Paul, 2010).

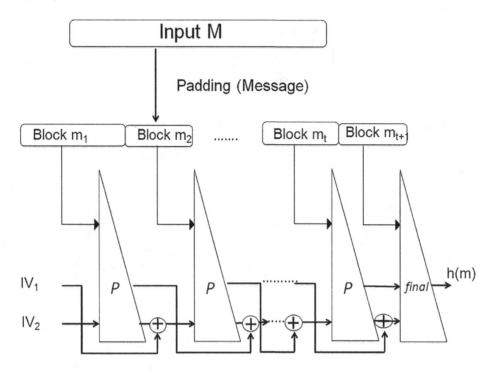

Figure 7. The sponge construction
(Guido Bertoni, et al., 2007).

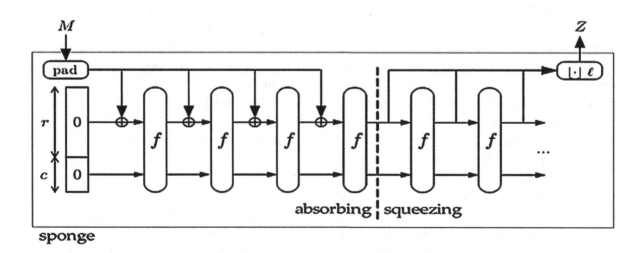

Figure 8. Classification of attack strategies
(Zheng, Pieprzyk, & Seberry, 1993).

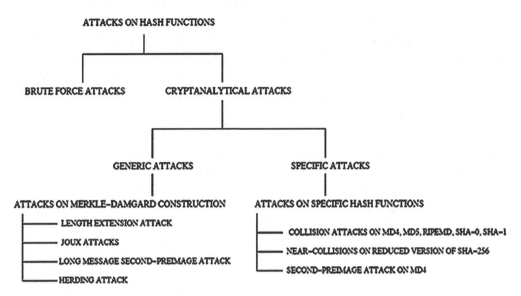

The sponge construction has been studied by many researchers to prove its security robustness. Bertoni et al. (Bertoni et al, 2007) proved that the success probability of any generic attack to a sponge function is upper bound by its success probability for a random oracle plus $N^2/2^{c-1}$ with N the number of queries to f. Aumasson and Meier (Aumasson & Meier, 2009) showed the existence of zero-sum distinguishers for 16 rounds of the underlying permutation f of Keccak hash function. Boura, Canteaut and De Cannière (Canniere, 2010) showed the existence of zero-sums on the full permutation (24 rounds).

4. Attack Strategies

Attacks on hash functions are based on a technical strategy by employing a challenger to conquer the hash function purpose. These technical strategies may vary and in many cases attacks target compression of a hash. A variety of attacks strategies' aimed to hash functions are categorized as depicted in Figure 8.

Strategies of attack on hash functions are mainly categorized into two categories: brute force attacks and cryptanalytical attacks.

4.1 Brute Force Attacks

Brute force attacks are a particular strategy used to try randomly computed hashes to obtain a specific hash digest. Hence, these attacks do not depend on the way the hash function was built (i.e. compression function). However, the safety of any hash function lies on the output hash digests length. Which means, the longer hash digest the more secure hash function. The brute-force attack is a trial and error method to obtain a desired hash function. As an example of a brute-force attack is a dictionary attack which contain a list of dictionary words to try them all in a consecutive manner. These brute-force attacks can always be attempted, however they are only considered as a break when the necessary number of tries to penetrate is considerably fewer than the designer estimation strength of the hash function in addition to a hash functions with ideal strength of similar parameters (Biham et al., 2005).

4.2 Cryptanalytical Attacks

A hash function cryptanalysis attempts to attack the of hash functions' properties mentioned above in Figure 2. The reason behind collisions that are found in hash functions come from the reflexive size of the message when related to the set size of the hash values. It is extremely essential to secure the hash function by complicating the findings of its computation. Note that finding collisions in a hash are way simpler to find than other security properties. Informally, there are numerous factors to break a hash functions, the most important of all is the lowest possible number of evaluations, then the random attacks of brute force. Finally, the ultimate strength estimated by the designer (theoretically). If all of these factors meet to violate at least one of the properties of the hash function then it is called "broken. For example, assume that the number of evaluations for a collision to occur is around 290 for a length of 256 bits. Hence, the probability of reaching such computation seem to be impractical especially with the hardware capability in hand, to break the hash function there is a need of 2^{128} assessment of the hash needed by the beginning of the attack. This theoretical break on the hash function is also termed an "academic break" on the hash function. Practically, it is easier to attack hash functions than encryption schemes due to the calculations made by the attacker depending on resources rather than the unawareness of the user to see the upper bound possibilities without the need to assume any secrets. Block ciphers differ from brute force attack in depending on the amount of computation endeavor the attacker seeks from the user. This limits the maximum the number of practical execution of the block algorithm (Zheng et al., 1993). As illustrated in Figure 8 cryptanalytical attacks on hash functions are categorized into two routes as explained below:

4.3 Generic Attacks (Attacks on Merkle-Damgård Construction)

Generic attacks are technical studies used to attack general hash function constructions (i.e Merkle-Damgård construction). The word *"generic"* means that the attack is not designed for a specific hash function (i.e. SHA-2). For example, if the hash function uses a certain block cipher, replacing this block cipher with another should not affect the complexity of a generic attack of that hash function. The generic attacks are classified into four types, discussed in the following sections.

4.3.1 Length Extension Attacks

An attacker can use the advantage of using the padding scheme for the messages in MD construction by applying length extension attack (it is also called extension attack). Length extension attack can be used to break secret prefix MAC scheme by calculating the authentication taps uncaring of knowing the secret key.

4.3.2 Joux Attack

It is also called Joux multi-collision attack that is used on MD hash function, where Antoine Joux have shown that finding single and multiple collisions are very close in difficulty. In the multi-collision attack (same digest where hashed from more than two messages), Joux assumed, getting into machine C with an initial state IV, results a couple of messages collided (Joux, 2004).

Also, Joux applied his multi collision in MD function to produce a collision in a concatenation of two independent hash functions. Particularly, this attack deemed to be the first spark to look forward to start searching for a new paradigm of mode of operation of hash function other than MD construction and hence announced SHA-3 competition.

4.3.3 Second Preimage Attacks with Long Message

In this algorithm, the attacker finds an S as Second Preimage for a given message M, where M $\neq$ S and H(M) = H(S) with an effort less than 2^t computation of H. In the Long Message Second Preimage Attack, the attacker tries to find a second preimage for a long target message M of 2^q+1 message blocks. The attacker does this by finding a linking message block M_{link}. Where, the digest of f_{IV} of the linking message block M_{link} matches one of the intermediate states Hi obtained in the hashing of M. The computation cost of this attack is about 2^{t-q} calls to the compression function f.

4.3.4 Herding Attack

This attack pertains to multi-collisions and to second preimage. It is used when an opponent places a deliberate value D to a hash function and exposes falsely the ownership of knowledge for a hidden future events and the value is the hash of that knowledge. After word, when the event matching happens, the opponent tries to herd the knowledge of those events to hash to the value previously was claimed (Kelsey & Kohno, 2006).

4.4 Specific Attacks on Specific Hash Functions

These attacks are based on the hash function itself as in Figure 8. The specific attacks are named Multi-Block Collision Attacks (MBCA) that are applied on MD5 (Wang & Yu, 2005), and what resembles it (Wang et al, 2005). MBCA technique applied on MD construction because it works on iterated function which finds two messages collided, each with a smallest length of two blocks. Moreover, by processing above one message block, collisions are found. In fact, multi-block collisions attack is applicable and valid on MD5, and what resembles it, since these hash functions collisions are randomly distributed and use more than single collision.

As Figure 8 shows the sub-categories of "attacks on specific hash functions" which are (collision attack on MD4, and resemblance to it; near collisions on reduced version of SHA-256 and second preimage attack on MD4) are only examples of specific attacks on these hash functions. Meaning that, attacks can be customized and applied based on the hash function behavior and architecture.

HASH FUNCTIONS APPLICATIONS

Application security such as certification, data integrity and authentication are subjects of interest for Hash functions. The following sections illustrate these applications.

1. Digital Signature

Giving an access to a valid sender, or a signer for an identity to manipulate a document or a message using an arithmetical method is called Digital Signature. Digital signatures are commonly used in Web-commerce, financial transactions and other cases where it is crucial to detect alteration of a message or a document. It uses private and public keys along with the hash digest to create the signature for a document. Digital Signature is meant to grants an privilege to personal document. It points out ownership of the document, a message or a record and isolate others from breaking such privacy (Goldwasser et al, 1988) .

2. Message Authentication Code (MAC)

MAC is akin to message digest in use. the design was made especially for applications to detect message tampering and forgery. MAC accepts a shared secret symmetric key (K) as input along with the arbitrary length and outputs MAC (sometimes called tag).

The process of the MAC algorithm is to access a message or a document, first it requires to figure out its message digest, then use the private key (K) to get the calculated MAC. Finally, the receiver gets the message along with the calculated MAC (Krawczyk, et al., 1997). Separately, the receiver calculates a new message authentication code value by using the symmetric secret key (K) and generate new hash digest. If the attached MAC with original message matches the new calculated MAC performed by the receiver then the message is authenticated and integrity verified.

MACs differ from digital signature as MAC uses a symmetric secret key and digital signature uses asymmetric key (public and private keys).

3. HMAC

A popular and specific implementation of message authentication codes is the Hash Message Authentication Code (HMAC). This scheme associates a private key and a cryptographic hash function to ensure secure data transfer over unsecure channels. As computers becoming more powerful, the need arises for complex hash functions. As a result, HMAC is a preferable to use with hash functions other than MAC due to its higher security. HMAC could be calculated using Cryptographic hash functions f, the resulting hash function is named with a prefix of HMAC-f.

4. Kerberos

Users of networks are more vulnerable and require an authenticated shield and well protected environment. Kerberos is a network authentication protocol that was designed and developed the Massachusetts Institute of Technology (MIT) in 1998 for client/server applications. Using Kerberos, a user can request an encrypted "ticket" from an authentication process so it can be used to request a specific service from a server.

5. Key Derivation

A Key Derivation Function (KDF) is an algorithm to derive a key of a given size from a secret value or other known information. That is used to derive keys from a secret value such as a value obtained by Diffie-Hellman key establishment. Keyed cryptographic hash function can be used for key derivation.

6. One Time Password

Cryptographic hash functions are used to compute One Time Password (OTP). OTP is a secret key which pertains to a private user. By using cryptographic hash functions, hashed passwords are saved instead of keeping the password itself. So that, if the file of passwords are revealed then the passwords still protected if the hash function is preimage resistance.

7. Pseudorandom Generator

A pseudorandom generator (PRG) is a result of applying cryptographic hash function. PRGs generates a short random seed that produces a pseudorandom bits which I turn used in truly random bits that cryptographic schemes rely on. Cryptographic with multipart objects use PRGs as a building block ex. Pseudorandom Function (PRF), bit commitment, etc (Blum & Micali, 1984).

8. Pretty Good Privacy

This famous program coves e-mail security over the internet by utilizing encryption and decryption of the e-mail. Hash Functions apply PGP to secure the accuracy of e-mail message.

9. Secure Socket Layer (SSL)/ Transport Layer Security (TLS)

SSL and TLS protocols are used to authenticate servers and clients over an untrusted network. SSL/TLS can help to secure data transferred using encryption. Also, SSL/TLS can authenticate servers as well as clients through secure communication.

AN OVERVIEW OF A SELECTED HASH FUNCTIONS

1. MD4 and MD5

In 1990 Message Digest 4 (MD4) was an innovative design initiated to become later on a super class for the next coming algorithms that evolved in 1991 such as MD5 and what resembled it which was developed as a result on enhancement of MD4. MD5 which was engineered by Ronald Rivestin was enriched by adding one more round to MD4 besides, compressing the input of a variable length of bits into 2^8 hash.

2. RIPLEMD

A cryptographic hash function named RIPEMD was first published in 1996 and developed by Hans Dobbertin, and et al. Its design was based on MD4. This consists of two equivalent forms of the MD4 compression function. RIPEMD produce 160-bits as a hash digest. . Enhanced copy of RIPEMD were developed due to the weakness that was found in RIPEMD-160 bits when Hans discovered a collision on two rounds of RIPEMD (Dobbertin et al, 1996). These versions are RIPEMD-128, RIPEMD-256 and RIPEMD-320. RIPEMD produce 128-bits of hash digest. The extended version of RIPEMD-128 is RIPEMD-256, which produce 256-bits as a hash digest. Also, the extended version of RIPEMD-160 is RIPEMD-320, which produce 320 bits as a hash digest.

3. SHA-x Family

3.1 Secure Hash Algorithm-0

Two famous Institutes, (NIST) together with (NSA) published the *Secure Hash Algorithm (SHA)* in 1993. At present, SHA is commonly referred to SHA-0. SHA-0 is an algorithm that produces a 160-bits hash digest. SHA-0 was developed to replace MD4 but it was withdrawn shortly after publication due to security issues.

3.2 Secure Hash Algorithm-1

SHA-0 was replaced by SHA-1 in 1995. Secure Hash Algorithm-1 or SHA-1 is a message digests algorithm, which is regarded the world's most popular hash function, which takes input a message of arbitrary length and produce output a 160 bits "fingerprint" of the input. However, the security level of this standard is limited to a level comparable to an 80-bit block cipher (Rijmen & Oswald, 2005). It is based on the design principle of MD4, and applies the Merkle-Damgård model of compression function.

3.3 Secure Hash Algorithm-2

NIST did publish three more hash functions around August, 2002, SHA-256, 384 and 512. These new hash functions family known as Secure Hash Algorithm-2 or simply SHA-2. SHA-2 was introduced due to the need of a larger key of a hash function to match the new *Advanced Encryption Standard (AES)* which introduced in 2001. In February 2004 another hash function joined to the SHA-2 family, SHA-224. SHA-224 and SHA-384 are the truncated versions of SHA-256 and SHA-512 respectively. The proposed system architecture of SHA-2 hash family can support efficiently the security needs of modern communication applications such as WLANs, VPNs and firewall (Sun et al, 2007).

3.4 Secure Hash Algorithm-3

In October 2012, NIST announced the winner of SHA-3 competition which started in 2008. Keccak was the winner of NIST competition and become the new SHA-3 standard. Keccak is a cryptographic hash function designed by Guido Bertoni, joan Daemen, Michael Peeters, and Gilles Van Assche. Keccak has completely different construction than SHA-0, SHA-1 and SHA-2 families. It supports at least four different output lengths n {224, 256, 384, and 512} in a high security levels (Andreeva et al, 2012). According to (Bertoni et al, 2009) the construction of Keccak sponge design is building the compression function from different permutation f operates components in the following:

1. Signify the length of message bit string by $|M|$, as a sequence of blocks in fixed length x, when calculated the ranges from 0 to $|M|_x$ -1.
2. Pad the message M in a sequence of x-bit blocks to signify by M|| pad [x] ($|M|$). Thus, padding rules have append a bit string to determined the bit length of M and the block length x.
3. It is a sponge hash functions to construct a function of [f, pad, r] where the permutation f has different length in input and fixed length of output, a padding rule "pad" and a bitrate r.
4. The permutation is a sequence of operations on the three-dimensional array The expression $a[x][y][z]$ with x, $y \in \mathbf{Z}_5$ and $z \in \mathbf{Z}w$, signifies the bit in position (x, y, z), follows by indexing starts from zero. The mapping between the bits of s and those of a is $s[w(5y + x) + z] = a[x][y][z]$. That terms in the x and y coordinates should be taken modulo 5 and expressions in the z coordinate modulo w. The source state has a fixed value and should never consider as an input (Taha et al, 2012).

CONCLUSION

This chapter presented an extensive study of cryptographic hash functions. The presented study surveys cryptographic hash functions from various aspects. It included the properties, classification, constructions, attacks, applications and an overview of a selected dedicated cryptographic hash functions. Practically, MD4, MD5 and SHA-0 considered broken hash functions. Theoretically, SHA-1 considered a broken hash function. But SHA-2 considered secure one. SHA-3 was presented due to the need for a long term security hash function which has a new promising sponge construction.

REFERENCES

Andreeva, E., Mennink, B., Preneel, B., & Škrobot, M. (2012). *Security Analysis and Comparison of the SHA-3 Finalists BLAKE*. Grøstl, JH, Keccak, and Skein.

Aumasson, J.-P., & Meier, W. (2009). Zero-sum distinguishers for reduced Keccak-f and for the core functions of Luffa and Hamsi. *rump session of Cryptographic Hardware and Embedded Systems-CHES, 2009*, 67.

Bertoni, G., Daemen, J., Peeters, M., & Assche, G. (2009). Keccak specifications. *Submission to NIST (Round 2)*.

Bertoni, G., Daemen, J., Peeters, M., & Van Assche, G. (2007). *Sponge functions*. Paper presented at the ECRYPT hash workshop.

Biham, E., Chen, R., Joux, A., Carribault, P., Lemuet, C., & Jalby, W. (2005). *Collisions of SHA-0 and Reduced SHA-1 Advances in Cryptology–EUROCRYPT 2005* (pp. 36–57). Springer.

Blum, M., & Micali, S. (1984). How to generate cryptographically strong sequences of pseudorandom bits. *SIAM Journal on Computing, 13*(4), 850–864. doi:10.1137/0213053

Boura, C. Canteaut, A. & De Canniere, C. (2010). *Higher-order differential properties of Keccak and Luffa.* Cryptology ePrint Archive, Report 2010/589.

Cramer, R., & Shoup, V. (2003). Design and analysis of practical public-key encryption schemes secure against adaptive chosen ciphertext attack. *SIAM Journal on Computing, 33*(1), 167–226. doi:10.1137/S0097539702403773

Damgård, I. B. (1990). *A design principle for hash functions.* Paper presented at the Advances in Cryptology—CRYPTO'89 Proceedings. doi:10.1007/0-387-34805-0_39

Diffie, W., & Hellman, M. (1976). New directions in cryptography. *Information Theory. IEEE Transactions on, 22*(6), 644–654.

Dobbertin, H., Bosselaers, A., & Preneel, B. (1996). *RIPEMD-160: A strengthened version of RIPEMD.* Paper presented at the Fast Software Encryption.

Goldwasser, S., Micali, S., & Rivest, R. L. (1988). A digital signature scheme secure against adaptive chosen-message attacks. *SIAM Journal on Computing, 17*(2), 281–308. doi:10.1137/0217017

Haber, S., & Stornetta, W. S. (1991). *How to time-stamp a digital document.* Springer.

Joux, A. (2004). *Multicollisions in iterated hash functions. Application to cascaded constructions.* Paper presented at the Advances in Cryptology–CRYPTO 2004. doi:10.1007/978-3-540-28628-8_19

Kelsey, J., & Kohno, T. (2006). *Herding hash functions and the Nostradamus attack Advances in Cryptology-EUROCRYPT 2006* (pp. 183–200). New York: Springer. doi:10.1007/11761679_12

Krawczyk, H., Canetti, R., & Bellare, M. (1997). HMAC: Keyed-hashing for message authentication. USA: RFC Editor.

Lucks, S. (2004). *Design principles for iterated hash functions*: Cryptology ePrint Archive, Report 2004/253, 2004, http://eprint. iacr. org

Maurer, U., Renner, R., & Holenstein, C. (2004). *Indifferentiability, impossibility results on reductions, and applications to the random oracle methodology Theory of cryptography* (pp. 21–39). New York: Springer.

Nandi, M., & Paul, S. (2010). Speeding up the wide-pipe: Secure and fast hashing. *Progress in Cryptology-INDOCRYPT, 2010,* 144–162.

Naor, M., & Yung, M. (1989). *Universal one-way hash functions and their cryptographic applications.* Paper presented at the Proceedings of the twenty-first annual ACM symposium on Theory of computing. doi:10.1145/73007.73011

Rijmen, V., & Oswald, E. (2005). *Update on SHA-1 Topics in Cryptology–CT-RSA 2005* (pp. 58–71). New York: Springer. doi:10.1007/978-3-540-30574-3_6

Rivest, R. L. (1991). *Cryptography. The Handbook of Theoretical Computer Science* (Vol. A). Cambridge, MA: The MIT Press.

Sun, W., Guo, H., He, H., & Dai, Z. (2007). *Design and optimized implementation of the SHA-2 (256, 384, 512) hash algorithms.* Paper presented at the ASIC, 2007. ASICON'07.

Taha, I., Alahmad, M., & Munther, K. (2012). Comparison and analysis study of sha-3 finallists. *International Conference on Advanced Computer Science Applications and Technologies* (26-28 Nov 2012), 7.

Wang, X., Yin, Y. L., & Yu, H. (2005). *Finding collisions in the full SHA-1.* Paper presented at the Advances in Cryptology–CRYPTO 2005. doi:10.1007/11535218_2

Wang, X., & Yu, H. (2005). *How to break MD5 and other hash functions Advances in Cryptology–EUROCRYPT 2005* (pp. 19–35). New York: Springer.

Zheng, Y., Pieprzyk, J., & Seberry, J. (1993). *HAVAL—a one-way hashing algorithm with variable length of output.* Paper presented at the Advances in Cryptology—AUSCRYPT'92.

KEY TERMS AND DEFINITIONS

Collision Resistant Hash Function: A hash function where finding any two inputs having the same hash digest is difficult.

Compression Function: H maps an input x of arbitrary finite bit length, to an output h(x) of fixed bit length n.

Cryptographic Hash Function: An algorithm that takes an arbitrary length of message as an input $\{0, 1\}*$ and produce a fixed length of an output called message digest $\{0, 1\}n$ (sometimes called an imprint, digital fingerprint, hash code, hash result, hash value, or simply hash).

Keyed Hash Functions: Accept a variable length message and a fixed length secret key as two inputs to the hash function design to produce a fixed length hash digest, $H: \{0,1\}^k \times \{0,1\}* \{0,1\}^n$.

One-Way Hash Function: A hash function where finding an input which hashes to a pre-specified hash digest is difficult.

Universal One-Way Hash Function: For randomly chosen input x, key k and the function Hk, it is hard to find y = x such that Hk(x) = Hk(y).

Unkeyed Hash Functions: Accepts a variable length message as a single input and produce a fixed hash digest, $H: \{0,1\}* \{0,1\}n$. It is also known as modification detection codes (MDCs).

Chapter 7
Crime Profiling System

Hussein Zedan
Applied Science University, Bahrain

Meshrif Alruily
De Montfort University, UK

ABSTRACT

Digital forensics aims to examine a wide range of digital media in a "forensically" sound manner. This can be used either to uncover rationale for a committed crime and possible suspects, prevent a crime from taken place or to identify a threat so that it can be dealt with. The latter is firmly rooted within the domain of intelligence counter measures. The authors call the outcome of the analyses subject profiling where a subject can be a threat or a suspect. In this Chapter the authors outline a process for profiling based on Self-organizing Map (SOM) and evaluating our technique by profiling crimes using a multi-lingual corpus. The development and application of a Crime Profiling System (CPS) is also presented. The system is able to extract meaningful information (type of crime, location and nationality), from Arabic language crime news reports. The system has two unique attributes; firstly, information extraction depends on local grammar, and secondly, automatic generation of dictionaries. It is shown that the CPS improves the quality of the data through reduction where only meaningful information is retained. Moreover, when clustering, using Self Organizing Map (SOM), we gain efficiency as the data is cleansed by removing noise. The proposed system is validated through experiments using a corpus collated from different sources; Precision, Recall and F-measure are used to evaluate the performance of the proposed information extraction approach. Also, comparisons are conducted with other systems.

INTRODUCTION

Digital forensics aims to examine a wide range of digital media in a 'forensically" sound manner. The ultimate goal is to identify, analyze and present facts and opinions about information. This can be used either to uncover rationale for a committed crime (and hence possible suspects), to prevent a crime from taken place or to identify a threat so that it can be dealt with. The latter is firmly rooted within the domain of intelligence counter measures. We call the outcome of the analyses 'subject profiling' where the subject here can be a threat or a suspect.

DOI: 10.4018/978-1-4666-6583-5.ch007

Copyright © 2015, IGI Global. Copying or distributing in print or electronic forms without written permission of IGI Global is prohibited.

In dealing with crimes (at the levels of their identification and prevention), the available resources that are to be mined and analyzed, are mainly in the form of unstructured texts (flat files). These are presented in a variety of languages, including Arabic. The volume of data in electronic form is rapidly increasing. According to McKnight (McKnight, 2005), there is around 90% of data is held in unstructured form, such as web pages, emails, police reports, etc. Current text mining techniques have been mostly developed and applied for the English language. However current threats are largely reported in languages other than English, e.g. Arabic, and that increasing efficiency and accuracy of mining processes is related to the size and richness of the carpi used.

In this Chapter, we develop a system which is able to recognize phrases that contain information related to crime in a given document and, during the information extraction stage, dictionaries are automatically created, which will assist in the information extraction process in a dynamic fashion. In addition, the extracted information will be utilized by SOM in order to perform clustering and visualization tasks.

The rest of the Chapter is organized as follows. The following section gives a background and a critical review of the related work. This chapter also presents the crime domain syntactic analysis, provides an overview of the framework's architecture, presents the experimental results,, the Performance evaluation results are given, and finally, presents the conclusion of this work.

BACKGROUND

With the advent of the Internet, the volumes of data in electronic form have become huge. As a result, a great deal of the information published on the Internet remains effectively hidden within large bodies of unstructured data.

The challenge that needs addressing is how to find specific knowledge about a particular subject with a high degree of accuracy. According to Noklestad (Noklestad, 2009), there are three different strategies: information retrieval, information extraction and question answering.

According to Fan et al. (Fan et al., 2006), the basic process in analyzing textual data is information extraction, and it is particularly useful when dealing with vast volumes of text. Extracting specific types of information from particular domains began in the late 1980s. The Defense Advance Research Project

Agency (DARPA) initiated a series of "Message Understanding Conferences" (MUC). DARPA's MUC described information extraction as "a task involving the extraction of specific, well-defined types of information from natural language texts in restricted domains, with the specific objective of filling pre-defined template slots and databases" (Ruch et al, 2005). In MUC-1 (1987) and MUC-2 (1989), messages about naval operations were studied. MUC-32 (1991) and MUC-4 (1992) focused on news reports about terrorist events, and MUC-5 (1993) and MUC-6 (1995) investigated news articles about joint ventures and management changes (Witten, 2004). In MUC-7 (1997), the task was to fill templates by identifying missile and rocket launch events from news articles published by the New York Times (Witten, 2004; Borthwick, 1999; Cowie and Lehnert, 1996). For example, in Figure 1, the task was to extract where the rocket was launched, the rocket's owner, the owner of the payload, and the date.

Rule-Based Approaches

Most of the systems developed for Arabic focus on the Named Entity Recognition (NER) technique (Attia et al, 2010; Abdul-Hamid and Darwish, 2010), the majority of which rely on predefined proper name gazetteers. Maloney and Niv (Maloney and Niv, 1998) developed a system, called TAGARAB, that uses a combination of a pattern

Figure 1. The outcome of information extraction for filling template slots

انطلقت بنجاح صباح امس الثلاثاء الأقمار الاصطناعية السعودية الثلاث، (سعودي كوم سات 1و2) و(سعودي سات 2)، من قاعدة (بيكانور) الفضائية في كازاخستان، على متن الصاروخ الروسي (دينبر).

The three Saudi satellites were launched successfully on Tuesday morning ((Saudi com SAT 1 and 2) and (SatCruiser 2)) form base (Bikanor) in Kazakhstan aboard a Russian rocket (Denber).

Template

Location: Kazakhstan	- كازاخستان
owner of rocket: Russia	- روسيا
owner of payload: Saudi	- السعودية
Date: Tuesday	- الثلاثاء

matching engine and morphological analysis as well as a words list to recognize information relating to names, dates, times, and numeric. Good results were achieved but it is an expensive process for it is applied for each token.

Mesfar (Mesfar, 2007) developed a system that combines morphological analysis, syntactic grammar and rules which recognizes proper names. As in the TAGARAB system, this is an expensive process because the whole text must undergo morphological analyses. In addition, large knowledge resources are used, which include many predefined gazetteers, such as a personal names list (containing 12,400 Arabic first names) and a locations list (consists of 5,038 entries), and a list of keywords (which has 872 trigger words).

NERA (Name Entity Recognition for Arabic), Shaalan and Raza (Shaalan and Raza, 2008), was developed to extract 10 named entities. They use a rule-based approach that relies on various fixed predefined dictionaries, such as for personal names (263,598 complete names, 175,502 first names and with 33,517 last names), locations (4,900 names) and organizations (273,491 names of companies). Also, there is a dictionary containing trigger words

(indicator words) for helping to identify entities, such as using job titles to indicate persons' names. It is noticeable that gazetteers are extensively used but building them renders the approach to be inefficient.

Al-Shalabi et al. (Al-Shalabi et al., 2009) presented an algorithm to extract proper nouns, using a set of keywords and special verbs together with some specific rules. However, it should be noted that the system is not able to extract proper nouns that do not appear directly after the keywords or the special verbs.

Elsebai et al. (Elsebai et al., 2009) adopted a rules-based approach that makes use of the outputs generated by the Buckwalter Arabic Morphological Analyzer (BAMA) for developing the Persons Names Arabic Extraction System (PNAES). Their system uses a set of keywords (introductory verbs and words) to indicate the phrases that might contain person names, i.e. there is no predefined person names gazetteer. Although this system is able to deal with names that appear not necessarily next to a keyword, unlike the above system quite complicated rules are created to cover all the probabilities of a person's name occurring in a text.

Abulei and Evens (Abuleil and Evens, 2004) developed an events extraction and classification system for Arabic information retrieval systems. Their developed system is based on a predefined keyword lists and a parser to extract the events, the dates and related proper nouns. Additionally, Abueil (Abuleil, 2007) proposed an algorithm for scanning and understanding events (natural disasters, bombings and deaths) in Arabic text in order to extract information related to them, such as event locations, event types and dates. The system uses different lists that are described as event elements. However, the system was only tested on a corpus compiled from one source. Furthermore, these lists were manually built, based on reading the texts, which is a key disadvantage.

Piskorski et al. (Piskorski et al., 2008) developed a multilingual news event extraction system. The system was able to extract violent and natural disaster events from online news. They use pattern matching ngine and a set of lexicons. The event extraction grammar was originally designed to be applied on the English language but the technique has been extended to work on other languages, such as French, Italian and Arabic. With regards to the Arabic language, the Arabic news articles were translated into English using translation systems, and then they implemented the event extraction grammar. The evaluation results were not reported for this system.

The performances of these systems are summarized in Table 1. Clearly, all the above systems use the rule-based approach. Also, common entities (person names, locations, organizations, dates and numbers) have been investigated except the two systems developed by Abulei and Evens (Abuleil and Evens, 2004) and by Abueil (Abuleil, 2007); they tried to recognize events in texts. Additionally, the described systems did not mention the data sparseness problem in the Arabic language, except (Shaalan and Raza, 2008). Furthermore, it seems that most dictionaries (gazetteers), especially the

Table 1. Precision, recall, and F-measure of above systems

System	Entity	Precision	Recall	F-Measure	Year
TAGARAB	Number	82.8	97.0	97.3	1998
	Time	91.0	80.7	85.5	
	Location	94.5	85.3	89.7	
	Person	86.2	76.2	80.9	
Mesfar	Number	97.0	94.0	95.5	2007
	Time	97.0	95.0	96.0	
	Location	82.0	71.0	76.0	
	Person	92.0	79.0	85.0	
Abueil	Event	86	81	84	2007
NERA	Time	97.25	94.5	95.4	2008
	Location	77.4	96.8	85.9	
	Person	86.3	89.2	87.7	
Al-Shalabi	Time	89.4	x	x	2009
	Location	91.6	x	x	
	Person	81.1	x	x	
PNAES	Person	93	86	89	2009
Traboulsi	Person	x	x	x	2009

keywords lists in the aforementioned systems, were built based on authors' observations or knowledge. In other words, there is no objective explanation or analysis phase carried out on the data being studied for identifying the keywords. However, this phase (data analysis phase) was discussed by Traboulsi (Traboulsi, 2009) in order to identify patterns of person names in Arabic texts. Three types of analysis (frequency, collocation and concordance) were conducted on huge corpora to identify the most important keywords, to discover the most frequent words collocating with keywords, and to obtain the concordance of the keywords. Consequently, the most frequent named entity structures were discovered, which led to the construction of a local grammar for recognizing person names, i.e. the other structures that may contain person names are discarded or neglected. As a result, the system might not be able identify of some person names entity. Also, no performance evaluation was conducted for this system.

Machine Learning Approaches

These have been adopted in Arabic NER research. Benajiba et al. (Benajiba et al., 2007) designed the Arabic Named Entity Recognition System (ANERsys) based on Maximum Entropy (ME). Annotated corpora were used as well as external resources such as dictionaries. Three different gazetteers were manually built: a location gazetteer (consisting of 1,950 names of continents, countries, cities, rivers and mountains); a person gazetteer (containing 2,309 names) and an organization gazetteer (consisting of a list of 262 names of companies, football teams and other organizations). As mentioned earlier, it is time consuming to build gazetteers. Also, in order for the system to be tested, several experiments must be first performed to train it and to derive a set of features for assisting in the recognition process. Moreover, Benajiba and Rosso (Benajiba and Rosso, 2008), changed the probabilistic model by using Conditional Random Fields

(CRF) instated of ME. Although, they achieved promising results through their improvement of ANERsys, their system still relies on an annotated corpus and the same predefined manually built gazetteers that were used with ME. Table 2 shows the evaluation results for ANERsys using ME and CRF. Also, Benajiba et al. [Benajiba et al., 2009] compared three machine learning approaches: Support Vector Machines (SVM), ME and CRF. The latter was the best and it yielded an overall F-measure of 83.

AbdelRahman et al. (AbdelRahman et al., 2010) integrated two machine learning techniques (bootstrapping semi-supervised pattern recognition and Conditional Random Fields (CRF)) for identifying 10 named entities, however, the developed system, as with the above systems, relies on predefined gazetteers (person (3,228), location (2,183), organization (403), job (70), device (253), car (223) and cell phone (184) to assist in recognizing the entities. Also, 16 different features are employed for implementing CRF as well as 232 different seeds. Table 2 lists the performance results of this system. Abdul-Hamid and Darwish (Abdul-Hamid and Darwish, 2010), created a system that is able to recognize named entities based on a set of features without using morphological or syntactic analysis or gazetteers. For implementing this work, Conditional Random Fields (CRF) was used. This technique was trained on a large set of surface features in order to avoid using Arabic morphological and syntactic features. Table 2 presents the evaluation results. It is noticeable that the above machine Table 2: Precision, recall and F-measure for machine learning systems learning approaches need an annotated corpus for them to be implemented. According to Ku (Ku et al., 2008), they also need large training data sets. Moreover, they often rely on different predefined gazetteers.

Table 3 presents a comparison of all the above systems in terms of method, type of corpus and whether or not they use gazetteers, POS and/or stemming.

Table 2. Precision, recall, and F-measure for machine learning systems

System	Entity	Precision	Recall	F-Measure	Year
ANERsys (using ME) (with gazetteers)	Location	82.17	78.42	80.25	2007
	Person	54.21	41.01	46.69	
	Misc.	61.54	32.65	42.67	
	Organisation	45.16	31.04	36.79	
(without gazetteers)	Location	82.41	76.90	79.56	
	Person	52.76	38.44	44.47	
	Misc.	61.54	32.65	42.67	
	Organisation	45.16	31.04	36.79	
ANERsys (using CRF)	Location	93.03	86.67	89.74	2008
	Person	80.42	67.42	73.35	
	Misc.	71.0	54.20	61.47	
	Organisation	84.23	53.94	65.76	
AbdelRahman (with pattern feature)	Location	96.05	80.86	87.80	2010
	Person	89.20	54.68	67.80	
	Organisation	84.95	60.02	70.34	
(without pattern feature)	Location	89.37	69.25	87.03	
	Person	87.01	53.23	66.05	
	Organisation	88.45	47.00	63.07	
Abdul-hamid and Darwish	Location	93	83	88	2010
	Person	90	75	81	
	Organisation	84	64	73	

Table 3. A comparison between the systems applied to Arabic text

System	Method	Stemming	Gazetteers	POS	Annotated Corpus
TAGARAB	Rule based	✓	✓	✓	x
Mesfar	Rule based	✓	✓	✓	x
NERA	Rule based	✓	✓	x	x
Al-Shalabi	Rule based	✓	x	x	x
PNAES	Rule based	✓	✓	✓	x
Abueil	Rule based	✓ for keywords	✓	x	x
Traboulsi	Rule based	✓	x	x	x
ANERsys	ME	✓ only prefixes	✓ x	x	✓
ANERsys	CRF	✓	✓	✓	✓
AbdelRahman	Bootstrapping + CRF	✓	✓	✓	✓
Abdul-hamid	CRF	✓	x	x	✓

Crime Domain and Text Mining Techniques

With regards to the crime domain, there have been several efforts to develop information extraction systems for automatically extracting meaningful crime-related information. Data mining techniques have been used in this domain and a comprehensive survey of the effectiveness of the various methods for crime data analysis is provided by Thongtae and Srisuk (Thongtae and Srisuk, 2008).

In the text mining field, Chau et al. (Chau et al., 2002) studied police narrative reports to extract five meaningful entities in order to facilitate crime investigation. The developed system is comprised of hand-crafted lexicons, rule-based and machine learning. The system was evaluated only on 36 documents collected from one source. Table 4 presents the evaluation results.

Also, Chau et al. (Chen et al., 2004) integrated the above system with some data mining techniques, such as association and prediction methods to develop a crime data mining system. Ku et al. (Ku et al., 2008) developed an information extraction system to extract crime-related information from different resources, such as police reports, newspaper articles and witness narrative reports written in the English language. Their system relies on rule-based and lexical look-up approaches. They manually built 88 gazetteer lists. Also, they employed the Gate open-source framework, which includes several modules, such as tokenizer, sentence splitter, Part-Of-Speech (POS) tagger, noun chunk, and JAPE rules for pattern matching. Table 5 shows the evaluation results for extracting crime events and crime scenes.

Moreover, Rilo (Rilo, 1993) developed a program called AutoSlog for extracting information in the terrorism domain. The system relies on concept nodes in order to extract information about terrorist incidents. AutoSlog is comprised of 13 concept nodes, and each one is triggered by predefined keywords (terrorist action words), such as 'bombed' and 'kidnapped', and is activated within a specific linguistic grammar (e.g. in passive form) in order to extract information, such as targets, perpetrators and victims. Also, it relies on a corpus tagged by POS tagger. In order to support crime investigation, other attempts have been made by governments and companies. The European Commission funded the AVENTINUS project which is a multilingual information extraction system. AVENTINUS is designed for multilingual drug enforcement authorities, improving multilingual communication and information processing (Schneider, 1998), and the rule-based approach is used for implementing the information extraction. Also, the Scene Of Crime Information System (SOCIS) was developed by a team from Sheffield and Surrey Universities (UK) in collaboration with four UK police forces (Surrey Police, Hampshire Constabulary, Kent County Constabulary and South Yorkshire Police) for crime scene photograph indexing and retrieval (Pastra et al., 2003). Moreover, the system performs information

Table 4. Evaluation results in terms of precision, recall, and F-measure

Entity	Precision	Recall	F-Measure
Person	74.1	73.4	73.7
Address	59.6	51.4	55.1
Narcotic Drug	85.4	77.9	81.4
Personal Property	46.8	47.8	47.2

Table 5. Evaluation results of extracting crime event and crime scene

Data Source	Entity	Precision	Recall	F-Measure
Police Narrative Reports	Event	100	67	80.2
	Scene	94	85	89.2
Witness Narratives	Event	100	57	72.6
	Scene	73	63	67.6

extraction using rule-based technique to extract all the names entities that might appear up in a caption: address, age, conveyance-make, date, drug, gun type, identifier, location, measurement, money, offence, organization, person and time. The system achieved 80% precision and 95% recall. Both systems (AVENTINUS and SOCIS) rely on predefined gazetteers.

Finally, the Locard Company developed an evidence tracking system, which offers management for all crime-related exhibits.

SYNTACTIC ANALYSIS

This section describes the development of the computational linguistic techniques for recognizing and extracting crime-related information (crime type, location (scene) and nationality). The syntactic analysis for the Arabic crime domain is performed in order to identify the context of the words used.

For implementing this intensive analysis, a huge corpus, which contains news reports on various crime incidents collected from different sources, is used. This corpus contains 502,609 tokens. In the analysis phase, frequency, collocation and concordance analyses are performed.

Syntactic Analysis: Frequency

All languages can be divided into two types: general and special (or restricted) language (or sub-language) (Almas and Kurshid, 2006). The specialist (or restricted) language has its own special vocabulary and idiosyncratic syntactic structures which varies from one domain to another. Much like the English language, Arabic texts are comprised of two types of linguistic units. Firstly 'closed class' words such as prepositions, determiners and conjunctions, which indicate the natural language. Secondly, 'open class' words such as verbs, nouns and adjectives, which indicate the topic, (Traboulsi, 2006).

More open class words are used in specialist texts; these words are often distinct and occur more frequently. The use of open class words together with well-defined words may reveal sentences governed by local grammar, which is described as syntactic restriction (Traboulsi, 2009).

Frequency analysis is able to present the most frequent words in the corpus being studied. Therefore, the first hundred open class words are selected after removing prepositions and conjunctions (closed class). As already mentioned, the open class words are rich in terms of the information that they carry because they reveal or indicate the topic of the document.

Table 6 lists the most frequent words that are either in a noun or verb form. Some words within Table 6 are considered highly informative. These words can be divided into three groups based on the type of information that they convey or indicate. Table 7 lists crime action words. Table 8 presents the word 'nationality', which is usually used to illustrate a person's nationality in Arabic texts. Finally, Table 9 shows the words that are often used for stating locations.

The nature of the event can be obtained directly through certain words, such as "murder' and "in theft" in Table 7. Moreover, the word "nationality" in Table 8 and the words related to location, such as "area", "city" and "province" in Table 9 is particularly useful for recognizing and extracting nationality and crime location because these two entities often occur in the context of the previous words.

The most significant result from this frequency analysis is that the way crime reports are written indicates that the type of crime most usually relies on using nouns instead of verbs, such as 'theft', which appeared twice in Table 7; in the first case "by theft", the proposition "in" is attached to it, and in the second, "the theft", the definite article "the" attached to it. . Moreover, place names are in noun form because they are proper nouns. With regards to nationality, in the Arabic language there is type of adjective called 'nisba', which

Table 6. Frequency distribution of the first 100 words after removing closed class words

Word	Translation	F	Word	Translation	F
تم	Completed	2406	التحقيقات	The probes	469
شرطة	Police	2165	القضية	The case	464
القبض	The arrest	2095	منزل	House	462
المتهم	The accused	1635	مبلغ	Amount	461
رجال	Men	1634	تمكنت	Able	460
الأمن	Security	1562	سيارة	Car	452
منطقة	Area	1175	طريق	Road	452
كان	Was	1172	جدة	Jeddah	441
مدير	Manager	1136	المحكمة	The court	438
التحقيق	The investigation	1038	الحادث	The incident	435
الأمنية	The security	1189	الفور	Immediately	428
امس	Yesterday	974	المنطقة	The area	426
قام	Did	900	قضية	Case	426
البحث	The search	887	اشخاص	Persons	421
الشرطة	The police	874	العقيد	The colonel	419
داخل	Inside	871	العصابة	The gang	416
النيابة	Public persecution	774	قتل	Murder	412
محمد	Mohammad	733	افراد	Members	407
التحريات	The investigations	726	وقال	And said	403
كانت	Was	719	بسرقة	In left	402
ضبط	Detect	680	الجنائية	The criminal	401
الجنسية	Nationality	678	الواقعة	The incident	400
الرياض	Riyadh	678	الأمر	The issue	398
احدى	One	672	عاما	Year	393
الواء	Major-general	664	الموقع	The location	392
الجنائي	The criminal	659	اعترف	Confessed	391
الجاني	The criminal	653	الاعلامي	The media	391
مركز	Centre	635	رئيس	Head	391
العامة	The general	633	سنة	Year	385
المجني	Victim	615	تعرض	Subjected	383
المباحث	The investigator	607	بشرطة	In police	382
المتهمين	The accused	594	مواطن	Citizen	382
الأول	The first	592	عثر	Found	379
امن	Security	587	زوجته	His wife	377
العام	The general	576	الناطق	Spokesman	374
محافظة	Province	574	دوريات	Patrols	367
الف	Thousand	558	الجهات	Officials	359
ريال	Riyal (currency)	558	وجود	Presence	359
الجناة	The criminals	532	الداخلية	The interior	356

continued on following page

Table 6. Continued

Word	Translation	F	Word	Translation	F
بمنطقة	In area	511	السيارة	The car	356
محكمة	Court	501	مستشفى	Hospital	351
تبين	Clarified	500	قسم	Section	348
مباحث	Criminal investigation	495	تمكن	Could	339
العمر	The age	489	سنوات	Years	339
المخدرات	The drugs	472	حي	District	338
شخص	Person	333	مصدر	Source	327
فريق	Team	333	الاشخاص	The persons	319
معلومات	Information	332	والبحث	And the investigation	318
عملية	Operation	329	النار	The fire	314
السرقة	The theft	327	مدينة	City	313

Table 7. The word that are found in the 100 most frequent words

Word	Translation
قتل	Murder
بسرقة	In theft
السرقة	The theft

Table 8. The word that is used to illustrate a person nationality

Word	Translation
الجنسية	The nationality

Table 9. The word that are often used to illustrate a place name in a text

Word	Translation
منطقة	Area
محافظة	Province
بمنطقة	In area
مدينة	City

is used to denote pertinence, such as origin and nationality (Halpern, 2009). It is derived from a noun by adding "iyy" in the masculine case or "iyyt" in the feminine case, as a suffix to the noun (Halpern, 2009; Condon et al, 2009). This type of adjective also exists in English, such as 'from Kuwait', from which the adjective 'Kuwaiti' can be derived, and from 'sun' the adjective 'sunny' is derived. In the Arabic, the nisba for "Britian" becomes "brytany" in the masculine case, and in the feminine case, it is " brytaniyyt". Therefore, these words can be considered as seeds for discovering the syntactic context of the event type, event location and nationality in order to identify the local grammar.

Syntactic Analysis: Collocation and Concordance

Collocation is to identify the most frequent collocation pairs of these words. This step is important because it can assist in determining the behavior of these words within sentences. As a result, the most frequent words that collocate with the words in the previous tables are discovered as well as their syntactic construction. Moreover, concordance analysis is carried out in order to identify

Table 10. Collocation results for "theft"

Theft		Positions												
Collocate	T	F	R	L	-5	-4	-3	-2	-1	+1	+2	+3	+4	+5
من	From	390	173	217	39	34	34	27	30	14	56	77	40	30
في	In	323	221	102	12	8	14	32	155	10	16	31	27	185
عن	About	109	86	23	3	8	3	8	64	6	4	6	2	5
على	On	86	67	19	15	14	11	5	22	0	2	5	5	7
بعد	after	46	28	18	4	6	10	1	7	0	4	4	8	2

the structural patterns that contain crime type, crime location and nationality. Consequently, the dominant patterns used for stating the crime event, crime location and nationality are obtained. The analyses for both are performed on words in Table 7, Table 8, and Table 9.

Crime Type

The collocation and concordance analyses of the crime action words in Table 7 were performed. It was found that these words often occur in the form of prepositional phrases and sometimes in the form of noun phrases. Because of the fact that a prepositional phrase is considered to be the complement of a head node (noun or verb), we investigated the head nodes that precede these prepositional phrases. It was found that the head nodes are transitive verbs, which are prevalent. Further, with regards to the noun phrases that contain a crime type, the transitive verbs are also

head nodes for them. Therefore, the local grammar for extracting the type of crime is constructed based on transitive verbs. These verbs are used as keywords when they are followed by specific prepositions, i.e. syntactic constraint is applied. As a result, the contexts of these verbs are analyzed in order to identify the prepositions that always collocate with them. A sample of the analysis phase for the crime action words and transitive verbs is presented in this section.

Table 10 shows the collocation results for "theft". I can be seen that the most frequent words are prepositions, namely "in", "an" and "from". These prepositions are considered the head nodes (governors) for this word because they occur immediately before it (Position -1), i.e. they assign the genitive case to the word "theft", and consequently, they form prepositional phrases. Table 11 shows the results of another analysis, where only the most frequent words that directly precede the word "theft" selected. It can be seen

Table 11. Collocation results of "theft" at Position-1

Theft		Positions												
Collocate	T	F	R	L	-5	-4	-3	-2	-1	+1	+2	+3	+4	+5
في	In	323	221	102	12	8	14	32	155	10	16	31	27	18
عن	About	109	86	23	3	8	3	8	64	6	4	6	2	5
قضية	Case	32	31	1	0	0	0	0	31	0	0	0	1	0
من	From	390	173	217	39	34	43	27	30	14	56	77	40	30
على	On	86	67	19	15	14	11	5	22	0	2	5	5	7
جرائم	Crimes	24	23	1	0	0	0	1	22	0	0	0	0	1

Table 12. Collocation results for "murder"

Murder		Positions												
Collocate	T	F	R	L	-5	-4	-3	-2	-1	+1	+2	+3	+4	+5
على	On	147	124	23	2	6	3	2	111	6	4	0	8	5
في	In	77	76	1	0	0	2	0	74	0	0	1	0	0
من	From	112	61	51	7	5	6	18	25	7	17	8	8	11
جريمة	Crime	25	22	3	2	0	0	1	19	0	1	1	0	1
بن	son	17	17	0	2	0	2	2	11	0	0	0	0	0

Table 13. Collocation results for "murder" at Position-1

Murder		Positions												
Collocate	T	F	R	L	-5	-4	-3	-2	-1	+1	+2	+3	+4	+5
عاى	On	147	124	23	2	6	3	2	111	6	4	0	8	5
جريمة	crime	77	76	1	0	0	2	0	74	0	0	1	0	0
في	in	112	61	51	7	5	6	18	25	7	17	8	8	11
في	in	25	22	3	2	0	0	1	19	0	1	1	0	1
قضية	case	17	17	0	2	0	2	2	11	0	0	0	0	0

Table 14. Most frequent verbs found in collocation results for "theft"

Theft		Positions												
Collocate	T	F	R	L	-5	-4	-3	-2	-1	+1	+2	+3	+4	+5
تخصصت	Specialized	34	34	0	0	0	1	33	0	0	0	0	0	0
اعترف	Confessed	18	18	0	4	9	4	1	0	0	0	0	0	0
تخصص	Specialized	17	17	0	0	1	2	14	0	0	0	0	0	0
تعرض	Subjected	14	12	2	1	5	4	2	0	1	0	1	0	0
اعترفوا	Confessed	13	13	0	4	2	3	4	0	0	0	0	0	0
تورط	involved	13	12	1	2	3	3	4	0	0	1	0	0	0

Table 15. Most frequent verbs found in collocation results for "murder"

Murder		Positions												
Collocate	T	F	R	L	-5	-4	-3	-2	-1	+1	+2	+3	+4	+5
اقدم	Conducted	41	40	1	0	3	10	27	0	0	0	1	0	0
قام	Did	12	2	10	0	1	0	1	0	0	1	5	4	0
شهدت	Had	17	17	0	7	6	3	1	0	0	0	0	0	0
اقدمت	conducted	9	8	1	0	1	0	7	0	0	1	0	0	0

Table 16. Most frequent verbs found in collocation results for "involved"

Involved		Positions												
Collocate	**T**	**F**	**R**	**L**	**-5**	**-4**	**-3**	**-2**	**-1**	**+1**	**+2**	**+3**	**+4**	**+5**
في	In	61	11	50	5	2	1	2	1	19	9	11	4	7
من	from	23	9	14	0	2	2	3	2	0	5	4	5	0
على	On	13	9	4	0	1	2	6	0	0	0	2	1	1
سرقة	Theft	13	1	12	0	0	0	1	0	0	4	3	3	2
عن	about	11	11	0	0	2	1	0	8	0	0	0	0	0

that not only prepositions precede this word; there are also nouns, for example, "case", "crime", "crimes", o\"operation", and they together form noun phrases, such as, "theft crime" and "theft operation".

According to these results, the word "theft" often occurs in the form of a prepositional phrase or noun phrase because it is often preceded by a preposition or a head noun. Similar result can be shown for "murder". Table 12 shows the collocation analysis of the word "murder".

Table 13 presents a further analysis, where only the most frequent words that immediately occur before the word "murder" are chosen.

It can be deduced that the two crime action words theft" and "murder" mostly appear in the form of prepositional phrases and sometimes in the form of noun phrases, i.e. they share the same context. This confirms our observation regarding the style in which these texts are written, describing event types by using nouns instead of verbs. As a consequence, the verbs that occur in collocation with the previous words were identified, and Table 14 and Table 15 show the most frequent verbs appearing in collocation with "murder", respectively. Table 14 and Table 15 show that the verbs mostly occur on the right side of the tokens "theft" and "murder" occurring most often at Position-2.

This result indicates that there is separation between these verbs and "theft" and "murder". However, all these verbs are transitive (with prepositions) except the verb had". This fact clarifies that the separation that occurs at Position -1 in Table

14 and Table 15 in front of the verbs is because Position -1 is for the prepositions that link these verbs to their complements. As a consequence, this result provides a strong motivation to further study the context of these transitive verbs.

Figure 2 presents a sample of the concordance analysis result for the verb "involved" / twrt / involved".

It can be seen that the verb in each sentence is followed by the preposition "in" to reach its complement, which contains a crime type. Also, it can be seen that the types of crime not only occur in the form of a prepositional phrase (preceded by a preposition), but also in noun phrase form because they are preceded by some nouns.

The analysis of the transitive verbs shows that the crime action words occur within the context of certain verbs in transitive constructions. These crime words occur after the associated prepositions of verbs, whether in the form of prepositional phrases or noun phrases. Furthermore, it has been found that each verb associates with a maximum of two prepositions. Moreover, the occurrence of the associated preposition, whether directly after the verb or not, is not important. As a result, the transitive construction can be an effective and useful tool for identifying and extracting types of crime. Accordingly, these can aid in building the local grammar for extracting the crime type patterns.

Figure 3 shows the local grammar for crime type. In Figure 3, the verb "subjected" always relates with the preposition "to" or ". Also, the

Figure 2. The concordance result of the verb "involved"

Kidnap (PP)	تورط في خطف أحد أبناء جلدتهم بهدف الحصول على مبلغ مالي	
Alcoholic distribution (PP)	تورط في ترويج خمر وإعداد مقر سكنه كموقع للعب القمار	
Rape (PP)	تورط في اغتصاب حدث	
Smuggling (NP)	تورط في ثلاث سوابق تهريب وأقر بتقاضي أكثر من	
Theft (NP)	تورط في جرائم سرق وسطو لمنازل ومدارس وكانت شرطة تلقت	
Killing (PP)	تورط في قتل زوجة أحد مواطنيه وانتقلت فرق الأمن الى مسرح	
Theft (PP)	تورط في سرق نصف مليون ريال فككت شرطة منطقة الرياض	
Forgery (NP)	تورط في عمليه تزوير وأشارت المعلومات الى أن القبض على	
Violence (PP)	تورط في الاعتداء على حدث بعد أن استدرجه وشقيقه واتجه بهما	
Theft (NP)	تورط في هذه سرق وكان مركز شرطة محافظة شقراء قد ألقى	
Burglary (PP)	تورط في السطو على " بنده " المجمعة ألقت الأجهزة الأمنية	

Figure 3. Crime types' local grammar

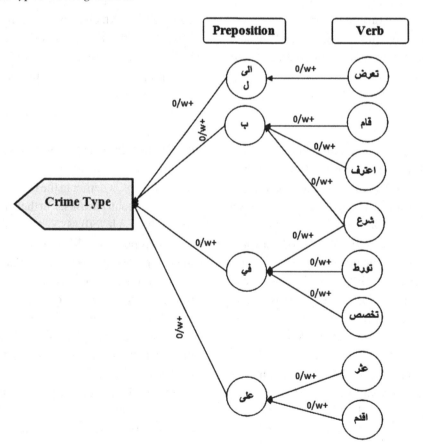

synonyms for the words "صوصخت", "طورت", "عرش" in English are "involved", "specialized" and "commenced", respectively. These three verbs come with preposition "يف", which means "in" in English but the verb "عرش" also has a dependency relationship with the preposition "ىب / bi / in". Moreover, the verb "ماق / qam", which means "did" and "فرتعا / aatraf / confessed" are associated with the preposition "ب / bi / in". The verbs "مدقا / aqdam / conducted" and "رثع / athar / found" have association with the preposition "ىلع / ala / on".

Nationality

As mentioned previously, the nationality type is one of the targets that need to be recognized and then extracted. It is has been found that the word "ةيسنجلا" / aljensyt / the nationality" is within the list of 100 tokens (see Table 6).

The frequency of "ةيسنجلا " (singular with the definite article "لا / al / the") occurs 676 times. Other forms of this word were found, and their frequencies were also counted. For example, the words "ةيسنجلا / jensyt / nationality" (singular without definite article) and " ىسنجلا syat / nationalities" (plural) occur 198 and 53 times, respectively. On the other hand, the word "تايسنجلا / aljensyat / the nationalities" (plural with definite article "لا / al / the") occurs 33 times.

The collocation and concordance analyses of all these words were performed. The results show that nationality is often represented by a word that immediately follows the above words with a syntactic constraint. The syntactic condition is that the words " ةيسنجلا / aljensyt / the nationality", "ةيسنج / jensyt / nationality", "تايسنج/jensyat / nationalities" and "تايسنجلا / aljensyat / the nationalities" must be assigned the genitive case by the preposition (governor) " نم / min / from". However, there is one exception: " ةيسنجلا / aljensyt / the nationality"; when this word is not preceded by the preposition "نم/ min / from", the word that occurs instead of the preposition is considered to indicate nationality.

The following is a sample of the collocation and concordance analyses that were performed on word words "ةيسنجلا/aljensyt/the nationality". Table 17 shows that the most frequent word collocating with " ةيسنجلا / aljensyt / the nationality" is the preposition "نم / min / from". This preposition occurs to the right (preceding) 406 times in various positions, and in 296 out of these 406 cases, it immediately precedes " ةيسنجلا / aljensyt / the nationality". Consequently, there is a dependency relationship between them. The other tokens, such as the prepositions "ىلع / ala / on", "يف / in" and the word "نب/ bin/ son of", are neglected because they have no strong relationship (i.e. Position-1) with the word being investigated.

On the other hand, the nationality word "ىدوعس/ saudi / Saudi" occurs 72 times immediately before "ةيسنجلا/ aljensyt / the nationality". As a result, another analysis was carried out to investigate the most frequent words immediately occurring before the word " ةيسنجلا/ aljensyt /

Table 17. Collocation results for "اجنسة / aljensyt / the nationality"

The Nationality		Positions											
Collocate	T	F	R	L	-5	-4	-3	-2	-1	+1	+2	+3	+4	+5
من	From	528	406	122	25	33	21	31	296	1	19	32	33	37
على	On	191	95	96	17	32	42	3	1	17	22	22	26	9
في	In	101	12	89	8	2	2	0	0	15	26	21	12	15
بن	Son	79	63	16	33	27	3	0	0	0	0	0	9	7
سعودي	Saudi	74	74	0	0	1	1	0	72	0	0	0	0	0

Table 18.Collocation results for "الجنسية / aljensyt / the nationality" at Position-1

The Nationality		Positions													
Collocate	T	F	R	L	-5	-4	-3	-2	-1	+1	+2	+3	+4	+5
من	From	528	406	122	25	33	21	31	296	1	19	32	33	37
سعودي	Saudi	74	74	0	0	1	1	0	72	0	0	0	0	0
هندي	Indian	31	31	0	0	0	0	0	31	0	0	0	0	0
باكستاني	Pakistani	27	27	0	0	0	0	0	27	0	0	0	0	0
نفس	same	17	14	3	0	0	0	0	14	0	0	0	0	3

the nationality". The results in Table 18 show that some nationalities appear with the suffix "ي / ya / y", such as "سعودى / saudi / Saudi", "هندى / hndi / Indian" and "باكستانى / bakstani / Pakistani". However, the preposition "من / min / from" is still at the top of the list.

The results of our investigation into the words that directly follow the word "الجنسية / aljensyt / the nationality" can be seen in Table 19. All these words represent different nationalities.

Therefore, we may deduce from these two analyses that a nationality can occur before or after the main word "" الجنسية / aljensyt / the nationality". It can be noticed that the nationalities in Table 18 have suffixes ending with "ي / iyy" but in Table 19 they end with "ةى / iyyt". In addition, according to the concordance analysis, it is found that the word that directly follows the word " " الجنسية / aljensyt / the nationality" is a nationality word when " الجنسية / aljensyt / the nationality" is assigned the genitive case by the proposition.

"من / min / from". In contrast, if it is not preceded by a preposition, the word that precedes it instead of that preposition is a nationality word.

Figure 4 presents a sample of the occurrence of the word " الجنسية / aljensyt / the nationality". Both cases can be seen, and the occurrence of nationality type before or after is controlled by the preposition "من / min / from", i.e. by the syntactic construction of " الجنسية / aljensyt / the nationality", whether or not it is in the genitive case.

Figure 5 depicts the nationality local grammar that was generated based on the syntactic analysis.

Crime Location

The words in Table 9, which are often used for stating a place name, are analyzed in this section. The words "منطقة / mantqt / area" and "بمنطقة/ bi-mantqt/ in area" are the same in terms of meaning but the word " بمنطقة / bi-mantqt / in area"

Table 19. Collocation result for "الجنسية / aljensyt / the nationality" at Position+1

The Nationality		Positions													
Collocate	T	F	R	L	-5	-4	-3	-2	-1	+1	+2	+3	+4	+5
اليمنية	The Yemeni	44	3	41	0	1	2	0	0	39	0	0	0	2
الأسيوية	The asian	39	0	39	0	0	0	0	0	39	0	0	0	0
الباكستانية	The Pakistani	29	0	29	0	0	0	0	0	29	0	0	0	0
الهندية	The Indian	33	0	33	0	0	0	0	0	29	0	0	0	4
البنغالية	The bangladeshi	22	2	20	0	0	2	0	0	20	0	0	0	0

Figure 4. The concordance lines for " الجنسية / *aljensyt / the nationality*"

	الجنسية	
في العقد الرابع من عمره بسجنه سبع سنوات	الجنسية	من المحكمة العامة بالرياض على احد الجناة سعودي
اليمنية كانوا ينوون تهريبها مثيا على الاقدام	الجنسية	المخدر وذلك بعد رصد لتحركات عدد من المهربين من
اثر تورطه في جريمة الرشوة وقالت وزارة	الجنسية	لمدة شهرين للمدعو / بشير بنجلاديشي
متورط في عدد من الجرائم منها سرقة سيار	الجنسية	اطاحت شرطة جدة بمتهم باكستاني
كان على خلاف مع القتيل ، وبحسب الناطق	الجنسية	« في منطقة المفرحات واتضح انه مقيم سوداني
الآسيوية على اثر تورطهم في تشكيل عصابة	الجنسية	منطقة الرياض من القاء القبض على ثلاثة اشخاص من
البنجلادشية يعملون في مطار الملك فهد الد	الجنسية	الجزئية بمحافظة القطيف على اقوال اربعة مقيمين من
في العقد الثالث من العمر لتورطه باطلاق	الجنسية	محافظة وادي الدواسر من ضبط احد الجناة سعودي
واحدات تلفيات فيه دون ان يصاب السائق	الجنسية	لاطلاق نار وهو واقف بحي الزوراء بقيادة سائق هندي
الباكستانية يتوافدون على الحوثيين محملين	الجنسية	المثير للشك ، فرصد رجال الشرطة افرادا وافدين من
في حي كيلو ثمانية الشعبي جنوب جدة مقتولة	الجنسية	عن ومسقوط وافدة في العقد الثالث من العمر افريقية
المنشورة صورته على جريمة (الرشوة) (	الجنسية	بيان وزارة الداخلية : اقدم محمد (سعودي
الاثيوبية في وقت متأخر من الليل وقاموا	الجنسية	تعرض شاب سعودي للاختطاف من قبل شخصين من

Figure 5. Nationality local grammar

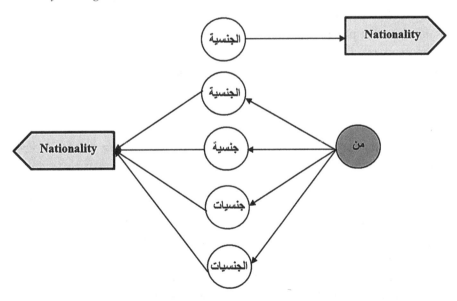

Table 20. Collocation results for "منطقة/ mantqt / area"

The Nationality		Positions												
Collocate	T	F	R	L	-5	-4	-3	-2	-1	+1	+2	+3	+4	+5
في	In	622	527	95	30	15	20	81	381	0	30	23	14	28
شرطة	Police	335	329	6	1	2	3	0	323	0	0	1	2	3
من	From	316	142	174	31	37	23	15	36	2	42	33	40	57
الرياض	Riyadh	302	7	295	5	0	1	1	0	286	2	0	3	4
بشرطة	In police	140	139	1	0	0	1	0	138	0	0	1	0	0

Table 21. Collocation results for "منطقة/ mantqt / area" at Position -1

The Nationality		Positions												
Collocate	T	F	R	L	-5	-4	-3	-2	-1	+1	+2	+3	+4	+5
في	In	622	527	95	30	15	20	81	381	0	30	23	14	28
شرطة	Police	335	329	6	1	2	3	0	323	0	0	1	2	3
بشرطة	In police	140	139	1	0	0	1	0	138	0	0	1	0	0
الي	To	145	98	47	12	8	7	12	59	0	8	13	13	13
لشرطة	To police	43	43	0	1	0	0	0	42	0	0	0	0	0

is attached to the preposition " ب / bi / in". This composition, as already described, is a prepositional phrase, which is a type of the genitive case.

Likewise, collocation and concordance analyses for the words in Table 9 were performed in order to investigate their contexts and to obtain a fuller picture. The results show that place names (crime locations) are often represented by words that immediately follow them. This is similar to the English compositions 'city of', 'province of' and 'region of', all of which constitute a construct state in terms of grammar. Accordingly, these words are chosen as keywords in order to recognize and extract a crime location. Although these words are often assigned the genitive case as objects of specific propositions in prepositional phrases, or as the second noun of specific construct heads in construct sats, there is no need to apply a syntactic constraint. The following analysis for the word منطق/ mantqt / area is presented.

Table 20 presents the results of the collocation analysis. The collocation analysis clearly shows that the word most frequently associating with"

منطق / mantqt / area" is the preposition "يف/ in"; it is to the right (preceding) and it occurs 381 times directly before the word" منطق / mantqat / area". Also, another preposition, "نم / min / from", can be seen, and it occurs 31 times in Position-1. The word " شرط/ shurtat / police", which is within the list of 100 tokens, appears 323 times out of 329 directly preceding the word "منطق/ mantqat /area". Moreover, the last row has the word "شرطب / bi-shurtat / in police", which is in reality a prepositional phrase because the preposition " ب / bi / in " is attached to the word " شرط / shurtat / police", forming one word (" شرطب / bi-shurtat / in police"). This word is also within the 100 words list, and it occurs 2,166 times in the corpus. On the other hand, the word " الرياض / alriyad / Riyadh", which is a city name, occurs 286 times immediately after the word being investigated.

Also, another two analyses were carried out to obtain the most frequent words at Position -1 and Position +1. The results are listed in Table 21 and Table 22.

Table 22. Collocation results for "منطقة / mantqt / area" at Position +1

The Nationality		Positions													
Collocate	T	F	R	L	-5	-4	-3	-2	-1	+1	+2	+3	+4	+5
الرياض	Riyadh	302	7	295	5	0	1	1	0	286	2	0	3	4
عسير	Asir	78	0	78	0	0	0	0	0	78	0	0	0	0
نجران	Najran	54	2	52	2	0	0	0	0	52	0	0	0	0
الباحة	Al Baha	44	0	44	0	0	0	0	0	44	0	0	0	0
جازان	Jazan	41	1	40	1	0	0	0	0	40	0	0	0	0

Position -1 in Table 21 shows the first three words (in, police and from) already seen in the above Table 20, and two new words, which are the preposition " الى / ila / to" and the word " لشرطة / li-shurtat / to police". The word " لشرطة /li-shurtat / to police" is a prepositional phrase because the preposition "ل/ li/ to" is attached to it, forming a single word. From the syntactic point of view, the words "bi-shurtat" and "li-shurtat" are considered governors and assign the genitive case to the word "منطقة / mantqt / area".

With regards to the words in Table 22 that occur at Position +1, i.e. immediately following "منطقة/ mantqt / area", all of them are the names of cities. This is similar to English where the phrases 'area of' and 'region of' are used before what we expect to be a place name. Moreover, in terms of grammar, they form a construct state because the word "منطقة / mantqt / area" inherits its definiteness from the name of the city that follows it.

The Figure 6, presents a sample of the concordance analysis. The results show that all the words immediately following "منطقة/ mantqt / area" are the names of cities, even though the word " منطقة / mantqt / area" is sometimes not preceded by the common words already seen, such as " بشرطة/ bi-shurtat / in police", " لشرطة / / li-shurtat / to police" and "في / in".

The analyses of the above words provide a full picture of their behavior within sentences. Furthermore, they show that their respective contexts contain place names. These names always immediately follow them, and therefore, these words are employed for extracting crime locations from a given text, by using them as keywords with no syntactic constraint. Figure 7 describes the location local grammar 21.

CRIME PROFILING SYSTEM (CPS)

The core of this work is the exploitation of the local grammar in order to extract crime type, crime location and nationality. The system consists of four stages, as follows:

1. Initial Preprocessing Stage.
2. Information Extraction Stage.
3. Intermediate Preprocessing Stage.
4. Clustering Stage.

The proposed architecture and its components are shown in Figure 8.

Initial Preprocessing Stage

This stage is comprised of four components:

- **Data Gathering:** Text mining research relies on the availability of a suitable corpus. As a result, many corpora have been created for specific purposes. For this research, the corpus has been collected from different Arabic newspapers published in different Arabic countries, such as Alriyadh, Aljazeera, Okaz, Sabq from Saudi Arabia,

Figure 6. The concordance lines for " منطقة / mantqt / area"

Figure 7. Location local grammar

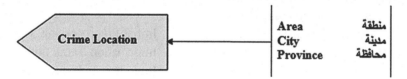

Elkhabar and Echoroukonline newspaper issues from Algeria, Addustour from Jordan, Ahram and Massai Ahram from Egypt, Alqabas and Alraimedia from Kuwait and Albayan and Alkhaleej from United Arab Emirates. The reason for compiling this corpus from different resources is to avoid the problem of bias, which could occur if the system is tested on documents that were collected from only one country.

- **Tokenization:** An important step in the processing of textual documents, which takes place before information extraction and clustering, is tokenization. It allows the unstructured text to be split into tokens,

which assists the system in processing the text. As a result, each textual le is represented through one vector.

- **Normalization:** Because there are spelling variations in the Arabic language, and because some letters that perform the same function are written in different forms, it is necessary to employ a normalization strategy. There are two normalization strategies; the rst is related to the letter "ا"; this may appear in text as "أ", "إ" or "آ", and these will be normalized to "ا". The second letter is "ة", which may appear as " ه", and this will be normalized to "ة". The reason behind this process is to make the corpus more consistent.

Figure 8. News-based crime profiling system architecture

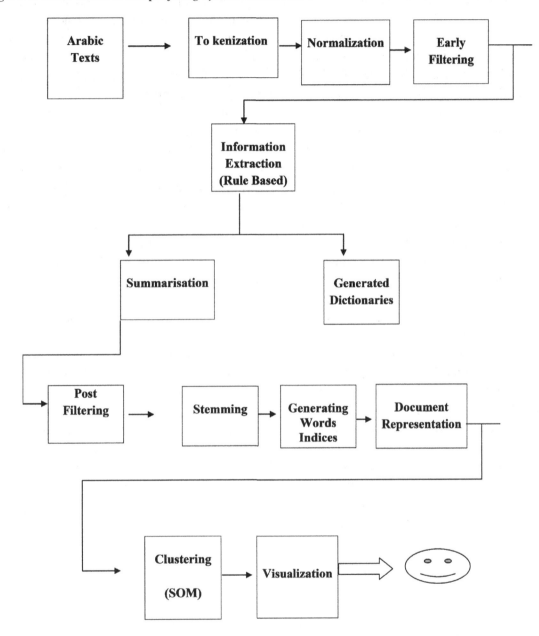

- **Early Filtering:** In most text mining systems, the functional words, such as prepositions and conjunctions, as well as punctuation marks, are usually removed during filtering. These stop words, which are found extensively in the text, have no useful meaning. In this framework, there are two filtering processes: early filtering and advanced filtering.

In the early filtering, all the stop words, punctuation marks and numbers are removed with the exception of some prepositions, as shown in Table 23; these are retained for the process that follows. These stop words are central to the operation of the system in that they play a significant role in recognizing the type of crime and nationality.

Information Extraction Stage

Information extraction is the process where relevant information is extracted from a document. This is achieved by using the developed local grammar. Moreover, the information extraction process creates a higher quality of data for the clustering process. This system performs three different tasks in order to extract three different types of information:

- **Type of Crime:** As we have shown above, the types of offence usually occur within the transitive grammatical structure. For extracting crime types, the system looks for words in a text that match the words in the verb list, and when a match occurs, the system will look for the first possible associated preposition that follows that verb. As a result, the system could avoid using annotated corpus by using prepositions to achieve the syntactic constraint. After that, the three words that immediately follow the preposition are extracted, and within these three words, the crime word should be present. Moreover, these extracted words are used to describe the document during the clustering stage that will follow. The reason that the three words after the preposition are extracted is to increase the probability of the crime word being identified.

In Arabic, the crime action word sometimes does not appear immediately after the preposition, as already seen in our concordance result of "روت / twarat / involve", i.e. it is preceded by a noun.

The following are representations of the possible positions of the noun.

In the first case, shown in Figure 9, the type of crime noun appears immediately after the preposition. Figure 10 illustrates where the type of crime noun does not appear immediately after the preposition because there is a word between, and Figure 11 illustrates the case where there are two words between the preposition and noun. Another point to consider in this grammatical construct is that sometimes the preposition does not always immediately follow the verb. An example of this is illustrated in Figure 12, where the preposition, which is followed by the type of crime noun, appears nine words after the verb. If these nine words were to be removed, the meaning can still be inferred from the head node (verb) and the preposition and noun (prepositional phrase).

As the Arabic language is rich in terms of morphology, whereby a word can be broken down into its base form and affixes, and usually it is the base, or root, of the word that is kept in dictionaries for extraction purposes. The proposed framework maintains a list of verbs in the past tense instead of the base or root form; this is because most news reports about crime are written in the past tense. The

Table 23. List of prepositions that are retained in this process

Arabic Preposition	Pronunciation	English Translation
على	Ala	On
في	Fi	In
إلى	Ela	To
ب	Bi	By
ل	Li	to

Figure 9. First case: crime type immediately follows the preposition

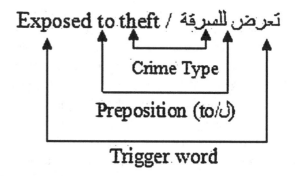

Figure 10. Second case: crime type after one word from the preposition

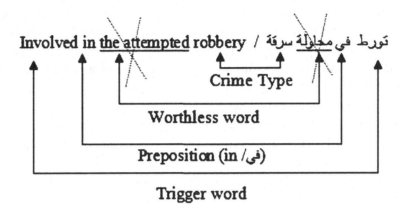

Figure 11. Second case: crime type after two words from the preposition

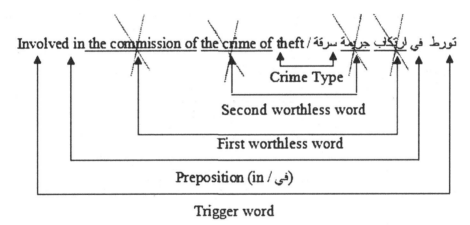

Figure 12. The associated preposition not directly following its verb

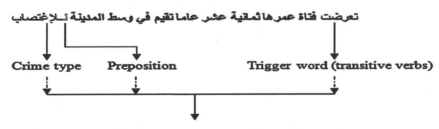

system uses N-gram to recognize many of the inflected forms of the verb by identifying the keyword from which the inflected forms are derived. These verbs can also produce nouns which are often followed by the same preposition that the verb takes. Examples of the keywords and their associated inflected forms are shown in Table. 24. The advantages of this approach are, firstly, not all of the words in the document need to be stemmed, as with other text mining systems, and secondly, it reduces the amount of required keywords in the list.

Also, there is no need for an annotated corpus, i.e. the framework has no linguistic components, such as PoS taggers. Instead, lists of intransitive verbs and their prepositions are provided to the system in order to extract the desired patterns.

- **Nationality:** For extracting nationality patterns from Arabic crime texts, the nationality local grammar previously presented is utilized. The system looks for words in a text that match the words in the nationality keyword list, and when a match occurs, the system checks the syntactic construction of the word to determine whether or not it is in a genitive construction. Therefore, the system will check whether the word is preceded by the preposition "من / min / from" in order to achieve the syntactic constraint. If the condition is achieved, then the word that immediately follows the keyword is extracted as a nationality. However, there is one exception; the word " الجنسية / aljensyah / the nationality" in singular

Table 24. Keywords and their inflected forms

Verb	Inflected Forms
تورط	التورط ـ المتورطين ـ تورطوا ـ تورطن ـ تورطا ـ تورطهم ـ متورطين
اعترف	اعترفا ـ اعترفوا ـ اعترفن ـ واعترف
تخصص	التخصص ـ تخصصوا ـ تخصصن ـ تخصصا ـ متخصصين ـ المتخصصين ـ المتخصصات
عثر	عثروا ـ عثرن ـ عثرا ـ فعثروا
اقدم	اقدموا ـ اقدمن ـ اقدما
تعرض	تعرضن ـ تعرضوا ـ التعرض ـ تعرضهم ـ المتعرضين

form with the article" ال / al / the" attached. When there is no preposition before it, the word that occurs instead of the preposition is identified as the nationality.

- **Location:** In order for the system to extract the place names, the location local grammar is used without syntactic constraint. Once matching occurs between any trigger word in the location keywords list and a word in the contents of the file, the word that follows the keyword is extracted and classified as a location name.

Using this linguistic technique serves to overcome the lack of any capital letter feature; this is not valuable in the Arabic language, so it cannot be used as a clue for extracting proper names, as in the English language.

Output from the Information Extraction Phase

The following are the two outcomes of the information extraction stage:

- **Summarization:** A summary is a condensed copy of the original document, containing only the essential information. The idea of summarization is to reduce the length of the document, retaining only key information and the overall meaning. It is from these summaries that the clustering will be produced according to the type of crime.
- **Generating Dictionaries:** It is an important aspect of this work is the automatic generation of dictionary: crime type and location and nationality.

Figure 13 presents the whole process of the early filtering stage with the information extraction stage. It shows the transformation phases for the text being processed through each process.

Intermediate Preprocessing Stage

The intermediate preprocessing stage is comprised of four processes, which are post filtering, stemming, generating words indices, and document representation. The main goal of this stage is to prepare the extracted data from the summarizing stage in adequate form in order to be processed in the clustering stage, where they can be visualized.

- **Post Filtering:** The post filtering process of the intermediate preprocessing stage is designed to remove the prepositions (see Table 23) that were retained for the information extraction stage but were not removed in the early filtering process. Therefore, the size of the data is reduced.
- **Stemming:** Once all crime reports are summarized and the dictionaries are automatically constructed, the summarized files and dictionaries are ready to be stemmed. As already explained, in order to obtain the root of a word, all suffixes, prefixes and/or infixes are removed. Table 25 shows three cases with the word "قرس / srq / steal" in Arabic, and how the system deals with them. Stemming in the proposed system is required because it makes it easier for the system to allocate numbers for generating the words' indices, which are used in the clustering process. Furthermore, it assists in applying the frequency analysis process in an efficacious manner.
- **Generating Word Index:** The clustering process only has the ability to process numerical data and therefore it is necessary to allocate to each word a specific number. Once the summarized files have been stemmed, each file is assigned a set of numbers, whereby each number corresponds to just one word within the file. Table 26 presents a sample of the crime action words with their unique numbers.

Figure 13. Initial preprocessing stage and information extraction stage

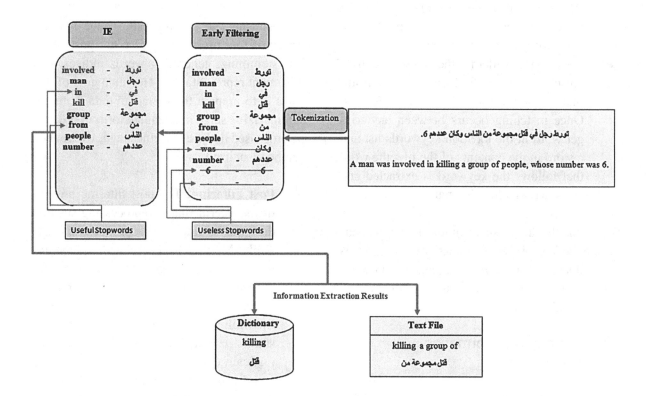

- **Document Representation:** Because the methods of classification or clustering are not able to directly process unstructured data, a document representation method is required so that textual documents can be handled effectively (Jing et a., 2002,; Amine et a., 2008). Therefore, texts need to be transformed into an appropriate form.

There are many methods for representing free texts, such as Vector Space Model (VSM), Bag of Phrase, N-gram, and ontology based representation (Amine et al., 2008). However, in the preprocessing phase, a typical document clustering process uses VSM (Freeman et al, 2002). In VSM all documents are transformed into vectors which are grouped into one matrix. Figure 14 depicts how each document is represented in the VSM.

It can be seen that each single column in the matrix represents a word and the number of words in the whole document collection defines the size of the vector. Once all the textual documents have been represented by their words, all the frequencies of the words are generated. The next step is to calculate the weight of each word. In fact, this step is very important because the weight of a word reflects its importance in a document. Term Frequency - Inverse Document Frequency (TF-IDF) is used for weight calculation.

The Term Frequency (TF) refers to the number of times a word occurs in a document. The Inverse Document Frequency (IDF) indicates the number of documents in which the word occurs.

The following is a TF-IDF equation [Amine et al., 2008]:

$$TFxIDF(tk; dj) = Occ(tk; dj) \times LogNb\_doc / Nb\_doc(tk)$$

Table 25. Stemming process for removing prefixes, infixes, and suffixes

Case	Before Stemming	Stemming Process	After Stemming
prefix	يسرق	سرق (ي)	
infix	سارق	رق (ا) س	سرق
suffix	سرقة	سرق (ة)	

Table 26. Each word of interest is assigned a unique number in order to convert textual data to numerical for facilitating clustering process

Word ID	Translation	Crime Action Word
1	smuggle	هرب
2	steal	سرق
3	rob	سلب
4	burgle	سطا
5	snatch	خطف
6	violate	عدى
7	distribute	راج
8	stab	طعن
9	shoot	طلق
10	forgery	زار
11	kill	قتل
12	smash	كسر
13	hit	ضرب
14	rape	غصب

where:

- Occ(tk; dj) represents the number of times the term tk appears in the document dj.
- Nb _doc indicates the total number of documents.
- Nb_doc(tk) is a variable that refers to the number of documents in which the tk term occurs.

Clustering Stage

For the clustering process, the Self Organizing Map (SOM) technique has been chosen to cluster the documents that were generated by the information extraction process, based on their similarity. The following is the SOM algorithm:

Figure 14. Vector space model

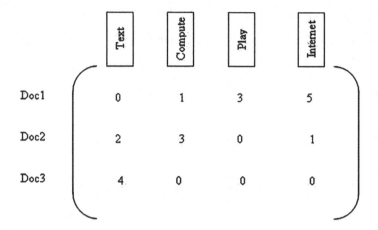

1. Initialize weight randomly.
2. Initialize neighbourhood ratio.
3. Set input pattern.
4. Calculate Euclidean distance.
5. Find the winner neuron (smaller distance).
6. Update winner and neighbour weight neurons.
7. Repeat Steps 3 to 7 until the convergence criterion is satisfied.

The first step is to randomly initialize the weight vectors of the output map. At each iteration, a sample vector is randomly chosen from the input data (known as the learning process). Through competitive learning, the Euclidean distance is calculated for choosing the Best Matching Unit (BMU). The wining neuron or BMU is the one most similar to the input pattern, that is, its weight is close to the input pattern.

As a result, all neurons on the output layer enter into competition with each other. The neuron on the output layer that has the smallest distance to the input pattern is the winner. Once the winning neuron has been selected, its weight and the weight of its neighbors are both updated in order to make them more similar to the input pattern. This process is repeated with other documents until accurate results are obtained or the maximum number of iterations (epochs) is reached.

EXPERIMENTS

In the following experiments, 401 crime reports collected from various online news sources and comprising of 57,595 tokens are used to test the performance of our CPS. Also, 401 crime news reports contains 71,882 tokens are used to perform the clustering in order to show how the proposed information extraction approach guides the Self Organizing Map (SOM) to gain improvement in clustering quality. Furthermore, based on extracting crime-related information from 80 news reports, statistical information about the crime status in the locations is provided.

Crime Type

In this experiment, the CPS crime type local grammar was assessed for its ability to recognize and extract the crime type from each report, and to generate a summary for each report. Table 27 shows the results of this experiment, which includes a number of 'true' and 'false' extracted entities from each dataset, together with their targets.

The extracted patterns are sent to crime type dictionary file. The system was able to automatically build a crime type dictionary with 794 tokens. The dictionary was filtered to remove certain stop words, and its size was accordingly reduced to 676 tokens. Furthermore, a frequency analysis was carried out after the filtering process, and this led to reducing the number of tokens to 380. In order to obtain the words only in their base form, their affixes were removed, and consequently, the size of the dictionary became 228 words.

Figure 15 shows a comparison of the content of the dictionary before and after the stemming process. It can be seen that the frequencies of the various forms of the word "سرقت/srqt/theft" were collated into one frequency, occurring 122 times.

Also, it can be noticed that the most frequent words either before or after the stemming are crime action words. Moreover, four crime action words ("غصب / gsb / rape", " خطف / ktf / snatch", "جار / raj / smuggle" and "خدر / kdr/ drug") rose to within the list of the 16 most frequent crime words following the stemming process.

The crime type dictionary was tested to see if it could identify any crime types that the crime type local grammar had failed to extract. Table 28 presents the results of this experiment. Accordingly, using the crime type dictionary assisted in recognizing more crime types, and therefore, the number of entities correctly identified increased to 481 (from 398 entities).

Consequently, only 15 types of crime were not extracted. However, the types of crime that were wrongly extracted also increased to 416 (from 360).

Location

The experiment here is dedicated to testing the CPS location local grammar in order to assess its ability to extract crime location from the given reports to generate summaries and to automatically build the location dictionary.

Figure 15. Sample of the crime type dictionary before and after the stemming process

Before Stemming				After Stemming			
	No	Word	Freq		No	word	Freq	
theft	1	سرقة	36		1	سرق	122	steal
theft	2	بسرقة	27		2	عدى	33	violence
theft	3	السرقة	21		3	قتل	32	kill
killing	4	قتل	20		4	كسر	22	smash
violence	5	بالاعتداء	14		5	سلب	19	rob
robbery	6	سلب	9		6	طلق	18	shoot
theft	7	لسرقة	8		7	ضرب	16	hit
hitting	8	للضرب	8		8	طعن	10	stab
theft	9	السرقة	7		9	خمر	9	wine
wine	10	خمر	7		10	غصب	9	rape
shooting	11	اطلاق	6		11	خطف	8	snatch
theft	12	بسرقتها	6		12	راج	8	smuggle
killing	13	بقتل	6		13	بلغ	6	report
smash	14	بكسر	6		14	جثة	6	dead body
smash	15	تكسير	6		15	خدر	6	drug
dead body	16	جثة	6		16	جهز	5	Prepare

Table 27. Crime type extraction results using crime type local grammar

Dataset	True	False	Goal
Riyadh	37	47	40
Sabq	70	76	76
Okaz	96	84	140
Ahram	49	47	64
Alwatan	67	52	80
Alamalyawm	62	36	72
Gokarsat	17	18	24
Total	398	360	496

Table 28. Crime type extraction results after utilizing crime type dictionary

Dataset	True	False	Goal
Riyadh	40	47	40
Sabq	74	82	76
Okaz	133	105	140
Ahram	64	60	64
Alwatan	80	59	80
Alamalyawm	68	41	72
Gokarsat	22	22	24
Total	481	416	496

Table 29. Location extraction results using location local grammar

Dataset	True	False	Goal
Riyadh	34	0	41
Sabq	50	0	68
Okaz	97	3	145
Ahram	53	5	74
Alwatan	59	0	67
Alamalyawm	50	0	53
Gokarsat	25	0	27
Total	368	8	475

Table 29 shows the number of extracted patterns, whether true or false, for each dataset, and the third column refers to the number of patterns that should be recognized in each dataset.

The CPS location local grammar was initially able to extract 376 tokens, which form the location dictionary. The frequency analysis process was also applied here. Consequently, the location dictionary contains only 131 different location names. As already mentioned, the dictionary is used when the CPS location local grammar fails to extract the crime location. In the following experiment, the location dictionary was tested to extract crime locations that had not been identified directly by the location local grammar. Table 30 lists the new results after utilizing the location dictionary. As can be seen, the assistance of the location dictionary has led to increasing the number of location entities that were correctly identified to 447 (from 368).

As a result, 28 crime locations were not recognized either by the local grammar or the dictionary. Also, using the dictionary increased the incorrectly recognized entities to 19 (from 8). Nationality the CPS nationality local grammar was tested in this experiment in 33 order to assess its ability to extract nationality entities from the same datasets used in the above experiments. Table 31 shows the results of this experiment.

The CPS was able to recognize 88 entities; 80 correct out of 210 entities. As a result, 8 entities were wrongly identified.

The system was able to generate the nationality dictionary; here, the number of tokens extracted was 88. The processes of removing affixes and a frequency analysis were then applied. As a result, the number of words that form this dictionary is only 21. Likewise, the nationality dictionary was tested to extract the missing entities that had not been identified by the nationality local grammar. The results of this experiment are presented in Table 32. Clearly, the number of nationality entities that were correctly identified after using the nationality dictionary improved to 185 (from

Table 30. Location extraction results after utilizing location dictionary

Dataset	True	False	Goal
Riyadh	38	2	41
Sabq	62	1	68
Okaz	137	4	145
Ahram	66	11	74
Alwatan	65	0	67
Alamalyawm	53	1	53
Gokarsat	26	0	27
Total	447	19	475

Table 31. Nationality extraction results using nationality local grammar

Dataset	True	False	Goal
Riyadh	11	1	17
Sabq	18	1	45
Okaz	28	5	65
Ahram	0	0	0
Alwatan	11	1	50
Alamalyawm	11	0	32
Gokarsat	1	0	1
Total	80	8	210

Table 32. Nationality extraction results after utilizing nationality dictionary

Dataset	True	False	Goal
Riyadh	17	3	17
Sabq	41	6	45
Okaz	63	10	65
Ahram	0	0	0
Alwatan	36	3	50
Alamalyawm	27	2	32
Gokarsat	1	0	1
Total	185	24	21

80). Also, it can be noticed that the total number of nationality entities that were incorrectly recognized increased to 24.

Two experiments were carried out on 401 documents in order to show how the information extraction process guides the Self Organizing Map (SOM) toward delivering acceptably accurate results. The corpus contains 71,882 tokens. The SOM was trained on the same documents, obtaining good results; the best learning rate, radius and iteration are 0.5, 30 and 1000, respectively. The size of the map is 6 x 6.

Clustering with Utilizing the CPS Information Extraction Stage

As explained earlier, the information extraction process was employed to extract the types and locations of the crimes as well as the nationalities, and then a summary for each file as well as three dictionaries were generated. In this experiment, we focus on the type of crime. The extracted crime type patterns from each document are used by the SOM to perform the clustering, instead of processing the whole of each document's content. Accordingly, after extracting the type of crime, the new size of the corpus is now 4,043 tokens (13KB), which is much smaller than the original size of 40KB (71,882 tokens). Figure 16 shows a sample of the document clustering results based on type of crime, using the extracted patterns obtained from the previous processes.

Clustering without Using the CPS Information Extraction Stage

For assessing this work in terms of the effectiveness of the clustering, another experiment was carried out on the same corpus, but this one did not rely on the information extraction process. The whole content of each file was stemmed and used for the clustering process through the SOM.

A Sample of the results of this experiment can be seen in Figure 17.

Figure 16. Clustering results with aid of the CPS information extraction (A: violence, B: theft, and C: fraud)

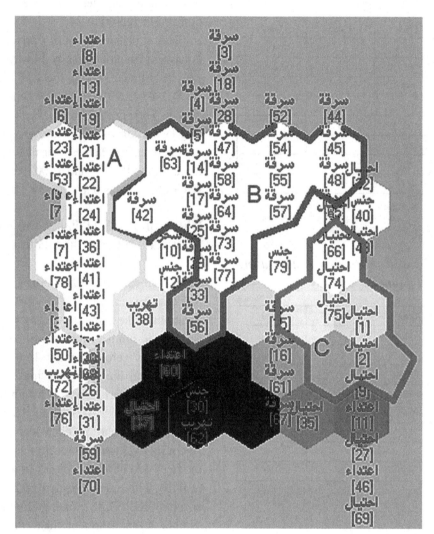

Crime Analysis

An additional benefit of this work is that this current system can be easily adapted to provide crime profiling for regions. In other words, it can be used to present a general picture about the security status of any area, based on local news reports. The system can offer statistical information about the highest and/or lowest type of crime.

Figure 18 shows that the crime of theft is the most common crime occurring in the Arab region; it is reported 31 times in our corpus (80 crime news reports). In addition, extracting the crime location can assist in identifying how safe a particular area is, and through combining such statistics, this system is able to provide information about the number of crimes occurring in a specific location.

Figure 19 depicts the number of crimes and their location in a pie-chart. It shows the numbers of crimes that happened in Saudi Arabia, Egypt, the United Arab Emirates, Jordan, Algeria, Kuwait and the USA.

Figure 17. Clustering results without aid of the CPS information extraction (A: violence, B: theft, and C: fraud)

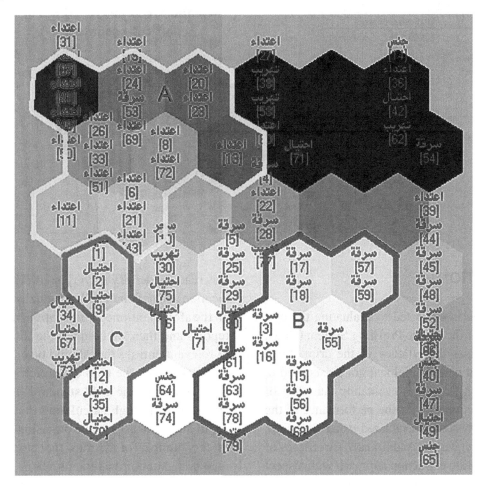

Figure 18. Averages for the different crime types, reported across the Arab countries mentioned above

Crime Type	Numbers recorded for different crimes
Theft سرقة	31
Violent اعتداء	27
Fraud احتيال	13
Sex جنس	4
Smuggling تهريب	3
Sorcery سحر	1
Total	79

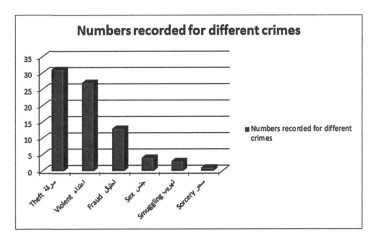

Figure 19. Numbers of crimes reported by location

Location	Numbers recorded for crimes in particular countries
Saudi - السعودية	26
Egypt - مصر	19
Emirates - الإمارات	13
Jordan - الأردن	6
Algeria - الجزائر	5
Kuwait - الكويت	3
USA - أمريكا	1

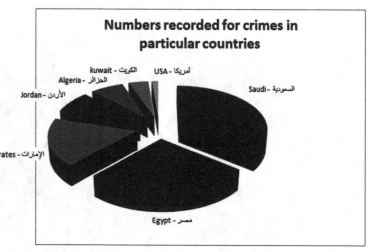

EVALUATION

This section is dedicated to evaluating the performance of the Crime Profiling System (CPS), i.e. it assesses the efficacy of the crime type, location and nationality local grammars used in this research as well as evaluating the effect of utilizing dictionaries on the performance of the CPS. The system is evaluated using precision, recall and F-measure. Additionally, the efficacy of the information extraction approach with respect to the performance of the Self Organizing Map (SOM) is evaluated through four parameters: data size, loading time, and computation time and quantization error.

Evaluating the Information Extraction

The performance of the CPS (in terms of its information extraction ability) is evaluated using standard precision, recall and F-measure, which are the most widely used evaluation measures in the information extraction community (Sitter et al., 2004), by comparing the answer le against a manually annotated 'gold standard' le. Accordingly, each of 401 crime news reports

was read to identify each type of crime, crime location and nationality. We manually annotated all the aforementioned information in the crime reports and then we counted the total number of relevant entities that should be extracted by the CPS. Thus, the CPS extraction results are compared with the gold standard (in order to evaluate it) through calculating the precision, recall and F-measure. The precision is defined as the number of entities that are correctly recognized out of the total number of retrieved entities, and recall is the number of entities found by the system out of the number of relevant entities existing in the corpus. The F-measure is the weighted harmonic mean of precision and recall. The equations for precision, recall and F-measure are as follows (Benajiba et al, 2009; Saha et al, 2008; Shaalan and Raza, 2007; van Rijsbergen, 1979):

Precision = *(number of correctly recognised entities) / (total number of recognised entities)*

Recall = *(number of correctly recognised entities) / (total number of correct entities)*

F-measure = *(2 × recall × precision) / (recall + precision)*

The performance results obtained after evaluating the CPS in terms precision, recall and F-measure for the crime type, location and nationality extraction processes are presented in the following sections.

Type of Crime

The system was able, directly (using the crime type local grammar) and through using the crime type dictionary, to extract a total number of 834 entities. The number of entities that were correctly recognized is 481 out of a total number of 496 relevant entities. The performance results achieved for the crime type extraction process through using the crime type local grammar and the crime type dictionary are presented in Tables 33 and 34. The results derived from the 401 crime news reports show that using the crime type dictionary has enabled the CPS to perform better (F-measure 69%).

These results indicate that the CPS was able to build a reliable crime type dictionary. This means that the performance of the crime local grammar seems satisfactory, either for building the dictionary or correctly recognizing the type of crime (by obtaining a recall score of 80%). The remaining unidentified entities result from the crime action words being outside the local grammar, i.e. they were used for describing the incident in the form of a verb. As can be seen, the assistance of the dictionary has led to improving the recall result to 97%. However, the precision value seems low, because the sentences' boundaries were neglected.

In other words, removing commas and full stops caused some confusion for the system while the text was being processed. As a result, when the system was searching for the preposition that should follow the verb (although not necessarily in all cases) in order to achieve the syntactic constraint (for the transitive construction), it proceeded into the following sentence in order to find that preposition, and this led to incorrect pattern extraction. The evaluation results vis-a-vis extracting crime type with or without the crime type dictionary have been compared with system developed by Abueil (Abuleil, 2007), which, to our knowledge, is the only system that has been developed for the Arabic language to extract events from within text (although not specific to any particular domain). It was chosen for comparison with the CPS because there is no system available that has been specifically developed for the Arabic crime domain.

However, to overcome this problem, we compared our CPS with the system created for the English crime domain by Ku et al. (Ku et al., 2008); both systems were discussed in section 2. Figure 20 shows the comparison between the three systems in terms of their performance in extracting

Table 33. The CPS evaluation results using crime type local grammar

Dataset	Precision (%)	Recall (%)	F-Measure (%)
Riyadh	44	93	60
Sabq	48	92	63
Okaz	53	68	60
Ahram	51	77	61
Alwatan	56	84	67
Alamalyawm	63	86	73
Gokarsat	49	71	58
Overall	53	80	63

Table 34. The CPS evaluation results after using crime type dictionary

Dataset	Precision (%)	Recall (%)	F-Measure (%)
Riyadh	46	100	63
Sabq	47	97	64
Okaz	56	95	70
Ahram	52	100	68
Alwatan	58	100	73
Alamalyawm	62	94	75
Gokarsat	50	92	65
Overall	54	97	69

Table 35. The CPS evaluation results using location local grammar

Dataset	Precision (%)	Recall (%)	F-Measure (%)
Riyadh	100	83	91
Sabq	100	74	85
Okaz	97	67	79
Ahram	91	72	80
Alwatan	100	88	94
Alamalyawm	100	94	97
Gokarsat	100	93	96
Overall	98	77	86

Table 36. The CPS evaluation results after using location dictionary

Dataset	Precision (%)	Recall (%)	F-Measure (%)
Riyadh	95	93	95
Sabq	98	91	95
Okaz	97	94	96
Ahram	86	89	87
Alwatan	100	97	98
Alamalyawm	98	100	99
Gokarsat	100	96	95
Overall	96	94	95

events. Although the performance comparison in terms of F-measure shows that systems developed by Abueil (Abuleil, 2007) and Ku et al. (Ku et al., 2008) obtained results better than our system (CPS), both systems use external predefined event gazetteers, which leads to obtaining high precision scores. On the other hand, the CPS does not utilize any external event list, rather it makes use of the automatically built crime type dictionary. However, the CPS outperforms the others in terms of the recall score.

Crime Location

As already seen in the previous section, the CPS was able to correctly recognize 447 entities out of 4475. Tables 35 and 36 show the evaluation results for the location extraction process, using the location local grammar and the location dictionary.

The precision and recall results show that the location local grammar was able to extract 77% of the location entities, with a 98% precision rate. On the other hand, using the location dictionary

Figure 20. Performance of CPS compared with other systems in terms of extracting crime type

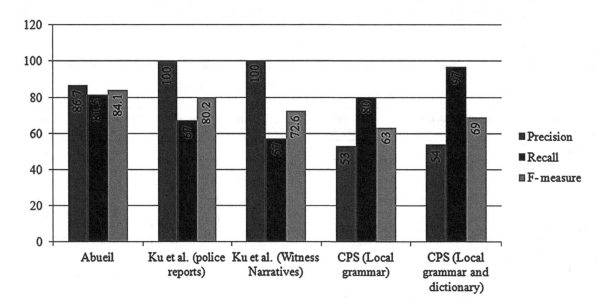

Figure 21. Comparison between CPS and other systems that used rule-based method in terms of extracting location

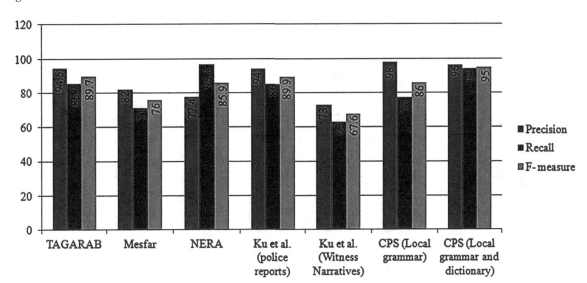

has led to increasing in the recall result to 94%, with a precision rate of 96%. It can be noticed that, after utilizing the location dictionary, the precision is slightly decreased; this is because of a lack of semantics. It is found that the location dictionary contains personal name entities; these were extracted and classified as locations by the location local grammar because they are also location names. As a result, incorrect recognition occurs when the dictionary, which neglects semantics, is used by the CPS.

Moreover, sometimes crime locations cannot be discovered by the location local grammar, and therefore the CPS fails to capture them. For example, in the sentence "فيدي تثحدث الجريمة / aljrimt hdthat dubai / the crime happened in Dubai", the city name "Dubai" cannot be identified because it does not follow these words:

"منطقة / mantqt / area", "بمنطقة / bi-mantqt / in area", "محافظة / mohafdat / province" or "مدينة / mdynt / city". However, the location dictionary overcomes this problem, and it increased the recall value to 94% (from 77%). Consequently, the F-measure score increased to 95% (from 86%).

The CPS performance in terms of extracting location entities with and without (i.e. only using the location local grammar) utilizing the location dictionary was compared with systems that utilize a rule-based approach (TAGARAB (Maloney and Niv, 1998 ; Mesfar (Mesfar, 2007); NERA (Shaalan and Raza, 2008) ; Ku et al., 2008), as in Figure 21.

Also, Figure 22 provides a comparison between the CPS (with and without using the location dictionary) with other systems that were developed based on machine learning approaches (ANERsys using Maximum Entropy (ME) (Benajiba et al, 2007); ANERsys using Conditional Random Field (CRF) (Benajiba and Rosso, 2008; AbdelRahman et al., 2010]).

The comparison accuracies of the CPS against these other systems show that, with the assistance of its dictionaries, the CPS is the second best system (after NERA (Shaalan and Raza, 2008) in terms of recall. However, predefined locations dictionary contains 4,900 names was utilized in NERA ([Shaalan and Raza, 2008). Moreover, the CPS is approximately equal to the top system AbdelRahman (AbdelRahman et al., 2010) in terms of

Figure 22. Comparison between CPS and other systems that used machine learning in terms of extracting location

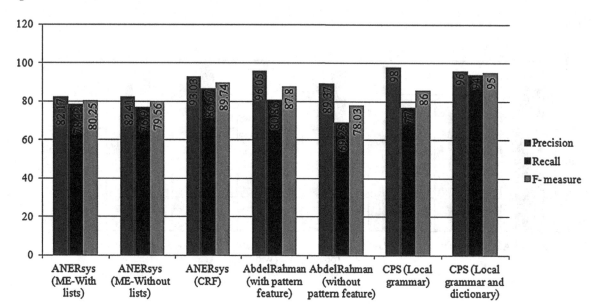

precision, although AbdelRahman (AbdelRahman et al., 2010) used predefined location dictionary (2,183 names). However, the CPS achieved the best performance result (F-measure 95%).

Nationality

As already seen, the nationality local grammar and nationality dictionary together were able to correctly recognize 185 entities out of 210, with 24 entities wrongly extracted. The results of the

performance evaluation for the CPS with using the nationality local grammar and nationality dictionary are listed in Tables 37 and 38. The results for precision and recall obtained by applying only the nationality local grammar in recognizing nationality entities in the above dataset are 91% and 38%, respectively.

Although a high precision value is obtained, the rate for recall is too low, i.e. many nationality entities were not identified. This means that certain entities appear to be outside the nationality local

Table 37. The CPS evaluation results using nationality local grammar

Dataset	Precision (%)	Recall (%)	F-Measure (%)
Riyadh	92	65	76
Sabq	95	40	56
Okaz	85	43	57
Alwatan	92	22	35
Alamalyawm	100	34	51
Gokarsat	100	100	100
Overall	91	38	54

Table 38. The CPS evaluation results after using nationality dictionary

Dataset	Precision (%)	Recall (%)	F-Measure (%)
Riyadh	85	100	92
Sabq	87	91	89
Okaz	86	97	91
Alwatan	78	54	64
Alamalyawm	92	72	81
Gokarsat	100	100	100
Overall	86	88	88

grammar. In some newspapers, it is found that a nationality word (e.g. Saudi, Indian or British) is coupled with the word "واقد/ wafd / expatriate", e.g. "هندی واقد / wafd hndy / Indian expatriate" instead of using the word "الجنسیة / aljnsyt / nationality", e.g. "الجنسیة هندی / hndyaljnsyt / Indian nationality". This has led to obtaining a low recall score.

However, the dictionary plays a crucial role here, and the results of utilizing the nationality dictionary show that the recall rate is increased to 88%. Therefore, the average F-measure value improved to 88% (from 54%). There is, to the author's knowledge, no system developed for extracting this type of entity in Arabic text.

Accordingly, Table 39 lists the overall performance results for the CPS. As can be seen, the performance of the CPS is improved through utilizing the dictionaries in terms of precision, recall and F-measure.

Clustering Performance

The Self Organizing Map (SOM) was used for the clustering and visualization tasks, and for assessing the effectiveness of the proposed approach on the SOM outputs (i.e. in terms of its clustering performance).

As already seen, the SOM was able to cluster 401 texts and to visualize them. The evaluation phase here is performed based on four parameters, as follows:

1. Data size;
2. Loading time;
3. Execution time;
4. Quantization error.

- **Data Size and Loading Time:** With regards to the size of data, the significant point here is that using the CPS led to a huge reduction in the quantity of data fed into the SOM. Although our system reduced the size of the corpus from 71,882

tokens (40KB) to only 4,043 tokens (13KB), the most important data (that the SOM used for the clustering task) were not affected. Thus, these 4,043 tokens can be considered as effectively representing the original 71,882 tokens.

The clustering experiment (utilizing the CPS information extraction stage) was assessed by comparing it with a clustering of the same documents but without the CPS information extraction stage, i.e. where the SOM processed the whole of each document's content. The loading time after using the CPS was 1.51 seconds, and in the other experiment (without the CPS) the loading time was 3.99 seconds, i.e. the loading time was reduced by more than a half with the CPS.

- **Execution Time:** As evident in Figure 23, the time spent in executing both experiments was measured and the two experiments (with/without the CPS information extraction stage) were repeated five times to ensure the validity of the result. It can be noticed that the second experiment (without the CPS information extraction stage) took longer than the first to process the data in order to perform the clustering. Therefore, the CPS increased the speed of the clustering process.

- **Quantization Error:** The average distance between each data vector and its BMU (quantization error) in the experiment that was supported by the CPS was between 0.462 and 0.47, but in the second

Table 39. The overall CPS evaluation results

	Precision (%)	Recall	F-Measure (%)
CPS (local grammar)	69	72	70
CPS (with dictionary)	71	94	81

Figure 23. The time taken by the SOM to perform the clustering tasks

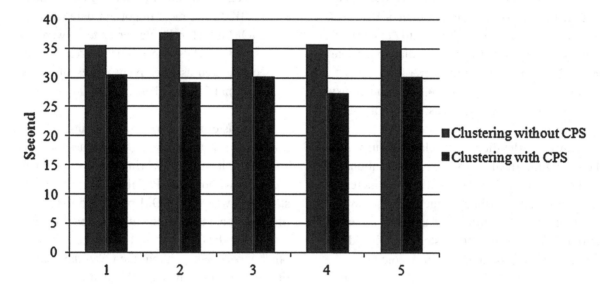

experiment (without the information extraction process), the quantization error was between 0.59 and 0.594.

Therefore, the performance of the SOM in the experiment that relied on the CPS information extraction represents an improved technique in terms of the quality of clustering; the information extraction process has a strongly positive effect on the performance of the SOM.

CONCLUSION

This paper has proposed a Crime Profiling System (CPS) for extracting meaningful information, i.e. crime type, crime location and nationality, by utilizing syntactic construction. Moreover, it has been shown that the system is able to extract this information from an unannotated corpus to generate summarizations, to automatically construct dictionaries and to cluster Arabic crime texts (employing the Self Organizing Map (SOM) technique). Also, the developed system can assist in crime analysis in terms of providing other useful information, e.g. general and specific crime trends (frequencies of crime within a particular area)

to law enforcement bodies or the general public, and performing spatial analyses by displaying the crime 'hot-spots' on the map.

The performance of the CPS for extracting the aforementioned crime-related information using both the local grammars and dictionaries were evaluated using standard precision, recall and F-measure. Moreover, the use of the automatically constructed dictionaries helped in improving its performance. The overall results obtained were: for precision 71%, recall 94% and F-measure 81%. Also, to evaluate the effectiveness of employing the CPS information extraction approach on the Self Organizing Map (SOM) clustering technique, four parameters (size of data, loading time, execution time and quantization error) were used.

This evaluation, performed through comparative experiments, was conducted between the SOM clustering technique with and the SOM clustering technique without using the CPS information extraction stage. The results show that the SOM is improved because only refined data containing meaningful keywords extracted through the information extraction process are inputted into it. As a result, a huge reduction in the quantity of data fed into the SOM is obtained, consequently, saving

Figure 24. The average distance between each data vector and its BMU (quantization error) in the two experiments

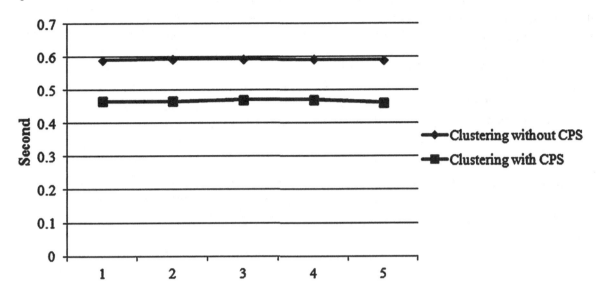

memory, data loading time and the execution time needed to perform the clustering. Therefore, the computation of the SOM is accelerated.

Finally, the quantization error is reduced, which leads to high quality clustering. The approach developed herein, for extracting crime information, does not rely on an annotated corpus, and speech taggers are not used in this task, rather, computational linguistic techniques, based on transitive and genitive construction, are used, i.e. the local grammars for crime type, location and nationality are applied to texts in order to extract the information. The prepositions that are often described as stopwords play a crucial role in obtaining the desired transitive and genitive constructions. Furthermore, traditional systems usually rely on manually built dictionaries, which is time consuming. The CPS is able to automatically generate crime type, location and nationality dictionaries from unlabeled data to assist in extracting patterns from texts. Also, the system produces higher quality extracted data, which in turn improves the quality of the clustering results. Also, a special corpus has been compiled for the Arabic crime domain.

Finally, future work will investigate improving the CPS further in order to extract more information about crime, such as type of perpetrator (e.g. group or individual) and the instruments used in crime incidents, such as weapons and vehicles. However, it seems clear that the same approach would be used to extract the above information, i.e. the transitive construction. In the frequency analysis, the words" قبض /qbd / arrested" and "عثر /athr / found" appeared, and they may assist in extracting the crime perpetrator and instrument entities if they are followed by the preposition"على/ ala / on". Experiments will be performed to examine these two verbs.

REFERENCES

AbdelRahman, S., Elarnaoty, M., Magdy, M., & Fahmy, A. (2010). Integrated machine learning techniques for arabic named entity recognition. *IJCSI International Journal of Computer Science Issues, 7*(3), 27–36.

Abdul-Hamid, A., & Darwish, K. (2010). Simplified feature set for arabic named entity recognition. In *Proceedings of the 2010 Named Entities Workshop, ACL 2010*, pages 110-115.

Abuleil, S. (2007). Using nlp techniques for tagging events in Arabic text. In Proceedings of the 19th IEEE International Conference on Tools with Artificial Intelligence - Volume 02, ICTAI '07, pages 440-443, Washington, DC, USA. IEEE Computer Society.

Abuleil, S., & Evens, M. (2004). Events extraction and classification for arabic information retrieval systems. In *Proceedings of the 16th IEEE International Conference on Tools with Artificial Intelligence, ICTAI '04*, pages 769{770, Washington, DC, USA. IEEE Computer Society.

Al-Shalabi, R., Kanaan, G., Al-Sarayreh, B., Khanfer, K., Al-Ghonmein, A., Talhouni, H., & Al-Azazmeh, S. (2009). Proper noun extracting algorithm for arabic language. In *International Conference on IT*, Thailand.

Almas, Y., & Kurshid, A. (2006). Lolo: a system based on terminology for multilingual extraction. In *Proceedings of the Workshop on Information Extraction Beyond the document*, pages 56{65. Sydney: Association for Computational Linguistics.

Amine, A., Elberrichi, Z., Simonet, M., & Malki, M. (2008). Evaluation and comparison of concept based and n-grams based text clustering using som. *INFOCOMP-Journal of Computer Science*, 7, 27–35.

Attia, M., Toral, A., Tounsi, L., Monachini, M., & van Genabith, J. (2010). An automatically built named entity lexicon for Arabic. In LREC 2010. Valletta, Malta, pages 3614-3621.

Benajiba, Y., Diab, M., & Rosso, P. (2009). Arabic named entity recognition: A feature-driven study. IEEE Transactions on Audio. *Speech and Language Processing*, 17(5), 926–934.

Benajiba, Y., & Rosso, P. (2008). Arabic named entity recognition using conditional random fields. In *Proceedings of 2008, Arabic Language and Local Languages Processing Workshop, LREC'08*, Marrakech, Morocco.

Benajiba, Y., Rosso, P., & Ruiz, J. (2007). Anersys: An Arabic named entity recognition system based on maximum entropy. In CICLing (pp. 1431-1453).

Borthwick, A. (1999). *A Maximum Entropy Approach to Named Entity Recognition*. PhD thesis, New York University.

Chau, M., Xu, J. J., & Chen, H. (2002). Extracting meaningful entities from police narrative reports. In *Proceedings of the 2002 Annual National Conference on Digital Government Research*, (pp. 1-5). Digital Government Society of North America.

Chen, H., Chung, W., Xu, J. J., Wang, G., Qin, Y., & Chau, M. (2004). Crime data mining: A general framework and some examples. *Computer*, 37, 50–56.

Condon, S., Sanders, G. A., Parvaz, D., Rubenstein, A., Doran, C., Aberdeen, J., & Oshika, B. (2009). Normalization for automated metrics: English and Arabic speech translation. In Proceedings of Machine Translation Summit XII, (Ottawa, Canada).

Cowie, J., & Lehnert, W. (1996). Information extraction. *Communications of the ACM*, 39(1), 81–91.

Elsebai, A., Meziane, F., & Belkredim, F. Z. (2009). A rule based persons names Arabic extraction system. In *Proceedings of the IBIMA*, Cairo, Egypt, volume 11, pages 53-59.

Fan, W., Wallace, L., Rich, S., & Zhang, Z. (2006). Tapping into the power of text mining. *Communications of the ACM*, 49, 76–82.

Freeman, R., Yin, H., & Allinson, N. (2002). Self-organising maps for tree view based hierarchical document clustering. In *Proceedings of the 2002 International Joint Conference on Neural Networks (IJCNN '02)*, (Vol. 2, pp. 1906 -1911).

Halpern, J. (2009). Word stress and vowel neutralization in modern standard Arabic. In *Proceedings of the Second International Conference on Arabic Language Resources and Tools*, Cairo, Egypt. The MEDAR Consortium.

Jing, L., Huang, H., & She, H. (2002). Improved feature selection approach tdf in text mining. In *Proceedings of the First International Conference on Machine Learning Cybernetics* (pp. 944-946). Beijing.

Ku, C. H., Iriberri, A., & Leroy, G. (2008). Natural language processing and e-government: crime information extraction from heterogeneous data sources. In *Proceedings of the 2008 International Conference on Digital Government Research*, (pp. 162-170). Digital Government Society of North America.

Maloney, J., & Niv, M. (1998). Tagarab: A fast, accurate arabic name recognizer using high-precision morphological analysis. In *Proceedings of the Workshop on Computational Approaches to Semetic Languages, COLING-ACL98*, (pp. 8-15). University of Montreal.

McKnight, W. (2005). In D. M. Review (Ed.), *Building business intelligence: Text data mining in business intelligence* (pp. 21–22).

Mesfar, S. (2007). Named entity recognition for Arabic using syntactic grammars. In Natural Language Processing and Information Systems (LNCS 4592, pp. 305-316). Berlin: Springer.

Noklestad, A. (2009). *A Machine Learning Approach to Anaphora Resolution Including Named Entity Recognition, PP Attachment Disambiguation, and Animacy Detection*. PhD thesis, University of Oslo.

Pastra, K., Saggion, H., & Wilks, Y. (2003). Intelligent indexing of crime scene photographs. *IEEE Intelligent Systems, 18*(1), 55–61.

Piskorski, J., Tanev, H., Atkinson, M., Van, E., & Goot, D. (2008). Cluster-entric approach to news event extraction. In *Frontiers in Artificial Intelligence and Applications* (Vol. 18, pp. 276–290). IOS Press.

Ruch, P., Perret, L., & Savoy, J. (2005). Features combination for extracting gene functions from medline. In ECIR, (pp. 112-126).

Saha, S. K., Chatterji, S., & Dandapat, S. (2008). A hybrid approach for named entity recognition in indian languages. In *Proceedings of the IJCNLP-08 Workshop on NER for South East Asian Languages* (pp. 17-24).

Shaalan, K., & Raza, H. (2007). Person name entity recognition for Arabic. In *Proceedings of the 5th Workshop on Important Unresolved Matters* (pp. 17-24).

Shaalan, K., & Raza, H. (2008). Arabic named entity recognition from diverse text types. In *Proceedings of the 6th international conference on Advances in Natural Language Processing, GoTAL '08* (pp. 440-451). Berlin, Heidelberg: Springer-Verlag.

Sitter, A. D., Calders, T., & Daelemans, W. (2004). *A formal framework for evaluation of information extraction. Technical report.* University of Antwerp, Dept. of Mathematics and Computer Science.

Thongtae, P., & Srisuk, S. (2008). An analysis of data mining applications in crime domain. In *Proc. IEEE 8th International Conference on Computer and Information Technology Workshops CIT Workshops 2008* (pp. 122-126).

Traboulsi, H. (2009). Arabic named entity extraction: A local grammar-based approach. In *Proceedings of the International Multiconference on Computer Science and Information Technology*, (pp. 139-143).

Traboulsi, H. N. (2006). Named Entity Recognition: A Local Grammar-based Approach. PhD thesis, School of Electronics and Physical Sciences, University of Surrey.

Van Rijsbergen, C. J. (1979). *Information Retrieval* (2nd ed.). London: Butterworths.

Witten, I. H. (2004). *Text Mining. Practical handbook of Internet computing*. Boca Raton, FL: CRC Press.

KEY TERMS AND DEFINITIONS

Clustering: A mechanism to classify data, information, and/or knowledge according to various similarity measures.

Information Extraction: The identification of information from a set of data coupled with knowledge.

Pattern Recognition: Techniques to identify a given pattern from a heterogamous corpus. This pattern could be in any media.

Profiling: Techniques to formulate to build a knowledge about a suspect. The outcome of which is a profile containing evidences, analyses, and argumentation.

Self-Organizing Map: A well-known and classic clustering technique.

Syntactic Analysis: A term used in a linguistic domain without the aid of grammar. Within the domain of computer languages, syntactic checks are done at a compilation stage.

Chapter 8
Proposals to Win the Battle Against Cyber Crime

Alaa Hussein Al-Hamami
Amman Arab University, Jordan

ABSTRACT

Through commercial networks and across the Internet, there are data files, millions of images and videos, and trillions of messages flow each day to drive the world economy. This vast electronic infrastructure is what our nation depends on. To commit crime by using a computer and communication to forge a person's identity, illegal imports or malicious programs, the computer here is used as an object or subject for the cybercrime. Most of the online activities are vulnerable to intrusion and can compromise personal safety just as effectively as common everyday crimes. This chapter concentrates on explaining and discussing the terms of cyber security, cybercrimes, and cyber-attacks. A history for each term has been given and the problems of cyber security have been discussed. Finally, a proposed solution has been suggested and future trends have been forecasted, and at the end of the chapter a conclusion will be given.

INTRODUCTION

A new theories and terms appear to change the concepts of the economics and the role of the organizations in society. Theories such as the "Blue Lake" and terms such as: Network Economics, Virtual Organizations, E-Government, E-Business, and Internet of Things are dependent, in general, on the Internet and Information Technology. New technology always brings new threats and here, security is the main concern for these technologies.

The advances of computers and communications have changed our life and habits. Everything now relies on those developed technologies (computer and Internet), communication (email, mobile phones), transportation (airplane navigation, car engine systems), shopping (e-commerce, credit cards, and online stores), medicine (medical records, equipment), entertainment (mp3s, digital cable) and the list goes on. We can see that our daily lives rely on computers. Also, much of our personal information is stored and processed on our own computers or on someone else's system. The

DOI: 10.4018/978-1-4666-6583-5.ch008

Copyright © 2015, IGI Global. Copying or distributing in print or electronic forms without written permission of IGI Global is prohibited.

objective of cyber security is to protect and defend that information by detecting, preventing, and responding to cyber-attacks (Ramkumar, 2014).

The Internet has 90% junk and 10% good security. When intruders find systems that are easy to break into, they simply hack into the system. Terrorists and criminals use information technology to plan and execute their cyber-criminal activities. The wide spread usage of computers and communications has facilitated the growth of crime and terrorism. Because of the increase in international interaction and the advanced communication, technology people need not be in one country to conduct such crime. Hackers can find security gaps in the system and can function from anywhere instead of their country of residence (Crime Desk, 2009).

The industries have invested considerable effort in managing the risks of terrorism and other deliberate criminal acts against facilities through their computer systems. Random attacks of worms, Trojans, viruses, etc. have occurred and they have adversely impacted computer systems including those operating manufacturing facilities, while few deliberately focused attacks on manufacturing systems have been reported,

THE HISTORY OF CYBERCRIME

Capacity of human mind is unfathomable. It is impossible to eliminate crime from the globe and there is no legislation has succeeded in doing that. People aware of their rights and duties and they know that the application of the laws is more stringent to check crime. Finally, it is not possible to eliminate cybercrimes from the cyber space.

Computers are a tool that criminals use much like a lock picking tool or a counterfeiting machine. Criminals have learned that computers provide an anonymity that has previously been unattainable in society. Criminals are criminals everywhere and at any time and their aims are to gain benefits (financial, social, etc) and at the end harming the society.

An advance in computers and communications that is so radical it not only changes the way that societies interact, it also has fundamental effects on the behavior of the human and criminal element within that society: introducing completely new and previously unheard of actions into our everyday life. Cyber Crime is one of the biggest radical changes in the society and criminal behaviors (Power, 2001).

The computer networks allow cyber criminals to conduct illegal activity from a remote computer far away from the crime position here it taking place by controlling another computer and make it to attack another computer. A criminal can access a computer network a continent away and steal credit card and banking information without having to be physically present at the scene. Criminals are using computers to conduct several crime acts such as: information theft, intellectual property theft, fraud, etc. using a computer and the communications as a subject or an object for illegal activity (Saini et al, 2012).

Cybercrime

Cybercrime may be said to be those species, of which, genus is the conventional crime, and where either the computer is an object or subject of the conduct constituting crime. Cybercrime is the most complicated problem in the cyber world.

Essentially, there are two separate and distinct components in cybercrime. One component is the exploiting weakness in the computer operating system or network (this method used by Hackers). The second component is the exploiting social fabric of a computer network (this method is called Social Engineering), whereby an intruder makes use of the computer network to infiltrate the trust of other users of that network for profit or gain. Although these different components of what constitute cybercrime may not seem overly important, they do have an impact when you look at the evolution and development of cybercrime (Kevin, 2011).

Large scale cybercrime centered on or around one-man operated criminals exploiting the weaknesses in the computer operating system or computer network. In most cases these crimes were committed by computer nerds who felt challenged to prove that they could beat the system. We used the term hacker for just such a nerd, but rarely was there a financial gain element to the criminal behavior. While a great deal of financial damage could actually result, not to mention the potential for the security risks that resulted, this one-man band criminal lacked the motive and intent of traditional criminal gangs (Stephen, 2011).

In short, cybercrime was infantile and largely seen as a practical joke or game by those who committed it. Criminal defense tactics at this time was also largely based on the fact that no real intentional damage was done and, in a large number of cases, the penalty for the crime was showing how the computer system had been hacked by the hacker.

Once we had all got over the fact that there was no millennium bug after all (probably the biggest cybercrime hoax of all time), cybercriminal had organized and focused their attention elsewhere. Yes, the geek element of hacking still existed - as still does today - but now hardened criminal gangs had worked out that the Internet was a safe domain, with much less risk, with which to operate and generate large profits. In short, criminal gangs had introduced a professional element into the world of cybercrime. No longer were we looking at geeky exploitation of weaknesses in computer operating/networking systems, things had now developed to criminal gangs making use of computer networks to infiltrate and take advantage of the trust of other users of that computer network for huge financial gains (Mirzoev et al, 2014).

Law makers and criminal defense lawyers began to see developments which reflected the radical change in the nature of cybercriminal activity. Primarily these included new cyber-crimes, such as:

- **Identity Theft:** The cybercriminal steals their victim's identity and then transacts, usually via the computers and the network communications in the name of the victim. More often than not this will include an element of credit card fraud.
- **Cyber-Extortion:** Where criminal gangs threatened to close down internet-based businesses (Web Site) if protection money was not paid. Worse still, threats can also be made to infiltrate the businesses security system to access financial or personal information stored therein that may then be used for financial gain.
- **Intellectual Property Theft:** Strangely many computer network users do not see the illegal downloading of software and intellectual property as constituting a criminal act. Billions of dollars are being lost each year on illegal software and intellectual property downloads that are putting sever financial constraints on the companies that manufacture these products, many of whom are young start-ups themselves. Nevertheless, unlike other forms of cyber-crimes, governments have been quick to respond to the actions of those who illegally download movies, music or software from the Internet and so, many argue, criminal defense procedures against such persons are probably the most successful and front-line of all.
- **Information Theft:** Similar to identity theft, only no prior approach is made to try and extort protection money and a computer network is infiltrated with the purpose of obtaining information relating to the users, whether they are an individual user of business.
- **Fraud:** Fraud has many guises on the Internet, from the famous e-mails promising millions in advance fees to the sale of unmarketable quality goods. What is usually fairly consistent is an unsolicited e-mail approach by the fraudster to their victim.

- **Exploitation of Children, etc.:** Unfortunately many view the act of cybercrime as either harmless fun (such as hacking) or for financial gain (such as credit card fraud). However, there is also a very real and extremely nasty side to cybercrime - taking advantage of weaker members of our society. Almost weekly we now hear of cybercriminal gangs who have been caught with child pornography or polluting the youth through indecent exposure.

- **Phishing and Vishing:** Both phishing and the more recent vishing is obtaining financial information, such as bank account records or credit card details, by sending what look like authentic messages to the recipient informing them they need to comply with certain procedures to reactivate their account. Once the information has been obtained, the criminal then defrauds the victim.

CLASSIFICATION OF CYBER

Current era is too fast to utilize the time factor to improve the performance factor. It is only possible due the use of Internet. The term Internet can be defined as the collection of millions of computers that provide a network of electronic connections between the computers. The Internet called as the network of the networks. There are millions of computers connected to the internet. Everyone appreciates the use of Internet but there is another side of the coin that is cybercrime by the use of Internet.

There are many terms and classifications concern the term Cyber, these are the following:

- **Cyber Crime:** It is a crime committed using a computer and the communications an object or subject of crime for illegal action to steal a person's identity, illegal imports, or malicious programs. Cybercrime

and conventional crime include conduct whether act or omission, which cause breach of rules of law and counterbalanced by the sanction of the state. The concept of cybercrime is not radically different from the concept of conventional crime.

Individuals need to know how to protect themselves and the persons for which they are responsible. Online activities are just as vulnerable to intrusion and can compromise personal safety just as effectively as common everyday crimes (Byun et al, 2014).

Any criminal activity that uses a computer either as an instrumentality (subject), target or means (object) for perpetuating further crimes comes within the ambit of cybercrime. Cybercrime is the most complicated problem in the cyber world. Cybercrime may be those species, of which, genus is the conventional crime, and where either the computer is an object of the conduct constituting crime (Thapa and Kumar, 2011).

There are some tips to be safe from Cybercrime such as: use antivirus software, insert firewalls, uninstall unnecessary software, maintain backup' and finally check security settings.

It is possible to categorize cybercrimes in two ways:

1. **The Computer as a Target:** Using a computer to attack other computers. E.g. Hacking, Virus/Worm attacks, DOS attack etc. In these crimes the computer is merely a tool. These crimes are categorized as following:
   a. **Forgery:** The intentional and unlawful input, alteration, deletion or suppression of computer data with the intent of violating law.
   b. **Fraud:** The intentional and unlawful causing of a loss of property to another person with fraudulent and dishonest intent to procure without right an economic benefit to oneself or others.

2. **The Computer as a Weapon:** Using a computer to commit real world crimes. E.g. Cyber Terrorism, IPR violations, Credit card frauds, EFT frauds, Pornography etc. Cyber Crime regulated by Cyber laws or Internet Laws. It means possession of illegal content in any form such as:

    a. Distribution of pornography via emails as other private Usenet forums.
    b. Misrepresenting or misusing names to gain advantage for financial edge.

- **Cyber Security:** Cyber security involves protection of sensitive personal and business information through prevention, detection, and response to different online attacks. Cyber security actually protects your personal information by responding, detecting and preventing the attacks. While cyber security is an established discipline for computer systems used for business management, it deals with the protection of valuable information stored on those systems from adversaries who want to obtain corrupt, damage, destroy or prohibit access to it.

Before submitting your name, email address, or other personal information on a web site, look for the site's privacy policy. Evidence that your information is being encrypted: to protect attackers from hijacking your information, any personal information submitted online should be encrypted. Many sites use SSL or Secure Socket Layer, to encrypt information.

If the seller releases patches for the software operating your device, install them as soon as possible. Installing them will prevent attackers from being able to take advantage. Use good passwords: select passwords that will be difficult for thieves to guess. Do not choose options that allow your computer to remember your passwords. Some personal Device Assistance (PDA's) and phones are equipped with wireless technologies, such as Bluetooth, that can be used to connect to other devices or computers. You should disable these features when they are not in use.

To protect your privacy, use updated software, use good passwords: select passwords that will be difficult for thieves to guess. Do not choose options that allow your computer to remember your passwords. Also you should disable remote connectivity when the equipment's are not in use. Evidence that your information is being encrypted: To protect attackers from hijacking your information, any personal information submitted online should be encrypted. Many sites use SSL or Secure Sockets Layer, to encrypt information for protecting your privacy.

The advantages of the Cyber security are: defending us from cyber-attacks and critical attacks such as: hacks and virus; it helps us to browse the safe website; Internet security processes all the incoming and outgoing data on our computer; the security developers will update their databases every week once. Hence the new virus also deleted (Mirzoev et al, 2014).

- **Cyber Attacks:** In these days of online processing and real time systems, most of the information is online and prone to intrusion threats. There are a huge number of cyber threats and their behavior is difficult to early detecting; hence difficult to restrict in the early phases of the cyber-attacks. The attacks are processed knowingly can be considered as the cybercrime and they have serious impact over the society in the form of economical disrupt, psychological disorder, threat to national defense etc. Elimination and restriction of cybercrimes is dependent on proper analysis of their behavior and understanding of their impact over various levels of society (Guitton, 2012).

- **Digital Crime:** Digital crimes differ in many aspects when compared to physical crime and so are the methods and techniques employed for investigation, Computers are considered as the primary evidence in digital crimes as they process the required information for investigation in the form of hardware, software and physical evidence as fingerprints from the peripheral devices.

Digital evidence is information left on computers, audio files, video files, and digital images left behind by the perpetrators after a cybercrime. This evidence is essential to investigate in computer and Internet crimes and it can prove for or against a theory on how a crime was committed. Digital evidence brings to light the communication between suspects and victims, online activities during a particular time period and other information that provides a digital dimension to the investigation. In computer intrusions the intruders will leave varied traces of their presence unknowingly in the form of system log, network logs, file systems and registry, which will be abundant information for the forensic analysts to analyze the case. In order to be useful in investigation digital evidence must be preserved and examined without being altered from the time it was collected to the time it was presented in the court of law. Authentication is required during evidence submission to substantiate the fact that the contents of the record have remained unchanged, information in the record was extracted from the target machine and the date of the record is accurate (Tamilarasi, 2013).

The most important feature of authentication is maintaining and documenting chain of custody in which each person who handled evidence may be required to testify that the evidence presented in the court of law is not tampered or altered from the original form. Evidence Integrity is implemented using hash functions to support the authentication process.

CYBER CRIME METHODOLOGY

There is a methodology typically followed by the cyber criminals when they are conducting their illegal activity. The methodology is based on cyber criminals experience gained through and subsequently breaking into computer systems.

Cyber criminals will "hack" into a victim computer or will use any public places to commit their illegal activity. Cyber criminals will typically need to use a computer network that is difficult to identify. This is done to make it difficult for law enforcement to identify the perpetrator of the cybercrime (Sindhu and Meshram, 2012).

Computers' Role

Before discussing the roles of computers in the cybercrime methodology, we have to define and explain some terms that are used in this methodology; these terms are the following:

- **Victim:** It is an object (computer) for the intrusion or unauthorized activity.
- **Instrumentality:** It is a subject computer used by the criminals to conduct illegal activity.
- **Evidence:** Any devices (computer) or software (log files) used to store evidence of the crime.

It is possible to see from the methodology the following functions:

1. Initially, intruders will collect information for the first time.
2. The intruders like to learn about the attacked network features.
3. The intruders need more information about the target victim's computer network such as: operating systems.

4. The intruders try to explore and identify the vulnerability that exists through conducting the host enumeration.

5. The intruders then succeeded to exploit the computer vulnerabilities.

6. The intruders also try to crack the password of the authorized users by installing password crackers.

7. After the intruders succeeded in compromising the network, they usually install sniffers to capture user id/passwords and other sensitive information.

8. The intruders may hide important data from law enforcement by using steganography.

CYBER CRIME EXISTENCE

Security systems are required to protect and safeguard computers against intrusions. Computer systems are vulnerable and the reasons for this vulnerability are the computers and systems itself. Some of these reasons are:

- **Software Complexity:** Operating systems are the heart of the computer and these in turn are composed of millions of codes. Due to the complexity of the operating systems, the developers leave gaps in these systems for future development. The cyber criminals take advantages of these gaps and hacks into the computer system.

- **Storage Capacity:** It is possible to store data in comparatively very small space because computer has unique characteristic of storing data. This affords to remove or derive of bulk of information either through physical or virtual medium makes it much easier.

- **Possibility of Breaching:** Computer systems are vulnerable and there is every possibility to breach the security system by the unauthorized access. This breaching is not due to human error but due to the complex

technology used to break in. By secretly implanted logic bomb, key beggars that can steal access codes, advanced voice recorders, retina imagers, etc. that can fool biometric systems and bypass firewalls can be utilized to get past many a security system.

- **Negligence:** Negligence is very closely connected with human conduct. It is therefore very probable that negligence leads to gain access by a cybercriminal while protecting the computer system.

- **Loss of Evidence:** It is a very common and obvious problem as all the data are routinely destroyed. Further collection of data outside the territorial extent also paralyses this system of crime investigation.

CYBER CRIME COMMITING

There are different modes and manners that criminals can commit their crimes; some of these attacks that can be used are the following:

- **Denial of Service:** It is the flooding of an entire network or victim, either by disabling them or by overloading them with messages so as to degrade performance. A more advance type is the Distributed Denial of Service (DDoS) attacks, where the attacker uses resources from a distributed environment against a target host.

- **Theft of Information:** Information is stored in a digital storage such as: hard disc, removable storage media, etc. It is so easy to steal this information either by appropriating the data physically or by tampering them logically through the virtual medium.

- **Data Diddling:** The intruders are altering raw data just before a computer processes it and then returning it back after the processing is completed.

- **Unauthorized Access to Computer Systems or Networks/Hacking:** This kind of offence is normally referred as hacking in the generic sense. The hackers here are looking for the gaps in the large systems such as operating system, networks, etc. These gaps are left intentionally by the developers for future maintenance. Hacker's term is different from "unauthorized access".

- **Email Bombing:** The victim email will be flooded by a large number of mails, which may be an individual or a company or even mail servers there by ultimately resulting into crashing.

- **Salami Attack:** This attack involves that the alteration is so small that it would normally go unnoticed. This kind of crime is normally prevalent in the financial institutions or for the purpose of committing financial crimes.

- **Virus/Worm Attacks:** Viruses are programs that attach themselves to a computer's program or a file and then copy themselves to other files and to other computers on a computer network. They usually altering, deleting, or destroying the data on a computer. Worms, unlike viruses do not need the host to attach themselves to. They merely make functional copies of themselves and do this repeatedly till they eat up all the available space on a computer's memory.

- **Logical Bombs:** These programs are created to do some action after getting a trigger; they are event dependent. These programs are put in action when a certain event (known as a trigger event) occurs such as a certain day, a certain date, or some action as update a file.

- **Trojan Attacks:** These programs are looks as innocent programs but they contain inside a devil programs. In software field this means unauthorized programs, which pas-

sively gains control over another's system by representing itself as authorized programs. The most common form of installing a Trojan horse is through e-mail.

- **Internet Time Thefts:** It is the thefts of the internet surfing hours of the victim by another person. This is done by gaining access to the login ID, privilege, and the password.

- **Web Jacking:** In this sort of attacks the hacker gains access and control over the web site of another person. He/she may even mutilates or change the information on the site. This may be done for fulfilling political objectives or for money.

TYPES OF CYBERCRIME

The Cybercrime can be classified in the following types:

- **Hacking:** It is an illegal intrusion into a computer system and/or network. It is also known as "Cracking". Government websites are the hot targets of the hackers due to the press coverage, it receives. Hackers enjoy the media coverage. Motive behind the crime called hacking:
  - Greed;
  - Power;
  - Publicity;
  - Revenge;
  - Adventure;
  - Desire to access forbidden information;
  - Destructive mindset;
  - Wants to sell n/w security services.
- **Child Pornography:** The Internet is being highly used by its abusers to reach and abuse children sexually, worldwide. As more homes have access to Internet, more children would be using the Internet and more are the chances of falling victim to the aggression of pedophiles. How they operate:

- Pedophiles use false identity to trap the children/teenagers pedophiles contact children/teens in various chat rooms which are used by children/teen to interact with other children/teen.
- Befriend the child/teen.
- Extract personal information from the child/teen by winning his confidence.
- Gets the e-mail address of the child/teen and starts making contacts on the victim's e-mail address as well.
- Start sending pornographic images/text to the victim including child pornographic images in order to help child/teen shed his inhibitions. A feeling is created in the mind of the victim that what is being fed to him is normal and that everybody does it.
- Extract personal information from child/teen at the end of it, the pedophile set up a meeting with the child/teen out of the house and then drag him into the net to further sexually assault him or to use him as a sex object.

- **Denial of Service:** It is flooding the bandwidth of the victim's network or fills his/her e-mail box with spam mail depriving him/her of the services he/she entitled to access or provide. Many DoS attacks, such as the Ping of Death and Teardrop attacks, exploit limitations in the TCP/IP protocols.
- **Virus Dissemination:** Malicious software attaches itself to other software (virus, worms, Trojan horse, web jacking, e-mail bombing, etc).
- **Computer Vandalism:** Damaging or destroying data rather than stealing or misusing them is called cyber vandalism. Transmitting Virus: These are programs that attach themselves to a file and then circulate. They usually affect the data on a computer, either by altering or deleting it against properties.

- **Cyber Terrorism:** Terrorist attacks on the Internet is by distributed denial of service attacks, hate websites and hate emails, attacks on sensitive computer networks, etc. The recent example may be cited of – Osama Bin Laden, the LTTE, and attack on America's army deployment system during Iraq war against government. Technology savvy terrorists are using 512 bit encryption, which is impossible to decrypt.
- **Software Piracy:** Theft of software through the illegal copying of genuine programs of the counterfeiting and distribution of products intended to pass for the original.
- **Fraud and Cheating:** Online fraud and cheating is one of the most lucrative businesses that are growing today in the cyber space.
- **Trafficking:** It may assume different forms. It may be trafficking in drugs, human beings, arms weapons, etc.

CYBERCRIME AND THE LAW

Cyber Criminals around the world lurk on the computer networks as an omnipresent menace to the financial strength of businesses, to the confidence of their customers, and as an emerging threat to society's' security.

The estimation for the cost of cybercrime is approximately around $50 billion annually. In North America, there are more than 60 million residents and they have online banking facilities. The cost of cyber-crimes in the USA alone is estimated not in million, but billions.

Clearly, then, with large scale criminal activity taking place on such a mammoth level the law intervenes and redress can be sought. Actually, no Criminal defense lawyers will be able to tell you that only approximately ten percent of all cyber-crimes are reported; and of those that are actually reported, less than two percent end up in some form of conviction on the part of the cybercriminal.

Should criminal defense procedures such actions and behavior by cyber criminals not encourage victims reporting cases? Conversely the argument goes the other way. Afraid of the risk of losing customer confidence in their network, major businesses that have fallen victim to cyber-crimes in the past have opted not to report. Nevertheless, even where victims have sought redress and restitution within the criminal defense system, the general consensus among victims has been that the law will provide little or no assistance to their case. More concerning, however, is cases where victims of the criminal gangs instigating the cybercrime have no recourse to criminal defense procedures that would otherwise protect their individual rights and freedoms, such as the alleged criminal gangs who operate in the former communist block selling the wares of child pornography over the Internet to clients in the West who believe they're safe from prosecution in their own homes.

Regardless of this factor, however, with 90 percent of American businesses surveyed stating that they had encountered computer-related security breaches in 2001, clearly cyber-crime has reached endemic proportions and the time has now come to address this issue. But what restitution within the criminal defense system would a victim of a cyber-crime currently have?

Currently there is little or no international legislation that contains criminal defense mechanisms against cyber-crimes. There are, however, a few multi-jurisdictional legislations, such as those in found within European Union law.

That said, there is a Convention on Cybercrime that a number of nations have become signatories to. Questions do, however, remain over whether or not this is toothless in the fight against cybercrime.

There are two things we can be fairly sure of:

1. Cybercrime is not going to go away of its own free will, there's simply too much money involved and criminal gangs are too organized to just walk away; and

2. Unless drastic measures are taken within the criminal defense system, the economic fallout from cybercrime is going to surpass all other organized criminal activity in a very short period of time.

The answer here is very probably three-fold:

1. **Improved Computer Security:** There is little doubt that businesses are not waiting on the criminal defense system to catch up with protecting their rights and taking it upon themselves to spend billions of dollars in improving their security systems. In many instances, those writing the improved computer security system packages have, themselves, previously been cyber criminals. Notable here are finance and credit card companies, who are leading the way in developing technology that is less friendly to cybercriminal activity.

2. **Changes in the Behavior of the Cybercriminal:** Notwithstanding the fact that businesses are spending billion in upgrading and improving their computer network systems, the cybercriminal themselves is also learning to adapt. Not sticking to tried and tested criminal behavior, that can easily be replicated by new emerging criminals, leading cyber criminals are adapting to new technology with new cybercrimes. Even now we are hearing of criminal activity involving WiFi networks, where the security systems are more infant. Moreover, criminals are also making use of the WiFi system itself to cover their tracks when carrying out illegal activities. A new comer on the block, Voice over Internet Protocol (VoIP), although not yet subject to major cybercriminal activity, is likely to be the next big thing that criminal gangs turn their attention to.

Consequently, changes and upgrades to technology and their security systems is a double-edge sword. On the one hand it is very much a way that businesses can stay ahead of the cybercriminal. On the other hand, it is also a way that cyber criminals can move into new untapped areas.

3. **Administrative Changes to the Criminal Defense Systems:** Although business can be seen to be making superhuman efforts to deter cyber-crimes via upgrades to their security systems and innovative changes to technology, the rights of individual users of the computer networks are still not being fully protected. Nor will these changes have much of an effect on individual computer network users, who are more vulnerable to cyber-fraud crimes than break-ins to their actual networks. In other words, the social element of computer cybercrime needs addressing. Here, changes to the law are going to be needed if cyber criminals are going to be deterred. However, with a global tool such as the Internet, with reach-ability from almost anywhere in the world, how will this work without?

Clearly a united front on criminal defense laws against cyber-crimes is going to be needed. If this cannot be implement on a global basis, then geographic areas are going to need to consider implementing these laws that across jurisdictional. The Council of Europe Convention on Cybercrime is an example of how this may be approached. However, with Internet technology and access now becoming more readily available to billions of people in South America and Asia, clear, concise and unified approach to the criminal activities of cybercriminal is going to need to the issue of the day if some form of criminal defense to cybercrime is going to be a success - either in the short-term or long-term. Implicit within these must be very strict laws to counter hard core criminal gang activities, such as crimes against children. To do otherwise would surely result in the Internet's image of being the last vestige of the wild, wild, west holding true - as a lawless environment where no criminal defense is required because no criminal action will be forthcoming.

THE CYBER SECURITY PROBLEMS

One of the biggest concerns is what if there is a hack into the critical systems in government, companies, financial institutions etc. This could lead to malware in critical systems leading to data loss, misuse or even killing the critical systems.

In the world of Cyber security, it is expected that some of the following things will be happened:

1. Threats will continue to become more intense. Global competition for business will include efforts to develop and acquire intellectual property. Therefore intellectual property and intellectual capital will become more valuable than ever before and the threat to them will rise.

2. Also, threats will continue to become more adaptive and subtle. Instead of knowing that a threat has a particular signature or fingerprint, it will have a changing signature and set of fingerprints, becoming more difficult to detect.

3. Attention to cyber security will rise. Savvier companies realize they need to protect their intellectual property. It won't be a question of compliance – it will be a question of survival.

4. Nations will increasingly cooperate to improve the global economy's cyber security. They will do this to make it more predictable and less susceptible to cyber terrorism and cyber vandalism, as well as protect the critical infrastructures of sovereign countries.

THE PROPOSED SOLUTIONS

Prevention is always better than cure. It is better to take certain precaution while operating the net. For instant, to prevent cyber stalking avoid disclosing any information pertaining to one. To overcome the previous cyber security problems we suggest the following solutions:

1. Security continues to become part of virtual infrastructure. As more and more organizations add virtualization technologies into their environment, particularly server and desktop virtualization, security will be more embedded in the native technologies, and less of an "add-on" after the implementation is complete. For server virtualization, new firewalls and monitoring capabilities are being integrated into some of the leading platforms now.

2. Wireless adoption will continue, branching out into a larger number of purpose-focused protocols that fit the needs of individual technology. Based on the failed protocols exposure, and the trend of Wi-Fi failure and improvement, we will see history repeating itself where vendors are quick to the market to capitalize on new opportunities, failing to critically examine the lessons from earlier wireless technologies.

3. Social media will provide the platform for the cybercrime. More organizations will adopt social media as a core aspect of their marketing strategy. They will struggle to balance the need to be active as part of online social communities while balancing compliance and litigation risks associated with such activities.

4. More cloud computing issues will be at the eye of the cyber attackers. Many organizations will soon discover that they do not have the flexibility they need for their business, and many others will discover that any security issues (from audit to compromise) are far more complex in the cloud. Security professionals will continue to apply extra security to scenarios that involve processing sensitive or regulated data in shared cloud environments.

5. Development of better computer-aided tools that will enable companies to asses more quickly and effectively a threat and select the right defense for it.

6. Situational awareness; it is an important innovation, which will enable companies to understand what's happening inside their enterprise as well as in the global environment. With situational awareness technology, they will be able to see threats as they evolve before they hit their operations.

7. Cloud development involves securing new architectures, like the cloud. Today organizations are beginning to adopt these architectures because they offer tremendous operational advantages, however they worry about security. With cloud security and Trusted Cloud capabilities, organizations will be able to develop secure new architectures.

8. Improved social engineering attacks will be the trend for the coming era. Attackers will increasingly make use of social-engineering tactics to bypass technological security controls, fine-tuning their techniques to exploit natural human predispositions.

9. Humans are the weakest link, regardless of how technology changes; attackers know they can always hack employees. In the year 2013 and 2014 these human attacks will only grow in sophistication and numbers.

10. Memory Scrapping will become more common in the coming time. This has been around for a long time, but is more aggressively targeting data such as credit card records, passwords, PIN's, keys, as of late.

THE FUTURE TRENDS

Because much of the information technology companies are privately owned, the focus would be on making customer happy as opposed to worry about the transnational crime. Some of the following cyber developments are expected to be seen on the horizon:

- One of the biggest concerns is what if there is a hack into the critical systems in government, companies, financial institutions etc. This could lead to malware in critical systems leading to data loss, misuse or even killing the critical systems. Since the communication flow is easy via the internet, the crime organizations might merge and cooperate even more than they are currently. We have to be ready for that.

- **Threats Become More Intense:** Global competition for business will include efforts to develop and acquire intellectual property. Therefore intellectual property and intellectual capital will become more valuable than ever before and the threat to them will rise.

- **Threats Become More Adaptive and Subtle:** Instead of knowing that a threat has a particular signature or fingerprint, it will have a changing signature and set of fingerprints, becoming more difficult to detect.

- **Attention to Cyber Security Will Rise:** Savvier companies realize they need to protect their intellectual property. It won't be a question of compliance; it will be a question of survival.

- **Improve the Global Economy's Cyber Security:** Nations will do this to make it more predictable and less susceptible to cyber terrorism and cyber vandalism. As well as protect the critical infrastructures of sovereign countries.

- **More International Cooperation:** Due to the existence of gang cyber criminals, there should be an International cooperation to fight the Cybercrime and consolidate their efforts to protect the nations through societies, security companies, and research & development.

- **Policies Will Emerge:** Policies must be set up by Governments and Companies to governance cyber security. These policies must be modern to cooperate with the new methods of cybercrime.

- **Situational Awareness:** It is an important innovation, which will enable companies to understand what's happening inside their enterprise as well as in the global environment. With situational awareness technology, they will be able to see threats as they evolve before they hit their operations.

- **Development of Better Computer-Aided Tools:** This will enable companies to asses more quickly and effectively a threat and select the right defense for it. This development involves securing new architectures, like the cloud.

- **Improved Social Engineering Attacks:** Attackers will increasingly make use of social-engineering tactics to bypass technological security controls, fine-tuning their techniques to exploit natural human predispositions.

- **Social Media Will Provide the Platform for the Cyber Crime:** More organizations will adopt social media as a core aspect of their marketing strategy. Organizations will struggle to balance the need to be active as part of on-line social communities while balancing compliance and litigation risks associated with such activities. Organizations will have a hard time controlling online social networking activities of their users. Attackers will continue to take advantage of the still-evolving understanding of online social networking safety practices to defraud people and organizations.

- **Humans Are the Weakest Link:** Regardless of how technology changes attackers know they can always hack employees. In the year 2013 and 2014 these human attacks will only grow in sophistication and numbers. Organizations and management will finally start doing something about it to secure the human.

- **Memory Scrapping:** This has been around for a long time, but is more aggressively targeting data such as credit card records, passwords, PIN's, keys, as of late. The reason they are successful is that they get around PCI/GLBA/HIPAA/ETC security requirements that data must be encrypted while in transit and at rest. Memory Scrapping Data in transit is decrypted on the system and often stored in memory during the lifetime of a process, or at least during a decryption routine. Depending on how a process cleans up after itself, it may stay resident even after the fact. The data is encrypted on the hard disk, but again, the RAM likely maintains the cleared version of the data.

- **Wireless Adoption:** Wi-Fi technology will continue to grow. But other protocols will also emerge with widespread adoption suiting the needs of embedded technology with a variety of focus areas including ZigBee, Wireless HART and Z-Wave, as well as propriety protocols.

- **More Cloud Computing Issues:** While there are many possible benefits to cloud computing, the honeymoon will end. Many organizations will soon discover that they do not have the flexibility they need for their business. Many organizations will discover that any security issues (from audit to compromise) are far more complex in the cloud.

- **Security in Virtual Infrastructure:** As more and more organizations add virtualization technologies into their environment,

security will be more embedded in the native technologies, and less of an "add-on" after the implementation is complete.

CONCLUSION

This chapter concentrates not only on the understanding of the cybercrimes but also explains the impacts over the different levels of the business. This will help the organizations to secure all the online information critical organizations which are not safe due to such cybercrimes. The understanding of the behavior of cyber criminals and impacts of cybercrimes on society will help to find out the sufficient means to overcome the situation.

Also this chapter tried to concentrate on the security problems, which are conducted by the cyber criminals and are faced by the nation. Some suggested solutions are given to help in solving these problems. At the end of the chapter, the Author tried to forecast some of the necessary future research that will help in stopping the cybercrimes or at least detect and give the evidence on those crimes.

REFERENCES

Byun, J. Y., Nasridinov, A., & Park, Y. H. (2014). Internet of Things for Smart Crime detection. *Contemporary Engineering Sciences*, 7(15), 749–754.

Crime Desk. (2009). Million Online Crimes in the year: Cyber Crime squad Established. londondailynews.com/million-online-crimes-year-cyber-crime-squad-established-p-117.html, Retrieved October 12, 2012 from http://www.the

Guitton, C. (2012). Criminals and Cyber Attacks: The missing Link between Attribution and Deterrence. [IJCC]. *International Journal of Cyber Criminology*, 6(2), 1030–1043.

Coleman, K. G. (2011). *Cyber intelligence: The huge economic impact of cyber crime.* Retrieved October 5, 2012 from: http://gov.aol.com/2011/09/19/cyber-intelligence-the-huge-economic-impact-of-cyber-crime

Mirzoev, T., Brannon, M., Lasker, S., & Millere, M. (2014). Mobile application threats and security. *World of Computer Science and Information Technology Journal*, 4(5), 57–61.

Power, R. (2001). 2001 CSI/FBI computer crime and security survey. *Computer Security Issues and trends*, 7(1), 1-18.

Ramkumar, R. (2014). Survey of Computer Crimes and their Impacts [IJSRD]. *International Journal of Scientific Research and Development*, 2(4), 840–844.

Saini, H., Rao, Y. S., & Panda, T. C. (2012). Cyber-Crimes and their impacts: A Review [IJERA]. *International Journal of Engineering Research and Applications*, 2(2), 202–209.

Sindhu, K. K., & Meshram, B. B. (2012). Digital Forensics and Cyber Crime Data mining. *Journal of Information Security*, 3(3), 1–6. doi:10.4236/jis.2012.33024

Northecutt, S. et al. (2011). *Security predictions 2012 & 2013: The emerging security threat.* Retrieved from http://www.sans.edu/research/security-laboratory/article/security-predict2011.

Tamilarasi, S. (2013). Forensic Investigative Methodologies for Digital Crime. [TIJCSA]. *The International Journal of Computer Science & Applications*, 2(3), 58–65.

Thapa, A., & Kumar, R., (2011). Cyber Stalking: Crime and challenge at the cyber space. *International Journal of Computing and Business research*, 2(1), 1-15.

KEY TERMS AND DEFINITIONS

Cyber Attacks: There are a huge number of cyber threats and their behavior is difficult to early detecting; hence difficult to restrict in the early phases of the cyber-attacks.

Cyber Crime: A crime committed using a computer and the communication as an object or subject of crime for illegal action to steal a person's identity, illegal imports, or malicious programs.

Cyber Security: The objective of cyber security is to protect and defend information by detecting, preventing, and responding to cyber-attacks.

Cyber Threat: Any attack to the security system, trying to delete or modified information.

Security Impacts: There is a security impact on the society behavior.

Chapter 9
Cyber Crimes:
Types, Sizes, Defence Mechanism, and Risk Mitigation

Hasan L. Al-Saedy
British Institute of Technology and E-Commerce, UK

ABSTRACT

The financial cost of cyber crime now has an annual cost estimated in the UK in eleven figures. In this chapter an ethic based definition of cyber crime is introduced and cyber crimes are classified. The impact of each class of cyber crime on society, individual, government and international security is highlighted. The cost of cyber crime is evaluated and a technique to prevent and mitigate the effect of these crimes on individual, government and international security and world peace is indicated. The forensic techniques and tools used in cyber crime evidence gathering and prosecuting procedure is also indicated. Finally, recommendations and suggestion are given to mitigate the impact of cyber crime on individuals, societies, world finance and international security.

INTRODUCTION

Email scam is considered as a crime in the west and the US law and regulation and probably there is no regulation in some countries to criminalize this sort of act, but this crime is ethically unacceptable in all societies worldwide, the definition could be based on the social convention or norms. Intercepting diplomatic mail by English speaking governments is an acceptable act among the five countries; however, the act is ethically unacceptable worldwide (Gurny, 2013). According to the above definition intercepted diplomatic mail is considered to be as cyber crime according what

been said as agreed upon convention and norms. The recent reported case of interception of the mail of a head of European state by the US government is a violation of norm and conventions. The US constitution doesn't allow the interception of the stored or transmitted data of US citizen, in theory, without legal warrant according to the fourth amendment 'The right of the people to be secure in their persons, houses, papers, and effects, against unreasonable searches and seizures, shall not be violated, and no warrants shall issue, but upon probable cause, supported by oath or affirmation, and particularly describing the place to be searched, and the persons or things to be seized'.

DOI: 10.4018/978-1-4666-6583-5.ch009

Copyright © 2015, IGI Global. Copying or distributing in print or electronic forms without written permission of IGI Global is prohibited.

It is clear evidence that the US government security agencies are violating the privacy of the US citizens and non US citizens. Snowden revealed facts in the UK Guardian newspaper is clear evidence of the US privacy violation.

In general, cyber crimes are crimes in which the internet, computer, email and mobile are used to engineer them. The designer of this sort of crimes takes the advantages of the weak security and policy measure in networking and communications technology to implement the crime (Sanders, 1994). A wide range of cyber crimes is in use these days (Home Office, 2010). It is not possible so far to estimate the real volume of these crimes as victims are usually decline to report these crimes for many reasons. Among these reasons are cultural backgrounds and for some are for brand name protection (Schneier, 1995). However, it is possible to estimate the proportional volumes of theses crimes from governments released report (Home Office, 2010). Among the sorts of crimes are the following:

Breaching of security, copyright violation, child pornography, child grooming, computer viruses, denial of services, malicious code, financial fraud, identity theft and phishing scam. A wide used definition of crime is a forbidden and punishable act. The definition of crime as used in this article is that a crime is *ethically* unacceptable act (Mackey, 2003).

From the classes of crime mentioned above it is possible to estimate the financial cost of some and not possible to estimate a cost for others. As an example it is not possible to allocate a cost for child pornography and child grooming, this is on one hand and on the other hand it is possible to allocate a cost for email scam and phishing.

Table 1 shows the type of cyber crimes and tools used in engineering of these crimes and their implication on economy, society and world security. It is important to highlight here the following facts about the nature of research in cyber crimes, among these facts are that knowing the proportional cost of the cyber crime will help in setting the research budgets and priorities. Also

Figure 1. UK cyber crimes

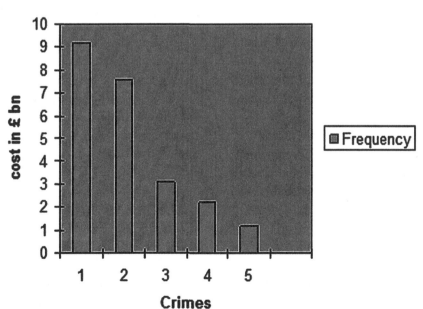

Table 1. Classes of major cybercrimes, used tools, and implication

Sequence	Type of Crime	Tool(s)	Implication
1	Child Pornography	Facebook, email, mobile and internet	Social
2	Child Grooming	Facebook, email, mobile and internet	Social
3	Privacy Violation	Facebook, twitter, government database and service providers	Social/Financial
4	Intellectual Property Theft	Classical and electronic media	Financial
5	Email Spam	Email	Financial
6	Email Scam	Email	Financial
7	Mobile Span	Mobile	Financial
8	Mobile Scam	Mobile	Financial
9	Phishing	Email, mobile and Web Technology	Financial
10	Viruses	Internet	Financial
11	Malicious Code	Computer and network	Financial
12	Network penetration	Network Software	Financial
13	Data Traffic interception	Network Software	Financial
14	Denial of Services	Internet	Financial
15	Defamation and Slander	Internet, Mobile, You tube	Social
16	Diplomatic mail interception	International communications channels	World Security
17	Scareware	Web Site	Financial
18	Email Hijacking	Email interception	Financial
19	Extortion	Email, mobile, social network	Financial
20	Espionage (Spying)	Email, Mobile, Telephone	Financial
21	Worm	Internet	Financial
22	Drugs Trafficking	Email	Social

setting a security plan in enterprises will help enhance the annual turnover of enterprises and again, discovering of a crime at an earlier stage will help reduce the cost of the crime (Newman, 2010).

The UK government estimate of the annual cost of cyber crimes is as much as 27 billion pounds (Cabinet Office and Detica, 2011), the cost of cyber crimes ordered from the most to the least expensive are as follows:

1. Intellectual property theft,
2. Espionage (spying),
3. Online theft,
4. Extortion,
5. Online fraud.

Figure 1 shows a histogram for the cost of the five highest crimes in cost.

(McGuire & Dowling, 2013) conducted a survey of public attitudes toward internet security in the UK environment. Table1 shows the classes of major cybercrimes, used tools and implication.

CLASSES OF MAJOR CYBER CRIMES, USED TOOLS AND IMPLICATION

The percentage of the reported crimes is very low compared with the real volumes of these crimes in all the above mentioned crimes.

BRIEF DESCRIPTION OF CYBER CRIMES WITH BRIEF REMARKS ABOUT THE DEFENSE MECHANISM

Child Pornography

It is about the sexual activities involving children, using Facebook, email and other media. The engineering of this sort of crimes is very simple, however, the detection and reporting of the crime is very rare. Western government has the mechanism to report and prosecute this sort of crimes. The media indicate that the reported and detected crimes are low compared with the revealed information then after. Many countries still have no procedure in place to report and prosecute suspects. It is the author's opinion that a proper investigation of the problem needs to be conducted, the investigation needs to cover all the side of the problem, these are the social, educational, psychological and reporting and prosecution procedures. The reported size of the problem is thin compared with real size of the problem. Children by nature are unable to defend selves a special cases are socially fragmented families. This is the case in western societies. The case is much worse in third world countries as the social security is very much less active and children leave school in early stage to join the labour markets. UN organizations need to demonstrate higher levels of responsibilities to develop the legal framework to protect the right of children.

Child Grooming

This is about establishing an emotional relation to a child by using electronic media, again electronics media is a potential tool used in engineering of these sorts of activities. Detection and reporting of this sort of crimes are small compared with the real size of the problem. No national or international procedure is available to detect and prosecute suspects. Again, in this case the reported cases are low compared with the real size of the problem,

also national and international efforts are needed to protect the children, help victims and prosecute suspects. It is important to add here that the family response toward the victim is unpredictable and it depends much on the norms and convention in local society. The large number of reported cases in the Middle East, in which victim's life was terminated, either by self or by close relatives.

Privacy Violation

This is to violate the privacy of a person by gaining some personal data from government or enterprise databases, many organizations collect date about citizens, expatriate and immigrants, the date is usually saved in databases with no policy in place for limiting the access to the data. Examples of these organizations that collect data about us are the National Health Service, the Home Office, supermarkets, transportation companies, hotels, internet service provider and mobile phone companies. Documents like the biometric passport and biometric identity carry personal details about the holder as name, nationality, date of birth and other personal details. Data in biometric documents are readable from a distance. The transport company like London transport have data about our everyday routine routs with no clear policy in place about the way they use this data. . Close circuit televisions are widely used by governments and private enterprises with no clear policy in place to regulate the access of the data. Again this is another risk for privacy and security with no clear policy in place to access the data. Mobile phone switching station databases are another risk for security and privacy; our everyday telephone calls are available to governments and private enterprises. Interception of telephone calls is very frequently reported in media in western society hardly been mentioned in third world countries. Again the size of reported cases is a fraction of the real volume of these privacy violation crimes. Privacy violation engineered by government intelligence agencies worldwide is usually undetected and unreported. In western society the law and regulation cover partly some of the above mentioned crimes, constitution of the majority of third world countries to avoid the regulation of the privacy right of citizens and if it is regulated it is hardly get activated (Stalling, 2011).

Intellectual Property Theft (Copyright Violation)

This is the violation of the copyright of idea, design, methodology, trade secrets and other forms of artistic and intellectual work. The majority of the third world countries have no copyright protection regulation and legal procedures of prosecution in place and accordingly the volume of this sort of crimes are unknown, but it is clear that the size of this sort of crimes is huge. Watermarking of document is effective way to protect the right of the author(s) (Aybet et al, 2009). An organized effort is needed to find an end to this sort of problems as the estimated size is very high. The reported size of the problem is an estimation based on assumptions. There is no real indicator of the real size of the problem. National and international effort is needed to limit this intellectual property theft. The Interpol and UN need to take the initiative to set an end to this problem.

Email Spam

This is the use of an email media to promote business by email junk material. Again, the engineering of this sort of crimes is simple; using the email filter could reduce the size of the problem. No clear procedure and regulation for reporting and prosecuting procures are available. Email user often deletes the spam email without reporting the case to authority. This sort of email is annoying and time consuming. Strict technical and legal regulation is needed to limit the use of this sort of email. No spam email should be sent without the consent of the receiver. Worst reported case in which the spam email carrying a malicious code or viruses (Stalling, 2004).

Email Scam

This is the use of the email as a tool to get some financial advantages from victims by the engineering of a fraud. The technology for engineering this sort of crime is the email, email filter is an acceptable tool for reducing the size of this problem (Nelson et al, 2008). The email Scam is a more serious crime than the email Span as the financial implication on individual is very serious. Email scam crimes are rarely reported as unclear procedures for reporting and prosecution is available. Financial organization refrains to declare the volume of these crimes for the sake of brand name protection and reputation. A very series reported cases in which scam email is used to organize kidnapping for many purposes, among the case was the kidnapping for the purpose of requesting a ransom from the family of the victim to secure the release of the victim. Again, no guarantee after the payment of the ransom the victim will be released unharmed.

Mobile Spam

This is the text or audio junk material sent to the mobile user by using the mobile phone network to promote a business or to propagate massages. Again, the mobile technology is used to engineer this sort of crimes, rarely reported. However, the media reports cases very frequently. Hiding the entity of the sender is often approached used to protect the sender from average users. Technically it is possible to recover the identity of the suspect. However, the majority of the user refrains to take the case very seriously and the suspect went unpunished. Mobile service providers, the police and international security organization need to work together to develop a legal framework to limit the size of these crimes.

Mobile Scam

This is similar to email Spam, fraud is designed to victimize the mobile user. It also used together with email scam in victimizing the email the mobile phone user. The volume of this crime is very large, most of the crimes are engineered overseas in internet café, the victims are from Europe and the USA, victims are asked to transfer money thought the Western Union Agent. Money transferred through Western union is very hard to trace. National and international cooperation are needed to limit the use of this sort of crimes.

Phishing

This is used to gain data about the victim by using web technology media to violate the victim privacy. Significant type of crimes is gaining access to the victim's bank account.

Reported detected phishing web sites in the UK was very large (Home Office, 2010). New approach introduced by Banks to limit the volume of these crimes. The technology is based on the use of zero-knowledge protocols (Al-Saedy, 2002), a calculator like machine is sent to clients to generate random number for every new financial transaction.

The approach introduces a secure authentication to limit this crime. Again, national and international effort is needed to limit the use of this sort of crime. Education of the users of the internet is a priority in these cases. It is important to make the idea as there is nothing as a free lunch as part of the internet user's culture. Web mining is a technique could be used to detect and stop the use of suspicious web sites. Newly introduced virus scanner to test website is an effective way to keep the user of browser save.

Careful analyses of the web site domain name will help in the detection of frauds. Using the same domain name with another extension is another approach. An example of this sort of phishing web site is that a web site is developed for domain.org to domain.com. It is also recommended to refrain to respond to email came from a free email provider like Yahoo, Hotmail, and others. Ask the sender to use the company official web site and email.

Viruses

Widely used crime is the spreading of viruses to contaminate the computer of the victims and damage the software and data on computer systems. A virus could be defined as a program inserts its code in executable programs and become active to contaminate other programs once the hosting program is getting active. Virus analyses search, and remove is a well establish business. Virus scans and cleans are an excellent defence mechanism to remove known viruses. New viruses need more time to engineer the anti-viral action. This problem is a very serious crime as the number of viruses is growing exponentially. To give an idea about the growing is that the number of viruses at the end of the last century was couple of thousands; today the number of viruses is more than a million. (Swenson, 2008). The exponential growth of the number of viruses is endless and an international effort is needed to set an end to this problem. The virus problem is very much associated with Microsoft Platform, less association with other platforms like Unix and Macintosh.

Malicious Code

Malicious code could be designed and deployed to a computer or network to destruct the data and violate the security of computer and network system. Hard to be discovered in the short time, regular auditing of the computer system activities could be a possible solution, but expensive solution. The virus is a special type of malicious programs. Malicious code not always replicates self in executable code like the virus spreading mechanisms. Malicious code could be designed for a specific purpose and for the specific targeted machine. The financial impact of the malicious code is very much depending on its action. In some reported cases malicious code is designed to destruct the whole file system of the victimized computer system. A reported case the malicious code was designed by a fired employee as revenge. The number of non-viral malicious crimes is not high compared with other types of the crimes as media rarely report malicious code cases.

Network Penetration

Network penetration action could be engineered by many approaches. Among these approaches is the use of network software to intercept the network traffic and get the user name and password of a legitimate user preferably the admin user name and password. Then the compromised user name and password is used to penetrate the networking system. Recovering from this sort of attack cost time and wasted resources. Open source network software, like Wireshark, could be used to engineer the attack. Machine learning as intelligent techniques is found to be effective to detect unusual network behaviour and intrusion detection (Witten & Frank, 2005). Recently, the media reported the penetration of a highly protected network as the CIA and Pentagon. The IP address of the suspect could be detected from the firewall logging records. Another defense mechanism is the honey pot network architecture. This is including the use of a dummy server to deceive the intruders and give time to the network administrators to handle the attack. In more than one occasion the US government request suspect from the UK government. The suspect could be handed to the US government and subject to the approval of the home secretary. However, no such cooperation is in place between other countries. It is the author's opinion that an international cooperation need to be regulated worldwide (Snader, 1994).

Data Traffic Interception

Interception of traffic of email and messages is very serious cyber crimes, Intercepted data could be used to engineer a wide range of cyber crimes. The Crimes could be social as well as financial and political. Regulation prevents government from intercepting the email of its own citizens is in place in Western countries, but no protection for citizens from the interception of foreign governments. In spite of the fact western government constitutionally refrain from interception of its own citizen, there is no guarantee that governments are actual refrain from interception of its own citizen. The recent reported case of a media agent was wire tape promenade figures are clear evidence of the violation of the privacy of citizens not by government body but also by a non-government agents. It is the author's opinion that governments and human right activist need to demonstrate a well organised effort to limit the violation of privacy. Much higher privacy violation went unreported and undetected world wide in underdeveloped countries.

Denial of Services

This is to engineer a flood of a large volume of requests from the victim computer or network and to block the availability of the legitimate use of the victimised computer. A networking tool is available to engineer this sort of attract. Easy to detect, hard to stop, now used as a tool to paralyse the financial and banking infrastructure between countries. The last reported case is that the Iranian government used this sort of attack against the US financial enterprises. The effectiveness of this attack has been unreported yet. An international effort is needed to regulate the use of the world internationals infrastructure.

Defamation and Slander

This is the communication of information by using email, Facebook and Twitter to harm the name and reputation of a victim. Legal procedures are available in western nations to stop this sort of activity, not available in the rest of the Worlds' nations. National and International effort is needed to criminalize the defamation crimes. It is very hard to set a cost for the level of the harm inflicted on the victim. Now days, the social media is used to propagate harmful information about prominent national figures, as actors, businessmen and politician. Media repatriated few cases of government action against suspects in the Middle East during what is known as the Arab spring. Victims often do not take action against suspected due to the cost involved in the prosecution. Finding a funding solution to prosecute suspect in some cases might be a solution. Legal firm offering no win no fee could be in theory a solution. No national regulation in place to reduce the numbers of this sort of crimes will encourage more to commit this sort of crimes.

Diplomatic Mail Interception

This is a very serious cyber crime, it could be traced to the first world war, the five English speaking countries are agreed and designed a network to intercept world diplomatic traffic, this is what is known as ECHELON system, the five English speaking countries participated in intercepting the whole world data traffic, the main player is the National Security Agency, a Swiss encryption company known as Crypto AG is also part of the game. Crypto AG exports encryption machines for more than one hundred countries worldwide. Crypto AG machines are designed to transmit the encryption key to ECHELON network. Also the international submarine cable connects the whole world is intercepted at switching points is reported.

The last reported case of Wikileak is a proof of the interception of the international traffic. This case could be summarised as the following:

The US government intercept international traffic and save the intercepted data as classified data, an army officer known as Bradley Manning (Now sentenced for 35 years in military prison) passed on the intercepted messages to Julian Assuange, Julian published the intercepted date on Wikileak (Now he is in the Ecuadorian Embassy for a year).

US government justified the interception of diplomatic traffic to defend its security. It is the author's opinion is that these sorts of action do great harm to world peace and security. Recent reported cases that the US government intercepts the diplomatic traffic of its allies and its enemies and this is very much reflected in Wikileak.

The most recent case of Prism Leak is evident; the recent revelation given by Edward Snowden to the Guardian in May 2013. The case was that the US Security agencies gather millions of phone records and monitoring the internet data. The main internet email suppliers are all active participants in these activities. (Greenwald et al, 2012).

Scare Ware

The victim is invited to visit a web site or download picture or video of unethical nature, cookies together with some video and pictures is recorded in the victim computer. Then the victim is threatened and forced to transfer money to certain bank account or he will face the reporting to employers or family members. An insignificant number of this sort of cyber crimes is reported in media. The best available solution is to ignore the threat, report the case to official body and use the system backup copy. Another alternative solution in a windows environment is back dated the system by using the system registry. Again, an organized international effort will limit the use of this sort of crimes.

Email Hijacking

Many approaches are used to hijack a victim's email, among these approaches is the interception of traffic, an open source tool could be used in the interception, Wireshark is an example. After the hijacking the email user name and password of the victim and changing the password to a new password, the email is used to gain financial benefit from the people in the user email contact list. People on the contact list of the victim will be asked to transfer money often through Western Union. A possible solution for this sort of problem is to ask the email service provider to block the email. Media reported recently Facebook hijacking case. Western union needs to organise its work to help tracking of suspect by local authority, also international and email service supplier cooperation is needed to limit this sort of crimes.

Extortion

This is an organized crime in which the victim is blackmailed and forced to offer money or property to the gang, Media like email, phone, cell phone and Facebook is used to design this sort of crimes. Environment of weak law and order always encourage criminals to use this approach of crimes. Many reported cases in the Middle East during what is known as the Arab spring are reported. Reported cases to local authority might escalate the action taken by the gang. It is hardly to find extortion crime in a stable environment. An international effort is needed to set an end to instability to find an end to security violation crimes like extortion.

Espionage (Spying)

This is the use of the media to conduct spying on governments and citizens. Media very frequently reports communication wiretapping on politicians and human rights activists. Installing close circuit television to monitor and recording is a normal security practice. No clear policy in place to limit the access and use of the collected video and audio data. Also there is nothing in the skyline and near future to see the control and use and access of the data. It is important to mention that the five English speaking countries do not criminalise the interception of diplomatic traffic but they criminalise the espionage (spying).

Worm

A malware computer program, the program replicates itself. Replicated worms heavily use the network circuit and block the network or reduce the bandwidth of the network and degrade the efficiency of the network and slow down the legitimate data traffic. Setting the network firewall to detect the signature of the worm and keeping the worm's signature up to date will mitigate the effect of the worm.

Drugs Trafficking

It is very hard to regulate the flow of goods and artifices nowadays in web commerce and web trading, almost all the types of goods are available to customers online. A huge flood of goods crosses the international borders every day. Among the artefacts and goods crossing the border are all time of drugs. An inconsistent international regulation about drug makes the regulation of the flow of the drug very difficult. Cretin drug is legal to be used in a given country and it is prohibited in another country. Another problem is making the regulation of the drug flow is the free trading agreements among countries like the European Union and among the states in the United States. An international effort is needed to regulate the flow of drugs.

ENGINEERING A CYBER CRIME

In most of the cases, the engineering of cyber crime is very simple, and the technology for detecting the crime is very simple. Cyber crimes like spam email, scam email and scam mobile message could be detected easily. The source message sender's details are usually available in the email header and the source IP address originated the message can easily be detected. Other types of cyber crimes could be investigated the same way.

The detection and prosecution of suspects will have a great influence on reducing the rate of the growth of this sort of cybercrimes.

Phishing is another simple approach of engineering cyber crimes, the majority of banks succeeds to stop this sort of crimes by introducing a random number generation calculator. This approach is useful to reduce the number of successful phishing crimes. The random number generator is used as zero knowledge protocol (Al-Saedy, 2002). Government search and detect software could reduce the number of Phishing crime drastically (Home Office, 2010). Service provider as the email, Face book and Twitter could cooperate to regulate the use of their resources to reduce or eliminate this sort of crimes.

The following is a brief description of the more technically serious cyber crimes; these are the information system attacks and malicious code:

Denial of Services

Denial of service attack can be implemented easily by deploring available network engineering tools to flood network with a huge number of SYN requests, three types of denial of service are in use, these are the SYN flood, the Smurf and distributed Denial of services. SYN flooding attack exploits the three way handshake of the TCP protocol used to initiate a communication session request. SYN packets are sent to the victim computer with an incomplete source of IP addresses. The victim computer under attack reserve memory space for each request and acknowledge the initiation of the communication session. As a result for this the memory of the victim computer is booked for unreal communication sessions and gets paralyzed. More serious SYN attack is the land attack in which the victim computer is used as the source of the SYN packets and an infinite loop of request and acknowledgement will paralyze the victim computer.

Smurf attack consumes the network communication circuit by abuse of the pink request using a spoofed IP addresses. Ping request are issued within the victim network. Each ping request broadcast and as a result a large number of responses from all nodes of the network are issued. This will jam the communications with the victim network and prevents the legitimate network communication.

Distributed Denial of Service is similar to the above attacked; the source of the attacks comes from more than one source. Denial of service attack could engineer by flood of short UDP packets.

Figure 2 is the block diagram of the three ways Handshake Protocol.

1. **Spoofing:** Spoofing attack is of four types these are the IP spoofing, ARP poisoning, Web spoofing and DNS spoofing. Spoofing means to modify the identity of the sender. A very simple example similar to the spoofing is that if I get your mobile SIM card I could pretend that I am you. In this attack the IP addresses are modified to deceive victims.
2. **Man-in-the Middle:** A man in the middle attack is a very serious attack in which the communications channel is intercepted and intruder gets the password of a ligament user of the system to gain some advantages.
3. **Replay:** It is a type of a man in the middle attack is used to get access to the computer system. A legitimate user name, IP address and password are recorded and used in an attack.

Figure 2. The three way Handshake Protocol

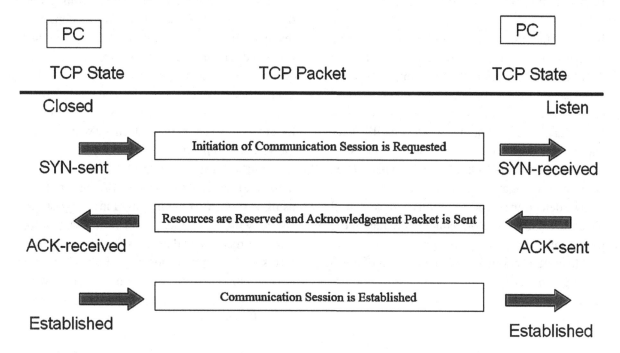

4. **TCP Session Hijacking:** Again, this is another type of man in the middle attack in which the TCP communication protocol session is hijacked by modifying the IP address of a legitimate user.

5. **Port Scanning:** In this sort of attack the source and destination ports of the TCP and UDP are scanned for data capturing and to compromise computer. UDP port is a good considerate for this sort of attack as the TCP port often be monitored.

6. **Ping of Death:** In this attack long echo packets are forwarded to the victim computer. The amount of bytes received will be higher than the capacity of the input buffer and more memory space is allocated to the received data resulting buffer overflow. As a result of this the operating system kernel gets damaged and the victim computer gets crashed.

Cyber Crimes: The Defence Mechanisms

Many technical defense mechanisms are available to be used, some of these mechanisms are preventives and other mechanisms are recovery and mitigation. However, there is no unique solution to security violations, system penetration and data traffic interception

Law regulations and user awareness are important issues to be considered to enhance the information system protection mechanism. Governments, international organization and the United Nations need to address the issue seriously.

In the above table few classes of cyber crimes, the media used are the internet, email, Facebook, tweeter and mobile. The victim's positive action to prosecute suspects is rare in most cases. The reason behind the negative action is the cost of prosecution, unclear procedure of prosecution nationally and internationally. It is the author's opinion is that leaving the criminals unpunished will encourage more criminals to join and commit more crimes. In spite of the fact the majority of the cyber crimes is rarely reported, official figures indicate an exponential increase in numbers of committed cybercrimes.

It is clear from the above that the technological solution to the cyber crimes is technically available, the author believes that the main problem is the lack of the mechanism to report, investigate and prosecute the suspects. A national web site and consultation forum could help a lot to mitigate the cybercrime problem.

Secure Socket Layer (SSL), Transport Layer Security and Pretty Good Privacy (PGP) and security technology protocols introduced during to mitigate the security risk of internet application threats to certain extent. Using these protocols will enhance the security and privacy level of the internet application.

SSL and later TSL are protocols developed to secure the communications over the internet. The protocols use algorithms. These algorithms are encryption/decryption, public key, error correction code and compression/decompression. PGP is a data encryption and decryption techniques used to offer both authentication and secrecy for email users.

Cyber Crimes Evidences Gathering and Prosecution

From the early eighties of the last century governments and enterprises noticed the need for software to data recovery in general and forensic evidence gathering. Now day cyber forensic software tools are available in the international market. Among the most popular tools are ProDiscover Basic, Access Data Ultimate Toolkit and Guidance Software EnCase. Features available on these tools are data Acquisition, validation, extraction, reconstruction and reporting.

Acquisition involves physical data copy, logical data copy and remote acquisition, validation includes hashing, filtering and analysing file headers. Extracting includes data viewing, keyword searching, decompressing, carving, decryption and bookmaking. Reconstruction includes a disk to a disk copy, an image to a disk copy, a partition to a partition copy and an image to a partition copy. Reporting is the tool used for report writing to summarises the forensic case investigated. (Nelson et al, 2008).

Open source software is also available for free download and use; the available features are limited compared with the professional forensics tools. An example of open source tools is WinHex, features available are hexadecimal editing, deleted file recovery and bootstrap sector copying.

The following is the national and international framework to limit cyber crimes. Responsibility to limit the cyber crimes are shared among the international community, the national governments, media provider and the media users. In Table 2 is the suggested national and international framework to limit cyber crimes.

CONCLUDING REMARKS

It is possible to reduce the number of cyber crimes committed world wide, if national and international serious efforts are deployed. It is the author's opinion that stopping this sort of crimes is not in the agenda of most technology leading counties. Neither western governments on one hand nor china on the other hand are willing to set an end to cyber war, Western governments take advantage of the security weakness of the communications media security and China on the other side get benefit from the communications media security weakness.

It is very difficult to estimate the size of cyber crimes as the number of reported cases is very low compared with the real size of these crimes.

Table 2. The national and international framework to limit cyber crimes

International	Developing the culture of multilateral respect of other countries privacy and security rights. The violation of security and privacy of other nations should be refrained. The privacy of the citizen of another nation should be respected.
	International organizations should take the initiative to organise conferences and forums to establish the culture and awareness of the importance of privacy and security.
	International organizations should support the research and development of the privacy and security over the media.
	International organizations should cooperate in protecting the whole world security and help in making the prosecution of suspects possible regardless of the suspect's nationality.
	Help in engineering the media security to stop further violation of security and privacy.
	Offer the support to the underdeveloped nations to enhance law and regulation of the security of the media
National	Develop a web based and hotline to offer advices, help and support to victims of the cyber crimes
	Cooperate actively with other nations to limit the effect of cyber crimes
	Educate citizen about the risk of media use and navigation
	Establish and publicizes the reporting and prosecuting of cyber crime
	Support victims to limit the effect of cyber crime on victims
	Protect children and aged people from abuse by other media users.
	Regulate the access for the data kept about the citizens
Media Provider	Set regulation to prevent the use of media in crime engineering
	Set regulations in place to limit the unauthorised access of the collected data
	Financial data and the names of current shareholders to be kept transparent
	Offers the mechanism to deal with suspected web sites
Media Users	Be aware that not to believe in the non-realistic offer received through the media
	Not to disclose personal information

It is evident that the size of the problem is beyond the available technical and financial resources of most governments.

Advances in technology will introduce new tools to engineer new types of cyber crimes. Criminalising the interception of data traffic in cyber space high seas will limit the cyber crimes. An international multilateral policy of refrain taken advantages of communications and networking security weakness will enhance the security and develop a universal data security protection culture. Also investigating the possibility of developing a well-structured and well secured internet infrastructure is another possibility to enhance cyber security. Introducing the basic concepts of cyber crime awareness at the school level will enhance the security awareness of people and society. More a prioritised investment in research and development in the field of security and privacy are also recommended.

It is the author's opinion that all types of classical crimes committed by classic mean soon will be committed by cyber tools. The technology of remote control of an embedded computer implanted in a patient's body to control heart betting is available. The technology could be abused to terminate the life of the patient from a distance. A robot could be programmed to commit all sorts of crimes committed now day by human being. This is a new challenge to forensic investigators.

ACKNOWLEDGMENT

The material of this chapter was presented and discussed at an international conference at the British Institute of Technology and E-Commerce, London, 28th August 2013; Colleagues gave excellent feedback comments to enhance the draft of this chapter. The author is grateful for their comments and remarks. However, the material solely reflects the opinion of the author. Comments and remarks of the following colleagues are appreciated:

1. Professor Mohammad Farmer, Director of the British Institute of Technology and E-Commerce.
2. Professor Gill Mitchell, Nano Technology Group, Reading University, England.
3. Professor Gilles Richard, Programme Leader, British Institute of Technology and E-Commerce.
4. Mr Bernardo Devire, LLM programme Leader, British Institute of Technology and E-Commerce.
5. Dr. Brian-Vincent Ikejiaku, LLM Senior Lecturer, British Institute of Technology and E-Commerce.
6. Dr. Abhijit Ganguly, MBA Programme Leader, British Institute of Technology and E-Commerce.

REFERENCES

Al-Saedy, H. (2002). Proofing identity to automatic teller machine – A zero knowledge protocol. In Proceedings of Portsmouth University min conference on computer technology (pp 30-35). Abu Dhabi, UAE: Portsmouth University.

Aybet, J., Al-Saedy, H., & Farmer, M. (2009). Watermarking spatial data in geographic information systems. In H. Jahankhani, A. G. Hessami, & F. Hsu (Eds.), *Global Security, Safety and Sustainability* (pp. 18–26). Berlin Heidelberg, Germany: Springer-Verlag.

Cabinet Office and Detica. (2011). *The Cost of Cyber Crime: A Detica report in partnership with the office of cyber security and information assurance in the cabinet office*. London, UK: Cabinet Office.

Greenwald, G., MacAskilly, E., Poltras, L., & Snowden, E. (2012). *The whistleblower behind the NSA surveillance revelations*. The guardian, Monday 10 June 2013. London. UK: The guardian.

Gurny, M. (2013). *Canada Navy Spy Case*, National Post. Reviewed, 13 August 2013. Canada: National Post.

Home Office. (2010). *Cyber Crime Strategy. Crown copyright*. London, UK: Home Office.

Mackey, D. (2003). *Web Security for Network and System Administrators*. Massachusetts, MA: Course Technology.

McGuire, M., & Dowling, S. (2013). *Cyber Crime: A review of the evidence. Research Report 75, Summery of key findings and implication*. London, UK: Home Office.

Nelson, B., Phillips, A., Enfinger, F., & Steuart, C. (2008). *Guide to Computer Forensics and Investigation* (3rd ed.). Massachusetts, MA: Course Technology.

Newman, R. (2010). *Security and Access Control Using Biometric Technologies*. Massachusetts, MA: Course Technology.

Sanders, C. (2007). *Practical Packet Analysis: Using Wireshark to solve real-world network problems*. California, CA: William Pollock Publisher.

Schneier, B. (1995). *Applied Cryptography: Protocols, Algorithms and Source Code in C*. New York, NY: Wiley.

Snader, J. C. (1994). *Effective TCP/IP Programming*. Reading, MA: Addison –Wesley.

Stalling, W. (2004). *Computer Network with Internet Protocols and Technology*. New Jersey, NJ: Prentice Hall.

Stalling, W. (2011). *Cryptography and Network Security: Principles and Practice*. New York, NY: Prentice Hall.

Swenson, C. (2008). *Modern Cryptanalysis: Techniques for Advance Code Breaking*. New York, NY: Wiley.

Witten, I. H., & Frank, E. (2005). *Data Mining: Practical Learning Tools and Techniques* (2nd ed.). New Jersey, NJ: Elsevier, Morgan Kaufman publisher.

KEY TERM AND DEFINITIONS

Cyber Crime: A conventional crime is a crime committed by conventional means; an example of conventional crimes is theft. Cyber crime is a crime committed by using the cyber media as internet, email and alike. An example of cyber crime is the email scam.

Cyber Security: This is the security of the electronic media like the internet, email, mobile phone and alike. Security includes secrecy and privacy.

Cyber War: This is the war between nations on the cyber space; this includes all types of attacks used to intercept the communications channels as the passive and active attacks, denial of services and spyware viruses.

Digital Forensic: Tools and techniques used in the investigation of cyber crimes. Example of cyber crime is intellectual property theft; an example of forensic tool is Encase.

Global Security: This refers to the security of the whole world; interception of communications channels is a way of interfering with other nation's affairs. Stopping this sort of activity will reduce the possibility of wars.

Identification and Verification: Techniques used to identify and verify individuals, an example of the tools and techniques used for identification and verification is biometric features as photograph and fingerprint.

Privacy: This is the right of individuals to keep personal information private. Regulation, law and constitution regulate the access to the data collected by government about citizens. The citizen also has the right to know about the information and data collected by the government about the citizen.

Chapter 10
Cyber Space Security Assessment Case Study

Hanaa. M. Said
University Ain Shams, Cairo, Egypt

Mohamed Hamdy
University Ain Shams, Cairo, Egypt

Rania El Gohary
University Ain Shams, Cairo, Egypt

Abdelbadeeh M. Salem
University Ain Shams, Cairo, Egypt

ABSTRACT

Cyberspace is known as the digital electronic medium for the knowing range of securing in the cyberspace. Therefore the importance of inferring the reference measure in the form of assessment procedure to improve the knowledge and making the decision for the e- government services. A series of the standards build on the application of data mining methods specifically represented as decision tress model, Logistic regression, association rules model, Bayesian network for making reference measurements, to measure the extent of securing the data, and the provided services. The authors discuss various types of cyber-attacks describing how data mining helps in detection and prevention of these attacks. A comparative analysis between a set of selected frameworks is presented. Finally this chapter imparts numbers of applications for the data mining Methodologies in Cyber Security. Results applied on the site of the authority for cleaning and beautifying Cairo governorate in Egypt.

INTRODUCTION

It is possible materially setting what is known as cyberspace or what is called also the cyberspace as being the electronic digital field extended through the different metallic, lighting and airy communication its channels in the net of the internet network. The extreme speed information with its technological expression, this space is related with its different concepts, that is because the non-availability of geography for the natural

place in the appearance of the geography for the information sailing in the different directions, at the same time that makes this phenomena of the cyberspace of the major features for the information age, it embodies practically the village society through its supposed space of open horizons which puts the human being in a digital world in its foundations and features .The new values talking about the arising of the supposed world as time and place space. They became like the new land as most of the capitals, the modern

DOI: 10.4018/978-1-4666-6583-5.ch010

Copyright © 2015, IGI Global. Copying or distributing in print or electronic forms without written permission of IGI Global is prohibited.

cultural and scientific movement prompted to it, also the means of amenities beside the crimes (Xiong et al, 2009).

The real cyberspace that is available on the internet. It is difficult, to conduct on them the assessment of quality which can be accepted for the extent of securing it. It can be expressed for this real cyberspace as if the series of the minor cyberspaces. Our objective is analysis, study securing one of the minor cyber space's which is the cyberspace for the authority of cleaning and beautifying Cairo, in the Arab Republic of Egypt (www.ccba.gov.eg) to Analysis the extent of the sufficiency for the suggested reasoning to measure the extent of securing data for the cyberspace. It is one of the important cyberspaces in the frame of the mechanism for the e-government services, and its effect on both the citizens, the investors and on the government, this cyberspace is related with

several electronic sites (Varun et al, 2008). The objective is to provide a framework for the system of managing the electronic service that is required to be secured, and which uses the classical means, and utilizing the tools of research for the data to enforce, these services, to provide them through a big set of readings, data, information and facts, discussing them by study, analysis and adapting them to the service of the chapter's objectives to get new services from the government, as it is clear from the Figure 1.

Risks can be caused by the electronic attacks, the role is enhance its scope enlarges in a world in which the internet network become fragile. The development of the programs and computers can be accessed easily, increasing the activity of information hikers who became having a profound experience in the field of the information technology. The field of the danger of those not for being

Figure 1. Site map of the Cairo Cleaning and Beautification Authority (www.ccba.gov.eg).

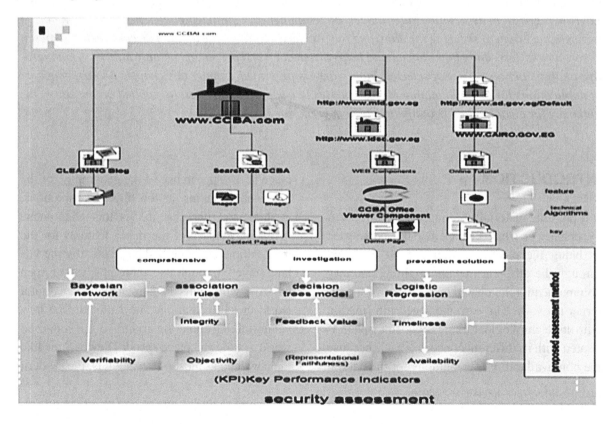

making movements danger and harmful compared with what they say for the existence of ignorance for their ability, meaning the non-predicting with their movements and its results (Verlag et al, 2012). the electronic attacks became as one of the effective ways without large costs, after that the world has become in front of a power equipped with the technology of the computer. They can by pressing the button of penetration and committing harmful technology, deeds against the others through the supposed world of cyberspace (Olivier et al, 2008).

The challenges of the space security that need to be encountered, on terms that the electronic government services that are introduced in need for coherent methodology and automatic one to achieve the space security, to face the threats which the cyberspace face from the group of tricking and spying that affect passively on the government organizations, The people, the infrastructure and on the work rendered by the government.

Dealing with these sites through the research for the data, which requires to fighting terrorism, As the ability to extract the results among the big attack of the data, has its private importance in the early discovery for the terrorist attacks and protection, that requires to study the risks for the different threats, the anti-arrangements, the illegal access to the private data for the explosions and for bombing also the access to this great information, known with the name of the cyber terrorism, Also the nuclear attacks, the biological and chemical attacks, the illegal access to the infrastructure against the gas lines, the electrical energy. The measurements against terrorism for protection against the access to this information, this section shows general view for how searching for the information through the sites can fight terrorism. We will notice that it used the internet network for mining and for the data. The quality of the exchanged data, its definition to extract the required data on the internet, exceeding the mere mining for the organized and exchanged data about the data and sorting the data (Ruben et al, 2012).

To ensure securing the data, protecting the information and the rendered service, it is the indicator for rendering the service of the e-government, making the necessary decision. For expecting the next values for the future, There is need for knowing the extent of verifying securing the data, its correctness, which is the hidden relation between the main indicators of the performance KPI (key performance indicators) data training (Sandeep et al, 2010) The decision maker needs to know what are lost of the data or what can be dependable of this KPI; it is part of the achieved efforts which depend on private ways, including some models of measuring, prediction for fighting terrorism.

The model is asset of the rules. The formulas and the equations that can be used for predicting the result, based on a set of the fields of entry or the variables the model is used to predict and to measure if there is violations or spying or an attack against the data among the possible risks to be good or bad. Based on the information that were known before when moving the data, the ability to predict this result is the central objective from the prediction analysis. And for understanding the process of modeling which is the used key (Sandeep et al, 2010).

Finding the factors affecting on the rate of securing the data, protecting the information, the safety of the government service rendered, which is identifying the difficulties that hinder the execution one of the main cases that encounters the people in charge in the government to achieve the accuracy of the data and the range of its safety, In addition to watching the levels of securing them through collecting the data, analysis and recognizing the major obstacles. That led to reducing the government performance level.

We will use the technology of research for the data thus this chapter shows general vision for how to measure the extent of securing the extraction of the required data through the electronic site, And becoming able to fight the cyber terrorism, As we depended on using a set of the models to measure the extent of the correctness and securing the data (Anirban et al, 2012).

The strategies of "decision tree", "logistic regression", "Bayesian network", and "association rules" are presented and explained in measuring the range of securing the data. Classifying and analysis the data for ensuring the non-violation to offer strategic information for the different rendered services. it enables the governorate for finding the major points for managing the effective government services, any type of the data that must be used, any type of data that has been moved in a proper way, what are the terms or the requirements that are used in the data organizing, arranging the knowledge from the time side or from the view of the priority and importance preform the view of the time for discovering them, compiling the processes based on the followed standards.

These help in choosing between several alternatives, if a violation for the information took place the infrastructure for dividing the knowledge, that will lead to the addition on the available net, on the light of the several made efforts, for the mechanism of this process, to search and analysis the data, testing its safety, In the frame of predicting the obstacles and the threats. It is the reason for applying a set of the models to measure the extent of the data correctness in two stages as the following: The first stage is (hybrid of auto regression and decision trees model), the second is (Bayesian network and association rules) to enable the decision maker about how to interact with the features of the value traits. The tools of extracting the data will be adopted (data mining) and applying them on an actual sample from the government to prove the feasibility of this objective at the same time appears the worldview and the general view for the solution (Chapman et al, 2000).

Data mining has many applications in security including cyber security; the various threats and counter-measures are discussed. In particular, we discussed non information related attacks such as bombings and explosions; information related attacks such as cyber terrorism; biological, chemical and nuclear attacks such as the spread of smallpox; and critical infrastructure attacks such as attacks on power and gas lines. Counter-terrorism measures include ways of protecting from no information related attacks, information related attacks, biological, chemical and nuclear attacks, as well as critical infrastructure attacks in this section we will provide a high level overview of how web data mining as well as data mining could help toward counter-terrorism (Dunham & Sridhar, 2006).

Existing studies on intelligence analysis have focused on analyzing news or forums for security incidents, but few have looked at blogs. We can improve information retrieval in blog search and keywords detection, and provide an analytical foundation for the future of security intelligence analysis of blogs. Information security violations such as access control violations as well as a discussion of various threats are presented. In this chapter we are mostly focused on data mining techniques that are being used for such purposes. We debate on the advantages and disadvantages of these techniques (Verlag & Ur-Rahman, 2012).

The rapid proliferation of blogs in recent years presents a vast new medium in which to analyst and detect potential cyber security threats in the blogosphere. In this chapter, we proposed blog data mining techniques for analyzing blog posts for various categories of cyber threats related to the detection of security threats, cybercrime, and information security (Xiong et al, 2009).

Data mining, popularly known as Knowledge Discovery in Databases (KDD), it is the nontrivial extraction of implicit, previously unknown and potentially useful information from data in databases (Olivier, et al, 2008). It is actually the process of finding the hidden information/pattern of the repositories (Fayyad, 1996).

Classification of data mining frameworks is based on to the type of data source mined. A huge amount of data is available where we need to classify these data, but these are available most of times in a similar fashion (Hoboken, 2005). We discuss a few of the challenges in this section.

Conceptual framework that clarifies the complete context affecting the outcome of a program or intervention, also the frameworks that describe the factors that influence a public- problem and their intervention are used to establish classifications for data mining systems according to different criteria. Conceptual frameworks are used in the sciences to select key variables for analysis. By constructing this kind of analytical frameworks as the foundation within programs are assumed to be designed, planed, and implemented. Monitoring and Evaluation of such programs' performance, real possibilities and limitations become clearer and more structured (Bernstein & Provost, 2001).

Cyber-terrorism is one of the major terrorist threats posed to our nation today. As we have mentioned earlier, there is now so much of information available electronically and on the web. Attack on our computers as well as networks, databases and the Internet could be devastating to businesses. It is estimated that cyber-terrorism could cause billions of dollars to businesses. Note that threats can occur from outside or form the inside of an organization. Outside attacks are attacks on computers from someone outside the organization. We hear of hackers breaking into computer systems. There are hackers who start spreading viruses and these viruses cause great damage to the files in various computer systems. But a more sinister problem is the insider threat. Just like non-information related attacks, there is the insider threat with information related attacks. There are people inside an organization who have studied the business practices and develop schemes to cripple the organization's information assets.

Also this chapter has conducted a comparison study between a number of available data mining frameworks and data classifications depending on their ability for classifying data correctly and accurately. The accuracy measure; the different methods of data mining are used to extract the patterns and thus the knowledge from this variety of data mining system (Flora et al, 2011).

This chapter describes 4 sections; the first section is the introduction as we can be able to get huge information about the literature survey. For assessing the security of the cyberspace the second section classifies how to use a useful technology style in measuring the extent of securing the data classifying and analyses the data to ensuring the non-violation when introducing the strategic information for the different rendered services through the minor cyber service. Moreover the concentrates on the means of research and measurements that are used and suggested How to use them are presented in the section 3. Also presenting the discussions about the different results, finally in section 4 we summarized and conclude the future work.

LITERATURE REVIEW

Data mining is the extraction of hidden predictive information from large databases; it is a powerful technology with great potential to help organizations focus on the most important information in their data warehouses (Campos et al, 2009). Data mining tools predict future trends and behaviors, helps organizations to make proactive knowledge-driven decisions. The automated, prospective analyses offered by data mining move beyond the analyses of past events provided by prospective tools typical of decision support systems. Data mining tools can answer the questions that traditionally were too time consuming to resolve. They prepare databases for finding hidden patterns, finding predictive information that experts may miss because it lies outside their expectations (Han et al, 2011).

Data Mining in Cyber Security is the process of posing queries and extracting patterns, often previously unknown from large related to security issues. Cyber security is the area that deals with protecting from cyber terrorism. Cyber-attacks include access control violations. In addition to improving on data mining and web mining techniques and adapting them for counter-terrorism, they will have to share the data as well as mine the data collaboratively. Here we are investigating ways to monitor the adversaries, for such monitoring to be effective and the monitor must avoid detection by the static and dynamic analyses employed by standard anti-malware packages for developing techniques that can dynamically adapt to new detection strategies and continue to monitor the adversary.

DATA MINING FRAMEWORKS

Frameworks are best understood as useful tools for understanding and analyzing a program. Designing frameworks is one way to develop a clearer understanding of the goals with emphasis on measurable objectives. Developing frameworks also helps to clearly define the relationships among factors key to the implementation and success. These factors may be internal or external to the program context.

Conceptual frameworks are used in the sciences to select key variables for analysis. By constructing this kind of analytical framework as the foundation within which your program will design, plan, and implement the Monitoring and Evaluation of program performance, real possibilities and limitations become clearer to everyone involved.

Conceptual frameworks are sometimes called "research" or "theoretical" frameworks. A conceptual framework is a useful tool for identifying and illustrating a wide variety of factors and relationships that may affect program success. Conceptual frameworks take a broad view of the program itself in order to clarify the relationship of its activities and its main goals to the context in which it operates. The design of the conceptual framework should show the interrelationships between all factors that are relevant to achieving the program's goals. These

factors can be systems, organizations, government or institutional policies, infrastructure, population characteristics, or other features of the operational landscape that may help or hinder the program's success.

Currently, many data mining and knowledge discovery Frameworks and data classification For everyone and different usage such as the Real-time (On line) Environment for Knowledge Analysis RTDMM (Xiong et al, 2009), other Xiong Deng et al, AKDT (Olivier and Marc, 2008), other Olivier Thonnard ET AL, DMCS (Bhavani and Thuraisingham, 2003), other Bhavani M.Thuraisingham, APSO (Sandeep et al, 2010), other Sandeep Rana et al, SCDI (Verleg et al, 2012), other Chandola DI et al L, ITICS, other Kutoma Wakunuma et al, GPLCA (Varun et al, 2008), other Kutoma Wakunuma et al, GPLCA (Baazaoui et al, 2005), Other Ap Jian Zhang1 ET etc. These Frameworks provide a set of methods and algorithms that help in better utilization of data and information available to users; including methods and algorithms for data analysis, cluster analysis, Genetic algorithms, Nearest neighbor, data visualization, regression analysis, Decision trees, Predictive analytics, Text mining, cyber security, Word wide web, Semantic web Data mining argent, Amplification Approach etc.

There are so many number of data mining models (Relational data model, Object Model, Object Oriented data Model, Hierarchical data Model/W data model) are available and each and every model we are using the different data .According to these data model the data mining system classify the data in the model Figure 2 and Table 1 shows the Classification of data mining Frameworks.

This classification must be discussed in detail according to the various frameworks. Classification of data mining frameworks according to the kind of Knowledge discovered and mining Technique are represented in Table 1.

Figure 2. Classification of mining frameworks

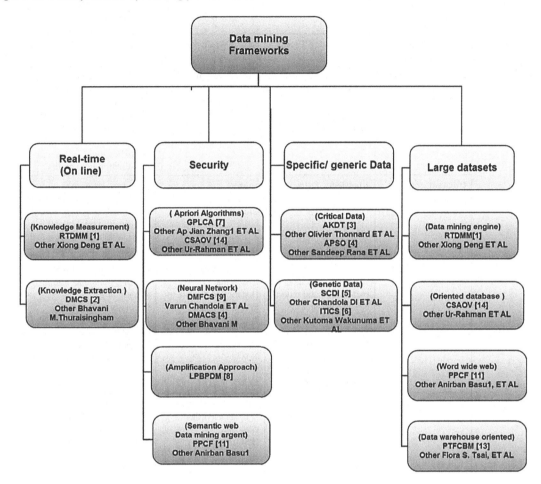

Description of Data Mining Frameworks

In this section, the framework's assumptions and notations will be presented. Moreover we elaborate the survey frameworks which is divided into nine sub-sections including data mining Frameworks tested by clustering, classification, regression, association rules, K-means, hierarchical model, frequently and priori algorithm.

The first step in the methodology consists of selecting a number of available open source data mining Frameworks to be tested. Many open data mining tools are available for free on the Web. After surfing the Internet, a number of Frameworks were chosen; including the Real-time Environment for Knowledge Analysis, Gaussian Process, the Summarization - Compressing Data, and Probabilistic Techniques. Table 2 shows the Frameworks tested using number of Analysis algorithms namely; Association rule Analysis, Classification, real-time, Clustering, Frequency, K-mean and Apriority Algorithms.

DISCUSSION

To make a complete framework we have to take in mind the following challenge many of these challenges cannot be solved by technology alone, but require us to understand the collective social dynamics as roots of problems and key to their solution to avoid Misuse of information Systems, to avoid

Table 1. Classification of data mining frameworks according to the kind of knowledge discovered and mining technique

Classification	Authors Knowledge	Knowledge Types	DM Tasks	DM Techniques/Applications
Support to Real-Time (Online)	(Xiong,et al., 2009)	Knowledge Conversion and Knowledge Measurement Transfer. Knowledge Measurement.	Association rule Analysis Classification real-time	Data Mining Tool Intelligent Miner Data Mining Techniques Association Analysis Sequential Patterns Analysis Knowledge Management System (KMS) for Disease Classification real-time(on line) model
	(Bhavani, et al, 2003)	Knowledge Extraction	online Classification; Clustering	providers database Agglomerative Classification; Principal Component Analysis; real-time(on line) model The Quintile Range Test and Polar Ordination Classification
Support to kDD	(Olivier Thonnard et al, 2003)	Knowledge Sets strings of data, models, parameters, and reports Knowledge Sharing Processes to Corporate Bond Classification first present the generic aspects of a domain-driven graph-based KDD methodology,	Classification Clustering Distance Metric for Frequency Data.	multi-dimensional knowledge discovery and data mining (KDD) methodology Ontology of Knowledge Management and Knowledge Sharing Financial Knowledge Management System (FKMS) Prototype for Financial Research Purposes
	(Sandeep Rana et al 2003)	analysis of data Knowledge Extraction	clustering algorithm K-mean and other classical (PSO)	The most popular clustering algorithm K-mean and other classical algorithms suffer from disadvantages of initial centric selection, Local optima, low convergence rate problem etc. Particle Swarm Optimization
	(Olivier,et al . 2008),	Knowledge Base	Classification	summarization of a dataset The first approach is an adaptation of clustering and the second Approach makes use of frequent item sets from the association analysis domain.
	(Kutoma, et al.2011)	Knowledge Seeding &Knowledge Cultivating	Classification	Extension Theory - Extenics Extension Data Mining (EDM) is combining Extenics with Data Mining

continued on following page

"pathological" collective behavior (panic, extremism, breakdown of trust, Cooperation, Solidarity etc.), to avoid conflicts or minimize their destructive effects, to improve social, environment, and political participation, Despite the substantial contributions that complexity science make in this connection, many of its implications have remained largely theoretical so far. This is basically due to the lack of data, the lack of computational power, and the lack of computationally tested institutional designs in the past. The challenge is to provide solutions to enhance national security but at the same time ensure privacy. There is now research at various laboratories on privacy enhanced sometimes called

Table 1. Continued

Classification	Authors Knowledge	Knowledge Types	DM Tasks	DM Techniques/Applications
Support to Security	(Jian Zhang1 et al 2003)	Knowledge Extraction Knowledge Measurement	modelled using a Gaussian process (GP)	Apriori Algorithms (Association Analysis) framework is significantly more effective in identifying the possible attackers than the currently deployed method
	(Sandeep, R, et al. 2010.),	classification models over randomized data	Apriori Algorithms (Association Analysis) K-means (Cluster Analysis)	Knowledge Extraction new definition of privacy breaches, and developed a general approach, called amplification, that provably limits Breaches. Amplification can be used to limit privacy breaches
	(Varun Chandola et al 2003)	A similarity measure. A data analyst can get a high level understanding of the Characteristics of the data set by analyzing the clusters.	Clustering	network analyst To understand the characteristics of the network traffic First, Cleaning of data has to be performed. Finally, the Data Mining Engine
	(Bhavani M 2003)	Knowledge Base	Classification Clustering	Decision Tree, Neural Network, Early Warning and Proactive, Control Systems (EW&PC) It proposes a technique that can efficiently handle both problems. Our main focus is to adapt three major data mining techniques: classification, clustering, and outlier detection to handle stream data.
	(Anirban Basu1 et al 2008)	Research Assets privacy preserving collaborative filtering Schemes pose challenges with practical implementations on real world cloud computing platforms.	Classification Analysis and collaborative filtering (CF).	Data Mining Agents Reasoning Pattern Recognition Knowledge-based System (KBS) Knowledge and Information Network (KIN) Approach Semantic Web Technologies
	(Ruben Torres et al 2009)	KM Styles & KM Performance	Clustering	Bayesian Network Classifier Rough Set Theory users of generic P2P systems
	(Flora S. Tsai, et al 2011)	Knowledge Sharing Knowledge Graph Knowledge Flows (KFs)	Clustering	Process Mining Technique Knowledge Flow Mining Group-based Knowledge Flows (GKFs) Collaboration and Teamwork Task (Worker's Log & Documents)
	(Ur-Rahman et al 1999)	Textual Databases (Textual Data Formats) Critical systems need to be built on secure foundations,	Dependency Modelling; Clustering	Text mining Clustering Apriori Association Rule Mining Multiple Key Term Phrasal Knowledge Sequences (MKTPKS)

Table 2. Classification of data mining frameworks according to the mining technique

Data Mining Techniques	Clustering	Classification	Regression	Association Rules	K-Mean	Real-Time	Hierarchical Model	Frequently	Priori
RTDMM	√	X	X	√	X	√	X	X	X
AKDT	√	X	X	√	X	X	X	√	X
DMCS	√	√	X	X	X	√	X	X	X
APSO	√	X	X	X	√	X	X	X	X
SCDI	X	√	X	X	X	X	X	X	X
ITICS	X	√	X	X	X	X	X	X	X
GPLCA	√	X	X	√	X	X	X	X	√
LPBPDM	X	X	√	X	X	√	X	√	√
DMFCS	X	√	X	X	X	X	X	X	X
DMACS.	√	√	X	X	√	X	X	X	√
PPCF	√	X	X	√	X	X	X	√	X
CCBS	√	X	X	√	X	X	X	√	X
CSAOV	√	X	X	√	X	X	X	X	√
PTFCBM	√	√	X	X	X	X	X	X	X

privacy sensitive data mining. The challenges include capture, mange, storage, search, sharing, analysis and visualization. The trend to larger data sets is due to the additional information derivable from analysis of a single large set of related data. Allowing correlations to be found to "spot business trends, determine quality of research, prevent diseases, combat crime, and determine real-time roadway traffic conditions, Data mining technologies have advanced a great deal (Tan et al, 2009). They are now being applied for many applications. The main question is, are they ready for detecting and /or preventing terrorist activities? Should we keep in mind the need to avoid socio-environment crises, systemic instabilities, and other contagious Cascade-spreading processes, to design cooperative, efficient, and sustainable socio-technical and environment Systems, to cope with the increasing flow of information, and how to prevent dangers from Malfunctions.

In this chapter has been conducted a comparison between different data mining frameworks for classification purposes. Nine different data sets were used to judge the frameworks tested using number of analysis algorithms namely; Association rule

Analysis, Classification, real-time online, Clustering, Frequency, K-mean and Apriority Algorithms This study has concluded that no framework is better than the other if used for a classification task, since the classification task itself is affected by the type of dataset and the way the classifier was implemented within the on line. However; in terms of classifiers' applicability, we concluded that the real-time {on line) is sufficient Framework for the require in terms of the ability to run the selected classifier followed by Gaussian Process, the Summarization-Compressing Data, and finally Probabilistic Techniques .

Real time Framework has achieved the highest performance improvements as a future research; we are planning to test the selected data mining Framework for other machine learning tasks; such as clustering, using test data sets designed for such tasks and the known algorithms for clustering and association. The future of security intelligence analysis of data mining system, Future applications of this stream of research may include automatically monitoring and identifying trends in cyber security threats that are present in blogs. The system should be able to achieve real-time detection of potential cyber threats by updating the analysis upon the posting of new blog entries. This can be achieved by applying techniques such as folding-in for automatic updating of new blog documents without re computing the entire matrix. Finally the resulting system can become an important tool for government and intelligence agencies in decision making and monitoring of real-time potential international terror threats present in blog conversations and the blogosphere.

CYBER TERRORIST ATTACKS

Various types of cyber terrorist attacks will be discussed and how data mining could detect and perhaps prevent such attacks will be examined:

1. **Non-Information Related Terrorism:** In this section we will provide an overview of various types of non-information related terrorism. Note that by information related terrorism we mean attacks essentially on computers and networks. That is, they are threats that damage electronic information.

2. **Terrorist Attacks and External Threats:** When we hear the word terrorism it is the external threats that come to our mind. .External threats these are threats occurring from the outside. In general, the terrorists are usually neither friends nor acquaintances of the victims involved. But there are also other kinds of threats and they are insider threats. We will discuss them in the next section.

3. **Insider Threats:** Insider threats are threats from people inside an organization attacking the others around them through perhaps not bombs and airplanes but using other sinister mechanisms.

4. **Transportation and Border Security Violations:** Transportation systems security violations can also cause serious problems. Buses, trains and airplanes are vehicles that can carry tens of hundreds of people at the same time and any secu-

rity violation could cause serious damage and even deaths. A bomb exploding in an airplane or a train or a bus could be devastating. Transportation systems are also the means for terrorists to escape once they have committed crimes.

5. **Information Related Terrorism:** This section discusses information related terrorism. By information related terrorism we mean cyber-terrorism as well as security violations through access control and other means. Trojan horses as well as viruses are also information related security violations, which we group into information related terrorism activities.

Cyber-Terrorism, Insider Threats, and External Attacks

Cyber-terrorism is one of the major terrorist threats posed to our nation today. As we have mentioned earlier, there is now so much of information available electronically and on the web. Attack on our computers as well as networks, databases and the Internet could be devastating to businesses. It is estimated that cyber-terrorism could cause billions of dollars to businesses. By crippling the computer system millions of hours of productivity could be lost and that equates to money in the end. Even a simple power outage at work through some accident could cause several hours of productively loss and as a result a major financial loss. Therefore it is critical that our information systems be secure.

Malicious Intrusions

We have discussed some aspects of malicious intrusions. These intrusions could be intruding the networks, the web clients and servers, the databases, operating systems, etc. Many of the cyber terrorism attacks that we have discussed in the previous sections are malicious intrusions. Essentially cyber terrorism includes malicious intrusions as well as sabotage through malicious intrusions or otherwise. Cyber security consists of security mechanisms that attempt to provide solutions to cyber-attacks or cyber terrorism. Money in the real world would translate to information assets in the cyber world. That is, there are many parallels between non-information related attacks and information related attacks.

Credit Card Fraud and Identity Theft

We are hearing a lot these days about credit card fraud and identity theft. In the case of credit card fraud, others get hold of a person's credit card and make all kinds of purchases, by the time the owner of the card finds out, it may be too late. The thief may have left the country by then. Information Security Violations

We provide an overview of the various information security violations. These violations do not necessarily mean that they are occurring through cyber-attacks or cyber terrorism. They could occur through bad security design and practices. Information security violations typically occur due to access control violations. That is, users are granted access depending on their roles which is called role-based access control) or their clearance level (which is called multilevel access control) or on a need to know basis. Access controls are violated usually due to poor design or designer errors. For example, suppose John does not have access to salary data. By some error this rule may not be enforced and as a result, John gets access to salary values. Access control violations can occur due to malicious attacks also. That is, someone could enter the system by pretending to be the system administrator and delete the access control rule that John does not have access to salaries. Another way is for a Trojan horse to operate on behalf of the malicious users and each time John makes a request, the malicious code could ensure that the access control rule is bypassed.

Security Problems for the Web

There are numerous security attacks that can occur due to the web. We discuss some of the web security threats in this section. Note that while we have focused on web threats in this section, the threats discussed are applicable to any information system such as networks, databases and operating systems. The threats include access control violations, integrity violations, sabotage, and fraud, denial of service and infrastructure attacks.

Bio-Terrorism, Chemical, and Nuclear Attacks

The previous two sections discussed non-information related as well as information related terrorist attacks. Note that by information related attacks we mean cyber-attacks. Non-information related attacks mean everything else. However we have separated bio-terrorism and chemical weapons attacks from non-information related attacks. We have also given special consideration for critical infrastructure attacks. That is, the non-information related attacks are essentially attacks due to bombs, explosions and other similar activities.

In this section we have only briefly mentioned the various biological, chemical and nuclear attacks. As we have stressed, we are not counter-terrorism experts; nor have we studied the various types of terrorist attacks in any depth. Our information is obtained from various articles and documentaries. Our main goal is to examine various data mining techniques and see how they could be applied to detect and prevent such deadly terrorist attacks (Botia et al, 1998).

Attacks on Critical Infrastructures

Attacks on critical infrastructures could cripple a nation and its economy. Infrastructure attacks include attacking the telecommunication lines, the electronic, power, gas, reservoirs and water supplies, food supplies and other basic entities that

Figure 3. Wheel of security protection; "the security wheel"

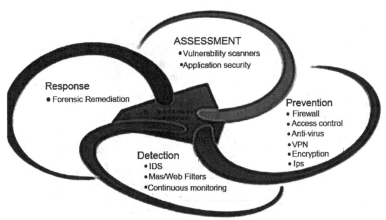

are critical for Attacks on critical infrastructures could occur during any type of attacks whether they are non-information related, information related or bio-terrorism attacks. For example, one could attack the software that runs the telecommunications industry and close down all the telecommunications lines. Similarly software that rules the power and gas supplied could be attacked. Attacks could also occur through bombs and explosives. That is, the telecommunication lines could be attacked through bombs. Attacking transportation lines such as highways and railway tracks are also attacks on infrastructures. Infrastructures could also be attacked by natural disaster such as hurricanes and earth quakes. Our main interest here is the attacks on infrastructures through malicious attacks both information related and non-information related.

Non Real-Time Threats vs. Real-Time Threats

The threats that we have discussed so far can be grouped into two categories; non real-time threats or real-time threats. In a way all threats are real-time as we have to act in real-time once the threats have occurred. However, some threats are analyzed over a period of time while some others have to be handled immediately. There are some other threats that do not have to be handled in real-time.

WHEEL SECURITY PROTECTION

The security protection wheel is a continual process, Used as an effective way to ensure the existence of the suitable measures to protect against the weak security areas and ensuring its working properly, The protection wheel pays an important role in applying the continual operation and the effective one, which includes the security policy, and represented in the 4 sections which are " the protection, the control, The tests, the improvement, to start the running of the protection wheel that takes place first by developing the protection policy that must be discussed as in the Figure 3.

1. Identifying the objectives of protection in the authority.
2. Identifying and documenting the required resources for its protection.
3. Identifying the infrastructure of the net with the plans and the stores.

Figure 4. Key performance indicators

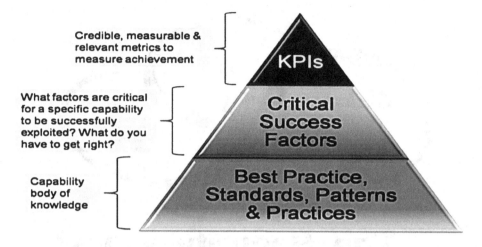

4. Identifying the critical resources that require the protection as resources for the researches and the financial and human resource

After developing the policy of protections, it will be made as the dimension for the protection wheel around which runs 4 branches including" the protection, the control. The experimental tests or the improvements, as it starts by planning for the preventive protection applying the fixation and preparing the arrangements for protection then for controlling, the testing then Improvement thus returning to the protection will take place, etc.

Proposed Assessment Method

As long as all the people follow the security protection wheel in the cyberspace thus we need to work assessment method that coincidence with the security protection wheel to achieve the concepts of research for the data. And that the assessment method is based on the basic concepts for the tests, with the objective of achieving the (assessment) for the extent of securing the data key performance indicators quality assessment.

Which are indicators for the main performance (KPI), (they are measurements that can be assessed quantity) that were approved in advance and reflect the different factors of success for the rendered

services through the minor cyberspace and will differ depending on the cyberspace whatever the measurements key the indicators of performance will be tested, and they must reflect the objectives of the cyberspace and that the indicators of performance must be the key for success we must know what are the standards of measurement. How to measure, and to achieve certain that the major performance indicators may change with the change of the objectives of the cyberspace. Or can be closer to achieve the objective .we can find in the Figure 4 that (KPI) represents how to use them methodology of safety and the standards that will be applied. in this chapter we are caring with two dimensions of measurement: they are (completely and correctness) completely covers asset of standards that cover and measure the security protection wheel for the basic features, and express about (KPI), (correctness) which is the extent for this to be the standards that assess the hypothesis of measuring the correctness and the adequacy.

In the Figure 5 we show the site map for the cyberspace site for the authority of beautifying Cairo (www.ccba.gov.eg). and how to use the props methodology with the cyber to measure the range of securing the data, knowing the points of weakness in the site, till we can correct them, By using the method for assessment.

Figure 5. Proposed model method assessment

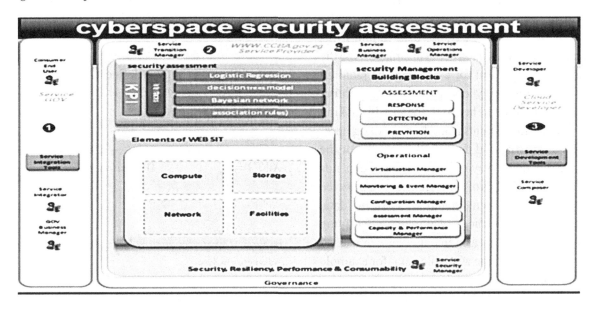

Figure 6. The proposed model

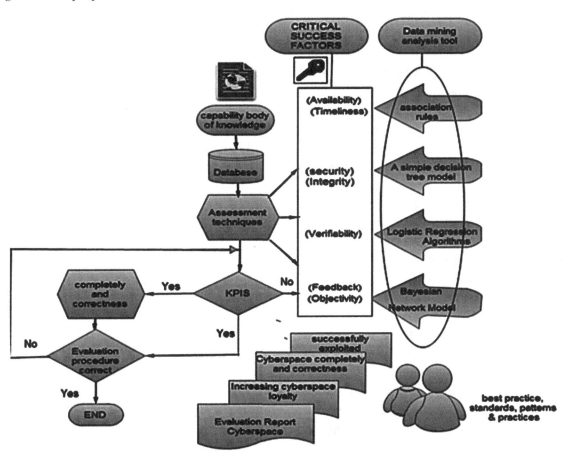

We will use how strategy of inferring. Analyze the data, searching for them in the cyberspace by one of the technology tools (data mining) this chapter shows the vision of the insurance. And the general arrangement for extracting the required data, through the cyberspace, enabling fighting terrorism to limit the harms in advance by making the relief arrangements from the view of comprehensive security and through the analysis of the results for the survey of the data . as it depends on using the models of measurement to assess the extent of the correctness and safety of the data, identifying the methods of research identifying the standards of measurements that can exceed the limitations of the available data, for example using the proposed model in the Figure 6 .

To measure the extent of the data correctness for the cyberspace, and that the infrastructure for the propped model for the cyberspace for the authority of beautifying Cairo, as the model will be built in steps represented in 2 states as the following

- **The First Stage:** Hybrid of auto regression and decision trees.
- **The Second Stage:** Bayesian network and association rules to enable the decision maker how to interact with the features of the traits of the value. And the extraction tools for the data will be adapted with data mining as it is shown in the Figure 7.

Testing and Verification of Availability (Availability) and (Timeliness) Using Association Rules

The terminology of availability is used also in the communications meaning the degree at which the cyberspace works in abiding state. Usually represents the fraction like, 9998 for the simple available A, It is the percentage of the expected value in the state of working and the stopping time (time down,)

$$A = \frac{E[UPtim]}{E[UPtim] + E[Downtim]}$$

As follows: x (t) if you define a function Status

$$1 = sys\ Function\ at\ Tim\ t$$

$$X(T) = \begin{cases} 1 \\ 0 \end{cases} \qquad 0 = otherwise$$

Table 3. Titrated measure how secure the minor cyberspace key

Define The Cyberspace Key	Cyberspace Key
Define it the continuous operation of the system which need different levels of availability.	Availability
The available information for the user must be in the suitable time not in late time with which will be difficult to utilize them.	Timeliness
It means the ability of the information to help the decision maker to make the procedures of prediction and correcting them.	Feedback Value
The information must be in safety and secured form and free of any intended tricking- using security policy for the information (protection).	Security (Representational Faithfulness)
Being far from the personal estimations and depending on the trusted evidences.	Objectivity
It means the existence of high degree of agreement by using similar measuring methods. And attaining the same results by the same accuracy.	Verifiability
Using the policy to guarantee the safety of the information when conducting the necessary measurements to ensure the safety of all the data.	Integrity
Save the data using the backup by using policy and means of storage is available.	Puck Up
Recover data that has been lost for any reason by using the means of storage is available.	Recovery
Achievement of general and complete satisfaction for the operation of the cyberspace.	Agree

Figure 7. Infrastructure cyberspace the Cairo Cleaning and Beautification Authority

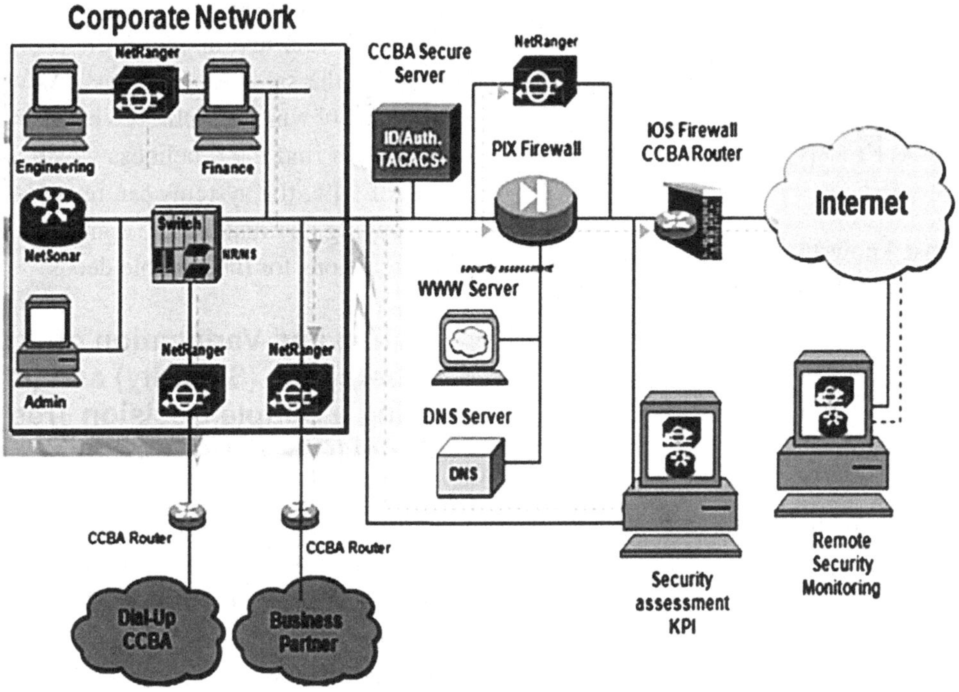

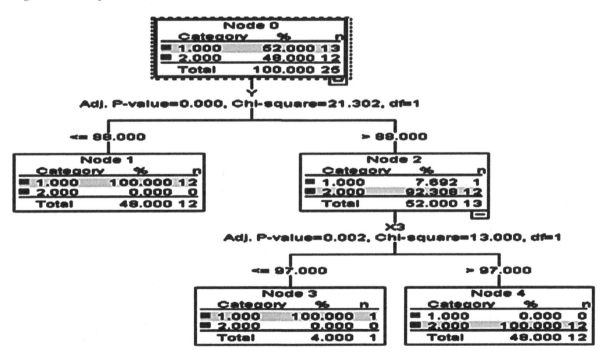

Figure 8. A simple decision tree model

The savings is as:

$$A(t) = \Pr\big|x(t) = 1\big|$$

$$\left\langle E\big|x(t)\big| = X.\Pr\,|\,x(t) = 1\,| \qquad t > 0 \right\rangle$$

And must know the average availability in the on-line and real-time as a static random, the average savings is expressed in the form

$$A_{c=\frac{1}{c}}\int_0^c A(t)dt, \quad c > 0$$

The represents the forbidden availability (steady state) as

$$A = \lim_{t \to \infty} A(t)$$

The average of the availability in the period on the real time line and being considered field and randomly . Then the average of the availability can be expressed in the following Fig

$$A_{\infty = \lim_{c\to\infty} A_c} = \lim_{c \to \infty} \frac{1}{c}\int_0^c A(t)dt \qquad c > 0$$

It is important to follow the state of the protection arrangements for the periodical control, to ensure the remaining of the cyberspace protected with all its effectiveness, as we can eliminate the

Table 4. Field name description

Field Name	Description
Input Variable	$x_{1,x_2,x_3,x_4 x_5}$ & Y
Security Rating	Security rating: 0= attack 1= security
Data Risk	Number of test range of security 1=< 88.00, 0 >88.00

weakness points and identifying the points of taking into consideration the arrangements for the protection and applying the previous equations on the sample of the data. As we find the availability which is achieved by the rate of 96% as we can find the timeliness which achieve the rate of 94%, the systems can reveal and prevent the spying and making the control and applying the reactions for the suitable deeds.

Testing and Verification of Security Cyberspace (Security) and (Integrity) Using a Simple Decision Tree Model (Chaid 1 Algorithms)

Using a simple decision tree model chaid algorithm security rating for classifying the data including the fields of entry or the variables, Decision tree; it is the structure of the tree on the shape of tree branches that represents sets of decisions . These decisions generate rules for classifying the set of the data. It includes limited forms for the branches of the branches, which includes the decision of classification, or the decline, it includes the space of the automatic discovery for the mistakes. See Table 4.

Is the coding Input data (0, 1) and is in the independent variables [x_ (1, x_2, x_3, x_4 x_5) & Y].

When looking to the Figure 8 the upper part of the first node of the tree, it gives us a summary for all the records in the set of the data. We can find the rate of 48% and represents 12 scores only in the cases of the set for the data sample representing the secured data that has protection, with the rate of 52%. And represents 13% scores for the risk and not secured, it needs to improve the performance for protection and security, it is exactly the first part of the analysis, so let us see if each tree can give us any evidence to what are the factors that may be responsible

We can see that the first division is according to the level of the input data. So it will be possible to assign or to determine the scores on terms that the income level in allow class

Table 5. Case processing summary

Data Security		N	Marginal Percentage
Wor	Y	13	52.0%
	No	12	48.0%
Variable	X1	6	24.0%
	X2	11	44.0%
	X3	8	32.0%
Valid		25	100.0%
Missing		0	
Total		25	
Subpopulation		25(a)	
a. The dependent variable has only one value observed in 25(100.0%)			

to (2 node) it is not surprising to see that this classification contains the highest rate of the non-secured data / it is a clear indicator for the data of this class, to contain high risks and needs a solution thus the rate of 52% for the data of this class represents a risk actually, if not supposedly, consequently, the prediction model practically cannot respond but that the model must be good and allow us to expect and to respond more likely for each score based on the available data by the same way if we looked to, the data which the node 2 refers to. We can find that the vast majority (92308%) appears unsecured represents a risk and needs to set a new mechanism security . so can improve the standards of security in this set of data to reduce the risk thus we learned that each score is an indicator for this model. We will identify the points of weakness by assigning certain node. See Table 5.

Assigning the new predictions either good or bad, depending on the most common response for this node, this process is known for assigning the predictions of the individual scores as it is the objective, by recording the same scores that are used for assessing the model. We can assess the extent of accuracy for the training data that know the result, this model is used for the tree of decisions that classifies the scores it's expected the response by using series of rules for taking the decision.

Preliminary Calculations for Verifiability Control Using Logistic Regression Algorithms

In the logistic decline, and that every field accrues two s for each class or the value of original field except for the last class, it is known as the reference class for each score, the value of the field in advance to the class of the attendee will be assigned at 1.0 and all the other fields will be assigned stemmed from the field 0,0 these fields which are derived are called the false fields, it is named the false recoding

For example the following data as x is a symbolic field with the possible value of C, B, A

Record #	X	X1'	X2'
1	B	0	1

In this data the accrue of the original group field, x in the two fields derivate from it is the indicator of the class A X2 is the indicator for the class B the last class IS C is the reference class. the scores which belong to this class equally x1,x2, the group of 0,0 model it found the threat each h score passed through the model of two sides of the logistic decline .

The expected value is calculated, and the degree of reliability. The expected value " the probably $z = 1$ the value of scores and calculated as shown in Table 6.

- Possibility of a "flexible value feedback" and "Objectivity" and "accuracy verifiability."

Table 6. Variable and parameter description

The Following Notation Is Used Through This Stated	
The number of observed cases	N
The number of parameters	P
n x 1 vector with element y .the observed value of the jth case of the dichotomous dependent variable.	Y
n x p matrix with element , the observed value of the ith case of the PARAMETER	X
PX 1 vector with element Bi, the coefficient for the jith parameter	B
n x 1 vector with element w, the weight for the jth case	W
Likelihood function	L
Log – lik lihod function	L
Information matrix	I

Confidence

$$\hat{\pi}_i = \frac{\exp\left(\hat{\eta}_i\right)}{1 + \exp\left(\hat{\eta}_i\right)}$$

$$\hat{\eta}_i = X_i'\hat{\beta}$$

IF $\hat{\pi} > 0.5$, *The predicted value is* 1 : *otherwise, the predicted value is* 0.

Confidence

For records with predicted value of y = 1, the confidence value is $\hat{\pi}$, for records with a predicted value of y = 0, the confidence value is $\left(1 - \hat{\pi}\right)$

$$\sum_{i=1}^{n} w_i \left(y_i - \pi_i\right) x_{ij} = 0$$, for the parameter

where

$x_{i0=1}$ *for* $i = 1, \ldots, n$.

Is the use of kind Newten Rafsson the algorithm for Verifiability? Cannot rely on convergence, the algorithms of Newten Rafsson type is used to get the verifiability/ we cannot depend on the proximity,

- The absolute difference estimated between the frequencies.
- The difference percent in the probability.
- Between the successive frequencies

The maximum limit for the number of the set frequencies to identify the accuracy of the data (verifiability) through the frequency, it is the smallest ranging from 10-8 for all cases. The probability of the occurring of the frequency is very near to zero. The stopping of the frequency or the message, the expectation of all the values either 1-zero and will be issued, getting the maximum limit for the estimates of probabilities and the matrix of the variation is the proxy estimated since before, The reverse of the first information matrix.

As Where: Remark: this example shows how to get the total percent as evidence in designing the model. It can be accuracy. I some cases it may be detective. The original; zero model was 72.6% accuracy in general, Meanwhile that the final model and the expectation to have full accuracy of 79.1% but as we saw, among the accuracy of the predictions the actual individualism of different class to a large scale,

The expected value for the scores is the output class with the biggest value,

Logarithmic Prospects

$$r_{ij} = \log\left(\frac{\pi_{ij}}{\pi_{ij}}\right) = x_i'\beta_j$$

for $j = 1, \ldots, j - 1$. *The* log *it for* reference category j, r, I, is   1.0.

Figure 9. Sample of model fitting information

Model Fitting Information

Model	Model Fitting Criteria	Likelihood Ratio Tests		
	-2 Log Likelihood	Chi-Square	df	Sig.
Intercept Only	34.617			
Final	.000	34.617	8	.000

Pseudo R-Square

Cox and Snell	.750
Nagelkerke	1.000
McFadden	1.000

$$\hat{\pi}_{ij} = \frac{\exp\left(r_{ij'}\right)}{1 + \sum_{k=1}^{i-1}\exp\left(r_{ij'}\right)} = \frac{\exp\left(x_i'\beta_j\right)}{1 + \sum_{k=1}^{i-1}\exp\left(x_i'\beta_k\right)}$$

The Results: it is probably to expect the occurrence of any changes for this classification on terms to calculate the probability of the occurrence for any of the previous standards through the calculation of exp) as it is shown in the table no 6 as we can find that:

1. The least probability for occurrence is 0.390 we find it in the variable of x4& the highest.

Probability for the occurrence is 4.494 we can find it in the variable y.

2. This model is considered a standard and measurement as we find 000= sig. It appears in the Fig 10, if attaching then identifying the possible choices then calculating the probability for all the classes' j in similar data.
3. Testing the flexibility (objectivity feedback value By using the Bayesian network model.

The Bayesian network model provides a brief way to describe the joint probably distribution for certain group of the random variables (x1 x2x3 x4 x5, y) Conditional probabilities for each variable show that the values of the data are divided into proportion to the origin of the node and the similar node, as an alternative for the analysis process, you can use them as an indicator for the evaluative figure to compare the accuracy of the model that was predicted based on the Fig, And is used as an indicator for the process of prediction and the probability to test the flexibility (feedback value and objectivity.)

*   As it is the case with the node of probability. The figure shows that each model produces similar results. but the model(the retrained model) is used for comparison of the data for these standards (the flexibility and objectivity) it is little better because it contains a higher level more than that of the confidence in its prospects,

Table 7. The notation used throughout this algorithm description

A directed acyclic graph	G
A Dataset	D
Target variable	$X_1, X_2, X_3, X_4, X_5, Y$

Figure 10. Sample of expected values

Parameter Estimates

Wor(a)		B	Std. Error	Wald	df	Sig.	Exp(B)	95% Confidence Interval for Exp(B)	
								Lower Bound	Upper Bound
No	Intercept	-174.349	256116.563	.000	1	.999			
	Y	1.503	2034.026	.000	1	.999	4.494	.000	.(b)
	X1	.303	625.467	.000	1	1.000	1.354	.000	.(b)
	X2	-.406	1117.323	.000	1	1.000	.667	.000	.(b)
	X3	1.373	4523.229	.000	1	1.000	3.948	.000	.(b)
	X4	-1.175	2069.738	.000	1	1.000	.309	.000	.(b)
	X5	.026	1861.721	.000	1	1.000	1.026	.000	.(b)
	[Gra=1.000]	14.383	35793.597	.000	1	1.000	1764094.730	.000	.(b)
	[Gra=2.000]	33.400	54032.791	.000	1	1.000	320059604887103.000	.000	.(b)
	[Gra=3.000]	0(c)	.		.	0	.	.	.
a. The reference category is: Y.									
b. Floating point overflow occurred while computing this statistic. Its value is therefore set to system missing.									
c. This parameter is set to zero because it is redundant.									

Figure 11. Bayesian network

- We can suppose that v forms a set of the classy random variables and that v=g e the Fig will be continual ring so we can find the direction of the node v and a set of the directive edges

- The model of Bayesian network consists of the Fig G besides the table of THE conditional probability for each specific node of the original node value

- Thus it will be possible to calculate the joint probable distribution for the random variables in the shape OF V AS producer for the conditional probabilities for all the nodes, due to the value of each node,

- A set of variables is given in the shape of V and a sample of the adjacent data as it is clear in the Figure 9 the Figure 11.Which shows the presentation of the task for installing the Bayesian network model. It is called for identifying the edges of the Fig the structural building for the e variables,

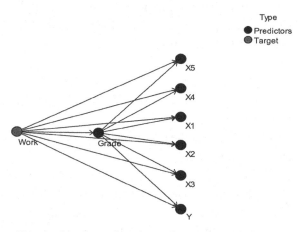

Figure 12. Sample of conditional probabilities of grade

Parents	Probability		
Work	1	2	3
1	0.38	0.31	0.31
2	0.08	0.58	0.33

By returning to the Figure 11 and the Table 9 we find that the probability of the occurrence for the flexibility (the flexibility and the subjectivity) when decoding the random variables x1, x2, x3, x4, x5, y and giving them one of the 2values (0,1) at 3 levels.

- The probably for the occurrence of the flexibility is the non, 38% in the first case.
- The probability of the occurrence of the non-objectivity which is, 58% in the first case.

The Figure 13 shows the probability and the expectation for the 3 dimensions and the distance that contains "v". random probabilities as it shows the dark blue color for non-probability of the occurrence for which the measurement is run and the light blue color which achieves the probability of the occurrence for the event, the Table 8 shows the probabilities and the expectations for the 3 dimensions and the distances

$$I\left(X_{i,}X_{j}\right)=\sum_{X_{i,}X_{j}}P_{r}\left(X_{i,}X_{j}\right)Log\left(\frac{P_{r}\left(X_{i,}X_{j}\right)}{P_{r}\left(X_{i}\right)P_{r}\left(X_{j}\right)}\right)$$

We start by replacing the information exchanged between the two predictors with the information exchanged between the two conditional predictions given the goal and know it.

$$I\left(X_{i,}X_{j}\mid y\right)$$
$$=\sum_{X_{i,}X_{j}}P_{r}\left(X_{i,}X_{j,}y_{k}\right)Log\left(\frac{P_{r}\left(X_{i,}X_{j}\mid y_{k}\right)}{P_{r}\left(X_{i}\mid y_{k}\right)P_{r}\left(X_{j}\mid y_{k}\right)}\right)$$

We can build the network by using the calculation between each pair of the variables by using the algorithms for building as the maximum level As it starts with the extended tree with the non-existence of the edges and the signs of the random variable as an approach, then will be found the variable of the non-controller, which its weight with one of the observable is the maximum limit.

Table 8. Possibilities and expectation triple dimensions and distances

Point Type	X	Y	V4
order set	0	0.7778	Grade
scale	0	6.2222	Bias
scale	0	5.4444	Y
scale	0	4.6667	X3
scale	0	3.8889	X5
scale	0	3.1111	X1
scale	0	2.3333	X2
scale	0	1.5556	X4
scale	1	5.25	Bias
scale	1	3.5	Hidden layer activation: Hyperbolic tangent Output layer activation: Soft max
scale	1	1.75	Hidden layer activation: Hyperbolic tangent Output layer activation: Soft max
set	2	3.5	Work

Figure 13. Predictor space

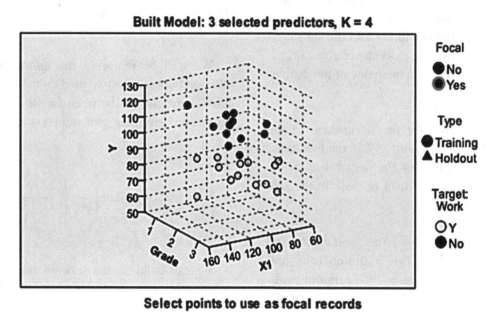

Table 9. Report of the proposed procedure modeling

The Factors	Achieve Percent	Percent Did Not Achieve
Availability	96%	Limited
Timeliness	94%	Limited
Security (Representational Faithfulness)	Limited and Poor	92.308%
Feedback Value	48%	52%
Objectivity	91.7%	0.58%
Verifiability	72.6%	Limited
Integrity	92.3%	Limited
Puck Up and Recovery and Agree	• We did not use these means and Measure the achieved and tested. • A future and we will supplement and follow-up research in this area	
Observation	We find that the Security needs to be improved and up gradation	

Figure 14. Sample of photos of the possibilities of the variable

Conditional Probabilities of X2

Parents		Probability				
Grade	Work	< 84.2	84.2 ~ 95.4	95.4 ~ 106.6	106.6 ~ 117.8	> 117.8
1	1	0.40	0.40	0.20	0.00	0.00
1	2	1.00	0.00	0.00	0.00	0.00
2	1	0.00	0.00	0.25	0.25	0.50
2	2	0.00	0.00	0.14	0.14	0.71
3	1	0.25	0.00	0.00	0.50	0.25
3	2	0.00	0.25	0.00	0.25	0.50

Then this variable will coincidence with this variable and adds its edge to the tree. this process is repeated till putting the sign on all the variables with setting standards for the measurement to the indicator of the assessment, so we can find the picture or the shape of the probabilities of the variable x2 which is shown clearly in the Figure11 as the following.

We can find in the Figure 14 cases for the probabilities as the following " in the first case the highest rate for the probability of the occurrence for the objectivity.40% and the second case with 1,% and the third case is 50% and the fourth case is,71% and the fifth case is 50% and the sixth case is 50%:

The Figure 15 shows the probabilities and the expectations that can build the net by using the non-directive tree for the result into one of the outputs, then choosing the node of the root and identifying the direction from all the edges to be outside it for each variable of the random variables, for the several predictions and the probabilities that can written or recorded to become indicator for the measurement,

In this tactic we find several results for the occurrence that appear better largely. Several if the degree of decline is < 0.998, or better, it is an encouraging matter, to ensure the improvement in

Figure 15. Sample of shows the variables and the average rating correct proportions

Classification for Work

Overall Percent Correct = 92.0%

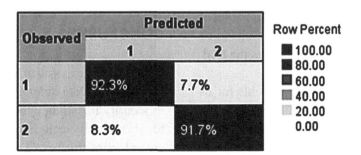

the model of analysis the classes then operating this technology to enable making the comparison between 2 or more models of the same type, the analytical output that indicates that the function of the Bayesian network can predict properly the rate of 97,85% from the cases that are still very good .

ANALYSIS OF THE RESULTS

Finally we can find in this chapter that the cyberspace needs to be improved and to enhance its sufficiency and taking the necessary arrangements to raise the efficiency of the security. As the data is exposed for the occurrence of violations at the rate of 92,308& we can find that (timeliness& integrity &objectivity availability were achieved by high rate of 91.7%, 72,6% 92,3% and we find that the (feedback value was achieved at the rate of medium. We find that the maximum limit for the number of the frequencies that are identified to set the accuracy of the data the less probability (verifiability) for occurrence, 309, we find it in the variable x4& and the highest probability for * verifiability) occurrence is 4.494 its clear in the Table 9.

Despite the above mentioned the table shows the outputs of the previous table as the function of assessment was of several values. And the expectation of diagnosing in each one case in correct and standardized shape. But in practicing it was not preferred to see the accuracy with 100%, but you can use the assistant analysis in identifying if the model of accurate and acceptable for the application of the cyberspace actually, or that there no other type of function or of sins nor linear that can apply, however with the set of different data, it is possible for the results to be easily different thus always it worthies the trial, with full set of choices,

We find also that it was not possible for us to use means of measurement for the extent if achieving some standards and testing them among those of the above mentioned in which is using

the policy of the pickup related with maintaining the data by using the policy of the relief coping by using means of secured storing using the policy of (recovery) related with retrieving the data that were lost for any reason by using the means the secured storing. The policy of the acceptable using (agree) related with achieving the satisfaction and the completeness when operating the cyberspace.

In the future we will complete and follow up the research in this field. Using the research for the data to be an active way in making the decision, it is expected in several cases what are the challenges that will be faced when operating and developing the system. According to this it will be possible to avoid several complaints by the users, it is clear that signing on all the challenges before facing them is impossible since the citizens used the technology, and that in several regions of the environment and the culture in the subsystems of the cyberspace, in the urban places, they must respond quickly and with sensitivity from the citizens to change the look to the gap between the objectives, and the actual achievements, the total, indicators for a long period of time, it is taken for granted that preparing or how to use the means of research measurements and testing the security of the data that are submitted recently and effective for the cyberspace may help in identifying the important indicators and the useful ones, from the practical side in addition to that I see that 3the government or any other system needs a new technology or modern ones to include the following up and knowing the challenges that face the cyberspace, and automatically identifying the directions of the used electronic security threats.

CONCLUSION

Cyberspace is exposed to the number of attacks at a rapid pace, Data mining has many applications in security including cyber security The threats to cyber security include attacking and destroying critical infrastructures Data mining techniques are being used to identify suspicious individuals and groups, and to discover which individuals and groups is concerned with protecting computer and network systems from corruption due to malicious software including Trojan horses and viruses. Data mining is also being applied to provide solutions and Predicting the Cyber Security Threats such as intrusion detection and auditing. In this chapter we focused mainly on data mining for cyber security applications.

Cyberspace Is like a battleground new of a threat added to the list of traditional threats facing the world, exceeding in its dimensions and its geographic and political boundaries, and receive repercussions on the future of national security and vital for States, Became the operations of penetration by the "hackers" capable of dumping hardware servers, computers with messages from multi-d systems of paralyzing functioning and stopped production systems.

This chapter presented many of the techniques and treatments and research topics based on the data available on the technologies of many government services and contemporary home depending on where these techniques work in different countries, and these institutions need to be large numbers of data relied upon by officials at the regulatory decision-making through the data sources involved in strategic decision-making through data storage, which has a value.

This chapter has been conducted a comparison between different data mining frameworks for classification purposes. Nine different data sets were used to judge the frameworks tested using number of analysis algorithms namely; Association rule Analysis, Classification, real-time online, Clustering, Frequency, K-mean and Apriority Algorithms This study has concluded that no framework is better than the other if used for a classification task, since the classification task itself is affected by the type of dataset and the way the classifier was implemented within the on line. However; in terms of classifiers' applicability, we concluded that the real-time {on line) is sufficient Framework for the require in terms of the ability to run the selected classifier followed by Gaussian Process, the Summarization - Compressing Data, and finally Probabilistic Techniques .

Real time Framework has achieved the highest performance improvements as a future research; we are planning to test the selected data mining Framework for other machine learning tasks; such as clustering, using test data sets designed for such tasks and the known algorithms for clustering and association. The future of security intelligence analysis of data mining system, Future applications of this stream of research may include automatically monitoring and identifying trends in cyber security threats that are present in blogs. The system should be able to achieve real-time detection of potential cyber threats by updating the analysis upon the posting of new blog entries. This can be achieved by applying techniques such as folding-in for automatic updating of new blog documents without re computing the entire matrix. Finally the resulting system can become an important tool for government and intelligence agencies in decision making and monitoring of real-time potential international terror threats present in blog conversations and the blogosphere.

The domain experts are required to determine the variety of data that should be collected in the specific problem domain, selection of specific data for data mining, cleaning and transformation of data, extracting patterns for knowledge generation and finally interpretation of the patterns and knowledge generation. Most of the domain specific data mining applications show accuracy above 90%. The generic data mining applications are having the limitations. From the study of various data mining applications it is observed that, no application called generic application is 100% generic. The intelligent interfaces and intelligent agents up to some extent make the application generic but have limitations. The domain experts play important role in the different stages of data mining.

The decisions at different stages are influenced by the factors like domain and data details, aim of the data mining, and the context parameters. The domain specific applications are aimed to extract specific knowledge. The domain experts by considering the user's requirements and other context parameters guide the system.

The results yield from the domain specific applications more accurate and useful. Therefore it is conclude that the domain specific applications are more specific for data mining. From above study it seems very difficult to design and develop a data mining system, which can work dynamically for any domain In addition to improving on data mining and web mining techniques and adapting them for counter-terrorism, we also need to focus of federated data mining. We can expect agencies to collaboratively work together. They will have to share the data as well as mine the data collaboratively. We can expect to see an increased interest in federated data mining. In this Research we have discussed just the high level ideas. We need to explore the details.

So that we can edit and manage and decision-making that is based on large numbers of data is indispensable for the use of techniques that include data processing may become unsuitable for use systems in many areas, this research suggests a number of emerging applications for cyberspace Special General Authority for cleanliness and beautification of Cairo and the methods to search for data in cyberspace Mutual extract the required data on the Internet and beyond the organization of data mining or exchanged between the data search and sort the data.

Determine the motive behind this research on the importance of data mining and its impact on cyber security on the Internet, and mining, in the presence of terrorism in the camera cyberspace, And is one of the terrorist threats Home facing our nation today, Which contribute to future research through the transaction, which relies heavily on the availability of the elements of safety and reliability systems contemporary as well as special abilities of this research approach in the field of image capture satellite remote.

FUTURE WORK

Future analysis of security intelligence system of analysis and data mining, and applications of the means of measuring the future of this flow of research may include monitoring and automatically identify trends in security threats online that are present in cyber. System should be able to achieve detection in real-time cyber threats possible by updating the analysis and loose were asked measurement. This can be achieved through the application of techniques such as automatic update of the means of measuring new and will be combined in more than one direction in the future of the concept proposed with modeling techniques to approach automatic so that the system is able to automatically detect and reduce risk management.

The future work would require the ability to reach a better decision through adaptive analysis. Through an in-depth analysis of the results collected from different cyberspace agencies an adaptive dimension to be applied to the cyberspace in order to reach better decision making. We also plan to add more adaptation features to our concept and implement them. Another future direction will be to combine the proposed concept with an automatic techniques modeling approach so that the system is able to automatically detecting and monitoring various types of cyber-attacks and prevention of these attacks

Results of this research are very useful to build a strategy for measuring the extent of securing data in order to improve the management of servants effective government, any type of data to be used, any type of data was transferred in a proper way, Could be this study remarkable as one of the first studies on the use of data mining tools in Cyberspace.

Finally, this chapter could become an important tool for the government and intelligence agencies in the decision-making and monitoring potential international terrorist threats in real time present at the talks and research and blogging.

REFRENCES

Anirban, B., Jaideep, V., Hiroaki, K., Theo, D., & Srijith, K. (2012). Privacy preserving collaborative filtering for SaaS enabling PaaS clouds. In *International Conference on Quality Software-QSIC 2003*. Retrieved from http://www.journalofcloud-computing.com/content/1/1/8

Baazaoui, Z., Faiz, S., & Ghezala, H. (2005). A Framework for data mining based multi-agent: An application to spatial data. In *Proceedings of World Academy of Science, Engineering and Technology* (volume 5, April 2005).

Bernstein, A., & Provost, F. (2001). An Intelligent Assistant for the Knowledge Discovery Process", Working Research of the Center for Digital Economy Research, New York University and also presented at the IJCAI, *2001 Workshop on Wrappers for Performance Enhancement in Knowledge Discovery in Databases*.

Bhavani, M., & Thuraisingham, Q. (2003). Data mining and cyber security. In International Conference on Quality Software - QSIC

Botia, J., Garijo, M., Velasco, J., & Skarmeta, A. (1998). A Generic Data mining System basic design and implementation guidelines. Retrieved from http://citeseerx.ist.psu.edu/viewdoc/summary?doi=10.1.1.53.1935

Cairo Cleaning and Beautification Authority. (2004). *Cairo Cleaning and Beautification Authority Website*. Retrieved from http://www.ccba.gov.eg/Default.aspx

Campos, M., Tengard, P., & Boriana, L. (2009). *DataMining*. Retrieved from www.oracle.com/technology/products/bi/odm/pdf/automated_data_mining_paper_1205

Chapman, P., Clinton, J., Kerber, R., Khabaza, T., Reinartz, T., Shearer, C., & Wirth, R. (2000). CRISP-DM 1.0: Step-by-step data mining guide. Denmark: NCR Systems Engineering Copenhagen.

Dunham, M., & Sridhar, S. 2006. Data Mining: Introductory and Advanced Topics. New Delhi, India: Pearson Education.

Fayyad, U., Piatetsky, G., & Smyth, P. (1996). From Data Mining to Knowledge Discovery in Databases. *AI Magazine, 17*(3).

Flora, S., Tsai, Y., Kap, L., & Chan, (2011). *Probabilistic techniques for corporate blog mining*. School of Electrical & Electronic Engineering, Nanyang Technological University, Singapore.

Han, J., Kamber, M., & Jian, P. (2011). *Data Mining Concepts and Techniques*. San Francisco, CA: Morgan Kaufmann Publishers.

Kutoma, W., & Yingqin, Z. (2012). Intelligence techniques in computer security and forensics: At the boundaries of ethics and law. *Computational Intelligence for Privacy and Security, 394*, 237–258.

Larose, D. (2005). *Discovering Knowledge in Data: An Introduction to Data Mining*. Hoboken, NJ: John Wiley & Sons, Inc.

Olivier, T., & Marc, D. (2008). Actionable knowledge discovery for threats intelligence support using a multi-dimensional data mining methodology. In *IEEE International Conference on Data Mining* Workshops.

Ruben, T., Marco, M., Maurizio, M., Munafo, S., & Rao, G. (2012). *Characterization of community based-P2P systems and implications for traffic localization*. Springer Science+Business Media.

Sandeep, R., Sanjay, J., & Rajesh, K. (2010). *A review on particle swarm optimization algorithms and their applications to data clustering.* Springer Science+Business Media.

Tan, P., Steinbach, M., & Vipin, K. (2009). Introduction to data mining. *New International Journal of Computer Science, Engineering and Information Technology, 2*(3).

Two Crows Corporation. (1999). *Introduction to Data Mining and Knowledge Discovery* (3rd ed.). Potomac, MD: Two Crows Corporation.

Ur-Rahman, H. (2012). Cyber Security: Assessing Our Vulnerabilities and Developing an Effective Defense. In C. S. Gal, P. B. Kantor, & M. E. Lesk (Eds.), ISIPS 2008 (LNCS 5661, pp. 20–33).

Varun, C., Eric, E., Levent, E., Gyäorgy, S., & Vipin, K. (2008). Data Mining for Cyber Security. In *IEEE/IFIP International Conference on Embedded and Ubiquitous Computing.*

Xiong, D., & Moustafa, M., Ghanem, & Yike, G. (2009). Real-time data mining methodology and a supporting framework. In *International Conference on Network and System Security* (pp. 522-527).

Chapter 11
Biometric Security

Muzhir Shaban Al-Ani
Anbar University, Iraq

ABSTRACT

The terms biometrics and biometry have been used to refer to the field of development of statistical and mathematical methods applicable to data analysis problems in the biological sciences. Recently biometrics refers to technologies and applications applied for personal identification using physical and behavioral parameters. Biometric security systems ensuring that only the authorized persons are permitted to access a certain data, because it is difficult to copy the biometric features pattern for a specific person. Biometrics is playing an important role in applications that are centric on identification, verification and classification. This chapter focuses on biometric security in their types, specifications, technologies and algorithms. Some algorithms of biometric security are also included in this chapter. Finally latest and future aspects of biometric system and merging technologies are also mentioned, including more details of system structures and specifications and what constitution will shape biometric security of in the future.

INTRODUCTION

Biometrics technology is the science and technology of measuring and analyzing biological data. In information technology, biometrics refers to technologies that measure and analyze the characteristics of human body, such as DNA, fingerprints, eye retinas and irises, voice patterns, facial patterns and hand measurements, for identification and authentication purposes.

The oldest effective characteristic that is used for recognition by humans is the face. Since the beginning of civilization, humans have used faces to identify objects and individuals. Other characteristics have also been used for individual recognition such as fingerprint, footprint ...etc. True biometric systems began to appear in the latter half of the twentieth century, by the time of the growth of computer systems. This field experienced and explosion of activity in the 1990s and began to surface in everyday applications in the early 2000s.

Information security is concerned with the assurance of confidentiality, integrity and availability of information in all forms. Many tools and techniques can support the management of information security. But biometric authentication system has evolved to support some aspects

DOI: 10.4018/978-1-4666-6583-5.ch011

Copyright © 2015, IGI Global. Copying or distributing in print or electronic forms without written permission of IGI Global is prohibited.

of information security. Biometric authentication supports the directions of identification, authentication and non-repudiation in information security.

A biometric is a general term used to describe a measurable physiological and/or behavioral characteristic that can be applied for automated recognition. A biometric system provides an automated method of person is recognizing based on the individual's biometric characteristics. Biometric modalities commonly implemented or studied biometrics patterns include fingerprint, face, iris, voice, signature, vein pattern, and hand geometry. Many other modalities are implemented in various stages of development and assessment (Ross et al, 2006).

Now a days the combination of biometrics and security leads to highlighting of a new modern field with huge application in everyday life. This chapter will concentrate on the theory and applications of using biometrics in security that is stronger in the merging of these two fields to generate new more applicable secure systems.

BACKGROUND OF BIOMETRIC SECURITY

Biometrics as a Key of Security

Biometrics technology is not a new concept; it is the oldest form of identification. As early as the 14th century, the Chinese were reportedly using fingerprint-like methods as a method of identifying of their children.

There are three basic, independent but related concepts of security (Jain et al, 1999):

- **Concept of Identification:** Who you are.
- **Concept of Authentication:** Proving whom you are.
- **Concept of Authorization:** What you are allowed to do.

Recently, huge data transfer all over the word every day, therefore identity theft and the loss of data and related intellectual property are growing problems. Now each have multiple accounts and use multiple passwords on an ever-increasing number of computers and Web sites. Maintaining and managing access while protecting both the user's identity and the computer's data and systems has become increasingly difficult. Security is the concept of authentication - verifying that the user is who he claims to be. Biometric based authentication applications refer to three types of authentication (Delac & Grgic, 2004).

- Something you know (most common used is a password or pin)
- Something you have (tokens such as a smart card), and finally
- Something you are (such as biometric).

Requirements for the Biometric Characteristic

In the development of biometric authentication systems, physical and behavioral characteristics for recognition are required many factors (Goswami & Chan, 2011; Scott & Nowak, 2004):

- **Uniqueness:** Dispose of biometric features, which are as unique as possible.
- **Universality:** Occur in as many people as possible.
- **Permanence:** Biometric features do not change over time.
- **Measurability:** Measurable with simple technical instruments.
- **User Friendliness:** Easy and comfortable to measure.

Biometric features can be described using five qualities (Anil & Chen, 2004):

- **Robustness:** The biometric characteristic should be stable over the time.

- **Distinctiveness:** The biometric characteristic should show great variation over the population (clearly recognize).
- **Availability:** The entire population should ideally have the measured biometric characteristic.
- **Accessibility:** The biometric characteristic should be easily acquired using sensors devices.
- **Acceptability:** The process of acquiring biometric measurement should be easy and user friendly.

Biometric Recognition System Components

A biometric recognition is a general term used to describe a measurable physiological and/or behavioral characteristic that can be used for automated individual recognition. A biometric system provides an automated method of recognizing an individual based on the individual's biometric characteristics. The biometric recognition system as shown in figure 1 must consists of the following

main parts (Gamboaa & Fred, 2004 ; Jain et al, 2004; Tripathi, 2011):

- **Sensor:** Converts the biometric characteristics into electrical signal and then into digital data.
- **Preprocessor:** Enhances the digital data and removes the noise to generate adequate data that are ready for processing.
- **Feature Extractor:** Represents the main part of the system to extract biometric features that are mainly used for recognition.
- **Template Database:** Stores the biometric data that are used for personal identification.
- **Matcher:** Makes a decision to certify between the enrollment and authentication data.

Biometric Data Entry

To extract the biometric features, the biometric data must be passes via a biometric devices consist of; a reader or scanning device, software that

Figure 1. Biometric recognition system

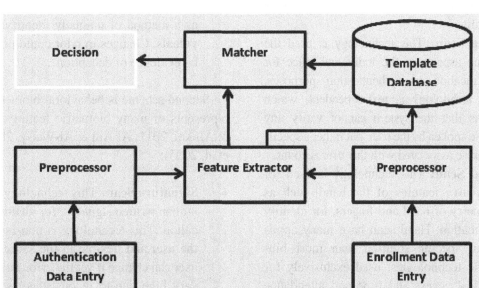

converts the scanned information into digital form and a database that stores the biometric data for comparison. To justify biometric data, we can say that there are two types of biometric identification schemes:

First scheme is Physiological Biometrics that represents of many biometrics (Tripathi, 2011; Baca et al, 2007; Julian, 2000):

- **Finger Scan:** This technology is used for unique fingerprint patterns present on the human finger to identify or verify the identity of the individual and this technology is very popular in the field and delivers high accuracy levels.

- **Facial Scan:** This technology is used for both authentication and identification. This technology is based on the analysis of facial features and it can be easily integrated in an environment that already uses image acquisition equipment.

- **Iris Scan:** This technology is based on using the unique features of the human iris for identification and authentication. This technology has been successfully implemented in ATMs and airports …etc. This technology promises high levels of accuracy and stability over the individual's lifetime.

- **Voice Scan:** This technology is used the unique aspects of the individual voice for identification or authentication purposes. This technology is text-dependent, which means that the system cannot verify any phrase spoken by the user, but rather a specific phrase associated with that user account.

- **Hand Scan:** This technology is used for distinctive features of the hand, such as geometry of hand and fingers, for identity verification. Hand scan have many application specific solution than most biometric technologies, used exclusively for physical access and time and attendance applications.

- **Retina Scan:** This technology is used for the distinct features of the retina for identification and authorization. It is considered one of the least used technologies in the field of biometrics, almost only used in highly classified government and military facilities and this technology delivers very high levels of accuracy.

- **DNA Matching:** A relatively new technology that relies on the analysis of DNA sequences for identification and authentication. The technology raises many concerns over "privacy issues, invasiveness and data misuse.

- **Vein Identification:** This technology uses vein patterns on the back of the hand for identification and authentication and ith has been recently applied in commercial products. This technology has the potential of delivering high accuracy, in addition to the advantage of being non-intrusive to the user.

- **Ear Scan:** This technology is a visual biometric that identify of an individual using the shape of the ear.

- **The Smell Scan:** It is the ability to identify individuals who may intend harm to the nation, the U.S. Department of Homeland Security looked into ways to use body odor as a method of uniquely identifying individuals. Changes in odor could potentially be evidence of deception.

Second scheme is behavioral biometrics that represents of many biometric features (Al-Ani & Al-Ani, 2011; Al-Ani & Al-Waisy, 2011; Jain et al, 2005):

- **Signature Scan:** This technology uses the human written signature for identity verification. This technology is non-invasive to the user and flexible in the sense that the user can change it yet the error rates can be very high due to inconsistencies in one's signature.

- **Keystroke Scan:** This technology uses a person's distinctive typing patterns for verification. This technique is combined with the traditional password scheme for increased security. It does not require any special hardware for data acquisition, since all data is gathered from the keyboard.

- **Gait Recognition:** This technology can be used to monitor people without their cooperation. This technology based on the analysis of the rhythmic patterns associated with walking stride. This is another new concept and it is currently under development.

Biometric Applications

Recently biometric recognition applications grow very fast that introduce in everyday life and most of these applications are concentrated on biometric authentication and security. These applications can be categorized into the following parts (Olzak, 2011; Xiao, 2010; Congdon, 2010):

- **Forensic Applications:** Criminal investigation; crime prevention; remains identification; parenthood determination.

- **Governmental Applications:** National ID; driver's license; border crossing; terrorist watch lists; welfare; casinos; access control.

- **Military Applications:** Identifying insurgents in Iraq and Afghanistan war zone using portable fingerprint and iris scan.

- **Enterprise Applications:** Access control; time/attendance control; biometric logon.

- **Consumer Applications:** Laptops; USB flash drives; cellphones; biometric locks; car ignition.

- **Financial Applications:** ATM; payment systems; account access.

- **Health Applications:** Access to a health registry; patients tracking and monitoring; drugs dispensing.

- **Education Applications:** Lunch and library entitlement; prevention of cheating on exams.

U. S. Department of Homeland Security

The Office of Biometric Identity Management (OBIM) supports the Department of Homeland Security's responsibility to protect the nation by providing biometric identification services that help federal, state, and local government decision makers accurately identify the people they encounter and determine whether those people pose a risk to the United States. OBIM supplies the technology for collecting and storing biometric data, provides analysis, updates its watch list, and ensures the integrity of the data. OBIM was created in March 2013, replacing the United States Visitor and Immigration Status Indicator Technology (US-VISIT) and streamlining operations. U. S. Department of Homeland Security enhancing security through biometric innovation, biometric services and biometric identification via US-VISIT. US-VISIT applies their services in three directions (US-VISIT, 2009; ArudouD, 2007 ; Jonathan, 2006).

US-VISIT: At the Forefront of Government-Driven Biometric Innovation

For more than 40 years, the U.S. government has driven biometrics research, developing early applications, such as automated fingerprint matching and digital fingerprint scanners. It has significantly deepened collaboration across its many agencies and with the private sector to advance biometric technology as a means to counter the increasing sophistication of criminals, terrorists and other dangerous people. After the September 11, 2001, Congress and the 9/11 Commission called for increased use of biometrics, and the White House created a cabinet-level subcommittee to coordinate policy to deploy biometric technology across many federal agencies. US-VISIT's biometric identification and analysis services are a successful application of years of government-driven innovation and increased focus since September 11. Today, US-VISIT continues to drive biometric innovations that further homeland security and help us to stay one-step ahead of those who seek to circumvent our security measures. This includes testing mobile biometric technology, exploring multimodal biometrics like iris and facial recognition and pushing industry to address the broad array of human factors that are critical to successful large-scale deployments of biometric technology.

US-VISIT's Biometric Services on the Front Lines

US-VISIT provides biometric identification and analysis services to decision makers across federal, state and local governments. US-VISIT supplies the technology for collecting and storing biometric data, provides analysis of the data to decision makers, and ensures the integrity of the data. The personal information collected by US-VISIT is used only for the purposes for which it was collected and as authorized or mandated by law.

- Department of State (State);
- U.S. Customs & Border Protection (CBP);
- U.S. Citizenship & Immigration Services;
- U.S. Immigration & Customs Enforcement (ICE);
- U.S. Coast Guard;
- Department of Justice & State and Local Law Enforcement;
- Investigation Support;
- Department of Defense (DOD) & Intelligence Community.

US-VISIT: Strengthening Security through Biometric Identification

The U.S. Department of Homeland Security is charged with protecting the United States from dangerous people. To meet this mission, authorized frontline decision makers must be able to accurately identify the people they encounter and assess whether they pose a risk to the United States. DHS's US-VISIT program provides biometric technology for identification and analysis services that enable the U.S. government to:

- Enhance the security of citizens and visitors,
- Facilitate legitimate travel and trade,
- Ensure the integrity of immigration system, and
- Protect the privacy of visitors.

US-VISIT has strengthened the United States' immigration and border security capabilities to a level that simply did not exist before. As we enhance the security of the United States with biometrics, other countries are seeking to collaborate with US-VISIT as they improve their immigration and border management systems. We are working with these countries to share best practices and develop standards that will improve security and facilitate travel worldwide.

FOCUS OF THE CHAPTER

The significant growth of the use of biological features in identification of people has led to a great revolution in this field of knowledge. Fingerprint recognition is one of the oldest techniques used in this area, this technology has evolved dramatically and became a very broad applications. So we will address in this section to offer two papers recently published by the author with a focus on the fingerprint recognition and identification and how to improve access to the best efficiency to personal identification based on biometric features.

Biometrics Fingerprint Recognition Using Discrete Cosine Transform (DCT)

Muzhir and et al (Al-Ani & Al-Aloosi, 2013) proposed a biometric recognition system based on the physiological fingerprint recognition that considered one of the most important identification biometrics technology. It is a successful way to determine the identity of the person that cannot be faked or stolen easily. This work aims to identify fingerprint images through several steps and extract their biometric features based on DCT technique. Fingerprint image is divided into sub-blocks that allow the evaluating of the statistical features from the DCT Coefficients. Matching process is implemented using the correlation between fingerprint images. The obtained results indicate an efficient recognition using DCT. These programs are implemented via MATLAB

environment. The work of the implemented system is divided into two main phases. First is the training phase, and second the testing phase (Baca et al, 2009).

DCT is implemented at the first five pictures belongs to each user. The data generated by the algorithm is stored in the database for further used by the second phase. The main object of this work is to design and implementation of fingerprint recognition system using the MATLAB environment that uses DCT in feature extraction stage. The implemented system consists of: Database capture stage, Preprocessing stage, Enhancement stage, Discrete Cosine Transform (DCT) and Matching stage as shown in Figure 2. In this study, the matching process was accomplished using correlation test and the obtained results showed that the ratio of matching for fingerprint images of the same person would have been acceptable (Al-Ani & Al-Aloosi, 2013 ; Lavanya & Raja, 2011).

Figure 2. Stages of implemented system

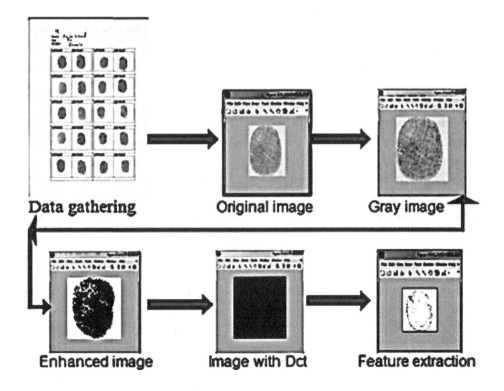

Figure 3. Components of fingerprint implemented system

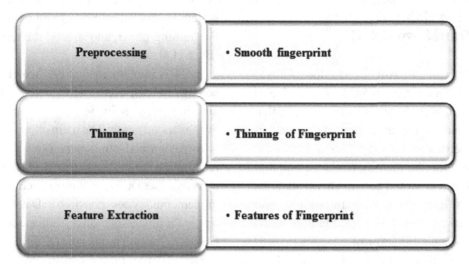

A Novel Thinning Algorithm for Fingerprint Recognition

Al-Ani (Al-Ani, 2013) studied the existing physiological fingerprint biometric technology algorithms in order to improve the performance of the proposed fingerprint algorithm to develop an efficient novel system of biometric features. The proposed fingerprint algorithm is concentrated on the improvement of the thinning process. Fingerprint enhancement and minutiae extraction approach based on optimal thinning. The output results indicate that there is significant improvement of the fingerprint recognition pattern.

In a fingerprint, the dark lines of the image are called the ridges and the white areas between the ridges are called valleys. This work is done applying several steps to achieve the proposed goal:

- Collect several fingerprint images for the same person in different situations.
- Construct a specific fingerprint database that stored fingerprint patterns.
- Classify the fingerprint according to their characteristics.
- Construct the algorithm to recognize the stored patterns.
- Test the implemented algorithm to check the system accuracy.

The system is implemented via several components as shown in Figure 3. Preprocessing process refers to the process of preparing the input images of fingerprint to be ready for the next step of the system that produces a good quality of the output fingerprint image. Preprocessing stage contains of the following steps:

1. Image acquisition that received images.
2. Converting the introduced input image into gray scale.
3. Removing the unwanted parts and noise from the input image.
4. Rearrange the image orientation into exact position.
5. Noise removal operation without any effect on fingerprint pattern.
6. Image resizing into exact size to be adapted for the next step.
7. Image enhancement that improve the quality of image.

Thinning process refers to the process of reducing the thickness of the lines as possible to be one pixel with minimum losses. This process is so important to identify the exact pattern of the fingerprint image. Fingerprint thinning process can be offered the following performance:

- The lines of output fingerprint image should be a single pixel as possible.
- The lines of output fingerprint image should not have any discontinuity as possible.
- The lines of output fingerprint image should be return to its center pixel as possible.
- Eliminate all redundancies and unwanted pixels as possible.

Feature extraction process depends on the previous processes and it is the main part of the overall system in which it extracts the required biometric features of the fingerprint pattern. Feature extraction process of fingerprint recognition system is very sensitive process and concentrated on illuminate the required characteristics of the Minutiae's; this can be implemented via Minutiae detection and Minutiae enhancement and Minutia extraction. Minutiae, in fingerprinting terms, are the points of interest in a fingerprint, such as bifurcations and ridge endings.

The statistical measures depend on both False Acceptance Ratio (FAR) and False Rejection Ratio (FRR) in addition to Real Acceptance Rate (RAR) are used to evaluate the system performance. For testing the proposed system, a set of random group males and females are used. Results of admitting the members of this set to a secure system were computed and presented. The evaluation criteria parameters that obtained are; Real Acceptance rate (RAR) = 0.88, False Acceptance Rate (FAR) = 0.02 and False Rejection Rate (FRR) = 0.10 (Pokhriyal & Lehri, 2010).

Efficient Watermarking Based on Robust Biometric Features

Al-Ani & et al (Al-Ani & AbdAl_ Baset, 2013) focused on fingerprints that are unique biometrics mainly used for the establishment of instant personal identity but they susceptible to accidental/intentional attacks because that must be secure biometric data from any attack using watermark technique. This approach used biometric image for features extraction from fingerprint images then embedded these features in face image applying watermarking technique via the calculation of average for all faces images that stored in database. This approach indicates a good result in watermarking process and data recovering process. This approach may apply in many applications such as credit card, enterprises records, personal identification card, secure passport … etc.

The proposed system can be summarized in the four steps as shown in the Figure 4.In step one Data collection from individual at 100 samples for 100persons (10 fingerprint image for each person) using scanner(Canon, 1410 mf, 300 dpi, color photo)and 10 face image by using camera with (14.1)resolution for each person. These data are saved in two databases (fingerprint image, face image) in which fingerprint images and face images are related to the same person. Each fingerprint image enter to preprocessing phase by applying many steps to enhance fingerprint image (read rgb images, resizing images, convert to gray scale, segmentation, edge detection). Feature extraction phase is implemented via discrete wavelet transform (DWT) that is a mathematical tool for hierarchically decomposing of an image. DWT provides both frequency and spatial description of an image, after the first level of decomposition, 4 sub-bands are obtained: LL1, LH1, HL1, and HH1. For each successive level of decomposition, the LL sub and of the previous level is used as an input to generate the second level. To perform second level decomposition, the

Figure 4. Block diagram of watermarking biometric system

```
┌──────────────────┐     ┌──────────────────┐     ┌──────────────────┐
│ Data Collection  │ ──> │  Preprocessing   │ ──> │     Feature      │
│                  │     │                  │     │    Extraction    │
└──────────────────┘     └──────────────────┘     └──────────────────┘
         │
         ▼
┌──────────────────┐     ┌──────────────────┐     ┌──────────────────┐
│  Watermarking    │ ──> │   Watermarking   │ ──> │ Decision Support │
│                  │     │    Detection     │     │     System       │
└──────────────────┘     └──────────────────┘     └──────────────────┘
```

DWT is applied to LL1 band that decomposes the LL1 band into four subbandsLL2, LH2, HL2, and HH2.The last step is biometric authentication of features by back the same watermarking method to retrieve features and matching with the base feature saving in database, where the matching is successfully done.

The proposed method has been simulated using the Matlab programming language. The entire images fingerprints were resized to 256*256 for biometric data and face images were resized to 128*128for watermarking. Five fingerprint images and five face images are used for training and testing. In this approach the features of biometric fingerprint image are embedded into face image to perform the watermarking process. The features are extracted using two methods; one method is done by applying DWT with two levels of LL sub band, and the second method is implemented without using DWT. When comparing these two methods, two robustness methods of watermarking are implemented, and these methods are greatly affected, but using DWT leads to faster implementation of run time program. Figure 5 shows the histogram of face image before and after watermarking (Al-Ani & Abd Al_Baset, 2013; Kashyap& Sinha, 2012).

Figure 5. Histogram implementation before DWT and after DWT

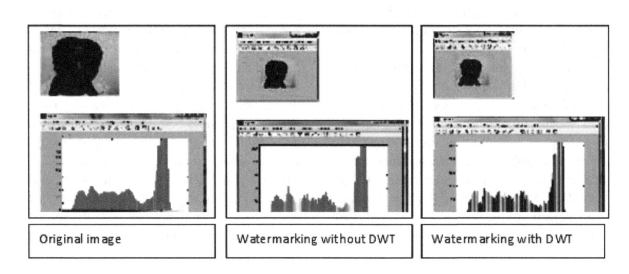

| Original image | Watermarking without DWT | Watermarking with DWT |

Figure 6. Hybrid biometric approach

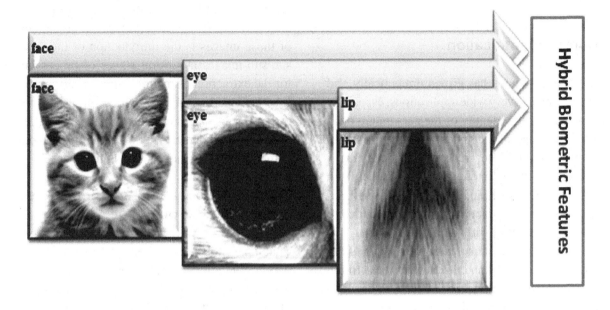

SOLUTIONS AND RECOMMENDATIONS

Semi-automated speaker biometric recognition systems as a sub subject of automated human biometric recognition began in the 1940s. Semi-automated and fully automated of many biometrics technologies such as fingerprint, hand writing, and facial recognition systems emerged in the 1960s as digital computers became more widespread and powerful. Fully automated systems based on hand geometry and fingerprinting were first deployed commercially in the 1970s, almost immediately leading to concerns over spoofing and privacy. Larger pilot projects for banking and government applications became popular in the 1980s. The fully automated systems for both government and commercial applications used many different technologies, including iris and face recognition are applied in the 1990s.

The design of biometric systems faced with their accuracy, means that always recognize with some level of error. Fingerprint recognition system is one that always leads to high level of accuracy, for this reason it is adapted for very wide range of real applications. If we can improve the system to reach high level of accuracy in fingerprint recognition, means we can approved that method of identification. The above section the author highlights two methods to implement fingerprint recognition system. These methods are concentrated on the enhancement of the image entry as well as image recognition and personal identification.

The combination of different types of biometrics leads to design a powerful biometric security system. In this case the system must be easy to use and not complex in adapting for real use. Figure6 shows a simple approach system for one shot in which you can capture three images first one is face image, the second one is eye image the third one is lip image. The combination of these features leads to non-similarity features and never repeatable.

FUTURE RESEARCH DIRECTIONS

Multibiometrics for Human Identification

Biometric systems has grown dramatically and introduced in a very wide applications, especially in achieving the identity of the person. Go deep into the design of the system depends biometric features of absolute secrecy is basically non-existent. So going into thus subject carries with it a lot of challenges and it depends on many factors, starting from data entry through to build the system and ending with the application.

Simple biometric authentication systems become easy to attack and this is what leads to big problems and challenges in this field, so began to go to mergers between different types of biological features of the human being in order to achieve better and strong identification. Thus, the subject must take into account, among other factors, including the complexity of the system and its ease of use and its applicability and speed of decision-making, in addition to adapt it to the nature of the input data and especially to the missing data.

When we talk about the future, we are talking about new biometric technologies and techniques effective in identifying biological features a rather flowing in the direction of integrating different set of features in order to achieve the biological identity of the person as well as the integration of a range of techniques in order to achieve higher accuracy in determining the identity of the person.

In this area we are talking about the two proposals for the use of multiple features in determining the identity of the person taking into consideration the lack of effect on a person's privacy.

First Proposal of Multibiometrics Face Recognition Image

This proposal relies on one picture shot to a person's face that possible fragmentation of that image into three main parts, a subset of the biometric features of the image and the image of the sub-parameters of the eye and the image of the sub-features of the lips. After the initial preprocessing of those images is the introduction of the three sub-sub-images at several stages of processing for the extraction of features of each sub-image. It is then overlap and merge those properties for the three sub-images in order to get the properties common to determine a person's identity without compromising privacy as shown in Figure 7.

Second Proposal of Multibiometrics Hand Recognition Image

This depends on the proposed capture one image to the hand of the person and the possible fragmentation of that image into three main parts, a subset of the image features hand shape (hand geometry) and sub-second image of the form of the blood vessels in the hand (palm print) and the third sub-image parameters of fingers (fingerprint). Then these images pass on the same sub-phases that have been presented in the first proposal, and then are overlapping and merging characteristics derived from the sub-images where the pool to be used in determining a person's identity without compromising the privacy of that person as shown in Figure 8.

On-Line Multi Biometric E-Passport

Many countries applied biometric passport that use biometric features in their passport and other countries use e-passport with traditional security. These passports are designed to be used through the population of the country only. The proposed multibiometrice passport depends on introducing three main biometrics features as shown above for human identification. The proposed passport introduce Radio Frequency Identification (RFID) automatic technology that works like wireless bar code system in which combine many parameters to generate a coding system. The encrypted code is stored on the Tag that embedded in the passport

Figure 7. First proposal depends on face recognition image

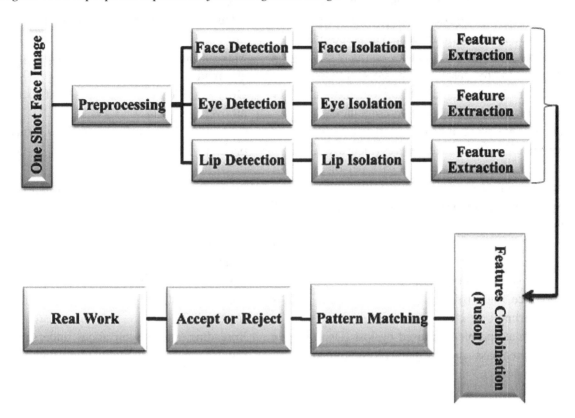

Figure 8. Second proposal depends on hand recognition image

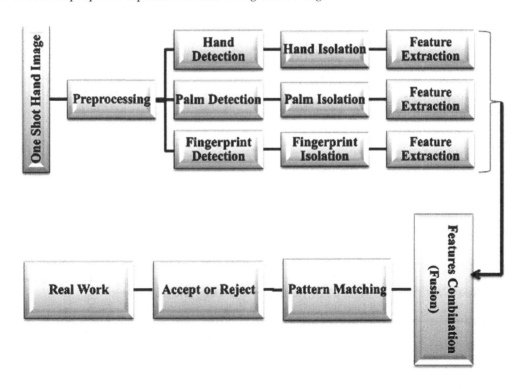

cover. To read the information on the chip, the e-passport reader energizes the chip circuitry by communicating through its antenna. The proposed multibiometric e-passport depends on many factors that used in the enrollment process and also these factors are compared with the database in the matching process. These factors combine each of date of issue, place of birth, birthday, country code number, and biometric features (face, eye & lip) to generate a unique code for each person as shown in Figure 9.

Advantages of multibiometrice passport are listed below:

- Increase security by providing a convenient security for e-passport.
- Reduce fraud by employing multibiometric technologies.
- Eliminate problems caused by lost IDs or forgotten passwords by using physiological attributes.

- Reduce password administration costs.
- Integrate a wide range of biometric solutions and technologies.
- Make it possible to implement e-passport automatically.
- Offer significant global e-passport to use all over the world.
- Considering a security measure to protect privacy.

Requirements of multibiometrice passport are listed below:

- Understanding that this project is an international one.
- Awareness of multibiometrice passport.
- Training of staffs for enrolling and matching data.
- Spreading information about understanding of the human interactions with this project.

Figure 9. Factors used for e-passport

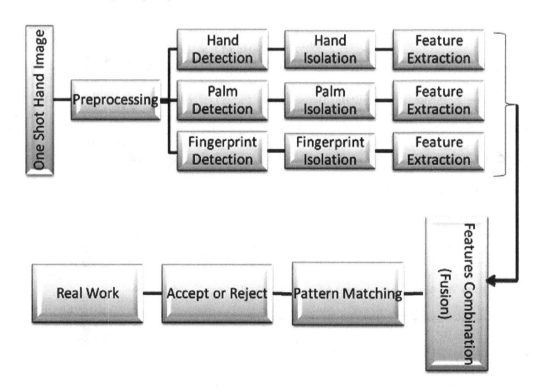

Figure 10. Multi biometric e-passport data

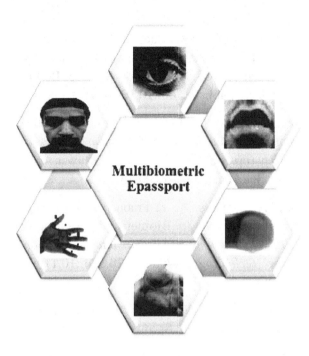

- Preparing the infrastructure to adapt multibiometrice passport.

The Multibiometric e-passport can be implemented by enrollment data as illustrated in Figure 10. These data can be collected via sensitive sensors that already transferred to many steps to ensure that data are accurately collected. Data entry may be repeated many times in order to ensure the high level of accuracy. A fusion process may implement in a certain step to integrate and cooperate all the features. A fusion process may occur in the starting step or ending step.

CONCLUSION

There is always resistance and challenges in adapting new technology. But these can be solved by continuing of training and learning about biometric passport. Now we live in an age of globalization and the digital age where the world has become a small village, and you can get the information in record time. Biological (Physiological & Behavioral) features and wide applications have become characteristic of this era where possible to say that we live in an age revolution biological features because of their importance in all features of life in the present age. The latest research indicates using a combination of biometric features for human identification is more effective, and far more challenging. Including biometric systems are used it is difficult to produce 100% error-free results and this may be due to different effects. The growth of biometrics applications leads to new fields and researches directions. Most of these directions concentrated on multibiometric applications and technologies so this explained one of the most important applications of multibiometric.

REFERENCES

Al-Ani, M. S. (2013). A Novel Thinning Algorithm for Fingerprint Recognition. *International Journal of Engineering Science, 2*(2), 43–48.

Al-Ani, M. S., & Abd Al Baset, K. (2013). Efficient watermarking based on robust biometric features. *Engineering Science and Technology: An International Journal, 3*(3).

Al-Ani, M. S., & Al-Aloosi, W. M. (2013). Biometrics fingerprint recognition using discrete cosine transform (DCT). *International Journal of Computer Applications, 69*(6), 0975 – 8887.

Al-Ani, M. S., & Al-Ani, I. H. (2011). Gait recognition based improved histogram. *Journal of Emerging Trends in Computing and Information Sciences, 2*(12).

Anil, K. J., & Chen, H. (2004). Matching of dental x-ray images for human identification. *Pattern Recognition, 37*, 1519–1532.

Arudou, D. (2007). *Fingerprinting: Amnesty/SMJ Appeal for Noon Nov 20 Public Appeal outside Justice Ministry*. Retrieved from http://www.debito.org/?s=doudou

Aus Jonathan, P. (2006). *Decision Making Under Pressure: The Negotiation of the Biometric Passports Regulation*. Retrieved from www.arena.uio.no/publications/

Baca, M., Cubrilo, M., & Rabuzin, K. (2007). Using biometric characteristics to increase its security. *Traffic &Transportation Scientific Journal on Traffic and Transportation Research*, *19*(6), 353–359.

Baca, M., Schatten, M., & Ševa, J. (2009). Behavioral and Physical Biometric Characteristics Modeling Used for Its Security Improvement. *Transport Problems*, *4*(4), 2009.

Congdon, K. (2010). *Are Biometrics the Key to Health IT Security?* Retrieved from http://www.healthcaretechnologyonline.com/article.mvc/Are-Biometrics-The-Key-To-Health-IT-Security-0001?VNETCOOKIE=NO

Delac, K., & Grgic, M. (2004). A Survey of Biometric Recognition Methods, In *Procceedings of the 46th International Symposium Electronics in Marine*. ELMAR-2004, (pp. 184-1 93). Zadar, Croatia.

Gamboa, H., & Fred, A. (2004). A behavioral biometric system based on human computer interaction. In SPIE, 5404-Biometric Technology for Human Identification (pp. 381-392). Orlando, USA.

Goswami, J. C., & Chan, A. K. (2011). *Fundamentals of Wavelets, Theory, Algorithms and Applications*. Hoboken, N.J: Wiley. doi:10.1002/9780470926994

Hoepman, J. H., Hubbers, E., Jacobs, B., Oostdijk, M., & Schreur, R. W. (2006). Crossing Borders: Security and Privacy Issues of the European e-Passport. In *Advances in Information and Computer Security, LNCS*. Netherlands: Springer Berlin Heidelberg publisher. doi:10.1007/11908739_11

Jain, A. K., Bolle, R., & Pankanti, S. (1999). *Biometrics: Personal Identification in Networked Society* (pp. 369–384). New York: Kluwer Academic Publisher. doi:10.1007/b117227

Jain, A. K., Ross, A., & Prabhakar, S. (2004). An Introduction to Biometric Recognition. *IEEE Transactions on Circuits and Systems for Video Technology*, *14*(1), 4–20. doi:10.1109/TCSVT.2003.818349

Julian, A. (2000). *Biometrics: Advanced Identity Verification*. London: Springer.

Kashyap, N., & Sinha, G. R. (2012). Image Watermarking Using 3-Level Discrete Wavelet Transform (DWT). *I. J. Modern Education and Computer Science*, *3*(3), 50–56. doi:10.5815/ijmecs.2012.03.07

Lavanya, B. N., & Raja, K. B. (2011). Performance Evaluation of Fingerprint Identification Based on DCT and DWT using Multiple Matching Techniques. *IJCSI International Journal of Computer Science Issues*, *8*(1), 2011.

Olzak, T. (2011). *Practical Application of Biometrics*. Retrieved from http://www.techrepublic.com/downloads/practical-application-of-biometrics/2393163

Pokhriyal, A., & Lehri, S. (2010). MERIT: Minutiae Extraction using Rotation Invariant Thinning. *International Journal of Engineering Science and Technology*, *2*(7), 3225–3235.

Ross, A., Nandakumar, K., & Jain, A. K. (2006). Handbook of Multibiometrics. New York, USA: Springer-Verlag.

Scott, C., & Nowak, R. (2004). Templar: A wavelet-based framework for pattern learning and analysis. *IEEE Transactions on Signal Processing*, *52*(8), 2264–2274.

Tripathi, K. P. (2011). A Comparative Study of Biometric Technologies with Reference to Human Interface. *International Journal of Computers and Applications*, *14*(5).

US-VISIT. (2009). *Final Rule: Enrollment of Additional Aliens, Additional Biometric Data and Expansion to More Land Ports*. Retrieved from http://www.dhs.gov/obim

Xiao, Q. (2010). *Applying Biometrics*. Retrieved from http://www.ottawa.drdc-rddc.gc.ca/html/biometrics-end.html

ADDITIONAL READING

Abhyankar, A., Hornak, L., & Schuckers, S. (2005). Bi-orthogonal wavelet based iris recognition, SPIE, Defense and Security Symposium, 5406, 2005.

Abhyankar, A., & Schuckers, S. A. C. (2004). Wavelet-based approach to detecting liveness in fingerprint scanners, *Proceedings of the SPIE Defense and Security Symposium, Biometric Technology for Human Identification*, April 2004. doi:10.1117/12.542939

Abhyankar, A., & Schuckers, S. A. C. (2009). Integrating a wavelet based perspiration liveness check with fingerprint recognition. *Pattern Recognition*, *42*(3), 452–464. doi:10.1016/j.patcog.2008.06.012

Al-Ani, M. S., & Al-Saidi, M. M. (2011). An Improved Proposed Approach for handwritten Arabic Signature Recognition. *Advances in Computer Science and Engineering, India*, *7*(1), 25–35.

Al-Ani, M. S., & Al-Waisy, A. S. (2011). Multiview face detection based on kernel principal component analysis and kernel support vector techniques. *International Journal on Soft Computing*, *2*(2).

Al-Ani, M. S., & Al-Waisy, A. S. (2012). Face Recognition Approach Based on Wavelet-Curvelet Technique. *Signal & Image Processing. International Journal (Toronto, Ont.)*, *3*(2).

Al-Ani, M. S., Mansor, F., & Kalid, W. (2012). *An Efficient Steganographic Algorithm Using Circular Hiding*. Iraqi Association of Information Technology.

Anwar, F., Rahman, A., & Azad, S. (2009). Multi-biometric Systems Based Verification Technique. *European Journal of Scientific Research*, *34*(2), 260–270.

Arun Ross, A., & Jain, A. K. (2004). Multimodal Biometrics: An Overview, *Proc. of 12th European Signal Processing Conference (EUSIPCO), (Vienna, Austria)*, pp. 1221-1224, September 2004.

Boles, W., & Boashash, B. (1998). A human identification technique using images of the iris and wavelet transform. *IEEE Transactions on Signal Processing*, *46*(4), 1998. doi:10.1109/78.668573

Chellin, G., Chandra, J., & Rajesh, R. S. (2009). Performance Analysis of Multimodal Biometric System Authentication. *International Journal of Computer Science and Network Security*, *9*(3).

Jain, A., Nandakumara, K., & Ross, A. (2005). Score normalization in multimodal biometric systems. *Pattern Recognition*, 2270–2285.

Maltonie, D., Maio, D., Jain, A. K., & Prabhakar, S. (2003). Handbook of Fingerprint Recognition. New York: Springer-Verlag.

Nageshkumar, M., Mahesh, P. K., & Shanmukha Swamy, M. N. (2009). An Efficient Secure Multimodal Biometric Fusion Using Palmprint and Face Image. *IJCSI International Journal of Computer Science Issues*, 2, 2009.

Orsag, F., & Drahansky, M. (2004). Biometric Security Systems: Fingerprint and Speech Technology. In *International Workshop on Biometric Technologies* (pp. 99-103), *Calgary*, CA.

Ratha, N. (2001). Enhancing security and privacy in biometrics-based authentication systems. *IBM Systems Journal*, 40, 613–614.

Ross, A. (2007). An Introduction to Multibiometrics. In *Proceedings of the 15th European Signal Processing Conference (EUSIPCO)*. Poznan Poland.

Ross, A., & Govindarajanb, R. (2005). Feature Level Fusion Using Hand and Face Biometrics, *SPIE Conference on Biometric Technology for Human Identification II*, Volume, 5779, pp.196-204(Orlando, USA) March 2005. doi:10.1117/12.606093

Snelick, R., Indovina, M., Yen, J., & Mink, A. (2003). Multimodal Biometrics: Issues in Design and Testing, *ICMI'03, November 5-7, 2003, Vancouver,* British Columbia, Canada. ACM 1-58113-621-8/03/0011.

Stylianou, Y., Pantazis,Y., Calderero, F., Larroy, P., Severin, F., Schimke, S., Bonal, R., Matta, F. &Valsamakis, A. (2005). GMM-Based Multimodal Biometric Verification, *Enterface'05, July18th -August 12th, MONS,* Belgium -Final Project Report.

Teoh, A., Samad, S. A., & Hussain, A. (2004). Nearest Neighborhood Classifiers in a Bimodal Biometric Verification System Fusion Decision. *Journal of Research and Practice in Information Technology*, 36(1).

Uludag, U., Pankanti, S., Prabhakar, S., & Jain, A. K. (2004). Biometric cryptosystems: Issues and challenges. *Proceedings of the IEEE*, 92(6), 2004. doi:10.1109/JPROC.2004.827372

KEY TERMS AND DEFINITIONS

Behavioral Biometrics: Types of human biometrics characteristics that depend on Behavioral characteristics include: gait, signature, and voice.

Biometric Authentication: Electronic identification of an individual on the basis of his or her unique biological or physiological characteristics (together called Biometric Signature) such as facial features, fingerprints, hand geometry, retinal patterns, voiceprint.

Biometric E-Passport: A combined paper and electronic identity document that uses biometrics to authenticate the citizenship of travelers. The passport's critical information is stored on a tiny computer chip, much like information stored on smartcards. The chip is able to hold digital signature data to ensure the integrity of the passport and the biometric data.

Biometric Identification: Biometric features that are used to verify the identity of the individual trying to access a computer system, network, credit card account, ATM, etc.

Biometric Recognition: The automated recognition of individuals based on their behavioral and biological characteristic. It is promoted as a way to help identify terrorists, provide better control of access to physical facilities and financial accounts, and increase the efficiency of access to services and their utilization.

Biometric Technologies: Appear to be useful tools for identification and verification in security initiatives. Biometric technology uses computerized methods to identify a person by their unique physical or behavioral characteristics.

Biometric Verification: The comparison of two or more items, or the use of supplementary tests, to ensure the accuracy, correctness, or truth of the information. In biometric this deals with biometric features.

Multibiometric: An authentication technology using different biometric technologies such as fingerprints, facial features, and vein patterns in the identification and verification process. The use of Multi-Biometrics takes advantages of the capabilities of each biometric technology while overcoming the limitations of a single technology.

Physiological Biometrics: Types of human biometrics characteristics that depend on physical characteristics include: DNA, ear, face, fingerprint, hand geometry, iris, and retina.

Chapter 12
Data Hiding Schemes Based on Singular Value Decomposition

Nidhal Khdhair El Abbadi
University of Kufa, Iraq

ABSTRACT

The security of information exchange is very important on the network. Authentication and information hiding have also become important issues. Information hiding techniques are acquiring an increasing importance due to the widespread diffusion of multimedia contents. The aim of this chapter is to focus on the Singular Value Decomposition (SVD) transform, with the aim of providing an exhaustive overview on those steganography, image cryptography and watermarking techniques leveraging on the important properties of such a transform. Despite the attention it has received in the last years, SVD in image processing and security is still in its infancy. Many SVD characteristics are still unutilized in image processing. In this chapter the author tries to highlight the basic properties of SVD and some of their applications in the field of security to encourage researchers to discover more about SVD properties which are not yet utilized.

INTRODUCTION

Due to the rising dependence on digital media and the unexpected expansion of the distribution opportunities over the Internet, techniques for hiding information into digital contents are achieving significant importance. Such techniques aim to provide the ability to communicate secretly and the capacity to protect copyrighted multimedia content against illegal distribution. Designing such schemes has become a topic of great importance and many researchers have spent much effort

in the last years to obtain an effective solution. However, despite many different approaches have been attempted, there is currently no scheme that can preserve imperceptibility of the hidden data while ensuring a high security against malicious attacks.

In networked environments, the safety of multimedia data can be investigated according to two aspects: the safety of static data and the data security during dynamic communication. The safety of static multimedia data can be inspected according to the following four aspects:

DOI: 10.4018/978-1-4666-6583-5.ch012

Copyright © 2015, IGI Global. Copying or distributing in print or electronic forms without written permission of IGI Global is prohibited.

1. **Storage:** Is the data centrally stored, or dispersed?
2. **Vulnerability:** How robustness is the data against theft or abuse?
3. **Confidence/Authenticity:** What constitutes authentic information? Can that information be tampered with?
4. **Linking:** Will the multimedia data be linked to other information, e.g., about originating and/or consuming party?

When inspecting the security of real-time multimedia communication, one should take into account the specific properties of both multimedia data and real-time communication. First, limited distortions in multimedia data cannot be perceived by end users. Thus some bit errors and packets loss that may occur during communication do not defect the overall visual/audio quality. Secondly, due to scheduling protocols of real-time multimedia communication, packet loss may happen. Thirdly, caused by the large amount of multimedia data, communication security trade-offs should be low enough.

The upcoming information processing architectures for ubiquitous computing is highly sensitive to security issues. For some networked scenarios, such as fingerprint collection in distributed environment, video monitoring and health care systems, the image integrity and authenticity is fatal to the success of these services. While most of the embedded systems working in such distributed environments are low-end devices in terms of their computing power, memory size and communication bandwidths. Therefore, new security policies have to provide, such that the given constraints of these devices are considered accordingly.

For the current digital age, digital forensic research becomes imperative. Counterfeiting and falsifying digital data or digital evidence with the goal of making illegal profits or bypassing laws is the main objective for the attackers. The forensic research focuses in many tracks; steganography, watermarking, authentication, labeling, captioning, etc. Many applications were developed to satisfy consumer requirements such as labeling, fingerprinting, authentication, copy control for DVD, hardware/ software watermarking, executables watermarks, and signaling (signal information for automatic counting) for the purpose of broadcast monitoring count (Sadek, 2012).

The SVD packs the maximum signal energy into few coefficients. It has the ability to adapt to the variations in local statistics of an image. However, SVD is an image adaptive transform; the transform itself needs to be represented in order to recover the data. Despite the attention it has received in the last years, SVD in image processing is still in its infancy. Many SVD characteristics are still unutilized in image processing. The present chapter highlights the basic properties of SVD and some of their applications in the field of security to encourage researchers to discover more about SVD properties which are not yet utilized (Liu & Tan, 2002).

Following some objectives of writing this chapter are:

1. Providing readers with knowledge about the SVD, and the usefulness of using SVD in image processing and specifically in security fields.
2. Prompting the researcher to discover new algorithms of using SVD in the fields of security and countermeasures such as steganography, watermarking, image encryption, stegoanalysis ... etc.
3. There are many SVD features not utilized. The SVD chapter may help to discover some of these features and utilize them in the fields of communication security in general.
4. Highlighting some novel uses of SVD in the fields of image and text cryptography (to the best of knowledge, there are no published papers in the field of using SVD in text encryption), steganography, the watermarks, stegoanalysis (which is also new field in using SVD), and some other new applications.

Figure 1. Decomposition of matrix by SVD

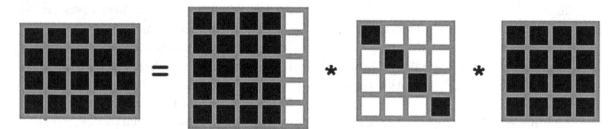

Using SVD in the fields of steganography, watermark, image encryption, and stegoanalysis is a new subject. There are few books discussed this issue, and I think this subject is very useful for postgraduate students, professors, researcher, and every one interested in the field of communication security.

SINGULAR VALUE DECOMPOSITION (SVD)

Singular value decomposition for square matrices was discovered by Beltrami in 1873 and Jordan in 1874, and extended to rectangular matrices by Eckart and Young in the 1930s. It was not used as a computational tool until the 1960s because of the need for sophisticated numerical techniques. In later years, Gene Golub demonstrated its usefulness and feasibility as a tool in a variety of applications. SVD is one of the most useful tools of the linear algebra with several applications in image compression, watermarking, and other signal processing areas. In the linear algebra, the singular valued composition (SVD) is a factorization of a real or complex matrix with many useful applications in signal processing and statistics. SVD is to be a significant topic in the linear algebra by many renowned mathematicians. It has many practical and theoretical values. Special features of SVD is that it can be performed on any real (m, n) matrix.

In the linear algebra the SVD is a factorization of a rectangular real or complex matrix analogous to the diagonalization of symmetric or Hermitian square matrices by using a basis of eigenvectors. SVD is a stable and an effective method to split the system into a set of linearly independent components, each of them bearing own energy contribution (Andrews & Patterson, 1976).

DEFINITION OF SVD

For any given matrix $A \in R^{m \times n}$ there exists decomposition $\mathbf{A} = \mathbf{U}\mathbf{S}\mathbf{V}^T$ such that

- U is an $m \times n$ matrix with orthonormal columns.
- S is an $n \times n$ diagonal matrix with non-negative entries.
- V^T is an $n \times n$ orthonormal matrix.

We can visualize this decomposition as in Figure 1.

The diagonal values of S are called 'Singular Values' of $\mathbf{A}$.

The column vectors of U are the 'Left Singular Vectors' of $\mathbf{A}$.

The column vectors of V are the 'Right Singular Vectors' of $\mathbf{A}$.

The SVD can be performed on matrices $A \in R^{m \times n}$, where m ≥ n (It can also be performed if $m < n$, but this is not interesting in the context of 3D Computer Vision). In the case that $m = n$ there will be only non-zero positive diagonal elements. In the case that $m > n$, $s_1, \ldots, s_n$ are non-zero positive, $s_n+1, \ldots, s_m$ are zero. The SVD can be performed, such that the diagonal values of S are descending i.e. $s_1 \geq s_2 \geq \ldots \geq s_n \geq 0$.

The diagonal values of S are the square roots of the eigenvalues of $\mathbf{A^TA}$ and $\mathbf{AA^T}$ (hence the non-negativity of the elements of $\mathbf{S}$).

The left singular vectors $\mathbf{u}_i$ are eigenvectors of $\mathbf{A^TA}$.

The right singular vectors $\mathbf{v}_i$ are eigenvectors of $\mathbf{AA^T}$.

For those who want to know even more properties of the SVD, I will shortly introduce them.

- The SVD explicitly constructs orthonormal bases for the null-space and the range of a matrix.
- U, S, V provide a real-valued matrix factorization of M, i.e., $M = USV^T$.
- U is an n × m matrix with orthonormal columns, $U^TU = I_m$, where I_m is the m× m identity matrix.
- V is an orthonormal k × k matrix, $V^T = V^{-1}$.
- S is a n×n diagonal matrix, with the non-negative *singular values*, $s_1, s_2, \ldots, s_n$, on the diagonal.
- By convention the singular values are given in the sorted order $s_1 \geq s_2 \geq \ldots \geq s_n \geq 0$.
- The rank of M is given by the number of singular values s_j that are non-zero.
- The singular values $s_1, s_2, \ldots, s_n$ are unique; however, the matrices *U and V* are not unique.

The important inherent properties of SVD from the view point of image processing applications which makes it popular to use are:

- Singular Values (*Svs*) are stable; i.e., any change to it doesn't affect the image quality.

- *Svs* are able to represent inherent algebra properties of digital image.
- SVD preserves both one-way and non-symmetric properties which are not available by using DCT or DFT transformations.
- The size of matrices can be square or rectangular in SVD.
- *Svs* are known to be invariant to some common attacks such as JPEG compression, noise addition, low pass filter (LPF), rotation, scaling and cropping.

COMPUTING SVD

The process of computing the SVD starts with a matrix (any image can be represented as a matrix). The matrix can be any size $n \times m$. An example would be:

$$A = \begin{pmatrix} 3 & 14 & 2 \\ 3 & 31 & 0 \\ 4 & 10 & 73 \end{pmatrix}$$

The first step in the SVD involves finding the transpose of the matrix A.

Definition 1: The transpose of an $m \times n$ matrix A is the $n \times m$ matrix A^T, whose columns are formed from the corresponding rows of A. The transpose of the example is:

$$A^T = \begin{pmatrix} 3 & 3 & 4 \\ 14 & 31 & 10 \\ 2 & 0 & 73 \end{pmatrix}$$

Definition 2: A 'symmetric matrix' is a matrix whose transpose is equal to the original matrix, i.e., $A^T = A$.

The second step in computing the SVD is to take the product of A^TA.

Definition 3: A dot product of two vectors is found by taking the sum of the products of the corresponding individual elements of the two vectors. Let

$$a = \begin{pmatrix} a_1 & a_2 & \dots & a_n \end{pmatrix}, \quad b = \begin{pmatrix} b_1 \\ b_2 \\ . \\ . \\ . \\ b_n \end{pmatrix}$$

The dot product of a and b is

$$a.b = a_1 b_1 + a_2 b_2 \dots + a_n b_n$$

Definition 4: A product (or matrix product) of the $m \times k$ matrix A and the $k \times n$ matrix B is the $m \times n$ matrix AB, whose *Ijth* entry is the dot product of the vectors A_i and B_j where A_i is the *ith* row of A and B_j is the *jth* column of B:

$$(AB)_{ij} = a_{i1} b_{1j} + a_{i2} b_{2j} + \dots + a_{ik} b_{kj}$$

The example yields:

$$A^TA = \begin{pmatrix} 34 & 175 & 298 \\ 175 & 1257 & 758 \\ 298 & 758 & 5333 \end{pmatrix}$$

The next step requires finding the eigenvectors and eigenvalues.

Definition 5: An 'eigenvector' of an $n \times n$ matrix A is a nonzero vector x such that $Ax = \lambda x$ for some scalar λ. A scalar λ is called an *eigenvalue* of A if there is a nontrivial solution x of $Ax = \lambda x$, i.e., if lambda has an eigenvector.

Note that a scalar λ is an eigenvalue of A if and only if the relation $(A - \lambda I) x = 0$ has a non-trivial solution.

The eigenvalues from the example above (A^TA) are $\lambda_1 = 5488.69$, $\lambda_2 = 1133.3$, and $\lambda_3 = 2.00893$. The related eigenvectors from the example above (A^TA) are,

$$vec_1 = \begin{pmatrix} 0.0605 \\ 0.1816 \\ 1 \end{pmatrix}, vec_2 = \begin{pmatrix} -0.5749 \\ -5.3145 \\ 1 \end{pmatrix}, vec_3 = \begin{pmatrix} 25.3412 \\ -2.9297 \\ -1 \end{pmatrix}$$

Definition 6: The 'norm', or length, of vector v is the nonnegative scalar $\|v\|$ which is defined by

$$\|v\| = \sqrt{v.v} = \sqrt{v_1^2 + v_2^2 + \dots + v_n^2}$$

The norm of the eigenvectors from the example is:

$$\| vec_1 \| = \sqrt{|0.0605|^2 + |0.1816|^2 + |1|^2}$$

$$= \sqrt{1.0366} = 1.01816$$

$$\|vec_2\| = 5.43821, \quad and \quad \|vec_3\| = 25.5396.$$

Definition 7: A 'unit vector' is a vector of length one. To *normalize* a nonzero vector is to divide it by its length. Observe that a normalized vector is a unit vector. The normalized eigenvectors from the example are:

$$v_1^T = \frac{vec_1^T}{|vec_1|} = \frac{\begin{pmatrix} 0.0605 & 0.1816 & 1 \end{pmatrix}^T}{0.01816}$$

$$= \begin{pmatrix} 0.5938 & 0.1784 & 0.9822 \end{pmatrix}^T$$

$$v_2^T = \frac{vec_2^T}{|vec_2|} = \begin{pmatrix} -0.1057 & -0.9772 & 0.1839 \end{pmatrix}^T,$$

and

$$v_3^T = \frac{vec_3^T}{|vec_3|} = \begin{pmatrix} 0.9926 & -0.1148 & -0.0392 \end{pmatrix}^T$$

Definition 8: A real 'positive semi definite matrix A' is a real symmetric matrix for which the eigenvalues are all non-negative.

Proposition 1: For any A, A^TA is positive semi-definite.

Definition 9: The 'singular values' of matrix A are the square roots of the eigenvalues of the positive semi-definite matrix A^TA and are denoted by $s_1,...,s_n$, arranged in non-increasing order. That is,

$$s_1 = \sqrt{\lambda_1} \geq s_2 = \sqrt{\lambda_2} \geq ... \geq s_n = \sqrt{\lambda_n},$$

where λI I is the *ith* eigenvalue of A^TA.

Note, because A^TA must be a positive semi-definite matrix, the singular values of A are real numbers. The singular values for the example are: s_1=74.0857, s_2= 33.6646 and s_3=1.4174.

Definition 10: Two vectors u and v in R^n are orthogonal to each other if $u .v = 0$.

Definition 11: A set $\{u_1, u_2, ..., u_n\}$ is an ortho-normal set if it is an orthogonal set of unit vectors.

Let the right singular vectors be the columns of the eigenvector matrix V.

V is the transpose of v_1, v_2, and v_3.

$$V = \begin{pmatrix} 0.0594 & -0.1057 & 0.9926 \\ 0.1784 & -0.9772 & -0.1148 \\ 0.9822 & 0.1839 & -0.0392 \end{pmatrix}$$

Definition 12: The 'column space' of $m \times n$ matrix A, written as Col A, is the set of all linear combinations of the columns of A. If $A = \{a_1, ..., a_n\}$, then Col A = Span $\{a_1, ..., a_n\}$. The 'rank' of A, denoted by rank A, is the dimension of the column space of A.

Definition 13: The left singular vectors can now be found by taking $u_i = \frac{1}{s_i} A v_i$ when $s_i = 0$.

For example:

$$u_1 = \frac{1}{s_1} A v_1$$

$$= \frac{1}{74.0857} \begin{pmatrix} 3 & 14 & 2 \\ 3 & 31 & 0 \\ 4 & 10 & 73 \end{pmatrix} \begin{pmatrix} 0.0594 \\ 0.1784 \\ 0.9822 \end{pmatrix} = \begin{pmatrix} 0.0626 \\ 0.7705 \\ 0.9951 \end{pmatrix}$$

$$u_2 = \frac{1}{s_2} A v_2 = \begin{pmatrix} -0.4049 \\ -0.9093 \\ 0.0959 \end{pmatrix}$$

$$u_3 = \frac{1}{s_3} A v_3 = \begin{pmatrix} 0.9122 \\ -0.4089 \\ -0.0258 \end{pmatrix}$$

Let U be the matrix of left singular vectors. In this example, this gives the matrix

$$U = \begin{pmatrix} 0.0626 & -0.4049 & 0.9122 \\ 0.0770 & -0.9093 & -0.4089 \\ 0.9951 & 0.0959 & -0.0258 \end{pmatrix}$$

To check the stability of the singular values, an experiment was conducted on 8 bit gray scale 512× 512 Lena image. In this experiment, original singular values were compared with singular values after applying various attacks on them. Table 1 shows the first four singular values of

Table 1. Various attacks on Lena image, its singular values

Image	S_1	S_2	S_3	S_4
Original Image	151.5234	42.2745	36.1516	27.9067
JPEG Compression(Q=20)	151.6007	42.2129	36.0787	27.6894
Rotation(15 Degree)	144.1636	48.0665	39.9409	28.7351
Scaling (512-256-512)	152.1418	42.1731	36.0141	27.7552
Scaling (512-1024-512)	152.7299	42.2633	36.1170	27.8758
Gaussian Noise (M=0, V= 0.01) Salt & Paper Noise (M=0 V=0.01)	158.5279 152.3987	40.7767 41.9533	35.4015 35.8831	27.3755 27.7077
Median Filter {3X3}	151.2235	42.2745	36.1516	27.9067
Histogram Equalization	151.5234	42.2745	36.1516	27.9067

the original and modified image after applying various attacks. The singular values do not change very much.

SVD IMAGE PROPERTIES

SVD is robust and reliable orthogonal matrix decomposition method. Due to SVD conceptual and stability reasons, it becomes more and more popular in signal processing area. SVD is an attractive algebraic transform for image processing. SVD has prominent properties in imaging. Although some SVD properties are fully utilized in image processing, others still needs more investigation and contribution. Several SVD properties are highly advantageous for images such as; its maximum energy packing, solving of least squares problem, computing pseudo-inverse of a matrix and multivariate analysis. A key property of SVD is its relation to the rank of a matrix and its ability to approximate matrices of a given rank. Digital images are often represented by low rank matrices, and therefore able to be described by a sum of a relatively small set of Eigen images. This concept rises the manipulating of the signal as two distinct subspaces. For a complete review, the theoretical SVD related theorems are summarized in the follows (Sadek, 2012).

- **SVD Subspaces:** SVD is constituted from two orthogonal dominant and subdominant subspaces. This corresponds to divide the M-dimensional vector space into dominant and subdominant subspaces. This attractive property of SVD is utilized in noise filtering and watermarking.

- **SVD Architecture:** For SVD decomposition of an image, singular value (*Svs*) specifies the luminance of an image layer while the corresponding pair singular vectors (SCs) specify the geometry of the image layer. The largest object components found in the image by using the SVD generally correspond to Eigen images associated with the largest singular values, while image noise corresponds to Eigen images associated with the *Svs*.

- **PCA vs. SVD:** Principle component analysis (PCA) is also called the Karhunen-Loéve transform (KLT) or the Hotelling transform. PCA is used to compute the dominant vectors representing a given data set and provide an optimal basis for minimum mean squared reconstruction of the given data. The computational basis of PCA is the calculation of the SVD of the data matrix, or equivalently the eigenvalues decomposition of the data covariance matrix.

- **SVD Multiresolution:** SVD has the maximum energy packing among the other transforms. In many applications, it is useful to obtain a statistical characterization of an image at several resolutions. SVD decomposes a matrix into orthogonal components with which optimal sub rank approximations may be obtained. With the multi-resolution SVD, the following important characteristics of an image may be measured, at each of the several level of resolution: isotropy, specify of principal components, self-similarity under scaling, and resolution of the mean squared error into meaningful components.

- **SVD Oriented Energy:** In SVD analysis of oriented energy both rank of the problem and signal space orientation can be determined. SVD is a stable and effective method to split the system into a set of linearly independent components, each of them bearing its own energy contribution. SVD is represented as a linear combination of its principle components, a few dominate components are bearing the rank of the observed system and can be severely reduced. The oriented energy concept is an effective tool to separate signals from different sources, or to select signal subspaces of maximal signal activity and integrity. Recall that the singular values represent the square root of the energy in corresponding principal direction. The dominant direction could equal to the first singular vector V_1 from the SVD decomposition. Accuracy of dominance of the estimate could be measured by obtaining the difference or normalized difference between the first two *Svs*.

WATERMARK

The idea of using singular values for watermarking was explored a few years ago by Liu and Tan (Liu, R., Tan, T., 2002). The main idea of this approach is to find the SVD of an original image and then modify its singular values to embed the watermark.

Digital watermarking technique is one of most important methods in information hiding and IPR (Intelligence Properties Right) protection and authentication. It is the process of embedding information into a digital signal in a way that is difficult to remove. The process of embedding a certain piece of information (technically known as watermark) into multimedia content including text documents, images, audio or video streams, based on which the watermark can be detected or extracted later to make an assertion about the data.

In visible digital watermarking, the information is visible in the picture or video. Typically, the information is text or a logo, which identifies the owner of the media. When a television broadcaster adds its logo to the corner of transmitted video, this also is a visible watermark.

In invisible digital watermarking, information is added as digital data to audio, picture, or video, but it cannot be perceived as such (although it may be possible to detect that some amount of information is hidden in the signal).

WATERMARK PROPERTIES

In general, a digital watermark should have several different properties. The most important are imperceptibility, robustness and security. Imperceptibility means that the watermarked data should be perceptually equivalent to the original, un-watermarked data.

In some applications, the watermark may be perceptible as long as it is not annoying or obtrusive; however, many applications require that the watermark be imperceptible. Security means that unauthorized parties should not be able to detect or manipulate the watermark. Cryptographic methods are typically employed to make watermarks secure.

Watermarking means embedding a piece of information into a multimedia content, such as a video, an audio or an image in such a way that it is imperceptible to a human observer, but easily detectable by a computer. Before the emergence of digital image watermarking, it was difficult to achieve copyright protection, authentication and data hiding, but now it is easy to achieve these goals by using watermarking techniques. Every watermarking algorithm consists of an embedding algorithm and a detection algorithm.

Embedded watermarks may have several properties such as robustness, fidelity, and tamper-resistance. The robustness means that the watermark must be robust to transformations that include common signal distortions such as digital-to-analogue conversion, analogue-to-digital conversion, and lossy compression. Fidelity means that the watermark should be neither noticeable to the viewer nor degrading for the quality of the content. Tamper-resistance means that the watermark is often required to be resistant to signal processing algorithms. These properties depend on the application. The watermark can be embedded in the spatial domain or in a transform domain.

The SVD mathematical technique provides an elegant way for extracting algebraic features from an image. The main properties of the Svs matrix of an image can be exploited in image watermarking. This matrix has a good stability. When a small perturbation occurs in an image, the variation of its Svs can be neglected. Using this property of the Svs matrix of an image, the watermark can be embedded to this matrix without a large variation in the obtained image.

Digital watermarking is a recent method of protecting digital multimedia data (audio, image and video) against unauthorized copying. A digital watermark is a signal added to the original signal, which can later be extracted or detected. The watermark is intended to be permanently embedded into the digital data so that authorized users can easily access it. At the same time, the watermark should not degrade the quality of the digital data.

The main driving force is the concern over protecting copyright: since audio, video and other works become available in digital form, the ease with which perfect copies can be made may lead to large-scale unauthorized copying, and this is of great concern to music, film, book and software publishing industries. At the same time, moves by various governments to restrict the availability of encryption services have motivated people to study methods by which private messages can be embedded in seemingly innocuous cover messages.

AUDIO WATERMARK

Before applying the SVD to an audio signal, the issue of how to organize the data into matrix form has to be addressed. The audio signal should first be split into frames whose length is denoted as *len*. The magnitude spectrum of the signal in each frame can then be computed. This spectrum will contain *len/2* frequency bins below the Nyquist frequency. If we put all of the frequency components of several consecutive frames into the same matrix, there should be redundancy, as generally, each component's magnitude would be similar to its value in the previous and the next frame. An alternative approach to organizing the Reduced Singular Value Decomposition RSVD input matrix is to put all the spectral components from one frame into a single matrix. For example, with a frame length of 1024 we just use the first 512 magnitude values and transform them into a 64×8 matrix. The magnitudes of the first 64 frequency bins will be put into the first column, the second 64 bin magnitudes into the second column and so on. The values in the first column will normally but not always be more significant than those in subsequent columns (Wang et al, 2010).

The steps of the SVD audio watermark embedding algorithm are summarized as follows:

1. The 1-D audio signal is transformed into a 2-D matrix ($\mathbf{A}$ matrix).
2. The SVD is performed on the $\mathbf{A}$ matrix.

$$\mathbf{A} = \mathbf{U}\mathbf{S}\mathbf{V}^{\mathrm{T}}$$

3. The chaotic encrypted watermark ($\mathbf{W}$ matrix) is added to the Svs of the original matrix.

$$\mathbf{D} = \mathbf{S} + k\mathbf{W}.$$

A small value of k of about 0.01 is required to keep the audio signal undistorted.

4. The SVD is performed on the new modified matrix ($\mathbf{D}$ matrix).

$$\mathbf{D} = \mathbf{U}_\mathrm{w}\,\mathbf{S}_\mathrm{w}\,\mathbf{V}^{\mathrm{T}}_\mathrm{w}.$$

5. The watermarked signal in 2-D format ($\mathbf{A}w$ matrix) is obtained using the modified matrix of Svs ($\mathbf{S}w$ matrix).

$$\mathbf{A}_\mathrm{w} = \mathbf{U}\,\mathbf{S}_\mathrm{w}\mathbf{V}^{\mathrm{T}}.$$

6. The 2-D $\mathbf{A}_\mathrm{w}$ matrix is transformed again into a 1-D audio signal.

To extract the possibly corrupted watermark from the possibly distorted watermarked audio signal, given $\mathbf{U}_\mathrm{w}$, $\mathbf{S}$, $\mathbf{V}_\mathrm{w}$ matrices, and the possibly distorted audio signal, the above steps are reversed as follows:

1. The 1-D audio signal is transformed into a 2-D matrix $\mathbf{A}_\mathrm{w}$. The * refers to the corruption due to attacks.
2. The SVD is performed on the possibly distorted watermarked image ($\mathbf{A}w$ matrix).

$$\mathbf{A}^*_\mathrm{w} = \mathbf{U}^*\,\mathbf{S}^*_\mathrm{w}\,\mathbf{V}^{*\mathrm{T}}.$$

3. The matrix that includes the watermark is computed.

$$\mathbf{D}^* = \mathbf{U}_\mathrm{w}\mathbf{S}_\mathrm{w}\mathbf{V}^{\mathrm{T}}_\mathrm{w}.$$

4. The possibly corrupted encrypted watermark is obtained.

$$\mathbf{W}^* = (\mathbf{D}^* - \mathbf{S})/k.$$

5. The obtained matrix $\mathbf{W}^*$ is decrypted.
6. The correlation coefficient between the decrypted matrix and the original watermark is estimated. If this coefficient is higher than a certain threshold, the watermark is present.

IMAGE WATERMARKING

In this section we present general algorithm to embed a gray scale image into another gray scale image of the same size using SVD (the same method for color image can apply for each color component Red, Green and Blue, and then later combine together as one image). Let the matrix $\mathbf{A}$, with elements aij, $i = 1, 2, \ldots, m$ and $j = 1, 2, \ldots, n$, represent the host image which needs to be watermarked. Let $\mathbf{W}$ represent the matrix of the image to be embedded. As a first step, we compute the SVD of both $\mathbf{A}$ and $\mathbf{W}$ (Agarwal & Santhanam, 2008).

$$A = Ua\ Sa\ V_a^T$$

For the watermark image

$$W = Uw\ Sw\ V_w^T$$

Now, we add the scaled eigenvector Vw of watermark to that of the original image,

$$V = Va + \propto Vw$$

where $\propto$ is the scaling factor, typically, $0 \leq \propto \leq 1$, so that the intensity of the watermark W is less compared to the original image A. Note that, within the framework of SVD, $Vw\ V_w^T = I$, where I is the identity matrix. Similar relation holds good for Va too. As $\propto \rightarrow 0$, the approximation that V is an orthogonal matrix, i.e., $VV^T \approx I$ gets better. This property is important in the next step for constructing the watermarked image. We get the watermarked image as,

$$Ac = Aa\ V^T.$$

Also, a modified to this algorithm, by apply the SVD to each component of the original image (A) (red, green and blue component)

SVD (A) = $U_i\ S_i\ V_i$ i= 1, 2, and 3. i= 1 for red component, 2 for green component and 3 for blue component.

We can perform the embedding procedure by the following steps.

$$S_{wj} = S_i + \propto T_i$$

$\propto$ is a scaling factor, which controls the strength of the watermark to be inserted. Because the embedded watermark can't degrade the host image quality, the value of $\propto$ should be small. During the process of SVD, three matrices U, V and S are produced.

(U1, V1); (U2, V2); (U3, V3) these matrices are the user's secret keys, which don't contain any information about three watermarks.

A method of desirable watermarking should satisfy the ownership of imperceptibility, where the integrated watermark is not visible for the observer. (A) Represent the Host image.

(T1, T2, T3) Represent the three watermarks for the protection of copyright, (A1, A2, A3) represent the three components of RGB image, (B1, B2, B3) represent the three components watermarked of RGB image, (B) The watermarked image.

Here, we define the value of scaling factor $\propto = 0.1$ and inject these watermarks into the RGB components of the host image (EL Gorfte et al, 2013).

VIDEO WATERMARKING

The watermark is a digital code embedded in the multimedia (audio, images, video, etc.) before transmission or broadcasting, which typically indicates the copyright owner. If different watermarks are appending to individual copies of the video, watermarking can be also used to indicate the identity of the legal receiver of each copy. This allows tracing back an illegally reproduced copy to the receiver of the copy from which the illegal copy is originated. As an important branch of watermarking algorithms, video watermarking is attracting more and more attention. In video watermarking, watermark can be embedded in the spatial and/or transform domains.

The embedding algorithm is based on transforming the host video using the SVD operator and then embedding the watermark information in the S, U, or V matrices diagonal-wise. We described in details in the following steps (Rajab et al, 2009):

Step 1: Divide the video clip into video scenes *Vsi*.
Step 2: Process the frames of each video scene using SVD described in steps 3 - 9 below.

Step 3: Convert every video frame *F* from RGB to YCbCr color space.

Step 4: Compute the SVD for the Y matrix for each frame *F*. This operation generates 3Matrices (U, S, V) such as: $Y = U_Y S_Y V_Y$

Step 5: Rescale the watermark image so that the size, of the watermark will match the size of the matrix which will be used for embedding either U, V or S.

Step 6: Embedding can be done in one of the three SVD matrices: *U, V, or S*, as follows:

Embedding in Matrix U Diagonal-Wise

1. Inverse each diagonal value $(u_{i,i})$ in The U matrix, such that $x = 1/u_{i,i}$
2. Embed the binary bits of the watermark W_{Vsi} into the integer part of x by substituting the watermark bit

W_i with the 7th bit of *x*.

3. Apply the inverse to each x, to get the modified values of U matrix, such that $u_{i,i}' = 1/x'$.
4. Apply inverse SVD on the modified coefficient matrix *U '*. Such as:

$$Y' = U_Y' S_Y V_Y^T$$

Embedding in Matrix V Diagonal-Wise

1. Inverse each diagonal value $(v_{i,i})$ in The V matrix, such tha $x = 1/v_{i,i}$
2. Embed the binary bits of the watermark W_{Vsi} into the integer part of x by substituting the watermark bit

W_i with the 7th bit of *x*.

3. Apply the inverse to each x, to get the modified values of V matrix, such that $v_{i,i}' = 1/x'$.

4. Apply inverse SVD on the modified coefficient matrix V '. Such as:

$$Y' = U_Y S_Y V_Y'^T$$

Embedding in Matrix S Diagonal-Wise

1. Embed the binary bits of the watermark W_{Vsi} into the integer part of each diagonal value of the S matrix $s_{i,i}$ by substituting the watermark bit W_i with the7th bit of $s_{i,i}$
2. Apply inverse SVD on the modified coefficient matrix S ' such as:

$$Y' = U_Y S_Y' V_Y^T$$

where Y' is the updated luminance in the YCbCr color representation. This operation produces the final watermarked video frame *F '*.

Step 7: Convert the video frames *F'* from YCbCr to RGB color space.

Step 8: Reconstruct frames into the final watermarked video scene V_{si}.

Step 9: Reconstruct watermarked scenes to get the final watermarked video clip.

HYBRID SVD

The schemes which are applied with or after cascading of any transform domain are called hybrid SVD based schemes. DCT, DWT, FFT are few most popular frequency domains which used with SVD to make watermarking schemes more robust.

SVD and DCT Based Algorithm

There are various types of hybrid watermarking schemes based on DCT and SVD has been proposed. In general in case of pure DCT based watermarking schemes the DCT transformation is applied to the original image and then frequency coefficients from lowest to highest are mapped in zig-zag sequence into some forms of quadrants or blocks. These DCT coefficients are modified to embed watermark. Whereas in case of SVD based watermarking SVD transformation is applied to the entire image and then the singular values of the image are modified to embed the watermark in host image. In hybrid DCT-SVD watermarking schemes both DCT & SVD features are combined, that means DCT transform is applied to the cover image and also to the watermark. DCT coefficients of cover image are mapped to some quadrants using zig-zag sequence. SVD is applied to each quadrant and also to the DCT coefficients of watermark, then the singular values of each quadrant modified with the singular values of DCT coefficients of watermark. The hybrid DCT-SVD based watermarking scheme when embedding watermark in lowest frequency shows robustness to some set of attacks, while embedding in higher frequency shows robustness to another set of attacks. In general a hybrid DCT-SVD watermarking scheme shows robustness against a set of attacks like Gaussian blur, Gaussian noise, JPEG compression, rescaling cropping, histogram equalization etc. but shows less robustness to rotation and translation operation.

SVD and DWT Based Algorithm

As in case of DCT, here in DWT the cover image is decomposed into four sub-bands i.e. LL, LH, HL, and HH. In hybrid SVD-DWT watermarking schemes, SVD is applied to the sub-bands and also to the watermark, then the singular values of the sub-bands are modified by embedding the singular values of watermark. Finally four sets of DWT coefficients are obtained and applying the inverse DWT using the modified DWT coefficients, watermarked image is being produced. Same as in DCT-SVD, watermarking scheme embedding watermark in various sub-band shows robustness to different kinds of set of attacks. In general hybrid DWT-SVD watermarking scheme

robust to a set of attacks including Gaussian blur, Gaussian noise, JPEG compression, JPEG 2000, compression, rescaling, cropping etc. But shows less robustness against sharpening, rotation, contrasting and histogram equalization, also when embedding watermark in LL band although the extracted watermark is best in visual quality but after embedding of watermark degrades the image quality to some extents.

STEGANOGRAPHY

The amazing developments in the field of network communications during the past years have created a great requirement for secure image transmission over the Internet. Steganography is a good solution to transmit the message in secure base, also it is possible to increase the security of steganography by combine it with encryption. Steganography is the science and art of hiding data of digital medium in other digital medium called 'cover object' in such a way that the existence of the message is concealed. The cover object along with the hidden message is known as the 'stego object' or 'steganogram'. Steganography is in contrast to cryptography where the existence of the hidden message is known, but the content is intentionally obscured.

There are several properties important in the creation and evaluation of an effective stego-algorithm. These include the following:

- **Capacity:** Measures the amount of payload that can be embedded in a fixed size of cover file. It is measured in bits (of payload) per byte (of cover). For example, in the LSB embedding scheme, the sender chooses as a cover image a gray scale, bit-mapped image, and replaces the least significant bit of each pixel with one bit of payload. Assuming each pixel occupies 8 bits, this scheme has a capacity of 1 bit/byte.

- **Perceptibility:** Describes the ability of a third party (not the intended recipient) to visually detect the presence of hidden information in the stego image (or audibly, in the case of audio data). Note that we do not require the third party to extract the information, just perceive its existence. We say that the steganography embedding algorithm is *imperceptible* when used on a particular image if an innocent third party interested in the content of the cover image, is unaware of the existence of the payload. Essentially this requires that the embedding process not degrade the visual quality of the cover image.

- **Detectability:** Describes the probability that a determined adversary, who suspects steganography, will be able to determine the existence of a payload, thus compromising the message's security. In other words, a stego algorithm provides low security if the payload is detectable in the stego image with a high probability.

- **Undetectability:** Obviously a much more difficult requirement to meet than is imperceptibility, but as the use of steganography increases, so will the use of steganalysis is. The concept of a 'safe bit-rate' is related to detectability of a stego algorithm. The safe bit-rate (SBR) is the maximum capacity of a stego algorithm when applied to a particular image that is not detectable by steganalysis. The SBR is therefore dependent not only on the algorithm used to embed the data, but the data itself as well as the steganalysis techniques available to detect it.

- **Robustness:** Characterizes the ability of the payload to survive the embedding and extraction process, even in the face of manipulations of the stego image such as filtering, cropping, rotating and compression.

- **Speed:** Reflects the computational effort required to embed and extract the hidden data. It is well-understood that there is always a tradeoff between capacity and visual imperceptibility, and capacity and detectability (Bergman & Davidson, 2005).

The message to be embedded will begin as a string of binary values $b_1 b_2 b_3 ...$ where $b_i \in \{0,1\}$. Next, these will need to be converted to signed bits using a transformation using either of the transformations $\left(b \to (-1)^b \ \ or \ \ b \to 2b \to -1 \right)$, making a message $p_1 p_2 p_3 ...$ where $pi \in \{-1,1\}$. The basic idea then is to embed the signed message into the image by changing the signs of certain entries in the matrix U (from the SVD of a matrix that describes part of an image) to correspond with the signed bit values *{pi}*. Each pixel of a gray scale image (cover) *M*, is a value in the range 0 to 255. To expand this to a colored image in a RGB format, each pixel would have three values in that range, ideally allowing the embedding of three times as many values.

The cover image is divided into a series of $n \times n$ blocks in some standard order.

Message bits are embedded into *A* by a simple four-step process:

1. Compute the SVD (U S V^T) of A.
2. Transform U to U'
   a. Set certain components u'ij = p_k . |u$_{ij}$|, where k the next bit from message.
   b. Chose remaining components to ensure that U' is still orthogonal.

The visual quality of *A* is primarily determined by its largest singular values and singular vectors. By assumption, those are the left-most values of *S* and the left-most columns of *U* and *V*. Part of this strategy is to leave those columns untouched in order to achieve imperceptibility in this method.

3. Compute $A' = U' S V^T$.
4. Clip and round the entries in A' to integers in the range 0...255. The resulting matrix A_E will be a block of stego image.

Extraction Algorithm A_E denotes the stego image and *SVD* is applied to retrieve the hidden message.

1. Compute the SVD_E, $U_E S_E V_E^T$ of A_E.
2. Extract payload bits from the signs of the entries in the triangular portion of U_E: $P_k = u_{Eij} / |u_{Eij}|$

For example: to embed the message: 0 0 1 1 0 1011 ...

- Keep first 2 columns unchanged.
- Construct UE by changing {uk2}, (see Figure 2):

$$u_{(E)k2} = \begin{cases} +|u_{k2}| & \text{if message bit is 1} \\ -|u_{k2}| & \text{if message bit is 0} \end{cases}$$

- Last entries z_{72} and z_{82}: calculated so that column 3 is orthogonal to columns 1 & 2.
- Next column: insert 4 bits; last 3 entries calculated so that column 4 is orthogonal to columns 1, 2 & 3.
- Etc.
- Reconstruct the block with the embedded bits:

$A_E = $ clip (round (U_E S V^T))

where U_E is the matrix constructed in previous, *S, V* are from original matrix (image) *A*.

- **Round:** Rounds to nearest integer; *clip*: values less than 0 get reset to 0; values larger than 255 get reset to 255.
- Do this for each block.

- Capacity for 8 × 8 block with two columns protected: 15 bits per 64 pixels = .234 bits/pixel bit embedding rate.
- 0.2 – 0.5 bits/pixel is typical for "good" stego algorithms. May not be "safe enough" to avoid detection.

With this algorithm, the error between the extracted message and the embedded message is typically 8% - 10% of the total bits embedded.

Most of the error comes from the fact that the change from *U* to U_E is large relative to the magnitudes of the entries in *U*. There are several solutions to reduce error.

STEGANALYSIS

Steganalysis is the art of discovering the very presence of hidden data in cover objects. Steganalysis can be broadly classified into two groups: algorithm specific (targeted) methods and universal (blind) methods. Algorithm specific steganalysis assumes that the steganographic method is known by the attacker. The attacker takes advantage of

Figure 2. How to embed a message in a column

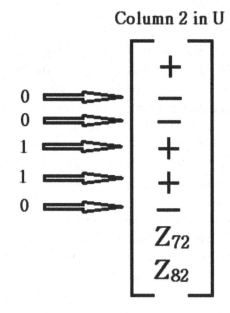

Column 2 in U

this prior knowledge to design methods to reveal the existence of the hidden data. The short coming of this type of steganalysis is that their satisfactory performance is restricted to a specific steganography. Universal steganalysis methods aim to overcome this problem. Instead of using any *a priori* information, they take into account all available steganography methods to devise a single steganalysis framework. It is supposed that a blind steganalysis method can detect any steganography if sufficient numbers of cover and stego images have been taken into account during the design process.

All universal steganalysis methods assumed that data-hiding destroys the underlined statistics of natural images. Therefore, a common characterization should be possible if the features incorporated to the classification process are sensitive to the embedding noise and insensitive to the image content. Universal steganalysis schemes can be divided into two categories: spatial domain and discrete cosine transform (DCT) domain. The methods belonging to the former one extract the features from the pixel information, while the latter ones attack on the DCT coefficients.

The SVD steganlysis method attacks steganographic content using the features derived from singular values. Let us assume a full rank matrix.

If any two rows or columns of this matrix are modified so that they become linearly dependent, it can be observed that the lowest singular value vanishes. If this process is repeated using the next row or column, the second lowest singular value becomes zero. This observation comes up with two main ideas which are the pillars of this method.

First, the reaction to the changes on the matrix content starts from the lowest singular value. Second, the lower valued singular values closeness to zero indicates a group of vectors closeness to the linear dependency. This observation can be used to model the soft relationship between the image rows and columns which will be disturbed by the embedding process.

Due to the aforementioned unequal effect of embedding noise on the singular values, it is necessary to adopt a function which can intensify the lower valued singular values for a powerful steganalysis and can attenuate the higher valued ones to normalize the different energy levels of different images. For this purpose, a function comprising the logarithm of the inverse power of singular values ($\log(s_x^{-1})$) is devised to derive features for the steganalysis. Since spatial domain represents a strong dependency between the pixels in the local neighborhoods the features are extracted from the sub-blocks representing the locality in the spatial domain rather than the entire image. It is obvious that when the block size increases the number of examined blocks decreases. This results in decreasing the dependencies which are considered. To alleviate this problem, the sub-blocks are overlapped proportionally to the block size in order to be able to take into account the correlations within and among sub-blocks. Consequently, the feature extraction algorithm is described as follows.

Step 1: Divide image A, into sub-blocks of size W×W, where W= 3,4,...,27 according to the following overlapping rules:

If W < 8, no overlapping

If 8<= W <= 13, 50% overlapping

If W>13, 75% overlapping

Step 2: For each particular, calculate the singular value vector S_v of each sub-block j

$$\text{SVD (sub-block}_j) = S_{vj} = (s_{1j},\ s_{2j},\ \ldots\ldots s_{wj})$$

Step 3: Calculate the natural logarithm of the inverse power of each singular value and add the singular values up with respect to the related sub-block j

$$SvB_j = \sum_{i=1}^{w} \log\left(s_{ij}^{-1}\right), \; j = 1, 2, \ldots T_w, \; s_{ij} \neq 0$$

where T_w is the total number of sub-blocks sizes of W×W

Step 4: Sum the final results obtained in Step 3 and normalize them with the number of total sub-blocks

$$F_w = \frac{1}{T_w} \sum_{j=1}^{Tw} S_v B_{j}, \; W = 3, \ldots, 27 \;.$$

Using this algorithm, we obtain 25 dimensional (25D) features for each image.

IMAGE ENCRYPTION

The field of encryption is becoming very important in the present era in which information security is of utmost concern. Security is an important issue in communication and storage of images, and encryption is one of the ways to ensure security. Image encryption has applications in internet communication, multimedia systems, medical imaging, telemedicine, military communication, etc.

Image information is different from the text data, it has larger amount of data, higher redundancy and stronger correlation between pixels. Traditionally developed encryption algorithm such as RSA, DES is suitable for text encryption but not suitable for image encryption directly because of two reasons.

The first one, that the image size is almost always much greater than that of text. Therefore, the traditional cryptosystems need much time to directly encrypt the image data. The other problem is that the decrypted text must be equal to the original text. However, this requirement is not necessary for image data. Due to the characteristic of human perception, a decrypted image containing small distortion is usually acceptable, encrypted image shows in Figure 3.

At present there are many image encryption algorithms are available but these algorithms doesn't satisfy the requirement of modern cryptographic mechanism and they are prone to attacks. In the recent years, the image encryption has been developed to overcome the above disadvantages.

1. The first step in this work is to create the necessary keys for encryption image (A)
2. Scrambling the pixels value is the second step, scrambling the image values as follow:

Figure 3. Image encryption

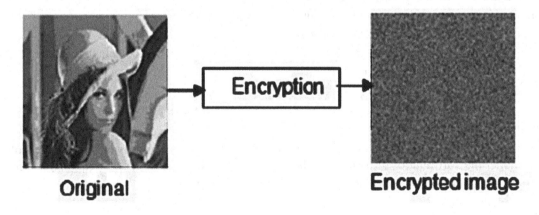

$A1 = Key1 * \max(A) - A, A2 = Key1 * \max(A1) - A1$

3. Appling SVD for both matrices resulting from the previous step.

SVD (A1) = UA$_1$, SA$_1$, VA$_1$

SVD (A2) = UA$_2$, SA$_2$, VA$_2$

4. Rebuild new matrix from the results of SVD process in step 3, this can be done by replacing the singular values (*Sv*) of A1 with singular values of A2.

C1 = UB$_1$ * SB$_2$ * VB$_1^T$

C2 = UB$_2$ * SB$_1$ * VB$_2^T$

5. For more complexes, the same steps above can be repeated to create new matrices.

Scrambling the elements in matrices (C1, C2) to get new matrices (D1, D2)

$D1 = C1 - C2, \quad D2 - KEY3 * D1 + C2$

6. Then, SVD applied for both matrices (D1, D2) and replaces the singular values of D1 with singular value of D2 as we did in previous steps to create new matrices (E1, E2)

[UD$_1$, SD$_1$, VD$_1$] = SVD   (D1)

[UD$_2$, SD$_2$, VD$_2$] = SVD   (D2)

So,

$E1 = UD1 * SD2 * VD1^T, \quad E2 = UD2 * SD1 * VD2^T$

7. Combine (E1, and E2) in one matrix

$F = \begin{bmatrix} E1E2 \end{bmatrix}$

8. Finally rescaling F, by using the following relation

$$FF = \frac{F - MI}{MA - MI}$$

where, MA is the maximum number in matrix (F), and MI is the minimum number in the matrix (F).

The decryption process is the inverse of the above steps.

SVD PREVIOUS RESEARCH

Nelson (Nelson et al, 2009) focused on the Ghost Circuitry Detection based on SVD in their research.

Ghost Circuitry (GC) insertion is an intentional hardware alteration of the design specification and IC implementation. The alterations only affect the circuit's functionality in a few specific circumstances and are hidden otherwise. GC is more difficult to detect than design bugs or manufacturing faults, since it is intentionally implanted to be unperceivable by the current debugging and testing methodologies and tools. The vast number of possibilities for inserting GC further complicates detection.

In a GC insertion attack, the adversary adds one or more gates such that the functionality of the design is altered. The gates can be added so that no timing path between primary inputs and flip-flops (FFs) and primary outputs and FFs is altered. However, leakage power is always altered. Even if the attacker gates the added circuitry, the gating requires an additional gate.

Manufacturing variation in power and delay behavior of gates is modeled by associating each gate with a scaling factor, α, which multiplies both delay and leakage current.

Measurements of total leakage power and path delay for various circuit inputs gives rise to linear equations with the scaling factors as the unknowns. Each set of measurements produces a linear system $Ga = m+e$ where a is the vector of scaling factors, also referred to as the α-values, and related to gate size.

- $m+e$ is a vector of measured values
- m would be the measured value if there is no measurement error
- e is the measurement error associated with each measured value
- G is derived from the expected power and/or delay characteristics of the gates.

For Ng number of gates in the circuit and Nm number of measurements, G is $Nm \times Ng$, a is $Ng \times 1$, and m is $Nm \times 1$.

More abstractly, one can imagine the circuit's gate characteristics split into two components represented by G and a. G represents the characteristics of gate classes, i.e. 2-input NANDs power and delay characteristics for a given input vector, and it is inherent the circuit design. This information is readily available and in our experiments we have used the values provided by for delay and for leakage power.

The vector a, which is a vector of α-values for all the gates in the circuit, represents the unknowns in the equation. In other words, a is the fingerprint for the circuit just as the α-value is the fingerprint for the individual gate. Due to manufacturing variability, gate sizes are not exactly matched to the design specifications. The size of each gate in the circuit of each fabricated IC can have a variety of values. All circuits accordingly will have a large variety of sizes for most or all of their gates, and hence the extremely large combinations of possibility for a results in a unique fingerprint for each circuit. Splitting each manufactured circuit into an invariant and into a variant component results in, $G,$ which is universal across all circuits of the same design for the same set of input vectors, and $a,$ which represents the unique characteristics of the fabricated circuit.

A large set of measurements are taken for the total circuit. As we can only access the input and output pins of the circuit, all the measurements made, represented by $m+e$, are made from a global circuit or path level and not at the individual gate level. Obviously, if we were able to measure these values at the gate level, we would easily be able to solve for each gate's α-value.

We do consider error in the formulation, as measurement error is possible when measuring total leakage power for the circuit and total delay along a path of the circuit from input to output pin. This is represented by e, which is the error that may be introduced in the measurement for each input vector or pair of input vectors.

A singular value decomposition $G = USV^T$ is used in the following way. $G+$, the pseudo-inverse of G, gives a least-squares solution to the system, a', an approximation of the scaling factors given the possibility of measurement errors being introduced.

The procedure for fingerprinting circuits, i.e., determining the α-values as accurately as possible is the following: (1) Choose a set of circuit inputs. (2) Compute G and $G+$. (3) Perform measurements on a circuit to produce $m+e$. (4) Compute the fingerprint $a' = G+(m+e)$. In this formulation, a' represents the fingerprint that we deciphered from the SVD. It does not necessarily match a, due to the measurement error and also due to gate correlations that hinder gate-level characterization.

Kamel and Sayeed (Kamel & Sayeed, 2008) used Data Glove Technique in signature verification Based on SVD. In the pitch of computer-generated milieus, information glove is an innovative measurement. The first considered to satisfy the strict supplies up-to-date indication apprehension and simulation specialists.

All proposals are relief and luxury of routine such as a minor method issue and several request motorists. Moreover, for truthful real-time simulation, the little cross-correlation and high data amount mark it the best.

The author attempt to modify the application of data glove such as be the sign proof tricky from indicator simulation, he completed routine of the obtainable numerous marks of liberty aimed at apiece finger and hand too.

Singular Value Decomposition is used in the planned system to outcome r remarkable vectors recognizing the greatest energy of glove data matrix **A**. This matrix is defined as a major subspace, it is excuse for maximum dissimilarity in the creative information. The dimensionality of the information can be compact.

Having known data glove sign ready its rth main subspace, the validity dismisses then be found by scheming the directions among the dissimilar subspaces.

Mention to the lively structures the data glove deliver information such as:

1. Outlines characteristic to an individuals' sign and hand size.
2. Time gone throughout the validation process.
3. Hand route reliant on progressing.

For that reason, the glove as implement for sign appreciation lets verification of people is not just over the biometric features of their signs, but took over the scope of their hands. Figure 4 shows the data glove with the place of the sensors.

Figure 4. Sensor mappings for 5DT data glove 14 ultra

Study a data glove of m sensors, apiece marks n examples each signature, creating an production data matrix, **A**$(m \times n)$. Typically $n >> m$, where m means the amount of dignified channels while n denotes the number of sizes. Numerous sign processing it has been created requests and regulator schemes that the singular value decomposition of matrix formed from observed data can be used to improve approaches of signal limit approximation and system documentation.

There are two sections for the model of the proposed signature verification technique:

Enrollment Section

- Use data glove to offer the system with ten frank examples of his/her signature.
- Obtainable of the composed ten frank examples choice the orientation signature.
- Excerpt the r-principal subspace of the orientation signature and apart from it in the file for equivalent.

Verification Section

- Use data glove to effort the signature of the employer (one sample).
- Compute the r-principal subspace of the demanded individuality consuming SVD.
- Competition the main subspace of the demanded individuality to the registered copies in the database over the parallel feature.
- Relate the parallel feature with the choice threshold for ACCEPT or REJECT.

In the way of the ith left remarkable course of the matrix **A**, The worried with determination restrained is equivalent to the ith singular value squared.

The rth principal subspace S_U^r is, among all r-dimensional subspaces of R^m, the one that senses a maximal oriented energy. Thus, the orthogonal breakdown of the drive via the singular value breakdown is official in the intelligence that it lets discovery subspaces of measurement *r* wherever the classification has slight and greatest energy. This breakdown of the ambient space, as straight sum of a space of greatest and slight energy for a assumed vector order, leads to a very stimulating abundant reflection.

Through the launching of the relation among the concerned with energy and SVD, it has been showed that the first *r* left singular courses intelligence the greatest drive of glove data matrix **A**. for that reason, the description for most of the variation in the original data.

This means that with *m* × *n* data matrix that is usually largely over determined with much more samples (columns) than channels (rows): *n* >> *m* the singular value decomposition allows to compact most signature characteristics into *r* vectors.

Thus, apiece signature will be recognized over its *r*th main subspace S_U^r, the validity of the strained signature can be got by scheming the viewpoint between its main subspace and the true one.

Gul and Avcibas used Forensic features based on SVD for Cell Phone source identification (Gul & Avcibas, 2007). For the cell-phones equipped with cameras, The documentation of the basis is suitable essential for allowed and safety causes through the always growing obtainability today.

Image source documentation needs a considerate of the physics and procedures of the image creation pipeline.

For nearly all numerical cameras the pipeline is alike, though greatly of the particulars are reserved as branded data of each builder.

Digital camera pipeline contain of a lens scheme, sampler filters, color filter collection, imaging instrument, and a numerical image computer.

There are alterations among numerical cameras and cell-phone cameras.

Whereas their imaging pipelines are like, there are important changes in excellence. The cell-phone cameras effect in minor excellence images owing to numerous details.

They need minor resolve, fixed f/number and minor opening halts. Their flashes are not healthy due to control compels and their analog-to-digital change (ADC) uses 10 bits instead of 12 bits as classically used in conservative numerical cameras.

Documentation method is created on the supposition that the image rows/columns will display the CFA exclamation and device blast typical in the form of comparative direct (in) dependency; as CFA exclamation presents inter pixel associations and device noise is additional in an scene self-governing way.

SVD is a very influential instrument in linear algebra. It rots a matrix *A*∈IR into the creation of two orthonormal matrices *U*∈IR, *V*∈IR and a slanting matrix *S*∈IR as follows:

$$A = USV^T$$

The diagonal rudiments of matrix *S* are nonnegative and organized in lessening instruction, these rudiments produce a vector called remarkable value vector

$$Sv = Diag(S)$$

Singular standards of a matrix direct the soft association between image rows/columns in statuses of linear dependence.

For additional exactly, singular standards tend to develop zero if the image rows and/or columns tend to develop comparatively linearly dependent. Two rows/columns, c1 and c2, of a matrix are named linearly reliant on if they can be defined as c2=*K*·c1 where *K* is an integer. Consequently, it can be described 'comparative linear dependency' between two rows/columns as the closeness of *K* to an integer.

A worthy perfect of the comparative linear dependency of image rows/columns lead to precisely identify the model of a cell-phone. It can be predictable that the different CFA outburst algorithms of dissimilar mobile phones as well as the noise shaped by the semiconductor devices present revealing properties both on local neighborhoods as well as on image macro blocks, including the image itself. Therefore a common characterization should compromise macro and micro statistics.

In order to obtain micro statistical features, images are first divided into sub-blocks of sizes $w \times w$ (w=3, 4…20). Then, each singular value is regularized with the sum of the remarkable values of the connected sub-block to reduce the dissimilar drive levels of dissimilar images.

For be able to income into explanation the associations within and between the image tablets, the blocks are overlay equivalently to the tablet size.

Macro Statistical Features

Macro statistical features are extracted from the entire image as well as from image macro blocks. The derivation of a singular value vector from an entire image, Sve, is straightforward. For image macro blocks the following procedure is applied to obtain a unique singular value vector:

- Divide the image A into four non-overlapping equal size sub-blocks ($A1$, $A2$, $A3$, $A4$).
- Find the mean sub-block As=0.25x ($A1+A2+A3+A4$) and subtract As from the image sub-blocks $Bj = Aj$-As, for j=1, 2, 3, 4.
- Calculate singular value vector, Svj, of each Bj for j=1, 2, 3, 4 and determine the average Sv, Sva=0.25Σj Svj.
- Normalize Sva with the sum of its elements Svn=(1/K)· Sva where K=Σi $Sva(i)$.

CONCLUSION

In this chapter we presented an introduction to SVD and its general applications, SVD thus, proves to be promising domain for security such as watermarking, steganography, encryption,

stegoanalysis. Also we introduced some of papers that used SVD in specific computer security. The algorithms presented in this chapter can be improved in several ways.

Due to the arrangement of the singular values in the matrix S (in a descending order), the SVD transformation has the property that the maximal variation among the objects is captured in the first singular value, as $s_1 > s_i$, for i $\geq$ 2. Similarly much of the remaining variations are captured in the second dimension, and so on. Thus, a transformed matrix with a much lower dimension can be constructed to represent the original matrix faithfully. This property makes the SVD particularly interesting for our application of high accuracy data hiding.

REFERENCES

Agarwal, R., & Santhanam, M. (2008). Digital Watermarking in the Singular Vector Domain. *International Journal of Image and Graphics*, *8*(3), 351–368. doi:10.1142/S0219467808003131

Andrews, H., & Patterson, C. (1976). Singular value decompositions and digital image processing. *Acoustics, Speech and Signal Processing. IEEE Transactions*, *24*(1), 26–53.

Bergman, C., & Davidson, J. (2005). Unitary embedding for data hiding with the SVD. In proceedings of Security, Steganography, and Watermarking of multimedia Contents (pp. 619-630), Bellingham, WA: SPIE.

El Gorfte, Z., Eddeqaqi, N., Bouzid, A., & Roukh, A. (2013). Multi-data embedding in to RGB Image with using SVD method. *International Journal of Computer Science Issues*, *10*(5), 190–195.

Gul, G., & Avcibas, I. (2007). Source Cell Phone Camera Identification Based on Singular Value Decomposition. In proceedings of Signal Processing and Communications Applications Conference (pp. 1-4). Eskisehir, Turket: IEEE.

Kamel, N., & Sayeed, S. (2008). SVD-Based Signature Verification Technique Using Data Glove. *International Journal of Pattern Recognition and Artificial Intelligence*, *22*(3), 431–443. doi:10.1142/S0218001408006387

Liu, R., & Tan, T. (2002). A SVD-Based Watermarking Scheme for Protecting Rightful Ownership. *Multimedia. IEEE Transactions*, *4*(1), 121–128.

Nelson, M., Nahapetian, A., Koushanfar, F., & Potkonjak, M. (2009). SVD-Based Ghost Circuitry Detection. In Information Hiding, Security and Cryptology, (pp. 221-234), Darmstadt, Germany, Springer Berlin Heidelberg.

Rajab, L., Al-Khatib, T., & Al-Haj, A. (2009). Video Watermarking Algorithms Using the SVD Transform. *European Journal of Scientific Research*, *30*(3), 389–401.

Sadek, R. (2012). SVD Based Image Processing Applications: State of The Art, Contributions and Research Challenges. *International Journal of Advanced Computer Science and Applications*, *3*(7), 26–34.

Wang, J., Healy, R., & Timoney, J. (2010). A Novel Audio Watermarking Algorithm Based On Reduced Singular Value Decomposition. In *proceeding of Intelligent Information Hiding and Multimedia Signal Processing (IIH-MSP), 2010 Sixth International Conference* (pp. 143 – 146), Darmstadt, Germany, IEEE. doi:10.1109/IIHMSP.2010.43

ADDITIONAL READING

Bhat, V., Sengupta, I., & Das, A. (2011). An Audio Watermarking Scheme Using Singular Value Decomposition and Dither-Modulation Quantization. *Multimedia Tools and Applications*, *52*(2-3), 369–383. doi:10.1007/s11042-010-0515-1

El Abbadi, N., Mohamad, A., & Mohammed, M. (2013). Blind Fake Image Detection. *International Journal of Computer Science Issues*, *10*(4), 180–186.

El-Bendary, M., El-Azm, A., El-Fishawy, N., Shawki, F., El-Tokhy, M., El-Samie, F., & Kazemian, H. (2011). SVD Audio Watermarking: A Tool to Enhance the Security of Image Transmission over ZigBee Networks. *Journal of Telecommunications and Information Technology*, (4), 99-107.

Golub, G., & Van Loan, C. (1996). *Matrix Computations* (3rd ed.). London, UK: The Johns Hopkins University Press.

Jagadeesh, B., Kumar, P., & Reddy, P. (2012). Genetic Algorithm approach for Singular Value Decomposition and Quantization based Digital Image Watermarking. *International Journal of Engineering Research and Applications*, *2*(2), 1229–1235.

Kalnins, Y., & Pakalnite, I. (2011). Singular Value Decomposition of Images with the Simple Elements. *Computer Modeling and New Technologies*, *15*(1), 49–54.

Milivojević, Z., & Stevanović, Z. (2013). Analysis on the Robustness SVD-Based Watermarking Algorithms. *International Journal of Computer and Information Technology*, *2*(4), 688–693.

Pomponiu, V., Cavagnino, D., Basso, A., & Vernone, A. (2010). Data Hiding Schemes Based on Singular Value Decomposition. In A. Al-Haj (Ed.), Advanced Techniques in Multimedia Watermarking: Image, Video and Audio Applications (pp. 254-288). Hershey, PA: Information Science Reference. doi:10.4018/978-1-61520-903-3.ch011

Shantikumar, Y., Devi, B., & Singh, Kh. (2013). A Review of Different Techniques on Digital Image Watermarking Scheme. *International Journal of Engine Research*, *2*(3), 193–199.

Singh, N., & Sharma, M. (2010). Singular Value Decomposition Technique for Digital Image Watermarking. In *Proceedings of National Conference on Advancements in Wireless and Optical Communication Technologies*, Maharashtra, India.

Swarnalipi, S., Majumder, S., Das, T., & Kumar, S. (2012). Binary Logo Watermarking Based on Multiresolution SVD. *In proceeding of International Conference on Computing and Control Engineering*, (page 61), Chennai, India: Coimbatore institute of information technology.

Wang, J. (2008). *Matrix Decomposition for Data Disclosure Control and Data Mining Applications*. Kentucky, USA: University of Kentucky Doctoral Dissertations.

KEY TERMS AND DEFINITIONS

Encryption: The process of encoding messages (or information) in such a way that third parties cannot read it, but only authorized parties can. Encryption doesn't prevent hacking but it prevents the hacker from reading the data that is encrypted.

Image Processing: Any form of signal processing for which the input is an image, such as a photograph or video frame; the output of image processing may be either an image or a set of characteristics or parameters related to the image.

Information Hiding: The process of embedding information into digital content without causing perceptual degradation.

Security: The field covers all the processes and mechanisms by which computer-based equipment, information and services are protected from unintended or unauthorized access, change or destruction.

Steganalysis: The art and science of detecting messages hidden using steganography; this is analogous to cryptanalysis applied to cryptography.

Steganography: The art and science of encoding hidden messages in such a way that no one, apart from the sender and intended recipient, suspects the existence of the message. It is a form of security through obscurity.

SVD: The singular value decomposition: is a factorization of a real or complex matrix, with many useful applications in signal processing and statistics.

Watermarking: The process of hiding digital information in a carrier signal; the hidden information should, but does not need to contain a relation to the carrier signal. Digital watermarks may be used to verify the authenticity or integrity of the carrier signal or to show the identity of its owners. It is prominently used for tracing copyright infringements and for banknote authentication.

Chapter 13
Malay Language Text-Based Anti-Spam System Using Neural Network

Hamid A. Jalab
University Malaya, Malaysia

Thamarai Subramaniam
University Malaya, Malaysia

Alaa Y. Taqa
Mosul University, Iraq

ABSTRACT

This unauthorized intrusion has cost time and money for businesses and users. The exponential growth of spam emails in recent years has resulted in the necessity for more accurate and efficient spam filtering. This chapter focuses on creating a text-based anti-spam system using back-propagation neural network for Malay Language emails that efficiently and effectively counter measure spam problems. The proposed algorithm consists of three stages; pre-processing, implementation and evaluation. Malay language emails are collected and divided into spam and non-spam. Features are extracted and document frequency as dimension reduction technique is calculated too. Classifiers are trained to recognize spam and non-spam emails using training datasets. After training, classifiers are tested to check whether they can predict spam (or non-spam) emails accurately with the testing datasets. The result of this classification in terms of accuracy, precision, and recall are evaluated, compared and analyzed, thus providing the best anti-spam solution to counter measure spam problem of Malay language emails.

INTRODUCTION

Email is one of the most popular communication tools that were ever invented. It has proliferated internet usage since it was introduced, and allows users to communicate with each other at low cost while providing an efficient message delivery system. However, the simplicity and low cost in sending an email has paved the way for unsolicited emails. Individual users and businesses can send

DOI: 10.4018/978-1-4666-6583-5.ch013

Copyright © 2015, IGI Global. Copying or distributing in print or electronic forms without written permission of IGI Global is prohibited.

thousands of emails to recipients at any given time. These emails, also known as spam, are unsolicited emails, which are neither requested nor required by the recipients. Spam either contains harmless marketing information or malicious codes such as viruses that could cause data loss, thus leading to inconvenience and/or economic loss to the recipients. Unsolicited emails are widely viewed as a serious threat to the internet as it clogs up the users' inboxes and cost businesses billions of dollars in wasted bandwidth (Cournane & Hunt, 2004). To combat spam, researchers and developers have created many anti-spam tools. The basic function of anti-spam tools is to filter emails by separating spam from genuine mail and adding them into a junk mail box. Various methods and standards are used to fight spam nuisances (Subramaniam, Jalab & et al, 2010).

There were many studies carried out on spam filtering that were effective and efficient on detecting and blocking spam email. However, these studies were mainly performed on English language email spam. Methods (preprocessing and Machine learning algorithms) used for English language spam detection will limit the performance of a classifier given the nature of different human languages (Özgür, Güngör & et al, 2004; Pang, Feng, & et al 2007). (Özgür et al., 2004) proposed dynamic spam filtering methods based on Artificial Neural Network and Bayesian algorithms for agglutinative language and for Turkish in particular (which is a complex morphology). They performed five different experiments by using Single Layer Perceptron (SLP), Multi-Layer Perceptron (MLP) and Bayesian with 3 different feature vector sizes. Their experiments showed that some non-Turkish words that occurred frequently in spam mail were better classified than most Turkish words.

(Dong, Cao & et al, 2006) indicated that segmenting Chinese words (email) restricts the performance of existing spam filter. They used Bayesian spam filter based on cross N-gram on CCERT Computer Emergency Response Term of which 940 were spam emails and 1400 were non-

spam Chinese language emails. These emails were then partitioned into 10 parts. 5 characters of crossed N-gram and three different feature selection methods were used: Mutual Information, Odd Ratio and X2 –statistic (*CHI*). Comparison of all 3 feature selection methods were reported based on $» = 1$ and $» = 9$. They concluded that the Odds Ratio selection scheme produced the best result and errors can be further reduced with the combination of rule-based methods.

(Pang & et al., 2007) used Support Vector Machine by adopting the tri-gram language model for word segmentation of Chinese emails and applied Discount Smoothing algorithms to overcome the sparse data problem. Automaton Machine identifies different factoid words. They experimented using LingSpam (English email) and CCERT data sets of Chinese emails, and made comparison between Maximum Entropy, Bayesian, Bayesian with Good-Turning, Bayesian with Absolute Smooth and Support Vector Machine.

(Anh, Anh & et al, 2008) specified that token segmentation of the Bayesian filter produced less effective performances for detecting Vietnamese language-based spam. Therefore, they proposed a Vietnamese segmentation for token selection based on language classification and Bayesian. They implemented two filters; token segmentation based on whitespaces and token selection based on the Vietnamese segmentation approach. The result showed that Vietnamese segmentation token selection coupled with Bayesian classifier generated more effective spam detection - 9% more accurate as compared to other segmentation techniques.

(Na Songkhla & Piromsopa, 2010) proposed a statistical rule-base for Thai language spam detection for Spam Assassin that can be shared among servers and easily maintained. They used Chulalongkorn University's Thai Word segmentation program that separated Thai words more accurately with low processing time and conditional probability (CP) to find spam-like patterns. They concluded that Spam Assassin's,

Thai statistical rule-base yielded better and more effective results when detecting Thai Language spam in terms of total detection and recall rates for every test set.

(Qiu, Xu, & et al, 2010) proposed Online Linear classifier; Perceptron and Winnow that were far more effective and efficient when filtering Chinese spam emails. These two classifiers were very adaptive and suitable for real dynamic environments. They used three corpora sets; 2005-Jun (CCERT), PU1 and Ling-Spam and concluded that all three test sets achieved a better accuracy using Winnow algorithms hence outperforming Naïve Bayesian.

In recent years, researchers study approaches that are capable of self-learn to differentiate spam from legitimate email. Thus the use of machine learning for spam control is escalating.

There are various machine learning approaches but this chapter concentrates on Back-propagation Neural Network (BPNN) algorithm. Neural Networks emulates the human brain cells have been applied for spam classification.

(Chuan, Xianliang & et al, 2005) proposed the use of Learning Vector Quantization (LVQ)-based neural network for spam email classification. Emails were classified into several subclasses for easy identification and Learning Vector Quantization (LVQ)-based NN outperformed the Back-Propagate network.

(Chuan & et al., 2005) proposed Self Organizing Map (SOM) for spam classifications and Automatically Defined Group (ADG) to extract correct judgment rules. They used 3007 emails classified as spam from Spam Assassin. SOM was used to classify these spams to obtain the visual distribution intuitively and the ADG extracted classification rules to judge spam correctly. Their experiment concluded that SOM improved classification process and ADG tremendously reduced false negatives.

(Wu, 2009) used a hybrid method of rule-based processing and back-propagation neural network for spam filtering. The study utilized spamming behaviors as features for describing emails. This information was then used to train the BPNN classifier. The system produced very low false positive and negative rates and had a better result in comparison to content-based classification. (Wu, 2009) proposed a new spam filtering system using Revised Back-Propagation Neural Network (RBP) which achieved a higher performance when combined with automatic thesaurus construction.

Increases in the number of users who are using the Malay language have catapulted spamming using Malay language text-based messages. Almost all government agencies in Malaysia (e.g. www.malaysia.gov.my) have computerized their processes and are using email as their main communication tool. Spammers are taking advantage of this and have increased sending spam emails using the Malay language. An effective machine learning classifier is required to reduce the Malay language spam. Most traditional anti-spam tools are capable of identifying English text-based messages but there are close to none to filter the Malay language text-based spam emails.

The main objective of this chapter is to design and implement the Malay language text-based anti-spam system using BPNN algorithm.

Spam is a growing problem, as email becomes the main communication tool. There is a lack of anti-spam applications that filter the Malay Language spam emails. This is the main motivation for this chapter. This chapter provides an insight of spam, spam impacts; various anti-spams approaches and demonstrates that machine learning approaches are able to classify spam more accurately. These will be significantly useful for other researchers who intend to pursue further research in this area. Furthermore, this chapter is a contribution to the Malay language anti-spam approach. The outline of the chapter is as follows: Back-propagation neural network classification technique presented in Section 2. Experimental results and discussion are shown in Sections 3. Finally the conclusion is presented in Section 4.

BACK-PROPAGATION NEURAL NETWORK CLASSIFICATION

Neural Network (NN), first introduced by McCulloch and Pitts (1943) has many applications such as signal processing, pattern recognition, medicine, speech production and speech recognition to name a few(Taqa & Jalab, 2010). Neural network classification has been increasingly used in text classification (Chen, Pan, & et al, 2012; Ghiassi, Olschimke & et al, 2012; Wu, 2009). Neural network emulates the functionality of a human brain in which neurons (nerves cell) communicate with each other by sending messages between them. Neural Network represents the mathematical model of these biological neurons.

It is a parallel distributed information processing structure consisting of a number of nonlinear processing units (neurons) (Ko, Tiwari, & et al, 2010) which can be trained to recognize features and identify incomplete features/data. Neural Network has great mapping capabilities or pattern association thus exhibiting generalization, robustness, high fault tolerance, and high speed parallel information processing (Alavala, 2008).

NN consists of input layer, hidden layers and output layer. Input layer contains input neurons which represent features, and hidden layer may consists of n number of layers that contain hidden neurons and output layer contain output neurons that represent categories or classes.

The input nodes indicate the number of attributes defining features $x_1, x_2, x_3, \cdots x_n$ and $w_1, w_2, w_3, \cdots w_n$ are the weight attached to the input links. The weights on the edges connecting nodes correspond to dependence relations. Output neurons indicated the number of classes i.e. spam or legitimate mail. The neurons receive input with corresponding weight and the total received inputs are then passed onto a non-linear filter φ called activation function that determines the output signal, which is then propagated to other neurons.

Activation function performs a mathematical operation on the output so that the output of a neuron in the network is between 0 and 1 (-1 and 1). Most common activation functions used in Neural Network are threshold function, piecewise-linear function and sigmoid function.

The learning NN algorithms methods can be broadly divided into supervised, unsupervised and reinforced learning methods (Goyal, 2007). A supervised learning is where a "teacher" is incorporated whereby each input pattern is associated with an output pattern. A comparison with generated output results and expected output results will determine the errors; the NN parameters are then adjusted accordingly to reduce the error convergence.

Performance Measurement

Classifiers need to be evaluated based on the performance of information retrieval (recall, precision and derived measures) and decision theory (false positives and false negatives) (Guzella & Caminhas, 2009). Accuracy, Spam Precision and Spam Recall are the most important performance parameters. "Recall" indicates the rate of the number of correctly classified spam against spam that is misclassified as non-spam and the number of spam recognized as spam. "Precision" represents the ratio between the numbers of correctly classified spam to the number of all marked spam. "Accuracy" represents the ratio between the number of correctly classified spam and non-spam to the total emails used for testing i.e. all emails that are correctly classified by the classifier. These parameters can be measured using the following equations.

$$Accuracy\left(A\right) = \frac{TP + TN}{TP + TN + FP + FN} \quad (1)$$

$$Precision\left(p\right) = \frac{TP}{TP + FP} \quad (2)$$

$$Recall\left(r\right)=\frac{TP}{TP+FN} \qquad (3)$$

Experimental Results

Performance tests for the system proposed by this chapter were implemented using Matlab 2013b on Intel(R) Core i7 at 2.2GHz, 4GB DDR3 memory, system type 64-bit and Window 7.

Classification process was carried out in stages as follows;

1. Collection of emails;
2. Tokenization process;
3. Features reduction process;
4. Features selection process;
5. Training process;
6. Testing process.

DATA COLLECTIONS

A total of 550 emails were used for this study of which 350 emails (250 spam emails and 100 non-spam emails) were used for training and 200 emails (100 spam emails and 100 non-spam emails) for testing. Due to the lack of availability for free Malay language spam dataset, a Google's Gmail account was setup for the purpose of collecting spam emails. This account was used to register with various websites such as porn sites, medicine/health sites, song downloading websites and alike to populate the inbox.

Even though the account received lots of emails, the number of the Malay language emails were small, thus total number of spam emails used were small. Non-spam emails were collected using the author's University Malaya email system, and personal emails. Only text-based emails were used for this study, emails containing images and other attachments were ignored.

The main challenges faced while collecting spam email were as follows:

- Many spam emails contained images or videos that were not useful for this study.
- Content of the spam emails received were in non-Malay language.
- Getting the same spam emails repeatedly.

Only subject field and message body were examined, the rest of email's details, videos and images (or any attachments) were ignored. The emails were converted into a text file format for the preprocessing. Conversion was accomplished by copying an email contents into Microsoft's Notepad application and saved as a text file (.txt). Figure 1 shows a sample of spam email used.

Tokenization Process

Tokenization is a process of separating the message of an email into a series of tokens. As mentioned earlier, only the subject and message body were considered for this study. Upon extracting these tokens (words), a vector space was created which contains all the words that appeared in the collected emails. Consequently, the vector space created upon completing tokenization contained a high level of content obscuration. This overwhelmed the classifiers during the classification process and caused the classifiers to produce less accurate results. Figure 2 shows sample tokens after the tokenization process applied on email1 (Figure 1).

Features Reduction Process

Since tokenized features from the emails may contain high levels of obscure text, noise, non-informative words, and symbols or simply produce a very large vector space, a features reduction process was needed to reduce the anomalies. In this chapter, document frequency was used as dimension reduction technique since it eliminated insignificant features that do not influence the classification process. A stop words list was created and

Figure 1. Sample spam email in Malay language

From: generasiperkasa@gmail.com generasiperkasa

To: marhanaf@googlegroups.com melayu lucah

Date: Wed, 25 Aug 2010 18:09:05 +0800

Subject: Promosi HEBAT Aidilfitri...HarumanHormon Istimewa PemikatLelaki /Wanita...!!!

Promosi HEBAT HarumanHormon Istimewa PemikatLelaki /

Wanita...SempenaMenyambutKedatanganAidilfitri...JanganLepaskan

Peluangini...!!

Produk-ProdukEksklusifUntukAnda...!!!

Portal SeksSensasi - PortaluntukmengintimkanPasanganSuamiIsteri

Dan jugaUntukGenerasiSensasiMasaKini..

http://generasiperkasa.com/

Figure 2. Sample of email tokenization output

Email After tokenization

Email 1: Subject

{ Promosi, HEBAT, Aidilfitri, Haruman, Hormon, Istimewa, Pemikat, Lelaki, /, Wanita, !!! }

Email 1: Body

{Promosi, HEBAT, Haruman, Hormon, Istimewa, Pemikat, Lelaki, /, Wanita, Sempena, Menyambut, Kedatangan, Aidilfitri, Jangan, Lepaskan, Peluang, ini, ...!!, Produk-Produk, Eksklusif, Untuk, Anda, ...!!!, Portal, Seks, Sensasi, -, Portal, untuk, mengintimkan, Pasangan, Suami, Isteri, Dan, juga, Untuk, Generasi, Sensasi, Masa, Kini, http://generasiperkasa.com/}

checked against the feature vector and if a stop-word was identified then it was removed from the vector. Document frequency and stop-word removal processes reduce the size of the vector space, thus improving the efficiency of the classifiers.

Stemming process was also applied on the feature vector to reduce the words to its basic form or root word. Prefix and suffix of the words were removed in the stemming process. Porter's stemming algorithm was used to strip the words because it is very robust and quite easy to implement (Willett, 2006).

Features Selection Process

Once the features were cleaned up, the number of occurrences of a feature in an email was measured. Word frequency was created using term frequency. The main idea of features selection was to maximize the accuracy of classifiers in predicting spam emails. This was done by only selecting important features that will influence the classification process. It allowed the reduction of data needed for training the classifiers. With the completion of the features selection process, stage 1 pre-processing tasks were completed.

Training Process

The training process consists of two phases; generate spam and non-spam dictionary and training process to derive the Back-propagation Neural Network architecture. Standard multilayer Back-propagation Neural Network classifier was trained using 4392 words from a database. The database was created with 1395 spam words and 2997 non-spam words (Table 1).

Highest Mutual Information score features were selected to generate the feature vector. Each word in the spam (non- spam) dictionary was then compared with spam (non -spam) email words by using the binary model. If the spam (non-spam) email word was available in the dictionary than assign 1 otherwise 0.

$$x = \begin{cases} 1, & \text{if ith word of feature occurs in email} \\ 0, & \text{otherwise} \end{cases}$$

$$(4)$$

The feature from spam and non-spam was combined into one dataset (database) and target value was set to 1 for spam and -1 for non-spam. This value was selected in order to have a larger gap to improve performances of the classifier. This data was used for training, validation and testing the proposed classifier.

The proposed Back-propagation Neural Network consisted of an input layer with 2200 neurons in which each neuron represented a feature from the feature vector (database), hidden layer with four neurons and output layer with one neuron which generated output ranging from -1 to +1. These values indicated the presence or absence of spam.

The Back-propagation Neural Network implementation in which the first layer had weights assigned from the input and subsequent layers had weights coming from the previous layer. Weight values associated with individual nodes were known as biases. The network's last layer was the output layer. Each layer's weights and biases were

Table 1. Sample of spam and non-spam dictionary

Sample of Spam Dictionary	Sample of Non-Spam Dictionary
bagus	abstrak
baik	academy
baju	acara
bakal	aceh
balas	acu
balik	adaptasi
bandar	adat
banding	adeg
bangga	adil
bank	administrator
bank-in	agama
banner	agamawan
bantu	agenda
barang	agensi
barat	agung
baris	ahad
baru	ahli
bawa	aids
bayang	akademi
bayar	akademik
beban	akar
bebas	akaunt
bekal	akhbar
belajar	akhirat
belanja	akibat
beli	akses
benar	aksi
benda	akta
benih	aktiviti
bentuk	amanah

initialized with "initnw". Adaption was done with training, which updated weights with the specified learning function. Performance was measured according to the specified performance function.

The next step was to train the network. The Back-propagation Neural Network neurons connection's weights were initialized with random values. The network's weights were repetitively adjusted by presenting spam and non-spam features as input with corresponding desired targets. The output was compared with the desired target, adjusted and propagated back into the network as new weight for input neurons. This process was conducted until the error measurement between the actual values of the classifier network and the desired output which was at a minimal level and correct output for every input was reached.

The Back-propagation Neural Network classifier was trained using the hyperbolic tangent sigmoid "tansig" transfer function on the hidden layers neurons and linear "purelin" transfer function on the output layer neuron. The learning rate used was 0.3 with the momentum constant at 0.6 and the maximum epoch was 500. Performance function was Mean Squared Error (MSE).

The gradient descent method was employed as the learning algorithm to minimize the training errors, which was defined as mean square difference between the desired value and the actual value. Gradient descent with momentum, implemented by "traingdm", which allowed a network to respond not only to the local gradient, but also to recent trends in the error surface. Acting like a lowpass filter, the momentum allowed the network to ignore small features in the error surface. Without the momentum a network can become stuck in a shallow local minimum. With momentum, a network can slide through such a minimum.

Testing Process

Upon completing the training of the network, Back-propagation Neural Network architecture along with its input (feature) weight was stored (saved). Then this trained network was used to test the new testing dataset. Spam and non-spam emails were fed into the Back-propagation Neural Network classifier to check whether the classifier was able to correctly identify these unknown

emails for which the network has not been trained on. This was accomplished by comparing the actual result of the classifier against the trained result.

Testing was accomplished using 100 spam and 100 non spam emails. These emails went through a similar preprocessing process such as tokenization, features reduction (stop-word removal, document frequency and stemming processes) and features selection process.

EVALUATION OF BACK-PROPAGATION NEURAL NETWORK TECHNIQUE

The effectiveness of the Back-propagation Neural Network classifier was measured in terms of accuracy, precision, recall, and specificity.

$$Specificity = \frac{TN}{TN + FP} \times 100\% \qquad (5)$$

Training performance of the network was determined by performing a validation performance analysis between the mean squared error (MSE) and the number of epochs. The best validation performance was 0.30531 at an epoch of 190.

Upon completing the testing process, true positive and true negative were derived from the Back-propagation Neural Network results. Misclassified emails were denoted as false negative and false positive. Based on the results, precision, recall, accuracy and specificity of the classifier were formulated.

Out of the 200 emails tested 98 and 96 emails were classified correctly by the classifier as spam and non-spam respectively. However, 3% of the emails tested were misclassified, of which 4 non-spam emails were misclassified as spam and 2 spam emails misclassified as non-spam. This misclassification generated 2.0% of false positive and 1.0% of false negative. Table 2 and Figure 3 show the results of Back-propagation Neural Network classification.

Table 2. Back-propagation neural network testing results

Output	Spam	Non Spam
Spam	98	2
Non Spam	4	96

Measuring the precision on the testing features determined the success of the classifier. As stated earlier, precision was measured and it was tabulated when the classifier correctly identified an email as spam or non-spam. After completing the testing process, Back-propagation Neural Network classifier produced a 96.1% precision rate with a recall rate of 98.0% and specificity of 96.0%. Due to false positive and false negative, which contributed 3.0% of error, the accuracy rate of the classifier reduced to 97.0%. Figure 4 shows the result obtained after applying the performances measurement parameter.

Back-propagation neural network achieved 97.0% accuracy. The main reasons for this were the high tolerance to noisy data and input parameters were adjusted (back-propagated) to reduce errors. Allowing back propagation and deriving a minimal error level made the BPNN more adaptive. False negative of BPNN was still high considering the fact that the cost of false negative was much higher than false positive, since users may delete spam emails without reading it which can cost them valuable non-spam (legitimate) emails. The false negative can be reduced if more training dataset was used and which can improve the precision rate and overall accuracy of BPNN classifier. Furthermore improvement of the feature reduction techniques may yield a better and more accurate result for BPNN.

Table 3 illustrates the comparison between proposed algorithms and four other algorithms (Awad & ELseuofi, 2011; Ruan & Tan, 2010; Subramaniam et al.). However, only three algorithms were selected (Naïve Bayesian, Neural Network and Rough Set) from their work but the other algorithms' (SVM, AIS, and KNN) results were omitted. The proposed back-propagation neural network classifier achieved better results compared to other works. While, (Ruan & Tan, 2010) employed BPNN using a two-element concentration based feature construction with benchmark corpus Ling and PU1.

Figure 3. Back-propagation neural network testing results

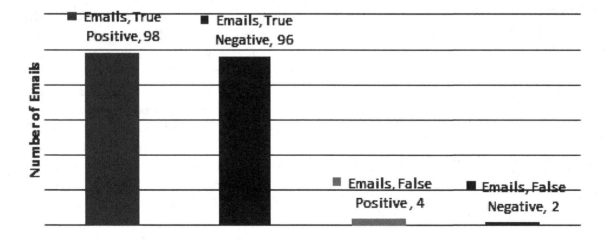

Table 3. Comparison between proposed algorithms other works

Algorithm	Precision	Recall	Accuracy
Naïve Bayesian (Awad & ELseuofi, 2011)	99.60	98.46	99.46
Naïve Bayesian(Subramaniam, Jalab, & Taqa, 2011)	95.10	97.00	96.00
Rough Set(Awad & ELseuofi, 2011)	98.70	92.26	97.42
Back propagation Neural network (Ruan & Tan, 2010)	97.09	96.97	97.37
Proposed Back propagation Neural network	96.10	98.00	97.00

Figure 4. Back-propagation neural network classifier performance measurements

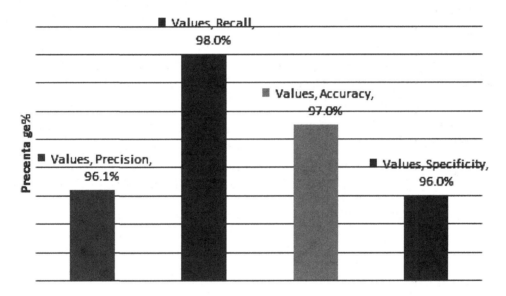

CONCLUSION

Spam problem is expected to accelerate and find its way into many Internet applications such as Facebook and Twitter. Various machine learning techniques have been applied to the English language corpus (e-mails). However, there are not many studies available on spam filtering systems for the Malay Language. In view of this, a back-propagation neural network classifier was selected for filtering the Malay language spam and to identify the best classifier

that is capable of accurately classifying spam emails. The results were evaluated based on performance measurement; recall, precision and accuracy rate, which are 97.0%, 96.1%, and 98.0% respectively. These results can be attributed to the capabilities of Back-propagation Neural Network in handling noisy data, and it is more adaptive with high tolerance. Further improvement can be made in order to increase the accuracy rate of the back-propagation neural network classifier. Following are some directions for future improvement:

- Include more features or increase number of emails used for training and testing. A benchmark dataset for Malay language should be created.
- Inclusion of images or other formats for classification.

Finally, Back-propagation Neural Network classifier is surely the best approach that should be engaged to filter Malay language text-based spam.

REFERENCES

Alavala, C. R. (2008). *Fuzzy logic and neural networks*. Hershey PA: IRM Press.

Anh, N. T., Anh, T. Q., & Binh, N. N. (2008). *Vietnamese Spam Detection based on language classification*. Paper presented at the Second International Conference on Communications and Electronics, 2008. ICCE 2008.

Awad, W., & ELseuofi, S. (2011). Machine Learning Methods for Spam E-Mail Classification. *International Journal of Computers and Applications*, *16*(1).

Chen, J., Pan, H., & Ao, Q. (2012). Study a Text Classification Method Based on Neural Network Model. *Advances in Multimedia, Software. Engineering and Computing*, *1*, 471–475.

Chuan, Z., Xianliang, L., Mengshu, H., & Xu, Z. (2005). A LVQ-based neural network anti-spam email approach. *Operating Systems Review*, *39*(1), 34–39. doi:10.1145/1044552.1044555

Cournane, A., & Hunt, R. (2004). An analysis of the tools used for the generation and prevention of spam. *Computers & Security*, *23*(2), 154–166. doi:10.1016/j.cose.2003.10.001

Dong, J., Cao, H., Liu, P., & Ren, L. (2006). *Bayesian Chinese spam filter based on crossed N-gram*. Paper presented at the Intelligent Systems Design and Applications, 2006. ISDA'06. Sixth International Conference. doi:10.1109/ISDA.2006.17

Ghiassi, M., Olschimke, M., Moon, B., & Arnaudo, P. (2012). Automated text classification using a dynamic artificial neural network model. *Expert Systems with Applications*, *39*(12), 10967–10976. doi:10.1016/j.eswa.2012.03.027

Goyal, R. D. (2007). *Knowledge based neural network for text classification*. Paper presented at the Granular Computing, 2007. GRC 2007. IEEE International Conference on. doi:10.1109/GrC.2007.108

Guzella, T. S., & Caminhas, W. M. (2009). A review of machine learning approaches to spam filtering. *Expert Systems with Applications*, *36*(7), 10206–10222. doi:10.1016/j.eswa.2009.02.037

Ko, M., Tiwari, A., & Mehnen, J. (2010). A review of soft computing applications in supply chain management. *Applied Soft Computing*, *10*(3), 661–674. doi:10.1016/j.asoc.2009.09.004

Na Songkhla, C., & Piromsopa, K. (2010). *Statistical Rules for Thai Spam Detection*. Paper presented at the Future Networks, 2010. ICFN'10. Second International Conference on. doi:10.1109/ICFN.2010.39

Özgür, L., Güngör, T., & Gürgen, F. (2004). Adaptive anti-spam filtering for agglutinative languages: A special case for Turkish. *Pattern Recognition Letters*, *25*(16), 1819–1831. doi:10.1016/j.patrec.2004.07.004

Pang, X.-L., Feng, Y.-Q., & Jiang, W. (2007). *A spam filter approach with the improved machine learning technology*. Paper presented at the Natural Computation, 2007. ICNC 2007. Third International Conference on. doi:10.1109/ICNC.2007.143

Qiu, Y., Xu, Y., & Wang, B. (2010). *An Online Linear Chinese Spam Emails Filtering System.* Paper presented at the e-Business and Information System Security (EBISS), 2010 2nd International Conference on. doi:10.1109/EBISS.2010.5473478

Ruan, G., & Tan, Y. (2010). A three-layer back-propagation neural network for spam detection using artificial immune concentration. *Soft Computing*, *14*(2), 139–150. doi:10.1007/s00500-009-0440-2

Subramaniam, T., Jalab, H. A., & Taqa, A. Y. (2010). Overview of textual anti-spam filtering techniques. *International Journal of the Physical Sciences*, *5*(12), 1869–1882.

Subramaniam, T., Jalab, H. A., & Taqa, A. Y. (2011). Naïve Bayesian Anti-spam Filtering Technique for Malay Language. Paper presented at the International Conference on Computer Engineering & Mathematical Sciences, Malaysia.

Taqa, A. Y., & Jalab, H. A. (2010). Increasing the reliability of skin detectors. *Scientific Research and Essays*, *5*(17), 2480–2490.

Willett, P. (2006). The Porter stemming algorithm: Then and now. P*rogram. Electronic Library and Information Systems*, *40*(3), 219–223.

Wu, C.-H. (2009). Behavior-based spam detection using a hybrid method of rule-based techniques and neural networks. *Expert Systems with Applications*, *36*(3), 4321–4330. doi:10.1016/j.eswa.2008.03.002

KEY TERMS AND DEFINITIONS

Automatically Defined Group (ADG): A rule extraction method used for classification.

Back-Propagation Neural Network (BPNN): Based on the function and structure of human brain or biological neurons. These network of neurons can be trained with a training dataset in which output is compared with desired output and error is propagated back to input until the minimal MSE is achieved.

False Negative (FN): Spam email that is classified as a non-spam email is referred to as False Negative (FN).

False Positive (FP): A non-spam email which is classified as spam is referred to as False Positive (FP).

Learning Vector Quantization (LVQ): A neural net that combines competitive learning with supervision. It can be used for pattern classification.

Mean Squared Error (MSE): A measure of performance of a point estimator. It measures the average squared difference between the estimator and the parameter.

Self-Organizing Map (SOM): One of the most popular neural network models. It belongs to the category of competitive learning networks. The Self-Organizing Map is based on unsupervised learning.

Single Layer Perception (SLP): A feedforward network based on a threshold transfer function. SLP is the simplest type of artificial neural networks and can only classify linearly separable cases with a binary target (1, 0).

Chapter 14
Virtualization Technology and Security Challenges

Ghossoon M. Waleed Al-Saadoon
Applied Science University, Bahrain

Ebrahim Al Naemi
Dolphin Energy Limited, Qatar

ABSTRACT

The aim of server virtualization is to eliminate the Hardware equipment in the Datacenter and maximize the utilization of the existing resources. This helps companies in achieving the business goals and objectives in cost effective manner and better support and integration. Virtualization technology changes the protection way of security, as most of hardware and software become after virtualization such as servers, switches, Logical Unit Numbers (LUNs) etc. and it's no longer trying to protect a physical hardware, (Hurwitz & et al, 2013). The overall objective of this chapter is to find out the solution for reducing the keep regular increasing recurring cost and risk involved in information technology management and maintenance. The chapter is about finding out the solution from which it's possible to ultimately lower the cost, speed deployment, provide additional disaster recovery options, and ease testing and developing, and provide unprecedented mobility, flexibility and reliability.

INTRODUCTION

Virtualization technology is possibly the single most important issue in IT and has started a top to bottom overhaul of the computing industry. The growing awareness of the advantages provided by virtualization technology is brought about by economic factors of scarce resources, government regulation, and more competition.

Virtualization is being used by a growing number of organizations to reduce power consumption, air conditioning needs, trim the building space and land requirements that have always been associated with server farm growth. Virtualization also provides high availability for critical applications, and streamlines application deployment and migrations. Virtualization can simplify IT operations and allow IT organizations to respond faster to business changing demands.

DOI: 10.4018/978-1-4666-6583-5.ch014

Copyright © 2015, IGI Global. Copying or distributing in print or electronic forms without written permission of IGI Global is prohibited.

The socio-political ramifications of global warming requiring good corporate citizens to meet greenhouse gas reduction targets, creates an added incentive for virtualization.

The availability of better virtual machine isolation through new Intel® Virtual Technology hardware support in commodity systems together with the broad availability of virtualization software provides a level of efficiency to meet these demands.

Today's IT intensive enterprise must always be on the lookout for the latest technologies that allow businesses to run with fewer resources while providing the infrastructure to meet today and future's customer needs. Virtualization utilizing Intel Virtualization Technology is the cutting edge of enterprise information technology.

SERVER CONSOLIDATION

It is not unusual to achieve 10:1 virtual to physical machine consolidation. This means that ten server applications can be run on a single machine that had required as many physical computers to provide the unique operating system and technical specification environments in order to operate. Server utilization is optimized and legacy software can maintain old Operating System (OS) configurations while new applications are running in VMs with updated platforms.

Although a server supporting many Virtual Memories (VMs) will probably have more memory, CPUs, and other hardware it will use little or no more power and occupy the same physical space reducing utilities costs and real estate expenditures.

Testing and Development

Use of a VM enables rapid deployment by isolating the application in a known and controlled environment. Unknown factors such as mixed libraries caused by numerous installs can be eliminated. Severe crashes that required hours of reinstallation now take moments by simply copying a virtual image.

Dynamic Load Balancing and Disaster Recovery

As server workloads vary, virtualization provides the ability for virtual machines that are over utilizing the resources of a server to be moved to underutilized servers. This dynamic load balancing creates efficient utilization of server resources.

Disaster recovery is a critical component for IT, as system crashes can create huge economic losses. Virtualization technology enables a virtual image on a machine to be instantly re-imaged on another server if a machine failure occurs.

Virtual Desktops

Multinational flexibility provides seamless transitions between different operating systems on a single machine reducing desktop footprint and hardware expenditure.

Virtualization of systems helps prevent system crashes due to memory corruption caused by software like device drivers. VT-d for Directed I/O Architecture provides methods to better control system devices by defining the architecture for Direct Memory Access (DMA) and interrupt remapping to ensure improved isolation of I/O resources for greater reliability, security, and availability.

Hardware virtualization or platform virtualization refers to the creation of a virtual machine that acts like a real computer with an operating system. Software executed on these virtual machines is separated from the underlying hardware resources. For example, a computer that is running Microsoft Windows may host a virtual machine that looks like a computer with the Ubuntu Linux operating system; Ubuntu-based software can be run on the virtual machine.

In hardware virtualization, the host machine is the actual machine on which the virtualization takes place, and the guest machine is the virtual machine. The words host and guest are used to distinguish the software that runs on the physical machine from the software that runs on the virtual machine. The software or firmware that creates a virtual machine on the host hardware is called a hypervisor or Virtual Machine Manager.

Different types of hardware virtualization include:

1. **Full Virtualization:** Almost complete simulation of the actual hardware to allow software, which typically consists of a guest operating system, to run unmodified.
2. **Partial Virtualization:** Some but not the entire target environment is simulated. Some guest programs, therefore, may need modifications to run in this virtual environment.
3. **Para Virtualization:** A hardware environment is not simulated; however, the guest programs are executed in their own isolated domains, as if they are running on a separate system. Guest programs need to be specifically modified to run in this environment.

Hardware-assisted virtualization is a way of improving the efficiency of hardware virtualization. It involves employing specially designed CPUs and hardware components that help improve the performance of a guest environment.

Hardware virtualization can be viewed as part of an overall trend in enterprise IT that includes autonomic computing, a scenario in which the IT environment will be able to manage itself based on perceived activity, and utility computing, in which computer processing power is seen as a utility that clients can pay for only as needed. The usual goal of virtualization is to centralize administrative tasks while improving scalability and overall hardware-resource utilization. With virtualization, several operating systems can be run in parallel on a single Central Processing Unit (CPU). This parallelism tends to reduce overhead costs and differs from multitasking, which involves running several programs on the same OS. Using virtualization, an enterprise can better manage updates and rapid changes to the operating system and applications without disrupting the user. "Ultimately, virtualization dramatically improves the efficiency and availability of resources and applications in an organization. Instead of relying on the old model of "one server, one application" that leads to underutilized resource, virtual resources are dynamically applied to meet business needs without any excess fat" (Bruce Hoard, 2012).

Hardware virtualization is not the same as hardware emulation. In hardware emulation, a piece of hardware imitates another, while in hardware virtualization; a hypervisor (a piece of software) imitates a particular piece of computer hardware or the entire computer. Furthermore, a hypervisor is not the same as an emulator; both are computer programs that imitate hardware, but their domain of use in language differs

Overview of the Problem

The main problem appears in the high cost of building a datacenter for a private company.

*   Dedicating a place and air-conditioning for the servers that intended to be used.
*   Difficulty in managing the whole datacenter from a single location with limited resources.
*   The time needed to order and build several servers.
*   Level of the security satisfaction or needed after the virtualization is in place.

These days' server and network equipment distributed throughout the globe creating power and cooling challenges at many of these locations. These conditions were leading to an increasing number of infrastructure investments being made at distributed sites while the data center remained underutilized. Some time there's not enough space for expansion of the infrastructure also.

Figure 1. Organization virtualization system (Kumar, 2010).

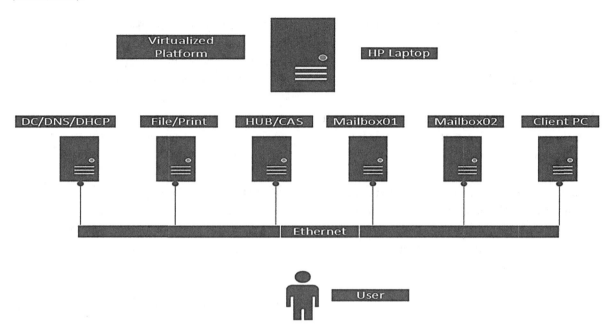

Sometimes most of the companies face an issue in managing the whole datacenter from a single location with limited resources. A number of the top virtualization challenges facing datacenters are caused by insufficient real-time information. Issues such as ensuring high availability, fulfilling service requests, capacity management, controlling virtual sprawl, isolating performance and configuration problems, managing across multiple data centers and increased infrastructure complexity, all become easier with the right information available at the right time

While reporting and monitoring can help simplify some of the complexities, it does little to help automate or proactively control the environment. Furthermore, these capabilities don't do much to get administrative teams out of the day-to-day manual tasks necessary to keep the infrastructure going and into the demanding task of building the private cloud (Litke, 2011).

DESIGN DESCRIPTION

Figure 1 shows the organization system for the virtualization.

Virtualization is a software technology which uses a physical resource such as a server and divides it up into virtual resources called Virtual Machines (VM's). Virtualization allows users to consolidate physical resources, simplify deployment and administration, and reduce power and cooling requirements. While virtualization technology is most popular in the server world, virtualization technology is also being used in data storage such as Storage Area Networks, and inside of operating systems such as Windows Server 2008 with Hyper-V (Litke, 2011).

Type of virtualization technologies:

- VMware,
- Citrix,
- IBM,
- Microsoft,
- Virtual Iron,
- Veeam.

BENEFITS OF VIRTUALIZATION

The following list is some of the Virtualization advantages:

Less Heat Buildup

Millions of dollars have gone into the research and design of heat dissipation and control in the data center. But the cold, hard fact is, all of those servers generate heat. The only way around that? Use fewer servers. How do you manage that? Virtualization. Virtualize your servers and you're using less physical hardware. Use less physical hardware and you generate less heat. Generate less heat in your data center and a host of issues go away.

Reduced Cost

Hardware is most often the highest cost in the data center. Reduce the amount of hardware used and you reduce your cost. But the cost goes well beyond that of hardware — lack of downtime, easier maintenance, less electricity used. Over time, this all adds up to a significant cost savings.

Faster Redeploy

When you use a physical server and it dies, the redeploy time depends on a number of factors: Do you have a backup server ready? Do you have an image of your server? Is the data on your backup server current? With virtualization, the redeploy can occur within minutes. Virtual machine snapshots can be enabled with just a few clicks. And with virtual backup tools like Veeam, redeploying images will be so fast your end users will hardly notice there was an issue.

Easier Backups

Not only can you do full backups of your virtual server, you can do backups and snapshots of your virtual machines. These virtual machines can be moved from one server to another and redeployed easier and faster. Snapshots can be taken throughout the day, ensuring much more up-to-date data. And because firing up a snapshot is even faster than booting a typical server, downtime is dramatically cut.

Greener Pastures

Let's face it: If you're not doing your part to help clean up the environment, you're endangering the future. Reducing your carbon footprint not only helps to clean up the air we breathe, it also helps to clean up your company image. Consumers want to see companies reducing their output of pollution and taking responsibility. Virtualizing your data center will go a long way toward improving your relationship with the planet and with the consumer.

Better Testing

What better testing environment is there than a virtual one? If you make a tragic mistake, all is not lost. Just revert to a previous snapshot and you can move forward as if the mistake didn't even happen. You can also isolate these testing environments from end users while still keeping them online. When you've perfected your work, deploy it as live.

No Vendor Lock-In

One of the nice things about virtualization is the abstraction between software and hardware. This means you don't have to be tied down to one particular vendor — the virtual machines don't really care what hardware they run on, so you're not tied down to a single vendor, type of server (within reason of course), or even platform.

Better Disaster Recovery

Disaster recovery is quite a bit easier when your data center is virtualized. With up-to-date snapshots of your virtual machines, you can quickly get back up and running. And should disaster strike the data center itself, you can always move those virtual machines elsewhere (so long as you can re-create the network addressing scheme and such). Having that level of flexibility means your disaster recovery plan will be easier to enact and will have a much higher success rate.

Easier Migration to Cloud

With a move to virtual machines, it is much closer to enjoying a full-blown cloud environment. You may even reach the point where you can deploy VMs to and from your data center to create a powerful cloud-based infrastructure. Beyond the actual virtual machines, that virtualized, technology gets you closer to a cloud-based mindset, making the migration all the more easy.

DRAWBACKS OF VIRTUALIZATION

The following are some of the Virtualization drawbacks:

High Risk in Physical Fault

It is great to host/run your very important five servers (as virtual) in one physical server. But, have you anytime imagined impact of these five servers by the single hardware failure in physical server? It will make all the five important servers go offline. It is definitely a big disadvantage and drawback in virtualization which must be considered in production environment while planning.

Yes, it can go with two physical servers with similar configuration and a centralized storage (Network Access Storage – NAS) to run these five virtual servers in cluster environment where single physical server failure will not impact the virtual servers. But, it involves in high cost and slight risk in centralized storage, two physical servers and smooth live server migration (which clustering should do automatically) in this setup. The cost involves in buying one more similar powerful server, network storage (NAS) and setting up them may be same as buying low end five physical servers which can be run independently. Figure 2 shows virtual servers on two servers.

For example, Figure 2 shows a server setup is the real world example. In fact, these two servers are hosting 15 virtual servers now. Hyper-v server virtualization software is running in cluster environment and these two servers are accessing a centralized storage. Therefore, if one physical server goes down for any reasons, the second server will take care of the all 15 servers.

But the issue is, these two servers are running next each other in one server chassis. If this chassis or power supply goes down, then the both physical servers with 15 virtual servers will go down at the same time.

It is a high risk of safety also, for example, if this rack or server gets fire (hope it will not), then these all 15 servers can't be accessible. If the backup is in storage, but it will take some time to restore in different hardware and start the servers.

Is Performance the Same?

It always has doubtful in this fact. Let's say that you have allocated 4GB RAM and 2 virtual CPUs of 3GHz to a virtual server which will be used as a web server in your office. The question is: will the server and application perform like running in a physical server with 4GB RAM and 2 CPUs of 3GHz?

There will be some certain performance drawbacks in virtual environment compared to similar hardware in physical environment. You must consider this factor while planning and allocating virtual servers (Valden, 2013).

Figure 2. 11 virtual servers on two servers
(Cunningham, 2010).

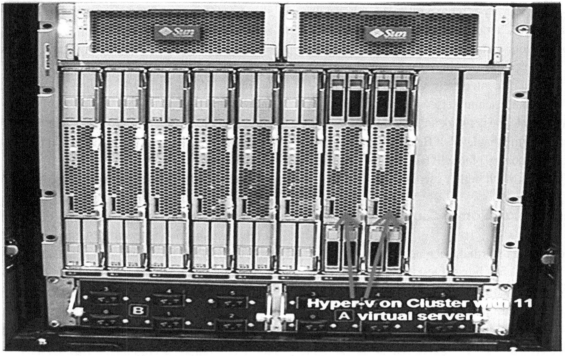

It Is Not Easy: Complicated

Yes, setting up and managing virtual environment with high critical servers in a production environment is not easy as managing physical servers. If you are expert in PC hardware, then you should be able to manage most of the server hardware and configuration aspects in Intel based servers. Unfortunately, that will not be the case in virtual environment. You must have special knowledge in VMware, Hyper-v or Xen server virtualization software to work with them.

You would find the similar setup in most of the physical server brands such as Dell, HP.etc. But, the server virtualization software like VMware, Hyper-v Xen are totally different software and you can't work with all in same knowledge. Special skills and knowledge are required to work with server virtualization products.

Not Supported by All Applications

Some of the core applications including few database applications are not ready for virtualization yet. Sometimes some applications or Operating Systems may face issues and act differently on virtual environment without giving any clues. You must consider this while planning your server Operating Systems and application implementation, make sure its certified and supported to virtualization 100%.

Securing the Virtual Datacentre

- **Secure Access Control:** Access to the Hypervisor should be password protected, limited to Identified administrators, and the IPs that are allowed to connect to the Hypervisor should be specified to avoid breaches.

- Controlling a hypervisor by a hacker can lead to a lot of damage or information stealing because gaining the access to the Hypervisor means gaining control of many resources.
- **Patch Management:** Patch management is a software to fix problems or update a computer program as well as fixing security vulnerabilities and bugs, and improving the performance.
- **Protecting Internal Network Resources:** Any network that communicates with external resources or uses Internet services should have a firewall to protect the internal infrastructure, identify the vulnerabilities, warns about breaches and block threats. Such as:
  - Forefront Threat Management Gateway (TMG).
  - Forefront protection for exchange for mail protection.

METHODOLOGY

The purpose of this chapter is to show the concept of virtualization for transforming the physical HW recourses to virtual through SW. There are lots of benefits which are already discussed above of virtualization. By using virtualization Its going to setup the whole infrastructure for a company name TEST.COM, which includes the Domain controller for authentication, DNS Server for name resolution, DHCP server for IP assignment, File server for sharing the document's over the LAN, Print server for sharing the printer to the user's, MailBox / HUB/CAS for the email setup for the company employee's.

With the help of virtualization it's going to be layered operating system resources and based on the need of every VM the resources will assigned to them.

The implementation of the virtual data center can be divided as followed:

Phase I: Setup the Hypervisor for creating the VMs.

Phase II: Installation the required Operating system on each VM.

Phase III: Installation of all the application or roles for the designated server accordingly based on the role what server is going to play in the infrastructure.

Phase VI: Setup the security policies for users that have been created.

Phase V: Testing the functionality of the Application's and high availability of the solution.

Phase IV: Securing the virtualized data center, managing inbound and outbound access and scheduling a regular security patching.

SETUP VIRTUALIZATION MECHANIZE

In regard for designing the solution is prepared for the following setup for the testing environment.

- HP laptop with VT enabled processor from BIOS.
- Windows 8 64 bit for host machine.
- Installing all the prerequisites for VMware workstation 7.
- Installing the VMware workstation on local HD of 1 TB.
- Creating the virtual network for internal and external communication of the Virtual machines.
- Creating the folder for the saving the VM's files.

Figure 3 shows creating a folder to save the VM's files.

IMPLEMENTATION

VMware Workstation as a Hypervisor 7.1.2 has the following steps as the following:_

Figure 3. Create folder to save the VM's files

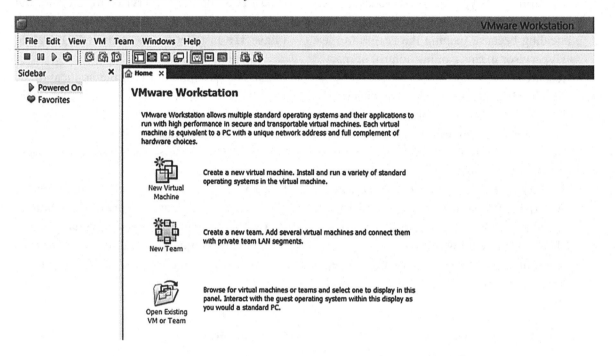

1. Installing Domain Controller/DNS/DHCP server.
2. Exchange Server 2010 Database Availability Group Overview.
3. Understanding Quorum for Exchange Server 2010 Database Availability Groups.
4. Understanding Quorum for Exchange Server 2010 Database Availability Groups.
5. Database Replication in Exchange Server 2010 Database Availability Groups.
6. Securing the network by managing Inbound and outbound access, this will be done in three important processes:
   a. Secure the console of the Hypervisor by protecting the access of it with a password. This can be done through the setting of the console.
   b. Patching management: Installing a program to schedule a regular update and install Security fixes. Security updates will be patched through SCOM.
   c. Installing TMG Threat Management Gateway 2010 as a firewall.

Installing Domain Controller/DNS/DHCP Server

- Creating New VM as in Figure 4.
- Choosing Windows operating system Server 2008 R2 x64 Bit.
- Giving the name of Virtual Machine name and location of the VM files.
- Giving the space for the VHD file which is 15 GB and keep the file as a single file for better performance of the VM.
- Final report represents the details of VM which is going to create.

Figure 5 shows the created VM which is going to host domain Controller/DNS/DHCP server.

Domain Controller

When you install Windows Server on a computer, you can choose to configure a specific server role for that computer. When you want to create a new forest, a new domain, or an additional domain

Figure 4. Creating new virtual machine

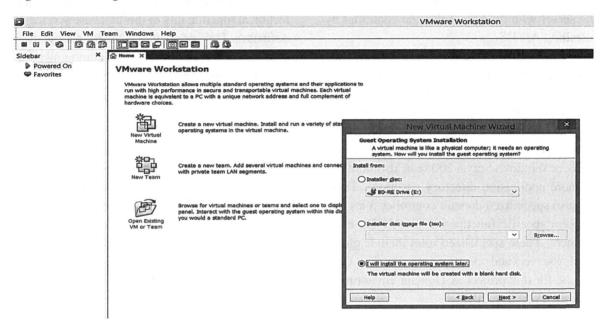

Figure 5. The creation of VM to host domain controller

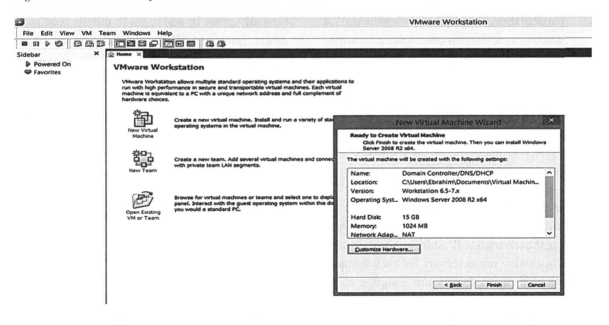

controller in an existing domain, you configure the server with the role of domain controller by installing AD DS.

By default, a domain controller stores one domain directory partition consisting of information about the domain in which it is located, plus the schema and configuration directory partitions for the entire forest. A domain controller that runs Windows Server 2008 R2, Windows Server 2008, or Windows Server 2003 can also store one or more application directory partitions. There are also specialized domain controller roles that perform specific functions in an AD DS environment. These specialized roles include global catalog servers and operations masters. Test.Com will be for this project as Domain environment (Microsoft Active, 2013).

- **DNS:** The Domain Name System (DNS) is a hierarchical distributed naming system for computers, services, or any resource connected to the Internet or a private network. It associates various information with domain names assigned to each of the participating entities. Most prominently, it translates easily memorized domain names to the numerical IP addresses needed for the purpose of locating computer services and devices worldwide. By providing a worldwide, distributed keyword-based redirection service, the Domain Name System is an essential component of the functionality of the Internet.

The Domain Name System distributes the responsibility of assigning domain names and mapping those names to IP addresses by designating authoritative name servers for each domain. Authoritative name servers are assigned to be responsible for their supported domains, and may delegate authority over sub-domains to other name servers. This mechanism provides distributed and fault tolerant service and was designed to avoid the need for a single central database.

The Domain Name System also specifies the technical functionality of this database service. It defines the DNS protocol, a detailed specification of the data structures and data communication exchanges used in DNS, as part of the Internet Protocol Suite (Microsoft, 2005).

- **DHCP:** The Dynamic Host Configuration Protocol (DHCP) is a network protocol used to conFigure devices that are connected to a network (known as hosts) so they can communicate on that network using the Internet Protocol (IP). It involves clients and a server operating in a client-server model.

The DHCP server maintains a database of available IP addresses and configuration information. When the server receives a request from a client, the DHCP server determines the network to which the DHCP client is connected, and then allocates an IP address or prefix that is appropriate for the client, and sends configuration information appropriate for that client. DHCP servers typically grant IP addresses to clients only for a limited interval. DHCP clients are responsible for renewing their IP address before that interval has expired, and must stop using the address once the interval has expired, if they have not been able to renew it. DHCP is used for IPv4 and IPv6. While both versions serve the same purpose, the details of the protocol for IPv4 and IPv6 are sufficiently different that they may be considered separate protocols. Figure 6 shows the Domain Controller /DNS/DHCP.

1. Assigning the OS DVD ISO image to the VM as shown in Figure 7.
2. Here DVD is assigned to the VM for installation.
3. Installation screen of Windows Server 2008 R2 after turn on of the VM.
4. Choosing the Standard edition 64 Bit for installing the DC/DNS/DHCP server roles.

Figure 6. Domain controller/DNS/DHCP

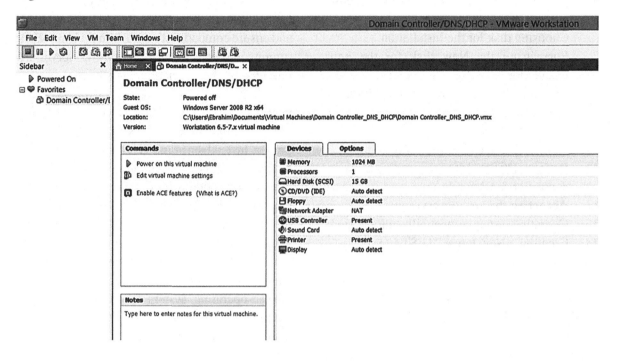

Figure 7. DVD ISO image

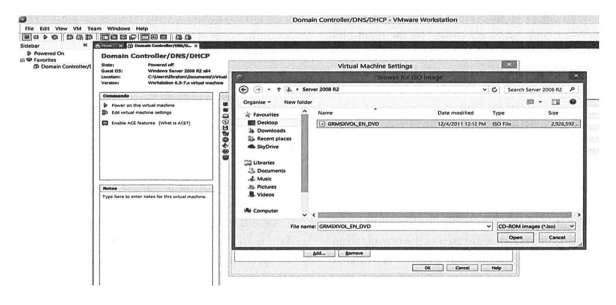

5. Accepting the Microsoft End user license agreement.
6. Choosing disk for the installation.
7. Formatting the New disk for the new installation.
8. Creating the disk partition for Windows installation.
9. Giving the name to the computer DC01.
10. Assigning static IP to the computer.
11. Running DCPROMO for installing Domain controller & DNS role.
12. Accepting the installation mode.
13. Operating system compatibility information.
14. Creating a New forest "TEST.COM"
15. Process is running.

Setting the Forest Functional Level to Windows Server 2008 R2

Domain controllers can run different versions of Windows Server operating systems, in Active Domain Services (ADDs). The functional level of a domain or forest depends on which versions of Windows Server operating systems are running on the domain controllers in the domain or forest. The advanced features are available in the domain or forest and can be controlled by the functional level of a domain or forest.

Ideally, the latest version of Windows can be run by all servers in an organization and take advantage of all the advanced features that are available with the newest software. But organizations often have a mixture of systems, generally running different versions of operating systems. Organizations are migrated to the latest version only as organizational requirements demand additional functionality, either for the entire organization or for a specific area of the organization.

Phased implementation of new versions of Windows Server and advanced features on domain controllers are supported by ADDs. This support is done by providing multiple functional levels, each of which is specific to the versions of Windows Server operating systems that are running

on the domain controllers in the environment. Configuration support for the AD DS features and ensure compatibility with domain controllers running earlier versions of Windows Server are provided by these functional levels.

AD DS does not automatically enable advanced features, even if all domain controllers within a forest are running the same version of Windows Server. Instead, an administrator raises a domain or forest to a specific functional level. When all domain controllers in the domain or forest are running an appropriate version of Windows Server, this will lead to safely enable advanced features. When an administrator attempts to raise the functional level, AD DS checks whether all domain controllers are running an appropriate Windows Server operating system to ensure the proper environment for enabling new Active Directory features as shown in Figure 8.

Installing Integrated DNS Server

Active Directory–integrated DNS enables Active Directory storage and replication of DNS zone databases. Windows 2008 DNS server, the DNS server that is included with Windows 2008 Server, accommodates storing zone data in Active Directory. When you configure a computer as a DNS server, zones are usually stored as text files on name servers — that is, all of the zones required by DNS are stored in a text file on the server computer. These text files must be synchronized among DNS name servers by using a system that requires a separate replication topology and schedule called a zone transfer However, if you use Active Directory–integrated DNS when you conFigure a domain controller as a DNS name server, zone data is stored as an Active Directory object and is replicated as part of domain replication. Only DNS servers that run on domain controllers can load Active Directory–integrated zones.

To use DNS integration within Active Directory, assign the zone type Active Directory-integrated when you create the zone. Objects that represent

Figure 8. AD DS check the domain controller

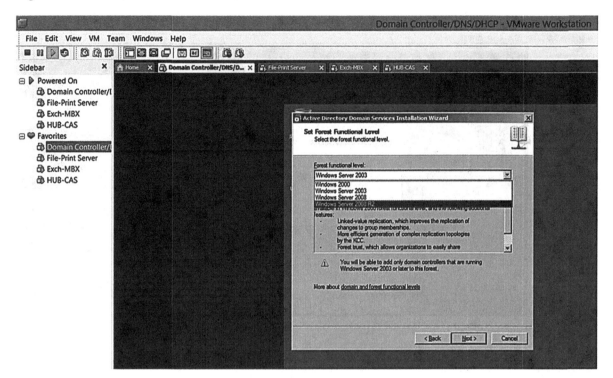

zone database records are created in the Microsoft DNS container within the System container (visible in the Advanced Features view in Active Directory Users and Computers), and the contents are replicated to all domain controllers in the domain. When you have Active Directory–integrated DNS zones, all Active Directory domain controllers that run Windows 2008 DNS server and are appropriately conFigured function as primary name servers.

When DNS data is stored in Active Directory, each DNS zone is an Active Directory container object (class *dnsZone*). The dnsZone object contains a DNS node object (class *dnsNode*) for every unique name within that zone. These unique names include the variations assigned to a specific host computer when it functions, for example, as a primary domain controller or as a Global Catalog server. The dnsNode object has a *dnsRecord* multivalued attribute that contains a value for every resource record that is associated with an object's name. Figure 9 shows the data storage.

Setting the Location for the Active Directory Folder

Summary for the settings of Active Directory and DNS server, as shown in Figure 10.

Configuring Mailbox Server

As creating the VM's steps are all same, so the VM creation steps are not shown again here. Only the print screen is deployed for the reference as shown in Figure 11.

The following steps are for the installation:

1. Installation of Exchange Server 2010. Setup launching.
2. Choosing the installation options.
3. Configuring &installing the prerequisites for Mailbox role.
4. Installation started for Mailbox role.
5. Installation completed page.

Figure 9. Stored data in active directory

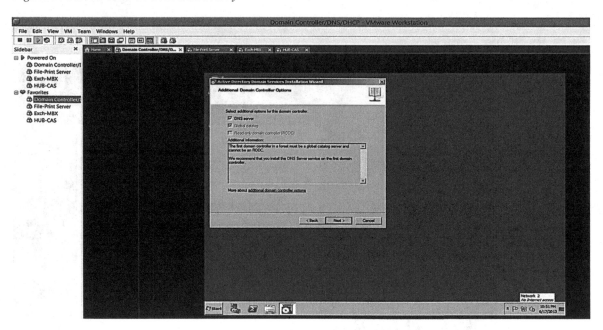

Figure 10. Summary for the settings of active directory and DNS server

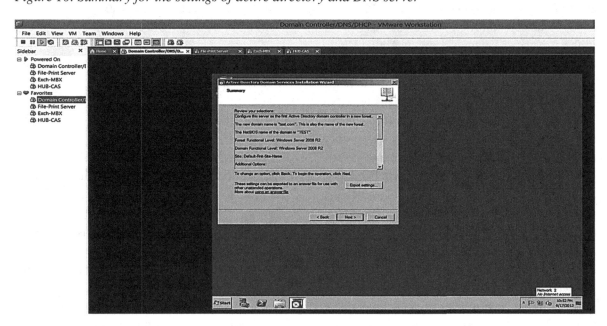

Figure 11. Configuring mailbox server

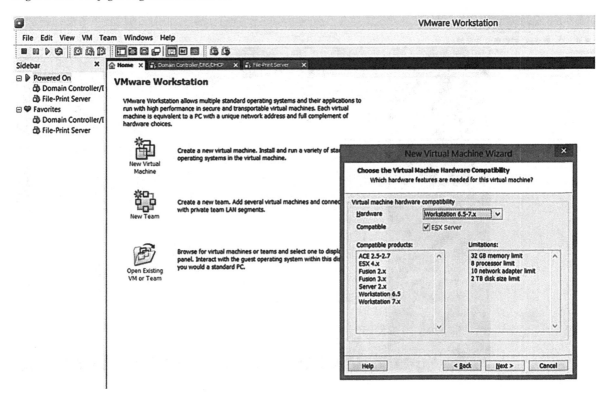

6. Creating the New mailbox database for the students under TEST.COM domain.

The creation of mailbox database is shown in Figure 12.

Exchange Server 2010 Database Availability Group Overview

Each server that is a member of the Database Availability Group (DAG) is capable of hosting active or passive copies of mailbox databases that reside on servers in the group. The DAG consist of up to 16 Exchange Server 2010 servers that are installed with the Mailbox server role.

Each Exchange Server 2010 servers configured with a single Mailbox database. For example, a Database Availability Group may consist of three Exchange Server 2010 servers. Each server that is a member of the DAG can host either an active

or passive copy of each of the three total mailbox databases as shown in Figure 13.

The foundation of an Exchange Server 2010 DAG is Windows Failover Clustering. Unlike traditional Exchange server clusters which existed in an active/passive state, and in which the entire cluster group needed to failover to an alternative node together. Each mailbox database can failover (or switchover, if it is a deliberate move) to another DAG member independent of the other mailbox databases in the DAG, with Exchange 2010 DAGs.

All, some or none of the active mailbox copies at any given time can be hosted by any given Mailbox server in the DAG. This capability provides two immediate advantages over previous clustering models:

- All of the Mailbox servers can be active and in use at all times to some capacity within the exchange 2010 DAG.

Figure 12. Creating the new mailbox database

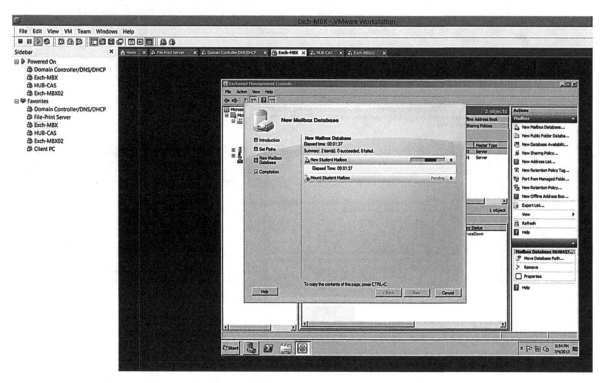

Figure 13. Exchange server 2010 database availability group example
(Cunningham, 2010).

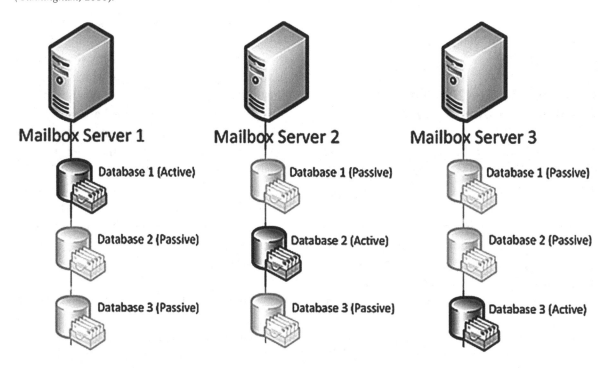

- Each mailbox database can failover/switchover when necessary without impacting the mailbox users connected to other mailbox databases within the DAG, for example when installing updates on DAG members.

Understanding Quorum for Exchange Server 2010 Database Availability Groups

The concept of quorum applies when the Database Availability Group utilizes an underlying Windows Failover Cluster. To make a decision, the quorum consider it as basically a voting process in which a majority of voting members must be present.

An odd number of members must be involved in the voting process for a majority decision to be made when using cluster. This applies to an Exchange Server 2010 DAG when you deploy a DAG with just two Mailbox servers as members (or any even number up to 16). Then neither server is able to determine by majority vote whether it should make its own copy of a given mailbox database active.

Another server in the same site is designated as a File Share Witness for the cluster to achieve quorum for a DAG with an even number of member servers. This is typically a Hub Transport server though it can technically be any compatible Windows server.

Database Replication in Exchange Server 2010 Database Availability Groups

The mailbox database replication occurs between Exchange Server 2010 DAG members in two ways.

RTM "file mode" replication is used in Exchange Server 2010. Each transaction log is written and then closed off (once it reaches 1Mb in size) with file mode replication. It is then copied to each member of the DAG that also holds a copy of that mailbox database. After the other members receive the file into their replay queue,

they replay the transaction log file into their own passive copy of the database.

File mode replication works fine but has an obvious shortcoming. Any transaction logs that have not yet been shipped to other servers in the DAG can be lost if the Exchange server hosting the active database copy fails. One of the other DAG members is able to bring their copy of the mailbox database online. Then will request missing emails be resent from the transport dumpster of Hub Transport servers within the site.

To bring mailbox database copies into sync with each other (e.g. during the initial sync process when a new database copy is added) when Exchange Server 2010 SPI file mode replication is used. Once they are in sync the DAG members switch to "block mode" replication. Each database transaction is written to the log buffer on the active server and also sent to the log buffer of DAG members hosting passive copies of the database when the mode is block replication.

Each DAG member builds their own transaction log files from their own log buffer when the log buffer becomes full. Block mode replication has an advantage over file mode replication in failure scenarios, because each DAG member is completely up to date with all changes to the active database.

The Public Folder databases can reside on Mailbox servers that are members of a Database Availability Group. They are not replicated by the DAG itself. Instead it is possible to use Public Folder replication to provide redundant copies of Public Folder databases.

Advantages of Exchange Server 2010 Database Availability Groups

- Exchange Server 2010 has just one high availability feature for Mailbox servers for all high availability deployment scenarios, unlike previous versions of Exchange Server (particularly Exchange Server 2007).

- The underlying Windows Failover Cluster is automatically created and configured for you when you create a Database Availability Group.
- Previous versions that required that clusters be established first before Exchange was installed, unlike Exchange Server 2010 when a DAG can be created at any time without requiring it to be removed and reinstalled from the server.
- Exchange Server 2010 DAG members can host other server roles, unlike Exchange Server 2007 that prevented clustered Mailbox servers from hosting other roles.

1. Setting up the witness server on HUB/CAS which is the preferred way of doing it. The folder location on the root of the system drive.
2. Defining the location of Quorum folder and server name.
3. DAG completed.
4. Adding the member in the DAG, which is Mailbox01 & Mailbox02.
5. Confirmation page for the member of DAG.
6. Configuring the Student database copy on another Mailbox server through the use of DAG.
7. Defining the copy of the Student Mailbox on Mailbox02 as a replica, so that if Mailbox01 goes down the Student database will come mounted automatically on Mailbox02 server.
8. Process running.
9. Adding the user mailbox name "Stduent01" for testing purpose.
10. Defining the mailbox store where this mailbox will reside.
11. Defining the achieve policy for the Student01 mailbox.
12. Process running for new mailbox.
13. New mail completion page.
14. Creating the new mailbox for new user "Student02".
15. Creating the new mailbox for a new user.
16. Creating the mailbox for "Student02".
17. Defining the mailbox store for "Student02".
18. Setting the archive setting for the user mailbox.
19. Process for new mailbox creation.
20. Getting logon with user "Student01" through outlook web access.
21. Choosing the language and time zone for the first time logon.
22. Displayed below is the email account of "Student01" which show's inbox items of the user. Now for the email functionality testing a email will be draft to user "student02" and will send.

TESTING AND FINDINGS

In this section the testing has been done on Exchange Mailbox server to ensure the high availability between the Mailboxes. Testing is also done to gather the data for virtualization overhead in regards to CPU/RAM/IO.

In findings, it found out that VMware is proved to be a best virtualization tool almost for all the application, even it is very light on the windows machines.

The setup for the VMware workstation is very simple and straight forward. It's also very easy to manage for deployment. Patching and maintenance of the VM is very easy through the VMware, even when the VM image profiles are many. The virtual switch solves the problem of configuring the Cisco or Juniper switches, because VMware have its own virtual switch with configure more of the settings automatically with only few clicks.

DAG Testing

As shown in Figure 14 the Student mailbox is mounted on Mailbox server "Mailbox01", for testing the high availability & functionality of the DAG, the Mailbox servers "Mailbox01" is restarted and the status of the mailbox goes mounted on Mailbox02.

Figure 14. Student mailbox is mounted on mailbox server "Mailbox01"

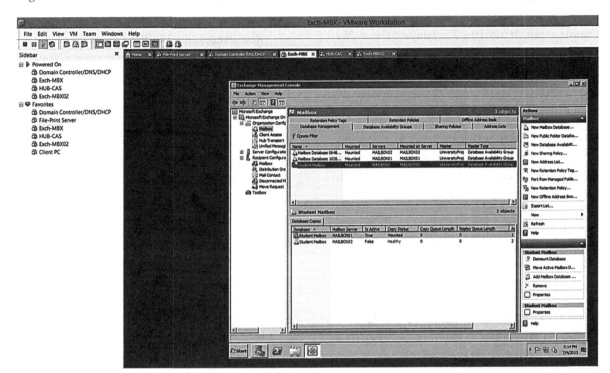

After the restart of the Mailbox01, now the Student data store is mounted on Mailbox02 which proves the high availability of the Mailbox server.

CONCLUSION

- Exchange 2010 OWA works a lilt slower on 1 gig network interface card on virtualization. So it's good to have higher NIC transfer rate.
- IE, Google chrome should be updated with JAVA latest update for running the script of Exchange 2010 OWA.
- Exchange log replication should be on separate HD for better performance.
- It's better to have dedicated NIC for Exchange log replication on Mailbox VM.
- It's better to have the NIC teaming on Exchange VM's and file server for better performance.
- It's recommended that the access of Hypervisor should be by identified IP and password protected.

- Regular Security updates mitigate threats and fixing vulnerabilities.

FUTURE WORKS

- One of the most important phases is installing EDGE server and forefront protection for Exchange as a mail protection.
- Iinstalling Antivirus on a dedicated VM and push the updates automatically to other VMs.
- Upgrading the VMware workstation to latest version.
- Configuring the CAS Server array.
- Configuring the HIB Server NLB.
- Installing and configuring Symantec endpoint protection.
- High availability on VM's level on workstation software.
- Planning for DR solution for Active directory, Exchange server.

REFERENCES

Cunningham, P. (2010). *Exchange Server 2010 Database Availability Group Installation Step by Step*. Retrieved from http://exchangeserverpro.com/exchange-server-2010-database-availability-group-installation-step-by-step/

Fogarty, K. (2009). *Server Virtualization: Top Five Security Concerns*. Retrieved July 3, 2013 from http://www.cio.com/article/492605/Server_Virtualization_Top_Five_Security_Concerns

Hoard, B. (2012). *5 Virtualization Challenges*. Retrieved June 21, 2013 from http://virtualization-review.com/articles/2012/08/01/5-virtualization-challenges.aspx

Hurwitz, J., Nugent, A., Halper, F., & Kufman, M. (2013). Big Data for Dummies. Security Issue. Hoboken: Wiley.

Kumar, K. (2010). *Virtualization Express*. Retrieved April 20, 2010 from http://www.virtualizationexpress.com/

Litke, J. (2011). *Overcoming Virtualization Challenges*. Retrieved June 24, 2013 from http://www.businessinsider.com/overcoming-virtualization-challenges-on-the-way-to-the-private-cloud-2011-3

Mcgraw-Hill. (2013). *Virualization Overview*. Retrieved from http://www.mhprofessional.com/downloads/products/0071614036/0071614036_chap01.pdf

Microsoft. (2005). *Active Directory Integration*. Retrieved July 2, 2013 from http://technet.microsoft.com/en-us/library/cc737383(v=ws.10).aspx

Microsoft. (2010). *Microsoft Active Directory-Integrated DNS*. Retrieved July 2, 2013 from http://technet.microsoft.com/en-us/library/cc978010.aspx

Torres, G. (2012). *Everything You Need to Know About the Intel Virtualization Technology*. Retrieved June 24, 2013 from http://www.hardwaresecrets.com/article/Everything-You-Need-to-Know-About-the-Intel-Virtualization-Technology/263

University of Cambridge. (2013). *Windows Server DNS Configuration Guidelines for Active Directory*. Retrieved from http://www.ucs.cam.ac.uk/support/windows-support/winsuptech/activedir/dnsconfig

Valden, T. (2013). *Hidden Truth About Virtualizing Business-Critical Applications: Benefits Realized, with Results to Prove It*. Retrieved from http://www.vmware.com/files/pdf/solutions/VMware-Hidden-Truth-About-Virtualizing-Business-Critical-Apps-WP-EN.pdf

Vanover, R. (2009). *Type 1 and Type 2 Hypervisors Explained*. Retrieved from http://virtualizationreview.com/blogs/everyday-virtualization/2009/06/type-1-and-type-2-hypervisors-explained.aspx [Accessed 4 July].

KEY TERMS AND DEFINITIONS

Disaster Recovery: A critical component for IT, as system crashes can create huge economic losses. Virtualization technology enables a virtual image on a machine to be instantly re-imaged on another server if a machine failure occurs.

Domain Name System (DNS): A hierarchical distributed naming system for computers, services, or any resource connected to the Internet or a private network. It associates various information with domain names assigned to each of the participating entities.

Exchange Server 2010: Each server that is a member of the DAG can host either an active or passive copy of each of the three total mailbox databases.

Mailbox: Each server that is a member of the DAG is capable of hosting active or passive copies of mailbox databases that reside on servers in the group.

Platform Virtualization: Platform virtualization or Hardware virtualization refers to the creation of a virtual machine that acts like a real computer with an operating system.

Virtual Machines: When software executed on the virtual machines is separated from the underlying hardware resources. For example, a computer that is running Microsoft Windows may host a virtual machine that looks like a computer with the Ubuntu Linux operating system; Ubuntu-based software can be run on the virtual machine.

Virtualization Technology: Changes the protection way of security, as most of hardware and software become after virtualization such as servers, switches, Logical Unit Numbers (LUNs) etc. and it's no longer trying to protect a physical hardware.

Chapter 15
The Impact of Big Data on Security

Mohammad Alaa Hussain Al-Hamami
Applied Science University, Bahrain

ABSTRACT

Big Data is comprised systems, to remain competitive by techniques emerging due to Big Data. Big Data includes structured data, semi-structured and unstructured. Structured data are those data formatted for use in a database management system. Semi-structured and unstructured data include all types of unformatted data including multimedia and social media content. Among practitioners and applied researchers, the reaction to data available through blogs, Twitter, Facebook, or other social media can be described as a "data rush" promising new insights about consumers' choices and behavior and many other issues. In the past Big Data has been used just by very large organizations, governments and large enterprises that have the ability to create its own infrastructure for hosting and mining large amounts of data. This chapter will show the requirements for the Big Data environments to be protected using the same rigorous security strategies applied to traditional database systems.

INTRODUCTION

The term Big Data has a relative meaning and tends to denote bigger and bigger data sets over time. In computer science, it refers to data sets that are too big to be handled by regular storage and processing infrastructures. It is evident that large datasets have to be handled differently than small ones; they require different means of discovering patterns, or sometimes allow analyses that would be impossible one small scale.

In the social sciences and humanities as well as applied fields in business, the size of data sets thus tends to challenge researchers as well as software or hardware. This may be especially an issue for disciplines or applied fields that are more or less unfamiliar with quantitative analysis. (Manovich, 2012) sees knowledge of computer science and quantitative data analysis as a determinant for what a group of researchers will be able to study. He fears a "data analysis divide" between those equipped with the necessary analytical training

DOI: 10.4018/978-1-4666-6583-5.ch015

Copyright © 2015, IGI Global. Copying or distributing in print or electronic forms without written permission of IGI Global is prohibited.

and tools to actually make use of the new data sets and those who will inevitably only be able to scratch the surface of this data.

New analytical tools tend to shape and direct scholars' ways of thinking and approaching their data. The focus on data analysis in the study of Big Data has even led some to the assumption that advanced analytical techniques make theories obsolete in the research process. Research interest could thus be almost completely steered by the data itself. But being driven by what is possible with the data may cause a researcher to disregard vital aspects of a given research object. (Boyd and Crawford, 2012) underline the importance of the (social) context of data that has to be taken into account in its analysis. The scholars illustrate how analyses of large numbers of messages ("tweets") from the micro blogging service.

Twitter currently used to describe aggregated moods or trending topics—without researchers really discussing what and particularly who these tweets represent: Only parts of a given population are even using Twitter, often in very different ways. As Boyd and Crawford point out, these contexts are typically unknown to researchers who work with samples of messages captured through Twitter. In addition, Big Data analyses tend only to show what users do, but not why they do it. In his discussion of tools for Big Data analysis, (Manovich, 2012) questions the significance of the subsequent results in terms of their relevance for the individual or society. The issue of meaning of the observed data and/or analyses is thus of vital importance to the debate around Big Data.

Many organizations are relying on multiple tools to produce the necessary security data. This will lead to a huge and a complex data feeds that must be analyzed, normalized, and prioritized. The scale of security data that needs analysis has simply become too big and complex to handle, and its takes a very long time. According to the Verizon 2013 Data Breach Investigations Report, 69% of breaches were discovered by a third party and not through internal resources and this is an example to clarify why the role of Big Data is important in security.

"BIG DATA" TERM

"Big Data" is a term that has quickly achieved widespread use among technologists, researchers, the media and politicians. Perhaps due to the speed of dissemination the use of the term has been rather nebulous in nature. The concept of Big Data can be framed by one of three perspectives. The first is a response to the technology problems associated with storing, securing and analyzing the ever-increasing volumes of data being gathered by organizations. This includes a range of technical innovations, such as new types of database and 'cloud' storage that enable forms of analysis that would not previously have been cost effective. The second perspective focuses on the commercial value that can be added to organizations through generating more effective insights from this data. This has emerged through a combination of better technology and greater willingness by consumers to share personal information through web services. The third perspective considers the wider societal impacts of Big Data, particularly the implications for individual privacy, and the effect on regulation and guidelines for ethical commercial use of this data. We now consider each of these perspectives on Big Data in more detail.

BIG DATA AND TECHNOLOGY INNOVATION

In its original form, Big Data referred to technical issues relating to the large volumes of data being created. While the rate at which data has been generated by information technology has always been increasing, recent growth produces some startling statistics (Qin and Li, 2013). Take the following two examples:

1. Ninety percent of all the data in the world has been produced in the past two years.
2. The sum of all information ever produced by humans by 1999, estimated at 16 Exabyte

(16 trillion megabytes) in 1999, will be the same as generated every nine weeks by the world's largest telescope, the Square Kilometer Array, when it opens later this decade.

At the same time as data volumes have increased, the cost of storing this information has reduced drastically. For example, in 2011, $600 would buy a disk drive with the capacity to store the entire world's recorded music. In providing these statistics we seek to highlight that the Big Data problem is not the volume of data itself, but the issues arising with analyzing and storing this data in a way that can easily be accessed. The costs of storing large volumes of data mean that, until recently, it has been common practice to discard information not strictly required for legal, regulatory or immediate business use. For example, hospitals and health care providers discard more than 90% of the data they generate, including nearly all real-time video data generated from operations.

In addition, two other factors, velocity and variety, are significant in Big Data. Velocity refers to the challenges in Downloaded from accessing stored data quickly enough for them to be useful. For most real-world uses, data need to be accessible in something close to real time. Offering fast access to massive amounts of data at a reasonable cost is a key limitation of existing technologies, both in terms of commonly used relational database software and the use of cheaper 'offline' tape storage devices. Variety refers to the type of information being stored. Previously, data stored tended to be highly structured in nature. By contrast, the types of data that tend to dominate modern data stores are unstructured, such as streams of data gathered from social media sites, audio, video, organizational memoranda, internal documents, email, organizational Web Pages, and comments from customers.

From a technology perspective, the solution to the Big Data problem has occurred through the intersection of several innovations. These include flash-based disk drives that allow much faster access to high volumes of information, and a new generation of non-relational database technologies that make it practical to store and access massive amounts of unstructured data. Fittingly, much of this new database technology has emerged from inside companies that run social media networks, including Google, Facebook, LinkedIn and Twitter.

BIG DATA AND COMMERCIAL VALUE

While technology has served as the enabler of Big Data services, the broader interest in Big Data has been driven by thoughts of the potential commercial value that it may bring. This is derived from the ability to generate value from data in ways that were not previously possible. For example, financial services are using high-performance computing to identify complex patterns of fraud within unstructured data that were not previously apparent. This has enabled the cost-effective provision of financial services in areas that would previously have been regarded as too risky to be sustainable. Another example is the use of personal location data, gained from a combination of smart phones, cell-tower tracking and GPS navigation data within vehicles. Such information is already being used to calculate fuel-efficient smart routing, report diagnostic information back to manufacturers or tracking applications to locate family members (Manyika *et al.* 2011).

In practical terms this gives organizations the ability to generate insights in minutes that might once have taken days or weeks – for example, by using diagnostic information to predict quality issues or develop new understandings of consumer behavior. The need to derive commercial value, and insight, from data is not new. Indeed, providing information to help support management insights can be considered a foundation of the market research sector. However, the key difference with Big Data strategies is not simply the provision of high-quality and more timely data into the decision-making process, but the enablement of continuous autonomous decision making via the use of automation. For example, the use of remote monitors for health conditions such as heart disease or diabetes, or 'chip-on-pill' technologies, could enable the automation of health decisions (Manyika *et al.* 2011).

THE 'DATA RUSH'

Since the 1990s and early 2000s, social scientists from various fields have relied more and more on digitized methods in empirical research. Surveys can be administered via Web sites instead of paper or via telephone; digital recordings of interviews or experimental settings make the analysis of content or observed behavior more convenient; and coding of material is supported by more and more sophisticated software. But in addition to using research tools that gather or handle data in digital form, scholars have also started using digital material that was not specifically created for research purposes. The introduction of digital technology in, for example, telephone systems and cash registers, as well as the diffusion of the Internet to large parts of a given population, have created huge quantities of digital data of unknown size and structure. While phone and retail companies usually do not share their clients' data with the academic community, scholars have concentrated on the massive amounts of publicly available data about Internet users, often giving insight into previously inaccessible subject matters. Subsequently, methodological literature began discussing research practices, opportunities, and drawbacks of online research.

Methodological Issues in the Study of Digital Media Data (Christians and Chen, 2004) discuss technological advantages of Internet research, but urge their readers to also consider its inherent disadvantages. Having huge amounts of data available that is "naturally" created by Internet users also has a significant limitation: The material is not indexed in any meaningful way, so no comprehensive overview is possible. Thus, there may be great material for many different research interests, but the question of how to access and select it cannot be easily answered. Sampling is therefore probably the issue most often and consistently raised in the literature on Internet methodology. Sampling online content poses technical or practical challenges.

Data may be created through digital media use, but it is currently impossible to collect a sample in a way that adheres to the conventions of sample quality established in the social sciences. This is partly due to the vastness of the Internet, but the issue is further complicated by the fact that online content often changeover time. On Web sites, content is not as stable or clearly delineated assign most traditional media, which can make sampling and defining units of analysis challenging. It seems most common to combine purposive and random sampling techniques.

The problems related to sampling illustrate that tried and tested methods and standards of social science research will not always be applicable to digital media research. But scholars take opposing sides on whether to stick with traditional methods or adopt new ones: Some suggest applying well-established methods tonsure the quality of Internet research. On the other hand, there are questions whether conventional methods would be applicable to large data sets of digital media. Communication scholars trained in conventional content analysis will find they need to adapt their methodological toolbox to digital media, at least to some degree. The incorporation of methods from other disciplines should be able to adequately study the structure of Web sites, blogs, or social network sites. Scholars may find more appropriate or complementary methods in; for instance, linguistics or discourse analysis. But methodological adaptation and innovation have their drawbacks, and scholars of new phenomena or data structures find themselves in an area of conflict between old and new methods and issues. While other scholars argue for a certain level of restraint toward experimenting with new methods and tools, researchers caught in the "data rush" seem to have thrown caution tithe wind, allowing themselves to be seduced by the appeal of Big Data.

BIG DATA MEANING

Researchers are already wrote about the belief or hope of scholars involved in Internet research that data collected through Web sites, online games, e-mail, chat, or other modes of Internet usage "represent::: well, something, some semblance of reality, perhaps, or some 'slice of life' on-line". Others illustrate that even the comparatively simple phenomenon of a hyperlink between two Web sites is not easily interpreted. What does the existence of just the connection, as such, between two sites tell a researcher about why it was implemented and what it means for the creators of the two sites or their users? Studying online behavior through large data sets strongly emphasizes the technological aspect of the behavior and relies on categories or features of the platforms that generated the data.

Yet, the behaviors or relationships thus expressed online may only seem similar to their offline counterparts. (Boyd and Crawford, 2012) illustrate that, for instance, network relationships between cell phone users may give an account of who calls whom how often and for how long. Yet, whether frequent conversation partners also find their relationship important for them personally or what relevance they attribute to it cannot be derived from (Christians and Chen, 2004) their connection data without further context. In addition, many authors' advice researchers to be wary of data collected from social media to a certain degree, because they may be the result of active design efforts by users who purposefully shape their online identities.

It is unclear how close to or removed from their online personas users actually are. This means that scholars should be careful to take data for what it truly represents (e.g., traces of behavior), but not infer too much about possible attitudes, emotions, or motivations of those whose behavior created the data—although some seem happy to make such inferences. Some researchers urge scholars to scrutinize whether a study can rely on data collected online alone or whether it should be complemented by offline contextual data.

OPPORTUNITIES OF BIG DATA RESEARCH

Data collected through use of online media is obviously attractive to many different research branches, both academic and commercial. We will briefly summarize key advantages in this section and subsequently discuss critical aspects of Big Data in more depth. Focusing on the social sciences, advantages and opportunities include the fact that digital media data are often a by-product of the everyday behavior of users, ensuring a certain degree of ecological validity. Such behavior can be studied through the traces it automatically left, providing a means to study human behavior without having to observe or record human subjects first. These canals allow examination of aspects of human interaction that could be distorted by more obtrusive methods or more artificial settings, due to observer effects or the subjects' awareness of participating in a study. Such observational data shares similarities with material used in content analysis since it can be stored or already exists in document form. Thus, content analysis methodology well-established in communication or other research fields can be applied to new research questions. When content posted on a platform is analyzed in combination with contextual data, such as time of a series of postings, geographic origin of posters, or relationships between different users of the same platform or profile, digital media data can be used to explore and discover patterns in human behavior, e.g., through visualization.

For some equally explorative research questions, the sheer amount of information accessible online seems to fascinate researchers because it provides (or at least seems to provide) ample opportunities for new research questions. Lastly, the collection of Big Data can also serve as a first step in a study, which can be followed by analyses of sub-samples on a much smaller scale. Groups hard to reach in the real world or rare and scattered phenomena can be filtered out of huge data sets proverbial needle in the digital haystack. This can be much more efficient than drawing, for instance, a huge sample of people via a traditional method, such as random dialing or random walking, when attempting to identify those who engage in comparatively rare activities (Nunan and Marialaura, 2013).

CHALLENGES OF BIG DATA RESEARCH

Although Big Data seems to be promising a golden future, especially to commercial researchers, the term is viewed much more critically in the academic literature. (Boyd and Crawford, 2012) discuss issues related to the use of Big Data in digital media research, some of which have been summarized above. In addition to more general political aspects of ownership of platforms and "new digital divides" in terms of data access or questions about the meaning of Big Data, its analysis also poses concrete challenges for researchers in the social sciences. One recurring theme in many studies that make use of Big Data is what we call its availability bias: Rather than theoretically defining units of analysis and measurement

strategies, researchers tend to use whatever data is available and the entry to provide an ex-post justification or even theorization for its use. This research strategy is in stark contrast to traditional theory-driven research and raises concerns about the validity and generality of the results.

SAMPLING AND DATA COLLECTION

The problem of sampling in Internet research has already been addressed previously and is mentioned in almost every publication on online research. While there are some promising approaches for applying techniques such as capture-recapture or adaptive cluster sampling to online research, the problem of proper random sampling, on which all statistical inference is based, remains largely unsolved. Most Big Data research is based on nonrandom sampling, such as using snowball techniques or simply by using any data that is technically and legally accessible. Another problem with many Big Data projects is that even with a large sampler complete data from a specific site, there is often little or no variance in the level of platforms or sites. If researchers are interested in social network sites, multiplayer games, or online news in general, it is problematic to include only data from Facebook and Twitter, World of Warcraft and Everquest II, or a handful of newspaper and broadcast news sites.

From a platform perspective, the sample size of these studies is tiny, even with millions of observations per site. This has consequences not only for the inferences that can be drawn from analyses, but also from a validity perspective: Expanding and testing the generalize-ability of the (Raghvendra, Langone et al., 2013) would not require more data from the same source, but information from many different sources. In this respect, the hardest challenge of digital media research might not be to obtain Big Data from a few, although certainly important, Websites or user groups, but from many different platforms and persons. Given the effort required to sample, collect, and analyze data from even a single source, and the fact that this can rarely be automated or outsourced, this "horizontal" 'expansion of online research remains a difficult task.

A third important aspect of Big Data collection is the development of ethical standards and procedures for using public or semi-public data. Researchers provide an excellent account of the problems facing them when making seemingly public data available to the research community. The possibility of effective de-anonymization of large data sets has made it difficult for researchers to obtain and subsequently publish data from social media networks such as YouTube, Facebook, or Twitter. Moreover, the risk of in advertently revealing sensitive user information has also decreased the willingness of companies to provide third parties with anonymized data sets, even if these companies are generally interested in cooperation with the research community. Researches who collect their data from publicly available sources are at risk as well because the content providers or individual users may object to the publication of this data for further research, especially after the data has successfully been de-anonymized. The post-hoc withdrawal of research data, in turn, makes replications of the findings impossible and therefore violates a core principle of empirical research.

Finally, basically all Big Data research is based on the assumption that use simplicity consent to the collection and analysis of their data by posting them online. In light of current research on privacy in online communication, it is questionable whether users can effectively distinguish private from public messages and behavior. But even if they can, since it is technically possible to recover private information even from limited public profiles, Big Data research has to solve the problem of guaranteeing privacy and ethical standards while also being replicable and open to scholarly debate.

BIG DATA MEASUREMENT

Concerns about the reliability and validity of measurement have been raised in various critical papers on Big Data research, most recently by (Boyd and Crawford, 2012). Among the most frequently discussed issues are

1. Comparatively shallow measures,
2. Lack of context awareness, and
3. A dominance of automated methods of analysis.

Clearly, these concerns and their causes are related to an implicit or explicit tendency toward data-driven rather than theory-driven operationalization strategies. In addition to the possible "availability bias" mentioned above, many prominent Big Data studies seem to either accept the information accessible via digital media as face-valid, e.g., by treating Facebook friendship relations as similar to actual friendships, or reduce established concepts in communication such as topic or discourse to simple counts of hash tags or re tweets.

While we do not argue that deriving measurement concepts from data rather than theory is problematic, per se, researchers should be aware that the most easily available measure may not be the most valid one and they should discuss to what degree its validity converges with that of established instruments. For example, both communication research and linguistics have a long tradition of content-analytic techniques that are, at least in principle, easily applicable to digital media content. Of course, it is not possible to manually annotate millions of comments, tweets, or blog posts. However, any scholar who analyzes digital media can and should provide evidence for the validity of measures used, especially if they rely on previously unavailable or untested methods.

The use of shallow, "available" measures often coincides with an implicit preference or automatic coding instruments over human judgment. There are several explanations for this phenomenon: First, many Big Data analyses are conducted by scholars who have a computer science or engineering background and may simply be unfamiliar with standard social science methods such as content analysis. Moreover, these researchers often have easier access to advanced computing machinery than trained research assistants who are traditionally employed as coders or raters. Second, Big Data proponents often point out those automatic approaches are highly reliable, at least in the technical sense of not making random mistakes, and better suited for larger sample sizes. However, this argument is valid only if there is an inherent advantage to coding thousands of messages rather than a smaller sample, and if this advantage outweighs the decrease of validity in automatic coding that has been established in many domains of content analysis research.

Some researcher find that supervised text classification is on average 20 percent less reliable than manual topic coding. Despite the vast amount of scholarship on these methods, the actual trade, although it is central to the question of whether and when, for example, we accept shallow lexical measures that are easy to implement and technically reliable as substitutes for established content-analytic categories and human coding.

DATA ANALYSIS AND INFERENCES

In addition to sampling, data collection, and measurement, the analysis of large data sets is one of the central issues around the Big Data phenomenon. If a researcher deals with Big Data in the original technical sense, meaning that data sets cannot be analyzed on a desktop computer using conventional tools such as Statistical Product and Service Solutions (SPSS) or Statistical Analysis System (SAS), he or she can investigate the possibilities of distributed algorithms and software that can run analyses on multiple processors or computing nodes.

An alternative approach would be to take a step back and ask whether an analysis of a subset of the data could provide enough information to test a hypothesis or make a prediction. Although in general, a larger sample size means more precise estimates and larger number of indicators or repeated observations lead to less measurement error, most social science theories do not require that much precision. If the sampling procedure is valid, the laws of probability and the central limit theorem also apply to online research, and even analyses that require much statistical power can still be run on a single machine. In this way, Big Data can safely be reduced to medium-size data and still yield valid and reliable results. The requirement of larger or smaller data sets is also linked to the question of what inferences one might like to draw from the analysis: Are we interested in aggregator individual effects, causal explanation or prediction? Predicting individual user behavior, for example on a Web site, requires both reliable and valid measurement of past behavior as well as many observations.

Longitudinal analyses of aggregate data, e.g., using search queries or large collections of tweets, do not necessarily require perfectly reliable coding or large sample sizes. If a blunt coding scheme based on a simple word list has only 50 percent accuracy, it is still possible to analyze correlations between time series of media content and user behavior as long as the amount of measurement error is the same over time. Moreover, whether a time series is based on hundreds or thousands of observations rarely affects the inferences that can be drawn on the aggregate level, at least if the observations are representative of the same population. If, on the other hand, a researcher is interested in analyzing the specific content of a set of messages or the behavior of a pre-defined group of online users. As in other disciplines such as psychology, education, or medicine, individual diagnostics and inferences require far more precision than the detection of aggregate trends.

Finally, one should ask how generalizable the findings of a study can or should be: In-depth analysis, both qualitative and quantitative, might allow for accurate predictions and understanding of a single individual, but it often cannot be generalized for larger samples or the general population. Observing a handful of Internet users in a computer lab can rarely lead to valid inferences about Internet users in general, simply because there is often too little information about individual differences or, more technically, between-person variance. Correlations on the aggregate level, on the other hand, cannot simply be applied to the individual level without the risk of an ecological fallacy, i.e., observing something in aggregate data that never actually occurs on the individual level.

INTERPRETATION AND THEORETICAL IMPLICATIONS

If researchers have undertaken analyses of Big Data, they need; of course, to interpret their results in light of the decisions they have made along the research process and the consequences of each of these decisions. The core question should be: What is the theoretical validity and significance of the data? Large samples of digital media are limited in some respects, so scholars have to be careful about what inferences are drawn from them. The problem of determining the meaning of some types of digital media data has already been alluded to above. The number of times a message gets forwarded ("retweeted") on Twitter, for instance, may show a certain degree of interest by users, but without looking at the content and/or style of tweet, "interest" could stand for popularity and support, revulsion and outrage, or simply the thoughtless routines of Twitter usage behavior.

As (Boyd and Crawford,2012) point out: No matter how easily available Facebook, YouTube, or Twitter data is, it is based on a small and certainly nonrandom subset of Internet users, and this is even more true when investigating specific Web sites, discussion boards, online games, or devices. If less than 5 percent of Internet users in a given country are active on Twitter, as in Germany, an analysis of trending topics on the micro blogging service can hardly represent the general population's current concerns.

In addition, a platform's interfaces (or ethical constraints) may not allow researchers to access information that would be most interesting to them, confining them to descriptive exploration of artificial categories. Visualizations based on such categories, for example connections between social media users, may allow the discovery of patterns, but without cases to compare them to, these patterns may not lead to insight. Likewise, we have already underlined that the mere occurrence of certain keywords in a set of social media messages does not constitute "discourse," per se. Such theoretical constructs should not be tweaked beyond recognition to fit the data structure of a given platform.

In sum, researchers should not compromise their original research interests simply because they cannot be as easily approached as others. If after careful scrutiny of the possibilities a certain platform or type of analysis really offers, the scholar decides that a Big Data approach is not advisable, a thorough analysis of smaller data sets may well produce more meaningful results. While similar problems exist in all empirical studies, such issues seem especially pressing in Big Data research.

THE BIG DATA IN CLOUD COMPUTING

With the development of Internet of Things, its technology has been widely used in to various fields, and has accumulated massive data. Since the emergence of Cloud Computing, with the continuous development of science and technology and advance by academia and industry, the applications of Cloud Computing are going on developing. Cloud Computing is moving from theory to practice. With the development of Cloud Computing, data center is also improved. Nowadays, data center is not only a site which manages and repairs servers, but also a center of many computers with high performance which could compute and store huge data.

Currently there are proposed many cleaning algorithms of Big Data that is mainly divided into regional object cleaning algorithm, the object cleaning algorithm based on information theory, based on discernibility matrix and on the basis of improved object cleaning algorithm. Many scholars mainly study on how to deal with inconsistent decision table and how to improve the efficiency of Big Data algorithm. The Big Data cleaning is the important way to resolve the massive data mining problem, and the Big Data cleaning algorithm combined the parallel genetic algorithm and co-evolutionary algorithm, to decompose of object cleaning task, which can improve the efficiency of Big Data algorithm (Zhang, Xue and et al, 2013).

To this end, such Big Data cleaning algorithm that assume all the data can be loaded into the main memory at one-time, which are infeasible for Big Data. Cloud computing is a new business computing model that was proposed in recent years, it is the development of distributed computing, parallel computing and grid computing. The pioneers of cloud computing is Google Inc., proposed a massive data storage and access capacity of large distributed file system GFS (Google File System), and providing a handle massive data parallel programming mode of Map Reduce, that provides a feasible solution for massive data mining. Cloud computing technology has been applied in the field of machine learning, but there is still no real application to Big Data cleaning algorithm.

BIG DATA IMPACTS BUSINESS ENTERPRISES

Data are generated in a growing number of ways. Use of traditional transactional databases has been supplemented by multimedia content, social sensors. Advances in information technology allow users to capture, communicate, aggregate, store and analyze enormous pools of data, known as "Big Data". However, the businesses that have depended upon database technology to store and process data. Big Data derives its name database systems are unable to capture. The actual size of Big Data varies by business sector, software tools available in the sector, and average dataset sizes within the sector. Best estimates of size range from few dozen terabytes to many peta bytes. In order to benefit from Big Data, be adopted, business executives must determine the suited to their information needs; eventually become non-competitive (Manyika & et al, 2011).

TYPES AND SOURCES OF BIG DATA

Executives need to be cognizant of the types of data three main types of data, regardless of data, structured data, and semi-structured data. Unstructured data are they were collected; no formatting is used (Coronel, Morris, & et al, 2013). Unstructured data are PDF's, e-mails, and documents formatted to allow storage, use, and generation of information (Coronel, Morris, & et al, 2013). Traditional transactional databases store structured data. Data have been processed to some extent aged text are examples of semi-structured data (Manyika et al., 2011). With traditional database management systems need to broaden their data horizons to include collection, storage, and processing of data collection of unstructured and semi-structured data is done through based technologies. Researchers describe sensors providing Big Data as being part of the Internet of Things. The Internet of Things is described as sensors and actuators that are embedded in physical objects. Some industries that are creating and using Big Data are those that have recently begun digitization of their data content; these industries include entertainment, healthcare, life sciences, video surveillance, transportation, logistics, retail, utilities, and telecommunications.

Journal of Technology Research The emergence of Big Data media, and myriad types of new data collection methodologies pose a dilemma for from the fact that the datasets are large enough that typical save, and analyze these datasets (Manyika et al., 2011). In new storage technologies and analysis methods need to new technologies and methodologies best Business executives ignoring the growing field of Big Data will they need to deal with whether or not a company is using Big Data structured data in the format in which Some Structured data are XML or HTML.

THE ROLE OF BIG DATA IN SECURITY

Many organizations are relying on multiple tools to produce the necessary security data. This will lead to a huge and a complex data feeds that must be analyzed, normalized, and prioritized. The scale of security data that needs analysis has simply become too big and complex to handle, and its takes a very long time. According to the Verizon 2013 Data Breach Investigations Report, 69% of breaches were discovered by a third party and not through internal resources and this is an example to clarify why the role of Big Data is important in security (Tankard, 2012).

Big Data security needs to be correlated with its business criticality or risk to the organization. Without a risk-based approach to security, organizations can waste valuable IT resources used for vulnerabilities that will cause in reality little or no threat to the business. Furthermore, big security data needs to be filtered to just the information that is relevant to specific stakeholders' roles and responsibilities. Not everyone has the same needs and objectives when it comes to leveraging Big Data.

To deal with big security data and achieve continuous diagnostics, progressive organizations are leveraging Big Data Risk Management systems to automate many manual, labor-intensive tasks. These systems take a preventive, pro-active approach by interconnecting otherwise silo-based security and IT tools and continuously correlating and assessing the data they generate. In turn, this enables organizations to achieve a closed-loop, automated remediation process, which is based on risk. These results in tremendous time and costs savings, increased accuracy, shorten remediation cycles, and overall improved operational efficiency.

Big Data Risk Management systems empower organizations to make threats and vulnerabilities visible and actionable, while enabling them to prioritize and address high risk security exposures before breaches occur. Ultimately, they can protect against and minimize the consequences of cyber-attacks.

SECURITY AWARENESS IN BIG DATA ENVIROMNEMTS

Data security can be addressed in an efficient and effective manner to satisfy all parties. Start Big Data security planning immediately and building security into Big Data environments will reduce costs, risks, and deployment pain.

Many organizations deploy Big Data environments alongside their existing database systems, allowing them to combine traditional structured data and new unstructured data sets in powerful ways. Big Data environments consists of reliable data storage using different infrastructure, that consist of Distributed File System, a column oriented database management system and a high-performance parallel data processing technique.

Big Data environments need to be protected using the same rigorous security strategies applied to traditional database systems, such as databases and data warehouses, to support compliance requirements and prevent breaches.

Security strategies which should be implemented for Big Data environments include (Manovich, 2012):

- **Sensitive Data Discovery and Classification:** Discover and understand sensitive data and relationships before the data is moved to Big Data environments so that the right security policies can be established downstream.
- **Data Access and Change Controls:** Establish policies regarding which users and applications can access or change data in Big Data environments.
- **Real-Time Data Activity Monitoring and Auditing:** Understand the: who, what, when, how and where of Big Data environments access and report on it for compliance purposes.
- **Data Protection:** Transform data in Big Data environments through masking or encryption.
- **Data Loss Prevention:** Establish an audit trail for data access and usage to ensure data is not lost.
- **Vulnerability Management:** Understand weaknesses and put policies in place to remediate.
- **Compliance Management:** Build a compliance reporting framework into Big Data environments to manage report generation, distribution and sign off.

FUNDAMENTIALS TO IMPROVE SECURITY IN BIG DATA ENVIRONMENTS

According to the Future of Data Security and Privacy, organizations can control and secure the extreme volumes of data in Big Data environments by following a three step framework (as shown in Figure 1):

The meaning of these fundamentals as the following:

1. **Define:** Most organizations are just starting down the path of implementing a Big Data environment, so they don't know which types of data (structured or unstructured) they want to include in a Big Data repository.

The planning phase presents the perfect opportunity to start a dialog across data security, legal, business and IT teams about sensitive data understanding, discovery and classification. A cross-functional team should identify where data exists, decide on common definitions for sensitive data, and decide what types of data will move into Big Data environments. Also, organizations should establish a life-cycle approach to continuously discover data across the enterprise.

Figure 1. The Future of data security and privacy: controlling big data
(Zhang, Xue et al., 2013).

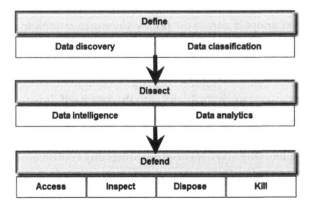

2. **Dissect:** Big Data environments are highly valuable to the business. However, data security professionals also benefit because Big Data repositories can store security information. Data security professionals can leverage Big Data environments to more efficiently prioritize security intelligence initiatives and more effectively place the proper security controls.

3. **Defend:** Aggregating data by nature increases the risk that an attacker can compromise sensitive information. Therefore, organizations should strictly limit the number of people who can access repositories.

Big Data environments should include basic security and controls as a way to defend and protect data. First, access control ensures that the right user gets access to the right data at the right time. Second, continuously monitoring user and application access is highly important especially as individuals changes roles or leave the organization. Monitoring data access and usage patterns can alert policies violations like an administrator altering log files. Typically attackers will leave clues or artifacts about their breach attempts that can be detected through careful monitoring. Monitoring helps ensure security policies are enforced and effective.

Organizations can secure data using data abstraction techniques such as encryption or masking. Generally, attackers cannot easily decrypt or recover data after it has been encrypted or masked. The unfortunate reality is that organizations need to adopt a zero trust policy to ensure complete protection.

There are several actions organizations can take today to better secure Big Data environments: move your controls closer to the data itself, leverage existing technologies to control and protect Big Data, ask legal to define clear policies for data archiving and data disposal, diligently control access to Big Data resources and watch user behavior.

BIG DATA SECURITY AND PRIVACY CHALLENGES

It is reasonable the huge amount of data is creating new security challenges. Big Data is very important because most organizations now are accessing Big Data and using it. In the past Big Data was been used just by very large organizations, governments and large enterprises that have the ability to create its own infrastructure for hosting and mining large amounts of data. These infrastructures were typically a private proprietary and were isolated to be accessed from outsiders. Nowadays, Big Data is cheap and available to all kinds of organizations through the public cloud infrastructure and this led to new security challenges.

The following list contains the top challenges for Big Data security and privacy (Steve, 2013):

1. Secure computations in distributed programming frameworks.
2. Security best practices for non-relational data stores.
3. Secure data storage and transactions logs.
4. End-point input validation/filtering.
5. Real-time security monitoring.
6. Scalable and compos-able privacy-preserving data mining and analytics.
7. Cryptographically enforced data centric security.
8. Granular access control.
9. Granular audits.
10. Data provenance.

Figure 2 shows the challenges for the Big Data security.

The challenges may be organized into four aspects of the Big Data ecosystem, as the following:

1. **Infrastructure Security:** This includes secure computations in distributed programming frameworks and Security best practices for non-relational stores.

Figure 2. Security and privacy challenges in Big Data ecosystem (Manyika, Brown et al., 2011).

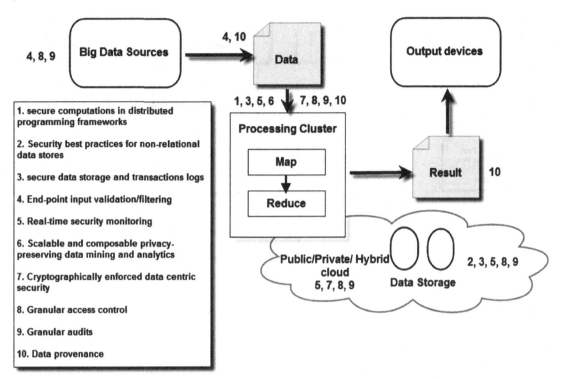

2. **Data Privacy:** It includes Privacy preserving data Mining and Analytics, Cryptographically enforced Data Centric Security and Granular Access Control.
3. **Data Management:** It contains secure data Storage and transaction logs and Granular Audits. Data Provenance.
4. **Integrity and Reactive Security:** It includes End-point validation and filtering. Real time security monitoring.

Figure 3 shows the four aspects of the Big Data ecosystem.

SECURITY ISSUES IN BIG DATA

Big Data offers a large store for data which make it a fine tool for the Intruders and attackers to violate the privacy for the people and to misuse this treasure of data.

1. Big Data Privacy

As the collection of unstructured data becomes more economically viable, and shifts in consumer usage of technology make a much wider range of data available, there is an incentive for organizations to collect as much data as possible. Yet, just because consumers are willing to provide data this does not mean that its use is free from privacy implications (Boyd, 2010). Four examples of these privacy challenges follow. The first arises from different sets of data that would not previously have been considered as having privacy implications concerns being combined in ways that threaten privacy. One example, albeit experimental, was discovered by researchers Downloaded and asked who used publicly available information and photographs from Facebook and, through application of facial recognition software, matched this information to identify previously anonymous individuals on a

Figure 3. The four aspects of Big Data ecosystem (Cloud Security, 2013).

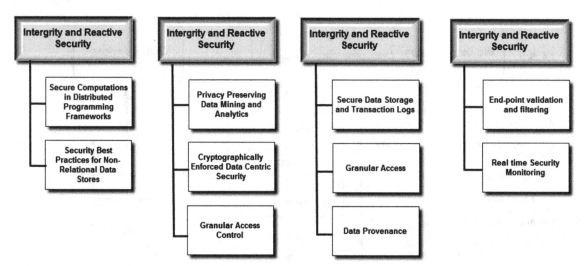

major dating site. In another example, anonymous 'de-identified' health information distributed between US health providers was found to be traceable back to individuals when modern analytical tools were applied. This creates an unintended use paradox. How can consumers trust an organization with information when the organization does not yet know how the information might be used in the future? The second challenge comes from security – specifically the issue around hacking or other forms of unauthorized access.

Despite increasing awareness of the need to maintain physical security, computer systems are only as strong as their weakest point, and for databases the weakest point is usually human. For all the advanced technical security used to protect the US diplomatic network, the Wikileaks scandal was caused by a low-level employee copying data on to a fake 'Lady Gaga' CD. For Big Data stores to be useful there needs to be a certain amount of regular access, often by a range of employees in different locations. While treating data like gold bullion and storing them in a vault may guarantee security, this is not a practical solution for most use cases; but what of security breaches? When a credit card is stolen it is relatively straightforward,

if time consuming, to cancel the card and be issued a new one. Yet a comprehensive set of information about one's online activities, friends or any other type of Big Data set is more difficult to replace.

In a sense, these are not simply items of data but a comprehensive picture of a person's identity over time. The third privacy challenge is that data are increasingly being collected autonomously, independent of human activity. Previously, there was a natural limit on the volume of data collected related to the number of humans on the planet, and the number of variables we are interested in on each individual is considerably fewer than the number of people on the planet. The emergence of network-enabled sensors on everything from electricity and water supplies through to airplanes and cars changes this dimension. Combining these sensors with nanotechnology it becomes possible to embed large numbers in new buildings to provide early warnings of dangers relating to the structural integrity of the building.

The volume of data, and the speed with which the data must be analyzed, means that there is the requirement for data to be collected and autonomously analyzed without an individual providing specific consent. This raises ethical concerns relating to the extent to which organizations can control the collection and analysis of data when there is limited human involvement. The final privacy challenge relates to the contextual significance of the data. Currently the ability of organizations to collect and store data runs far ahead of their ability to make use of it. As a function of storing any, and all, unstructured data regardless of potential use cases this means that combinations of data for which there are currently no capabilities to analyze could become subject to privacy breaches in the future.

2. Using Steganography with Big Data

With the advance of computer and Internet technologies, protecting personal information becomes an important issue. Traditional Cryptography for symmetric encryption schemes and non-symmetric encryption schemes can provide high-level data security, but they are not flexibility for all kinds of media. Steganography also called "Information Hiding" is the covert communication which embeds secret information into a meaningful media with imperceptibly and only the authorized users can extract the hidden data. The meaningful media used to hidden secret message is called the cover media, and the encoding result is called the stego media. Generally, an information hiding scheme should satisfy the followings two issues. Firstly, the hiding capacity should be as large as possible. Secondly, the visual quality of the embedding result should not distinguishable from the cover media (Chuang and Chen, 2012).

Digital image is the most popular camouflage media and the main reason is image pixels can be distortion. Images are very easy to make imperceptible modification. When an image pixel is tiny modified, it is not easily awarded something difference by the human eyes. Recently, some researches concerning the information hiding scheme on the text documents. The embedding payload of a text document is less than a digital image because it is not easy to find the redundancy information in a text document. In generally, text hiding schemes can be classified into two types, content format and language semantic. The content format methods adjust the width of tracking, the height of leading, number of white spaces, etc. The language semantic methods change the meaning of a phrase or a sentence in a text document.

The traditional text hiding schemes embed secret information at between-word and between-character by adding tabs or white spaces. However, the adjusted white spaces of between-word may look like strange. Therefore, we intend to design a text hiding scheme using Big-5 code. The secret is first converted into binary and then embedded into whitespaces between-word and between-character of a cover text by placing a Big-5 code either 20 or 7F.

We can propose a method for using a steganography in text as an example, to embed secret into a cover text, we shall adjust the content of a cover text. We need to add a white-space in each between-word and between-character. Secret messages are sequentially converted into 0's and 1's binary stream. One white-space of between-word and between-character in a cover text is used to hide one secret bit. If we want to embed a secret bit 0, the Big-5 code of white-space 20 is applied. If we want to embed a secret bit 1, the Big-5 code of blank character 7F is applied. After finishing the secret embedding, we add an end of-code 7F to indicate no secret of input. The hiding capacity of a cover text can be determined before data embedding. We can calculate the total number of white-spaces in a cover text. Assume a cover text contains w characters; the embedding payload of a cover text is (w-1) bits.

3. The Ethics of Big Data

We never, ever in the history of mankind have had access to so much information so quickly and so easily. Concerns over privacy, and the collection and use of personal information, have been closely associated with the growing influence of technology in society. As long ago as 1890, legal scholars raised concerns over the commercial application of new photographic technologies in the newspaper industry. On the potential impacts of the future use of information technologies in commerce, the prescient observation has been made: 'what is whispered in the closet shall be proclaimed from the house-tops'. These concerns have grown significantly since commercial use of the internet first became widespread in the mid-1990s.

For many people, the question of how personal data are used for marketing purposes has become a defining social feature of the internet. Yet the same technology has also created significant new opportunities for market researchers to collect and analyze information to generate more timely and relevant insights. To date, these two perspectives have existed side by side, albeit sometimes uneasily, with market researchers able to leverage the internet as an important research tool within the framework of existing ethical approaches.

However, the trend towards Big Data presents a number of challenges in terms of both the ways that personal information is collected and consumer relationships with this information. Because of its key role in collecting, analyzing and interpreting data, many of the problems, and opportunities, of Big Data are also those of market research. For market research to prosper it requires the continuing cooperation of respondents, both in terms of providing data for research studies and in giving permission for these data to be analyzed. In an environment where there are issues around increasing non-cooperation by respondents, it is essential for market researchers to be at the forefront of understanding emergent ethical and privacy issues critical where regulatory change poses a potential threat to market researchers' ability to collect data in the future.

On the other hand, progressions offered by Big Data present significant opportunities for generating new insights into consumer behavior. The ability to triangulate multiple data sources and perform analyses of these massive data sets in real time enables market researchers to gather a range of insights that may not be possible using existing market research techniques.

USING BIG DATA FOR BUSINESS RESEARCH

The following areas represents an opportunity as a source of new insight for business and market researchers by using Big Data, but also has the potential to create significant challenges in terms of privacy and the use of personal data.

1. The Social Graph

Much of the growth in data is driven by the voluntary sharing of information between members of social networks. Rather than focus on individual responses, Big Data allows a picture to be built of group-level interactions and the nature of the bonds that Downloaded from warc.com5bring these people together – a concept that has been labeled the 'social graph'. The relationship is symbiotic: in order to create value in their social graph, users need to contribute information about their lives, but in doing so they also increase the digital exhaust of information that is available about them.

Yet, the boundaries of this social graph are imprecise. The challenge of continuously identifying and labeling 'friends', particularly those where there are weak social ties, creates the potential for social uncertainty. The labels for these virtual world connections such as 'followers' or 'friends', may not be analogous to their physical-world meanings. It is this source of ambiguity that presents ethical challenges. Understanding how an individual's online social graph relates to real-world meaning is thus likely to be essential in effectively leveraging it.

2. Data Ownership

With Big Data the nature of the organizations that collect the largest stores of personal information is changing. In general, it is not central governments or traditional large corporations that are storing information, but rather a breed of smaller high technology firms such as Facebook, Twitter, LinkedIn, Google and others. On the one hand, this provides researchers access to sources of data that may not previously have been available. While there is little incentive for governments to monetize their data commercially, the business models of the majority of consumer-facing web services are built around, to put it simply, driving commercial value from customer data. For example, Twitter will now make a feed of several years' historical content available to anyone wishing to use it for research or analysis purposes. This raises the question of the long-term ownership of personal data that consumers make available online. Even those companies that do not currently sell access to their data stores could themselves be potentially sold in the future, and policies for the use of data changed.

3. Big Data Memory

The capability for Big Data technology to enable the storage, and recall, of large volumes of information gives a temporal dimension to the storage of personal information. Information recorded today, even if not public now, can be recalled instantly in decades' time. For example, the emerging focus of Facebook on a 'timeline' has created challenges that activities people partake in while at college may reflect badly on them when they enter the world of work. While analyzing data and building effective models of consumer behavior has always been a part of market research, Big Data provides the promise of more accurate and far-reaching models. Thus Big Data enables the ability to rewind and fast-forward people's lives, but in doing so may remove the ability for individuals to forget and be forgotten.

4. Passive Data Collection

Much information collection is now automatic and passive. Existing approaches to market research are typically reliant on some form of active opt-in. Big Data makes use of passive technologies, such as location-based information from mobile phones, data from autonomous sensors, or facial recognition technology in retail stores. This creates the potential for powerful new variables to be included in consumer research. At the same time the individual may no longer have specific knowledge and awareness that data are currently being collected about them. Even if permission has been given initially, these services are not asking for permission every time such contextual data are gathered.

5. Respecting Privacy in a Public World

While privacy concerns have been raised over the use and creation of Big Data, these have been outpaced by individuals' use of social networks. The value inherent in the social graph provides some form of counterbalance to the potential privacy Downloaded from warc.com6issues. Put another way, for all the privacy implications, people derive great benefit from services such as mobile applications and social networks – many of which are available at no charge. Beyond this, for many social groups, contributing to Big Data stores becomes a socially necessary form of communication in a world where avoiding social networking sites serves the potential to exclude people from their communities. This creates a paradox in that, while individuals can opt out of having their personal data collected, to do so may result in increasing their exclusion from the digitally connected world in which they reside.

6. Personal Data and Business Research

For many sectors the ability to collect data and turn it into insight has a key role in developing more innovative and successful products and services. However, for market research, the importance of access is instrumental to the ability to deliver the product. The history of marketing activity provides us with many examples of situations where regulators have responded reactively to public perceptions of over-zealous, or unethical, marketing activity. From the promotion of ineffective 'patent 'medicines in the 19th century through to tobacco and alcohol in the 20th century, in sectors that generate negative externalities regulatory pressure is never far behind. Given the criticality of online data collection to market research, and the potential for personal data to become a similarly hot topic of the 21st century, for the successful realization of the potential of Big Data in market research it is also necessary to be proactive in responding to potential privacy issues, even if these have yet to reach the public imagination.

BUSINESS INTELLIGENCE AND ANALYTICS: FROM BIG DATA TO BIG IMPACT

Business Intelligence and Analytics (BI&A) has emerged as an important area of study for both practitioners and researchers, reflecting the magnitude and impact of data-related problems to be solved in contemporary business organizations. This introduction to the Management Information System (MIS) Quarterly Special Issue on Business Intelligence Research first provides a framework that identifies the evolution, applications, and emerging research areas of BI & A.BI&a 1.0, BI & a 2.0, and BI&A 3.0 are defined and described in terms of their key characteristics and capabilities. Current research in BI&A is analyzed and

challenges and opportunities associated with BI&A research and education are identified. We also report a bibliometric study of critical BI&A publications, researchers, and research topics based on more than a decade of related academic and industry publications. Finally, the six articles that comprise this special issue are introduced and characterized in terms of the proposed BI&A research framework.

Business Intelligence and Analytics (BI&A) and the related field of Big Data analytics have become increasingly important in both the academic and the business communities over the past two decades. Industry studies have highlighted this significant development. For example, based on a survey of over 4,000 Information Technology (IT) professionals from 93 countries and 25 industries, the IBM Tech Trends Report (2011) identified business analytics as one of the four major technology trends in the 2010s. In a survey of the state of business analytics by (Bloomberg Business week, 2011), 97 percent of companies with revenues exceeding $100 million were found to use some form of business analytics. A report by the McKinsey Global Institute (Manyika et al. 2011) predicted that by 2018, the United States alone will face a shortage of 140,000 to 190,000 people with deep analytical skills, as well as a shortfall of 1.5 million data-savvy managers with the know-how to analyze Big Data to make effective decisions. Hal Varian, Chief Economist at Google and emeritus professor at the University of California, Berkeley, commented on the emerging opportunities for IT professionals and students in data analysis as follows:

BIG DATA AND MOBILE PHONES

By analyzing patterns from mobile phone usage, a team of researchers in San Francisco is able to predict the magnitude of a disease outbreak half way around the world. Similarly, an aid agency sees early warning signs of a drought condition in a remote Sub-Saharan region, allowing the agency to get a head start on mobilizing its resources and save many more lives.

Much attention is paid to the vital services that mobile phone technology has brought to billions of people in the developing world. But now many policy-makers, corporate leaders and development experts are realizing the potential applications, like the examples above, for the enormous amounts of data created by and about the individuals who use these services.

Sources such as online or mobile financial transactions, social media traffic, and GPS coordinates now generate over 2.5 quintillion bytes of so-called "Big Data" every day. And the growth of mobile data traffic from subscribers in emerging markets is expected to exceed 100% annually through 2015.

The data emanating from mobile phones holds particular promise, in part because for many low-income people it is their only form of interactive technology, but it is also easier to link mobile – generated data to individuals. This data can paint a picture about the needs and behavior of individual users rather than simply the population as a whole.

To turn mobile-generated data into an economic development tool, a number of ecosystem elements must be in place. For those individuals who generate the data, mechanisms must be developed to ensure adequate user privacy and security. At the same time, business models must be created to provide the appropriate incentives for private-sector actors to share and use data for the benefit of the society. Such models already exist in the Internet environment. Companies in search and social networking profit from products they offer at no charge to end users because the usage data these products generate is valuable to other ecosystem actors. Similar models could be created in the mobile data sphere, and the data generated through them could maximize the impact of scarce public sector resources by indicating where resources are most needed. We can see that data collected through mobile device usage can spur

effective action in two primary ways: by reducing the time lag between the start of a trend and when governments and other authorities are able to respond to them, and by reducing the knowledge gap about how people respond to these trends.

Ecosystem actors have much to gain from the creation of an open data commons. Yet the sharing of such data especially that tied to individuals raises legitimate concerns that must be addressed to achieve this cross-sector collaboration.

As ecosystem players look to use mobile-generated data, they face concerns about violating user trust, rights of expression, and confidentiality. Privacy and security concerns must be addressed before convinced to share data more openly.

When individuals have multiple SIM cards, it is impossible to aggregate data from each SIM back to the same individual. This data is most useful if it can be attached to demographic indicators, which allow the data to tell a story about the habits of a segment of the population. Improved methods of tying subscriptions to demographic information are needed to ensure data generated by mobile devices is as individualized as possible.

Individuals, facing security and privacy concerns, often resist sharing personal data. In addition, many private-sector firms do not see an incentive to share data they regard as proprietary. Governments often cannot forces contractors to share data collected in the execution of public contracts or make all government data available for use by academia, development organizations, and companies. All players must see material benefits and incentives in data sharing that outweigh the risks.

CONCLUSION

The opportunities for large-scale digital media research are obvious—as are its pitfalls and downsides. Thus, researchers should differentiate between alternative research approaches carefully and be cautious about the application of unfamiliar tools, analytical techniques, or methodological innovation. With no or few references to compare one's results to, findings will be difficult to interpret and online researchers should "hold themselves to high standards of conceptual clarity, systematically of sampling and data analysis, and awareness of limitations in interpreting their results" assert that methodological training should be part of the answer to the challenges of digital media research. Manovich argues for advanced statistics and computer science methods, which could likely help in furthering an understanding of the underlying algorithms of online platforms as well as analytical tools. Yet, a reflection on and an understanding of what comes before the first data is collected or analyzed is equally or possibly even more important.

Big Data security needs to be correlated with its business criticality or risk to the organization. Without a risk-based approach to security, organizations can waste valuable IT resources used for vulnerabilities that will cause in reality little or no threat to the business. Furthermore, big security data needs to be filtered to just the information that is relevant to specific stakeholders' roles and responsibilities. Not everyone has the same needs and objectives when it comes to leveraging Big Data.

New data structures and research opportunities should not be ignored by media and communication scholars, and there are many relevant and interesting research questions that are well suited to Big Data analysis. On the other hand, established practices of empirical research should not be discarded as they ensure the coherence and quality of a study. After all, this is one of the key contributions that social scientists can bring to the table in interdisciplinary research. It should go without saying that a strong focus on theoretically relevant questions always increases the scientific significance of the research and its results. Yet, some developments in digital media research, particularly those related to Big Data, seem to warrant affirmation of this fundamental principle.

REFERENCES

Agrawal, D., Das, S., & El Abbadi, A. (2010, September). Big data and cloud computing: New wine or just new bottles. *Proceedings of the VLDB Endowment*, *3*(2), 1647–1648. doi:10.14778/1920841.1921063

Anderson, C. (2008). The end of theory: The data deluge makes the scientific method obsolete Wired. Retrieved from http://www.wired.com/science/discoveries/magazine/16-07/pb_theory/

Bailenson, J. N. (2012). Contribution to the ICA Phoenix closing plenary: The Internet is the end of communication theory as we know it. *62nd annual convention of the International Communication Association, Phoenix, AZ. Retrieved from* ttp://www.icahdq.org/conf/2012/closing.asp

Barnes, S. (2006). A privacy paradox: Social networking in the United States. *First Monday*, *11*(9). http://firstmonday.org/htbin/cgiwrap/bin/ojs/index.php/fm/article/ view/1394/1312 doi:10.5210/fm.v11i9.1394

Batinic, B., Reips, U.-D., & Bosnjak, M. (Eds.). (2002). *Online social sciences*. Seattle, WA: Hogrefe& Huber.

Bollier, D. (2010).The promise and peril of Big Data. *Washington, DC: Aspen Institue. Retrieved November 30, 2012, from* http://www.aspeninstitute.org/sites/default/files/content/ docs/pubs/The_Promise_and_Peril_of_Big_Data

Boyd, D. (2010). Privacy and Publicity in the context of big data. *Presented at WWW Conference, Raleigh, North Carolina, 29 April.*

Boyd, D., & Crawford, K. (2012). Critical questions for big data: Provocations for a cultural, technical, and scholary phenomenon. *Information Communication and Society*, *15*(5), 665–679. do i:10.1080/136911BX.2012.678878

Busemann, K., & Gscheidle, C. (2012). Web 2.0: Habitualisierung der Social Communities [Web 2.0: Habitualization of social community use]. *Media Perspektiven*, (7–8), 380–390.

Changqing, J. I. (2012). Big data processing in cloud computing environments. In *Proceedings of the 2012 International Symposium on Pervasive Systems, Algorithms, and Networks, I-SPAN 2012* (pp. 17–23).

Cheng, H. (2012, April). Identity based encryption and biometric authentication scheme for secure data access in cloud computing. *Chinese Journal of Electronics*, 21(2), 254–259.

Chew, C., & Eysenbach, G. (2010). Pandemics in the age of Twitter: Content analysis of tweets during the 2009 H1N1 outbreak. *PLoS ONE*, 5(11), e14118. doi:10.1371/journal.pone.0014118 PMID:21124761

Christians, C. G., & Chen, S.-L. S. (2003). Introduction: Technological environments and the evolution of social research methods. Johns, M. D., Chen, S.-L. S., & Hall, G. J. (Eds.), Online social research: Methods, issues, & ethics (pp. 15–23). New York, NY: Peter Lang.

Chuang, J. C., & Chen, H. Y. (2012). Data hiding on text using big-5 code. *International Journal of Security and Its Applications*, 6(2).

Cloud Security Alliance. (2013). Expanded Top Ten Big Data Security and Privacy challenge. https://cloudsecurityalliance.org/research/big-data/, Accessed on 15 Jan. 2014.

Colin, T. (2012). Big Data Security, Digital Pathways. *Network Security*, (July): 2012.

Coronel, C., Morris, S., & Rob, P. (2013). *Database Systems: Design, Implementation, and Management* (10th ed.). Boston: Cengage Learning.

Daniel, N., & Di Domenico, M. (2013). Market research and the ethics of Big Dat. *International Journal of Market Research*, 55(4), 2013.

Dodge, M. (2005). The role of maps in virtual research methods. In C. Hine (Ed.), *Virtual Methods: Issues in social research on the Internet* (pp. 113–127). Oxford, UK: Berg.

Feng, Z., Hui-Feng, X., Dung-Sheng, X., Yong-Heng, Z., & Fei, Y. (2013). *Big Data Cleaning Algorithms in Cloud Computing*. Retrieved from; doi:10.3991/ijoe.vqi3.2765

Mall, R., Langone, R., & Suykens, J. A. K. (2013). Kernal Spectral Clustering for Big Data Networks. *Entropy*, 15, 1567-1586. doi:3390/e15051567

Manovich, L. (2012). Trending: The Promises and the Challenges of big social data. In M. K. Gold (Ed.), *Debates in the Digital Humanities* (pp. 460–475). Minneapolis: University of Minneapolis Press.

Manyika, J., Chui, M., Brown, B., Bughin, J., Dobbs, R., Roxburgh, C., & Byers, A. H. (2011). *Big Data: The next frontier for Innovation, Competition, and Productivity*. Retrieved from http://www.mckinsey.com/insights/mgi/research/technology_and_innovation/.

Qin, H. F., & Li, Z. H. (2013). Research on the Method of Big Data Analysis. *Information Technology Journal*, 12(10), 1974–1980.

Van Till, S. (2013). Will Big Data Change Security? *securityMagazine.com*, April 2013.

Wang, H. (2012). Virtual machine-based intrusion detection system framework in cloud computing environment. *Journal of Computers*, 7(10), 2397–2403.

Yang, T. (2012). Mass data analysis and forecasting based on cloud computing. *Journal of Software*, 7(10), 2189–2195.

KEY TERMS AND DEFINITIONS

Big Data: Refers to data sets that are too big to be handled by regular storage and processing infrastructures.

Structured Data: Data that resides in fixed fields within a record or file.

Unstructured Data: Refers to information that either does not have a pre-defined data model or is not organized in a pre-defined manner.

Variety: Refers to the type of information being stored. Previously, data stored tended to be highly structured in nature.

Velocity: Refers to the challenges in Downloaded from accessing stored data quickly enough for them to be useful.

Chapter 16

16–Directional Geographical Traceback with Generalization to Three Dimensional Multidirectional Geographical IP Traceback

S. Karthik
SNS College of Technology, India

A. Rajiv Kannan
College of Engineering, India

ABSTRACT

Distributed denial-of-service attacks are a serious threat to the stability and availability of the Internet. Several traceback schemes are available to mitigate these attacks. Along with several IP traceback schemes, a latest one is the DGT in which the tracking is relying on geographical information. Segment direction ratios (SDR) a novel scheme to overcome the directional limitations of 2^3 DGT is proposed. This scheme is generalized to 2^n DGT ($n \geq 4$).The concepts of DR, DRS and NDRS at a Router point is introduced based on uniqueness theorem. Three dimensional, multi-directional geographical traceback, using direction ratio algorithm (DRA) is proposed to remove the limitations. To overcome directions, dimensions and storage space deficiency, three dimensional multidirectional geographical IP traceback direction ratio sampling algorithm (DRSA) traceback is proposed.

INTRODUCTION

DoS/DDoS attacks deny regular internet services, from being accessed by legitimate users, either by blocking the services completely, or, disturbing it totally, so as to cause consumer baulking. Several traceback schemes are available to mitigate these attacks. DGT 8, the eight directional geographical traceback scheme proposed by (Zhiqiang .G & Nirwan .A 2005) is one of them.

DOI: 10.4018/978-1-4666-6583-5.ch016

Copyright © 2015, IGI Global. Copying or distributing in print or electronic forms without written permission of IGI Global is prohibited.

IP traceback is the process of identifying the actual sources of attack, so that the attackers can be held accountable and mitigating the attacks (Angelos et al., 2004), either by isolating the attack sources, or by filtering packets far away from the victim.

Among several IP traceback schemes, a recent one is the DGT where the tracking is based on geographical information.

This scheme as proposed by (Zhiqiang .G & Nirwan .A 2005) had three major limitations:

1. Being limited to 2^3 (=8) directions, it had a directional limitation.
2. Being a two dimensional scheme it was more of an ideal, approximation than the real spherical; this dimensional limitation was a serious one.
3. Traceback is affected in all IP traceback schemes by marking the packet header during its flight from the source to destination. All marking schemes have accepted the impossibility of ensuring sufficient unused space in the packet header for complete marking, especially when the length of the path is not known a priori.

Being limited to only 8 directions this scheme suffers from directional limitations and may not work well when the interfaces between the routers is more than 8.

In reality, obviously, the interface between routers is manifold. A novel scheme of 2^n DGT ($n \geq 4$) to make DGT purposeful and useful by eliminating

1. Directional limitations;
2. Dimensional limitations;
3. Deficiency in packet header space.

In this chapter, by proposing 2^n ($n \geq 4$) directional, two dimensional DGT using Segment Direction Ratios, they eliminated the directional limitations. The choice of number of directions, for

implementing the scheme, it was noted, depended on ensuring sufficient unused space on the packet header. Thus the importance of header space was, though implicitly, accepted.

Then dimensional limitations were removed by the proposal of 3 dimensional, multi-directional geographical traceback, using Direction Ratio Algorithm (DRA). The use of the d(n) function, where n $\in$ N (set of natural numbers) allowed us to have many directions. Indeed, we have listed the 13 directions of d(1), and the 49 directions of d(2) in Figures 14 and 15 respectively.

In packet header the space needed to append a d.r is 6 bits for d(1) members and 9 bits for d(2) and d(3) elements. In fact d(3) offers as many as 109 directions for a router's successors.

In all this, what is evident is the limited nature of the header space on a packet. It is impossible to eliminate this deficiency. It can be overcome by modified marking scheme like Direction Ratio Sampling Algorithm.

THE MERITS OF DGT SCHEMES

DGT schemes rely on the geographical layout of the routers in the internet path and the directions between transmitting routers.

These schemes possess many desirable features, such as fast convergence, light weight, good scalability and attack mitigation capability. Also with data received through a single packet from the attacker, the victim can traceback the geographical location of the attack router. In this chapter, using the method of segment direction ratios (SDR) a novel scheme to overcome the directional limitations of 2^3 DGT is proposed. This scheme is generalized to 2^n DGT ($n \geq 4$).

The Concept of SDR

As in (Zhiqiang G. & Nirwan A. 2005) literature, the assumption of a two dimensional square grid with routers at selected grid points is made. The

Figure 1. Router edge R_iR_j having direction cosines (Cos α, Cos β)

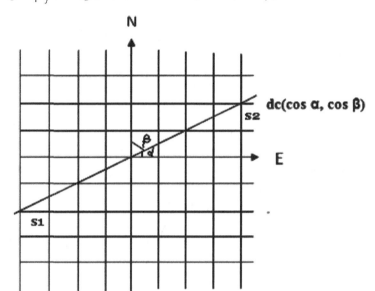

edge between 2 routers is thus a line in two dimensions, whose directions are specified by its direction cosines (Cos α, Cos β) where α, β are the angles which the line of the routers makes with axes of reference OE, ON where E is the east and N the north direction. It is shown in Figure 1. The direction cosines of any line always satisfy $Cos^2a + Cos^2b = 1$.

Since most $Cos\theta$ values are cumbersome irrationals in [-1, 1], the concept of direction ratios was introduced. Direction ratios (d.r) are proportional quantities to direction cosines (d.c); are integers denoted by (a, b) where in general $a^2 + b^2 \neq 1$ and a, b are coprimes. In Figure 2, the d.r of the line segment AB are (2, 1) and hence

Figure 2. For edge between routers at A and B with $SDR = \left(x_2 - x_1, y_2 - y_1 \right)$

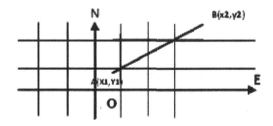

the dc of the line are $\left(\dfrac{2}{\sqrt{5}}, \dfrac{1}{\sqrt{5}} \right)$. It is found by segment that the edge AB between 2 adjacent routers, with coordinate $A\left(x_1, y_1 \right)$ and $B\left(x_2, y_2 \right)$ with respect to OE, ON axes of reference. The coordinates are in units of the grid size. The segment direction ratios (SDR) of AB is $\left(x_2 - x_1, y_2 - y_1 \right)$ where $\left| x_2 - x_1 \right|, \left| y_2 - y_1 \right| \leq 2$ and coprimes.

It is easy to see that $\left(x_2 - x_1, y_2 - y_1 \right)$ are only the grid steps to be taken in the $\pm$OE, $\pm$ON directions (depending on the sign of the SDR) to reach B from A. They are the projections of the edge AB on OE, ON with appropriate sign attached.

For the choice of $\left| x_2 - x_1 \right|, \left| y_2 - y_1 \right| \leq 2$ there are 16 directions possible called D_1 to D_{16} where D_1, D_5, D_9, D_{13} directions are respectively OE, ON, OW, OS directions. The Figure 3 gives the SDR in bits of the 16 directions used in 2^4 DGT. Figure 4 also gives the summary of the SDR bits of the 16 directions D_1 to D_{16}.

The SDR concept allows a natural extension of 2^3 DGT (with limited 8 directions) to 2^n DGT (n $\geq$ 4). This is possible if $\left| x_2 - x_1 \right|, \left| y_2 - y_1 \right|$ to take coprime integer values less than or equal to (n-2).

Figure 3. DGT 16 SDR in bits

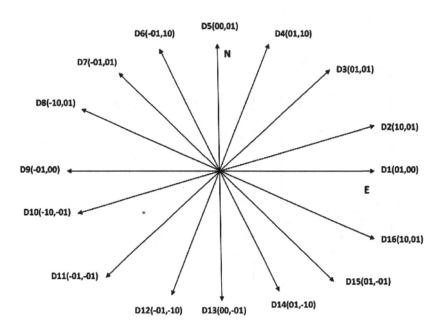

Figure 4. DGT 16 SDR in decimal and binary forms

Direction	Decimal	Binary
D_1	(1,0)	(01,00)
D_2	(2,1)	(10,01)
D_3	(1,1)	(01,01)
D_4	(1,2)	(01,10)
D_5	(0,1)	(00,01)
D_6	(-1,2)	(-01,10)
D_7	(-1,1)	(-01,01)
D_8	(-2,1)	(-10,01)
D_9	(-1,0)	(-01,00)
D_{10}	(-2,-1)	(-10,-01)
D_{11}	(-1,-1)	(-01,-01)
D_{12}	(-1,-2)	(-01,-10)
D_{13}	(0,-1)	(00,-01)
D_{14}	(1,-2)	(01,-10)
D_{15}	(1,-1)	(01,-01)
D_{16}	(2,-1)	(10,-01)

Figure 4 summarizes the SDR bits of the 32 directional interfaces $D(D_1)$, to D_{32} Specifications of 2^5 DGT SDR of Figure 5 (only quadrant I directions D_1 to D_9 are shown) are $|x_2 - x_1|, |y_2 - y_1| \leq 3$ and coprimes. For 2^5 DGT, full SDR list is given in Figure 6, in both decimal and binary forms.

2^4 DGT Procedure

When a packet arrives at router R_i and is destined for router R_j, where the direction d_{ij} is one of D_1 to D_{16}, the only task the router R_i has to perform is to add the ordered SDR values of d_{ij} to the corresponding ordered subfields in the IP header and subtract 1 from the TTL value.

Thus, for the implementation of DGT 16, it requires 2 subfields in the IP header, to keep track of the cumulative grid step movements, from router to router through their SDR.

In this way, when a packet arrives at the victim, the geographical location of the attack router can be obtained from the data in the SDR subfields, regardless of the source IP address which may be incorrect or compromised.

Figure 5. 2^5DGT SDR of Quadrant I

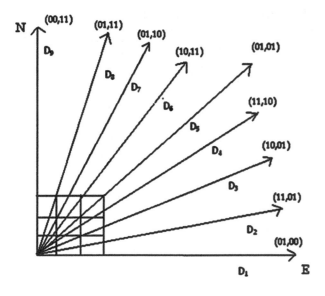

Encoding Requirements for DGT 16

Assuming that the length of the Internet paths seldom exceed 32 hops, the cumulative SDR value (CSDR) cannot exceed in magnitude the integer 64, for DGT 16.

Hence $2(1+7) = 16$ bits are needed in the IP header for the CSDR totals.

To calculate the total number of hops, between the attack router and the victim router, as the difference of initial TTL value and the final TTL value, the initial TTL value has to be stored (or at least the last 5 bits of it) in the IP header.

Assuming that the IP header has $(16+8+1)$ 25 bits, for DGT 16, here the 8 bits segment for storage of initial TTL value is used. Location of the attacker, from the CSDR, together with the hop count enables the victim to process the traceback.

Limitations of DGT 16

Differential Interface Limitation

1. *A limitations of DGT 16 is the inequality (though marginal) among the interfaces. But, this is the cost one has to pay to satisfy*

the integer requirements of the SDR and for generalization to 2^n DGT.

2. *2^3 DGT suffers from directional and dimensional limitations.* 2^4 DGT scheme and its generalization below remove only the directional limitations. The dimensional limitations still exists.

Generalization of 2^4 DGT to 2^n DGT (n ≥ 4)

The concept of SDR allows us to extend 2^4 DGT to 2^n DGT (n ≥ 4) without any restriction in an elegant manner. The only addition requirement that arises is the increased CSDR upper limits; consequently more bit space in the IP header for the two subfields is needed.

Specifically 2^n DGT restricts SDR of segment joining $A(x_1, y_1)$ and $B(x_2, y_2)$ to the constraint $|x_2 - x_1|, |y_2 - y_1| \leq n - 2$ and coprimes. Ultimately the number n of the scheme DGT 2^n depends on the IP header bit capacity as is evident from Figure 7.

THREE-DIMENSIONAL, MULTI-DIRECTIONAL GEOGRAPHICAL TRACEBACK

Though the directional constraint of DGT is eliminated by the concept of SDR, the dimensional constraint remains. This constraint is eliminated by the concept of Three Dimensional DGT.

The dimensional constraint is redressed, generalizing DGT to three dimensions, where the true spherical topology of the earth is taken into consideration for the traceback.

All the advantages (like robustness, fast convergence, independence etc.,) of the two dimensional DGT are fully available in the three dimensional scheme as well. The basic assumption about the traffic and the network are the same as in the study of (Zhiqiang G. & Nirwan A. 2005).

Figure 6. DGT 32 SDR in decimal and binary forms

Direction	Decimal	Binary	Direction	Decimal	Binary
D_1	(0,1)	(00,01)	D_{17}	(0,-1)	(00,-01)
D_2	(3,1)	(11,01)	D_{18}	(-1,-3)	(-01,-11)
D_3	(2,1)	(10,01)	D_{19}	(-2,-1)	(-10,-01)
D_4	(3,2)	(11,10)	D_{20}	(-2,-3)	(-10,-11)
D_5	(1,1)	(01,01)	D_{21}	(-1,-1)	(-01,-01)
D_6	(2,3)	(10,11)	D_{22}	(-3,-2)	(-11,-01)
D_7	(2,1)	(10,01)	D_{23}	(-2,-1)	(-11,-01)
D_8	(1,3)	(01,00)	D_{24}	(-3,-1)	(-11,-01)
D_9	(0,1)	(00,01)	D_{25}	(0,-1)	(00,-01)
D_{10}	(-1,3)	(-01,11)	D_{26}	(1,-3)	(01,-11)
D_{11}	(-2,1)	(-10,01)	D_{27}	(2,-1)	(10,-01)
D_{12}	(-2,3)	(-10,11)	D_{28}	(2,-3)	(10,-11)
D_{13}	(-1,1)	(-01,01)	D_{29}	(1,-1)	(01,-01)
D_{14}	(-3,2)	(-11,10)	D_{30}	(3,-2)	(11,-10)
D_{15}	(-2,1)	(-10,01)	D_{31}	(2,-1)	(11,-01)
D_{16}	(-3,1)	(-11,01)	D_{32}	(3,-1)	(11,-01)

Figure 7. 2^n DGT specifications

N	2^n	SDR bit length	Max step moves on grid	Max CSDR value	IP header CSDR length
3	8	1	1	32	2(1+6)
4	16	2	2	64	2(1+7)
5	32	3	3	96	2(1+7)
6	64	4	4	128	2(1+8)

Figure 8. Topology of the Earth

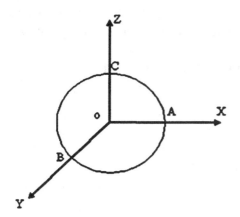

Figure 9. Direction angles of a line in space

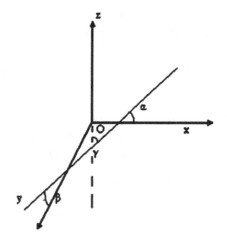

Geographical Topology of the Earth

Topology of the Earth is shown in Figure 8. Referred to rectangular axes, OX, OY, OZ, the earth can be, geographically considered as a sphere, having the Equation (1.1)

$$X^2 + Y^2 + Z^2 = a^2 \qquad (1.1)$$

where 'a' is the radius of the Earth and the points A, B, C having coordinates (a, 0, 0), (0, a, 0) and (0, 0, a) respectively.

Making the transformation

$$X = ax, \; Y = ay, \; Z = az \qquad (1.2)$$

(1.2) gives,

$$x^2 + y^2 + z^2 = 1 \qquad (1.3)$$

where the metric unit is the radius of the Earth.

Alternatively, assuming the ellipsoidal topology of the earth in the form

$$\frac{X^2}{a^2} + \frac{Y^2}{b^2} + \frac{Z^2}{c^2} = 1 \qquad (1.4)$$

where under the transformation

$$X = ax, \; Y = by, Z = cz \qquad (1.5)$$

(4.4) gives,

$$x^2 + y^2 + z^2 = 1 \qquad (1.6)$$

Hence, in this traceback study, all the routers R_i, are at chosen points $P(x_i, y_i, z_i)$ on (1.3) where

$$x_i^2 + y_i^2 + z_i^2 = 1 \text{ for all i.}$$

Concept of Direction Ratio Set at a Router Point

The directions of a line in space is indicated by their direction cosines (Cosα, Cosβ, Cosγ) where α, β, γ are the angles which the line makes with the positive directions of the axes of reference shown in Figure 9.

$$Cos^2\alpha + Cos^2\beta + Cos^2\gamma = 1 \qquad (1.7)$$

for all direction cosines (d.c).

The dc, in general, being cumbersome rationals/irrationals in [-1, 1], are not suited for IP traceback.

Hence they used proportional quantities to d.c, called direction ratios (d.r) denoted by (a, b, c) where a, b, c are integers with

$$\gcd\left(a,b,c\right)=1 \qquad (1.8)$$

Direction Ratio serve the purpose of d.c admirably; are convenient to handle and at any instant the corresponding d.c can be retrieved as ($\frac{a}{r},\frac{b}{r},\frac{c}{r}$)where

$$a^2+b^2+c^2=r^2 \qquad (1.9)$$

where r is the radius of the earth.

Direction Ratio Set (DRS) at a router R_0 is the D_i of direction ratios

$$D_i=\left\{\left(a_i,b_i,c_i\right),\ I\left(i\right)=1\ to\ n\right\} \qquad (1.10)$$

of its immediate neighbors R_1 to R_n from R_0 as shown in Figure 10. Note that all router points R_i for i=0 to n, all lie on the unit sphere.

Figure 10. DR set from router R_0

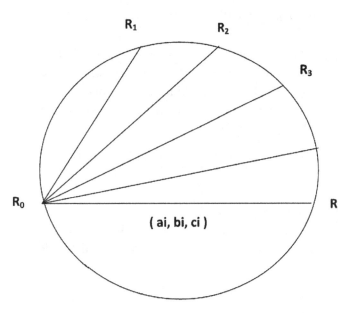

(ai, bi, ci)

In contrast to two dimensional DGT, we can prove that, for any specific direction ratio (a_i, b_i, c_i) at router R_0, there is a unique router R_i on the unit sphere.

Uniqueness Theorem

Statement

If $\left(x_0,y_o\left(y_0\right),z_o\left(Z_0\right)\right)$ are the coordinates of router R_o (R_0), then there is a unique router R_i with coordinates $\left(x_i,y_i,z_i\right)$ on the unit sphere in the directions R_o (R_0), R_i, with d.r $\left(a_i,b_i,c_i\right)$ where,

$$x_i=x_o+a_ir, y_i=y_o+b_ir, z_i=z_o+c_ir \qquad (1.11)$$

with

$$r=\frac{-2\left(a_ix_o+b_iy_o+c_iz_o\right)}{\left(a_i^2+b_i^2+c_i^2\right)} \qquad (1.12)$$

Proof

R_0R_i is a line segment on the unit sphere with end point R_0 $\left(x_0,y_0,z_0\right)$ and with d.r of the line being (a$_i$, b$_i$, c$_i$). The Figure 11 shows an One-to-One correspondence of $\left(a_i,b_i,c_i\right)$ and R_i (from a point R_0).

Hence, the equation of the line can be taken as

$$\frac{x-x_0}{a_i}=\frac{y-y_0}{b_i}=\frac{z-z_0}{c_i}=r \qquad (1.13)$$

$R_i\left(x_i,y_i,z_i\right)$ being a point on line (1.13) then,

$$x_i=x_0+a_ir,\ y_i=y_0+b_ir,\ z_i=z_0+c_ir \qquad (1.14)$$

but R_i lies on the sphere

$$x^2+y^2+z^2=1 \qquad (1.15)$$

Figure 11. One-to-one correspondence of $\left(a_i, b_i, c_i\right)$ and R_i (from a point R_0)

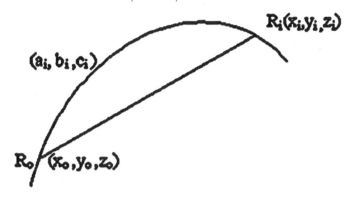

$$\left(x_0 + a_i r\right)^2 + \left(y_0 + b_i r\right)^2 + \left(z_0 + c_i r\right)^2 = 1$$
(1.16)

Simplifying (1.15), and using the fact

(1.17)

$$x_0^2 + y_0^2 + z_0^2 = 1$$
it yields a unique value of r given by,

$$r = \frac{-2\left(a_i x_o + b_i y_o + c_i z_o\right)}{\left(a_i^2 + b_i^2 + c_i^2\right)}$$
(1.18)

Thus, there is a One-to-One correspondence between the d.r $D_i = (a_i, b_i, c_i)$ and the points $R_i = (x_i, y_i, z_i)$ on the sphere with respect to the router point R_0 (x_0, y_0, z_0) except when

$$a_i x_0 + b_i y_0 + c_i z_0 = 0$$
(1.19)

when D_i direction is that of the tangent line at R_0.

This uniqueness makes the three dimensional IP traceback, a robust one, converging on a single packet.

Neighborhood Direction Ratio Set at a Router Point

In space, from any router point R_0, there are infinite directions, all of which by Uniqueness theorem, give distinct, infinitely many, possible router points R_i on the unit sphere.

It is needless/ impossible, for routers to know the d.r of all its neighbors. To reduce the router overhead, the concept of Neighborhood Direction Ratio Set (NDRS) has introduced.

In general, the direction ratio triads of integers $\left(a_i, b_i, c_i\right)$ are allowed to take values given by,

$$0 \le |a_i|, \ |b_i|, \ |c_i| \le n, n \in N$$
(1.20)

(N is the set of natural numbers).

Then d(n), number of directions from R_0, for a choice of n, satisfies the inequality

$$\left(2n - 1\right)^3 < d\left(n\right) < \left(2n + 1\right)^3$$

Due to the weeding out of redundant direction ratios from the total set.

The choice of n, and hence d(n), depends on the field width reserved for each d.r triad in the packet header. It is easily verified that for a field width allotment of 3(m+1) bits for a d.r triad, the range is

$$0 \leq |a_i|, \ |b_i|, \ |c_i| \leq n$$

where

$$n = 2^m - 1$$

and

$$(2n-1)^3 < d(n) < (2n+1)^3$$

Specifically, for a field width of 6 bits for a d.r triad, (including 3 sign bits),

$$0 \leq |a_i|, \ |b_i|, \ |c_i| \leq 1$$

and

$$1 < d(1) < 27$$

As the result of this, d(1)=13, and the 13 d.r are in Figure 12 is shown below,

Similarly d(2)=49 and the d.r of the 49 directions are listed below in Figure 13

Direction Ratio Algorithm

Assuming that, for every router, the NDRS has been uniformly chosen, so that uniform field width is needed for the d.r marking, the traceback procedure is as follows (for 13 directions it requires 6 bits/d.r and for 49 directions it requires 9 bits/d.r.).

Figure 12. d (n) for n=1

D_i	d.r
D_1	(1,0,0)
D_2	(0,1,0)
D_3	(0,0,1)
D_4	(1,1,0)
D_5	(-1,1,0)
D_6	(1,0,1)
D_7	(-1,0,1)
D_8	(0,1,1)
D_9	(0,-1,1)
D_{10}	(1,1,1)
D_{11}	(-1,1,1)
D_{12}	(1,-1,1)
D_{13}	(1,1,-1)

Let $D_i = (a_i, b_i, c_i)$ be the d.r triad at router R in the direction (of the successor router R_i) RR_i. Then the Direction Ratio Algorithm (DRA) is as follows:

1. Marking Procedure at Router R

For each packet w, append D_i (the d.r of the successor) to w.

2. Path Reconstruction at Victim V

For any packet w from an attacker, extract Direction Ratio List (D_1, D2…) from the suffix of w.

Unique traceback is now possible using the results (1.11) and (1.12)

Figure 13. d (n) for n=2

D_i	d.r		D_i	d.r
D_1	(1,0,0)		D_{26}	(-1,1,2)
D_2	(0,1,0)		D_{27}	(1,-1,2)
D_3	(0,0,1)		D_{28}	(1,1,-2)
D_4	(1,1,0)		D_{29}	(-1,2,1)
D_5	(-1,1,0)		D_{30}	(1,-2,1)
D_6	(1,0,1)		D_{31}	(1,2,-1)
D_7	(-1,0,1)		D_{32}	(-2,1,1)
D_8	(0,1,1)		D_{33}	(2,-1,1)
D_9	(0,-1,1)		D_{34}	(2,1,-1)
D_{10}	(1,1,1)		D_{35}	(2,2,1)
D_{11}	(-1,1,1)		D_{36}	(2,1,2)
D_{12}	(1,-1,1)		D_{37}	(1,2,2)
D_{13}	(1,1,-1)		D_{38}	(-2,2,1)
D_{14}	(0,1,2)		D_{39}	(2,-2,1)
D_{15}	(0,2,1)		D_{40}	(2,2,-1)
D_{16}	(1,2,0)		D_{41}	(-2,1,2)
D_{17}	(2,1,0)		D_{42}	(2,-1,2)
D_{18}	(1,0,2)		D_{43}	(2,1,-2)
D_{19}	(2,0,1)		D_{44}	(-1,2,2)
D_{20}	(0,-1,2)		D_{45}	(1,-2,2)
D_{21}	(-1,2,0)		D_{46}	(1,2,-2)
D_{22}	(-1,0,2)		D_{47}	(0,-2,1)
D_{23}	(1,1,2)		D_{48}	(-2,1,0)
D_{24}	(1,2,1)		D_{49}	(-2,0,1)
D_{25}	(2,1,1)			

If $(D_{n-1}, D_{n-2}, ..., D_0)$ are the n suffixes of w during the n hops from R_n to R_0 then the path is reconstructed as in Figure 14.

Limitations of DRA

DRA is both robust and extremely quick to converge (on a single packet) and is independent. For 13 directions/router, the field/d.r is as small as 6 bits/hop. Yet there are limitations.

Apart from the router overhead incurred by appending data to packets in flight, since the length of the path is not known apriori, it is impossible to ensure that there is sufficient unused space in the packet header for the complete list of d.r of the path.

In this chapter, this problem can be addressed by d.r sampling by the routers on the path, one at a time, instead of recording the entire path list of d.r.

DIRECTION RATIO SAMPLING ALGORITHM TRACEBACK BASICS

It requires an address field (R), a direction ratio field (DR) and a distance field (S), in the packet header to implement this algorithm.

In this chapter, assuming that the IP header has (16 + 8 + 1) = 25 bits, for DRSA, 10 bits each for the address field and the DR field and 5 bits for the distance field was allotted. This is acceptable since the routers are numbered serially: the 10 bit field can accommodate the last 3 digits of the serial number and is sufficient for RN (mod 1000) where RN is the router number. Also a 9

Figure 14. PathTraceback

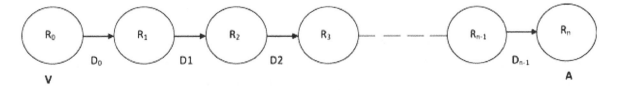

Figure 15. IP header format for DRSA

10	10	5
RN mod (1000)	DR (a, b, c)	S
R Field (RF)	DR Field (DRF)	Distance Field (SF)

bits are sufficient for d(2) (=49) members, 10 bits are sufficient for the DR field. Since any IP path never exceeds 32 hops, a 5 bit distance field is sufficient and the layout is shown in Figure 15.

Here RN is the router number of router R_i at $\left(x_i, y_i, z_i\right)$ and D_j is the d.r $\left(a_j, b_j, c_j\right) \in d(2)$ of the successor router R_j from R_i.

Note that $R_i(D_j) = R_j$ and by uniqueness theorem, there is One-to-One correspondence between D_j (from R_i) and successor R_j.

Three Dimensional Multidirectional Geographical IP Traceback: Direction Ratio Sampling Algorithm

The marking procedure at a router R_i of every packet w from the attacker is as follows: Let x be a random number in (0,1) and p, a chosen probability level. If x < p, then if the packet is unmarked, then write RN (mod 1000) of the router in the RF and D_i in DRF, 0 in SF. Otherwise (if the packet is already marked or x ≥ p) then only increment the distance field SF.

After sufficient number of samples are drawn, then using the property $R_i(D_j) = R_j$ and the distance field count, the attack path can be reconstructed. The victim uses the DRF (along with RF) sampled data in these packets to create a graph, leading to the source(s) of the attack.

RESULTS AND DISCUSSION

If we constrain p to be identical at each router, then the probability of receiving a marked packet, from a router d hops away is $p(1-p)^{d-1}$ and this function is monotonic in the distance variable

d from the victim. Because the probability of receiving a sample is geometrically smaller, the further away it is from the victim, the time of this algorithm to converge is dominated by the time to receive a sample from the farthest router.

Let us assume that samples from all of the d routers, (in the path from A to V) appear with the same likelihood as the furthest router. Since these probabilities are disjoint (mutually exclusive), the probability that a given packet will deliver a sample from some router is at least dp $(1-p)^{d-1}$ by addition law of mutually exclusive events. As per the well-known coupon collector problem, the number of trials required to select one of each of d equiprobable victims, is d $(\ln(d)) + O(1)$ Therefore, the number of packets X, required by the victim to reconstruct a path of length d, has the bounded expectation

$$E(x) = \frac{\ln(d)}{p(1-p)^{d-1}} \qquad (1.21)$$

From (1.21) it is known that E(x) is optimally minimum for $p = \frac{1}{d}$ since $\frac{dE}{dp} = 0$ and $\frac{d^2 E}{dp^2} > 0$ for $p = \frac{1}{d}$.

Thus min $\left(E(x)\right) = \frac{d^2 \ln(d)}{(d-1)^{d-1}} = k$ (say) for $p = \frac{1}{d}$, where d is the attack path length and hence the victim can typically reconstruct the path after receiving k packets.

For d =10, k ≤ 75 and hence the victim can typically reconstruct the path after receiving 75 packets from the attacker.

COMPARISON OF DGT 16 WITH OTHER TRACEBACK SCHEMES

Comparison with DGT 8

DGT 16 and DGT 8 being like schemes (the former, removing the directional constraints of the latter) they have equivalent advantages with respect to computational burden, scalability and mitigation capability of the attack, except for the fact that 16 directions are available now, with nil or negligible additional computations.

Quantitative Comparison with Other Schemes like PPM and SPIE

DGT as one hand and PPM & SPIE on the other, being totally different types of traceback schemes, only qualitative comparison are possible. The results as reported by (Zhiqiang .G & Nirwan .A 2005) gives superiority with respect to computational load, scalability and mitigation capability parameters.

SUMMARY

Two dimensional DGT to three dimensional DGT on a unit sphere and in the process, eliminated the dimensional constraint of basic DGT.

In Three dimensional DGT, the number of directions for NDRS of a router can be increased multifold by increasing the value of the parameter $n \in N$ in $d(n)$. For as small a value as $n=2$, $d(n) = 49$. The concepts of DR, DRS and NDRS along with the uniqueness theorem are true for all values of n.

The DRA traceback is qualitatively robust, with fast convergence and independence.

The storage issue is addressed through Direction Ratio Sampling Algorithm (DRSA) traceback, so as to make DGT free from the three limitations of directions, dimensions and storage space deficiency.

The DRSA algorithm can discern efficiently, multiple attacks also. When attackers from different sources, produce disjoint edges in the tree structure of reconstruction, the number of packets needed to construct each path is independent of other paths.

The limitations imposed by restricting the number of directions at a router to d(2) at every stage and using RN (mod 1000) instead of the full serial number of the router are marginal in nature.

In conclusion, DRSA is a robust scheme of three dimensional, multi-directional geographical IP traceback.

Thus DGT removing

1. Directional limitations,
2. Dimensional limitations,
3. Packet header space management through DRSA.

REFERENCES

Al-Duwairi, B., & Govindarasu, M. (2006). Novel Hybrid Schemes Employing Packet Marking and Logging for IP Traceback. *IEEE Transactions on Parallel and Distributed Systems*, *17*(5), 403–418. doi:10.1109/TPDS.2006.63

Angelos, D. K. (2004). SOS: An Architecture for Mitigating DDoS Attacks. *IEEE Journal on Selected Areas in Communications*, *22*(1), 176–188. doi:10.1109/JSAC.2003.818807

Belenky, A., & Ansari, N. (2003). *Accommodating Fragmentation in Deterministic Packet Marking for IP Traceback* (pp. 1374–1378). IEEE – GLOBECOM. doi:10.1109/GLOCOM.2003.1258463

Chen, Z., & Lee, M.-C. (2003), An IP Traceback Technique against Denial-of-Service Attacks. In *Proceedings of the IEEE, Annual Computer Security Applications Conference* (pp. 96–104). doi:10.1109/CSAC.2003.1254314

Gao, Z., & Ansari, N. (2005). Directed Geographical Traceback. In *Proceedings of the IEEE International Conference on Information Technology: Research and Education* (pp. 221-224).

Haining, W., & Kang, G. S. (2003). Transport-Aware IP Routers: A Built-In Protection Mechanism to Counter DDoS Attacks. *IEEE Transactions on Parallel and Distributed Systems*, *14*(9), 873–884. doi:10.1109/TPDS.2003.1233710

Huang, C., Li, M., Yang, J., & Gao, C. (2005). A real-time traceback scheme for DDoS attacks. In *Proceedings of the IEEE International Conference on Wireless Communications, Networking and Mobile Computing* (pp. 1175 – 1179).

Jing, Y. N., Tu, P., Wang, X. P., & Zhang, G. D. (2005). Distributed-log-based scheme for IP traceback. In *Proceedings of the IEEE International Conference on Computer and Information Technology (CIT)*.

Li, J., Sung, M., Xu, J., & Li, L. (2004), Large scale IP Traceback in High Speed Internet: Practical techniques and theoretical foundation. In *IEEE Symposium on Security and Privacy* (pp. 115 –129).

Li, Q., Feng, Q., Hu, L., & Ju, J. (2005). Fast Two Phrases PPM for IP Traceback, In *IEEE-International Conference on Parallel and Distributed Computing, Applications and Technologies* (pp. 286–289).

Mirkovic, J., Prier, G., & Reiher, P. (2002). Attacking DDoS at the source. In *Proceedings of the IEEE International Conference on Network Protocols* (pp. 312–321).

Mirkovic, J., Prier, G., & Reiher, P. (2003). Source-End DDoS Defense. In *IEEE International Symposium on Network Computing and Applications* (pp. 171–178).

Muthuprasanna, M., & Manimaran, G. (2005), Space-Time Encoding Scheme for DDoS Attack Traceback. In *Proceedings of the IEEE – Globecom* (pp. 1842-1846). doi:10.1109/GLOCOM.2005.1577967

Muthuprasanna, M., Manimaran, G., Alicherry, M., & Kumar, V. (2006). Coloring the Internet: IP Traceback. In *Proceedings of the IEEE International Conference on Parallel and Distributed Systems*, Vol. 1.

Park, K., & Lee, H. (2001). *On the Effectiveness of probabilistic Packet Marking for IP traceback under Denial Service attack* (pp. 338–347). IEEE INFOCOM.

Savage, S., Wetherall, D., Karlin, A., & Anderson, T. (2001). Practical Network Support for IP traceback. *IEEE/ACM Transactions on Networking*, *9*(3), 226–237. doi:10.1109/90.929847

Savage, S., Wetherall, D., Karlin, A., & Anderson, T. (2001). Network Support for IP Traceback. *IEEE/ACM Transactions on Networking*, *9*(3), 226–237. doi:10.1109/90.929847

Snoeren, A. C., Partridge, C., Sanchez, L. A., Jones, C. E., Tchakountio, F., Schwartz, B., & Strayer, W. T. et al. (2002). Single Packet IP Traceback. *IEEE/ACM Transaction Networking*, *10*(6), 721–734. doi:10.1109/TNET.2002.804827

Song, D. X., & Perrig, A. (2001). Advanced and Authenticated Marking Schemes for IP Traceback. In IEEE INFOCOM'01 (pp. 878 – 886) Anchorage, AK.

Sung, M., & Xu, J. (2003). IP Traceback-Based Intelligent Packet Filtering: A Novel Technique for Defending against Internet DDoS Attacks. *IEEE Transactions on Parallel and Distributed Systems*, *14*(9), 861–871. doi:10.1109/TPDS.2003.1233709

Terence, K. T. L., John, C. S. L., & David, K. Y. Y. (2005). You can run, but you can't hide: An effective statistical methodology to trace back DDoS attackers. *IEEE Transactions on Parallel and Distributed Systems, 16*(9), 799–813. doi:10.1109/TPDS.2005.114

Wang, B. T., & Schulzrinne, H. (2004). A Denial-of-Service-Resistant IP Traceback Approach. In *Proceedings of the IEEE International Conference on Internet Computing* (pp. 351–356).

Xiang, Y., & Zhou, W. (2005), A Defense System against DDoS Attacks by Large-Scale IP Traceback. In *Proceedings of the IEEE, International Conference on Information Technology and Applications* (pp. 431–436). doi:10.1109/ICITA.2005.10

Yang, X., Pei, C., Zhu, C., & Li, Y. (2005), AMS Based Reconstruction Algorithm with Two-dimensional Threshold for IP Traceback. In *Proceedings of the Sixth International Conference on Parallel and Distributed Computing Applications and Technologies* (pp. 781–783).

KEY TERMS AND DEFINITIONS

CoPrime: Two integers a and b are said to be coprime if the only positive integer that evenly divides both of them is 1 - they have no common positive factors other than 1.

Direction Ratio Sampling Algorithm (DRSA) Traceback: A robust scheme of three dimensional, multi-directional geographical IP traceback.

Equiprobable: A philosophical concept in probability theory that allows one to assign equal probabilities to outcomes when they are judged to be equiprobable.

IP Traceback: The process of identifying the actual sources of attack.

Neighborhood Direction Ratio Set: In space, from any router point R_0, there are infinite directions, all of which by Uniqueness theorem, give distinct, infinitely many, possible router points R_i on the unit sphere.

Segment Direction Ratio: A novel scheme to overcome the directional limitations of 2^3 DGT and generalized to 2^n DGT ($n \geq 4$).

Topology of the Earth: The Earth can be geographically considered as a sphere.

Chapter 17
A New Approach in Cloud Computing User Authentication

Alaa Hussein Al-Hamami
Amman Arab University, Jordan

Rafal A Al-Khashab
Amman Arab University, Jordan

ABSTRACT

Cloud computing provides the full scalability, reliability, high performance and relatively low cost feasible solution as compared to dedicated infrastructure. These features make cloud computing more attractive to users and intruders. It needs more and complex security measures to protect user privacy and data centers. The main concern in this chapter is security, privacy and trust. This chapter will give a discussion and a suggestion for using cloud computing to preserve security and privacy. The malicious hacker and other threats are considering the major cause of leaking security of the personal cloud due to centralized location and remote accesses to the cloud. According to attacks, a centralized location can be easier target rather than several goals and remote access is insecure technologies which offer a boundary of options for attackers to infiltrate enterprises. The biggest concern is attackers that will use the remote connection as a jumping point to get deeper into an organization.

INTRODUCTION

The concept of cloud computing is based on a collection of many old and few new concepts in several research fields like Service-Oriented Architectures (SOA), distributed and grid computing as well as virtualization. Cloud computing concept is not a new thing, and it is a combination of several concepts from virtualization, distributed application design, grid computing, utility computing and clustering. The cloud computing is a set of multiple resources (hardware and software) available via the Internet and managed by the provider. The customer gets all or some of these resources according to usage system, the main concepts of cloud computing declared in Figure 1.

The organization pay for access to cloud computing services then these services are present to customer according to the client usage, the storage space, processing capabilities, number of the clients allowed them to work and other factors. The main idea of the cloud is how the customers

DOI: 10.4018/978-1-4666-6583-5.ch017

Copyright © 2015, IGI Global. Copying or distributing in print or electronic forms without written permission of IGI Global is prohibited.

Figure 1. Main concepts of cloud computing

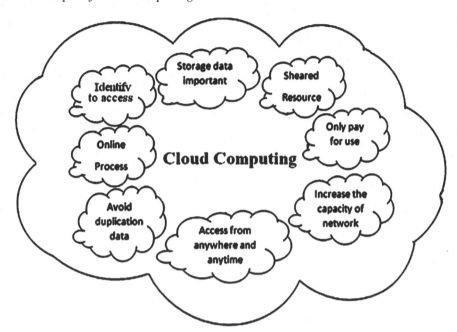

satisfied their requirements and pay only for the actual used without needing any details about process. Cloud computing is a way to increase the capacity of a network without investing in new infrastructure, training new personnel, or licensing new software (Kumar & et al, 2012).

It can be the ability to rent a server or a thousand servers and run a geophysical modeling application on the most powerful system available anywhere. It can store and secure amounts of data that accessed only by authorized applications and users. It is the ability to use applications on the Internet that store and protect data while providing a service and it can be the ability to use a handful of web services to integrate photos, maps, and Global Positioning System navigation system (GPS) information to create a mash up in customer's web browsers (Sun, 2009).

Other interest of cloud computing, most of the organizations which do not use the cloud computing, need to have data available at all the times. To achieve this target, without increase cost, determine centralized server or any additional requirements, the organization should have cop-

ies of their data at many servers throughout their offices. To avoid this duplication of data by using the cloud computing, when the organization used public, private, community or even the hybrid cloud service of their own, this means all the data exist in the cloud and everyone would be able to access the data easily (Chowdhury & et al, 2013).

Cloud computing allows providers to develop, deploy and run applications that can easily grow in capacity, work rapidly, and never fail, without any concerns on the properties and the locations of the underlying infrastructures (Dwivedi & et al, 2013). Cloud vendors effectively sell computation and storage resources as commodities, some cloud vendors and third parties sell higher-level resources, such as the Google Application platform, relational DBMSs or the Sales Force application. The customer controls the virtual machine's capacity (computational and storage) by sending the cloud vendor a service request to add or subtract resources as needed. The time to gain or release capacity (for small fractions of the provider's inventory) is typically measured in minutes, not months (Mohana & et al, 2013).

Cloud is not just about technology, it also represents the fundamental change in how information technology is provisioned and used. The providing security is major challenging issue in cloud computing, therefore the enterprises before adapting to the cloud computing have to consider its benefits, risks and effects on their organizations and customers who are dealing with the networking environment (Buyya & et al, 2008; Nafi & et al, 2013).

The authentication mechanisms in identification and access control, it is achieved by three methods: the first method refers to the identification of human by their physical characteristics called biometric such as DNA, fingerprints, retinas and irises, voice patterns, facial patterns and hand measurements. The second method can be defined between two parties. One of these parties is determined which method to identify authorized user like ATM card, smart card and mobile phone. The third method is one of the widely used mechanisms to authenticate

authorized user. In this method the user is able to select something and he/she is the only one who knows that information like password, PIN and pattern.

In this chapter we use the password to identify authorized user, this method is weak, when the user reuse the same password in multiple log-in and that can be easily broken by hackers, while using multiple password will increase security for the people who face generally difficulties in remembering multiple passwords. So we need accurate method to provide high security and easy use to user. See Figure 2.

SECURITY ISSUES IN CLOUD COMPUTING

Security issue refers to the protection of data, network, computer programs, computer power and other elements of computerized information system. Security problem is getting complicated

Figure 2. Cloud authentication

because you do not need to be an expert to launch an ordinary attack, thus, the security aims mainly to prevent or at least minimize the attacks (Turban & et al, 2012).

Any security model defines through subjects and objects, as well as in the cloud computing environment, the security defines through subjects such as users of the cloud, attacker trying to gain control, the cloud controller, cluster controllers, node controllers, and process running on various node controllers as well as the system itself, and defines through objects such as files, programs, resources, etc. that available in the cloud system (Dhage & et al, 2011).

Cloud computing is like any new technology. It has some risk in the cloud computing is the resources shared between different organizations and individual users in open environment, and these resources can be handled by all other users of the cloud. So the resources become more vulnerable to attack and it is very easy for an intruder to access, misuse and destroy the original form of data and an intruder can also interrupt the communication (Nafi & et al, 2013).

We should focus on security issue when any user is using the cloud services or two users are sharing the same cloud services. The security issues associated with cloud computing is divided into two broad categories: security issues faced by cloud providers such as the organizations which providing service through the cloud, and security issues faced by their customers. In case of the provider security, the provider must ensure that their infrastructure is secure, also that their clients' data and applications are protected. While in the case of the customer security, the customer must ensure that the provider has taken the suitable security measures to protect their information (Munir, 2013).

Security is a key concern while considering the move to the cloud application that have very sensitive and confidential information would be better off being behind the corporate firewall. Technical mechanisms for data security in the cloud are still evolving and still the top most inhibiter of cloud adoption (Subashini, 2011).

Thus before migration to the cloud, one should focus on some important attacks on cloud computing (Munir, 2013; Global, 2010):

- **Denial of Service (DoS) Attacks:** A large cloud services provider is arguably a bigger target and more attractive for those who wish to cause maximum distribution through attacks such as distributed Denial of Service because it is shared by many users, which makes DoS attacks much more damaging.

- **Zombie Attack:** Through the Internet, an attacker tries to get the attention of the victim by sending requests from innocent hosts in the network. These types of hosts are called zombies. In the Cloud, the requests for Virtual Machines (VMs) are accessible by each user through the Internet. An attacker can flood the large number of requests via zombies. This type of attack can effect of cloud service because it will cause DoS (Denial of Service) or DDoS (Distributed Denial of Service) to the servers.

- **Backdoor Channel Attack:** It is a passive attack, which allows hackers to gain remote access to the compromised system. Using backdoor channels, hackers can be able to control victim's resources and can make it a zombie for attempting a DDoS attack. It can also be used to disclose the confidential data of the victim.

- **Side Channel Attacks:** Cloud system is responsible on service request; this type of attack tries to inject a malicious service or new virtual machine into the Cloud system and can provide malicious service to users. An attacker could attempt to compromise the cloud by placing a malicious virtual machine in close proximity to a target cloud server and then launching a side channel attack. If this attack succeeds to do this, then valid requests are redirected to the malicious services automatically.

- **Authentication Attacks:** Authentication is a weak point in hosted and virtual services and is frequently targeted. There are many different ways to authenticate users; for example, based on what a person knows to allow the user to enter the cloud application. The mechanisms used to secure the authentication process and the methods used are a frequent target of attackers.

- **Man-in-the-Middle Attacks:** This attack is commonly taking place when different cloud users across the cloud are communicating with each other or sharing the resources from the cloud environment. This attack is carried out when an attacker places himself between any two users and tries to hack the information during the transmission. Anytime attackers can place themselves in the communication's path, there is the possibility that they can intercept and modify communications.

- **Phishing Attack:** Phishing attacks are well known for manipulating a web link and redirecting a user to a false link to get sensitive data. In Cloud, it may be possible that an attacker use the cloud service to host a phishing attack site to hijack accounts and services of other users in the Cloud.

In the area of cloud computing different security models and algorithms are applied, in this chapter focus on Authentication attacks to show users that their information is secure and they have authority to know who access their information in the cloud and required strong authentication between application components so that is transmitted only to authorized parties.

CHARACTERISTICS OF CLOUD COMPUTING

Cloud Computing has several characteristics such as:

1. **Reduce Run Time and Response Time:** For application that use the cloud essentially for running batch jobs, cloud computing makes it straightforward to use 1000 servers to accomplish a task in 1/1000 the time that a single server would require, and reduce time to take hours to setup, install, and configure the applications in organization (Sun, 2009).

2. **Reduced Cost:** The most important characteristic in cloud computing is to reduce the cost and that has several directions (Ullah, 2012):-

    a. **Reduce Hardware Cost:** All the work is done in the cloud and it will reduce the cost for purchasing high cost equipment for the organization having thousands of employees. The employees only need a terminal to connect to the cloud in order to perform most of the computation.

    b. **Reduce Software Costs:** The proprietary software is no longer needed to purchase. The amount is paid to the cloud provider as when it is needed to use the high cost software instead of buying it. Also reduces the software cost which needed to run and manage any organization's server.

    c. **Maintenance and Upgrading Cost:** It is possible for the employers to quickly remove associated computer costs when the number of employees is reduced. It is easy to migrate, or upgrade the current operating system, hardware etc. with a new one, because the organization only needs to pay for the services which they want to upgrade instead of investing again and purchasing the high cost software and hardware.

3. **Independence Device and Location:** One of the benefits of cloud computing is that, although the organization is not aware of the physical location of the data and what device to use it, but they view the data to be presented in one location. Independence Device and location enables users to access systems using a web browser regardless of their location or what device they are using. The portability of the application is that users can use it from home, work, or at client locations. These characteristics are increased the employees access to information from anywhere they are (Ullah, 2012; Rawat, 2012).

4. **Resource Pooling:** Resources such as network bandwidth, virtual machines, memory, processing power, storage capacity, etc. are pooled together to serve multiple customers using a multi-tenant model with different physical and virtual resources dynamically assigned and reassigned according to consumer demand (Rawat, 2012 ; Massadeh, 2013).

5. **Reliability:** Reliability is improved if multiple redundant sites are used, which makes well-designed cloud computing suitable for business continuity and disaster recovery and if we use cloud computing then, that data will be stored in the cloud and we do not need to think of our data (Kumar, 2012).

6. **Performance:** Performance is monitored and consistent and loosely coupled architectures are constructed using web services as the system interface.

7. **Maintenance:** Maintenance of cloud computing application is easier, because they do not need to be installed on each user's computer and can be accessed from different places.

8. **Back-Up Facility:** Cloud computing provides an automatic data backed – up facility as opposed to a desktop computer or notebook computer does set to automatically save important data on server (Ullah, 2012).

9. **Reduces the Risks of Theft:** As the data resides on the cloud, so, if a company's notebook or any other computing equipment is stolen, then there will be less chances of losing the company's proprietary and sensitive data, and it will also reduce the chances of greater financial impact (Ullah, 2012).

10. **Availability and Collaboration:** If the user gets services from cloud using internet then he/she is not responsible for the underlying infrastructure of the service i.e. if the system is properly working or any system is failed completely or faulty, every such concern is managed by the could itself by its distributed nature so user get a quality service. And if a company has all its important data or computation on the cloud, then it is very easy to access your data from anywhere if you have only a computer terminal and it is connected with the internet. Similarly it also allows the participant to share and work on the same instance of the data. It is easy for the organization to expand its branches (Ullah, 2012).

11. **On-Demand Self-Service:** Customers can automatically provision computing capabilities and resources on their own when needed without necessitating any human intervention (Massadeh, 2013).

12. **Elasticity and Scalability:** The cloud is elastic. This means that resource allocation can get bigger or smaller depending on demand. And the cloud is scalability which means the increase or decrease capacity depending on the demand, also the application can scale when adding users or when application requirements change (Massadeh, 2013).

CLOUD COMPUTING SERVICE MODEL (ARCHITECTURAL LAYERS OF CLOUD COMPUTING)

The main concept in the cloud computing is provide different services to the customers, these services divided into three categories: software as a service, platform as a service and infrastructure as a service, as shown in Figure 3.

Software as a Service (SaaS)

SaaS is the top layer in this model; it means the capability of the customer is using a provider's application running on a cloud infrastructure, a single instance of the application runs on the cloud services and multiple end users or client organization. The benefit of SaaS that the customer can remotely accessible to special-purpose software through the internet, the customer dose not mange or control the underlying cloud infrastructure including network, servers, operating system, storage, or even individual application capabilities (Rawat, 2012 ; Kaur, 2012, ; Tiwari, 2012).

Figure 3. Types of cloud computing service model

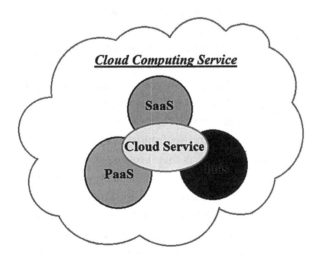

Platform as a Service (PaaS)

PaaS is the middle layer in this model, it is means the capability of the customer is deploying onto the cloud infrastructure consumer-created or acquired application created using programming language, libraries, services and tools supported by the provider. The benefit of PaaS that is encapsulates a layer of software and providers, and it can be used to build higher-level services, the customer does not manage or control underlying cloud infrastructure including network, servers, operating system, or storage, but has control over the deployed application and possibly configuration setting for the application-hosting environment (Rawat, 2012; Kaur, 2012; Tiwari, 2012).

Infrastructure as a Service (IaaS)

IaaS is the lowest layer in this model, it means the capability of the customer is provisioning processing, storage, networks and other fundamental computing resources where the consumer is able to deploy and run arbitrary software, which can include operating system and applications. The benefit of IaaS is delivering the basic storage and compute capabilities as standardized services over the network, the customer dose not manage or controls the underlying cloud infrastructure but has control over operating system, storage, and deployed applications, and possibly limited control of select networking components (Rawat, 2012; Kaur, 2012; Tiwari, 2012).

CLOUD COMPUTING DEPLOYMENT MODEL

The customer when moving to the cloud computing should use one of the types cloud computing deployment model; these types are different from one to other based on the purpose of it. IT organization can choose to deploy application on public, virtual, private, personal, community or hybrid clouds as shown in Figure 4. The organization is choosing one of these deployment models based on the characteristics to optimized of it, and may use more than one model to solve different problems (Sun, 2009 ; Boampong, 2012).

Public Clouds

The cloud infrastructure is provisioned for open use by the general public; it owned, managed and operated by service provider (business, academic, government organization or some combination of item). The resources, such as storage and application, from different customers are likely to be mixed together on the cloud's servers, storage system, and network. These resources are made available to multiple customers by a service provider via internet. This type of cloud is typically low-cost or pay-on-demand and has highly scalable services (Sun, 2009; Rawat, 2012; Boampong, 2012).

Private Clouds

The cloud infrastructure is provisioned for exclusive use by a single organization comprising multiple customers; it can be built, managed and operated by the company's own IT organization, by a cloud provider (third party), or some combination of them. Private cloud are built for the exclusive use of one client, this model gives companies high level of security, quality of service and control over how application or data are deployed on it.

Community Clouds

The cloud infrastructure is provisioned for exclusive use and it is controlled and shared by several organization and support a specific community that has shared interests, such as mission, policy and security requirements. It may be owned, managed and operated by one or more of the organization in the community, a third party or some combination of them, and it may exist on or off premises, and the member of the community share access to the data and application in the community cloud (Sun, 2009; Rawat, 2012; Boampong, 2012).

Figure 4. Types of cloud deployment model service

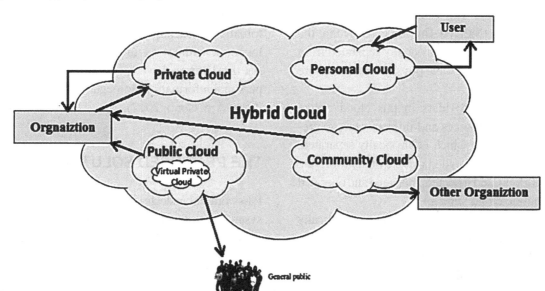

Hybrid Clouds

The cloud infrastructure is a combine of two or more distinct cloud infrastructure like public, private and community. That remains unique entities, but is bound together by standardized or proprietary technology that enables data and application portability. Application with less stringent security, legal, compliance and service level requirements can be outsourced to the public cloud, while keeping business-critical services and data in a secured and controlled private cloud.

Hybrid clouds introduce the complexity of determining how to distribute applications across both a public and private. Among the issues that need to be considered is the relationship between data and processing resources. If the data is small, or the application is stateless, a hybrid cloud can be much more successful than if large amounts of data must be transferred into a public cloud for a small amount of processing.

Virtual Private Cloud

The cloud infrastructure is provisioned for exclusive use in specific portion of public cloud infrastructure; this cloud is virtually partitioned rather than completely physically separated from the larger cloud. The main idea of this Virtual Private Cloud (VPC) definition is really that the VPC is not completely physically separated from the larger cloud and some physical infrastructure sharing remains.

The service providers in this cloud utilize public cloud resources and infrastructure to create infrastructure which is physically separated, it would simply be called private or semi-private virtual cloud, and it owned, managed and operated by a public cloud vender.

Virtual private cloud was introduced specifically for those customers interested in taking advantage of the benefits of cloud computing but who have concerns over certain aspects of the cloud. Common concerns involve privacy, security and the loss of control over proprietary data. In response to this customer need, many public cloud vendors designed a VPC offering a part of a vendor's public infrastructure but having dedicated cloud servers, virtual networks, cloud storage and private ID addresses, reserved for a VPC customer.

The VPC is an on demand configurable pool of shared computing resources in a public cloud, isolated between the tenants of the public cloud and not shared with any other customer. The isolation between tenants of a public cloud is performed via access control mechanism (Boampong, 2012).

The cloud infrastructure is provisioned for personal use, this cloud help any user to access the digital files located in home use from anywhere in the world and from any device and time.

It can be owned, managed and operated by user who create personal cloud, and only user who own cloud can access to this cloud serves and responsibility who looking to own files and maintain on it. But it is also possible to grant permission to others such as family and friends.

In this chapter, we use personal cloud because this type provides each user fully isolated virtual network and can store any type and any size of file online in centralized location, releases space on PCs, smart phones and tablets. And files can be accessed from any device with an internet connection.

The personal cloud allows user to data automatically backup in a safe, secure and nearby location, without having to wonder whether or not third parties have access to own private and personal information (Iomega, 2013; Srinivasan, 2011; Ardissono, 2012).

THE PROPOSED SOLUTION

Password authentication is a common approach to the system security and widely used to authenticate an authorized user, and the user is usually accomplished by employing usernames and passwords when using web browser to access the cloud. The security is reduced when users reuse the same password for different clouds or for different log-in in the same cloud, at the same time; we know that people generally have difficulty remembering multiple passwords.

In this chapter, we will propose more efficient security model for cloud computing that helps users can freely choose single password for multiple uses in the cloud. The process in this chapter is generating new password every log-in instead of single password, in other words, it is generating multiple passwords from one password.

The proposed model includes three main components, these are:-

1. **Cloud User:** The individual user can store his/her data and applications in the cloud, and can accessing them from anywhere and anytime.

2. **Third Party:** Who manages cloud server and provide authentication between user and cloud.

3. **Cloud Application:** An application that allows the user to enter cloud computing and have full control over cloud.

The proposed framework for cloud computing model is consisting of two procedures:

1. Authentication procedure.
2. Privacy procedure.

Figure 5 shows the proposed cloud model and the main steps in each procedure.

Figure 5. The proposed cloud model

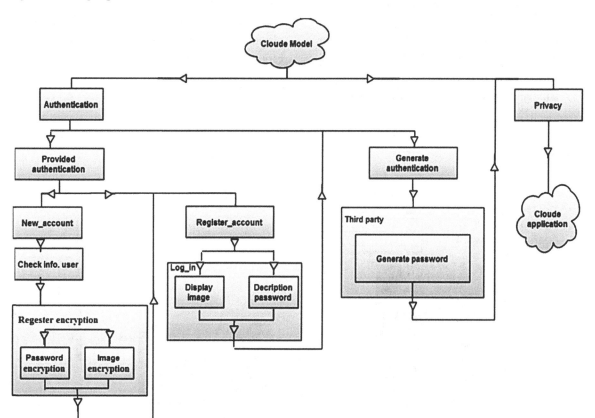

Authentication Procedure

The first procedure used to provide authentication between user and cloud, this procedure includes:

1. **Provided Authentication:** Includes two stages: the first stage is for the new user stage, When the user is registered his/her user-name, password and own image in the new-account interface, it is assigned new-account for the new user by using a register algorithm. This algorithm used to encrypt user password and user image then saves them in the database. The model uses this algorithm to protect password from hacker in the database, also it is increase authentication and defines authorized user, as shown in Figure 6. The other stage is for the registered user stage. The system will check user name and password to decide the authorization of the user. The system will decrypt and display pic-algorithm. The Image Display algorithm will be used when the model is ensure the user password, this algorithm used to show six images in different sequence in the interface log-in and the user determines the correct image.

2. **Generate Authentication:** This is an internal stage, third party is responsible on this stage, and making two points: the first point is to prove authentication by the third party by comparing between two images that selected by the user with image saved in the database to the same user for check the user authority. The second one is designed to generate new authentication to increase the trust between user and cloud by generating multiple passwords from one password to each log-in cloud, the model displayed a notice to the user by sending email contains the new password, as shown in Figure 7.

Privacy Procedure

There are many service providers for personal cloud storage. In this chapter, we use one of the cloud computing service providers. The provider cloud is called just cloud to construct our personal cloud storage. Many of the process are accrued in this provider.

Figure 6. New user stage

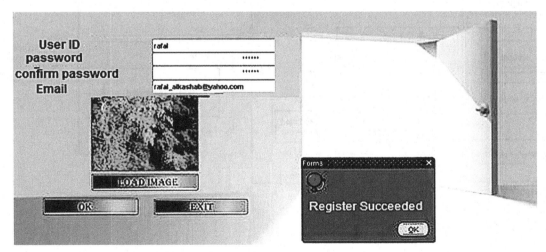

Figure 7. Generate authentication stage

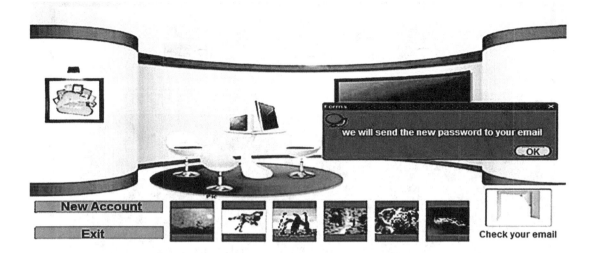

The log-in cloud is the last stage in our model, include main interface between user and cloud. When user enters user- name and new password that generated from first procedure in the cloud interface, it permits user to full control to all data and application found in the cloud, and many of the process are accrued in this provider. The important process is providing the privacy for important file before uploading to the cloud, and for the sharing file when the user wants to share some files with other users as flowing below:

1. **Privacy of Backup Files:** We provide privacy of backup files by using methods to closing important folder before loading to the cloud, when the user needs to show this folder in the cloud must know which methods are used to close folder.

The proposed model use password method to closing folder by writing a set of DOS coding, and written required password in this code in TXT. The TXT is saving as (locker.bat), when click on the locker icon will appear the private folder; the cloud user puts all secret files in this folder and hides this folder from appearing by click on the locker icon. Stages of this method appear in Figure 8.

2. **Privacy of Sharing Files:** After the user determines which folder should be share, the user chooses the type of sharing files as shown in Figure 9.

The sharing files in cloud computing with other users include:

a. **Share Folder:** Share file with only one user by sending the link sharing file to the user's email.
b. **Public Link:** Put the link of sharing file in public link and any user can show this file.
c. **Post:** Share file by social media like Facebook and Twitter.

The previous type is deployment files by link in to user email; we provide privacy of this like by hidden link in to picture or statement as shown in the Figure 10.

The user sent this picture or statement to the other user, so only the other user is know the hidden link that can show the share file. Figure 11 shows an example of retrieving the Hidden Link.

Figure 8. Stages of hide folder

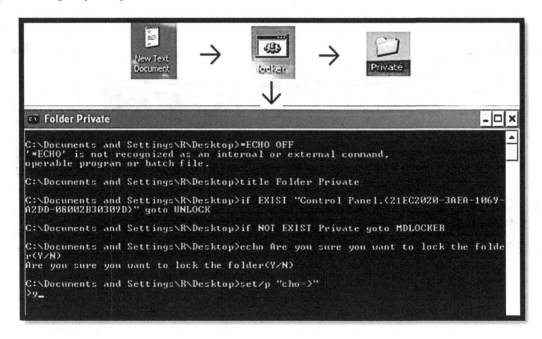

Figure 9. Share files type

Figure 10. Stages of hidden link

CONCLUSION

The concept of cloud computing is still unclear to many, in this chapter we trying to clear the basic concepts of cloud computing such as general mean-ing of cloud, security issue related it, characteristic, deployment and service model of cloud computing.

While the cloud computing have several ben-efits, migration to the cloud needs allows users to know that their information is secured and safe from threats and attacks on the cloud. In this chap-ter we made efforts to provide authentication to show cloud users that their information is secure and they have authority to know who access his information in the cloud.

When we designed the proposed model, we focus on two points, the first point is to prove authentication through image as determined by user, this image is used to proof if the cloud user is authorized or not. The second point is to generate authentication through using multiple password technique in the cloud; it is a new research field which is gaining interest from cloud users because the probability of brute force attack for breaking the password can be reduced when increase gen-erated multiple passwords from single password.

After the user has access to the cloud comput-ing, we offer some ideas to provide data privacy inside the cloud, and suggest methods to actual execute for this ideas in future work.

Figure 11. Stages of retrieve hidden link

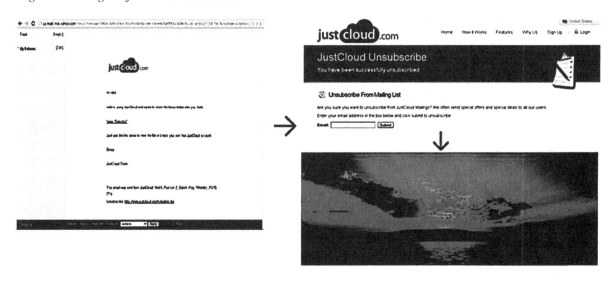

FUTURE DEVELOPMENTS

At the end of the chapter, we offer some suggestion for future work to provide more trust between user and cloud, this suggestion is summarized in:

1. The possibility of adding one of the biometric authentication types to the identification of humans by their characteristics in addition to the image like finger print and Iris recognition, to more identification of the user.
2. It is possible to achieve the ideas that presented in privacy session in this chapter by:
   a. Before Backup to the cloud, determine specific part in the cloud by the user, and the user is upload all important data and application to this part. Then identify privilege of the part cloud to determine which users can access to this part, and determine type of privilege to authorized users from administrator like show, alter, add and delete.
   b. Before sharing any link in the cloud with other users, the link is hidden in the text or image by one type of the steganography like Least Significant Bit. Then share text or image with the users, so only authorized user knows which steganography method is used through seeing the link.
3. It is possible to enhance the implemented model according to the characteristics of the new deployments model by adding more features and expanding the model.

REFERENCES

Ardissono, L., Goy, A., Petrone, G., & Segnan, M. (2012). From service clouds to user-centric personal clouds. In *IEEE International Conference on Cloud Computing*.

Boampong, P., & Wahsheh, L. (2012). Different facets of security in the cloud. In *Proceedings of the 15th Communications and Networking Simulation Symposium*.

Buyya, R., Yeo, C., & Venugopal, S. (2008). Market-oriented cloud computing: vision, hype, and reality for delivering IT services as computing utilities. In *10th IEEE International Conference on High Performance computing and Communication*. doi:10.1109/HPCC.2008.172

Chowdhury, C. R., Chatterjee, A., Sardar, A., Agarwal, S., & Nath, A. (2013). A Comprehensive study on cloud green computing: To reduce carbon footprints using clouds. *International Journal of Advanced Computer Research*, *3*(8).

Dhage, S. N., Meshram, B. B., Rawat, R., Padawe, S., Paingaokar, M., & Misra, A. (2011). Intrusion Detection System in Cloud Computing Environment, *International Conference and Workshop on Emerging Trends in Technology*, (2011). doi:10.1145/1980022.1980076

Dwivedi, S. K., Kushwaha, D. S., & Ankit, M. (2013). Security issues and resource planning in cloud computing. *International Journal of Engineering and Computer Science*, *2*(2).

Gregg, M. (2010). *10 Security Concerns for Cloud Computing*. Retrieved from http://www.globalknowledge.be/content/files/documents/386696/386784

Iomega. (2010). *The coming personal cloud: cloud storage for the rest of US*. white paper. Retrieved from http://iomega.com/resources/pdf/pdf_30.pdf

Kaur, N., Gagandeep, S., & Kaur, M. (2012). A Cloud Computing Against Unified Ontology. *International Journal of Computer & Technology*, *3*(2).

Kumar, A., Ranjan, A., & Gangwar, U. (2012). An understanding approach towards cloud computing. *International Journal of Emerging Technology and Advanced Engineering*, 2(9).

Massadeh, S. A., & Mesleh, M. A. (2013). Cloud Computing in Higher Education in Jordan. *World of Computer Science and Information Technology Journal, 3*.

Sun Microsystems. (2009). Introduction to Cloud Computing Architecture (1st ed.). Retrieved from https://java.net/jira/secure/attachment/29265/cloudcomputing.pdf

Mohana, R. S., Thangaraj, P., Kalaiselvi, S., & Krishnakumar, B. (2013). Cloud computing for biomedical information management. *International Journal of Scientific Engineering and Technology*, 2(4).

Munir, K., & Palaniappan, S. (2013). Secure cloud architecture. *Advanced Computing: An International Journal, 4*.

Nafi, K. W., Kar, T. S., Hoque, S. A., & Hashem, M. M. (2012). A newer user authentication, file encryption and distributed server based cloud computing security architecture. *International Journal of Advanced Computer Science and Applications, 3*.

Rawat, S. S., & Sharma, N. (2012). A new way to save energy and cost-cloud computing. *International Journal of Emerging Technology and Advanced Engineering*, 2(3).

Srinivasan, J., Wei, W., Ma, X., & Yu, T. (2011), EMFS: Email-based personal cloud storage. In *IEEE Sixth International Conference on Networking, Architecture, and Storage*. doi:10.1109/NAS.2011.55

Subashini, S., & Kavitha, V. (2011). A survey on security issues in service delivery models of cloud computing. *Journal of Network and Computer Applications*, *34*(1). doi:10.1016/j.jnca.2010.07.006

Tiwari, P., & Mishra, B. (2012). Cloud computing security issues, challenges and solution. *International Journal of Emerging Technology and Advanced Engineering*, 2(8).

Turban, E., King, D., Lee, J., Liang, T., & Turban, D. (2012). *Electronic Commerce 2012: A Managerial and social networks perspective* (7th ed.). United States of America: Pearson.

Ullah, S., & Xuefeng, Z. (2012). Cloud Computing Research Challenges, In *5th IEEE International Conference on BioMedical Engineering and Informatics*.

KEY TERMS AND DEFINITIONS

Authentication: It refers to any mechanisms by which a system allows or denials the access to the data and keep them stored at cloud sites that accessible only by users who own the data.

Cloud Computing: It involves the movement of Information Technology services – applications, infrastructure and platform – via the Internet, deployment models and managed by provider.

Cloud Security: Cloud needs more and complex security measures to protect user privacy and data centers.

Data Centre: Is a facility used to house computer systems and associated components, such as telecommunications and storage systems.

Privacy: It is the right to be free from secret surveillance and to determine whether, when, how, and to whom, one's personal or organizational information is to be revealed.

Service Models: These services divided into three categories: Software as a service (SaaS), Platform as a service (PaaS) and Infrastructure as a service (IaaS).

Virtualization: It refers to creation of a virtual (rather than actual) version of something, including but not limited to a virtual computer hardware platform, operating system (OS), storage device, or computer network resources.

Chapter 18
Trust Determination in Wireless Ad Hoc Networks

Hussein Al-Bahadili
University of Petra, Jordan

ABSTRACT

Wireless ad hoc networks are susceptible to attacks by malicious nodes that could easily bring down the whole network. Therefore, it is important to have a reliable mechanism for detecting and isolating malicious nodes before they can do any harm to the network. Trust-based routing protocols are one possible mechanism as they locate trusted routes dynamically to conform to network environment. However, such algorithms require reliable and effective trust determination algorithm. This chapter presents a detail description and evaluation of the trust determination algorithm, namely, the Neighbor-Weight Trust Determination (NWTD) algorithm. The performance of the algorithm is evaluated through simulation using the Mobile Ad hoc Network (MANET) simulator (MANSim). The simulation results demonstrated the effectiveness and reliability of the algorithm in isolating any maliciously behaving node(s) in a timely manner.

INTRODUCTION

Wireless ad hoc network is defined as a set of wireless mobile nodes communicate with one another for a purpose of data (message) exchange without relying on any pre-existing infrastructure or centralized control(Murthy & Manoj, 2004). Early ad hoc research papers assumed a friendly and cooperative environment and focused on problems such as wireless channel access, multi-hop routing, power consumption, while ignoring any network security issues. Network security involves securing computer network infrastructure from

being attached by adversary or malicious nodes and ithas become a primary concern in order to provide protected communication between nodes in a potentially hostile ad hoc environment (Djenouriet al., 2005; Yang et al., 2004).

Wireless ad hoc networks are very vulnerable to and heavily suffer from maliciously behaving nodes or malicious nodes, which could easily degrade the network stability by exhibiting one or more of the following behavior: packet drop, battery drained, buffer overflow, bandwidth consumption, illegal node entering, stale packets, packet delaying, link break, message tampering,

DOI: 10.4018/978-1-4666-6583-5.ch018

Copyright © 2015, IGI Global. Copying or distributing in print or electronic forms without written permission of IGI Global is prohibited.

message modification, denying from sending message, route modification, node isolation, stealing information, session capturing, etc. Therefore, it is important to have a reliable mechanism for detecting and isolating malicious nodes before they can do any harm to the network. One of these mechanisms is the trust-based routing protocols (Gonzalez et al., 2011; Ferdous et al., 2010; Hughes et al., 2003). In which only trusted nodes are accepted for forwarding control/data packets, so that each node to be part of the routing table, it should have a trust above a certain minimum acceptable trust (MAT). The main requirement and challenge to these protocols is the availability of an appropriate trust determination algorithm.

One of the earliest approaches for trust determination is Marsh's formalism (Marsh, 1994). Marsh uses the outcomes of direct interactions among nodes to calculate situational and general trust. Situational trust is the level of trust in another for a specific type of situation, while general trust refers to overall trustworthiness irrespective of the situation. After each interaction, a node considers whether the other node fulfilled its obligations. If so, then trust increases, but trust decreases if commitments are broken. This formalism is the base of many subsequent models, which supplement trust based on direct interactions with other information sources to update decision-making. Throughout the years, a number of trust determination algorithms have been developed; however, still more powerful algorithms are required to meet network security needs (England et al., 2012; Cordasco et al., 2008; Liu et al., 2004).

This chapter describes and evaluates the performance of the new trust determination algorithm, namely, the Neighbor-Weight Trust Determination (NWTD) algorithm (El-Zayyat et al., 201), which is based on the weighted voting concept (COMAP, 2011). In this algorithm, each node in the network is timed to periodically broadcast message stoat's one-hop neighbors containing the IDs of its one-hop trusted nodes and their trusts. Each node will receive a number of messages, most probably, equal to the

number of its one-hop neighbors. After receiving these messages, each receiving node extracts the IDs and trusts of each node on the message; and consequently, a node may receive different trusts for the same one-hop neighbor from other nodes. Afterwards, the receiving node calculates the new trust for each of its one-hop neighbors by averaging the node trusts' that is received from other one-hop neighbors using the weighted-average formula. The weight here is the weight of the node one-hop neighbors, therefore it is referred to as the NWTD algorithm. The node itself participates in the averaging process by giving itself a trust one and 100% weight.

The algorithm defines two types of nodes: the master and monitoring nodes. A master node is any trusted node in the network that can take the responsibility of testing new arriving nodes, determines their initial trust, and then broadcasts the initial trust to its one-hop neighbors. Each node in the network must define a master node for itself by applying a certain criteria on its one-hop neighbors and on itself; therefore, the network may have one or more master nodes. If a node could not find a master node for itself, it can be a master node for itself. A monitoring node is any node in the network that has the capacity to detect the malicious behavior of other nodes within its neighborhood, reduces the trust of the detected malicious nodes, and then uses the updated trust in the forthcoming trust determination process. The algorithm allows for one or more monitoring nodes to be active at the same time.

The NWTD algorithm is implemented and integrated with the mobile ad hoc network simulator (MANSim) (Al-Bahadili, 2010), which is used to evaluate the performance of the algorithm. In particular, in this work, MANSim is used to simulate three main scenarios. The first one simulates a network environment with no malicious nodes; the second scenario simulates a network with one monitoring and one malicious node; and the third scenario simulates a network with one monitoring and two malicious nodes.

This section introduces the general domain of this chapter. The rest of this chapter is organized as follows. Section 2 reviews some of the most recent work on trust determination. Section 3 describes the NWTD algorithm. The implementation of the NWTD algorithm and the simulation environment used in this chapter are described in Section 4. The results and discussions are presented in Section 5. Finally, in Section 6, based on the results obtained from the different scenarios, conclusions are drawn, and a number of recommendations for future work are pointed-out.

LITERATURE REVIEW

Many trust determination models have been developed for peer-to-peer systems (Barolli et al., 2013; Song et al., 2005), which are based on sharing recommendation information to establish trust and reputation. Applying these models to ad hoc networks faces two main problems; these are: significant network overhead due to the additional information exchanged, and requirement of a trusted third party (or a computationally expensive public key infrastructure (PKI)), which are against the nature of ad hoc networks. However, later on, many trust determination models have been developed for ad hoc networks.

Sabater & Sierra (2002) and Ramchurn et al. (2005) proposed approaches that are based on this Marsh formalism (Marsh, 1994), namely, ReGreT and FIRE, which add reputation information provided by third parties and knowledge of social structures to arrive at overall trust assessments. However, whilst powerful, such sophisticated models are not appropriate for ad hoc networks, where resources are limited and knowledge of social relationships between nodes is unlikely to be accessible.

Hughes et al. (2003) proposed a dynamic trust-based resources (DyTR) system, which applies a dynamic notion of trust to wireless ad hoc network resources. DyTR continuously assesses the trustworthiness of entities over time based on system events and controls network resources according to current levels of trust. For dynamic trust assessment, DyTR utilizes a socio-cognitive model of trust, a formal model of the essential concepts and characteristics of trust in human society, and subjective logic for reasoning about trust-relevant system events.

Liu et al. (2004) designed and formulated a novel trust-based routing protocol for secure transactions in MANETs. This model represents nodes by opinion, which is updated during a routing information exchange process. If a node performs healthy behaviors, its credibility from the viewpoints of other nodes is increased; otherwise, the credibility will be decreased, and this node will be eventually denied by the whole network. The performance of the protocol was evaluated through simulations. The results demonstrated that the whole MANET system can be maintained at a satisfactory security level with reasonable short convergence time and significant lower computation overheads. More importantly, the security level can be easily customized to meet the diverse demands from applications over MANETs.

Nekkanti & Lee (2004) developed a routing protocol that basically behaves depending upon the trust factor and the level of security assigned to the information flow to decide what level of encryption is applied to the current routing information at a source/intermediate node. So based on trust factor, the routing information will be low, medium, and high level encrypted. This protocol saves the node's power and time by avoiding unnecessary encoding, which are very much valuable in cases of emergencies where the information is as valuable as the time.

Pirzada & McDonald (2006) developed a trust determination mechanism, where nodes calculate situational trust according to observed events and then use an aggregated general trust for routing decisions. Nodes record information about others for various event types: acknowledgements, packet precision, gratuitous route replies, blacklists, HELLO packets, destination unreachable messages and authentication objects. For each type, the proportion of positive events is taken to correspond to the situational trust. Situational trust values are then aggregated using a weighted product to give overall trust. Pirzada and McDonald obtained promising simulation results.

Sun et al. (2006) presented an information theoretic framework to quantitatively measure trust. They developed four axioms and based on these axioms, they presented two trust models: entropy-based and probability-based models, which satisfy all the axioms. Simulations showed that the proposed models can significantly improve the network throughput as well as effectively detect malicious behaviors in ad hoc networks.

Manickam & Shanmugavel (2007) developed a fuzzy-based trusted AODV routing protocol with varying number of malicious nodes. In this protocol, each node verifies the trust of the neighbor from which it receives the control packet. They used Mamdani fuzzy model to compute the trust value for its neighbors and stores it in the neighbor table. Nodes will interact only with the trusted neighbors. Simulation results demonstrated that the performance of their protocol is better than AODV in terms of routing overhead ratio, throughput, latency and packet loss under similar attack conditions.

Cordasco & Wetzel (2008)compared the performance of two MANET routing protocols; these are: the Secure AODV (SAODV) and Trusted AODV (TAODV), which address routing security through cryptographic and trust-based means respectively. They provided performance comparisons on actual resource-limited hardware, and discussed design decisions for future routing protocols.

Park et al. (2008) presented a cluster-based trust model, which uses the reputation from a neighboring node to the calculation of the trust value. They used the trust value of a trustees as a weight to perform more sophisticated calcula-

tion of the trust value. All nodes in the cluster can fully trust the selected head, if entire nodes in the cluster participate in the head competition. Then, the head node issues the certificate that shows the trust level of each member node. If a node moves from one cluster to another, the trust level of the node is determined by the certificate issued by the previous cluster-head. Each cluster has a cluster head, which is responsible for issuing trust certificate. However, a node acting as a cluster head is extraneous requirement for ad hoc concept in which processing and battery resources are limited.

Ferdous et al. (2010) developed a novel scheme for trust management in MANETs, namely, the Trust Management (NTM) scheme that is based on the nodes' own responsibility of building their trust level and node-level trust monitoring. They developed a mathematical framework of trust in NTM, and they presented their scheme with notations, algorithms, analytical model and prove of its correctness. Zhang et al. (2010) presented a trust establishment and management framework for hierarchical wireless sensor networks. They demonstrated that the framework helps to minimize the memory, computation and communication overheads involved in trust management in wireless sensor networks.

Gonzalez et al. (2011) compared the performance of three well-established reputation-based trust approaches and discussed some potential attacks against them. Guo et al. (2011) presented a trust management framework (TMF) for MANETs. The framework calculates a node's trust value based on observations from neighbor nodes by using Grey theory and Fuzzy sets. The TMF chooses multiple rather than a single parameter to obtain trust values. They claimed that the TMF can detect abnormal trust behavior, and discover which parameter for forming trust values of a mobile node is abnormal. They demonstrated that the TMF can be considered as an effective trust framework for MANETs.

Saini & Gautam (2011) proposed an approach to establish trust among nodes, which can be evaluated by monitoring the nodes for their behavior. The values are defined for trust is dynamic in nature and depends on the behavior of nodes.

Xia et al. (2012) presented a dynamic trust prediction model to evaluate the trustworthiness of nodes, which is based on the nodes' historical behaviors, as well as the future behaviors via extended fuzzy logic rules prediction. They also integrated their trust predication model into a unicast source routing protocol for MANETs, namely, the Trust-based Source Routing (TSR) protocol. Their results demonstrated that TSR improves packet delivery ratio and reduces average end-to-end latency.

Gowda & Hiremath (2013) presented a highly reliable secure routing scheme based on node-to-node packet forwarding. The simulation framework is design in java for formulating the node-to-node packet-forwarding scheme, and the simulation results demonstrated that scheme can provide highly reliable data exchange on secure routing medium with extremely less communication overhead and high packet delivery ratio. Patil et al. (2013) proposed a new approach that to consider all issues and challenges for establishing reputation into common place and to propose a reputation Index Protocol that remunerate its objective. The approach may develop a revolutionary concept in ad hoc networks to maintain security, integrity and robustness among participating nodes. The scope of the work is to extend further the reputation Index Protocol that can ensure the end-to-end communication in public domains.

THE NWTD ALGORITHM

This section presents a detail description of the NWTD algorithm. It is well-recognized that any trust model should resolve the following issues:

1. Determine a trust value for any new arriving node, so that it will be either trusted by other nodes in the network or not.
2. Periodically determine/update the trust of all nodes in the network.
3. Broadcast the newly determined trusts to other nodes in the network with minimum overheads.

Furthermore, since the model will be used in a dynamic and multivariable ad hoc environment, it is important to introduce some configuration parameters that should be carefully adjusted at each node to suit the environment and to optimize the performance of the trust determination model. In general, these parameters are:

1. **Minimum Acceptable Trust (MAT):** It is the minimum trust anode should have in order to be trusted by other nodes in the network. In this model, it is numeric value between 0 and 1.
2. **Minimum Trustable Participants (MTPs):** It is the minimum number of trustable neighbors that should participate in determining the trust of any other node in the network. For example if it is set to 3, then in order for Node i to determine the trust of Node j ($T_{i,j}$), Node i should get trusts for Node j from at least two other trustable nodes as it already has a trust for Node j.
3. **Trust Update Time (TUT):** It is the minimum duration before updating nodes' trust.

Trust Determination

The main concept behind the NWTD algorithm is that each node in the network periodically broadcasts (shall be referred to as broadcasting node) an extended HELLO (EHELLO) message to its one-hop neighbors, which has the same format of standard HELLO message broadcasted by the network routing protocol plus additional data appended at the end of the message. The additional data includes:

Figure 1. Structure of trust table showing trusts of Node s(j) as determined by Node s(i)

s(i) \ s(j)	s(1)	s(2)	s(3)	s(4)	s(5)	...	s(n)
s(0)	$T_{s(0),s(1)}$	$T_{s(0),s(2)}$	$T_{s(0),s(3)}$	$T_{s(0),s(4)}$	$T_{s(0),s(5)}$		$T_{s(0),s(n)}$
s(1)			$T_{s(1),s(3)}$		$T_{s(1),s(5)}$		$T_{s(1),s(n)}$
s(2)	$T_{s(2),s(1)}$		$T_{s(2),s(3)}$	$T_{s(2),s(4)}$,			$T_{s(2,s(n)}$
s(3)	$T_{s(3),s(1)}$	$T_{s(3),s(2)}$		$T_{s(3),s(4)}$	$T_{s(3),s(5)}$		
s(4)							
s(5)	$T_{s(5),s(1)}$						
...							
s(n)	$T_{s(n),s(1)}$	$T_{s(n),s(2)}$					

1. The number of one-hop neighbors.
2. The ID and trust of each of the one-hop neighbors.

On the other hand, each node in the network that receives these EHELLO message(s) from its one-hop neighbor(s) (shall be referred to as the receiving node). When a node receives these extended EHELLO message(s) from its one-hop neighbor(s), it performs the following tasks:

1. Compares the trust of the broadcasting node with the pre-defined MAT. If it is equal to or greater than MAT, then accept message, otherwise discard the message.
2. Extract the IDs and trusts of the one-hop neighbors of the broadcasting node that pass the test in (1).
3. Construct a table listing the one-hop neighbor(s) and the trusts they have for each other as shown in Figure 1. The node is fully trusted by itself (i.e., $T_{x,x}=1$)
4. Determine the trust of the one-hop neighbors using the mathematical model described below.

5. Remove from the routing table any node for which the determined trust is less than MAT.
6. Broadcast the newly determined trusts to all one-hop neighbors and waits for broadcasts from its neighbors.

Node $s(0)$ calculates the trust of each of its one-hop neighbors as follows:

1. Calculates the average trust of the one-hop neighbor, x using the following equation:

$$\bar{T}_{s(0),s(j)} = \frac{1}{k_j} \sum_{i=0}^{k_j} T_{s(i),s(j)}, \quad (j=1 \; to \; n)\left(k_j \geq MTP\right)$$

(1)

where

$T_{s(i),s(j)}$: Trust of Node $s(j)$ as determined by Node $s(i)$, where both Nodes $s(i)$ and $s(j)$ are one-hop neighbors of Node $s(0)$.

$\bar{T}_{s(0),s(j)}$: Average trust of Node $s(j)$ as calculated by Node $s(0)$.

k_j: Number of nodes that have trust for Node $s(j)$.

n: Number of the one-hop neighbors of Node $s(0)$.

MTP: The Minimum Trustable Participants.

2. Calculates the new trust of Node $s(j)$ as the sum of the product of the trust of Node $s(j)$ as determined by Node $s(i)$ and the weight of Node $s(i)$ as determined by Node $s(0)$, which is mathematically expressed as:

$$T_{s(0),s(j)} = \sum_{i=0}^{k_j} w_{s(0),s(i)}^{s(j)} \cdot T_{s(i),s(j)},$$
$$\left(j = 1 \ to \ n \right)\left(k_j \, {}^3 MTP \right)$$

(2)

where $w_{s(0),s(i)}^{s(j)}$ is the weight of Node $s(i)$ as determined by Node $s(0)$ for a particular Node $s(j)$, and it is calculated as:

$$w_{s(0),s(i)}^{s(j)} = \frac{\overline{T}_{s(i),s(j)}}{\sum_{m=0}^{k_j} \overline{T}_{s(m),s(j)}},$$
$$\left(i = 0 \ to \ k_i, \ j = 1 \ to \ n \right)\left(k_j \, {}^3 MTP \right)$$

(3)

The average trusts serve to compute the weights of the nodes that contribute in determining the new trust of their one-hop neighbors, which means that the one-hop neighbors share their ideas before deciding the trust of any of their one-hop neighbors, and the contribution of each neighbor depends on its weight as determined by the receiving node. This is similar to the weighted voting concept (COMAP, 2011). This is of course more reliable way of determining the trust than just accepting the average trust as the new trust.

Master Node

A master node is a node in the network that is responsible for testing a new arriving node in order to determine an initial trust for it; and propagate the outcome of this test to its one-hop neighbors. Each node in the network must define a reference master node for itself by applying a certain criteria on its one-hop neighbors and itself. Thus, the network may have more than one master node. If a node could not define a master node for itself, it can act as a master node for itself.

The main characteristics of a master node are:

1. It is one-hop neighbor for both the new node and node searching for a master node.
2. It must be trusted by the new node.
3. If there is more than one node having the same characteristics, then the one with the smallest ID should be selected as the master node.

Let us consider a scenario with five nodes. Nodes A, B, C and D trust each other and also trusted by their one-hop neighbors. They are all in same range except for Node D, which is in range only with Node C. New Node X arrives to the network. It is one-hop neighbor for Nodes A, B, C and D as shown in Figure 2. All four nodes can detect that there is a new node arriving to the network. When detected, each node will compare

Figure 2. Master node selection scenario

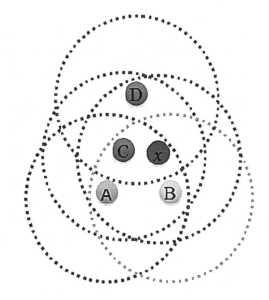

its table of one-hop neighbors with the neighbor table received from Node X in order to choose a master node.

For example, Node A will choose itself as a master node, Nodes B and C will choose Node A as a master node and Node D will choose Node C as a master node. The reason why Node D chooses Node C as a master node is that it doesn't see Node A or Node B. But Node C will not become master node as it already knows that Node A will test Node X. Therefore, it will just wait for the result and then forward it to the Node D.

In the current version of the NWTD, the master node performs two types of test on any new arriving node, namely, the FirstTest and the SecondTests. In the FirstTest, the master node randomly chooses a destination node with a known and reachable route. It informs the destination that test will start. Then, it sends a route request (RREQ) message for that destination through Node X(FirstTest()). The first RREQ has intentionally increased sequence number, so that the new node shouldn't reply. If it replies it indicates a malicious behavior (Test1()). While, the second RREQ has a normal sequence number and the new node should reply back telling the master node that it has a route to the destination. However, if it doesn't reply, this indicates a malicious behavior (Test2()).

This test will be repeated for a number of times, if possible with different destinations, and the success and fail ratios are calculated. The success ratio (S_r) is calculated as the number of successful test divided by the total number of tests, and the fail ratio (F_r) is calculated as the number of failed tests divided by the total number of tests; so that $S_r+F_r=1$. If S_r of the new node is less than a pre-set value, then it is announced as a non-trusted node. Figure 3 outline the pseudocode for the procedures FirstTest(), Test1(), and Test2().

If the new node made a success then a second phase of testing will begin (SecondTest()). In the SecondTest, the master node sends data packet to some destination via the new node. At the same time, the master node sends the hash value of the

Figure 3. The pseudocode for procedures First-Test(), Test1(), and Test2()

```
FirstTest()
    Failed=0
    For (trials<nTests)
        If (Test1() == False)
            Failed++
        End If
        If (Test2() == False)
            Failed++
        End If
    If (Failed ≥ 25% of Trials)
        BlockNode ();
    Else
        SecondTest()
    End If

Test1()
    SendRREQ(IncreasedSeqNumber)
    ReceiveRREQ()
    If (RREP Received)
        Return False;
    Else
        Return True;
    End If

Test2()
    SendRREQ(NormalSeqNumber)
    ReceiveRREQ()
    If (RREP received)
        Return True;
    Else
        Return False;
    End If
```

transmitted data packet to the destination by using its old route (not going through the new node).

The SecondTest will also be repeated for a number of times. Each time, the destination calculates the hash of the received data packet and compares it with the hash received from the master. If they match then it is a successful test. However, if the data is not received or the hashes don't match, this indicates a malicious behavior (Testee()) or failed test. In this case, the new node is announced by the Mater node as a non-trusted node. If both phases have completed successfully then the master node announces that the new node is fully-trusted. Figure 4 outlines the pseudocode for the procedures SecondTest() and Testee(). These tests should be performed periodically between nodes to ensure the stability of the network.

Monitoring Node

In addition to the master node discussed above, in the NWTD algorithm, as many nodes as possible should be designated as monitoring nodes. The monitoring nodes should be equipped with all capabilities to:

1. Monitor and classify the behavior of its one-hop neighbors into positive and malicious behaviors.
2. Update the trust of its one-hop neighbors accordingly, i.e., upgrade the trust of the positively behaving neighbors, and degrade the trust of the maliciously behaving neighbors.
3. Use the updated trust of its one-hop neighbors in the forthcoming trust determination procedure described above.

The monitoring node can update the trust of any of its one-hop neighbors using the following simple linear equation:

Figure 4. The pseudocode for procedures SecondTest() and Testee()

```
SecondTest()
    packet = GenerateDataPacket()
    hash = CalculateHash(packet)
    Destination = Testee
    OriginalRoute = RoutingTable(Testee)
    TestedRoute = RetrieveRouteFrom(RREP)
    Send(hash, OriginalRoute)
    Send(data, TestedRoute)
    Response = ReceiveResponse(Testee)
    If (Response == False)
        Return False;
    Else
        Return True;
    End If
```
```
Testee()
hash = ReceiveHash()        // Receive a hash from master node
packet = ReceivePacket()  // Receive a packet from tested node
If (packet.IsReceived)
    newHash = CalculateHash(packet)
    If (hash == newHash)
        Send(True)        // Send response to the master node
    Else
        Send(False)
    End If
Else
    Send (False)
End If
```

338

$$T_{updated} = \alpha \cdot T_{current} \qquad (4)$$

where $T_{current}$ and $T_{updated}$ are the trust of the one-hop neighbor before and after the update; and α is the update factor ($\alpha>0$). For the above equation, α should be greater 1 ($\alpha>1$) for positively behaving nodes, and less than 1 ($\alpha<1$) for maliciously behaving nodes. The value of α can be determined dynamically by the monitoring node for each of its one-hop neighbors separately; which means different values of α can be determined for different nodes at the same time depending on their behavior. Furthermore, a more complicated relationship can be used to estimate $T_{updated}$, where in general the relationship for $T_{updated}$ can be expressed as:

$$T_{updated} = f(\alpha, T_{current}) \qquad (5)$$

It is important to recognize that any node in the network can act a monitor node as long as it has the capabilities to monitor the behavior of its neighbors, classify their behaviors into positive and malicious behaviors and update their trust accordingly. Furthermore, it can be easily seen that the new trust of any node depends on a number of factors, such as:

1. The number of one-hop neighbors who have trust for the node.
2. The actual trusts of the node as determined by its one-hop neighbors.
3. The weight of the one-hop neighbors who have trust for the node as determined by the receiving node.

IMPLEMENTATION AND SIMULATION ENVIRONMENT

In order to evaluate the performance of the NWTD algorithm, it is implemented and integrated with the Mobile Ad hoc Network Simulator (MAN-Sim), which is a network simulator written with C++ programming language for evaluating the performance of various MANETs protocols (Hussein Al-Bahadili, 2010). In particular, three main functions are developed and integrated with MANSim, these are:

1. TrustDetermination(), where the trust determination model described in Section 3.1 is implemented.
2. InitialTrust. As we have discussed in Section 3.2 that the master node is responsible for testing and determining the initial trust of any new arriving node, and broadcast this initial trust to its one-hop neighbors. This function simulates the function of the master nodes, where it determines the trust of the one-hop neighbors for each of the nodes in the network using the following initial trust distribution function:

$$T_{i,j} = 0.5 + 0.5\xi \qquad (6)$$

where $T_{i,j}$ is the trust of Node j as determined by Node i, and ξ is a random number between 0 and 1. According to the above equation the initial trust lies between 0.5 and 1. However, $T_{i,j}$ can be determined using any other linear or non-linear function.

3. TrustUpdate(), where the trust update procedure described in Section 3.3 is implemented.

Simulation Environment

The simulation environment that will be used throughout this chapter simulates a network area of 150x150m with 49 nodes distributed across the network semi-regular node distribution. Each node is assumed to have a transmission range or transmission radius (R) of 30m. The actual nodes locations across the network are shown in Figure 5. This distribution is chosen because it is easy to predict the NWTD performance variation according to the nodes behavior. Furthermore, using the same nodes distribution keeps the focus on the effect of nodes behavior and how it is handled by the NWTD algorithm.

In order to focus on the node logical behavior rather than its physical behavior, the nodes are assumed to be fixed (non-mobile) throughout the simulations. After describing the network configuration and nodes mobility, let us describe the nodes' behavior that will be investigated in this Chapter. First, it should be clear that there are infinite number of nodes' behaviors can be expected and simulated using MANSim. However, we shall limit these possible simulations to few ones that we believe are appropriate for

demonstrating the effectiveness and reliability of the NWTD algorithm in identifying malicious behavior fairly.

Each simulation starts with specifying the following main attributes for each node in the network:

- Location;
- Transmission radius (R);
- Speed (u);
- Initial trusts;
- Simulation time (T_{sim}).

The simulation time is divided into discrete intervals (loops). During each loop, each node in the network calculates new trusts for its one-hop

Figure 5. Nodes distributed in 150x150m network area for all scenarios

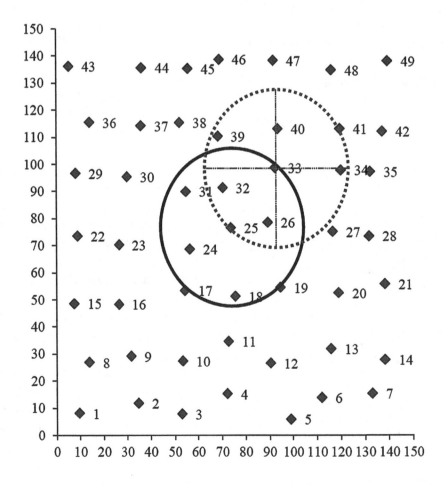

neighbors. In addition, the monitoring nodes may update (degrade or upgrade) the trust of its one-hop neighbors based on their behavior. Therefore, we refer to the number of discrete intervals as number of updates (U). In this work, each simulation is carried-out for 25 updates, which is enough to demonstrate the trust variation.

In general, the implementation of the NWTD algorithm is developed in a very flexible way to enable the user to estimate the trust of the nodes in the network for as many trials as required by the user. The user also has the option to set and investigate the performance of the algorithm considering different numbers of monitoring and malicious nodes.

RESULTS AND DISCUSSION

In order to evaluate the performance of the NWTD algorithm in identifying and isolating a malicious node, the MANSim simulator has been used to simulate three different scenarios considering the simulation environment described in Section 4.1; these are:

Scenario #1: No Malicious Nodes

It simulates a neighborhood that confined no malicious nodes.

Scenario #2: One Monitoring and One Malicious Nodes

It simulates a neighborhood that confined one monitoring node (Node 25) and one malicious node (Node 31).

Scenario #3: One Monitoring and Two Malicious Nodes

It simulates a neighborhood that confined one monitoring node (Node 25) and two malicious nodes (Nodes 31 and 26).

Scenario #1: No Malicious Nodes

In this scenario, it is assumed that all nodes across the network are behaving positively (i.e., $\alpha_{i,j}=1$). The trust of one-hop neighbors of Node 25 ($T_{25,x}$) (e.g., Nodes: 18, 24, 26, 31, 32, 33) are estimated and plotted in Figure 6.

Scenario #2: One Monitoring and One Malicious Nodes

In this scenario, it is assumed that all nodes across the network are behaving positively (i.e., $\alpha_{i,j}=1$) except for Node 31, which presents some malicious behavior as recognized by the monitoring node (Node 25). The trust of some neighbors of Node 25 ($T_{25,x}$) are estimated considering three different update factors ($\alpha_{25,31}$) of 0.9, 0.8, and 0.7. The results obtained for these three different cases are shown in Figures 7, 8, and 9, respectively.

Scenario #3: One Monitoring and Two Malicious Nodes

This scenario simulates exactly the same network configuration in Section 4.1. However, it assumes and simulates different nodes behavior in which two of the first hop-neighbors of Node 25 are acting maliciously, namely, Nodes 31 and 26 who are detected by Node 25. Due to their malicious behavior, Node 25 reduces their trusts obey the same update factor. In particular, we shall consider two different cases, in the first case, the trust of Nodes 31 and 26 are reduced by 20% (i.e., $\alpha_{25,31}=\alpha_{25,26}=0.8$), and in the second by 30% ($\alpha_{25,31}=\alpha_{25,26}=0.7$).

The variation of $T_{25,31}$ and $T_{25,26}$ for $a_{25,31}=a_{25,26}=0.8$ and $a_{25,31}=a_{25,26}=0.7$ (two malicious nodes) are shown in Figures 10 and 11, respectively. The figures also show the variation of $T_{25,31}$ and $T_{25,26}$ for $a_{25,31}=0.8$ and $a_{25,31}=0.7$ (one malicious node) for the sake of comparison between Scenarios 2 and 3.

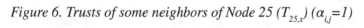

Figure 6. Trusts of some neighbors of Node 25 ($T_{25,x}$) ($\alpha_{i,j}=1$)

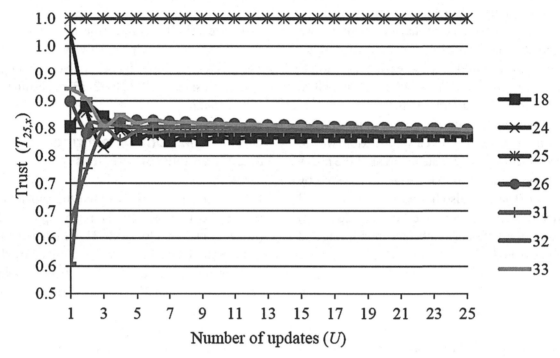

Figure 7. Trusts of one-hop neighbors of Node 25 ($T_{25,x}$) ($\alpha_{25,31}=0.9$)

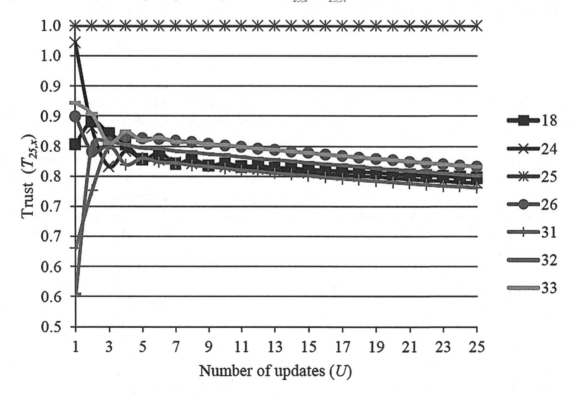

Figure 8. Trusts of one-hop neighbors of Node 25 ($T_{25,x}$) ($\alpha_{25,31}$=0.8)

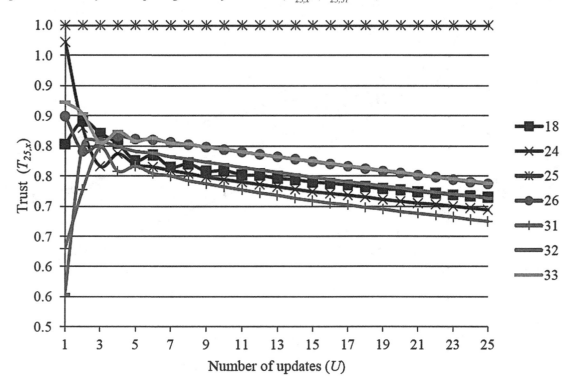

Figure 9. Trusts of some neighbors of Node 25 ($T_{25,x}$) ($\alpha_{25,31}$=0.7)

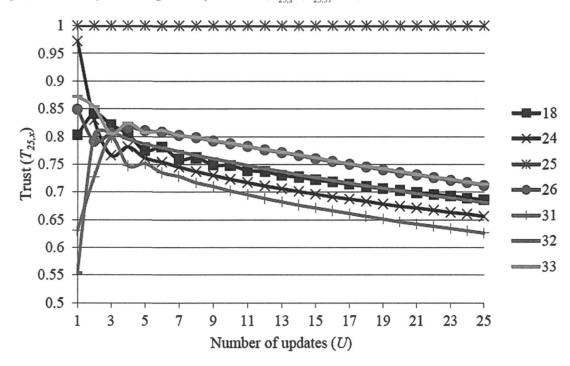

Figure 10. Variation of $T_{25,31}$ for various $\alpha_{25,31}$ and $\alpha_{25,26}$

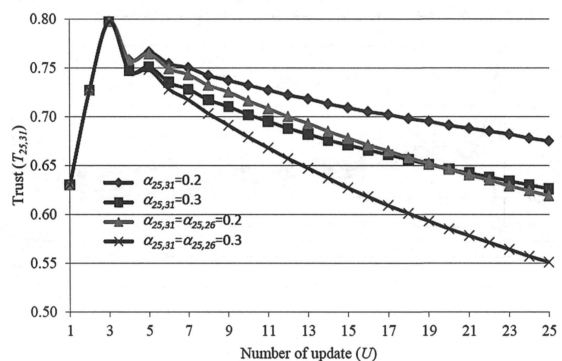

Figure 11. Variation of $T_{25,26}$ for various $\alpha_{25,31}$ and $\alpha_{25,26}$

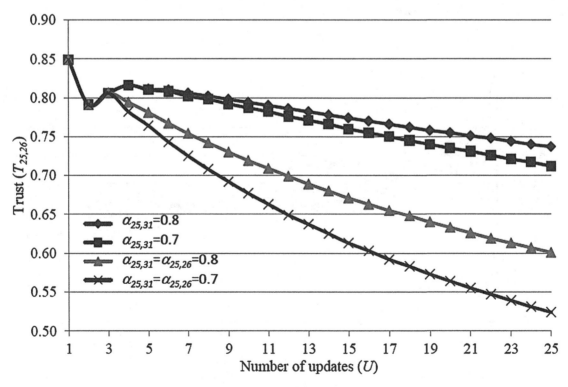

The main outcomes of the above scenarios:

- The trust of Node 25 is always equal to 1 as the node is usually fully trust by itself. This trivial output is a way of validating the algorithm accuracy and MANSim accurate computations.
- For Scenario #1, after an initial fluctuation for few updates, the trust of the nodes almost stabilizes and none of the nodes introduce any changes in the trusts of the nodes within its neighborhood.
- For Scenario #2 after an initial fluctuation for few updates, the trusts of the nodes almost stabilize with some decreasing rates for all nodes. The reduction rate depends on the nodes locations with respect to Nodes 25 and 31, and the update factor. For example, after 25 updates, Node 18 has a trust of 0.786, 0.748, 0.715 and 0.686 for $\alpha_{25,31}$ 1.0, 0.9, 0.8, and 0.7, respectively. This means that the trusts decreases as $\alpha_{25,31}$ increases. This is because the reduction in the trust of Node 31 reduces its weight and consequently the trust of any nodes received through it as explained in the NWTD algorithm.
- It has been found that if MAT=0.5, Node 25 requires around 50 updates to isolate Node 31 with $\alpha_{25,31}$=0.6 and around 40 updates with $\alpha_{25,31}$=0.5. If it is assumed that the duration of the trust update is 30 sec, then with $\alpha_{25,31}$=0.6 it requires around 20 min to isolate Node 31, which may look very long time.
- For Scenario #3, it can be clearly seen from Figures 10 and 11 that the NWTD algorithm with one monitoring node can monitor more than one malicious node at a time. Furthermore, it requires less converges time or number of updates to isolate the malicious nodes. This can be explained as follows: Node 25 reduces the trust of Nodes 31 and 26 each update, and they will contribute indirectly to reduce the trust of their

neighbors (e.g., Node 32), and consequently the weight of their neighbors. As a result of that these neighbors contribute to further reduction in the trust of the Nodes 31 and 26. For example, after 25 updates, $T_{25,31}$ is equal to 0.626 when only Node 31 acting maliciously ($\alpha_{25,31}$=0.7), and equal to 0.551 when both Nodes 31 and 26 are acting maliciously ($\alpha_{25,31}=\alpha_{25,26}$=0.7). Also, $T_{25,26}$ is equal to 0.712 when only Node 31 acting maliciously ($\alpha_{25,31}$=0.7), and equal to 0.524 when both Nodes 31 and 26 are acting maliciously ($\alpha_{25,31}=\alpha_{25,26}$=0.7).

- It must be well remembered that when a node trust less than MAT, the node will be isolated by its neighbors, which means terminate its effect on the network. However, in our implementation of the NWTD algorithm, the computation continues without discarding or isolating the malicious node.
- The values of U (which indicates the malicious node active time), $\alpha_{25,31}$ and MAT should be carefully selected to ensure stable network operation and quickly isolating any malicious node.
- It can be deduced from the above discussion that the convergence time or the number of updates required to isolate any malicious node within the network can be reduced by increasing the number of monitoring nodes who can recognize the malicious behavior of the node and then reduces its trust and broadcasts the updated trust to their neighbors, which, for example, can be easily achieved in high density networks.

CONCLUSION

The NWTD algorithm is an efficient and effective algorithm that can be used reliably to determine the trust of mobile nodes in wireless ad hoc network, and consequently isolating any malicious node that has its trusts downgraded to less than a preset minimum acceptable trust. The active time of the malicious node can be adjusted to the minimum acceptable level as it depends on the number of monitoring nodes, α and MAT.

The main recommendations for future work may include performing further investigations to evaluate the performance of the NWTD algorithm for variable nodes density and speed, and various and variable malicious and monitoring behavior models. Furthermore, implement the NWTD algorithm fully as part of a data routing protocol (e.g., AODV, DSR, etc.) in a MANET network using NS-2 simulator to estimate the time delay, throughput, load, and power consumption.

REFERENCES

Al-Bahadili, H. (2010). On the use of discrete-event simulation in computer networks analysis and design. In E. Abu-Taieh and A. El-Sheikh (Eds.), Handbook of Research on Discrete-Event Simulation Environments: Technologies and Applications (pp. 418-442). Hershey, PA: Information Science Reference.

Barolli, L., Spaho, E., Xhafa, F., & Younas, M. (2013). Performance evaluation of an integrated fuzzy-based trustworthiness system for p2p communications in jxta-overlay. *Neurocomputing*, *122*, 43–49.

Cordasco, J., & Wetzel, S. (2008). Cryptographic versus trust-based methods for manet routing security. *Electronic Notes in Theoretical Computer Science*, *197*(2), 131–140.

Djenouri, D., Khelladi, L., & Badache, N. (2005). A Survey of security issues in mobile ad hoc and sensor networks. *IEEE Communications Surveys and Tutorials*, *7*(4), 2–28.

El-Zayyat, K., Al-Bahadili, H., & Zobai, T. (2010). A novel neighbor weight-based trust determination model for wireless ad hoc networks. Proceedings Of The International Conference On Theoretical And Mathematical Foundations Of Computer Science (Tmfcs-10) (pp. 116-126), Orlando, Florida, USA, 12-14 July.

England, P., Shi, Q., Askwith, B., & Bouhafs, F. (2012). A Survey on trust management in mobile ad-hoc networks. In *the 13th Post Graduate Symposium on the Convergence of Telecommunications, Networking, and Broadcasting*. Liverpool, UK, June 25-26, 2012.

Ferdous, R., Muthukkumarasamy, V., & Sattar, A. (2010). A node-based trust management scheme for mobile ad-hoc networks. In *2010 4th International Conference on Network and System Security* (pp. 275–280).

Gonzalez, J. M., Anwar, M., & Joshi, J. B. D. (2011). Trust-based approaches to solve routing issues in ad-hoc wireless networks: A Survey. In *2011 IEEE 10th International Conference on Trust, Security and Privacy in Computing and Communications* (pp. 556–563).

Gowda, S. R., & Hiremath, P. S. (2013). Secure routing schema for MANET with probabilistic node to node forwarding. *International Journal of Computer Science*, *10*(3).

Guo, J., Marshall, A., & Zhou, B. (2011). A new trust management framework for detecting malicious and selfish behaviour for mobile ad hoc networks. In *2011 IEEE 10th International Conference on Trust, Security and Privacy in Computing and Communications* (pp. 142–149).

Hughes, T. D. P., Denny, J., Muckelbauer, P. A. D. P., & Etzl, J. (2003). Dynamic trust applied to ad hoc network resources. In *Autonomous Agents*. Multi-Agent Systems Conference.

Liu, Z., Joy, A. W., & Thompson, R. A. (2004). A dynamic trust model for mobile ad hoc networks. Presented At The *10th IEEE International Workshop on Future Trends of Distributed Computing Systems* (pp. 80–85).

Manickam, J. M. L., & Shanmugavel, S. (2007). Fuzzy based trusted ad hoc on-demand distance vector routing protocol for MANET. In *International Conference on Advanced Computing and Communications* (pp. 414–421).

Marsh, S. P. (1994). *Formalising trust as a computational concept.* Unpublished doctoral dissertation, University of Stirlin, UK.

Murthy, C. S. R., & Manoj, B. S. (2004). *Ad hoc wireless networks: Architectures and protocols.* Michigan: Prentice Hall.

Nekkanti, R. K., & Lee, C. (2004). Trust based adaptive on demand ad hoc routing protocol. In *Proceedings Of The 42nd Annual Southeast Regional Conference* (pp. 88–93). New York: ACM.

Park, S.-S., Lee, J.-H., & Chung, T.-M. (2008). Cluster-Based Trust model against attacks in ad-hoc networks. In *Third International Conference on Convergence and Hybrid Information Technology,* (Vol. 1, pp. 526–532).

Patil, K., Bhanodia, P., & Joshi, S. (2013). A novel paradigm RIP (reputation index protocol) for MANET. *International Journal of Engineering Research & Technology, 2*(1).

Pirzada, A. A., & Mcdonald, C. (2006). Establishment in pure ad-hoc networks. *Journal of Wireless Personal Communications, 37,* 139–168.

Ramchurn, S. D., Huynh, D., & Jennings, N. R. (2005). Trust In multi-agent systems. the knowledge engineering. *RE:view, 19*(01).

Sabater, J., & Sierra, C. (2002). Reputation and social network analysis in multi-agent systems. In *1ˢᵗ International Joint Conference on Autonomous Agents and Multi-Agent Systems* (pp. 475–482). Bologna, Italy, July 15-19.

Saini, R., & Gautam, R. K. (2011). Establishment of dynamic trust among nodes in mobile ad-hoc network. In *2011 International Conference on Computational Intelligence and Communication Networks* (pp. 346–349).

Song, S., Hwang, K., Zhou, R., & Kwok, Y.-K. (2005). Trusted P2P transactions with fuzzy reputation aggregation. *IEEE Internet Computing, 9*(6), 24–34.

Sun, Y. L., Member, S., Han, Z., & Liu, K. J. R. (2006). Information theoretic framework of trust modeling and evaluation for ad hoc networks. *IEEE Journal on Selected Area in Communications, 24,* 305–317.

Xia, H., Jia, Z., Li, X., Ju, L., & Sha, E. (2012). Trust prediction and trust-based source routing in mobile ad hoc networks. *Journal of ad hoc networks, 11*(7), 2096–2114.

Yang, H., Luo, H., Ye, F., Lu, S., & Zhang, L. (2004). Security in mobile ad hoc networks: Challenges and solutions. *IEEE Wireless Communications, 11*(1), 38–47.

Zhang, J., Shankaran, R., Orgun, M. A., Varadharajan, V., & Sattar, A. (2010). *A dynamic trust establishment and management framework for wireless sensor networks* (pp. 484–491). IEEE.

KEY TERMS AND DEFINITIONS

Malicious Node: A malicious node is defined as node seeking to deny service to other nodes in the network.

MANSim: A network simulator written with C++ programming language for evaluating the performance of various wireless ad hoc network protocols.

Network Security: Network security involves securing computer network infrastructure from being attached by adversary or malicious nodes and it has become a primary concern in order to provide protected communication between nodes in a potentially hostile ad hoc environment.

Trust Determination Techniques: Trust determination techniques are defined as the techniques that determine the trusts of all nodes on the network.

Trust: Trust is defined as the level of confidence that anode participating in a wireless network places on another node in the same network for forwarding control/data packets.

Trust-Based Routing Protocols: Trust-based routing protocols are protocols that only accepts nodes with a trust above a certain minimum acceptable trust (MAT) in their routing table and use them for forwarding control/data packets, so that each node to be part of the routing table, it should have a trust above a certain MAT.

Wireless Ad Hoc Network: A wireless ad hoc network is defined as a set of wireless mobile nodes communicate with one another for a purpose of data (message) exchange without relying on any pre-existing infrastructure or centralized control.

Chapter 19
Security in Mobile Computing

Venus W. Samawi
Amman Arab University, Jordan

ABSTRACT

These days, peoples expected to move around carrying their mobile devices, talking to friends, completing their work, accessing emails etc. His/her pictures, work, study, even relationship (friends, and family) all is in the mobile device. Therefore, mobile devices (especially smart phones) become an ideal target for different attacks. Mobile computing also becomes important in enterprises and organizations. Therefore, it is important to illustrate the state of art on vulnerabilities and threats on mobile device. This chapter is addressed to explain mobile computing concept, features, architecture, operating systems, and risks to mobile devices. Mobile operating system structureand characteristicsare demonstrated. The author also illustrates mobile security issues, and type of threats to mobile devices. Finally, features and security models of two popular smartphone operating systems, Android and iOS, are illustrated. It was found that the security models of these two smartphones is immature and do not meet the enterprises security policies.

INTRODUCTION

Recent advances of hardware and software in mobile computing contributed to the improvement of services delivered by institutes, enterprise and government organizations. Business that had to stop when the employees leave their desks now is supplemented by using mobile devices (smartphones, PADs, wireless ultra-books and laptops). Most of the corporate employees in these organizations use mobile devices to access, find, share information, and perform email communication at any time and from any place. In this chapter, we will emphasis on smartphones due to the explosive growth and increasing usage of these devices.

The main aspect of mobile computing is portability, which requires software (mobile application requirements, and data encryptions), hardware (mobility devices and components), and mobile communication issues (network infrastructure, protocols, and communication properties) (Agrawal et al, 2003; Nosrati et al, 2012). Mobile devises should be equipped with a suitable operating system to run its services and to act as a platform that organizes the mobile device functionalities.

DOI: 10.4018/978-1-4666-6583-5.ch019

Copyright © 2015, IGI Global. Copying or distributing in print or electronic forms without written permission of IGI Global is prohibited.

Although we benefit from numerous services provided by mobile computing, we must understand that we are the victims of security vulnerabilities (Agrawal et al, 2003). Mobile computing needs extra security issues compared with other computer networks. This is due to the additional constraints caused by wireless transmission and mobility characteristics.

In this chapter, we are keen on answering the following questions: What does mobile computing mean? What are its main characteristics? Does it need special form of operating system? Is it more vulnerable to attacks? What are the main security issues in mobile computing? What are the main security problems that need to be solved?

MOBILE COMPUTING

Mobile computing is a term that refers to a set of computing operations that allows information accessing anytime, from any place, using any mobile device (laptops, tablets, or smartphones). If the information to be accessed is local, then the user is working under disconnected mode operation. When the device is connected to a network through wireless or wired connection, in this case the user is working under connected mode. Nowadays, mobile devices play an essential role in human daily lives. This is attributed to the availability of different forms of mobile communications (viz. 3G, 4G, GPRS, Bluetooth and Wi-Fi) that enable users to access various ubiquitous services regardless of time (Deepak & Pradeep, 2012). The main challenges faced by the mobile devices are limitation of their resources (viz. battery life, storage, and bandwidth) which affect the service qualities and communications (viz. mobility and security).

The availability of small powerful computing devices, improved telecommunication and specialized software helped the prevalence process of mobile computing (Deepak, 2012). The main mobile computing characteristics are common

with other technologies. But they are of special importance to the mobile computing (Agrawal et al, 2003; Deepak & Pradeep, 2012; Nosrati et al, 2012).

- **Portability:** The ability of the device to operate consistently during its move. It can operate at any time and in any place. Therefore, rechargeable batteries are needed to support working for several hours without needing any external charger

- **Data Connection:** The networking infrastructure that allows digital connection to the Internet for transmitting and receiving data. Mobile connectivity could be cellular connection (GSM, CDMA or GPRS, 3G, and 4G networks), WiFi connection (accessed through a private business network or through public hotspot), or Satellite Internet access.

- **Social Interactivity (Interactivity):** The collective cooperation and data exchanging between users. Here, data denotes files transfer, emails, facsimile, and accessing WWW. Interactivity is more important for mobile devices, since they have less computing power than other types of technology.

- **Individuality:** A basic component in mobile computing, which providing communication services between individuals. Basically, mobile devices are designed for individuals

Mobile computing devices suffer from series of specific problems and limitations. In brief, could be described as follows (Nosrati et al, 2012; Deepak & Pradeep, 2012):

- **Scarcity of Bandwidth:** In mobile computing, users need to access Internet on the move. In this case, we need sort of wireless connectivity (cellular, WiFi, or Satellite), which could be a weak point. If we are not near any of these connections, accessing the internet will be very limited.

- **Security Standards:** Most people nowadays keep their private sensitive information on their mobile devices. They connect to a public network via Virtual Private Network (VPN) which is considered unsafe to connect to. If WiFi network is accessed, it is also risky since Wi-Fi Protected Access (WPA) and Wireless Encryption Protocol (WEP) security can be easily intercepted.
- **Powerconsumption:** Mobile devices use expensive rechargeable batteries as power source. The main problem is when the battery runs out, and there is no nearby source of power for charging.
- **Transmission Interferences:** Signal strength in mobile devices affected by various factors. Network coverage (the nearest point of reference), weather, geographical location and terrain interfere with signal reception. Also, the presence in tunnels or in some buildings may cause poor signal receipt.
- **Potential Health Hazards:** Lack of concentration resulting from using mobile devices (especially texting) during car driving may cause traffic accidents. Cell phones signal could interfere with sensitive medical devices. Mobile phone radiation and its effect on health are questionable.
- **Human Interface with Device:** Screens and keyboards of mobile devices tend to be small, making them hard to be used. Other input methods (viz. speech or handwriting recognition) need training.

Different types of mobile devices are introduced, such as Personal Digital Assistant (PAD), smart phone, tablet computer, Ultrabook, and wearable computer. The emphasis is on smartphones since they become such pervasive and affordable.

To control smartphone services (texting, taking photos, calling, etc.), an operating system is needed. Types, features, and lack points of different smartphones operating systems will be illustrated in the next section.

MOBILE OPERATING SYSTEMS

An operating system is a collection of software which acts as an interface between hardware and user. It is used to manage system resources (software and hardware) (Silberschatz et al, 2013; Jindal & Mayank, 2012). As any computing device, mobile phones need an operating system (called Mobile OS) to control its resources and services (viz. manage wireless broadband and local connectivity, mobile multimedia formats, different input techniques, power management, calling, texting, taking photos etc.) Mobile Operating System, 2013; Fing et al, 2012).

At early years of mobile phones, mobile operating systems were simple due to the limited capabilities of the mobile phones. Nowadays, smartphones have many of personal computer features such as GPU (graphical processing unit which is also called visual processing unit), high-resolution screens, cameras, high speed CPUs, large storage space, multitasking etc. Therefore, more complex mobile operating systems are needed to support these features and provide application development capability. It is also important for the mobile operating system to provide proper development environment to support external developers and users to write software for smartphones. In this case, a full feature SDK (Software Development Kit) is needed in addition to well defined API's. Open-sourced (Linux based) mobile operating system provides an easy way to create inexpensive specialized applications. For competitive purposes, smartphone companies are willing to choose proper mobile operating system that comes with its own new features (Husted et al, 2011; Mobile Operating System, 2013). Smartphones combines

Figure 1. Smartphone platform

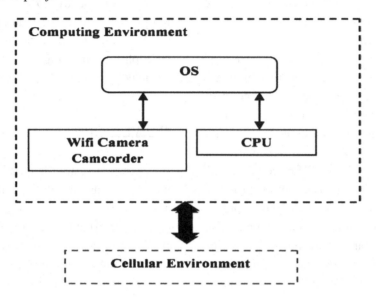

two environments (computing environment, and cellular environment) in one device. The computing environment is similar to a laptop environment, which is responsible of user interface, graphical rendering, and arithmetic computation. On the other hand, the cellular environment features are analogous to the features of traditional phones. Cellular environment consists of baseband chip which is responsible of interacting with cellular network. When making a phone call, the operating system delivers the audio stream to the baseband chip for processing and transmission. Figure 1 shows the general smartphone platform (Husted et al, 2011).

In this chapter, an overview of two popular mobile operating systems with their security issues will be illustrated: Android and iOS (as they have the highest sale market according to Q3 2013).

ANDROID OPERATING SYSTEM

Android is Linux-based open-source operating system with higher-level APIs (written in C).It is used by mobile devices such as smartphones and tablets. Android developed by the Open Handset

Alliance led by Google Inc. Google unveiled Android technology in November 2007 Mobile Operating System, 2013). Its technology (operating system, software, and application) is constantly developed and maintained by the Android Open Source Project (AOSP) (Jindal & Mayank, 2012). Android operating system is considered a flexible, open source back end operating system, which gives the developers the ability to access all aspects of phone operations. The application programs are written in Java, and are executed by Dalvik virtual machine (DVM) using just-in-time compilation. Just-in-time compilers translate the generated Java bytecode to Dalvikdex-code (Kumar, 2014).

Although Android is built on open-source Linux kernel, it is not entirely open source. It is open source to some limit at user and system levels. The user (phone owner) is able to make modification at application level, but he is not able to modify elements at any other operating system level. Taking into account, that some of its applications (viz. Android Market, Google Maps, and Google Docs) and the hardware level are closed source. Accessing source code that interfaces with the device drivers (viz. camera, camcorder, and other hardware devices in the system) and boot-loaders is not allowed. Although, these access limitations in open sources violates the notion of an open platform, but are used by the cellular systems. The access limitations affect causes some security limitations on both application and system level. Some security technologies are used to protect application part from Malware, but cannot mitigate vulnerabilities at system level since it is close source (Mobile Operating System, 2013; Husted et al, 2011).

Figure 2 shows the architecture of Android platform. The platform is mainly partitioned into application layers (application, and application framework), library and run time layer, and the system layer with modified Linux kernel with low-level device drivers and power management. Binder IPC driver is added by Google as a form of protected interprocess communication. The library layer provides most of Android functionality through set of service libraries (Android specific libc (Bionic), surface manager which handle user interface (UI) windows, SGL and OpenGL ES provide 2D and 3D graphics, SSL(Secure Sockets Layer) for internet security, WebKitOpen source web-browser, and SQLite which enhances data storage) that are interfaced using Java. The Android runtime libraries hold the Dalvik (a Java derivative)Virtual Machine (DVM), and the core libraries(written in Java language, and provide most of the functions available in Android libraries)(Husted et al, 2011; Heger, 2011; Jindal & Mayank, 2012; Kumar, 2014). Application layer is built on top of application framework layer. It contains built-in applications and user applications. Any built in application can be replaced by a user application. Each application runs in its own protected user space, using its own DVM instance. The application framework provides tools (such as activity manager, content providers, resource manager, and notification manager) that could be used by all application. Activity manager manage application life cycle. Activity manager tracks the installed applicants. Content providers support

sharing data with other applications. Resource manager is responsible for managing resources. Notification manager manages notification alerts (Husted et al, 2011; Jindal & Mayank, 2012). Developers could use Java Native Interface to write libraries in native code, which could be accessed by Java interfaces (Jindal & Mayank, 2012).

iOS OPERATING SYSTEM

iPhone OS (iOS) is a mobile operating system which is derived from Mac OS X and is therefore a Unix operating system. It is introduced to the world by Apple Inc. in 2007 for iPhone, and then extended to support iPad, Apple TV, and iPod Touch. iOS is only licensed for installation on Apple hardware(Nosrati et al, 2012; Mobile Operating System, 2013). iOS developed a user interface for small screen and limited input devices. It provides multi-touch gestures (such as swipe, tap, pinch) to perform interface actions, as well as physical gestures (viz. shaking and rotating the device orientation (Mobile Operating System, 2013; Nosrati et al, 2012). The amaze thing about iOS is that it seems to be similar to the operating system released in 2007, although its features evolved rapidly making from Apple's mobile devices one of the popular devices. The new versions of iOS (iOS5 and iOS6) are easily understood by novel user, and provide powerful application development tool (SDK). Apple limited the source of application to be installed (i.e. the applications are only allowed to be installed from Apple Store; Jindal & Mayank, 2012; Nosrati et al, 2012).

The main architecture of the iOS is shown in Figure 3. On the top of the hardware, there are four layers (Core OS, Core Services, Media, and Cocoa Touch) (Nosrati et al, 2012; AppleD, 2013). The Core OS layer includes the fundamental services and low-level features (viz. system support—threads, sockets, IO, DNS, math, memory, general security services, certificates,

Figure 2. Android architecture hierarchy

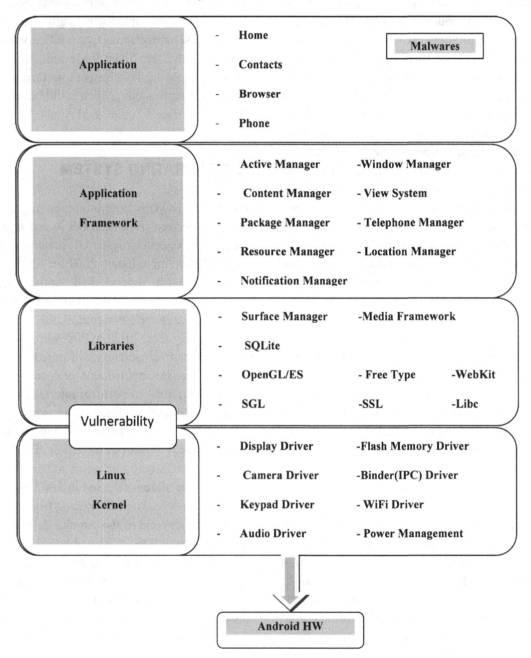

private-public keys, encryption, external hardware management, Bluetooth, and sound and image processing). It is considered the base on which other technologies are built upon. Even if these features are not directly used by the applications, they could be used by other frameworks. The framework of Core OS layer is used when we need to deal with security (explicitly), or when trying to interconnect with a hardware accessory (Mobile Operating System, 2013;AppleD, 2013). The Core Services layer provides the basic system services used by all applications (viz. accounts, contacts, networking, data management, location, iCloud, calendar events, store purchasing, XML support, SQLite used to embed lightweight SQL without running a separate DB server process, and social media). Media Layer provides technologies (such as graphics, audio, and video) which helps in constructing a very amazing multimedia applications. Finally, Cocoa Touch layer includes frameworks used to construct iOS application, multitasking, touch-base input, push notifications, interface views, and access to device data. To design any application, we should explore this layer's technologies to check if they meet all the requirements to construct the application (Mobile Operating System, 2013; AppleD, 2013; AppleG, 2009).

SECURITY ISSUES IN MOBILE COMPUTING

Smartphones has become an important part of mobile users as they provide anytime and anywhere service which is accomplished by combining mobiles with wireless network. These wireless networks are public networks, which require careful use of VPN. VPN can easily be attacked due to the huge number of interconnected networks. Mobile device capabilities are radically evolved. New applications are developed daily making these devices an integral part in people life. Smartphones help users to achieve both working tasks and personal life tasks. The increasing importance of smartphones functionality makes them more vulnerable to threats (Fedler et al, 2012; Agrawal et al, 2003). Threats could be lost devices, Web-based and network-based threats, Malware propagation, social engineering attacks, resource and service availability abuse, malicious and unintentional data loss, and attacks on the integrity of the device's data (Nachenberg, 2011; AV-Comparatives, 2013; Wang et al, 2012; La Polla et al, 2013).

- Smartphones are target for thieves or loss; security software (theft protection feature) is needed to make it difficult for thieves to access data. Theft protection features such as lock the phone with password to provide secure access control, and remote location detection which allows the owners to find their phones in case they loss it. Theft protection features are controlled either by sending command from other phone to activate some actions, or through web interface. Web interface may cause multiple device administration from one account.

- Web-based and network-based threats are launched by malicious websites. These websites will send ill-behaved payload to the attacked smartphone browser. The malicious instructions then will try to install malware on the system or steal confidential data, such as credit card numbers, passwords, etc.

- To protect smartphones from malwares, they should be scanned for malicious software using the malware protection function. Malwares signatures must be kept up-to-date.

- Social engineering attacks are accomplished by utilizing social engineering to deceive users into revealing confidential information, or persuade a user to install malware on the smartphone.

- Resource and service availability abuse the most popular abuses are sending spam emails from intermediary devices, and then use of the intermediary devices to launch denial of service attacks on either third-party websites or on the mobile carrier's data network.

- Data integrity threats the attacker attempts to modify or corrupt data without the data owner permission.

- Data loss which could be accidental or malicious. This could happen, for example, when someone synchronize his smartphone with home PC of other person, to add music or other multimedia content to

Figure 3. iOS architecture hierarchy

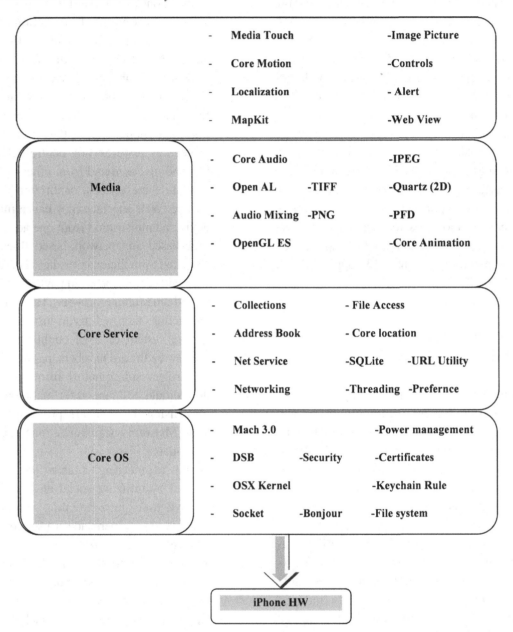

his device, the confidential data may be mistakenly backed up onto the user's home computer and become a target for hackers

To manage security on mobile smartphones, security policy is needed, authentication and encryption is required, official and/or approved application is important, secure connections (VPN, IPsec, etc.). Awareness training for naïve users is essential. Although smartphones should provide security model, but user could help in securing their phones by following some easy ways (Agrawal et al, 2003; Ernst & Young, 2012):

1. Use reliable security tools to protect your phone from malwares and Increase security. (AppleD, 2013)
2. When you want to installing software applications, choose applications from confidant sources.
3. Most smartphones provides password, screen auto-lock, location detection, activate these features to protect the phone for a period of time in case of loss or theft.
4. Try to keep sensitive data away from your smartphone since it is easy to lose your smartphone.
5. Perform regular backup, especially if there is important data on your smartphone data. Sync the smartphone with your computer and keep data backup of the smartphone.
6. When we are not using Bluetooth, Turn it off. Virus can attack smartphone through Bluetooth.
7. Pay attention to some signs that could help in suspecting attacks. For example, warm battery even the phone is not in use, cell phone lights up unexpectedly, sudden beeps or clicks during phone calls. In such cases, consult security professional.

AS mentioned before, in this chapter we will focus on Android and iOS. When considering mobile security both operating systems share few common strategies with their original operating systems. Although iOS is built on Apple OSX operating system, and Android is based on Linux they employ improved security models to make inherently secure platform instead of forcing users to depend on third parity security software(Nachenberg, 2011).The security model of iOS and Android is constructed based on(Nachenberg, 2011; Fedler et al, 2012):

- **Authentication and Access Control:** Idle-time screen locking, user ID and password, biometrics (such as voice, and fingerprint) are the most popular access control techniques that are used to protect devices.

- **Source of Application:** It is important to know the source of the application that needs to be installed. Therefore, each application should be stamped with the identity of its author which should be approved using a digital signature. This will help users to decide if they will install the application or no. Sometimes, the publisher analyzes the applications to be sure that it is secure before publishing them. This will increase the confidence of an application.

- **Data Encryption:** Data encryption is very important protect confidential data from being reveled by un-authorized person in case of device loss or theft.

- **Data Isolation:** Isolation techniques are needed to limit the application ability and prevent it from accessing sensitive data or systems on mobile device.

- **Authorization Access Control:** Authorization-based access control specify set of permissions to each application. Each application is limited to only access resources (date or system) within the permissions scope. If the applications try to perform actions out of the scope of these permissions, they will be blocked.

According to the above security pillars, could we consider iOS and Android secure platforms? This question will be discussed and answered in the next sections.

SECURITY IN ANDROID

Android is an open source mobile operating system (Google releases the source code of Android project). The major idea of considering open source is that it leads to detect faults and improves the security level platform (Fedler et al, 2012). It is a multi-processing mobile operating system, where each application runs its own process. Security between system and applications is imposed at process level by standard Linux. Authorization-access control security feature is used as permission mechanism to restrict the operation performed by a process, and URI permissions to access specific piece of data (Jindal & Mayank, 2012). Since Android is an open source, application are available to be installed, these applications are provided by different developer (in addition to Google's official "Play Store", application is provided by a third-parity marketplace). It was found that most malicious codes are disseminated by applications provided by third-parity application store. Therefore, users must install applications from trustworthy marketplace. Malware distributed through third-party stores has been designed to steal data from the host device (Agrawal et al, 2003; Jindal & Mayank, 2012).

Android's security model includes set of security actions provided by Linux kernel (system level security). These actions grant a secure mechanism for inter-process communication, user-based permissions model, process isolation, and the ability of deleting unimportant or possibly insecure segment of the kernel. In multiple system users, users are prevented from accessing each other's resources and exhausting them (Fedler et al, 2012; Nachenberg, 2011)]. The operating system platform in Android prohibits device owners from administering the device through running user land applications using permission-based sandbox (Husted et al, 2011).

Application security features are also provided by Android's security model (mandatory application sandbox). Each application has unique user ID, and run as a separate process. At the process level, Linux kernel will not allow process interaction, and also limits their access to the Android operating system. In this case, users will have permission based access control before the application is even downloaded. For file system permissions, also each application (or user) has its own files which cannot be altered or even read by another file (unless a developer explicitly exposes files to another) (Fedler et al, 2012). Applications

could, obtain list of applications installed on the device, read the user's SD flash card, launch other applications on the system (Web browser, maps, etc.). Android applications could optionally encrypt their data, If application developers did not explicitly perform data encryption, the data produced by the application is saved in an unencrypted form) (Fedler et al, 2012; Nachenberg, 2011; Jindal & Mayank, 2012).

Android's security model is majorly based on three pillars. Authentication-access control, process isolation, and permission- access control. For authentication-access control, Android provides password number of failed login attempts before the device wipes its data. Android 3.0 provides password expiration notion, administrators could force users to perform regular password updating (Nachenberg, 2011; Jindal & Mayank, 2012).

Android imply strong 'process isolation' policy, where applications are isolated from each other's, and they are prevented from accessing or altering the kernel, which a positive point (Nachenberg, 2011; Husted et al, 2011).

When considering 'permission-access control', most Android applications can do very little without user permission. The user will accept or deny application requests. This seems to be very strong policy, but the robustness of this policy will depend on the user technical ability to make such decisions (Nachenberg, 2011; Jindal & Mayank, 2012).

Threats to Android

Mobile computing is vulnerable to different form of threats (such as malwares, stolen or lost data). Most smartphones faces high malware threats. Android in particular is becomes more vulnerable to malware attacks tripled at the 2nd quarter of 2012 (as Kaspersky Labs). One of the popular malicious code is Zitmo (mobile version of Zeus malware), which steal information defeating the SMS-based banking 2-factor authorization. Another is Nickspy Trojan which is disguises as Google plus application, but actually records phone conversation on to audio file. Connecting insecure WiFi may cause steeling data, for example, Faceniff is version from Firesheep Firefox extension which perform packet sniffing to intercept unencrypted cookies (reveal user's login credentials).Android has auto-update service enabled by the user, this facility help in removing a malware infection by overwriting the infected application. This is useful unless the security of the operating system sandbox in the mobile is violated by hackers(Agrawal et al, 2003).

Android's provenance approach guarantees that only digitally signed applications could be installed on the device. But attackers can use unknown digital certificates to sign their applications (threats) and distribute them through the Internet without Google certification, which is a big problem (Nachenberg, 2011).

SECURITY IN iOS

Build a secure platform on mobile devices, regardless of user experience, is an important issue. Therefore, iOS is constructed to provide a high level of security without compromising the user capability. Apple iOS is built on layers of security, (design security at its core), which enables iPhone to protect confidential data and provide secure access to corporate services. iOS provides secure storage of application based on strong encryption for data during transmission process, which mitigate man-in-the-middle attack. Hardware encryption for data on device is mandatory (users cannot disable device encryption by mistake). iOS devices use the user passcode to generate a the encryption key which is used to protect mail and important data on the mobile. iOS also provides authentication-access–control through passcode policies. When a device is lost, users can initiate a remote wipe command to delete confidential information. At application level, iOS use sandboxed approach to protect applications during runtime. Application signing is required to

approve the applications (prevent tampering with application) (Apple, 2012; Apple, 2014). iPhone OS security APIs are placed in the Core Services layer based on services located in the kernel (Core OS layer) (Jindal & Mayank, 2012) . iOS security model is majorly base on four security pillars, authentication-access–control, process isolation (sandboxing), data encryption, and application (Nachenberg, 2011; Jindal, 2012) .

For authentication-access–control, iOS provides password configuration, and account auto-lockout option. The administrator can choose the passcode strength, determine number of failed login attempts before the device wipes itself, and specify how often the passcode should be updated (Apple, 2012; Apple, 2014).

iOS provides powerful process isolation feature, where applications are prevented from interfering each other, or accessing the operating system. This means, no applications can view or modify other application, or even find out the presence of other applications. Applications are also prevented from accessing the operating system, installing privilege drivers on the device, or obtaining root-level access to the device. Furthermore, iOS isolates applications from the phone's SMS, email in/out-boxes, and email attachments (Nachenberg, 2011; Apple, 2012; Apple, 2014).

A hybrid encryption model is employed by iOS. All data stored in the device or flash are encrypted. To mitigate the encryption process effect on the battery power, hardware-accelerated AES-256 encryption is applied. iOS also encrypt email using secondary encryption level (Apple, 2014).

The main goal of Apple's provenance approach is mitigating malware attacks. Applications developers should register with Apple to join the iOS developer program. Developers could distribute their applications using one of two publishing approaches. When using the first approach, developers who want to sell their iOS application to users must digitally sign the application with Apple-issued digital certificate. Apple's certification process takes one to two weeks. When the application is certified, it will be put for sale on the App Store. The second approach concerns corporations who wish to publish privately-developed application to their internal workforce. They should register with Apple's iOS developer enterprise program. In this case, the applicant corporation must be certified by Dun and Bradstreet, to guarantee that the established corporation has clean track record. When the corporation becomes a member of this program, enterprises could distribute the developed applications in-house using internal corporate website. Each application has to be digitally signed by the enterprise before being distributed to the internal workforce. Additionally, internally developed applications can only be used on digital certificated devices (provisioning profile should be installed on the device via the enterprise) (Apple, 2014; Nachenberg, 2011).

In addition to the four pillars mentioned above, iOS security model provides a limited permission-access-control feature. Basically, iOS's control accessing system services or data using a built-in isolation policy (explicitly allow or block). There are only four system resources that could be accessed by applications. In this case, the application will need user permission before accessing the resources. Users are asked for permission whenever an application try to access location data from the device's GPS, receive notification alerts from the Internet (used by cloud-based services to send notifications to applications on the user's iPhone), start a phone call, or send an SMS or email message.

Threats to iOS

Applications for smartphones have grown exponentially; in return, malwares that attack smartphones also grow exponentially. Although iOS marketplaces provide security checks, poorly-written applications still the main cause of data loss. A report published by Arxan (a private software security company) said that "more than 90% of top paid mobile applications have been hacked, few applications use security defenses that keep user data protected". LinkedIn application on iOS devices, for example, jeopardized user data by mistakenly enabling privileged access to calendar data, transmit passwords, meeting note, and other information (kept in calendar entries) without user knowledge (Agrawal et al, 2003; Nachenberg, 2011; Apple, 2014).

In iOS, anti-viruses may not have the ability to read programs in memory for protection purposes, which mean malicious code, will be executed (Nachenberg, 2011).

Since iOS provide high process isolation, an attacker could have control of a single process (e.g. the Safari process) but is not allowed to take administrator-level control (Nachenberg, 2011).

Overall, iOS's security model is considered to be well designed. Although iOS's encryption system is a bit power consuming, but it provides strong protection for confidential data (transmitted or stored in the device), and enables device wipe. Apple checks every publicly available application. But this checking approach is not foolproof, which means it can be avoided by a certain attackers. iOS's permission model limits the probability that application can specify the device's location, send SMS messages, or starts phone calls without the user permission. Finally, there is no centralized repository of shared data in iOS, which might cause a serious risk.

Android vs. iOS

The main deference between Android and iOS security features could be summarized in Table 1 (Ernst & Young, 2012). It is clearly seen that iOS provide security features more than Android. iOS concentrate on code signing, and securing and managing data more than Android. This makes Android more vulnerable to malware attacks.

SOLUTIONS AND RECOMMENDATIONS

Smartphones are resource-constrained devices (viz. battery life, storage, and bandwidth) with embedded sensors. They, almost always, need network connection (such as Bluetooth, Wi-Fi, etc.). These characteristics have impacts on smartphone security models.

Taking in consideration, the limited battery power, which will be consumed if all security defense lines are activated at once. As a suggestion, since cloud computing could be combined with mobile device (Mobile Cloud Computing MCC), it is recommended that most security work should be done by the cloud, leaving little security work to be done by the mobile site.

Table 1. Comparison of the security features

Features	Android	iPhone
Remote wipe capability	✓	✓
Encrypted backup files	✓	✓
Authentication	✓	✓
Virtualization	✗	✓
Corporate managed Email	✗	✓
Type safe programming	✓	~
Application sandbox	~	~
Corporate policy enforcement	~	~
Full disk and memory encryption	✗	~
End to en data encryption	✗	~
Firewall	✗	✗

✓ = Implemented, X = Not Implemented, ~ = Partially Implemented.

FUTURE RESEARCH DIRECTIONS

Security in mobile computing is a challenging task, since its security platform should handle security problems in network, operating system, devices, unsecure applications, and naive usage all together.

We are interested in Android as it is a popular open source mobile device, with a vulnerability problem. In my opinion, data loss is the main problem in Android. This problem should be handled by forcing data encryption. But as well known the available data encryption algorithm that provides robust security is expensive from time, and battery power consuming. Therefore, encrypting all data on mobile deice is not a good idea. What is needed is a separation between sensitive and insensitive data, where only sensitive data is forced to be encrypted. On the other hand, what is needed is robust data encryption algorithm which compromise between security level and the battery power consumption is needed, which must be embedded in system level to enforce sensitive data encryption.

Enterprises started to debate security issues in mobile devices, especially smartphones, which become part of their employee daily life style. Consequently, developing a robust business security model which corresponds with smartphones characteristics and satisfies enterprises security policy becomes indispensable issue.

CONCLUSION

Securing mobile computing is important to develop secure applications. But we should always remember that perfect mobile security is a dream. Every mobile Operating System tries to provide unique features for their users, and be enterprise-friendly. Since the security issues are considered essential for enterprises, the mobile devices must come up with robust security model to be enterprise-friendly. By reviewing the security models of two popular mobile operating systems (Android and iOS), it was found that iOS is considered more enterprise-friendly, since it comes with relatively secure and manageable platform. Although iOS provide data encryption feature, which has great effect on its security model, but it affect battery lifetime. On the other hand, market performance of Android is impressive, and it is an open source operating system where users develop new ideas every day. Being an open source with strong market make Android a victim to different sort of attacks. This means, Android suffers from security and manageability problems, which affect its use in enterprises. We can conclude that it is a bit early to make smartphones part of enterprise. It is difficult (even with best available mobile security model) to feel secure, when all confidential information is on mobile device.

REFERENCES

Agrawal, D. P., Deng, H., Poosarla, R., & Sanyal, S. (2003). Secure mobile computing. In Distributed Computing IWDC 2003, (LNCS 2918, 265-278).

Apple Developer. (2013). *iOS technology overview*. Retrieved March 20 2014, from https://developer.apple.com/library/ios/documentation/miscellaneous/conceptual/iphoneostechoverview/iOSTechOverview.pdf

Apple General. (2009). *iPhone OS technology overview*. Retrieved March 20 2014, from www.ithaca.edu/barr/Student/CS390/docs/iPhoneOSTechOverview.pdf

Apple Inc. (2012). *Deploying iPhone and iPad security overview*. Retrieved March 20 2014, from https://ssl.apple.com/ca/ipad/business/docs/iOS_Security_Mar12.pdf

Apple Inc. (2014). *iOS security*. Retrieved March 22 2014, from https://ssl.apple.com/ca/ipad/business/docs/iOS_Security_Mar12.pdf

AV-Comparatives. (2013). *Mobile security review*. Retrieved March 20 2014, from www.av-comparitves.org

Deepak, G., & Pradeep, B. S. (2012). Challenging issues and limitations of mobile computing. *International Journal of Computer Technology & Applications, 3*(1), 177–181.

Ernst & Young. (2012). *Mobile device security: Understanding vulnerabilities and managing risks*. Retrieved January 22 2014, from http://www.ey.com/Publication/vwLUAssets/Mobile_Device_Security/$FILE/Mobile-security-devices_AU1070.pdf

Fedler, R., Banse, C., Krauss, C., & Fusenig, V. (2012). *Android OS security: Risks and limitations a practical evaluation* (Tech. Rep.). Fraunhofer Research Institution for Applied and Integrated Security. Retrieved January 22 2014, from http://www.aisec.fraunhofer.de/content/dam/aisec/Dokumente/Publikationen/Studien_TechReports/deutsch/AISEC-TR-2012-001-Android-OS-Security.pdf</eref>

Fing, L. X., Wang, Y. W. J., Jiang, K., & Liu, B. W. (2012). Mobile operating system architecture trends. *Intel Technology Journals, 16*(4), 178–198.

Heger, D. A. (2011). *Mobile Devices: An introduction to the Android operating environment design, architecture, and performance implications*. Retrieved January 22 2014, from http://www.dhtusa.com/media/AndroidInternals.pdf

Husted, N., Saïdi, H., & Gehani, A. (2011). Smartphone security limitations: conflicting traditions. *Proceedings of the 2011 Workshop on Governance of Technology, Information, and Policies*, (pp. 5–12). *New York, NY, USA: ACM*. doi:10.1145/2076496.2076497

Jindal, G., & Mayank, J. (2012). A comparative study of mobile phone's operating systems. *International Journal of Computer Applications & Information Technology, 1*(3), 10–15.

Kumar, S. (2014). *Architecture Android development tutorial. Architecture of Android.* Retrieved March 10 2014, from http://www.androidaspect.com/2014/01/android-development-tutorial.html

La Polla, M., Martinelli, F., & Sgandurra, D. (2013). A survey on security for mobile devices. *IEEE Communications Surveys and Tutorials*, *15*(1), 446–471. doi:10.1109/SURV.2012.013012.00028

Nachenberg, C. (2011). *A window into mobile device security: Examining the security approaches employed in Apple's iOS and Google's Android.* Retrieved January 15 2014, from http://www.symantec.com/content/en/us/about/media/pdfs/symc_mobile_device_security_june2011.pdf

Nosrati, M., Karimi, R., & Hasanvand, H. (2012). Mobile computing: Principles, devices and operating Systems. *World Applied Programming Journal*, *2*(7), 399–408.

Saeedipour, R. (2013). *Computer organization and platform technologies course.* Retrieved March 10 2014, from http://people.eecs.ku.edu/~rassul/spring2014/classes/it310/misc/mobile_operating_systems.pdf

Silberschatz, A., Galvin, P., & Gagne, G. (2013). *Operating system concepts* (9th ed.). USA: John Wiley, Reading.

Wang, Y., Streff, K., & Raman, S. (2012). Security threats and analysis of security challenges in smartphones. *Computer*, *99*, 1–8.

KEY TERMS AND DEFINITIONS

Android: An open source mobile operating system which is based on Linux operating system. Android is developed by the Open Handset Alliance led by Google Inc. It is used by mobile devices such as smartphones and tablets.

iOS: A mobile operating system developed by Apple Inc., and it is exclusive for Apple devices (iPhone, iPad, etc.).

Mobile Computing: A term that refers to a set of computing operations that allows information accessing at any time, from any place, using a mobile device.

Mobile Operating System: An operating system dedicated for mobile devices. It is to manage mobile system resources and services.

Mobile Security Model: Used to manage security on mobile smartphones, where security policy should be enforced, authentication and encryption is required, approved application is mandatory, in addition to maintain secure connections (VPN, IPsec, etc.).

Mobile Threats: Mobile computing is vulnerable to different form of threats (such as malwares, stolen or lost data, etc.).

Smartphones: Small portable devices which combine computing environment and cellular environment in one device.

Chapter 20
The Security Impacts on Social Media Platforms

Mohammad Alaa Hussain Al-Hamami
Applied Science University, Bahrain

ABSTRACT

Because of its importance, social media became a main target in cyber war and for criminals as well. The attacker can gain a lot of valued information from social media. This chapter will discuss the security impacts on social media and their effects on individuals, companies, and governments. This chapter, also will explain risks of using Internet, the importance of social media for attackers, what could go wrong in social media, examples of methods used by attackers, why attackers success in their attacks, social media problems from a legal point of view, social media security environment, general security model for social media web sites, data that could be mined, points of attack, security defenses against attacks, methods of security attacks, reasons of attacking social media, social media programming flaws, social media security strategy and policy, social media privacy and governments, social media security new trends, and the best practice in social media.

INTRODUCTION

Social media refers to the use of web-based and mobile technologies to turn communication into an interactive dialogue. It is any online platform where people gather to share opinions and relate with one another (OSCE, 2013). Social media becomes a main part in our life. In the past we used different web sites and different applications for communications and exchange information such as: emails, chatting, news, entertainment, etc, but thanks to social media that make it possible to do all these activities now through using a single site.

Social media is not important only for individuals but also becomes important to companies and organization because it doesn't only provide the ability for users to communicate with each other but also enable them to find like-minded individuals "power of the masses". Social media helps in shifting power from organization to clients as the masses are able to channel and exert their influences.

Firms no longer rely on traditional media (print, radio, TV, etc.) to enforce public perception of their services and products. By harnessing social media information, organizations can use

DOI: 10.4018/978-1-4666-6583-5.ch020

Copyright © 2015, IGI Global. Copying or distributing in print or electronic forms without written permission of IGI Global is prohibited.

it to help in identifying their most influential clients, drive participation in service and product development, and improve their images (Social Networking, 2013).

Although there are many advantages of social media, but at the same time it can be a target for security threats and attacks such information leaks and also a malware attack vector. In this chapter we will explain the main security concerns in social media and the importance of social media networks for attackers and their incentive, and the best practice to use social media in a safety way.

TYPES OF SOCIAL MEDIA PLATFORMS

Social media can be categorized as the following:

- **Social Networks:** Allow users to build and maintain relationships with others. In this kind of social media, only your contacts on your private network can see your posts. Examples are Facebook and Google+.
- **Forums and Online Communities:** Social media platforms focused on a specific audience or topic. Chat rooms and online forum are examples for this type of social media.
- **Blogs:** Allows users to easily publish and share content, similar to a personal journal. Web blogs nowadays are widely used.
- **Micro Blogging:** Allows users to post short messages, typically 140 characters or less like SMS. Twitter is an example for this kind.
- **Multimedia Sharing:** Allows users to post and share multimedia content with others. Examples are YouTube for videos, for shared for different kinds of files and Instagram for images and short videos.
- **Location Services:** Allow users to share their where about with others. Although there are security concerns of using this

kind of social media regarding to privacy, but at the same time this kind is so effective for business and marketing and it could be used in works that need to be allocate like voluntary jobs. Four square is good example for this kind.
- **Bookmarks:** Allows users to share web sites of interest with others.

RISKS OF USING THE INTERNET

Although the rapid development of information technology, security attacks on the Internet and its applications are still an easy task, several reasons contribute to this issue (Peixian, 2013):

- The tools necessary to perform an attack on the Internet is fairly cheap.
- The Internet till now doesn't offer much security.
- Eavesdropping and using false identity is simple.
- Stealing data is undetectable in most cases.
- Popular PC operating systems offer little or no security against security attacks.
- User awareness for security risks is threateningly low.

The previous points are encouraging attackers to attack social media platforms and take advantages from these attacks.

THE IMPORTANCE OF SOCIAL MEDIA FOR ATTACKERS

Social media can be a source of valued and private information; they can also become a malware attack vector when they are not used in the right way. Users and companies trust their contacts for not sending bad links, not trying to infect their computers, and taking good care of their private data. The real cleverness comes from masking those bad links look good. For example a normal user will probably click on a *yahoo.com* link but might be more careful with a *virus.net* link.

URL shorteners are a main security concern and should be taken very seriously. These online redirection services hide a URL in order to make it shorter and easier. Malicious URLs don't look dangerous before clicking on them; after that click though, it is often too late.

As have been mentioned before, the necessary tools to perform an attack on the Internet is fairly cheap. The criminal only needs a computer and an Internet connection to start his attack. Also the low cost of entry to a social media platform attracts the broader criminal population and attackers because the payoff of a successful attack is unimaginable.

Attacks against social media networks are increasing rapidly and mostly every day in the news we hear about a successful attack on a social media network.

WHAT COULD GO WRONG IN SOCIAL MEDIA?

When you are using social media and you don't have much security awareness, the following things may happen to you (Sancho, 2013):

- Your account or profile is hacked and somebody else is using it.
- You added someone to your social media network that you thought you know but in fact you don't.
- You added someone to your social media network you thought was trustworthy but he or she in fact turns out not to be.
- Lake of awareness to use privacy controls and options in social media networks will lead you to share private information with people you never know.

EXAMPLES OF ATTACKING STYLES IN SOCIAL MEDIA

Criminals and attackers try to use everything that could trick users and companies to retrieve their personal information and sometimes destroy them. The following are some of the attacking styles that attackers can use (Sancho, 2013):

- Creating a fake celebrity profile or account and allowing people to add them to their network.
- Creating a duplicate profile or account and re-inviting all of their friends or followers.
- Creating a profile, adding themselves to a medium size group or community, and inviting a number of members of the group (universities, schools, etc.). Then joining a second group and starting again.
- Creating a female profile and publishing a pretty picture of her, then letting people add her to their network.

WHY DO ATTACKERS SUCCEEDED IN THEIR ATTACKS?

A lot of social media users don't realize that their network should be a circle of trust and by adding someone they do not know they're opening their data to un-trusted parties. Security is a chain and its strength depends on the weakest ring in this chain. Also some social media platforms sometimes don't have privacy controls in place, or the ones they have do not protect all users' data.

One of the problems is the user often does not obligated to select who can access his data and is often dissuaded from using the available controls because they appear too complex or time consuming. Many users simply do not bother themselves to configure these controls because of laziness or lack of knowledge. This means that whether by the social media design or the user's lack of awareness, personal data is needlessly exposed to strangers, search engines, and the wider online world.

SOCIAL MEDIA LEGAL CHALLENGES

Cybercrimes involve criminal activities that are similar in the real world such as theft, fraud, forgery, defamation and mischief. In a simple way it can be said that cyber crime is illegal actions where in the computer and network is either a tool or a target or both. The abuse of computers has also given birth to a gamut of new age crimes that are addressed by the Information Technology.

Most of the known issues in the Internet and social media as well link to the need to protect users, companies' personality and image. This includes social concepts such as reputation, false allegations, privacy, copyright, insult and discriminations of all sorts. Fundamentally, with regard to legal and awareness requirements, social media platforms should be familiar with compliance and governance mandates and security frameworks. Implementing legal rules in the Internet and Social media is a big challenge.

The following points could be considered as challenges in the Internet and social media from a legal point of view (Garrigues, 2013):

1. **Violation User's Information Protection Rights:** The inclusion by the users of personal details regarding to themselves or other users in a social media involve a risk of violation in information protection subject.
2. **Identity Fraud:** The huge amount of information related to a user in social media represents a threat to his safety and privacy by considering the possibility of unauthorized usage of information to steal the user identity.
3. **Absence of Unified Rules at the International Level:** Absence of international standard regulation to use the social media can only increase the lack of security for the users.

THE SOCIAL MEDIA SECURITY ENVIRONMENT

Figure 1 shows the Social Media Security Environment which consists of the following:

- **Data:** The raw material for social media. It's the information in raw or unorganized form such as alphabets, numbers, or symbols that refer to or represent conditions, ideas, or objects.

Figure 1. Social Media Security Environment (University, 2013).

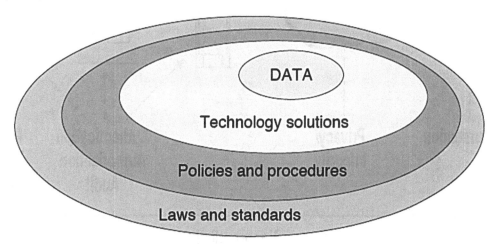

- **Technology Solutions:** It's the broad range of information technology services, such as hardware, software, networking, programming, website design, consulting, project management, and a full range of technology to meet any needs.
- **Policies and Procedures:** A policy is a statement of purpose implemented by procedures. Procedures are how a policy is implemented. Procedures have to be compatible with the organizations goals, policies, legal and environmental regulations.
- **Laws and Standards:** Laws are a system of rules and guidelines which are enforced through social organizations to govern behavior. Standards are documents that provide requirements, specifications, guidelines or characteristics that can be used

to ensure that materials, products, procedures, processes and services are appropriate for their purpose.

GENERAL SECURITY MODEL FOR SOCIAL MEDIA WEB SITES

The general security model for the social media web site is shown in Figure 2.

- **Authentication:** The ability to identify the identity of a person or entity with whom you are dealing in social media.
- **Confidentiality:** The ability to ensure that messages and data are available only to those who are authorized to view them in social media.

Figure 2. The general security model
(Turban & et al, 2006).

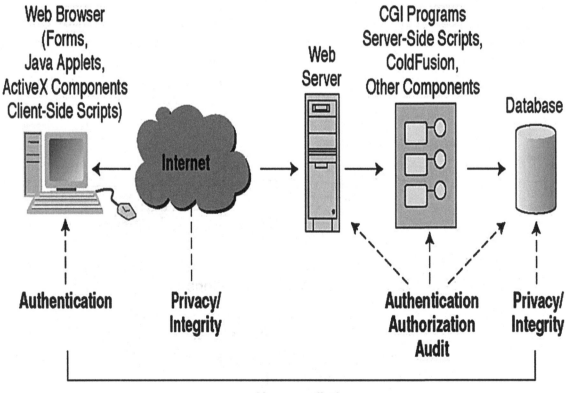

- **Privacy:** The ability to control the use of information in social media about oneself.
- **Integrity:** The ability to ensure that information being displayed on a social media, transmitted or received over the Internet has not been altered in anyway by an unauthorized party.
- **Availability:** The ability to ensure that a social media continues to function as intended.
- **Non-Repudiation:** The ability to ensure that social media participants do not deny (i.e. repudiate) their online actions.

DATA THAT COULD BE MINED IN SOCIAL MEDIA

Social media contains a wealth of information. This information is a treasure for attackers and criminals. Underground forums in the dark corners of the internet always try to mine and collect personal information to sell them to attackers and criminals. Any attack will be more effective by having additional information about the target victim and having the needed information about a person or a company can give attackers and Criminals ideas to perform valued attacks.

The following list contains types of data that could be mind:

1. **User Identifiers and Attributes:** Such as account ID, user name, academic title, academic degree, sex -gender, birth maiden name, relationship status, birthday, sign of the zodiac, hometown, country, time zone, political views, or religious views.
2. **Contact Information:** Such as address, city, zip, country, website, email, mobile phone, land phone, fax, Skype ID, ICQ ID, AIM ID, Yahoo ID, Windows Live ID, or Google Talk ID.

3. **Work:** Such as status, employer, position - title, company website, address, city, zip code, state, country, industry, description, wants, haves, time period from, time period to, or business organization.
4. **Education:** College - university, class year, attended for, degree, college - graduate school, concentration, second concentration, third concentration, degree, high school, or class year.
5. **Personal Information and Interests:** Such as activities, interests, hobbies, favorite music, favorite TV show, favorite movies, favorite books, favorite quotes, about me, pictures, uploaded pictures, picture tags, audio, uploaded audio, audio tags, video, upload videos, or video tags.
6. **Location, Connection, and Usage Information:** Such as location, contacts, number of contacts, messages, number of messages, events, number of events, gust book entries, number of gust book entries, online status, login time, usage, IP address, network, operating system, browser screen size, or language.

POINTS OF ATTACKS IN SOCIAL MEDIA

There are many points of attacks in social media available for attackers. Figure 3 shows these attack points.

The following resources can be used by an attacker in social media:

- **User:** The attacker tries to attack social media user using different kinds of attacks such as social engineering.
- **Workstation**: Workstation is the device that could be used by a user such as PC's, laptops and mobiles to deal withsocial media web sites. The attacker may scan workstation to attempt his attack.

Figure 3. Attack points
(e-Commerce, 2013).

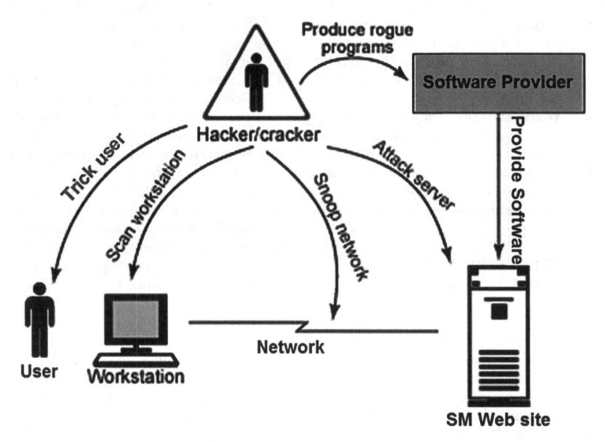

- **Network:** the network is the most point that interact attackers because it's hard to secure it. The network can be eavesdropping by the attacker.
- **Social Media Web Site:** Social media web site can be violated by attacking the server that is hosting the web site.
- **Software:** Software that is used to build the social media web site can be attacked by malicious software such as viruses, Trojan horse, applets and scripts.

SECURITY DEFENSES AGAINST ATTACKS

The security defenses procedures against attacks are shown in Figure 4.

- **User:** Education is the best method to protect the user from been tricked by the attacker.
- **Workstation:** Personal firewall like internet security software is a solution to protect workstation from attackers.

Figure 4. The security defenses
(Developer, 2013).

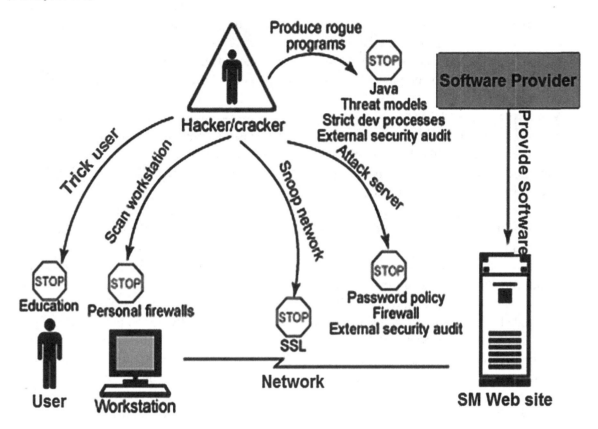

- **Network:** Using Secure Socket Layer (SSL) and encryption is the best method to protect the transmitting data in the network.
- **Social Media Web Site:** Using password policy, firewall, and external security audit will protect the social media web site.
- **Software:** Java treat models, accurate development processes, and external security audit will protect software from being harmed.

KINDS OF ATTACKS IN SOCIAL MEDIA

There are varieties of methods to be used by attackers in social media. Some of these methods are the following (Developer, 2013; Information, 2013; Social Network, 2013):

- **Hacking:** Hacking in is an illegal log in process into a computer system or a network or both. Many hackers like to leave their prints such as a message or a photo on the hacked system. Social media platforms are a main target for hackers because they got a lot of attention in press coverage. The other kind of hackers called crackers are more dangerous and malicious because they aim to damage computer systems, steal or destroy information and pull down web sites.
- **Viruses:** Viruses are programs designed to replicates themselves and infect computer systems according to a specific event or action. Viruses cause different level of damages such as displaying a message when using a keyboard, deleting files, or affecting system performance.

- **Trojan Horse Programs:** Trojan horses are programs that appear to be useful software but in fact they are not. Trojans can cause a lot damages such as deleting information, copying themselves to e-mail address lists and open up computers to additional attacks, etc.

- **Vandals:** Social media and web sites have come alive through the development of such software applications like ActiveX and Java Applets. A vandal is a software application or an applet that causes damages in different levels. These applications can be a main source of attacks. Vandals may destroy files or damage computer systems.

- **Reconnaissance Attacks:** Reconnaissance Attacks are unauthorized information gathering process done by attackers to collect the needed information that is used to compromise social media. Software tools like sniffers and scanners are used to locate the resources and trying to discover weaknesses in networks, hosts, and systems.

- **Access or Denial of Service Attacks:** This kind of attacks attempt to attack networks in different areas such as authentication services and File Transfer Protocol (FTP) functionality to gain different information from e-mail accounts, databases. DoS attacks can prevent access to a part of or all of social media resources. This kind of attacks done by sending large amounts of unmanageable data to a machine that is connected to a network to block traffic from getting through.

- **Data Interception:** This kind of attacks eavesdrops on the transmitted information or even trying to alter the data that are being transmitted in the network.

- **Cyber Terrorism:** This kind of attacks are evolving and include the terrorist attacks on the Internet and social media like denial of service attacks, shouting down websites, hating social media accounts and e-mails etc.

- **Software Piracy:** The illegal copying process of programs or distribute software products without getting permission from their owners.

- **Social Engineering:** Social engineering is the act of obtaining private information through non-technical means like communicating with social media users using false identities to gathering passwords or personal information.

- **Cyber-Bullying:** Cyber-Bullying is bullying that takes place using electronic technology and the Internet. Electronic technology includes devices and equipment such as cell phones, computers, and tablets as well as communication tools including social media sites, text messages, chat, and websites. Examples of cyber-bullying include mean text messages, rumors sent by email or posted on social media web sites, and embarrassing pictures, videos, websites, or fake profiles.

- **Sexual Attacks:** This kind of attacks uses social media to share forbidden content and to induct victims. In some cases the attackers don't use their real identity to fool their victims.

- **Child Pornography:** Social media are being highly used by abusers to reach and abuse children sexually worldwide. Pedophiles use fake identity to trick children and teenagers to extract personal information from them. Attackers may send pornographic text or images and trying to convince the victim that is normal and that everybody are doing it. The danger of this attack is pedophile may try to meet the child or the teenager in the real world to attempt his attack.

- **Spam:** Spam is referring to the unwanted e-mails like advertising messages. Spam is usually can be annoyance because it cost time and storage space.

- **Rogue Applications:** Most social media platforms allowed adding or installing third-party applications such as games or Profile Viewer Apps. These applications may have full access to user accounts and personal information. A rogue application is built by an attacker to fraud and cheat social media users. This kind of software look indecent but in fact they do harmful actions like obtaining users information and spread spam's etc.

- **Physical Attacks:** This kind of attacks cased physical harm or damage to social media users or to their property such as stealing, stalking, blackmailing, and any other physical damages. Because the nature of social media, users could be at risk of such attacks.

REASONS OF ATTACKING SOCIAL MEDIA

Using the previous kinds of security attacks, the attacker can gain the following advantages from the attack success (Sancho, 2013):

- **Advertise:** Spamming people by commenting on their accounts, sending e-mails, sending web site links and products.

- **Collect Contact Information:** Gain information like e-mail addresses and telephone numbers. Social media networks that displays contact information can serve different kinds of attacks like spamming and fraud.

- **Phishing and/or Malware Installation:** Attackers can build phishing pages identical to a social medialogin pages to trick users. The user will enter his user name and password to log in, in this way the attacker will have the victim's username and password, and the attack maybe does not stop at this point. One of the scenarios is

after logging in, the fake page will run executable file that take advantage of browser and install a Trojan horse software. An example for this scenario a malware known as "KOOBFACE" that have been successful spreading on a number of social media networks.

SOCIAL MEDIA PROGRAMMING FLAWS

Social media can have errors and programming flaws that could compromise their security measures. This had been happened to famous social media platforms and could happen again in the future. Poor security, weak administration, and bad programming can all help attackers to collect user information and help them to stage a bigger attack against any number of users (Sancho, 2013).

Facebook suffered from security flaws that allow, anyone to access the basic information of any user whatever the security settings were. This attack has been created by casual users after Facebook ignored the users' warnings for days (Kaplan, 2013).

Twitter had cross-site scripting attacks performed against it. The attackers could change the status of any user who accesses the attacker's account. This will allow the attacker to make users tweet bad links so their followers will in danger (Jennings, 2013).

My Space had been attacked in 2007 by a JavaScript that copy itself to the viewer's profile with a message "Sami is my hero." This was caused by a security flaw that could make the victim run any command like redirecting the page to a malicious website (Mook, 2013).

These three examples are not the only cases of security flaws on social media networks. In fact, such flaws are identified frequently.

Social media platforms keep developing their security features and enhancing their existing ones. But like any development process, they are also continued to update their platforms and add new options. The new options should keep up with the security features or they will suffer from security weaknesses.

SOCIAL MEDIA SECURITY STRATEGY AND POLICY

Social media platforms should use security Strategy and policy. The implemented strategy and policy should control the access to the social media and prevent unauthorized users from entering restricted areas.

Passwords usually used to prevent users from entering the restricted areas, but this will be active only if the passwords remain private. Social media users must be regulated by the policies as well.

Policies will be useless if all of the involved parties do not know and understand them. It is necessary to have effective mechanisms to deal with the existing policies, policy changes; (Security Aspects, 2013).

The following are some basic rules for companies, users, and passwords in social media:

Basic Rules for Companies

- Use external security experts (ethical hackers) to evaluate the security of the company accounts and profiles in social media.
- Standards, such as the Federal Information Processing Standard (FIPS), describe guidelines for implementing features like password policies.
- Centralize your social media channels. Centralize control and publishing of accounts in a single tool that you can secure and protect.
- Determine who is authorized to post in your social media accounts. Use a strategy to clarify who has the permission to deal with thousands or millions of your followers.

- Social media education is essential. Be sure that whoever communicates through social media has some basic training on how to deal with it in a good manner.

Basic Rules for Users

- Be logical when you choose your passwords, easy passwords could be detect and cracked. For example passwords like "love me" or "123456" will be predicted get and cracked easily.
- Be careful when you deal with links that you receive from your friends. Treat links in messages on social media as you would links in e-mail messages.
- Be aware about what you have posted about yourself. Hackers may hack accounts by clicking the "Forgot your password?" link in the login page. To hack your account, attackers try to search for the answers of your security questions, such as your birthday date, home town, etc. Make up your own password questions if the social media network allows that, and don't make them easy to be found by a quick search.
- Don't trust that a message is really from who it says it's from. Attackers can send messages that look like they're from your friends, but in fact they aren't. If you suspect that a message is fraudulent, use an alternate method to contact your friend to find out.
- Do not allow social media to use your e-mail address book. When you join a new social media network, most of times you will receive an offer to enter your e-mail address and password to find out if your contacts are already in the network. This information might be used to send e-mail messages to anyone in your contact list or even anyone you've sent an e-mail message. Social media platforms should explain that they're going to do that, but most of them do not.

- Type URL address of the social media web site directly into the browser or use bookmarks. If you click a link to a social media network through e-mail or another website, you might be entering your account name and password into a fake page where your personal information could be stolen.
- Be wise about who you are accepting as a friend in social media. Attackers might create fake profiles in order to steal your information.
- Choose your social media carefully. Evaluate the social media network that you are planning to join and make sure you will read and understand the privacy policy. Find out if it will scan and use the content without informing users.
- You should know that everything you post in the social media is permanent. Even if you can delete your account, anyone on the Internet can easily print photos or text or save images and videos to a computer and search engines could find your information even after you delete your profile.
- Be careful about installing application in social media. Many social media platforms allow you to use third party applications that you could use them in different ways. Attackers sometimes use these applications to steal your information and even to hack your account.
- Think twice before you use social media at work. Find out if your company has a policy about using social media through your company network. When you sign up for a social media network, you should use your private e-mail address, not your company e-mail address.
- Aware your kids about how to use social media in a safety way. Let your kids be aware about the danger of social media and how to use it in a safety way.

Some Rules for Passwords

- Don't use the same passwords for a long time, change passwords regularly.
- Make passwords as meaningless as possible.
- Never disclose passwords to anyone.
- Use biometrics such as fingerprints, eye prints, or voice prints.

SOCIAL MEDIA PRIVACY AND GOVERNMENTS

Social media networks are important not just because they became the main communication channel in these days, but they are also important because they contain huge and wealth information that belong to individuals, organizations and governments.

Every social media network has a privacy policy, when a user tries to create an account in the network the privacy policy will be as a contract between the user and the network. This contract provides for the items illustrate the social network commitment to protecting user's data and comply with what is stipulated and agreed between the parties. The user must agree to those items before creating and configuring his account.

In this age, virtual world become important as the real world. Governments are trying to protect themselves in the both worlds, especially since the threats coming from the virtual world has become outweigh the threats that could be exposed in the real world. So governments became clearly press the social media networks to get some data of their users, and in some cases governments may use judicial orders to get these data.

The government requests for the data of its citizens may be acceptable and legal, especially if the request is accompanied by a court order is not inconsistent with the privacy policy that belong to the network, and this what social networks such as Twitter, Facebook and Google tries to justify over transparency reports, especially if these requests related to the orders of criminal jurisdiction or terrorism related issues.

But the topic remains much more complicated, as governments may request data in some cases for users are not citizens of those governments. In addition, a lot of other issues need to be solved, clarified, and considered in the following points:

- There is a real need for a unified international legal text to protect user data privacy and also to protect governments as well.
- The request for a user data should not conflict with the privacy policy of the network.
- Access to data belongs to a citizen without taking permission from the state to which he/she belongs by other states is violation of sovereignty.
- How to trust requests and do not mind as a kind of spyware? It can be assumed that some governments may fabricate the court orders or even sometimes using court orders that does not exist for the purpose of spyware. It has already been revealed espionage operations carried out by some governments relating to Internet users, and without judicial orders or any direct charges! PRISM (Wikipedia, 2013) is the recurrent example for this issue.
- If personal information has been disclosed to a particular destination and proved the innocence of the information owner how it will be compensated for the violation that took place mainly can compensation?
- Is there a guarantee the information that is obtained by a specific request will not be used in other business not related to the original request?

SOCIAL MEDIA SECURITY NEW TRENDS

Social media had been considered as a revolution not only in the IT filed but it had also changed the life style of human. The massive development and the international adoption of social media networks will make them an effective weapon for individuals, organizations and even countries. This will bring security threats and attract attackers with different Motives to keep attacking social media platforms. Security systems must develop their methods to stand against attacks, and this is not an easy task. The following are predictions on future security trends of social media networks (Security Aspects, 2013):

Social Media Terrorism

Social media networks help terrorists to get new members and it's the perfect place to meet with each other and discuss their plans. It's easy to build groups and communities and how to start terrorist cells, so that they no longer need to travel to the target to carry out reconnaissance. Micro blogging Social media like Twitter could be used as an effective communication tool for communicating and coordinating terrorist attacks in real time.

Terrorists are widely starts using social media platforms in their activities. Terrorists also could use social media as online training camps to evade detection and avoid prosecution.

Social Media Forensics

Security systems will need to develop their tools and processes to detect and investigate criminal activities on social media and ensure the protection of information and collect all the needed evidence. Information discovery demands the ability to search for information as soon as a user creates or posts it.

Social media forensic framework must focus on the analysis of an online user (profile or account) and its activities. It will have to include the investigation of the suspect or victim relationships and social media communities, the usage pattern on social media networks, uncovering past relationships and forensic analysis of social media applications.

Take More Advantage of Social Media Add-On Applications

Most social media platforms allow installing and using applications that bring third party tools and games. Rogue applications become a main tool for attackers because they are popular and also they are easy to create and implement. Applications could be used as a spyware or viruses to attack social media users.

Also the motivations for attackers to use such applications are till now social media don't use effective security models to scan and detect malicious applications.

Social Media Attacks Using Semantic Web

Social media networks identify friends or followers based on existing relationships or common interests in a group or community. An attacker could use such characteristics to get huge information from social media. Malicious software built with support from Semantic Web attributes would be able to easily identify users' connections and quickly spread across social graphs.

BEST PRACTICE

To use social media in a safety way, we should consider the following points (Johnson, 2012; Tips, 2013):

1. Education is the most important thing. Users should educate themselves to use social media in a safety way and to know about the security threats, users also should read the privacy policy of social media platforms. This kind of education requires a collaborative knowledge of technology and its applicability in social media.

2. Upgrade your operating systems with the latest patches to avoid the exploitation of vulnerabilities in various components of installed software.

3. Use antivirus and/or internet security software for your computer system and keep them up to date.

4. Choose the right security options for your internet browser. Users also should secure their browsers by installing appropriate filters such as No Script in Mozilla, to defeat the malicious scripts when rendered in browsers.

5. Choose the right configuration for your account in social media. Users should configure their profiles by applying the appropriate restrictions provided by standard social media platforms to protect privacy.

6. Publish only the information that you are comfortable with, depending on what you want to accomplish. For example publish your age but not your exact birthday. To meet your high school friends, publish your year of graduation not your date of birth.

7. Don't click unknown or suspicious hyperlinks. Users should try to investigate the origin of hyperlinks on social media to avoid traps.

8. If you are going to use the social media to meet new people and therefore plan to add unknown persons, set up a special account with a special e-mail address and minimize the amount of personal information you share. Use sense of humor to add only people that look trusty to your contact list.

9. Users should report suspicious messages and e-mails directly to the security teams of social media platforms. This will help social media platforms to apply filters on their infrastructure.

CONCLUSION

We should admit that the Internet and its applications become the most important technology for individuals and organizations, and we all agree that social media become a main part in our Business and life style. But at the same time, because of the Internet importance and its applications such as social media web sites and platforms, they became a main target for attackers, and without the needed security social media will die because it will be useless.

There is a real war in the cyber world; this war is between countries, business organizations, and even between good and bad guys. Although social media platforms update their security features regularly, they are still can't face the tremendous kinds of attacks. Every day we hear about hundreds of new attacks and hacking accidents. In other words attackers somehow become smarter and more creative than the security defenses systems, so why is that?

The main reason for successful attacks on Internet web sites and social media networks from my point of view is that attackers do not work according to standards to perform their attack, they are keeping developing their methods and they are adapting their techniques with the technological environment, so they have the flexibility to enhance their attacks. On the other hand security systems including security measures, security services and techniques are still working according to standards, these standards are enforced by governments to keep security and encryption under control, and this is limiting the security defenses systems flexibility to develop and enhance their methods against attacks. Security needs a new re-thinking and new philosophy to stand against attacks. And working according to standards is not useful anymore.

The other reasons for successful attacks on web sites and social media networks are:

1. The Internet is evolving in a fast manner but it doesn't offer much security measures. If we compare the importance of the Internet with its security features we can say only one word, "weak!".
2. Many users and social media platforms view strong security as an impediment to efficient and user-friendly operation of use.
3. Starting a security attack using the Internet is so easy and fairly cheap, the attacker only needs a computational device and an Internet connection to start an attack, and the attacker could get a lot of advantages with a successful attack.
4. Popular operating systems for clients and servers still offer little or no security at all against viruses or other malicious software.
5. Web sites and social media networks have been made by humans and they can have security flaws and errors that could compromise their security measures.
6. Although social media networks keep adding more security options and refining existing ones, but at the same time they are also continue to innovate on their platforms and add exciting new features. These new features need to be aligned with the security options or they will too suffer from security weaknesses.
7. Weak administration and controlling can help attackers to hack accounts, steal user's information, or help attackers to stage bigger attacks.
8. Some social media platforms don't have enough privacy controls, or the ones they have do not protect all user information.
9. Business organizations should use strong security policies. These policies should be clear for the employees and the customers

as well because these policies essentially useless if all of the involved parties do not know and understand them.

10. Eavesdropping and acting under false identity in social mediais very simple and stealing information is undetectable in most cases.

11. User awareness for security risks is threateningly low. The user also don't use the available security controls because they appear too complex or time consuming.

12. The user doesn't choose appropriate passwords nor use passwords rules and policies such as changing passwords regularly, making passwords as meaningless as possible.

RECOMMENDATIONS

Security is a war between two sides, a side that want to protect information and the other side who want to take advantage by attacking this information. Social media platforms are a treasure for attackers because of the huge amount of information that been store inside them and also because they become a main communication tool, so hacking an important account is also attractive for attackers.

The following recommendations could be used to enhance social media networks security:

1. Using biometric measures like finger prints or Cornea is a perfect way to identify users, especially the devices that are used to connect with social media have the capabilities to deal with biometric.

2. Use multi-level security not just relaying on username and passwords, mixing more than one security technique in the login process will be a great choice. Most of the hacking attacks are successful because of using weak passwords.

3. Tracking the usage pattern of accounts on social media is a good way to be sure the user account didn't been hacked, any user

has a pattern of using social media and if a big change happen in this pattern that will be suspicious.

4. Using public key encryption in the verification process will make social media much secured.

5. Social media platforms should use strong encryption algorithms to protect users' data.

6. Social media platforms should try to invest the MAC address for devices that are used for dealing with social media in their security measures.

7. Social media should use dummy servers (honey pot) for the online transactions and store the important information in protected servers that is hard for attackers to reach.

REFERENCES

de Paula, A. M. G. (2013). Security Aspects and Future Trends of Social Networks. Retrieved from http://www.ijofcs.org/V05N1-PP07-SECURITY-SOCIAL-NETS.pdf

Festoon Media. (2013). *Social Networking: Why Use it for Your Business?* Retrieved April 22, 2013, from http://www.festoonmedia.com/whitepapers/images/Social_Networking.pdf

Granda, P. A. L., Mouriz, N. S., & Ruiloba, S. C. M. (2013). Legal problems of social networks. Retrieved January 15, 2013, from http://www.w3.org/2008/09/msnws/papers/NETWORKS_LEGAL_PROBLEMS.PDF

Jennings, R. (2009). Twitter reels from Mikeyy's XSS 'sploits. Retrieved June 18, 2013, from http://blogs.computerworld.com/twitter_stalk-daily_mikeyy_xss_worm

Johnson, D. (2013). *How to protect your company's social media.* Retrieved March 26, 2013, from http://www.cbsnews.com/8301-505143_162-57576041/how-to-protect-your-companys-social-media/

Kaplan, D. (2009). *Facebook bloggers reveal way to peek at private profiles*. Retrieved March 20, 2013, from http://www.scmagazineus.com/Facebook-bloggers-reveal-way-to-peek-at-private-profiles/article/138867/

Khusial, D., & McKegney, R. (2013). e-Commerce security: Attacks and preventive strategies. Retrieved March 2, 2013, from http://www.ibm.com/developerworks/library/co-0504_mckegney/index.html

Microsoft. (2013). *11 Tips for social networking safety*. Retrieved July 10, 2013, from http://www.microsoft.com/security/online-privacy/social-networking.aspx

Mook, N. (2006). *Cross-Site Scripting Worm Hits MySpace*. Retrieved May 20, 2013, from http://www.betanews.com/article/CrossSite-Scripting-Worm-Hits-MySpace/1129232391

OSCE. (2013). *2013 Social Media Guidebook*. Retrieved April 20, 2013, from http://www.osce.org/fom/99563

Peixian, L. (2013). Issues of Security and Privacy in Electronic Commerce. Retrieved February 15, 2013, from http://www.cs.virginia.edu/~pl9a/resume/ECommerce.doc

Sancho, D. (2013). *Security Guide to Social Networks*. Retrieved March 11, 2013, from http://www.trendmicro.com/cloud-content/us/pdfs/security-intelligence/white-papers/wp_security_guide_to_social_networks.pdf

Turban, E., King, D., & Viehland, D. (2006). Electronic Commerce: A Managerial Perspective (4th ed.). USA: Prentice Hall.

University of Michigan-Flint. (2013). *E-Business Transactions and Security*. Retrieved September 21, 2013, from http://www.umflint.edu/~weli/courses/mgt581/note/transaction.html

University of North Texas Information and Learning Technologies Center. (2013). Common Security Risks. Retrieved May 10, 2013, from http://www.cob.unt.edu/ciltc/securityrisks.php

Wang, E. (2013). Social network security: A brief overview of risks and solutions. Retrieved April 14, 2013, from http://www1.cse.wustl.edu/~jain/cse571-09/ftp/social.pdf

Wikipedia. (2013). *PRISM (surveillance program)*. Retrieved September 28, 2013, from http://en.wikipedia.org/wiki/PRISM_(surveillance_program)

KEY TERMS AND DEFINITIONS

Cybercrimes: Illegal actions wherein the computer and network is either a tool or a target or both.

Information Privacy: The ability to control the use of information in social media about oneself.

Location, Connection, and Usage Information: Such as location, contacts, number of contacts, messages, number of messages, events, number of events, gust book entries, number of gust book entries, online status, login time, usage, IP address, network, operating system, browser screen size, or language.

Multimedia Sharing: Allows users to post and share multimedia content with others. Examples are YouTube for videos, 4shared for different kinds of files and Instagram for images and short videos.

Security Attacks: Any action that compromises the security of information owned by an organization.

Social Engineering: The act of obtaining private information through non-technical means.

Vandal: A software application or an applet that causes damages in different levels.

Chapter 21
Security in Digital Images:
From Information Hiding Perspective

Mohammed A. Otair
Amman Arab University, Jordan

ABSTRACT

Due to the swift growth of the using of the digital multimedia in the internet these days, the security in digital images has become a very important issue. Lately, significant attentions are given by many researchers in the field of the security for digital images, and several image encryption techniques have been developed to improve the security levels of these images. Different techniques can be applied to protect intellectual property rights for digital images and prohibit illegal copying. The aim of this chapter is to introduce the most important techniques that have been developed to implement the security in digital images such as digital watermarking and image steganography.

INTRODUCTION

Image processing can be defined as "the manipulation of an image for the purpose of either extracting information from the image or producing an alternative representation of the image" (Rafael & Richard, 2002). Image processing has several stimuli that may be categorized into the following:

- To implement the security levels to face attacks versus the images such as: copyright violations or image integrity.
- To eliminate undesirable components those are distorting the image or to improve the pictorial information in order to be interpreted by human.

- To elicit useful description and representation by showing the images in a more evident shape.

Digital images have been lately implemented in many several fields and disciplines. However, with some types of computer programs, those images and its data can be duplicated or modified easily. If these duplications or modifications are illegal, then they will make us questionable when considering the digital images as proof in a legal issue. The differentiations between digital images and the nature of texts, the traditional textual security techniques are not adequate to be implemented on the digital images for two major causes (Alireza & Woo, 2011):

DOI: 10.4018/978-1-4666-6583-5.ch021

Copyright © 2015, IGI Global. Copying or distributing in print or electronic forms without written permission of IGI Global is prohibited.

- The size of text format is mainly much smaller than image. Thus, to secure and encrypt the data of image, the traditional techniques of cryptosystems require much time to be implemented.
- When the text is decrypted, then the resulted text must be matched with the original text. However, this issue and rule is not necessary to be always true with the images.

With the growing use of multimedia applications such as image processing applications, the security has espoused a significant manner on the storage of images and communication. In the literature of the security of multimedia information system, there is no comprehensive or thorough review for two causes (Shiguo et al., 2009):

- The variety and intricacy of security issues and the congruous protection in the multimedia information system could be varied.
- The nature of multimedia systems is emerging continually, which fetch emerging security threats and their solutions continually as well.

The sharing of digital data became easier than ever because propagation and existence of: computer networks, storage tools, and imaging devices. Such type of sharing data; however, the questions on "how sensitive information can be protected?" have increasingly needed to be answered. For instance, when the user of digital camera in the mobile-phone needs to enhance and improve his private picture with one of the online image processing applications. The user who owns the picture concerns the privacy of his picture. At the other side, the online application (image processing website) concerns the issues of the protection by improvement the technologies against any attacks. The goals of image security are mainly found to ensure the following issues:

1. The originality of the image, and proprietorship of the creator or the sender of the image.
2. The safety of the data image, by ensuring that the image had not been changed.
3. Privacy, by protecting the proprietorship and content of the data.

Recently, digital media protection will be a mandatory issue with the growing of distributed multimedia systems. This is specifically significant for the protection and implementation of some types of intellectual rights such as copyright. The protection of copyright includes the authorization of image proprietorship, and it may include the recognition of unauthorized or illegal copies of a digital image. In order to prohibit the unauthorized or illegal distribution or copying the digital media like images, many number techniques were needed. In the case of placing the digital images on the internet imposes them at danger of steal and replacement especially when no protection techniques were used.

One of the most important techniques which enforce such sensitive data, images and copyrights is an image watermarking (Chang et al., 2002 ; Ruanaidh et al., 1996 ; Shih & Wu, 2005). Another science or technique to do the same task is cryptography by securing data which dismantles it using some encryption algorithms (Highland, 1997; William, 2003). Steganography is developing and a very robust technique for securing data because it does not provide evidence to doubtful. It can be defined as "an art and science of hiding data in other innocuous medium" (Artz, 2002 ; Wang & Wang, 2004 ; Altaay et al, 2012).

Three mandatory characteristics must me imposed by security of images, as mentioned in (Fridrich et al, 2002):

- **Confidentiality:** The images will be used and accessed by only the authorized persons.
- **Reliability:** Can be taken from two perspectives:

Figure 1. The overall disciplines of information hiding (Chaddad et al, 2010).

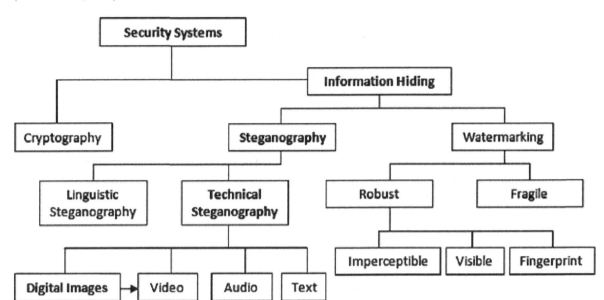

- ○ **Integrity:** An unauthorized person will never alter the image;
- ○ **Authentication:** It can be examined if the image belongs exactly to the right and authorized source or person.
- **Availability:** An image should be able to be accessed and exercised by the authorized persons in the normal situations within reasonable time.

Background

This chapter provides an analysis and criticizes the various current techniques under the two main information hiding techniques: watermarking and steganography. Different popular criteria and guidelines depicted from the literature. Figure 1 shows the most techniques, types, and classifications that will be discussed in this chapter.

This chapter swivels about the watermarking and steganography in digital images and does not introduce of steganography such as: linguistic, audio, video. Additionally, cryptography will not present because its carrier and the secret data are

a text based, with some minor extensions to the digital images. So, it is beyond the field of this chapter.

Digital Watermarking

In order to protect digital images, concealed confirmation notes and copyright comments can be added by the technique of digital watermarking (Rafael & Richard, 2002; Cox et al, 2002). In image watermarking, information in images can be embedded based on some characteristics of the images such as the redundancy of the images and the perceptual feature of human. Because of the low vulnerability of the human visibility to slight modifications and the elevated resilience of digital images, a very few number of persons can percept these slightly added modifications.

It is very important to embed hidden information within an image to make sure that the protection of the copyright is achieved. Only entitled person with the protection of the copyright can access this information of the image. The best method to do this is to put the information of

Figure 2. General image watermarking procedure

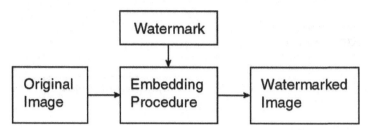

copyright into the image by intelligently adjusting the chrominance and luminance values of the specific pixels. Keeping the watermark secret and its location could provide an additional protection. If this information found by an unauthorized person, then he will never understand its meaning.

To protect the digital images, many techniques are found such as: authentication, encryption can be utilized along with the image. Figure 2 depicts the procedure of general embedding watermarking technique.

The optimal characteristics of a digital watermark have been mentioned in many papers (Cox et al, 1997; Swanson et al, 1996 ; Pitas, 1996). These characteristics involve:

1. To prohibit retardation of the original image, a watermark should be not noticed by humans.
2. A watermark should not be statistically discovered or eliminated.
3. The extraction process of watermark should be short and simple. At the other side, the detection process should be time consuming.
4. The detection process of watermark should be very precise. In other words, minimize the possibility of false positives (detecting spurious watermark) and minimize the possibility of false negatives (missing real watermark).
5. Several watermarks can be generated, in order to mark too many number of images.
6. Watermarks should be arduous to several types image processing such as: compression, additive noise, and filtering.

7. The right proprietor of the image should be determined by the watermark.

Several watermarking techniques as in (Berghel & O'Gorman, 1996; Cox et al, 1995; Macq & Quisquater, 1995) have to recognize a perfect differentiation via many watermarking characteristics such as: the computational cost, robustness and quality.

Watermarking and steganography are very similar from different perspectives. Both of them require to entrenched information within a cover message with slight to no devolution of the object. However; watermarking -in order to achieve a robustness characteristic- needs a further requirement. An optimal steganographic system would entrench a huge magnitude of information, quite securely without noticeable devolution to the object. However; at the other side, an optimal watermarking system would entrench a magnitude of information. This added information should not be changed or eliminated without producing the object quite unusable.

Digital Image Watermarking Classification

Most of the significant classifications of watermarking based on several watermarks (Petitcolas et al, 1999) are given as follow:

1. **Visible Watermarks** When the user cannot read the image, the watermark is considered as invisible watermarking (the watermarked image cannot be read using the same as the original image).

2. **Invisible Watermark:** Invisible watermarking, where the watermark is invisible to the user (it cannot be read through regular image reading).

3. **Fragile Watermark:** It can be defined as tamper-proof watermarks. This type of watermark is crashed once it is processed. It is intended to be crashed when it exposure to any shape of processing or even copying. It means that if the watermark is not found, then means that this copy of the image is an illegal copy.

Classification of Image Watermarking Techniques

The frequency sensitivity can be referred to the response of the eye for some frequency changes such as: spatial, time, or spectral. Spatial frequencies are distinguished as textures or patterns, and spatial frequency sensitivity is always defined as the sensitivity of the human vision to luminance alters (Friedman, 1993). It has been shown that a human eye is being very sensitive to luminance alters in the mid-range spatial frequencies, and this sensitivity minimized at lower and higher spatial frequencies. The techniques of the digital image watermarking may be classified into two main categories:

1. **Spatial Domain Techniques:** These techniques of watermarking can also be implemented using color separation. The watermark will be displayed in only one of the color bands, in such cases. This will make the visibility of the watermark is perfect and it will be very hard to discoverable under normal situations. However, the hidden mark displays instantly when the colors are detached for specific processing tasks such as printing. This makes the document which contains the mark not useful for the printer and the watermark can be eliminated from the color band. These types of techniques are mainly used in the commercial field like journalists.

2. **Frequency Domain Techniques:** In compared with the spatial-domain techniques, the frequency-domain techniques are more broadly implemented. The main objective in this classification is to embed or insert the watermarks into the spectral coefficients for the image. The mainly used transforms as in (Friedman, 1993) are: the Discrete Cosine Transform (DCT), Discrete Fourier Transform (DFT), and Discrete Wavelet Transform (DWT). The characteristics of the human visual system is better seized by the spectral coefficients is considered as the main reason for watermarking in the frequency domain. By other words, the low-frequency coefficient is considerably perceived and the high-frequency is believed inferior. To gain a trade-off between robustness and imperceptibility, most techniques embed watermarks in the midrange frequencies.

Figure 3 shows the operational fields of Digital Image Watermarking. The spatial domain will come after the wavelet or frequency transformation domain from the robustness and compatibility perspectives based on the common standards of image compression. The frequency domain involves different types of transformations such as: Discrete Wavelet Transform (DWT), Discrete Cosine Transform (DCT) and Discrete Fourier Transform (DFT).

Characteristics of Watermarking

In the digital image watermarking, the concepts: characteristics, properties, requirements or attributes can be used interchangeably. The applications and their purposes of the digital image watermarking will determine their characteristics. These characteristics should be considered once the watermarking system is designed. The main characteristics of the digital image watermarking are given as in (Ming-Shing & Din-Chang, 2001 ; Sin-Joo & Sung-Hwan, 2001):

Figure 3. Digital image watermarking classifications (Jobenjit & Shivani, 2013).

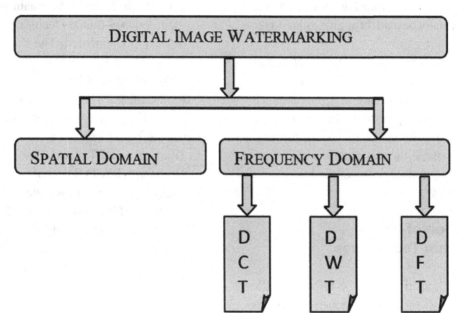

1. **Invisibility:** When a watermark is embedded within the image, then it will be invisible and the content will contain the hidden watermark inside. A hidden watermark can be discovered by only the owner or an authorized person. These watermarks are used for different applications such as: author or content authentication and it could be used for detecting illegal copying.

2. **Robustness:** An embedded watermark should not be affected or destroyed by an image processing or forgery attacks. Even if an attack removed the visible watermark, then it could be restored by the backup invisible watermark. The original image incorporates the visible watermark into, whereas the watermarking system adds an invisible watermark to this image. Consequently, it can be considered as a watermark within another one which creates binary watermarked images. Thus, a robust watermarking can be developed using this technique. In order to achieve more robustness levels, watermark could be added to different locations inside the image. So, it could be retrieved and restored easily if more than one or more watermarks were removed.

3. **Security:** Generally, a watermark must be confidential and not discoverable by any user except the owner or an authorized person. Moreover, there watermarks should be accessed by those authorized persons. Using cryptographic keys a very important characteristic can be achieved in the watermark and security at the same time. So, the algorithm of digital watermark and its details could be propagated globally. A signal of specific watermark is associated with a particular number which uses to express and embed a watermark. This particular number is must be kept secretly and it could be used to make sure who is the authorized and the owner of digital image. The invisibility will be foible or weak when there are many constraints and restrictions on the robustness. Consequently, when the watermarking system is being designed there should be a significant consideration and trade-off between the invisibility and robustness (Brajesh et al, 2013).

Applications of Digital Image Watermarking

There are many number of image watermarking applications, the main applications as indicated in (Hartung et al, 2005 ; Jobenjit & Shivani, 2013) are given in the following:

1. **Fingerprints:** In such applications, information about the authorized receiver is embedded into the image. Several watermarks are embedded into each published image in the fingerprint application and enable the owner of the image to control and place the images that are unauthorized acquired or altered. Linking distinct information about each published copy of the digital image or content is known as fingerprinting, and a suitable solution for such applications is a watermarking because it could not be visible, known or even isolated from the contents (Kougianos et al, 2009). Adding or embedding information about the legal usability of the image will prevent an illegal copying or using of that content (Keshav & Dheerendra, 2010).

2. **Image and Content Authentication:** In these applications, the main objective is to discover alterations to the image. Different image attributes like edges could be used in order to compare with the existing images to detect any differences. A message authentication technique can be applied as a digital signature to solve these types of problems which derives from cryptography science. Digital signature mainly performs several types of content summary. Tampering could be detected and considered when any portion of these summaries had been altered. The rule of digital signature here is to make the detection process.

3. **Medical Applications:** On the MRI and X-ray images (reports), the patients' names are printed by a visible of watermarking techniques. The patient can gain benefits and take the right treatment by the significant task that offered from these reports. If two reports for different patients are mixed up, then this may result a catastrophe (Coatrieux et al, 2006).

4. **Copyright Protection:** A watermark can be embedded into the image to achieve a copyright of information. If there is a disagreement on the proprietorship, then to know who is the right owner? The watermark will be extracted as evidence and it will be used to resolve this trouble (Jain & Xiang, 2005).

5. **Broadcast Monitoring:** This kind of monitoring is applied mainly in the advertising field in order to ensure that the material broadcasted as the commitment and agreement between different parties such the client advertisement firm (Yusof & Khalifa, 2007).

6. **Tamper Detection:** Tamper detection can be detected by using fragile watermarks. If this watermark is crashed or even altered, it denotes existence of tampering and then this will make a digital content is questionable.

7. **Content Description:** Captioning and labeling of the host image and other further information can be embedded into this type of watermark. For such types of applications, the watermark capacity should be comparatively huge and it does not include constraints or restrictions on the robustness requirement.

Drawbacks of Existing Watermark Systems

1. The main trouble of most of the watermarking systems is that there is no system can face most the image attacks or manipulations. These systems are completely sophisticated to be performed timely.

2. **Digital Fingerprints:** The main issues with concern to this application are: Legal Issues, Security Concerns, and Technological Compatibility.

3. **Encryption:** Electronic devices are used to store encrypted information of criminals, or they used secure channels.

Attacks on Digital Image Watermarking

A watermarked image could be modified by mistake or intention. Thus, the robust feature should be found with the watermarking system in order to discover and elicit the watermark. A modification or alteration is considered as an attack that can be performed to distort the quality of the image by adding some deformations. The classifications attacks of the digital image watermarking can be categorized into: non-geometric and geometric attacks. If the watermark is weak, then the attack will be successful and the watermark will be considered as a watermark with a very low acceptable limit (Jobenjit & Shivani, 2013).

1. **Geometric Attacks:** A group of parameters that can be implemented on the image are known as geometric attack. In other words this type of attacks is mainly basic geometric mutations or transformations within an image. Geometric attack may involve: cropping, rotation, scaling, translation, warping, etc.
2. **Non Geometric Attacks:** It involves different signal image processing steps such as: printing, averaging, filtering, sharpening, brightness, scanning, gamma correction, addition of noise, compression of image, etc.

Image Steganography

Steganography is a hiding information technique for digital media such as images in order to hide the presence some or all of the information. In this case, cover media is the digital media without hidden information; whereas the stego media is with (Birgit, 1996). Steganography can converge both authorized and unauthorized weal. The target of communication in steganography is a concealed message and the cover data means how it can be sent. The secret and hidden information as along with the cover data could take any shape of the media such as: audio, image, video or even text. It is well know that the Information security is a very critical subject in all computerized systems around the world and it will remain. Digital Steganography as in (Shuozhong, 2005 ; Bailey & Curran, 2005 ; Kahn, 1996) is considered as of the major trigger that can be used to implement the securing level on the data. Using steganography, the secret information are hidden within signals as an insignificantly information.

The steganography depends on the reality of the observation and senses of the human that are not enough in compare with computerized systems. Thus, the human senses such as: hearing or vision does not have the ability to discover very slight or teeny alterations in visual or auricular scenes that makes a steganography a very strong technique to hide the important information (Birgit, 1996).

Steganography (Cox et al, 2007) is implemented as a secure communication channel by hiding the secret information into some multimedia materials (such as images) and then sending them to recipients insignificantly. Only the intended recipient who engaged the transmitter has the ability to discover these multimedia materials and then grab the secret information from. The main difference between Steganography and watermarking is that the multimedia material (such as images) can be detected to know if it was altered and doubtful by a third party. This phenomenon is called steganalysis. This third part has the ability also to decide to eliminate these illegal modifications if they are occurred. The steganography algorithms will be considered a robust algorithm when it has the strong resistance level to the primary and ultimate steganalysis techniques.

A cover image is used in steganography as the carrier of concealed message and should have regular and unhurt presence without arousing any type of mistrust. The cover image could be called as stego image if it has the hidden message and then use it for discovering the message at the recipient side (Jamil, 1999; Munuera, 2007 ; Sanjay & Kanak, 2012). The secret key that could be simple or composite, with the usability to insert message into the cover image and discovering message which embedded from the stego image is called stego key. This key can be created by achieving some computations based on some criteria such as (the size of the cover image and its texture) or it can be generated randomly. The general procedures of steganography are presented in Figure 4. The features of the cover image that are using to conceal the message in it are referred as embedding domains. Transform domain techniques or spatial domain techniques can use these features and characteristics. In the past, the image pixels are altered and manipulated straightly for embedding. However and recently, before the images really embedding, the message should be transformed mathematically (Ratankirti et al, 2013).

As mentioned that the main idea in steganography is that it depends on the reality that human does not have the ability to know if an image file or a sound or even a portion of text really comprises concealed information. Steganography is a very efficient technique for protecting information especially when the unauthorized receiver

of information or assailant does not understand or discover that the digital media (images) given before them really includes concealed information because when this is discovered, steganography unlock itself up to assault and forfeits its most powerful feature: innocuousness, which represents the detection feature of steganography.

Classification of Image Steganography

The existing steganographic methods were classified in (Brajesh, et al, 2013) as follows:

1. **Transform-Based Steganographic Methods:** In these methods, the signals will be mapped to other types of domain like Fourier transformation or even DCT (Pevny & Fridrich, 2007); the gained co-efficient are modified.
2. **Palette-Based Steganographic Methods:** The steganographic message will be hidden within the indices or the palette bits. The number of colors should be taken in account to be sure it will not exceed its allowable limit, when the image file format has been used.

Figure 4. General skeleton of steganography (Sanjay & Kanak, 2014).

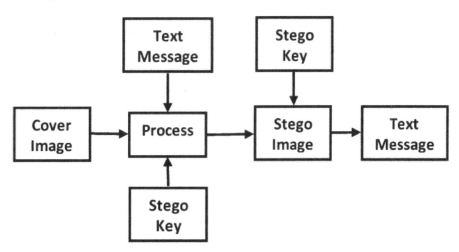

3. **Spatial Domain-Based Steganographic Methods:** Least Significant Bits (LSB) is the mainly used steganography type in many applications like uncompressed file like BMP or TIFF. In a specific layer, the modification on the least significant bit will result a hidden secret message.

The Requirements of Steganographic Techniques

Three main requirements could be applied to estimate and evaluate the steganographic performance techniques as listed and discussed in (Bin, et al, 2011):

- **Security:** Active or passive attacks may be considered as the most trouble with the steganography. If the presence of the secret message can only be evaluated with a possibility less than or equal random appraising key in the existence of several steganalytic systems, then under these systems, steganography could be evaluated as a secure technique. However, in the other cases steganography will claim as insecure.

- **Capacity:** In order to be valuable in carrying secret message, the concealing capacity supplied by steganography technique must be a high as much as possible. The capacity may be provided in ultimate measurement like the secret message size, or it may be a comparative value (e.g. the bits in each pixel, or the secret ratio message) which is known a data embedding rate.

- **Imperceptibility:** Visual artifact scenes could be served by stego images. It will be better when the stego image has a very high value of fidelity when compare to others under the same circumstances of the capacity and security. If the consequent stego image seems unhurt, then this characteristic has to be persuaded for the custodian not having the authentic cover image in order to contrast.

Types of Attacks on Image Steganography

Steganalys is be defined as the attacking steganography science in a combat that never stops. It simulates the existing founded or developed science of Cryptanalysis. A steganalysis system can be created by steganographer in order to evaluate the robustness of his algorithm. Steganalysis can be performed via implementing several techniques or step of image processing such as: translating, cropping, rotating, and filtering. Additionally, it can be performed deliberately by specific program that explores the structure of stego image and evaluates its statistical characteristics such as first and second order statistics (Chaddad et al, 2010). Based on available information for analysis, there are various types of attacks. They can be categorized into six main categories as in (Gangadhar et al, 2013):

1. **Stego-Only Attack:** The stego-image is only available for analysis.
2. **Cover Attack:** The authentic cover and stego images are both obtainable.
3. **Message Attack:** At some point, the concealed message at sometimes could be known to the attacker. But it could be useless for the attacker.
4. **Chosen Stego Attack:** Where the stego-image and steganography tool are already known.
5. **Chosen Message Attack:** Steganalyst generates a stego-image from steganography tool from a chosen message.
6. **Known Stego Attack:** algorithm is known and both the authentic image and stego-image are obtainable.

Steganalsysis can be mainly categorized into universal and specific steganalsysis based on to the tools of targeted steganographic. Universal steganalsysis is known as blind or universal blind steganalsysis, while specific steganalsysis is found to discover some specific steganalsysis. Without steganography algorithms, universal steganalsysis can discover the presence of secret message and workable than the other type of steganalsysis.

CONCLUSION

Steganography is an approach and science that can be used to secure information by hiding messages within some types of covers and suitable multimedia carrier that will never known by attackers. These cover files could take any file format of digital data such as audio or image files. It depends on the proposition that if the attribute is visible, then this means that there is an obvious point of attack, thus the main target is mainly to hide the very presence of the embedded data.

Over the past decade, digital image watermarking is an increasing research topic that has received considerable interest from the researchers. For copyrights of different electronic materials and media, the watermarking is a very significant domain. With proliferation of digital images on the Internet, sometimes a watermarking is mandatory option. Digital watermarking is the processing of information along with a digital signal. A watermark is a minor image, which is embedded into the host or original image, and results a protected image. It behaves as a digital signature, providing the image a type of originality or proprietorship and it makes the image very resistance to the attacks.

REFERENCES

Alireza, M. S., & Woo, C. S. (2011). *Secure Image Processing on Mobile Devices Using J2ME*. Master's Thesis, University of Malaya, Malaysia.

Altaay, A. J., Shahrin, S. B., & Mazdak, Z. A. (2012). *An Introduction to Image Steganography Techniques*. International Conference on Advanced Computer Science Applications and Technologies, IEEE, 2012,122-126, Malaysia.

Artz, D. (2002). Digital Steganography: Hiding Data within Data. *IEEE Internet Computing Magazine, 5*(3), 75–80. doi:10.1109/4236.935180

Bailey, K., & Curran, K. (2005). *Steganography (paperback)*. New York, NY: Book Surge publishing.

Berghel, H., & O'Gorman, L. (1996). Protecting ownership rights through digital watermarking. *IEEE Computer, 29*(7), 101–103. doi:10.1109/2.511977

Bin, L., Junhui, H., Jiwu, H., & Yun, Q. S. (2011). A Survey on Image Steganography and Steganalysis. *Journal of Information Hiding and Multimedia Signal Processing, 2*(2), 142–172.

Birgit, P. T. (1996). Information hiding terminology-results of an informal plenary meeting and additional proposals, In *Proc. of the First International Workshop on Information Hiding*, 1174, 347-350.

Brajesh, M., Rizwan, B., & Vidit, P. (2013). Information Security Through Digital Image Steganography Using Multilevel and Compression Technique. *International Journal of Computer Science & Information Technology, 3*(1), 26–29.

Chaddad, A., Condell, J., Curran, K., & Paul, M. (2010). Digital Image Steganography: Survey and Analyses of Current Methods. *Signal Processing, 90*(3), 727–752. doi:10.1016/j.sigpro.2009.08.010

Chang, C. C., Hwang, K. F., & Hwang, M. S. (2002). Robust authentication scheme for protecting copyrights of images and graphics. In *IEEE Proceedings on Vision, Image and Signal Processing, 149*(1), 43–50.

Coatrieux, G., Lecornu, L., Sankur, B., & Roux, C. (2006). A review of digital image watermarking in health care. In *Annual International Conference of the IEEE, Engineering in Medicine and Biology Society*. New York.

Cox, I. J., Kilian, J., Leighton, F., & Shamoon, T. (1997). Secure Spread Spectrum Watermarking for Multimedia. *IEEE Transactions on Image Processing*, *6*(12), 1673–1687. doi:10.1109/83.650120 PMID:18285237

Cox, I. J., Kilian, J., Leighton, T., & Shamoon, T. (1995). Secure spread spectrum watermarking for multimedia. *NEC Research Institute, Technical Report 95-10*.

Cox, I. J., Miller, M., & Bloom, J. (2002). *Digital Watermarking*. San Francisco: Morgan Kaufmann Publishers.

Cox, I. J., Miller, M., Bloom, J., Fridrich, J., & Kalker, T. (2007). *Digital Watermarking and Steganography* (2nd ed.). Ney York, NY: The Morgan Kaufmann Series in Multimedia Information and Systems.

Fridrich, J., Miroslav, G., & Rui, D. (2002). *Lossless Data Embedding for All Image Formats*. Proc. SPIE Photonics West, Security and Watermarking of Multimedia Contents, 572–583, Friedman, G. L. (1993). The Trustworthy Digital Camera: Restoring Credibility to the Photographic Image. *IEEE Transactions on Consumer Electronics*, *39*(4), 905–910.

Gangadhar, T., Arun, K., & Madhusudhan, M. (2013). A survey on digital image steganography and steganalysis. *IOSR Journal of Electronics and Communication Engineering*, *8*(1), 56–60.

Hartung, F., Kutter, M., Katzenbeisser, S., & Fabien, A. P. (2005). *Information Hiding Techniques for Steganography and Digital watermarking*. Norwood, MA: Artech House.

Highland, H. J. (1997). Data encryption: A non-mathematical approach. *Computers & Security*, *16*(5), 369–386. doi:10.1016/S0167-4048(97)82243-2

Jain, L., & Xiang, J. (2005). *A review study on Digital Watermarking*. In *International Conference on Information and Communication Technologies*, Egypt.

Jamil, T. (1999). Steganography: The art of hiding information is plain sight. *IEEE Potentials*, *18*(1), 10–12. doi:10.1109/45.747237

Jobenjit, S. C., & Shivani, K. (2013). A Review on Digital Image Watermarking. *International Journal of Emerging Technology and Advanced Engineering*, *3*(12), 482–484.

Kahn, D. (1996). *The History of Steganography*. *Proceedings of the First International Workshop On Information Hiding, Lecture Notes in Computer science*, 1-5.

Keshav, S. R., & Dheerendra, S. T. (2010). Digital watermarking scheme for authorization against copying or piracy of color image. *Indian Journal of Computer Science and Engineering*, *1*(4), 295–300.

Kougianos, E., Saraju, P. M., & Rabi, N. M. (2009). Hardware assisted watermarking for multimedia. *Computers & Electrical Engineering*, *35*(2), 339–358. doi:10.1016/j.compeleceng.2008.06.002

Macq, B. M., & Quisquater, J. J. (1995). Cryptology for digital TV broadcasting. *Proceedings of the IEEE*, *83*(6), 944–957. doi:10.1109/5.387094

Ming-Shing, H., & Din-Chang, T. (2001). Hiding Digital Watermarks Using Multi resolution Wavelet Transform. *IEEE Transactions on Industrial Electronics*, *48*(5), 875–882. doi:10.1109/41.954550

Munuera, C. (2007). Steganography and error-correcting codes. *Signal Processing Elsevier*, *87*(6), 1528–1533. doi:10.1016/j.sigpro.2006.12.008

Petitcolas, F. A., Anderson, R. J., & Kuhn, M. G. (1999). Information hiding - A survey. *Proceedings of the IEEE, 87*(7), 1062–1078. doi:10.1109/5.771065

Pevny, T., & Fridrich, J. (2007). *Merging Markov and DCT features for multi-class JPEG steganalysis*. In: *Proc. of SPIE*, San Jose, CA. doi:10.1117/12.696774

Pitas, I. (1996). A Method for Signature Casting on Digital Images. *Proc. IEEE Int. Conf. on Image Processing*, 3: 215-218. doi:10.1109/ICIP.1996.560422

Rafael, C. G., & Richard, E. W. (2002). *Digital Image Processing* (2nd ed.). New Jersey: Prentice Hall.

Ratankirti, R., Suvamoy, C., Anirban, S., & Narayan, C. D. (2013)... *Evaluating Image Steganography Techniques: Future Research Challenges. IEEE, 2013*, 309–314.

Ruanaidh, J. J., Dowling, W. J., & Boland, F. M. (1996). Watermarking digital images for copyright protection. *IEEE Proceedings on Vision, Image and Signal Processing, 143*(4), 250–256.

Sanjay, B., & Kanak, S. (2012). Techniques of Steganography for Securing Information: A Survey. *International Journal on Emerging Technologies, 3*(1), 48–54.

Sanjay, B., & Kanak, S. (2014), A High End Capacity in Digital Image Steganography: Empowering Security by Mottling through Morphing, *Proceedings of the 2014 International Conference on Communications, Signal Processing and Computers*, 151-156.

Shiguo, L., Dimitris, K., & Giancarlo, R. (2009). Recent Advances in Multimedia Information System Security. *Informatica, 33*, 3–24.

Shih, F. Y., & Wu, Y. T. (2005). Robust watermarking and compression for medical images based on genetic algorithms. *Information Sciences, 175*(3), 200–216. doi:10.1016/j.ins.2005.01.013

Shuozhong, W. (2005). *Digital Steganography and steganalysis information war Technology in internet times* (pp. 70–72). Bejing: Tsinghua University, Press.

Sin-Joo, L., & Sung-Hwan, J. (2001). A Survey of watermarking techniques applied to multimedia. *IEEE Transactions on Industrial Electronics, 1*, 272–277.

Swanson, M., Zhu, B., & Tewfik, A. (1996), Transparent Robust Image Watermarking, *Proc. IEEE Int. Conf. on Image Processing*, 3, 211-214. doi:10.1109/ICIP.1996.560421

Wang, H., & Wang, S. (2004). Cyber warfare: Steganography vs. steganalysis. *Communications of the ACM, 47*(10), 76–82. doi:10.1145/1022594.1022597

William, S. (2013). *Cryptography and Network Security: Principles and Practices* (6th ed.). New York, NY: Prentice Hall.

Yusof, Y., & Khalifa, O. O. (2007), *Digital watermarking for digital images using wavelet transform*. In *Telecommunications and Malaysia International conference on Communications*.

KEY TERMS AND DEFINITIONS

Cryptography: The art of protecting information by transforming it (encrypting it) into an unreadable format, called cipher text.

Digital Watermarking: A kind of marker covertly embedded in a noise-tolerant signal such as audio or image data. It is typically used to identify ownership of the copyright of such signal.

Discrete Cosine Transform (DCT): A finite sequence of data points in terms of a sum of cosine functions oscillating at different frequencies.

Image Processing: The manipulation of an image for the purpose of either extracting information from the image or producing an alternative representation of the image.

Image Steganography: The art or practice of concealing a message, image, or file within another message, image, or file.

Information Hiding: A technique to prevent system design change. If design decisions are hidden, certain program code cannot be modified or changed.

Steganalysis: The study of detecting messages hidden using steganography; this is analogous to cryptanalysis applied to cryptography.

Compilation of References

AbdelRahman, S., Elarnaoty, M., Magdy, M., & Fahmy, A. (2010). Integrated machine learning techniques for arabic named entity recognition. *IJCSI International Journal of Computer Science Issues*, 7(3), 27–36.

Abdul-Hamid, A., & Darwish, K. (2010). Simplified feature set for arabic named entity recognition. In *Proceedings of the 2010 Named Entities Workshop, ACL 2010*, pages 110-115.

Abuleil, S. (2007). Using nlp techniques for tagging events in Arabic text. In Proceedings of the 19th IEEE International Conference on Tools with Artificial Intelligence - Volume 02, ICTAI '07, pages 440-443, Washington, DC, USA. IEEE Computer Society.

Abuleil, S., & Evens, M. (2004). Events extraction and classification for arabic information retrieval systems. In *Proceedings of the 16th IEEE International Conference on Tools with Artificial Intelligence, ICTAI '04*, pages 769{770, Washington, DC, USA. IEEE Computer Society.

Agarwal, R., & Santhanam, M. (2008). Digital Watermarking in the Singular Vector Domain. *International Journal of Image and Graphics*, 8(3), 351–368. doi:10.1142/S0219467808003131

Agrawal, D. P., Deng, H., Poosarla, R., & Sanyal, S. (2003). Secure mobile computing. In Distributed Computing IWDC 2003, (LNCS 2918, 265-278).

Agrawal, D., Das, S., & El Abbadi, A. (2010, September). Big data and cloud computing: New wine or just new bottles. *Proceedings of the VLDB Endowment*, 3(2), 1647–1648. doi:10.14778/1920841.1921063

Ahmad, I., Abdulah, A. B., Alghamdi, A. S., Alnfajan, K., & Hussain, M. (2011). Feature subset selection for network intrusion detection mechanism using genetic eigen vectors. In *Proceedings of the 2011 International Conference on Telecommunication Technology and Applications. IACSIT Press*: Singapore.

Ajith, A., Prachi, D., Aggarwal, A., Sharma, S. C., & Sateesh, P. (2013). Distributed port-scan attack in cloud environment. IEEE, 27-31.

Al-Ani, M. S., & Abd Al Baset, K. (2013). Efficient watermarking based on robust biometric features. *Engineering Science and Technology: An International Journal, 3*(3).

Al-Ani, M. S., & Al-Aloosi, W. M. (2013). Biometrics fingerprint recognition using discrete cosine transform (DCT). *International Journal of Computer Applications*, 69(6), 0975 – 8887.

Al-Ani, M. S. (2013). A Novel Thinning Algorithm for Fingerprint Recognition. *International Journal of Engineering Science*, 2(2), 43–48.

Al-Ani, M. S., & Al-Ani, I. H. (2011). Gait recognition based improved histogram. *Journal of Emerging Trends in Computing and Information Sciences*, 2(12).

Alavala, C. R. (2008). *Fuzzy logic and neural networks*. Hershey PA: IRM Press.

Al-Bahadili, H. (2010). On the use of discrete-event simulation in computer networks analysis and design. In E. Abu-Taieh and A. El-Sheikh (Eds.), Handbook of Research on Discrete-Event Simulation Environments: Technologies and Applications (pp. 418-442). Hershey, PA: Information Science Reference.

Al-Bakri, S. H., Mat Kiah, M. L., Zaidan, B. B., & Gazi, M. A. (2011). Securing peer-to-peer mobile communications using public key cryptography: New security strategy. *International Journal of the Physical Sciences, 6*(4), 930–938.

Al-Duwairi, B., & Govindarasu, M. (2006). Novel Hybrid Schemes Employing Packet Marking and Logging for IP Traceback. *IEEE Transactions on Parallel and Distributed Systems, 17*(5), 403–418. doi:10.1109/TPDS.2006.63

Al-Haidari, F., Sqalli, M. H., & Salah, K. (2012). Enhanced EDoS-Shield for Mitigating EDoS Attacks Originating from Spoofed IP Addresses. In *Security and Privacy in Computing and Communications, IEEE 11th International Conference*, (pp. 1167–1174). Liverpool, UK.

Alireza, M. S., & Woo, C. S. (2011). *Secure Image Processing on Mobile Devices Using J2ME*. Master's Thesis, University of Malaya, Malaysia.

Al-Janabi, S. T., & Saeed, H. A. (2011). A Neural Network Based Anomaly Intrusion Detection System. 2011 Developments in E-systems Engineering, (pp. 221-226) IEEE Computer Society.

Al-Khanjari, Z., Alanee, A., Kraiem, N., & Jamoussi, Y. (2013). Proposing a real time internal intrusion detection system towards a secured development of e-government web site. *European Scientific Journal*, (3), 27-37.

Almas, Y., & Kurshid, A. (2006). Lolo: a system based on terminology for multilingual extraction. In *Proceedings of the Workshop on Information Extraction Beyond the document*, pages 56{65. Sydney: Association for Computational Linguistics.

Al-Saedy, H. (2002). Proofing identity to automatic teller machine – A zero knowledge protocol. In Proceedings of Portsmouth University min conference on computer technology (pp 30-35). Abu Dhabi, UAE: Portsmouth University.

Al-Shalabi, R., Kanaan, G., Al-Sarayreh, B., Khanfer, K., Al-Ghonmein, A., Talhouni, H., & Al-Azazmeh, S. (2009). Proper noun extracting algorithm for arabic language. In *International Conference on IT*, Thailand.

Altaay, A. J., Shahrin, S. B., & Mazdak, Z. A. (2012). *An Introduction to Image Steganography Techniques*. International Conference on Advanced Computer Science Applications and Technologies, IEEE, 2012,122-126, Malaysia.

Amine, A., Elberrichi, Z., Simonet, M., & Malki, M. (2008). Evaluation and comparison of concept based and n-grams based text clustering using som. *INFOCOMP-Journal of Computer Science, 7*, 27–35.

Anderson, C. (2008). The end of theory: The data deluge makes the scientific method obsolete Wired. Retrieved from http://www.wired.com/science/discoveries/magazine/16-07/pb_theory/

Anderson, J. P. (1980). Computer Security Threat Monitoring and Surveillance. Fort Washington, USA: Technical Report, James P. Anderson Co.

Andreeva, E., Mennink, B., Preneel, B., & Škrobot, M. (2012). *Security Analysis and Comparison of the SHA-3 Finalists BLAKE*. Grøstl, JH, Keccak, and Skein.

Andrews, H., & Patterson, C. (1976). Singular value decompositions and digital image processing. *Acoustics, Speech and Signal Processing. IEEE Transactions, 24*(1), 26–53.

Angelos, D. K. (2004). SOS: An Architecture for Mitigating DDoS Attacks. *IEEE Journal on Selected Areas in Communications, 22*(1), 176–188. doi:10.1109/JSAC.2003.818807

Anh, N. T., Anh, T. Q., & Binh, N. N. (2008). *Vietnamese Spam Detection based on language classification*. Paper presented at the Second International Conference on Communications and Electronics, 2008. ICCE 2008.

Anil, K. J., & Chen, H. (2004). Matching of dental x-ray images for human identification. *Pattern Recognition, 37*, 1519–1532.

Anirban, B., Jaideep, V., Hiroaki, K., Theo, D., & Srijith, K. (2012). Privacy preserving collaborative filtering for SaaS enabling PaaS clouds. In *International Conference on Quality Software-QSIC 2003*. Retrieved from http://www.journalofcloudcomputing.com/content/1/1/8

Apple Developer. (2013). *iOS technology overview*. Retrieved March 20 2014, from https://developer.apple.com/library/ios/documentation/miscellaneous/conceptual/iphoneostechoverview/iOSTechOverview.pdf

Apple General. (2009). *iPhone OS technology overview*. Retrieved March 20 2014, from www.ithaca.edu/barr/Student/CS390/docs/iPhoneOSTechOverview.pdf

Apple Inc. (2012). *Deploying iPhone and iPad security overview*. Retrieved March 20 2014, from https://ssl.apple.com/ca/ipad/business/docs/iOS_Security_Mar12.pdf

Apple Inc. (2014). *iOS security*. Retrieved March 22 2014, from https://ssl.apple.com/ca/ipad/business/docs/iOS_Security_Mar12.pdf

Ardissono, L., Goy, A., Petrone, G., & Segnan, M. (2012). From service clouds to user-centric personal clouds. In *IEEE International Conference on Cloud Computing*.

Artz, D. (2002). Digital Steganography: Hiding Data within Data. *IEEE Internet Computing Magazine*, *5*(3), 75–80. doi:10.1109/4236.935180

Arudou, D. (2007). *Fingerprinting: Amnesty/SMJ Appeal for Noon Nov 20 Public Appeal outside Justice Ministry*. Retrieved from http://www.debito.org/?s=doudou

Askguru. (2011). Retrieved March 12, 2011 from http://askguru.net/newreply.php?tid=11752&pid=46273

Attia, M., Toral, A., Tounsi, L., Monachini, M., & van Genabith, J. (2010). An automatically built named entity lexicon for Arabic. In LREC 2010. Valletta, Malta, pages 3614-3621.

Aumasson, J.-P., & Meier, W. (2009). Zero-sum distinguishers for reduced Keccak-f and for the core functions of Luffa and Hamsi. *rump session of Cryptographic Hardware and Embedded Systems-CHES, 2009*, 67.

Aus Jonathan, P. (2006). *Decision Making Under Pressure: The Negotiation of the Biometric Passports Regulation*. Retrieved from www.arena.uio.no/publications/

AV-Comparatives. (2013). *Mobile security review*. Retrieved March 20 2014, from www.av-comparitves.org

Awad, W., & ELseuofi, S. (2011). Machine Learning Methods for Spam E-Mail Classification. *International Journal of Computers and Applications*, *16*(1).

Aybet, J., Al-Saedy, H., & Farmer, M. (2009). Watermarking spatial data in geographic information systems. In H. Jahankhani, A. G. Hessami, & F. Hsu (Eds.), *Global Security, Safety and Sustainability* (pp. 18–26). Berlin Heidelberg, Germany: Springer-Verlag.

Baazaoui, Z., Faiz, S., & Ghezala, H. (2005). A Framework for data mining based multi-agent: An application to spatial data. In *Proceedings of World Academy of Science, Engineering and Technology* (volume 5, April 2005).

Baca, M., Cubrilo, M., & Rabuzin, K. (2007). Using biometric characteristics to increase its security. *Traffic &Transportation Scientific Journal on Traffic and Transportation Research*, *19*(6), 353–359.

Baca, M., Schatten, M., & Ševa, J. (2009). Behavioral and Physical Biometric Characteristics Modeling Used for Its Security Improvement. *Transport Problems*, *4*(4), 2009.

Baig, M. N., & Kumar, K. K. (2011). Intrusion detection in wireless networks using selected features. *International Journal of Computer Science and Information Technologies*, *2*(5), 1887–1893.

Bailenson, J. N. (2012). Contribution to the ICA Phoenix closing plenary: The Internet is the end of communication theory as we know it. *62nd annual convention of the International Communication Association, Phoenix, AZ*. Retrieved from ttp://www.icahdq.org/conf/2012/closing.asp

Bailey, K., & Curran, K. (2005). *Steganography (paperback)*. New York, NY: Book Surge publishing.

Bakry, A. H., & Bakry, S. H. (2005). Enterprise resource planning: A review and a STOPE view. *International Journal of Network Management*, *15*(5), 363–370. doi:10.1145/1110960.1110967

Barhoo, T. S., & ElShami, E. (2011). Detecting WLANs' DoS Attacks Using Back propagate Neural Network. *Journal of Al Azhar University-Gaza*, *13*, 83–92

Barnes, S. (2006). A privacy paradox: Social networking in the United States. *First Monday*, *11*(9). http://firstmonday.org/htbin/cgiwrap/bin/ojs/index.php/fm/article/view/1394/1312 doi:10.5210/fm.v11i9.1394

Barolli, L., Spaho, E., Xhafa, F., & Younas, M. (2013). Performance evaluation of an integrated fuzzy-based trustworthiness system for p2p communications in jxta-overlay. *Neurocomputing, 122*, 43–49.

Bashar, A., Almohammad, , & Gheorghita, G. (2011). Information hiding in SOAP messages: A steganographic method for web services. *International Journal for Security Research, 1*(1/2), 61–70.

Batinic, B., Reips, U.-D., & Bosnjak, M. (Eds.). (2002). *Online social sciences*. Seattle, WA: Hogrefe& Huber.

Belenky, A., & Ansari, N. (2003). *Accommodating Fragmentation in Deterministic Packet Marking for IP Traceback* (pp. 1374–1378). IEEE – GLOBECOM. doi:10.1109/GLOCOM.2003.1258463

Benajiba, Y., Rosso, P., & Ruiz, J. (2007). Anersys: An Arabic named entity recognition system based on maximum entropy. In CICLing (pp. 1431-1453).

Benajiba, Y., & Rosso, P. (2008). Arabic named entity recognition using conditional random fields. In *Proceedings of 2008, Arabic Language and Local Languages Processing Workshop, LREC'08*, Marrakech, Morocco.

Benjamin, V. A., & Hsinchun, C. (2013). Machine learning for attackvector identification in malicious source code, *Intelligence and Security Informatics (ISI), 2013 IEEE International Conference,* Seattle, Washington USA: IEEE Conference publications, 21–23.

Bensefia, H., & Ghoualmi, N. (2011). A New Approach for Adaptive Intrusion Detection, In *2011 Seventh International Conference on Computational Intelligence and Security*. doi:10.1109/CIS.2011.220

Berghel, H., & O'Gorman, L. (1996). Protecting ownership rights through digital watermarking. *IEEE Computer, 29*(7), 101–103. doi:10.1109/2.511977

Bergman, C., & Davidson, J. (2005). Unitary embedding for data hiding with the SVD. In proceedings of Security, Steganography, and Watermarking of multimedia Contents (pp. 619-630), Bellingham, WA: SPIE.

Bernstein, A., & Provost, F. (2001). An Intelligent Assistant for the Knowledge Discovery Process", Working Research of the Center for Digital Economy Research, New York University and also presented at the IJCAI, *2001 Workshop on Wrappers for Performance Enhancement in Knowledge Discovery in Databases*.

Bertoni, G., Daemen, J., Peeters, M., & Assche, G. (2009). Keccak specifications. *Submission to NIST (Round 2)*.

Bertoni, G., Daemen, J., Peeters, M., & Van Assche, G. (2007). *Sponge functions*. Paper presented at the ECRYPT hash workshop.

Bhavani, M., & Thuraisingham, Q. (2003). Data mining and cyber security. In International Conference on Quality Software - QSIC

Bidgoli, H. (2003). *The Internet Encyclopedia*. John Wiley & Sons, Inc.

Biham, E., Chen, R., Joux, A., Carribault, P., Lemuet, C., & Jalby, W. (2005). *Collisions of SHA-0 and Reduced SHA-1 Advances in Cryptology–EUROCRYPT 2005* (pp. 36–57). Springer.

Bin, L., Junhui, H., Jiwu, H., & Yun, Q. S. (2011). A Survey on Image Steganography and Steganalysis. *Journal of Information Hiding and Multimedia Signal Processing, 2*(2), 142–172.

Birgit, P. T. (1996). Information hiding terminology-results of an informal plenary meeting and additional proposals, In *Proc. of the First International Workshop on Information Hiding*, 1174, 347-350.

Blum, M., & Micali, S. (1984). How to generate cryptographically strong sequences of pseudorandom bits. *SIAM Journal on Computing, 13*(4), 850–864. doi:10.1137/0213053

Boampong, P., & Wahsheh, L. (2012). Different facets of security in the cloud. In *Proceedings of the 15th Communications and Networking Simulation Symposium*.

Bollier, D. (2010).The promise and peril of Big Data. *Washington, DC: Aspen Institue. Retrieved November 30, 2012, from*http://www.aspeninstitute.org/sites/default/files/content/ docs/pubs/The_Promise_and_Peril_of_Big_Data

Borthwick, A. (1999). *A Maximum Entropy Approach to Named Entity Recognition*. PhD thesis, New York University.

Bortolus, D. (2012). *What Is ERP Technology?* Retrieved from http://www.ehow.com/about_6665167_erp-technology_.html

Botia, J., Garijo, M., Velasco, J., & Skarmeta, A. (1998). A Generic Data mining System basic design and implementation guidelines. Retrieved from http://citeseerx.ist.psu.edu/viewdoc/summary?doi=10.1.1.53.1935

Boura, C. Canteaut, A. & De Canniere, C. (2010). *Higher-order differential properties of Keccak and Luffa*. Cryptology ePrint Archive, Report 2010/589.

Boyd, D. (2010). Privacy and Publicity in the context of big data. *Presented at WWW Conference, Raleigh, North Carolina, 29 April.*

Boyd, D., & Crawford, K. (2012). Critical questions for big data: Provocations for a cultural, technical, and scholary phenomenon. *Information Communication and Society, 15*(5), 665–679. doi:10.1080/136911BX.2012.678878

Brajesh, M., Rizwan, B., & Vidit, P. (2013). Information Security Through Digital Image Steganography Using Multilevel and Compression Technique. *International Journal of Computer Science & Information Technology, 3*(1), 26–29.

Buchanan, W. J., Naylor, M., Mannion, M., Pikoulas, J., & Scott, A. (2011). *Agent Technology*. Retrieved July 5, 2013 from http://buchananweb.co.uk/research/agent2.PDF

Busemann, K., & Gscheidle, C. (2012). Web 2.0: Habitualisierung der Social Communities [Web 2.0: Habitualization of social community use]. *Media Perspektiven,* (7–8), 380–390.

Buyya, R., Yeo, C., & Venugopal, S. (2008). Market-oriented cloud computing: vision, hype, and reality for delivering IT services as computing utilities. In *10th IEEE International Conference on High Performance computing and Communication.* doi:10.1109/HPCC.2008.172

Byun, J. Y., Nasridinov, A., & Park, Y. H. (2014). Internet of Things for Smart Crime detection. *Contemporary Engineering Sciences, 7*(15), 749–754.

Cabinet Office and Detica. (2011). *The Cost of Cyber Crime: A Detica report in partnership with the office of cyber security and information assurance in the cabinet office.* London, UK: Cabinet Office.

Cairo Cleaning and Beautification Authority. (2004). *Cairo Cleaning and Beautification Authority Website.* Retrieved from http://www.ccba.gov.eg/Default.aspx

Campos, M., Tengard, P., & Boriana, L. (2009). *DataMining.* Retrieved from www.oracle.com/technology/products/bi/odm/pdf/automated_data_mining_paper_1205

Chaddad, A., Condell, J., Curran, K., & Paul, M. (2010). Digital Image Steganography: Survey and Analyses of Current Methods. *Signal Processing, 90*(3), 727–752. doi:10.1016/j.sigpro.2009.08.010

Chang, C. C., Hwang, K. F., & Hwang, M. S. (2002). Robust authentication scheme for protecting copyrights of images and graphics. In *IEEE Proceedings on Vision, Image and Signal Processing, 149*(1), 43–50.

Changqing, J. I. (2012). Big data processing in cloud computing environments. In *Proceedings of the 2012 International Symposium on Pervasive Systems, Algorithms, and Networks, I-SPAN 2012* (pp. 17–23).

Chao, Y., Yimin, S., & Guofei, G. (2012). Active User-Side Evil Twin Access Point Detection Using Statistical Techniques. Information Forensics and Security. IEEE Transactions.

Chapman, P., Clinton, J., Kerber, R., Khabaza, T., Reinartz, T., Shearer, C., & Wirth, R. (2000). CRISP-DM 1.0: Step-by-step data mining guide. Denmark: NCR Systems Engineering Copenhagen.

Chau, M., Xu, J. J., & Chen, H. (2002). Extracting meaningful entities from police narrative reports. In *Proceedings of the 2002 Annual National Conference on Digital Government Research,* (pp. 1-5). Digital Government Society of North America.

Cheng, H. (2012, April). Identity based encryption and biometric authentication scheme for secure data access in cloud computing. *Chinese Journal of Electronics, 21*(2), 254–259.

Chen, H., Chung, W., Xu, J. J., Wang, G., Qin, Y., & Chau, M. (2004). Crime data mining: A general framework and some examples. *Computer, 37,* 50–56.

Chen, J., Pan, H., & Ao, Q. (2012). Study a Text Classification Method Based on Neural Network Model. *Advances in Multimedia, Software. Engineering and Computing, 1*, 471–475.

Chen, Z., & Lee, M.-C. (2003), An IP Traceback Technique against Denial-of-Service Attacks. In *Proceedings of the IEEE, Annual Computer Security Applications Conference* (pp. 96–104). doi:10.1109/CSAC.2003.1254314

Chew, C., & Eysenbach, G. (2010). Pandemics in the age of Twitter: Content analysis of tweets during the 2009 H1N1 outbreak. *PLoS ONE, 5*(11), e14118. doi:10.1371/journal.pone.0014118 PMID:21124761

Chou, T. C. (2011). Cyber security threats detection using ensemble architecture. International Journal of Security and Its Applications, 5(2), 17–32.

Chowdhury, C. R., Chatterjee, A., Sardar, A., Agarwal, S., & Nath, A. (2013). A Comprehensive study on cloud green computing: To reduce carbon footprints using clouds. *International Journal of Advanced Computer Research, 3*(8).

Christians, C. G., & Chen, S.-L. S. (2003). Introduction: Technological environments and the evolution of social research methods. Johns, M. D., Chen, S.-L. S., & Hall, G. J. (Eds.), Online social research: Methods, issues, & ethics (pp. 15–23). New York, NY: Peter Lang.

Christopher, A., & Audrey, D. (2002). Managing Information Security Risks. USA: Addison Wesley.

Chuang, J. C., & Chen, H. Y. (2012). Data hiding on text using big-5 code. *International Journal of Security and Its Applications, 6*(2).

Chuan, Z., Xianliang, L., Mengshu, H., & Xu, Z. (2005). A LVQ-based neural network anti-spam email approach. *Operating Systems Review, 39*(1), 34–39. doi:10.1145/1044552.1044555

Cissyr. (2013). Retrieved July 17, 2012 from http://www.cis.syr.edu/~wedu/Teaching/cis758/LectureNotes/Security_Overview.docCissyrCissyr

Cloud Security Alliance. (2013). Expanded Top Ten Big Data Security and Privacy challenge. https://cloudsecurity-alliance.org/research/big-data/, Accessed on 15 Jan. 2014.

Coatrieux, G., Lecornu, L., Sankur, B., & Roux, C. (2006). A review of digital image watermarking in health care. In *Annual International Conference of the IEEE, Engineering in Medicine and Biology Society*. New York.

Coleman, K. G. (2011). *Cyber intelligence: The huge economic impact of cyber crime.* Retrieved October 5, 2012 from: http://gov.aol.com/2011/09/19/cyber-intelligence-the-huge-economic-impact-of-cyber-crime

Colin, T. (2012).Big Data Security, Digital Pathways. *Network Security*, (July): 2012.

Condon, S., Sanders, G. A., Parvaz, D., Rubenstein, A., Doran, C., Aberdeen, J., & Oshika, B. (2009). Normalization for automated metrics: English and Arabic speech translation. In Proceedings of Machine Translation Summit XII, (Ottawa, Canada).

Congdon, K. (2010). *Are Biometrics the Key to Health IT Security?* Retrieved from http://www.healthcaretech-nologyonline.com/article.mvc/Are-Biometrics-The-Key-To-Health-IT-Security-0001?VNETCOOKIE=NO

Cordasco, J., & Wetzel, S. (2008). Cryptographic versus trust-based methods for manet routing security. *Electronic Notes in Theoretical Computer Science, 197*(2), 131–140.

Coronel, C., Morris, S., & Rob, P. (2013).*Database Systems: Design, Implementation, and Management* (10th ed.). Boston: Cengage Learning.

Cournane, A., & Hunt, R. (2004). An analysis of the tools used for the generation and prevention of spam. *Computers & Security, 23*(2), 154–166. doi:10.1016/j.cose.2003.10.001

Coursehero. (2013). Retrieved August 14, 2013 from http://www.coursehero.com/file/4039109/SecurityOverview

Cowie, J., & Lehnert, W. (1996). Information extraction. *Communications of the ACM, 39*(1), 81–91.

Cox, I. J., Kilian, J., Leighton, F., & Shamoon, T. (1997). Secure Spread Spectrum Watermarking for Multimedia. *IEEE Transactions on Image Processing, 6*(12), 1673–1687. doi:10.1109/83.650120 PMID:18285237

Cox, I. J., Miller, M., & Bloom, J. (2002). *Digital Watermarking.* San Francisco: Morgan Kaufmann Publishers.

Cox, I. J., Miller, M., Bloom, J., Fridrich, J., & Kalker, T. (2007). *Digital Watermarking and Steganography* (2nd ed.). Ney York, NY: The Morgan Kaufmann Series in Multimedia Information and Systems.

Cramer, R., & Shoup, V. (2003). Design and analysis of practical public-key encryption schemes secure against adaptive chosen ciphertext attack. *SIAM Journal on Computing, 33*(1), 167–226. doi:10.1137/S0097539702403773

Crime Desk. (2009). Million Online Crimes in the year: Cyber Crime squad Established. londondailynews. com/million-online-crimes-year-cyber-crime-squad-established-p-117.html, Retrieved October 12, 2012 from http://www.the

Cunningham, P. (2010). *Exchange Server 2010 Database Availability Group Installation Step by Step*. Retrieved from http://exchangeserverpro.com/exchange-server-2010-database-availability-group-installation-step-by-step/

Dabbagh, M., Ghandour, A. J., Fawaz, K., & Hajj, W. (2011). Slow port scanning detection, In *Proceedings of the Information Assurance and Security (IAS), 7th International Conference IEEE* (pp. 228-233). doi:10.1109/ISIAS.2011.6122824 doi:10.1109/ISIAS.2011.6122824

Damgård, I. B. (1990). *A design principle for hash functions*. Paper presented at the Advances in Cryptology—CRYPTO'89 Proceedings. doi:10.1007/0-387-34805-0_39

Daniel, N., & Di Domenico, M. (2013). Market research and the ethics of Big Dat. *International Journal of Market Research, 55*(4), 2013.

Das, S. K. (2012). *Seminar Report on Intrusion Detection System*. Retrieved August 21, 2012 from: http://www.123seminarsonly.com/Seminar-Reports/006/73557476-Intrusion-Detection-System.doc

de Paula, A. M. G. (2013). Security Aspects and Future Trends of Social Networks. Retrieved from http://www.ijofcs.org/V05N1-PP07-SECURITY-SOCIAL-NETS.pdf

Deepak, G., & Pradeep, B. S. (2012). Challenging issues and limitations of mobile computing. *International Journal of Computer Technology & Applications, 3*(1), 177–181.

Delac, K., & Grgic, M. (2004). A Survey of Biometric Recognition Methods, In *Procceedings of the 46th International Symposium Electronics in Marine*. ELMAR-2004, (pp. 184-1 93). Zadar, Croatia.

Depren, O., Topallar, M., Anarim, E., & Ciliz, M. K. (2005). An intelligent intrusion detection system (IDS) for anomaly and misuse detection in computer networks. *Expert Systems with Applications, 29*(4), 713–722. doi:10.1016/j.eswa.2005.05.002

Detection. (2011). Retrieved June 10, 2011 from http://int-detection.fotopages.com

Dhage, S. N., Meshram, B. B., Rawat, R., Padawe, S., Paingaokar, M., & Misra, A. (2011). Intrusion Detection System in Cloud Computing Environment, *International Conference and Workshop on Emerging Trends in Technology*, (2011). doi:10.1145/1980022.1980076

Diffie, W., & Hellman, M. (1976). New directions in cryptography. *Information Theory. IEEE Transactions on, 22*(6), 644–654.

Djenouri, D., Khelladi, L., & Badache, N. (2005). A Survey of security issues in mobile ad hoc and sensor networks. *IEEE Communications Surveys and Tutorials, 7*(4), 2–28.

Dobbertin, H., Bosselaers, A., & Preneel, B. (1996). *RIPEMD-160: A strengthened version of RIPEMD*. Paper presented at the Fast Software Encryption.

DoD. (1985). *Trusted Computer System Evaluation Criteria*. DoD 5200.28-STD, Department of Defense. Retrieved from http://fas.org/irp/nsa/rainbow/std001.htm

Dodge, M. (2005). The role of maps in virtual research methods. In C. Hine (Ed.), *Virtual Methods: Issues in social research on the Internet* (pp. 113–127). Oxford, UK: Berg.

Dong, J., Cao, H., Liu, P., & Ren, L. (2006). *Bayesian Chinese spam filter based on crossed N-gram*. Paper presented at the Intelligent Systems Design and Applications, 2006. ISDA'06. Sixth International Conference. doi:10.1109/ISDA.2006.17

Douligeris, C., & Serpanos, D. N. (2007). *Network Security: Current Status and Future Directions*. New York, USA: John Wiley & Sons, Inc. doi:10.1002/0470099747

Dunham, M., & Sridhar, S. 2006. Data Mining: Introductory and Advanced Topics. New Delhi, India: Pearson Education.

Dwivedi, S. K., Kushwaha, D. S., & Ankit, M. (2013). Security issues and resource planning in cloud computing. *International Journal of Engineering and Computer Science, 2*(2).

Eipgov. (2012). Retrieved May 5, 2012 from: http://www.eip.gov.eg/Upload/ConferenceDocs/4/4.pdf

El Gorfte, Z., Eddeqaqi, N., Bouzid, A., & Roukh, A. (2013). Multi-data embedding in to RGB Image with using SVD method. *International Journal of Computer Science Issues, 10*(5), 190–195.

Elsebai, A., Meziane, F., & Belkredim, F. Z. (2009). A rule based persons names Arabic extraction system. In *Proceedings of the IBIMA*, Cairo, Egypt, volume 11, pages 53-59.

El-Zayyat, K., Al-Bahadili, H., & Zobai, T. (2010). A novel neighbor weight-based trust determination model for wireless ad hoc networks. Proceedings Of The International Conference On Theoretical And Mathematical Foundations Of Computer Science (Tmfcs-10) (pp. 116-126), Orlando, Florida, USA, 12-14 July.

England, P., Shi, Q., Askwith, B., & Bouhafs, F. (2012). A Survey on trust management in mobile ad-hoc networks. In *the 13th Post Graduate Symposium on the Convergence of Telecommunications, Networking, and Broadcasting.* Liverpool, UK, June 25-26, 2012.

Ernst & Young. (2012). *Mobile device security: Understanding vulnerabilities and managing risks.* Retrieved January 22 2014, from http://www.ey.com/Publication/vwLUAssets/Mobile_Device_Security/$FILE/Mobile-security-devices_AU1070.pdf

Esposito, S., Fallavollita, P., Corcione, M., & Balsi, M. (2013). Experimental Validation of an Active Thermal Landmine Detection Technique. *Geoscience and Remote Sensing Society, IEEE Transactions, 99.*

Fan, W., Wallace, L., Rich, S., & Zhang, Z. (2006). Tapping into the power of text mining. *Communications of the ACM, 49,* 76–82.

Fayyad, U., Piatetsky, G., & Smyth, P. (1996). From Data Mining to Knowledge Discovery in Databases. *AI Magazine, 17*(3).

Fedler, R., Banse, C., Krauss, C., & Fusenig, V. (2012). *Android OS security: Risks and limitations a practical evaluation* (Tech. Rep.). Fraunhofer Research Institution for Applied and Integrated Security. Retrieved January 22 2014, from http://www.aisec.fraunhofer.de/content/dam/aisec/Dokumente/Publikationen/Studien_TechReports/deutsch/AISEC-TR-2012-001-Android-OS-Security.pdf</eref>

Feng, Z., Hui-Feng, X., Dung-Sheng, X., Yong-Heng, Z., & Fei, Y. (2013). *Big Data Cleaning Algorithms in Cloud Computing.* Retrieved from; doi:10.3991/ijoe.vqi3.2765

Ferdous, R., Muthukkumarasamy, V., & Sattar, A. (2010). A node-based trust management scheme for mobile ad-hoc networks. In *2010 4th International Conference on Network and System Security* (pp. 275–280).

Ferraiolo, D., Sandhu, R., Gavrila, S., & Kunh, D. (2001). Proposed NIST Standard for Role-Based. *ACM Transactions on Information and System Security, 4*(3), 224–274. doi:10.1145/501978.501980

Festoon Media. (2013). *Social Networking: Why Use it for Your Business?* Retrieved April 22, 2013, from http://www.festoonmedia.com/whitepapers/images/Social_Networking.pdf

Fing, L. X., Wang, Y. W. J., Jiang, K., & Liu, B. W. (2012). Mobile operating system architecture trends. *Intel Technology Journals, 16*(4), 178–198.

Flora, S., Tsai, Y., Kap, L., & Chan, (2011). *Probabilistic techniques for corporate blog mining.* School of Electrical & Electronic Engineering, Nanyang Technological University, Singapore.

Fogarty, K. (2009). *Server Virtualization: Top Five Security Concerns.* Retrieved July 3, 2013 from http://www.cio.com/article/492605/Server_Virtualization_Top_Five_Security_Concerns

Freeman, R., Yin, H., & Allinson, N. (2002). Self-organising maps for tree view based hierarchical document clustering. In *Proceedings of the 2002 International Joint Conference on Neural Networks (IJCNN '02),* (Vol. 2, pp. 1906 -1911).

Fridrich, J., Miroslav, G., & Rui, D. (2002). *Lossless Data Embedding for All Image Formats*. Proc. SPIE Photonics West, Security and Watermarking of Multimedia Contents, 572–583, Friedman, G. L. (1993). The Trustworthy Digital Camera: Restoring Credibility to the Photographic Image. *IEEE Transactions on Consumer Electronics*, *39*(4), 905–910.

Gamboa, H., & Fred, A. (2004). A behavioral biometric system based on human computer interaction. In SPIE, 5404-Biometric Technology for Human Identification (pp. 381-392). Orlando, USA.

Gangadhar, T., Arun, K., & Madhusudhan, M. (2013). A survey on digital image steganography and steganalysis. *IOSR Journal of Electronics and Communication Engineering*, *8*(1), 56–60.

Gao, Z., & Ansari, N. (2005). Directed Geographical Traceback. In *Proceedings of the IEEE International Conference on Information Technology: Research and Education* (pp. 221-224).

Gehrmann, C., Mitchell, C., & Nyberg, K. (2004). Manual Authentication for wireless devices. *CryptoBytes*, *7*(1), 29–37.

Ghiassi, M., Olschimke, M., Moon, B., & Arnaudo, P. (2012). Automated text classification using a dynamic artificial neural network model. *Expert Systems with Applications*, *39*(12), 10967–10976. doi:10.1016/j.eswa.2012.03.027

Glass, R. L. (1998). Enterprise Resource Planning - Breakthrough or Term. *The Data Base for Advances in Information Systems*, *29*(2), 13–16. doi:10.1145/298752.298755

Goldwasser, S., Micali, S., & Rivest, R. L. (1988). A digital signature scheme secure against adaptive chosen-message attacks. *SIAM Journal on Computing*, *17*(2), 281–308. doi:10.1137/0217017

Gonzalez, J. M., Anwar, M., & Joshi, J. B. D. (2011). Trust-based approaches to solve routing issues in ad-hoc wireless networks: A Survey. In *2011 IEEE 10th International Conference on Trust, Security and Privacy in Computing and Communications* (pp. 556–563).

Goswami, J. C., & Chan, A. K. (2011). *Fundamentals of Wavelets, Theory, Algorithms and Applications*. Hoboken, N.J: Wiley. doi:10.1002/9780470926994

Gowda, S. R., & Hiremath, P. S. (2013). Secure routing schema for MANET with probabilistic node to node forwarding. *International Journal of Computer Science*, *10*(3).

Goyal, R. D. (2007). *Knowledge based neural network for text classification*. Paper presented at the Granular Computing, 2007. GRC 2007. IEEE International Conference on. doi:10.1109/GrC.2007.108

Granda, P. A. L., Mouriz, N. S., & Ruiloba, S. C. M. (2013). Legal problems of social networks. Retrieved January 15, 2013, from http://www.w3.org/2008/09/msnws/papers/NETWORKS_LEGAL_PROBLEMS.PDF

Greenwald, G., MacAskilly, E., Poltras, L., & Snowden, E. (2012). *The whistleblower behind the NSA surveillance revelations*. The guardian, Monday 10 June 2013. London. UK: The guardian.

Gregg, M. (2010). *10 Security Concerns for Cloud Computing*. Retrieved from http://www.globalknowledge.be/content/files/documents/386696/386784

Guijarro, M., Rubén, F.-F., & Pajares, G. (2011). A multi-agent system architecture for sensor networks. In F. Alkhateeb (Ed.), *Multi-Agent Systems: Modeling, Control, Programming, Simulations and Applications*. InTech; doi:10.5772/14309

Guitton, C. (2012). Criminals and Cyber Attacks: The missing Link between Attribution and Deterrence. [IJCC]. *International Journal of Cyber Criminology*, *6*(2), 1030–1043.

Gul, G., & Avcibas, I. (2007). Source Cell Phone Camera Identification Based on Singular Value Decomposition. In proceedings of Signal Processing and Communications Applications Conference (pp. 1-4). Eskisehir, Turket: IEEE.

Guo, J., Marshall, A., & Zhou, B. (2011). A new trust management framework for detecting malicious and selfish behaviour for mobile ad hoc networks. In *2011 IEEE 10th International Conference on Trust, Security and Privacy in Computing and Communications* (pp. 142–149).

Guojun, Z., Liping, C., & Weitao, H. (2011). The Design of Cooperative Intrusion Detection System, IEEE *Computer Society, 2011 Seventh International Conference on Computational Intelligence and Security, pp.764-766.* doi:10.1109/CIS.2011.173

Gupta V., Krishnamurthy S., & Faloutsos M, (2011). *Denial of Service Attacks at the MAC Layer in Wireless Ad Hoc Networks.* This material is based upon work supported by the National Science Foundation under Grant No. 9985195, DARPA award N660001-00-18936

Gurny, M. (2013). *Canada Navy Spy Case*, National Post. Reviewed, 13 August 2013. Canada: National Post.

Guzella, T. S., & Caminhas, W. M. (2009). A review of machine learning approaches to spam filtering. *Expert Systems with Applications, 36*(7), 10206–10222. doi:10.1016/j.eswa.2009.02.037

Haber, S., & Stornetta, W. S. (1991). *How to time-stamp a digital document.* Springer.

Hahn, A., Ashok, A., Sridhar, S., & Govindarasu, M. (2013). Cyber-physical security testbeds: Architecture, application, and evaluation for smart grid. Smart Grid IEEE Transactions, 4(2), 847–855.

Haining, W., & Kang, G. S. (2003). Transport-Aware IP Routers: A Built-In Protection Mechanism to Counter DDoS Attacks. *IEEE Transactions on Parallel and Distributed Systems, 14*(9), 873–884. doi:10.1109/TPDS.2003.1233710

Haldar, N. A., Abulaish, M., & Pasha, S. A. (2010). An Activity Pattern Based Wireless Intrusion Detection System, IEEE Computer Society, In *2012 Ninth International Conference on Information Technology- New Generations*, pp. 846-847.

Halpern, J. (2009). Word stress and vowel neutralization in modern standard Arabic. In *Proceedings of the Second International Conference on Arabic Language Resources and Tools*, Cairo, Egypt. The MEDAR Consortium.

Hamed, S. M. (2005).*Design and Implementation of a Secure Distributed Agent System.* PhD thesis, University of Technology, Iraq.

Han, J., Kamber, M., & Jian, P. (2011). *Data Mining Concepts and Techniques.* San Francisco, CA: Morgan Kaufmann Publishers.

Hartung, F., Kutter, M., Katzenbeisser, S., & Fabien, A. P. (2005). *Information Hiding Techniques for Steganography and Digital watermarking.* Norwood, MA: Artech House.

Hashem, S. H. (2013). Efficiency Of SVM And PCA To Enhance Intrusion Detection System. *Journal Of Asian Scientific Research, 3*(4), 381–395.

Heger, D. A. (2011). *Mobile Devices: An introduction to the Android operating environment design, architecture, and performance implications.* Retrieved January 22 2014, from http://www.dhtusa.com/media/AndroidInternals.pdf

Highland, H. J. (1997). Data encryption: A non-mathematical approach. *Computers & Security, 16*(5), 369–386. doi:10.1016/S0167-4048(97)82243-2

Hoang, L., & Uyen, T. (2012). A study of different types of attacks in mobile ad hoc networks. In *Electrical & Computer Engineering (CCECE), 2012 25th IEEE Canadian Conference*, (pp. 149-161). Montreal Canada.

Hoard, B. (2012). *5 Virtualization Challenges.* Retrieved June 21, 2013 from http://virtualizationreview.com/articles/2012/08/01/5-virtualization-challenges.aspx

Hoepman, J. H., Hubbers, E., Jacobs, B., Oostdijk, M., & Schreur, R. W. (2006). Crossing Borders: Security and Privacy Issues of the European e-Passport. In *Advances in Information and Computer Security, LNCS.* Netherlands: Springer Berlin Heidelberg publisher. doi:10.1007/11908739_11

Holsbeck, M. V., & Johnson, J. Z. (2004). *Security in an ERP World.* Retrieved from http://www.net-security.org/article.php?id=691

Home Office. (2010). *Cyber Crime Strategy. Crown copyright.* London, UK: Home Office.

Huang, C., Li, M., Yang, J., & Gao, C. (2005). A real-time traceback scheme for DDoS attacks. In *Proceedings of the IEEE International Conference on Wireless Communications, Networking and Mobile Computing* (pp. 1175 – 1179).

Hughes, J. R., & Beer, R. (2007). *A Security Checklist for ERP Implementations.* (educause.edu) Retrieved from http://www.educause.edu/ero/article/security-checklist-erp-implementations

Hughes, T. D. P., Denny, J., Muckelbauer, P. A. D. P., & Etzl, J. (2003). Dynamic trust applied to ad hoc network resources. In *Autonomous Agents*. Multi-Agent Systems Conference.

Hurwitz, J., Nugent, A., Halper, F., & Kufman, M. (2013). Big Data for Dummies. Security Issue. Hoboken: Wiley.

Husted, N., Saïdi, H., & Gehani, A. (2011). Smartphone security limitations: conflicting traditions.*Proceedings of the 2011 Workshop on Governance of Technology, Information, and Policies*, (pp. 5–12). *New York, NY, USA:ACM*. doi:10.1145/2076496.2076497

Ijarcsse. (2012). Retrieved May 25, 2012 from: http://www.ijarcsse.com/docs/papers/Volume_3/7_July2013/V3I7-0225.pdf

Iomega. (2010). *The coming personal cloud: cloud storage for the rest of US*. white paper. Retrieved from http://iomega.com/resources/pdf/pdf_30.pdf

Isa, M., Hashim, H., Manan, J. A., Mahmod, R., & Othman, H. (2012). Integrity Verification Architecture (IVA) Based Security Framework for Windows Operating System. In *Trust, Security and Privacy in Computing and Communications, IEEE 11th International Conference*, (pp. 1304-1309). Liverpool, UK.

Jain, A. K., Bolle, R., & Pankanti, S. (1999). *Biometrics: Personal Identification in Networked Society* (pp. 369–384). New York: Kluwer Academic Publisher. doi:10.1007/b117227

Jain, A. K., Ross, A., & Prabhakar, S. (2004). An Introduction to Biometric Recognition. *IEEE Transactions on Circuits and Systems for Video Technology, 14*(1), 4–20. doi:10.1109/TCSVT.2003.818349

Jain, L., & Xiang, J. (2005). *A review study on Digital Watermarking*. In *International Conference on Information and Communication Technologies*, Egypt.

Jamil, T. (1999). Steganography: The art of hiding information is plain sight. *IEEE Potentials, 18*(1), 10–12. doi:10.1109/45.747237

Jennings, R. (2009). Twitter reels from Mikeyy's XSS 'sploits. Retrieved June 18, 2013, from http://blogs.computerworld.com/twitter_stalkdaily_mikeyy_xss_worm

Jindal, G., & Mayank, J. (2012). A comparative study of mobile phone's operating systems. *International Journal of Computer Applications & Information Technology, 1*(3), 10–15.

Jing, L., Huang, H., & She, H. (2002). Improved feature selection approach tdf in text mining. In *Proceedings of the First International Conference on Machine Learning Cybernetics* (pp. 944-946). Beijing.

Jing, Y. N., Tu, P., Wang, X. P., & Zhang, G. D. (2005). Distributed-log-based scheme for IP traceback. In *Proceedings of the IEEE International Conference on Computer and Information Technology (CIT)*.

Jobenjit, S. C., & Shivani, K. (2013). A Review on Digital Image Watermarking. *International Journal of Emerging Technology and Advanced Engineering, 3*(12), 482–484.

Johnson, D. (2013). *How to protect your company's social media*. Retrieved March 26, 2013, from http://www.cbsnews.com/8301-505143_162-57576041/how-to-protect-your-companys-social-media/

Jonny, C., Abhinav, S., & Edward, B. (2012). A knowledge-based system approach for sensor fault modeling, detection and mitigation. *Elsevier, 39*(12), 10977–10989.

Joux, A. (2004). *Multicollisions in iterated hash functions. Application to cascaded constructions*. Paper presented at the Advances in Cryptology–CRYPTO 2004. doi:10.1007/978-3-540-28628-8_19

Julian, A. (2000). *Biometrics: Advanced Identity Verification*. London: Springer.

Kahn, D. (1996). *The History of Steganography.Proceedings of the First International Workshop On Information Hiding, Lecture Notes in Computer science*, 1-5.

Kamel, N., & Sayeed, S. (2008). SVD-Based Signature Verification Technique Using Data Glove. *International Journal of Pattern Recognition and Artificial Intelligence, 22*(3), 431–443. doi:10.1142/S0218001408006387

Kaplan, D. (2009). *Facebook bloggers reveal way to peek at private profiles*. Retrieved March 20, 2013, from http://www.scmagazineus.com/Facebook-bloggers-reveal-way-to-peek-at-private-profiles/article/138867/

Kashyap, N., & Sinha, G. R. (2012). Image Watermarking Using 3-Level Discrete Wavelet Transform (DWT). *I. J. Modern Education and Computer Science*, *3*(3), 50–56. doi:10.5815/ijmecs.2012.03.07

Kaur, N., Gagandeep, S., & Kaur, M. (2012). A Cloud Computing Against Unified Ontology. *International Journal of Computer & Technology*, *3*(2).

Kelsey, J., & Kohno, T. (2006). *Herding hash functions and the Nostradamus attack Advances in Cryptology-EUROCRYPT 2006* (pp. 183–200). New York: Springer. doi:10.1007/11761679_12

Keshav, S. R., & Dheerendra, S. T. (2010). Digital watermarking scheme for authorization against copying or piracy of color image. *Indian Journal of Computer Science and Engineering*, *1*(4), 295–300.

Khan, B., Khan, M. K., Mahmud, M., & Alghathbar, K. S. (2010). Security Analysis of Firewall Rule Sets in Computer Networks, Emerging Security Information Systems and Technologies *(SECURWARE), 2010 Fourth International Conference, IEEE Conference publications*, Venice Italy, 51-56.

Khusial, D., & McKegney, R. (2013). e-Commerce security: Attacks and preventive strategies. Retrieved March 2, 2013, from http://www.ibm.com/developerworks/library/co-0504_mckegney/index.html

Ko, M., Tiwari, A., & Mehnen, J. (2010). A review of soft computing applications in supply chain management. *Applied Soft Computing*, *10*(3), 661–674. doi:10.1016/j.asoc.2009.09.004

König, B., Alcaraz Calero, J. M., & Kirschnick, J. (2012). Elastic monitoring framework for cloud infrastructures. IET Communications, 6(10), 1306–1315. doi:10.1049/iet-com.2011.0200 doi:10.1049/iet-com.2011.0200

Kotzanikolaou, P., Mavropodi, R., Douligeris, C., & Chrissikopoulos, V. (2006). Secure distributed intelligent networks. *Elsevier Computer Communications*, *29*(3), 325–336.

Kougianos, E., Saraju, P. M., & Rabi, N. M. (2009). Hardware assisted watermarking for multimedia. *Computers & Electrical Engineering*, *35*(2), 339–358. doi:10.1016/j.compeleceng.2008.06.002

Krawczyk, H., Canetti, R., & Bellare, M. (1997). HMAC: Keyed-hashing for message authentication. USA: RFC Editor.

Ku, C. H., Iriberri, A., & Leroy, G. (2008). Natural language processing and e-government: crime information extraction from heterogeneous data sources. In *Proceedings of the 2008 International Conference on Digital Government Research*, (pp. 162-170). Digital Government Society of North America.

Kumar, K. (2010). *Virtualization Express*. Retrieved April 20, 2010 from http://www.virtualizationexpress.com/

Kumar, K. a. (2000). ERP Experiences and Evolution, *43*(4).

Kumar, S. (2014). *Architecture Android development tutorial. Architecture of Android*. Retrieved March 10 2014, from http://www.androidaspect.com/2014/01/android-development-tutorial.html

Kumar, A., Ranjan, A., & Gangwar, U. (2012). An understanding approach towards cloud computing. *International Journal of Emerging Technology and Advanced Engineering*, *2*(9).

Kutoma, W., & Yingqin, Z. (2012). Intelligence techniques in computer security and forensics: At the boundaries of ethics and law. *Computational Intelligence for Privacy and Security*, *394*, 237–258.

La Polla, M., Martinelli, F., & Sgandurra, D. (2013). A survey on security for mobile devices. *IEEE Communications Surveys and Tutorials*, *15*(1), 446–471. doi:10.1109/SURV.2012.013012.00028

Lakhina, S., Joseph, S., & Verma, B. (2010). Feature reduction using principal component analysis for effective anomaly–based intrusion detection on NSL-KDD. *International Journal of Engineering Science and Technology*, *2*(6), 1790–1799.

Lalli, & Palanisamy. (2013). Modernized intrusion detection using enhanced apriori algorithm. *International Journal of Wireless & Mobile Networks, 5*(2).

Larose, D. (2005). *Discovering Knowledge in Data: An Introduction to Data Mining*. Hoboken, NJ: John Wiley & Sons, Inc.

Lavanya, B. N., & Raja, K. B. (2011). Performance Evaluation of Fingerprint Identification Based on DCT and DWT using Multiple Matching Techniques. *IJCSI International Journal of Computer Science Issues, 8*(1), 2011.

Lee, W., Stolfo, S. J., & Mok, K. W. (1999). A data Mining Framework for Building Intrusion Detection Models, In *Proceeding of IEEE Symposium on Security and Privacy*, pp 120-132.

Letsch, T. (2001). *Agents and system agents 2001-02-21*. Retrieved October 10, 2013 from http://www.tagents.org/thesis/node3.html

Li, Q., Feng, Q., Hu, L., & Ju, J. (2005). Fast Two Phrases PPM for IP Traceback, In *IEEE-International Conference on Parallel and Distributed Computing, Applications and Technologies* (pp. 286–289).

Li, J., Sung, M., Xu, J., & Li, L. (2004), Large scale IP Traceback in High Speed Internet: Practical techniques and theoretical foundation. In *IEEE Symposium on Security and Privacy* (pp. 115 –129).

Litke, J. (2011). *Overcoming Virtualization Challenges*. Retrieved June 24, 2013 from http://www.businessinsider.com/overcoming-virtualization-challenges-on-the-way-to-the-private-cloud-2011-3

Liu, Z., Joy, A. W., & Thompson, R. A. (2004). A dynamic trust model for mobile ad hoc networks. Presented At The *10th IEEE International Workshop on Future Trends of Distributed Computing Systems* (pp. 80–85).

Liu, R., & Tan, T. (2002). A SVD-Based Watermarking Scheme for Protecting Rightful Ownership. *Multimedia. IEEE Transactions, 4*(1), 121–128.

Lucks, S. (2004). *Design principles for iterated hash functions*: Cryptology ePrint Archive, Report 2004/253, 2004, http://eprint. iacr. org

Mackey, D. (2003). *Web Security for Network and System Administrators*. Massachusetts, MA: Course Technology.

Macq, B. M., & Quisquater, J. J. (1995). Cryptology for digital TV broadcasting. *Proceedings of the IEEE, 83*(6), 944–957. doi:10.1109/5.387094

Majeed, S. K., Hashem, S. H., & Gbashi, I. K. (2013). Propose HMNIDS hybrid multilevel network intrusion detection system. *IJCSI International Journal of Computer Science Issues, 10*(5).

Mall, R., Langone, R., & Suykens, J. A. K. (2013). Kernal Spectral Clustering for Big Data Networks. *Entropy, 15,* 1567-1586. doi:3390/e15051567

Maloney, J., & Niv, M. (1998). Tagarab: A fast, accurate arabic name recognizer using high-precision morphological analysis. In *Proceedings of the Workshop on Computational Approaches to Semetic Languages, COLING-ACL98,* (pp. 8-15). University of Montreal.

Manickam, J. M. L., & Shanmugavel, S. (2007). Fuzzy based trusted ad hoc on-demand distance vector routing protocol for MANET. In *International Conference on Advanced Computing and Communications* (pp. 414–421).

Manovich, L. (2012).Trending: The Promises and the Challenges of big social data. In M. K. Gold (Ed.), *Debates in the Digital Humanities* (pp. 460–475). Minneapolis: University of Minneapolis Press.

Manyika, J., Chui, M., Brown, B., Bughin, J., Dobbs, R., Roxburgh, C., & Byers, A. H. (2011). *Big Data: The next frontier for Innovation, Competition, and Productivity*. Retrieved from http://www.mckinsey.com/insights/mgi/research/technology_and_innovation/.

Marsh, S. P. (1994). *Formalising trust as a computational concept*. Unpublished doctoral dissertation, University of Stirlin, UK.

Massadeh, S. A., & Mesleh, M. A. (2013). Cloud Computing in Higher Education in Jordan. *World of Computer Science and Information Technology Journal, 3*.

Maurer, U., Renner, R., & Holenstein, C. (2004). *Indifferentiability, impossibility results on reductions, and applications to the random oracle methodology Theory of cryptography* (pp. 21–39). New York: Springer.

Mcgraw-Hill. (2013). *Virualization Overview*. Retrieved from http://www.mhprofessional.com/downloads/products/0071614036/0071614036_chap01.pdf

McGuire, M., & Dowling, S. (2013). *Cyber Crime: A review of the evidence. Research Report 75, Summery of key findings and implication*. London, UK: Home Office.

McKnight, W. (2005). In D. M. Review (Ed.), *Building business intelligence: Text data mining in business intelligence* (pp. 21–22).

Mesfar, S. (2007). Named entity recognition for Arabic using syntactic grammars. In Natural Language Processing and Information Systems (LNCS 4592, pp. 305-316). Berlin: Springer.

Microsoft. (2005). *Active Directory Integration*. Retrieved July 2, 2013 from http://technet.microsoft.com/en-us/library/cc737383(v=ws.10).aspx

Microsoft. (2010). *Microsoft Active Directory-Integrated DNS*. Retrieved July 2, 2013 from http://technet.microsoft.com/en-us/library/cc978010.aspx

Microsoft. (2013). *11 Tips for social networking safety*. Retrieved July 10, 2013, from http://www.microsoft.com/security/online-privacy/social-networking.aspx

Ming-Shing, H., & Din-Chang, T. (2001). Hiding Digital Watermarks Using Multi resolution Wavelet Transform. *IEEE Transactions on Industrial Electronics, 48*(5), 875–882. doi:10.1109/41.954550

Mirkovic, J., Prier, G., & Reiher, P. (2002). Attacking DDoS at the source. In *Proceedings of the IEEE International Conference on Network Protocols* (pp. 312–321).

Mirkovic, J., Prier, G., & Reiher, P. (2003). Source-End DDoS Defense. In *IEEE International Symposium on Network Computing and Applications* (pp. 171–178).

Mirzoev, T., Brannon, M., Lasker, S., & Millere, M. (2014). Mobile application threats and security. *World of Computer Science and Information Technology Journal, 4*(5), 57–61.

Mobach, D. G. A., Overeinder, B. J., Wijngaards, N. J. E., & Brazier, F. M. T. (2001). *Managing Agent Life Cycles in Open Distributed Systems*. Retrieved from http://www.soc.napier.ac.uk/~bill/research/dist_c26.PDF

Mohammad, M. N., Sulaiman, N., & Muhsin, O. A. (2011). A novel intrusion detection system by using intelligent data mining in weka environment. *Procedia Computer Science, 3*, 1237–1242. doi:10.1016/j.procs.2010.12.198

Mohana, R. S., Thangaraj, P., Kalaiselvi, S., & Krishnakumar, B. (2013). Cloud computing for biomedical information management. *International Journal of Scientific Engineering and Technology, 2*(4).

Monk, E. F., & Wagner, B. J. (2013). *Concepts in Enterprise Resource Planning*. USA: Cengage Learning.

Mook, N. (2006). *Cross-Site Scripting Worm Hits MySpace*. Retrieved May 20, 2013, from http://www.betanews.com/article/CrossSite-Scripting-Worm-Hits-MySpace/1129232391

Munir, K., & Palaniappan, S. (2013). Secure cloud architecture. *Advanced Computing: An International Journal, 4*.

Munuera, C. (2007). Steganography and error-correcting codes. *Signal Processing Elsevier, 87*(6), 1528–1533. doi:10.1016/j.sigpro.2006.12.008

Murthy, C. S. R., & Manoj, B. S. (2004). *Ad hoc wireless networks: Architectures and protocols*. Michigan: Prentice Hall.

Muthuprasanna, M., & Manimaran, G. (2005), Space-Time Encoding Scheme for DDoS Attack Traceback. In *Proceedings of the IEEE – Globecom* (pp. 1842-1846). doi:10.1109/GLOCOM.2005.1577967

Muthuprasanna, M., Manimaran, G., Alicherry, M., & Kumar, V. (2006). Coloring the Internet: IP Traceback. In *Proceedings of the IEEE International Conference on Parallel and Distributed Systems*, Vol. 1.

Na Songkhla, C., & Piromsopa, K. (2010). *Statistical Rules for Thai Spam Detection*. Paper presented at the Future Networks, 2010. ICFN'10. Second International Conference on. doi:10.1109/ICFN.2010.39

Nachenberg, C. (2011). *A window into mobile device security: Examining the security approaches employed in Apple's iOS and Google's Android*. Retrieved January 15 2014, from http://www.symantec.com/content/en/us/about/media/pdfs/symc_mobile_device_security_june2011.pdf

Nafi, K. W., Kar, T. S., Hoque, S. A., & Hashem, M. M. (2012). A newer user authentication, file encryption and distributed server based cloud computing security architecture. *International Journal of Advanced Computer Science and Applications, 3*.

Nandi, M., & Paul, S. (2010). Speeding up the wide-pipe: Secure and fast hashing. *Progress in Cryptology-INDOCRYPT, 2010*, 144–162.

Naor, M., & Yung, M. (1989). *Universal one-way hash functions and their cryptographic applications.* Paper presented at the Proceedings of the twenty-first annual ACM symposium on Theory of computing. doi:10.1145/73007.73011

NCSC. (1988.). *National Computer Security Center, "Glossary of Computer Security Terms".* Retrieved from http://csrc.nist.gov/publications/secpubs/rainbow/tg004.txt

Neelakantan, N. P., Nagesh, C., & Tech, M. (2011). Role of feature selection in intrusion detection systems for 802.11 networks. *International Journal of Smart Sensors and Ad Hoc Networks, 1*(1).

Nekkanti, R. K., & Lee, C. (2004). Trust based adaptive on demand ad hoc routing protocol. In *Proceedings Of The 42nd Annual Southeast Regional Conference* (pp. 88–93). New York: ACM.

Nelson, M., Nahapetian, A., Koushanfar, F., & Potkonjak, M. (2009). SVD-Based Ghost Circuitry Detection. In Information Hiding, Security and Cryptology, (pp. 221-234), Darmstadt, Germany, Springer Berlin Heidelberg.

Nelson, B., Phillips, A., Enfinger, F., & Steuart, C. (2008). *Guide to Computer Forensics and Investigation* (3rd ed.). Massachusetts, MA: Course Technology.

Newman, R. (2010). *Security and Access Control Using Biometric Technologies.* Massachusetts, MA: Course Technology.

Noklestad, A. (2009). *A Machine Learning Approach to Anaphora Resolution Including Named Entity Recognition, PP Attachment Disambiguation, and Animacy Detection.* PhD thesis, University of Oslo.

Northecutt, S. et al. (2011). *Security predictions 2012 & 2013: The emerging security threat.* Retrieved from http://www.sans.edu/research/security-laboratory/article/security-predict2011.

Nosrati, M., Karimi, R., & Hasanvand, H. (2012). Mobile computing: Principles, devices and operating Systems. *World Applied Programming Journal, 2*(7), 399–408.

Office of Nuclear Security and Incident Response. (2011). Intrusion Detection Systems and Subsystems: Technical information for NRC licensees. Washington, D.C: U.S. Nuclear Regulatory Commission.

Ojaa, M., Tammb, B., & Taveterc, K. (2001).. . *Agent-Based Software Design., 7*(1), 5–21.

Ojugo, E., Eboka, A. O., Okonta, O. E., Yoro, R. E., & Aghware, F. O. (2012). Genetic Algorithm Rule-Based Intrusion Detection System. Journal of Emerging Trends in Computing and Information Sciences, 3(8), 1182–1194.

Olivier, T., & Marc, D. (2008). Actionable knowledge discovery for threats intelligence support using a multi-dimensional data mining methodology. In *IEEE International Conference on Data Mining* Workshops.

Olzak, T. (2011). *Practical Application of Biometrics.* Retrieved from http://www.techrepublic.com/downloads/practical-application-of-biometrics/2393163

OSCE. (2013). *2013 Social Media Guidebook.* Retrieved April 20, 2013, from http://www.osce.org/fom/99563

Özgür, L., Güngör, T., & Gürgen, F. (2004). Adaptive anti-spam filtering for agglutinative languages: A special case for Turkish. *Pattern Recognition Letters, 25*(16), 1819–1831. doi:10.1016/j.patrec.2004.07.004

Paez, R., Uribe, M. Y., & Torres, M. (2013). Internal Security on an IDS based on agents. International Journal of Network Security and Its Applications, 5(4), 129–142. doi:10.5121/ijnsa.2013.5410 doi:10.5121/ijnsa.2013.5410

Pang, X.-L., Feng, Y.-Q., & Jiang, W. (2007). *A spam filter approach with the improved machine learning technology.* Paper presented at the Natural Computation, 2007. ICNC 2007. Third International Conference on. doi:10.1109/ICNC.2007.143

Park, S.-S., Lee, J.-H., & Chung, T.-M. (2008). Cluster-Based Trust model against attacks in ad-hoc networks. In *Third International Conference on Convergence and Hybrid Information Technology*, (Vol. 1, pp. 526–532).

Park, Y. P., & Salvatore, J. (2012). Software Decoys for Insider Threat. Anomaly Detection at Multiple Scales The Defense Advanced Research Projects Agency (DARPA). New York, USA: Columbia University.

Park, K., & Lee, H. (2001). *On the Effectiveness of probabilistic Packet Marking for IP traceback under Denial Service attack* (pp. 338–347). IEEE INFOCOM.

Pastra, K., Saggion, H., & Wilks, Y. (2003). Intelligent indexing of crime scene photographs. *IEEE Intelligent Systems*, *18*(1), 55–61.

Patil, K., Bhanodia, P., & Joshi, S. (2013). A novel paradigm RIP (reputation index protocol) for MANET. *International Journal of Engineering Research & Technology*, *2*(1).

Peddabachigaria, S., Abraham, A., Grosanc, C., & Thomas, O. (2005). Modeling intrusion detection system using hybrid intelligent systems. *Journal of Network and Computer Applications*, *30*(1), 114–132. doi:10.1016/j.jnca.2005.06.003

Peixian, L. (2013). Issues of Security and Privacy in Electronic Commerce. Retrieved February 15, 2013, from http://www.cs.virginia.edu/~pl9a/resume/ECommerce.doc

Petitcolas, F. A., Anderson, R. J., & Kuhn, M. G. (1999). Information hiding - A survey. *Proceedings of the IEEE*, *87*(7), 1062–1078. doi:10.1109/5.771065

Pevny, T., & Fridrich, J. (2007). *Merging Markov and DCT features for multi-class JPEG steganalysis*. In: *Proc. of SPIE*, San Jose, CA. doi:10.1117/12.696774

Pirzada, A. A., & Mcdonald, C. (2006). Establishment in pure ad-hoc networks. *Journal of Wireless Personal Communications*, *37*, 139–168.

Piskorski, J., Tanev, H., Atkinson, M., Van, E., & Goot, D. (2008). Cluster-entric approach to news event extraction. In *Frontiers in Artificial Intelligence and Applications* (Vol. 18, pp. 276–290). IOS Press.

Pitas, I. (1996). A Method for Signature Casting on Digital Images. *Proc. IEEE Int. Conf. on Image Processing*, 3: 215-218. doi:10.1109/ICIP.1996.560422

Pokhriyal, A., & Lehri, S. (2010). MERIT: Minutiae Extraction using Rotation Invariant Thinning. *International Journal of Engineering Science and Technology*, *2*(7), 3225–3235.

Power, R. (2001). 2001 CSI/FBI computer crime and security survey. *Computer Security Issues and trends*, *7*(1), 1-18.

Proctor Paul, E. (2001). *The Practical Intrusion Detection Hand Book*. Nottingham, England: Prentice Hall.

Qin, H. F., & Li, Z. H. (2013). Research on the Method of Big Data Analysis. *Information Technology Journal*, *12*(10), 1974–1980.

Qiu, Y., Xu, Y., & Wang, B. (2010). *An Online Linear Chinese Spam Emails Filtering System*. Paper presented at the e-Business and Information System Security (EBISS), 2010 2nd International Conference on. doi:10.1109/EBISS.2010.5473478

Rafael, C. G., & Richard, E. W. (2002). *Digital Image Processing* (2nd ed.). New Jersey: Prentice Hall.

Rajab, L., Al-Khatib, T., & Al-Haj, A. (2009). Video Watermarking Algorithms Using the SVD Transform. *European Journal of Scientific Research*, *30*(3), 389–401.

Ramchurn, S. D., Huynh, D., & Jennings, N. R. (2005). Trust In multi-agent systems. the knowledge engineering. *RE:view*, *19*(01).

Ramkumar, R. (2014). Survey of Computer Crimes and their Impacts[IJSRD]. *International Journal of Scientific Research and Development*, *2*(4), 840–844.

Ramteke, S. P., Karemore, P. S., & Golait, S. S. (2013). Privacy preserving and access control to intrusion detection in cloud system. *International Journal of Innovative Research in Computer and communication Engineering*, *1*(1), 21–29.

Ratankirti, R., Suvamoy, C., Anirban, S., & Narayan, C. D. (2013)... *Evaluating Image Steganography Techniques: Future Research Challenges*. IEEE, *2013*, 309–314.

Rawat, S. S., & Sharma, N. (2012). A new way to save energy and cost-cloud computing. *International Journal of Emerging Technology and Advanced Engineering*, *2*(3).

Reddy, E. K., Reddy, V. N., & Rajulu, P. G. (2011). A Study of Intrusion Detection in Data Mining, *Proceedings of the World Congress on Engineering 2011* Vol III WCE *2011, July 6 - 8, London, U.K.*

Rijmen, V., & Oswald, E. (2005). *Update on SHA-1 Topics in Cryptology–CT-RSA 2005* (pp. 58–71). New York: Springer. doi:10.1007/978-3-540-30574-3_6

Rivest, R. L. (1991). *Cryptography. The Handbook of Theoretical Computer Science* (Vol. A). Cambridge, MA: The MIT Press.

Robin, S. (2013). Intrusion Detection and Protection Systems, Intrusion Detection. Technical University of Denmark.

Ross, A., Nandakumar, K., & Jain, A. K. (2006). Handbook of Multibiometrics. New York, USA: Springer-Verlag.

Ross, J. A. (2001). *Security Engineering: A Guide to building Dependable Distributed Systems.* New York, USA: John Wiley.

Ruanaidh, J. J., Dowling, W. J., & Boland, F. M. (1996). Watermarking digital images for copyright protection. *IEEE Proceedings on Vision, Image and Signal Processing, 143*(4), 250–256.

Ruan, G., & Tan, Y. (2010). A three-layer back-propagation neural network for spam detection using artificial immune concentration. *Soft Computing, 14*(2), 139–150. doi:10.1007/s00500-009-0440-2

Ruben, T., Marco, M., Maurizio, M., Munafo, S., & Rao, G. (2012). *Characterization of community based-P2P systems and implications for traffic localization.* Springer Science+Business Media.

Ruch, P., Perret, L., & Savoy, J. (2005). Features combination for extracting gene functions from medline. In ECIR, (pp. 112-126).

Sabater, J., & Sierra, C. (2002). Reputation and social network analysis in multi-agent systems. In *1st International Joint Conference on Autonomous Agents and Multi-Agent Systems* (pp. 475–482). Bologna, Italy, July 15-19.

Sadek, R. (2012). SVD Based Image Processing Applications: State of The Art, Contributions and Research Challenges. *International Journal of Advanced Computer Science and Applications, 3*(7), 26–34.

Saeedipour, R. (2013). *Computer organization and platform technologies course.* Retrieved March 10 2014, from http://people.eecs.ku.edu/~rassul/spring2014/classes/it310/misc/mobile_operating_systems.pdf

Saha, S. K., Chatterji, S., & Dandapat, S. (2008). A hybrid approach for named entity recognition in indian languages. In *Proceedings of the IJCNLP-08 Workshop on NER for South East Asian Languages* (pp. 17-24).

Saini, H., Rao, Y. S., & Panda, T. C. (2012). Cyber-Crimes and their impacts: A Review[IJERA]. *International Journal of Engineering Research and Applications, 2*(2), 202–209.

Saini, R., & Gautam, R. K. (2011). Establishment of dynamic trust among nodes in mobile ad-hoc network. In *2011 International Conference on Computational Intelligence and Communication Networks* (pp. 346–349).

Sancho, D. (2013). *Security Guide to Social Networks.* Retrieved March 11, 2013, from http://www.trendmicro.com/cloud-content/us/pdfs/security-intelligence/white-papers/wp_security_guide_to_social_networks.pdf

Sandeep, R., Sanjay, J., & Rajesh, K. (2010). *A review on particle swarm optimization algorithms and their applications to data clustering.* Springer Science+Business Media.

Sanders, C. (2007). *Practical Packet Analysis: Using Wireshark to solve real-world network problems.* California, CA: William Pollock Publisher.

Sandhu, R., Ferraiolo, D., & Kuhn, R. (2000). *The NIST Model for Role-Base Access Control: Towards A Unified Standard.* Retrieved from http://csrc.nist.gov/rbac/sandhu-ferraiolo-kuhn-00.pdf

Sanjay, B., & Kanak, S. (2012). Techniques of Steganography for Securing Information: A Survey. *International Journal on Emerging Technologies, 3*(1), 48–54.

Sanjay, B., & Kanak, S. (2014), A High End Capacity in Digital Image Steganography: Empowering Security by Mottling through Morphing, *Proceedings of the 2014 International Conference on Communications, Signal Processing and Computers,* 151-156.

Sanmorino, A., & Yazid, S. (2013). DDoS Attack detection method and mitigation using pattern of the flow, *Information and Communication Technology (ICoICT), 2013 International Conference,* Indonesia: IEEE Conference publications, 12–16.

Savage, S., Wetherall, D., Karlin, A., & Anderson, T. (2001). Practical Network Support for IP traceback. *IEEE/ACM Transactions on Networking*, *9*(3), 226–237. doi:10.1109/90.929847

Schneier, B. (1995). *Applied Cryptography: Protocols, Algorithms and Source Code in C*. New York, NY: Wiley.

Scott, C., & Nowak, R. (2004). Templar: A wavelet-based framework for pattern learning and analysis. *IEEE Transactions on Signal Processing*, *52*(8), 2264–2274.

Seminarproject. (2010). Retrieved April 8, 2011 from http://seminarprojects.com/Thread-mobile-agent-based-distributed-intrusion-detection-system.

Shaalan, K., & Raza, H. (2007). Person name entity recognition for Arabic. In *Proceedings of the 5th Workshop on Important Unresolved Matters* (pp. 17-24).

Shaalan, K., & Raza, H. (2008). Arabic named entity recognition from diverse text types. In *Proceedings of the 6th international conference on Advances in Natural Language Processing, GoTAL '08* (pp. 440-451). Berlin, Heidelberg: Springer-Verlag.

Sharma, A., & Ojha, A. (2010). Implementation of cryptography for privacy preserving data mining. *International Journal of Database Management Systems*, *2*(3), 57–65. doi:10.5121/ijdms.2010.2306

She, W., & Thuraisingham, B. (2007). Security for Enterprise Resource Planning Systems. *Information Systems Security*, *16*(3), 152–163. doi:10.1080/10658980701401959

Shiguo, L., Dimitris, K., & Giancarlo, R. (2009). Recent Advances in Multimedia Information System Security. *Informatica*, *33*, 3–24.

Shih, F. Y., & Wu, Y. T. (2005). Robust watermarking and compression for medical images based on genetic algorithms. *Information Sciences*, *175*(3), 200–216. doi:10.1016/j.ins.2005.01.013

Shuozhong, W. (2005). *Digital Steganography and steganalysis information war Technology in internet times* (pp. 70–72). Bejing: Tsinghua University, Press.

Silberschatz, A., Galvin, P., & Gagne, G. (2013). *Operating system concepts* (9th ed.). USA: John Wiley, Reading.

Sindhu, K. K., & Meshram, B. B. (2012). Digital Forensics and Cyber Crime Data mining. *Journal of Information Security*, *3*(3), 1–6. doi:10.4236/jis.2012.33024

Sin-Joo, L., & Sung-Hwan, J. (2001). A Survey of watermarking techniques applied to multimedia. *IEEE Transactions on Industrial Electronics*, *1*, 272–277.

Sitter, A. D., Calders, T., & Daelemans, W. (2004). *A formal framework for evaluation of information extraction. Technical report*. University of Antwerp, Dept. of Mathematics and Computer Science.

Snader, J. C. (1994). *Effective TCP/IP Programming*. Reading, MA: Addison –Wesley.

Snoeren, A. C., Partridge, C., Sanchez, L. A., Jones, C. E., Tchakountio, F., Schwartz, B., & Strayer, W. T. et al. (2002). Single Packet IP Traceback. *IEEE/ACM Transaction Networking*, *10*(6), 721–734. doi:10.1109/TNET.2002.804827

Song, D. X., & Perrig, A. (2001). Advanced and Authenticated Marking Schemes for IP Traceback. In IEEE INFOCOM'01 (pp. 878 – 886) Anchorage, AK.

Song, Y. S., Locasto, M. E., Stavrou, A., Keromytis, A. D., & Stolfo, S. J. (2010). On the infeasibility of modeling polymorphic shellcode. Re-thinking the role of learning in intrusion detection systems (pp. 179–205). New York: Springer.

Song, S., Hwang, K., Zhou, R., & Kwok, Y.-K. (2005). Trusted P2P transactions with fuzzy reputation aggregation. *IEEE Internet Computing*, *9*(6), 24–34.

Sprott, D. (2000). Componentizing the Enterprise Application Packages. *Communications of the ACM*, *43*(3).

Srinivasan, J., Wei, W., Ma, X., & Yu, T. (2011), EMFS: Email-based personal cloud storage. In *IEEE Sixth International Conference on Networking, Architecture, and Storage*. doi:10.1109/NAS.2011.55

Stallings, W. (2004). *Network security essentials: Applications and standards* (4th ed.). Upper Saddle River, NJ: Prentice-Hall.

Stalling, W. (2004). *Computer Network with Internet Protocols and Technology*. New Jersey, NJ: Prentice Hall.

Stalling, W. (2011). *Cryptography and Network Security: Principles and Practice*. New York, NY: Prentice Hall.

Subashini, S., & Kavitha, V. (2011). A survey on security issues in service delivery models of cloud computing. *Journal of Network and Computer Applications, 34*(1). doi:10.1016/j.jnca.2010.07.006

Subramaniam, T., Jalab, H. A., & Taqa, A. Y. (2010). Overview of textual anti-spam filtering techniques. *International Journal of the Physical Sciences, 5*(12), 1869–1882.

Subramaniam, T., Jalab, H. A., & Taqa, A. Y. (2011). *Naïve Bayesian Anti-spam Filtering Technique for Malay Language*. Paper presented at the International Conference on Computer Engineering & Mathematical Sciences, Malaysia. Taqa, A. Y., & Jalab, H. A. (2010). Increasing the reliability of skin detectors. *Scientific Research and Essays, 5*(17), 2480–2490.

Suebsing, A., & Hiransakolwong, N. (2011), Euclidean-based Feature Selection for Network Intrusion Detection, *2009 International Conference on Machine Learning and Computing IPCSIT* vol.3*(2011), IACSIT Press, Singapore*.

Sumit, M., Matthews, M., Anupam, J., & Tim, F. (2012). A Knowledge-Based Approach to Intrusion Detection Modeling (pp. 1–7). IEEE Computer Society.

Sun Microsystems. (2009). Introduction to Cloud Computing Architecture (1st ed.). Retrieved from https://java.net/jira/secure/attachment/29265/cloudcomputing.pdf

Sun, W., Guo, H., He, H., & Dai, Z. (2007). *Design and optimized implementation of the SHA-2 (256, 384, 512) hash algorithms*. Paper presented at the ASIC, 2007. ASICON'07.

Sung, M., & Xu, J. (2003). IP Traceback-Based Intelligent Packet Filtering: A Novel Technique for Defending against Internet DDoS Attacks. *IEEE Transactions on Parallel and Distributed Systems, 14*(9), 861–871. doi:10.1109/TPDS.2003.1233709

Sun, Y. L., Member, S., Han, Z., & Liu, K. J. R. (2006). Information theoretic framework of trust modeling and evaluation for ad hoc networks. *IEEE Journal on Selected Area in Communications, 24*, 305–317.

Swanson, M., Zhu, B., & Tewfik, A. (1996), Transparent Robust Image Watermarking, *Proc. IEEE Int. Conf. on Image Processing, 3*, 211-214. doi:10.1109/ICIP.1996.560421

Swenson, C. (2008). *Modern Cryptanalysis: Techniques for Advance Code Breaking*. New York, NY: Wiley.

Taha, I., Alahmad, M., & Munther, K. (2012). Comparison and analysis study of sha-3 finallists. *International Conference on Advanced Computer Science Applications and Technologies* (26-28 Nov 2012), 7.

Tamilarasi, S. (2013). Forensic Investigative Methodologies for Digital Crime. [TIJCSA]. *The International Journal of Computer Science & Applications, 2*(3), 58–65.

Tan, P., Steinbach, M., & Vipin, K. (2009). Introduction to data mining. *New International Journal of Computer Science, Engineering and Information Technology, 2*(3).

Tanenbaum, A. S., & Wetherall, D. J. (2010). *Computer Networks* (5th ed.). Upper Saddle River, NJ: Prentice-Hall.

Terence, K. T. L., John, C. S. L., & David, K. Y. Y. (2005). You can run, but you can't hide: An effective statistical methodology to trace back DDoS attackers. *IEEE Transactions on Parallel and Distributed Systems, 16*(9), 799–813. doi:10.1109/TPDS.2005.114

Thapa, A., & Kumar, R., (2011). Cyber Stalking: Crime and challenge at the cyber space. *International Journal of Computing and Business research, 2*(1), 1-15.

Thongtae, P., & Srisuk, S. (2008). An analysis of data mining applications in crime domain. In *Proc. IEEE 8th International Conference on Computer and Information Technology Workshops CIT Workshops 2008* (pp. 122-126).

Thuraisingham, B. (2006). *Assured information sharing: Technology challenges and directions*. UTD Technical Report UTDCS-43-06, the University of Texas at Dallas.

Tiwari, P., & Mishra, B. (2012). Cloud computing security issues, challenges and solution. *International Journal of Emerging Technology and Advanced Engineering, 2*(8).

Tom, W. (2000). *Agent-based system architecture and organization*. Retrieved from http://www.enel.ucalgary.ca/People/far/Lectures/SENG697/PDF/tutorials/2002/Agent-Based_System_Archit

Torres, G. (2012). *Everything You Need to Know About the Intel Virtualization Technology.* Retrieved June 24, 2013 from http://www.hardwaresecrets.com/article/Everything-You-Need-to-Know-About-the-Intel-Virtualization-Technology/263

Traboulsi, H. N. (2006). Named Entity Recognition: A Local Grammar-based Approach. PhD thesis, School of Electronics and Physical Sciences, University of Surrey.

Traboulsi, H. (2009). Arabic named entity extraction: A local grammar-based approach. In *Proceedings of the International Multiconference on Computer Science and Information Technology,* (pp. 139-143).

Tripathi, K. P. (2011). A Comparative Study of Biometric Technologies with Reference to Human Interface. *International Journal of Computers and Applications, 14*(5).

Tulasi, R. L., & Ravikanth, M. (2011). Impact of feature reduction on the efficiency of wireless intrusion detection systems. *International Journal of Computer Trends and Technology.*

Turban, E., King, D., & Viehland, D. (2006). Electronic Commerce: A Managerial Perspective (4th ed.). USA: Prentice Hall.

Turban, E., King, D., Lee, J., Liang, T., & Turban, D. (2012). *Electronic Commerce 2012: A Managerial and social networks perspective* (7th ed.). United States of America: Pearson.

Two Crows Corporation. (1999). *Introduction to Data Mining and Knowledge Discovery* (3rd ed.). Potomac, MD: Two Crows Corporation.

Ullah, S., & Xuefeng, Z. (2012). Cloud Computing Research Challenges, In *5th IEEE International Conference on BioMedical Engineering and Informatics.*

University of California Irvine. (1999). *KDD Cup 1999 Data.* Retrieved July 14, 2013 from http://kdd.ics.uci.edu/databases/kddcup99/kddcup99.html

University of Cambridge. (2013). *Windows Server DNS Configuration Guidelines for Active Directory.* Retrived from http://www.ucs.cam.ac.uk/support/windows-support/winsuptech/activedir/dnsconfig

University of Michigan-Flint. (2013). *E-Business Transactions and Security.* Retrieved September 21, 2013, from http://www.umflint.edu/~weli/courses/mgt581/note/transaction.html

University of North Texas Information and Learning Technologies Center. (2013). Common Security Risks. Retrieved May 10, 2013, from http://www.cob.unt.edu/ciltc/securityrisks.php

Ur-Rahman, H. (2012). Cyber Security: Assessing Our Vulnerabilities and Developing an Effective Defense. In C. S. Gal, P. B. Kantor, & M. E. Lesk (Eds.), ISIPS 2008 (LNCS 5661, pp. 20–33).

US-VISIT. (2009). *Final Rule: Enrollment of Additional Aliens, Additional Biometric Data and Expansion to More Land Ports.* Retrieved from http://www.dhs.gov/obim

Vaarandi, R., & Podinš, K. (2010). Network IDS Alert Classification with Frequent Itemset Mining and Data Clustering, In *The 2010 International IEEE Conference on Network and Service Management, pp. 451-456.*

Vaarandi, R. (2011). Real-Time Classification of IDS Alerts with Data Mining Techniques. In *Proceedings of the 28th IEEE conference on Military communications (MILCOM'09), pp.1786-1792.*

Valden, T. (2013). *Hidden Truth About Virtualizing Business-Critical Applications: Benefits Realized, with Results to Prove It.* Retrieved from http://www.vmware.com/files/pdf/solutions/VMware-Hidden-Truth-About-Virtualizing-Business-Critical-Apps-WP-EN.pdf

Van Rijsbergen, C. J. (1979). *Information Retrieval* (2nd ed.). London: Butterworths.

Van Till, S. (2013). Will Big Data Change Security? *securityMagazine.com,* April 2013.

Vanover, R. (2009). *Type 1 and Type 2 Hypervisors Explained.* Retrieved from http://virtualizationreview.com/blogs/everyday-virtualization/2009/06/type-1-and-type-2-hypervisors-explained.aspx [Accessed 4 July].

Varun, C., Eric, E., Levent, E., Gyäorgy, S., & Vipin, K. (2008). Data Mining for Cyber Security. In *IEEE/IFIP International Conference on Embedded and Ubiquitous Computing.*

w3.org. (2012). *Web services architecture*. Retrieved from http://www.w3.org/

w3.org. (2013). *XML*. Retrieved from http://www.w3.org/XML/

Wang, E. (2013). Social network security: A brief overview of risks and solutions. Retrieved April 14, 2013, from http://www1.cse.wustl.edu/~jain/cse571-09/ftp/social.pdf

Wang, J., Healy, R., & Timoney, J. (2010). A Novel Audio Watermarking Algorithm Based On Reduced Singular Value Decomposition. In *proceeding of Intelligent Information Hiding and Multimedia Signal Processing (IIH-MSP),2010 Sixth International Conference* (pp. 143 – 146), Darmstadt, Germany, IEEE. doi:10.1109/IIHMSP.2010.43

Wang, X., Yin, Y. L., & Yu, H. (2005). *Finding collisions in the full SHA-1*. Paper presented at the Advances in Cryptology–CRYPTO 2005. doi:10.1007/11535218_2

Wang, B. T., & Schulzrinne, H. (2004). A Denial-of-Service-Resistant IP Traceback Approach. In *Proceedings of the IEEE International Conference on Internet Computing* (pp. 351–356).

Wang, H. (2012). Virtual machine-based intrusion detection system framework in cloud computing environment. *Journal of Computers*, *7*(10), 2397–2403.

Wang, H., & Wang, S. (2004). Cyber warfare: Steganography vs. steganalysis. *Communications of the ACM*, *47*(10), 76–82. doi:10.1145/1022594.1022597

Wang, X., & Yu, H. (2005). *How to break MD5 and other hash functions Advances in Cryptology–EUROCRYPT 2005* (pp. 19–35). New York: Springer.

Wang, Y., Streff, K., & Raman, S. (2012). Security threats and analysis of security challenges in smartphones. *Computer*, *99*, 1–8.

Warnier, M., Brazier, F. M. T., & Oskamp, A. (2008, March). Security of distributed digital criminal dossiers. *Journal of Software*, *3*(3).

Warnier, M., Oey, M. A., Timmer, R. J., Overeinder, B. J., & Brazier, F. M. T. (2009). Enforcing integrity of agent migration paths by distribution of trust. *International Journal of Intelligent Information and Database Systems*, *3*(4).

Weyns, D. (2010). *Architecture-Based Design of Multi-Agent Systems*. Springer.

Wikipedia. (2013). *PRISM (surveillance program)*. Retrieved September 28, 2013, from http://en.wikipedia.org/wiki/PRISM_(surveillance_program)

Willett, P. (2006). The Porter stemming algorithm: Then and now. P*rogram. Electronic Library and Information Systems*, *40*(3), 219–223.

William, S. (2013). *Cryptography and Network Security: Principles and Practices* (6th ed.). New York, NY: Prentice Hall.

Witten, I. H. (2004). *Text Mining. Practical handbook of Internet computing*. Boca Raton, FL: CRC Press.

Witten, I. H., & Frank, E. (2005). *Data Mining: Practical Learning Tools and Techniques* (2nd ed.). New Jersey, NJ: Elsevier, Morgan Kaufman publisher.

Wood, A. D., & Stankovic, J. A. (2002). Denial of service in sensor networks. *IEEE Computer*, *35*(10), 54–62. doi:10.1109/MC.2002.1039518

Wu, C.-H. (2009). Behavior-based spam detection using a hybrid method of rule-based techniques and neural networks. *Expert Systems with Applications*, *36*(3), 4321–4330. doi:10.1016/j.eswa.2008.03.002

Xia, H., Jia, Z., Li, X., Ju, L., & Sha, E. (2012). Trust prediction and trust-based source routing in mobile ad hoc networks. *Journal of ad hoc networks, 11*(7), 2096–2114.

Xiang, Y., & Zhou, W. (2005), A Defense System against DDoS Attacks by Large-Scale IP Traceback. In *Proceedings of the IEEE, International Conference on Information Technology and Applications* (pp. 431–436). doi:10.1109/ICITA.2005.10

Xiao, Q. (2010). *Applying Biometrics*. Retrieved from http://www.ottawa.drdc-rddc.gc.ca/html/biometrics-end.html

Xiaohui, L., & Chun, C. (2011). The Study on Privacy Preserving Data Mining for Information Security.*International Conference on Future Information Technology (IPCSIT)*, Vol. 13.

Xiong, D., & Moustafa, M., Ghanem, & Yike, G. (2009). Real-time data mining methodology and a supporting framework. In *International Conference on Network and System Security* (pp. 522-527).

Yang, H., Luo, H., Ye, F., Lu, S., & Zhang, L. (2004). Security in mobile ad hoc networks: Challenges and solutions. *IEEE Wireless Communications*, *11*(1), 38–47.

Yang, T. (2012). Mass data analysis and forecasting based on cloud computing. *Journal of Software*, *7*(10), 2189–2195.

Yang, X., Pei, C., Zhu, C., & Li, Y. (2005), AMS Based Reconstruction Algorithm with Two-dimensional Threshold for IP Traceback. In *Proceedings of the Sixth International Conference on Parallel and Distributed Computing Applications and Technologies* (pp. 781–783).

Yusof, Y., & Khalifa, O. O. (2007), *Digital watermarking for digital images using wavelet transform*. In *Telecommunications and Malaysia International conference on Communications*.

Zeng, B., & Yao, L. & ZhiChen, C. (2010).A network intrusion detection system with the snooping agents. In *Computer Application and System Modeling (ICCASM)*. IEEE Conference Publications, 3, 232-236.

Zhang, F. (2011). Mitigating Distributed Denial-of-Service Attacks: Application-Defense and Network-Defense Methods, Computer Network Defense (EC2ND), *2011 Seventh European Conference, IEEE Conference publications*, Gothenburg Sweden, 58-69.

Zhang, G., & Gu, U. (2011). The research and implementation of intelligent intrusion detection system based on artificial neural network. IEEE, 5, 3178-3182.

Zhang, J., Shankaran, R., Orgun, M. A., Varadharajan, V., & Sattar, A. (2010). *A dynamic trust establishment and management framework for wireless sensor networks* (pp. 484–491). IEEE.

Zheng, Y., Pieprzyk, J., & Seberry, J. (1993). *HAVAL—a one-way hashing algorithm with variable length of output*. Paper presented at the Advances in Cryptology—AUSCRYPT'92.

Zhou, Q., & Zhao, Y. (2013). The design and implementation of intrusion detection system based on data mining technology. *Journal of Applied Sciences. Engineering and Technology*, *5*(14), 3824–3829.

About the Contributors

Alaa H. Al-Hamami is presently Professor of Database Security and Dean of Computer Sciences and Informatics College, Amman Arab University, Jordan. He had his Ph.D and M.Sc. from East Anglia University and Loughborough University of Technology, UK, respectively. He is a reviewer for several national and international journals and a keynote speaker for many conferences. He is supervising a lot of Ph.D, M.Sc., and Diploma theses. His research is focused on distributed databases, data warehousing, data mining, cryptography, steganography, and network security. Prof. Al-Hamami published seventeen books in computer philosophy and other computer topics, and more than 160 research papers, in addition to several chapters in IGI and Springer publications. He is Chief Editor and Editor for several magazines in addition to his participation in project research evaluations.

Ghossoon M. Waleed Al-Saadoon is presently an expert of Security Network and Database; she is a Director of Academic Staff performance development Unit, since 2010 till now, Applied Science University, Kingdom of Bahrain. Dr. Al-Saadoon has a Ph.D, M.Sc., and Higher Diploma in Computer Science. She got her B.Sc. in Computers and Statistics. She occupied several positions in different levels as: Head of Management Information System (MIS) Department, ASU, Bahrain, Faculty member at the Computer &Communication Engineering School, University Malaysia Perlis UniMap 2007-2009. Also she was a Dean Deputy of the Institute for Post graduate Studies of Informatics (ICCI), Iraq. Administrator for academic staff for postgraduate studies. Dr. Al-Saadoon have published more than 25 research paper in several International journals. Dr. Al-Saadoon has supervised Postgraduate Students in Ph.D & M.Sc. courses, and Higher Diploma in Iraq, Malaysia and Bahrain. Dr. Al-Saadoon has been a reviewer and editorial member for many journals and conferences such as: *IEEE TMC: IEEE Transactions on Mobile Computing*, and Member in the ICED2008 conference, technical program committee, reviewer in the ICED2008 and many others. Dr. Al-Saadoon has been awarded from *Marquis Who's Who in the World*, selected as one of the original publisher in America for the year 2013. Also awarded by Ministry of Science Technology and Innovation (MOSTI) for selection her as one of the 500 recognized people, Malaysia 2009.

* * *

Mohammad Abdulateef AlAhmad received a Ph.D in Computer Science from International Islamic University of Malaysia in Jan 2014, a M.Sc. in Computer Engineering from College of Computer Science and Engineering, Gulf University, Bahrain in Jan, 2011, and a B.Sc. in Computer Engineering from College of Electrical and Computer Engineering, University of the Pacific, Stockton, CA, USA Dec 22, in 2002. He has published more than 9 papers in high quality journals. Dr. AlAhmad supervised many undergraduate and postgraduate projects and degrees.

Muzhir Shaban Al-Ani has received Ph.D. in Computer & Communication Engineering Technology, ETSII, Valladolid University, Spain, 1994. He was Assistant of Dean at Al-Anbar Technical Institute (1985). Head of Electrical Department at Al-Anbar Technical Institute, Iraq (1985-1988), Head of Computer and Software Engineering Department at Al-Mustansyria University, Iraq (1997-2001), Dean of Computer Science (CS) & Information System (IS) faculty at University of Technology, Iraq (2001-2003). He joined Electrical and Computer Engineering Department, College of Engineering, Applied Science University, Amman, Jordan, as Associate Professor. He joined Management Information System Department, Amman Arab University, Amman, Jordan, as Associate Professor, then he joined computer science department at the same university. He joined in 15 September 2009 Computer Sciences Department, Anbar University, Anbar, Iraq, as a Professor. His research of interests include digital signal processing, parallel processing, digital filters, digital image processing, image compression, computer vision, information hiding, steganography, computer networks, wireless networks, next generation cellular mobile communications, MIS, MIT, e-activities, m-activities, biometric recognition and related works.

Hussein Al-Bahadil is an Associate Professor at Petra University. He received his Ph.D and M.Sc degrees from University of London (Queen Mary College) in 1991 and 1988 respectively. He received his B.Sc in Engineering from the University of Baghdad in 1986. He is a visiting researcher at the Centre of Osmosis Research and Applications, Faculty of Engineering and Physical Sciences, University of Surrey, UK. He has published many papers in different fields of science and engineering in numerous leading scholarly and practitioner journals, and presented at leading world-level scholarly conferences. He published four novel algorithms in computer networks, data compression, network security, and web search engines. He supervised more than thirty Ph.D and M.Sc theses. He edited a book titled *Simulation in Computer Network Design and Modeling: Use and Analysis*, which was published by IGI-Global. He has published more than ten chapters in prestigious books in information and communication technology. He is also a reviewer for a number of books. His research interests include computer networks design and architecture, routing protocols optimizations, parallel and distributed computing, cryptography and network security, data compression, software and Web engineering.

Mohammad Alaa H. Al-Hamami received a Ph.D in Computer Science and Information Technology, and a M.Sc. and B.Sc. in Computer Science. He is a specialist in social media and information systems security. He is currently working as an Assistant Professor in Management Information Systems Department, College of Administrative Sciences, Applied Science University, Kingdom of Bahrain. Al-Hamami is Board Leaders Member of Social Media Club (SMC) Bahrain Chapter and Member of the Bahrain Internet Society (BIS). He was supervising many undergraduate final projects and graduate students (M.Sc. Thesis). Al-Hamami also participates in many conferences and seminars in the field of information security, social media, e-government and information technology. He has published around thirty three scientific researches and papers in many journals and scientific magazines, as well as six books in steganography, data structure, and C++ language.

Wasim A. Al-Hamdani is a Professor of Cryptography and Info Sec, Ph.D.in computer Science, 1985, University of East Anglia, UK, M.Sc. in Computer Science, 1981, Loughborough University of Technology, UK and B.Sc. Math, 1976, University of Basrah, Iraq. Dr. Al-Hamdani played a leading role at KSU in developing the Cyber security program at graduate and undergraduate studies; He was at the University of Technology in Baghdad from 1985 to 1999. He has published six textbooks dealing with computer science and cryptography. Dr. Al-Hamdani concentrated his research in cryptographic algorithms, computer and information security. Currently he is engaged in information security research and teaching. Dr. Al-Hamdani has contributed many chapters in research textbooks and published more than 350 research paper and projects.

Zuhoor Al-Khanjari has over 19 years of experience in teaching and research. She is currently HoD, Department of Computer Science (DCS), College of Science, Sultan Qaboos University (SQU), Muscat, Oman. She is an Associate professor in Software Engineering (SE). She received her B.Sc. in 1993 in Mathematics & Computing from Sultan Qaboos University, and both M.Sc. in 1995, and Ph.D in 1999 in Software Engineering from the University of Liverpool, UK. She is chairing the Software Engineering Research Group and E-Learning in Department of Computer Science. She Chaired the College E-Learning Committee. She was the College Assistant Dean for Postgraduate Studies and Research during 2003-2006. She participates in the evaluation committees for IT international awards, the editorial boards of IT international journals and conferences, and other professional bodies and societies. She published 24 journal and 37 conference papers in international journals and conference proceedings. Also she published a book chapter related to utilizing e-learning in software engineering education. Her research interests include software engineering, software testing and security, data base management, and e-learning.

Meshrif Alruily has gained his Bachelor degree from King Saud University (Saudi Arabia) before he joined the Software Technology Research Laboratory, De Montfort University (UK) where he was awarded his Ph.D in Computer Science. He is currently an Assistant Professor at KSU.

Hasan L. Al-Saedy works as a professor of information security and lead M.Sc. programs in information Technology of UK universities delivered at the British Institute of Technology and E-Commerce. Professor Hasan obtained his MPhil and Ph.D degrees from Westminster University and Southampton University (UK), both degrees are in computer Science (Picture Processing and Pattern Recognition) in 1977 and 1981 respectively. He worked with many universities in the Middle East, Africa and the UK. He gave consultation to many organizations in the field of communications and network security. Also he developed a wide range of protocols and algorithms for many organizations worldwide. His research interests include machine learning, data warehousing and data mining, cyber security and cyber forensics, biometrics and radio frequency access control. He has published more the 50 research papers in international conference proceedings and peer reviewed scientific, engineering and business journals. . Professor Al-Saedy regularly participates and organizes conferences and seminars within the field of computer science in general and in cyber security in particular.

Imad Fakhri Alshaikhli has research interests in cryptography, steganography, genetic algorithms, neural networks, and biometrics. Dr. Al-Shaikhli received his Ph.D in Computer Science, India, (2000), his M.Sc. in Computer Science, Iraq, (1991), and his B.Sc Mathematics, Iraq (1985). He is working in IIUM university in Malaysia since 2010 and he has occupied many positions like Dean, college of computer eng. & sciences- Gulf University-Bahrain since 2006-2010, Head of the dept. of computer information systems at Al-Rafidain university college (2003- 2005) and Head of Software Engineering department at the same university. He has published many scientific papers in national and international journals and conferences.

Nidhal Khdhair El Abbadi received his B.Sc. in Chemical Engineering, B.Sc. in computer science, M.Sc. and Ph.D in computer science. Dr. El Abbadi worked in industry and many universities, he is general secretary of colleges of computing and informatics society in Iraq, member of editorial board of the *Journal of Computing and Applications*, and a reviewer for a number of international journals. He has published many papers and three books (*Programming with Pascal, C++ from beginning to OOP*, and *Data Structures in Simple Language*). His research interest are in image processing, security, and steganography, He is currently working as an Associate Professor in Computer Science in the University of Kufa – Najaf, Iraq.

Rania Elgohary is an assistant professor at the Faculty of Computer and Information Sciences, Ain Shams University, Cairo, Egypt. Rania Elgohary got her B.SC. in Accounting and Foreign Trade, Faculty of Commerce and Business Administration, Helwan University, Cairo, Egypt, and also a B.Sc. complementary in computer science from Faculty of Computer and Information Sciences, Ain Shams University, Cairo, Egypt, and a Masters degree from Ain Shams University, Egypt in computer and information sciences, Information Systems Department, with a thesis titled: *Deliberation Process Mechanisms for Software Development*. Dr. Rania got a Ph.D degree from University of Ain Shams, Cairo, Egypt. Dr. Rania Elgohary is known and well recognized authority in the domain of development and the applications of software engineering. Her research interests include software engineering, E-Business, stock Market Exchange, surveillance systems and information security.

Mohamed Hamdy is an assistant professor with more than 14 years experience in both research and teaching in many fields of computer networks and computer science in general. He gets this experience in leading universities in MENA and Europe. He got his B.Sc. and M.Sc. degrees in Computer Science at Ain Shams University in Egypt and formed a solid background and a set of research and teaching skills. During his Ph.D at the University of Jena in Germany, he has conducted a set of highly ranked and reputed research groups in several occasions. He acquired high managerial skills as working on the top IT strategic management at Ain Shams University as director for a large enterprise network like Ain Shams University Network. He managed to provide several strategic vision and solutions for many challenges in this job.

Soukaena Hassan Hashem is interested in networking security, data mining, artificial intelligences (swarm intelligence) and Web and search engines. She has published many books in computer philosophy and other computer topics in addition to several papers. Dr. Hashem supervised many postgraduate students. Dr. Hashem received her Ph.D in 2006 her M.Sc. in 2002 and her B.Sc. in 2000 all in Computer Sciences from the Computer Sciences Department at the University of Technology.

Hamid A. Jalab received his Bachelor's degree in Electrical Engineering from University of Technology-Baghdad, Iraq, and his M.Sc. and Ph.D degrees in Computer Systems from Odessa National Polytechnic University. He is currently a senior lecturer at the Faculty of Computer Science and Information Technology in University of Malaya, Malaysia. His areas of research interest include signal processing, digital image processing, neural networks and information security. His research work has been published in several international journals and conference publications.

A. Rajiv Kannan is presently Professor in Computer Science and Engineering from Anna University, Chennai. He was awarded Ph.D in Computer Science and Engineering by Anna University, Chennai. Presently he is also working as Professor & HoD in the Department of Computer Science & Engineering, KSR College of Engineering, Affiliated to Anna University, Chennai. Prof. Kannan started his career as Assistant Professor at KSR College of Engineering, Tiruchengode, Namakkal. He is a life member in Indian Society for Technical Education (ISTE), a member of the Institute of Electrical and Electronics Engineering (IEEE), and Computer Society of India (CSI). His research interests include network security, wireless systems and data mining. In particular, he is currently working in a research group developing new Internet security architectures and active defense systems against DDoS attacks. Prof. Kannan published more than 25 papers in refereed international journals and 15 papers in conferences and has been involved many international conferences as Technical Chair and tutorial presenter. He has also acted as editor and reviewer of many journals.

S. Karthik received his M.Sc. in Applied Science – Computer Technology from Periyar University, M.E and Ph.D in Computer Science and Engineering from Anna University, Chennai. Presently he is working as Professor and Dean in the Department of Computer Science & Engineering, SNS College of Technology, Affiliated to Anna University, Chennai. He started his career as Senior Lecturer and head at Maharaja Engineering College, Avinashi, Coimbatore, Coimbatore. He is life member in Indian Society for Technical Education (ISTE), Senior Life Member in International Association of Computer Science and Information Technology (IACSIT) and member of the Institute of Electrical and Electronics Engineering (IEEE), Computer Society of India and International Association of Engineers. His research interests include network security, Web services and wireless systems. In particular, he is currently working in a research group developing new Internet security architectures and active defense systems against DDoS attacks. He published more than 46 papers in refereed international journals and 25 papers in conferences and has been involved many international conferences as technical chair and tutorial presenter. Prof. S. Karthik has acted as Chairman of various Research Selection Committees, Research Project Monitoring Committees and other Administrative Committees of his Institute and other Universities. He has also acted as editor and reviewer of many journals.

Rafal A. Al-Khashab recived her B.Sc. in Computer Science, from the College of Science, University of Mosul, Iraq (2010) and her M.Sc. in Computer Science from College of Computer Sciences and Informatics, Amman Arab University, Jordan (2014). Miss Al-Khashab joined the Iraqi Middle East Investment Bank as an IT Administrator for six months in 2011. Then she joined Al-Ala'mia Academy for Training in Jordan as a Lecturer since Feb. 2013 till now. She started her research activity by publishing a paper on cloud computing databases.

Ebrahim Al Naemi received his Bachelor's degree in Information Systems Management from University of Applied Science University in 2014. Mr. Al Naemi research interests include virtual machines, security management, packet analysis and information security. Mr. Al Naemi has worked in private companies in Qatar and has participated in many workshops and training courses in the security and network of virtual machines. Mr. Al Naemi is now mainly interested in cloud computing security and is also interested in computer science especially in the fields of virtual machines, Windows servers, client and server access controls and similar subjects.

Assad Abdulrahman Nayyef has over 10 years of experience in teaching and research. He is currently a lecturer in the Department of Computer Science (DCS), College of Science, Sultan Qaboos University (SQU), Muscat, Oman. He received his B.Sc. in Computer Science / Information Systems from Al_Rafidain University in Iraq, and his M.Sc. in 2005 in Data Security from Iraqi Commission for Computers and Informatics Institute for Postgraduate Studies, Baghdad, Iraq. He is a Professional Ambassador for Oman National CERT (Safety Ambassador Program information in eOman). He published 7 journal and conference papers in international journals and conference proceedings. His research interests include internal intrusion detection, embedded internal sensors in cloud computing, embedded security systems, information hiding, and software testing and security.

Mohammed A. Otair is an Associate Professor in Computer Information Systems and Computer Center Manager at Amman Arab University-Jordan. He received his B.Sc. in Computer Science from IU-Jordan and his M.Sc. and Ph.D. in 2000 and 2004, respectively, from the Department of Computer Information Systems-Arab Academy. His major interests are mobile computing, data mining and databases, neural network learning paradigms, Web-computing, and e-learning. He has published more than 40 publications.

Hanaa. M. Said is the IT general manger of Information & Computer Center at Cairo Cleaning & Beautification Authority, Egypt. Dr. Hanaa is responsible for Supervision of all administration tasks for the departments: Center of Information, Documents and Decision Support, Administration of Documents Department, Information and Statistics Department, Publishing Department, Decision Supporting Department. Dr. Hanna got his B.Sc. in Communications Engineering, Faculty of Engineering, Helwan University, in 1987. His telecommunications & electronic, project was the design of a microprocessor. He received his Diploma of Computer Science from Ain Shams University with very good grades, Master's degree in science at the Information Systems College of Computing & Information Technology. In July 2011 Grade: "Excellent" From Arab Academy for Science, Technology & Maritime Transport. Ph.D degree from Faculty of computer science at Ain Shames University Faculty of Computing & Information Science Information Systems Department Topic: *Ontological Engineering Approach for Cyber Security in Cloud Computing.*

Abdel-Badeeh M Salem was a Professor of Computer Science in the Faculty of Computer and Information Sciences, Ain Shams University, Cairo, Egypt since 1989. He is a professor emeritus since October 2007. He was a Director of Scientific Computing Center at Ain Shams University (1984-1990). His research includes intelligent computing, expert systems, biomedical informatics, and intelligent e-learning technologies. He has published around 300 papers in refereed journals and conference proceedings in these areas. He has been involved in more than 300 conferences and workshops as a plenary speaker, member of international program committees, workshop/invited session organizer and Session Chair. He is author and co-author of 15 Books in English and Arabic Languages. He is the Editor-in-Chief of the *International Journal of Bio-Medical Informatics and e-Health* (IJBMIeH), *Egyptian Computer Science Journal (ECSJ)*, and Associate Editor of the *International Journal of Applications of Fuzzy Sets and Artificial Intelligence (IJAFSAI).*

Venus W. Samawi is an Associate Professor at Amman Arab University, Department of Computer Information Systems. She received her B.Sc. from University of Technology in 1987, her M.Sc. and Ph.D. degrees from Computer Science Department in Al-Nahrain University (previously Saddam University) in 1992 and 1999 respectively. Dr. Samawi supervises postgraduate Ph.D students in system programming, pattern recognition, and network security. She also leads and teaches modules at both B.Sc. and M.Sc. levels in computer science. Dr. Samawi was a reviewer in four IEEE conferences (ICIEA 2009, 2011, 2012, and ICFCN'12). Her special areas of research include AI, neural networks, genetic algorithms, and image processing.

Thamarai Subramaniam, received her Bachelor's degree in Computer Science from University of Nottingham Trent in 2003, and her Master's of Science degree in Computer Science from the Faculty of Computer Science and Information Technology in University of Malaya, Malaysia in 2012. Thamarai Subramaniam had been teaching in various education institutions for pass 20 years. Her research areas include text-based anti-spam processing, image analysis, digital image processing, information security, and artificial neural networks. Additionally her research work has been published in several international journals and international conference publications.

Alaa Y. Taqa received her Bachelor's degree in Computer Science from University of Mosul - Iraq in 1989, her M.Sc. degree in Computer Science from Informatics Institute for Postgraduate Studies-Baghdad-Iraq in 2001, and her Ph.D degree in Computer Science from College of Computer Sciences and Mathematics - University of Mosul - Iraq in 2007. She was a Visiting Research Fellow at the Faculty of Computer Science and Information Technology in University of Malaya, Malaysia in 2010. She is currently a lecturer at the Education Collage for pure Sciences in University of Mosul; Iraq. Her areas of interest include artificial intelligence techniques, text processing, image analysis, and information security. Her research works have been published in several local and international journals and conference publications.

Hussein Zedan is the Dean of Scientific Research and Postgraduate Studies at Applied Science University (ASU), Bahrain. His research interests include formal methods, verification, semantics, critical systems, re-engineering, computer security, CBD, and IS development. Before joining ASU, he was the Technical Director of the Software Technology Research Laboratory at De Montfort University (UK). He was awarded the degrees of M.Sc. and Ph.D. from Bristol University (UK), both in Mathematics. He worked at many British universities including Bristol, Oxford and York universities.

Index

Printed in the United States
By Bookmasters